D0618399

Social Work and Social Welfare

An Introduction

Hisham F. Ibrahim/Photodisc Green/Getty Images
(The credit is for the photo on page ii.)

SIXTH EDITION

Social Work and Social Welfare

An Introduction

Rosalie Ambrosino
University of Texas at San Antonio

Robert Ambrosino
University of Texas at Austin

Joseph Heffernan, Emeritus
University of Texas at Austin

Guy Shuttlesworth, Emeritus
University of Texas at Austin

THOMSON

BROOKS/COLE

Australia • Brazil • Canada • Mexico • Singapore
Spain • United Kingdom • United States

Social Work and Social Welfare: An Introduction, Sixth Edition

Rosalie Ambrosino, Robert Ambrosino, Joseph Heffernan, and Guy Shuttlesworth

Social Work Editor: Dan Alpert
Development Editor: Tangelique Williams
Assistant Editor: Ann Lee Richards
Editorial Assistant: Stephanie Rue
Technology Project Manager: Julie Aguilar
Marketing Manager: Meghan McCullough
Marketing Assistant: Teresa Marino
Marketing Communications Manager: Shemika Britt
Project Manager, Editorial Production: Tanya Nigh
Creative Director: Rob Hugel
Art Director: Vernon Boes

Print Buyer: Linda Hsu
Permissions Editor: Bob Kauser
Production Service: ICC Macmillan Inc.
Photo Researcher: Laura Molmud
Copy Editor: Carolyn Acheson
Cover Designer: Roger Knox
Cover Image: © Jose Ortega, Images.com
Cover Printer: RR Donnelley, Crawfordsville
Compositor: ICC Macmillan Inc.
Printer: RR Donnelley, Crawfordsville

© 2008, 2005 Thomson Brooks/Cole, a part of The Thomson Corporation. Thomson, the Star logo, and Brooks/Cole are trademarks used herein under license.

ALL RIGHTS RESERVED. No part of this work covered by the copyright hereon may be reproduced or used in any form or by any means—graphic, electronic, or mechanical, including photocopying, recording, taping, web distribution, information storage and retrieval systems, or in any other manner—without the written permission of the publisher.

Printed in the United States of America
1 2 3 4 5 6 7 12 11 10 09 08 07

Thomson Higher Education
10 Davis Drive
Belmont, CA 94002- 3098
USA

For more information about our products, contact us at:
Thomson Learning Academic Resource Center
1-800-423-0563
For permission to use material from this text
or product, submit a request online at
http://www.thomsonrights.com.
Any additional questions about permissions can be
submitted by e-mail to thomsonrights@thomson.com.

Library of Congress Control Number: 2007920001

ISBN-13: 978-0-495-09512-5
ISBN-10: 0-495-09512-5

Brief Contents

v

Contents

PART **THREE**

Fields of Practice and Populations Served by Social Workers   163

CHAPTER **6**
Social Work Practice with Agencies and the Community   144

CHAPTER **7**
Poverty, Income Assistance, and Homelessness   167

Preface

This sixth edition of this book is written at a critical time for the United States and the entire world. As we move toward the eighth year of the new millennium, the United States faces many challenges both at home and abroad. An often-debated topic is what the role of the United States should be in fostering relationships around the world as a means of promoting the social well-being of world citizens. Civil wars stemming from ethnic conflicts and the human rights violations they bring about, coupled with famines and other natural disasters, impact the United States daily. All of this raises critical issues regarding how to balance our need to address important domestic issues against our leadership role in an increasingly complex world.

Current domestic policy issues that cannot be ignored or swept under the rug include what to do with the millions of Americans who either are uninsured or under-insured, how to reduce poverty, how to address the growing homeless population, what to do about the lack of parity in mental health care, how to guarantee the fair and equitable treatment of the country's rapidly growing immigrant population, what commitment should be made to keeping the nation's children free from harm, how to implement and sustain juvenile and criminal justice reforms, and how to create a civil society in which *all* persons are appreciated and valued.

At the dawn of the 20th century, the roots of social work were just beginning to take hold. It was one of the most prolific eras for social and economic justice in the history of the social work profession. The settlement house movement was in full force. Social workers (mainly women) were making significant contributions to the development of social welfare policy that affected the lives of immigrants, the poor, the homeless, delinquent youth, the medically indigent, individuals in need of mental health services, and many others. It was a time of massive social and economic change. Social workers sought to bring order out of chaos, to connect private troubles to public causes, and to help the disenfranchised create better lives for themselves. Most of all, it was a period of hope—hope for a better future for all of humanity.

The 21st century is off to a rocky start. The time is more critical now than ever for social workers to advocate for policies and programs they believe will address the issues referenced above and to provide services and support to the vulnerable populations most likely to be affected by world events. This book is about the many social welfare issues facing the United States and the world today and the many roles that social work professionals play in responding to those issues.

Although approaches to social welfare have changed over time, the needs to which the social work profession responds remain much the same—not because the social work profession has been ineffective in addressing these needs but, rather, because the response to social welfare needs is tied closely to the prevailing social values. It can be argued that there is a rhythm of social responses to social welfare problems. This rhythm is affected by the events of history, the state of the economy, the prevailing political ideology, and the will of the people.

At this time in history, the social welfare needs of the United States have taken a back seat to other issues, such as waging a global war on terrorism, reducing taxes, and downsizing government. Yet, the problems of poverty, homelessness,

AIDS, substance abuse, child abuse and neglect, teen pregnancy, youth violence, immigration, and an inadequate and unjust health-care system remain and will not simply disappear by ignoring them. Because these problems tear at the very fabric of our society, they once again will stand high on the country's social agenda and receive the bulk of public attention.

In this text we hope to help students develop a frame of reference to understand social welfare and an approach to address social issues that will serve them well in times of commitment as well as retrenchment. We have reworked much of the previous edition of the text to reflect changes in the social work profession, as well as in the social welfare policy arena. In keeping with the current Council on Social Work Education's Educational Policy and Accreditation Standards, the text takes a generalist practice perspective in addressing social welfare issues, within the context of the systems/ecological framework—the overarching framework used by generalist practitioners to address social welfare needs at the individual, family, group, organization, community, and societal levels.

Part One of the text, Understanding Social Work and Social Welfare, provides an introduction to the nature of social welfare and the profession of social work. In chapter 1 we focus on the historical context of social welfare to show how the past has shaped present-day social welfare problems, the evolution of society's views of people in need, and the roles of social workers in responding to those needs. Chapter 2 explores the social work profession, contrasting social work with other helping professions and showing the importance of collaboration in working with individuals, families, groups, and communities. In chapter 3, we introduce key underpinnings of the social work profession, including the systems/ecological framework, the concept of generalist practice, and the strengths perspective, all used by social workers in assessing client needs and working with clients and other helping professionals to develop appropriate strategies of

intervention. In chapter 4 we highlight key social justice issues such as the impact of racism, sexism, homophobia, and other forms of oppression on individuals and the ways the allocation of resources reinforces these forms of oppression and injustices.

In the chapters in Part Two, Social Work Practice, you will learn intervention methods that social workers use. These chapters have been streamlined to enhance the beginning social worker's understanding of both micro and macro levels of practice. Chapter 5 covers methods that social workers use in working with individuals, families, and groups. Chapter 6 focuses on social work at the macro level, including work in the community and in policy, administration, and research.

In Part Three, Fields of Practice and Populations Served by Social Workers, you will study the fields of practice and populations with which social workers are involved. You will be considering the issues raised within the broad perspective of social welfare, the nature of the social work profession, the systems/ecological framework, and the impact of oppression and social and economic injustice on at-risk populations. Chapter 7 focuses on poverty and income assistance. Because homelessness is primarily a result of poverty and economic conditions, a discussion on homelessness is included. In chapter 8 you will learn about mental health, substance abuse and developmental disabilities, and policies and programs intended to address the impacted individuals and their families. Chapter 9 explores health care, including a discussion of who is more likely to be in good health and why, and critical issues in current health care delivery. Chapters 10 and 11 address the needs of and services to children, youth, and families with an emphasis on family issues such as divorce, child maltreatment, and problems associated with adolescence, and policy and program responses to address these concerns. In chapter 12 you will learn about the needs and services of older adults and the critical need for social workers as our population continues to age. Chapter 13 explores the criminal justice system, including differences in the adult and juvenile justice systems. Chapter 14 is directed to social work in rural settings, pointing out key factors that social workers must keep in mind when working in rural areas.

Social workers increasingly must consider the impact of their work on their clients, discussed in chapter 15. In this chapter you also will learn about social work opportunities in the workplace. Because social workers must incorporate a global worldview into their interventions wherever they practice, and because social workers are playing ever more important roles in international circles, the discussion on international social work has been expanded and incorporated into chapter 16. Content on immigration has been expanded in this chapter because immigration issues are central to the social and economic future of the United States and because the 2,000-mile border shared with Mexico is a major entry point into the United States for immigrants from Mexico and Central and South America.

As you read this text and engage in classroom discussions about the material, note that from the beginning of time, our society has been shaped by the discussion of conflicting ideas. This text presents multiple perspectives about many social welfare issues—for example, poverty and welfare reform, health care, diversity, reproductive rights of women, domestic violence, and youth crime. You also will find that social workers have multiple perspectives about these issues. Social work is a diverse profession, and like members of the broader society, social workers do not agree on the ways these issues are framed and the best approaches to address them. We hope that you will consider the ideas presented in this text and those of your student colleagues and your professor— and listen to these different voices with an open mind. More important, we hope that you will treat clients that you serve with dignity and respect, even though their values and other perspectives may differ from yours.

A number of features will help students and instructors get the most out of this book. At the end of each chapter is a list of key terms, as well as discussion questions that can be used in the classroom or individually to help students strengthen their critical thinking skills. We also include a list of Internet sites by which to locate specific journal articles on subjects of interest using *Info-Trac College Edition*®.

This text is a collaborative work among four colleagues. Where consensus was possible, we sought it; where it was not possible, we sought to identify the diverse views about the established wisdom of social work. Each of us contributed to the book from the perspectives of our own education and professional experience in addition to social work: child development, education, human behavior, and psychology in the case of Rosalie Ambrosino; political science and economics in the case of Joe Heffernan; sociology and history in the case of Guy Shuttlesworth; and educational psychology, policy, and administration in the case of Robert Ambrosino. Although the text is interdisciplinary in this sense, it is disciplined by the continuity and the certainty of unresolved social issues to which social work skills are relevant.

We hope that a number of you using this text will be persuaded, or have your choices reinforced, to join the social work profession. We urge those of you considering a career in social work to talk with your course instructors about the BSW degree. We also recommend that you visit social agencies and undertake some volunteer experiences in conjunction with your course. Most important, however, we hope this book in some way will contribute to your social conscience no matter what career you choose, and encourage you to recognize social work as a dynamic, challenging profession whose values, principles, and practices intersect with a wide variety of other professions.

As we continue to struggle with social welfare issues that have existed in various forms for centuries, we urge you to look back on the early roots of social work—to remember the profession's significant contributions to making the world a better place to live. We urge you to build on the many accomplishments of the social work profession that took root at the turn of the last century and to translate what was learned there into the very different and ever-changing world of today. We urge you to rekindle the flame of hope that burned so brightly in those early days of the profession. We urge you to seek to advance what the social work profession stands for in everything you do. Finally, regardless of the profession you choose, we urge you to leave a legacy, no matter how large or small, for others to follow you into the future and continue to make the world a better place to live.

Rosalie Ambrosino
Robert Ambrosino
Joseph Heffernan
Guy Shuttlesworth

Acknowledgments

Four "referent" groups played an important role in strengthening this book: our families, our student and faculty colleagues in Austin and San Antonio, and our colleagues in the profession. We owe our gratitude to our families—Jean, Megan, Will C., Catie, Coleman, and Jimmy—for their support and understanding when the book took priority. A special note of thanks goes to our children and grandchildren who have enriched our lives immeasurably with their open minds and zest for life—and ultimately for whom this book was written, as they are the inheritors of the world we leave behind.

We also thank the diverse group of reviewers whose comments contributed significantly to the quality of this sixth edition. We very much appreciate the thoughtful guidance they provided in our making revisions from the fifth edition.

The referent group of greatest relevance has been our students. We owe special appreciation to them for helping us frame the issues in the text by asking the "hard questions" and challenging us to remember that social welfare issues are timeless and complex. Their comments in classes over our collective years of teaching have helped to shape our views of what they want and need to know to become better social workers and citizens in our complex society. The most rewarding part of teaching is to watch our students begin to see connections between the past and the present, as well as the myriad of factors that shape social welfare issues and their impact on the diverse populations within the United States. We have incorporated many of their ideas into this sixth edition.

Last but not least, we express our gratitude to our project manager, Lynn Lustberg, for her persistence and encouragement in the book's preparation and publication. Also, a special thanks to the production guidance and abilities—and the patience—of Dan Alpert, Stephanie Rue, Ann Lee Richards, Vernon Boes, and Tanya Nigh of Thomson Publishing Company and to others who helped with this publication along the way.

Understanding Social Work and Social Welfare:

Key Concepts and Perspectives

Bruno Vincent/Reportage/Getty Images

Part One of this book is an introduction to the nature of social welfare and social work—what social welfare encompasses and what social workers who function in social welfare settings do. The information in these four chapters constitutes a historical and theoretical framework for understanding subsequent chapters.

Chapter 1, *Social Welfare, Past and Present*, provides the historical context of social welfare—how the past has shaped present-day social welfare problems and society's views toward people in need. The chapter begins with a discussion of early welfare policies and legislation and traces these influences to contemporary social welfare institutions.

Chapter 2, *Social Work and Other Helping Professions*, explores the relationships between social welfare as a broad system intended to maintain the well-being of individuals within a society and the profession of social work. The discussion covers the diverse roles and functions of social work professionals, contrasting the profession of social work with other helping professions and examining ways by which they can work together. For those who are interested in careers in one of the helping professions, the chapter indicates educational pathways and credentialing for various roles.

Chapter 3, *The Systems/Ecological Perspective*, suggests a theoretical framework for understanding subsequent chapters. A systems/ecological perspective is the basis for considering individuals within the broader environment. This framework encompasses a broad societal perspective, a family perspective, and an individual perspective. Examples are provided to show how social work practitioners apply the framework and its concepts. The chapter also covers generalist social work practice and the strengths perspective, explaining how these perspectives fit within a systems/ecological context.

Chapter 4, *Diversity and Social Justice*, addresses the ways by which racism, sexism, homophobia, and other forms of oppression and discrimination disenfranchise vulnerable groups in our society. Specific examples illustrate the long-range effects of social injustice at the individual, group, organizational, community, and societal levels related to color, gender, class, and sexual orientation. The promotion of social and economic justice and work toward eliminating oppression at all levels of the environment are implicit roles of the social work profession.

Together, these chapters comprise an overview of the major concepts upon which the profession of social work is based, and they lay the groundwork for the remaining chapters. They are intended as an overview, a prelude to what follows. Concepts introduced in these chapters also provide the foundation for understanding content in later chapters. For those majoring in social work, these concepts and their application will become second nature. You will use them daily, probably without even realizing it.

As you read the chapter in this section and engage in classroom discussions about the material, note that from the beginning of time, our society has been shaped by the discussion of conflicting ideas. These initial chapters present multiple perspectives about many social welfare issues—for example, poverty and welfare reform, diversity, reproductive rights of women, and same-sex marriage. You also will find that social workers have multiple perspectives about these issues. Social work is a diverse profession, and like members of the broader society, social workers do not agree on the ways these issues are framed and the best approaches to address them. We hope that you will consider the ideas presented in this text and those of your student colleagues and your professor—and listen to these different voices with an open mind. More important, we hope that you will treat clients you serve with dignity and respect, even though their values and other perspectives may differ from yours.

CHAPTER 1

Social Welfare, Past and Present

Consider what your life would be like if you were living in an earlier time—or a time in the future. What would be the same? What would be different? Why? How would personal and religious values and beliefs of the time, the economy, and the group in power shape your life and the choices available to you? Have you ever thought about how the personal and religious values and beliefs, the economy, and groups in power in earlier years of the United States impact your life now and the choices available to you?

Social welfare policy in the United States has undergone tremendous change since the time of the early settlers. Yet, much of social welfare as we know it today reflects the mainstream belief system in place during colonial American times—a system borrowed from Elizabethan England—which in turn largely reflects the English Poor Laws of the early 1600s. Many of the provisions of the English Poor Laws—such as an emphasis on personal responsibility, local control of decision making, promotion of family

values, limited government involvement in social welfare programs, the equating of work to religious salvation, and a distinction between the "deserving" poor and the "undeserving" poor—are embedded in contemporary social welfare policies.

The landmark welfare reform legislation passed in 1996 created a burgeoning underclass of working poor. For many, working at a job, even two jobs, no longer guarantees a life free from poverty and even a small share of the American dream. Can this trend be reversed, or is the fundamental belief system about social welfare in the United States so entrenched that limited incremental change is the best we can expect? What lessons can be learned from the American social welfare experience? What are the implications of failing to meet the basic needs of a large segment of the population? Resolving these and similar questions is central to the social work profession. Failing to resolve them is simply not an option.

There is no consensus regarding the nature, focus, and development of social policy or the responsibility—if any—of government in developing programs to assist those in need. In the following discussion we identify some of the more salient factors involved in developing

a comprehensive approach to social welfare in the United States. But first, a few basic questions are in order: What is social welfare? Who gets it? Who pays for it? Does it create dependency? Why is our social welfare system organized as it is?

Social welfare in our society long has been a matter of dispute and controversy. Often, the controversy results from a misunderstanding of the policies that govern social welfare, as well as misinformation about people who are entitled to receive social welfare benefits. Many people view those who receive public assistance (commonly called "welfare") as lazy and unwilling to work. This presumes that poverty, mental illness, and unemployment signify personal failure or personal neglect. Others view recipients of public assistance as victims of a rapidly changing society that provides little help in enabling people to become self-sufficient. It is understandable, then, that people with divergent views would have different opinions about the nature and scope of social welfare programs and the people they serve.

Determining *who* is in need represents one of the fundamental decisions involved in developing any public social welfare program. This judgment is almost always based, at least in part, by how much we think a person deserves help. Frequently, a distinction is made between the deserving poor and the undeserving poor. Many people are more accepting of the needs of older people and those with disabilities and chronic illnesses than the needs of seemingly able-bodied persons.

Today, who we consider deserving is defined more often than not by whether the person is able to work. We often assume that people who are poor have chosen that lifestyle, are lazy, or lack motivation to rise out of poverty. These assessments often fail to consider how changing social systems contribute to outcomes that result in poverty for a substantial portion of the population. Even those who work at two or more jobs can be poor.

Why does poverty in the United States persist? What can and should be done about it, and who should be responsible for addressing the problem? What resources should be brought to bear, and who should pay for them?

A Definition of Social Welfare and Its Relationship to Social Work

What is social welfare? A broad definition may well include all organized societal responses that promote the social well-being of a population. This would include education, health, rehabilitation, protective services for adults and children, public assistance, social insurance, services for those with physical and mental disabilities, job-training programs, marriage counseling, psychotherapy, pregnancy counseling, adoption, and numerous other related activities designed to promote social well-being.

In the *Encyclopedia of Social Work*, P. Nelson Reid (1995) defines social welfare in this way:

> Social welfare . . . is perhaps best understood as an idea, that idea being one of a decent society that provides opportunities for work and human meaning, provides reasonable security from want and assault, promotes fairness and evaluation based on individual merit, and is economically productive and stable. The idea of social welfare is based on the assumption that human society can be organized and governed to produce and provide these things, and because it is feasible to do so, the society has a moral obligation to bring it to fruition. (p. 2206)

The term **social welfare,** then, refers to the full range of organized activities of public and voluntary agencies that seek to prevent, alleviate, or contribute to solving a selected set of social problems. For some who view social welfare broadly—from the concept that a society pools its resources for the general welfare of all—social welfare encompasses public facilities such as libraries, public parks, and hospitals. Others include social support to corporations, sometimes called "corporate welfare," or the extensive investment that some countries such as the United States make to businesses in addition to investment in people with need. Still others view social welfare more narrowly, to consist of programs that address issues such as poverty and child maltreatment.

The length and breadth of the list of social problems typically depend on the values perspective of the person compiling the list, the historical time in which the list is developed, and the perceived economic resources available to meet the social welfare problems listed. As you read on, consider how individual and professional values shape one's views about what constitutes social welfare.

Social work is the primary profession that works within the social welfare system and with those the system serves. Social workers implement planned social change activities prescribed by social welfare institutions. They facilitate change by working with individuals, families, groups, organizations, and communities and at the societal level to improve social functioning. Social workers advocate for social and economic justice within the social welfare system, making needed resources available to members of vulnerable populations—children, elderly people, those with disabilities, and those living in poverty.

Social workers within the social welfare system assist abused and neglected children and their families, pregnant and parenting teens, the homeless and others living in poverty, individuals with health and mental health problems, youth and adults within the criminal justice system, employees in the workplace, refugees across the world, and individuals with a myriad of other needs. They organize neighborhoods and communities to strengthen or create programs and policies to better meet human needs, and advocate for change in a variety of roles at state, national, and global levels. Individuals involved in other helping professions work closely with social workers in planned change at all levels. The roles of social work professionals and other helping professions in the social welfare system are discussed in chapter 2.

The Value Base of Social Welfare

Values are assumptions, convictions, or beliefs about what is good and desirable or the way things ought to be. A person's values are shaped by his or her socialization experiences. Many values are dominant and supported by the majority of the population. For example, most people agree that life is sacred. Nearly everyone believes that killing another person with wanton disregard for that person's life is a criminal offense. Other values related to the sanctity of life, however, are not shared so readily. For example, our society differs on issues such as assisted suicide and capital punishment.

The development of social welfare over time reflects differences in values as they relate to social responsibility for those in need. Values alone, however, do not determine social policy. Availability of resources, coupled with economic, religious, and political influences, results in ever-evolving policies of social responsibility for vulnerable members of a society.

One dominant value that has guided the development of our social welfare system is **humanitarianism,** derived largely from Judeo-Christian philosophy and teachings (Marson & MacLeod, 1996). Our society also is influenced by the economic doctrine of **laissez-faire,** based on limited government involvement, individualism, and personal responsibility. From a laissez-faire perspective,

1. problems of the poor and the disenfranchised are perceived as a matter of personal failure that government welfare programs would only perpetuate,
2. work is considered to be the only justifiable means of survival because it contributes to the productive effort of society, and
3. social responsibility for vulnerable members of society would be carried out through

volunteerism aimed at encouraging personal responsibility and self-sufficiency rather than formal government intervention.

A different perspective maintains that we all are members of society and, by virtue of that membership, are entitled to share in its productive effort. Those who hold this belief argue that people become poor or needy as a result of changing social institutions such as economic globalization or the shift from a manufacturing economy to a service-based economy. Individuals are not the cause of these conditions but, rather, are swept along and victimized by them. For example, members of some ethnic groups face barriers such as inferior educational resources, limited (and usually menial) job opportunities, poor housing, and inadequate health resources. An analysis from this perspective would not blame these conditions on individual group members but, instead, identify factors such as institutional discrimination and oppression.

Those who conceptualize social welfare have differing values perspectives. Some focus on whether one's view is liberal or conservative, or on a continuum somewhere in between. From a conservative perspective, individuals are responsible for taking care of themselves, with little or no government intervention. This perspective suggests that government should provide a safety net only for those with the greatest need. From the liberal perspective, government is responsible for ensuring the availability of social and economic structures, including equitable access to support for those who cannot meet their own needs (Karger & Stoesz, 2004).

Another perspective contrasts residual and institutional social welfare. The residual perspective views social welfare as serving only those with the most problems or greatest need. This perspective often is associated with a values system that supports individualism and an expectation that people can, and should, take care of themselves and that those who are unable to

care for themselves are deficient in some way. In contrast, an institutional perspective holds that everyone has needs throughout the life cycle, and society is responsible for supporting those needs by providing services and benefits (Kirst-Ashman, 2006).

Thus, perspectives regarding societal responsibility for vulnerable members of society vary widely. As you follow the discussion of historical influences that have converged to shape our present social welfare structure, see whether you can identify the values positions that have contributed to the formulation of social policy.

Our English Heritage

In England, before mercantilism, care for the poor was a function primarily of the Church. By extending themselves through charitable efforts to those in need, parishioners fulfilled a required sacred function. The Church's resources usually were sufficient to provide the relief that was made available to the poor.

The feudal system itself provided a structure that met the needs of most of the population. The only significant government legislation during this time was passed as a result of the Black Death—bubonic plague—which began in 1348 and killed approximately two-thirds of the English population within 2 years. In 1349, King Edward III mandated the Statute of Laborers Act, which required all able-bodied individuals to accept any type of employment within their parish. Furthermore, it laid the groundwork for residency requirements by forbidding able-bodied persons from leaving their parish. (This later became an intrinsic part of American social welfare legislation.)

Some 150 years later, with the breakdown of the feudal system and the division of the Church during the Reformation, organized religious efforts no longer could cope with the increasing needs of the poor. Without the Church or the feudal manor to rely on in times of need, the poor were left to fend for themselves. This frequently led to malnutrition, transience, poor health, broken families, and even death.

As Europe struggled with the transition from an agricultural society to an industrial one, the numbers of dislodged persons increased. Many of the poor found their way into cities, lured by the prospect of work in manufacturing facilities. The Industrial Revolution, however, was still in its early stages, and jobs were insufficient to accommodate the growing population. Further, most of those who were seeking jobs were illiterate and lacked the skills necessary to work in a manufacturing environment. Turned away by the cities, large bands of poor unemployed people wandered the countryside begging for whatever meager assistance they could get. A sense of lawlessness often accompanied them. Local officials were pressed to find suitable solutions for the homeless, the poor, and dependent children. Unable to address the problems on their own, local officials turned to Parliament for a solution.

Parliament responded by passing the **Elizabethan Poor Law** (Elizabeth 43) in 1601. This legislation is significant because it attempted to codify earlier legislation as well as establish a national policy regarding the poor. The Elizabethan Poor Law delineated "categories" of assistance, a practice retained in our current social welfare legislation.

1. *Individuals considered to be "worthy."* These were individuals for whom impoverishment was not viewed as a fraudulent attempt to secure assistance. They included the aged, the chronically ill, individuals with disabilities, and orphaned children. The worthy poor typically were placed in almshouses (poorhouses), where they received minimal care. This practice was called *indoor relief* because it provided services to the poor within institutions. In some instances children were placed with families and often were required to work for their keep.

2. *The able-bodied poor.* For those classified in this way, programs were less humane. Some of the able-bodied were placed in prisons, others were sent to workhouses, and still others served as indentured servants in local factories or as slave laborers on local farms. Unlike the worthy poor, the able-bodied poor were assumed to be malingerers who lacked the motivation to secure gainful employment. The treatment they received was designed to deter others from following in their footsteps, as well as to punish them for their transience and idleness.

The Elizabethan Poor Law was enacted primarily to standardize the way the poor were to be managed, not because of altruism and concern for them. This law is significant because it established the guiding philosophy of public assistance legislation in England until 1834 and in the United States until the Social Security Act was passed in 1935. Its influence also can be seen in the Personal Responsibility and Work Opportunity Act of 1996 (commonly called "welfare reform"). The important components of the Elizabethan Poor Law (Axinn & Stern, 2004, p. 10) in relation to U.S. policies toward the poor are the establishment of

- clear (but limited) government responsibility for those in need,
- government authority to force people to work,
- government enforcement of family responsibility,
- the principle of local responsibility, and
- strict residence requirements.

More than 200 years later, the Poor Law Reform Act of 1834 was passed in reaction to concerns that the Elizabethan Poor Law of 1601 was not being implemented as intended. The prevailing belief then was that liberalized supervision of the programs for the poor had served as a disincentive for work and, in effect, had created dependency on the program. The Poor Law Reform Act mandated that all forms of outdoor relief (assistance to people in their homes) be abolished and that the full intention of the provisions of the Poor Law of 1601 be rigidly enforced. Furthermore, the act established the "principle of least eligibility," which prescribed that no assistance be provided in an amount that left the recipient better off than the lowest-paid worker. This principle also served as a basic tenet of early American social welfare legislation and public welfare programs today.

Social Welfare in Colonial America

Early American settlers brought a religious heritage that emphasized charity and the mutual interdependence of people. They also brought with them the heritage of the Elizabethan Poor Law. America in colonial times was an undeveloped and often hostile land that required early settlers to work hard to survive. The country had no formal government network for providing assistance on any significant basis. Those in need were aided by their neighbors or by members of religious organizations. As the population increased, many colonies passed laws requiring new arrivals to demonstrate their ability to sustain themselves or, in the absence of such ability, locate sponsors who were willing to pledge their support for them. For the most part, transients were "warned out" and returned to their place of residence or back to England (Axinn & Stern, 2004). Times were difficult, the Puritan work ethic was embedded deeply, and little surplus was available to distribute to those in need. The names of habitual paupers were posted routinely at the townhouse in many towns and villages.

Because much of colonial America was based on a feudal system, with indentured servants in the mid-colonies (more than half of all colonists

came to this country as indentured servants) and slavery in the southern colonies, the pauper class clearly lacked freedom. Often overlooked, however, was a set of harsh laws—reasonably enforced up until the time of independence—requiring masters to meet the basic survival needs of servants and slaves. Ironically, in the maturation from a plantation to a pre-industrial economy, economic uncertainty also increased. Consequently, public relief was the largest expenditure in the public budgets of most major cities at the time of the American Revolution.

The rigid restraint of the Poor Law philosophy was consistent with the extreme scarcity in the colonial economy. Colonial law stressed **indoor relief,** in which assistance was provided in the homes of others for those who could not care for themselves. In effect, though, the truly poor (paupers) often were segregated within almshouses as punishment for being poor and were put to tasks that at least paid for their meager keep. The apprenticeship of children reflected a belief in family controls for children and emphasized work and training for productive employment. Also, the deification of the work ethic and the belief that pauperism was a visible symbol of sin permitted a harsh response to those in need as a means of saving their souls.

Changing Patterns after the Revolution

Between the time of the American Revolution and the Civil War, several broad patterns of welfare emerged, all of which were consistent with the basic tenets of the Elizabethan Poor Law. The American separation of church and state doctrine forced the connection between parish and local welfare office to be severed. Nevertheless, many states—most, in fact—retained a religious connection, with the requirement that at least one member of the welfare board be a "licensed preacher." Local governments accepted grudgingly the role of welfare caretaker and adopted rigid residency requirements.

The most important shift in this period was from indoor relief to **outdoor relief**—providing cash assistance that allowed individuals to remain in their own homes. Outdoor aid, with its reliance on in-kind aid and work-relief projects, was more adaptable to the volatile economics of the first half of the 19th century.

Another significant movement during this period was the shift away from public-sector to private-sector welfare, or so-called voluntary welfare. The responsibility for welfare, therefore, was left to charitable institutions rather than remaining a public concern.

Caring for the Urban Poor

As the new nation grew, cities began to appear on the eastern seaboard. The immigrants who arrived regularly often had difficulty finding jobs, and a large population of displaced poor began to emerge. People who were interested in those who were less fortunate sought avenues for meeting their needs. Attaching the poor to subsistence-level employment usually was the goal, but concern arose over meeting their basic needs until they could derive income through employment. While almshouses often were used to care for the chronic poor, outdoor relief was increasingly accepted as a suitable way to care for the poor.

One of the earliest organizations to seek a formal solution to the problems of poverty was the New York Society for the Prevention of Pauperism, established in 1817. Following the precedent established by Thomas Chalmers in England, the society divided the city into districts and assigned "friendly visitors" to work in each district to assess and respond to the needs of the poor (Axinn & Stern, 2004). In 1843, the Association for Improving the Conditions of the Poor was established in New York City to coordinate relief efforts for the unemployed. One significant technique the association introduced—and which the social work profession widely practices today—was the requirement that relief could not be dispensed until the individual's needs were assessed so agencies providing relief could do so more effectively.

Perhaps the most effective relief organization for the poor was the Charity Organization Society (COS) of Buffalo, New York. A private organization modeled after the COS in London, it was founded by wealthy citizens who embraced the work ethic, yet had compassion for the deserving poor. The COS sought to infuse efficiency and economy in programs serving the poor, as well as organize charities in an effort to prevent duplication of services and reduce dependency on charitable efforts. Like the Association for Improving the Conditions of the Poor that preceded it, the COS emphasized the necessity of assessing the condition of the poor and added the dimension of engaging "friendly visitors" with clients in an effort to guide, rehabilitate, and help prepare for self-sufficiency. The COS had little sympathy for chronic beggars, viewing them essentially as hopeless derelicts.

Caring for Specific Populations

Many other private charities emerged during the 1800s to address special problem areas such as care of orphan children and of the deaf, blind, and mentally ill. For the most part, these services were sponsored by state or local governments and provided largely in institutional settings that were physically removed from the community. Shortly thereafter, a growing number of socially active citizens expressed grave concern over the treatment that residents of these institutions received.

Dorothea Dix, a philanthropist and social reformer, traveled throughout the United States observing the care given the "insane" and was appalled by what she saw. She sought to convince President Franklin Pierce to allocate federal and land grant monies for establishing federal institutions to care for individuals with mental illness. Although she initially was unsuccessful in changing the system, Dix was successful in raising public awareness about the problems of people with mental illness, and her work set the tone for an era of significant reform during the mid- to late-1800s.

Toward the latter part of the 19th century, several states developed centralized agencies to oversee the activities of charitable institutions. State charity agencies sought better quality of care for institutional inmates, as well as greater efficiency and economy in providing relief to the poor. With the federal government assuming only limited responsibility for selected groups (veterans, for example), state agencies became the primary public resource for addressing the problems of the poor and debilitated (Day, 2005).

A new wave of immigrants from southern Europe entering the United States in the late 1800s and early 1900s added to the burden of unemployment, homelessness, and poverty. **Jane Addams,** a social worker, was instrumental in creating the settlement house movement as a resource for preparing immigrants to live in a new society. Patterned after Toynbee Hall in London, Addams established **Hull House** in 1869 in one of the worst slum neighborhoods of Chicago. By addressing the problems of deficient housing, low wages, child labor, juvenile delinquency and disease, Hull House and other settlement houses became major social action agencies.

Here we must point out the ideological conflict between the COS movement and the settlement house movement, as well as the contributions of each to contemporary social work practice. COS proponents believed that urban poverty was rooted in moral and character deficiencies and

that poverty could be abolished by helping poor people recognize and correct their flawed character. The COS movement embraced social Darwinism as its theoretical underpinning for helping (or not helping) the poor, and labeled this process "scientific charity." The focus of COS workers was on clients' self-support, but only after a thorough investigation and determination of their worthiness. The primary emphasis of COS agencies was on helping the poor find social and economic salvation through work (Axinn & Stern, 2004).

The settlement house movement was guided by a completely different set of principles. Clients of settlement houses were viewed as able, normal individuals. No effort was made to separate the "worthy" poor from the "unworthy" poor. The emphasis was on providing neighborhood services and community development. The settlement house movement embraced a philosophy that combined individual achievement with satisfying social relations and social responsibility. Settlement house workers took a holistic perspective of the person in society. The overall mission of the settlement house movement was social reform (Axinn & Stern, 2004).

Both the COS and the settlement house movements left an indelible mark on contemporary social work practice. The COS movement was the forerunner of clinical social work, with its concentration on individuals and families, scientific methods to determine need, and specialized training of social service providers. The settlement house movement was the forerunner of nonclinical social work, with a primary emphasis on individuals as part of their community, social needs assessment, community organizing, social reform and political action, understanding and appreciating the strengths of cultural diversity, and research on the community (Axinn & Stern, 2004).

The current debate in social work circles about whether nonclinical social work is indeed legitimate social work has its roots in the ideological differences inherent in these two early approaches to social welfare. You should be aware of these differences because of their direct impact on how social welfare policy is formulated and carried out.

Another social welfare policy issue debated in the 1800s—and still debated today—is whether social welfare services should be provided by public or by private entities. During the 1800s, the parameters of public versus private welfare programs were defined more clearly. Public welfare benefit programs relied on taxation for funding. Private welfare programs were funded through the voluntary contributions of individuals or philanthropic organizations. No clearly defined limits determined what types of benefits either public or private (voluntary) agencies would offer. As a result, services often overlapped. Public agencies were administered by government agencies at local, state, or federal levels. Private agencies often had religious or philanthropic sponsorship or received contributions from citizens.

Public and private agencies alike provided a myriad of services throughout the 1800s and into the 1900s. Following World War I, the nation entered a period of significant social change and prosperity. The economy improved, and the nation was euphoric. This mood ended abruptly in 1929 with the economic downturn that led to the **Great Depression.** In short order, conditions became grave. Businesses that had been considered stable ceased production, banks declared bankruptcy, and millions of workers lost their

The Great Depression created immense hardship for millions of Americans. Families who became homeless formed tent cities in many areas of the country, supporting each other to survive.

Courtesy of the Franklin D. Roosevelt Library and Museum. #53227 jobs. Savings were depleted as banks collapsed and businesses failed, and a large portion of the American population was left penniless, homeless, and without resources as unemployment increased.

As jobs became scarce, the unemployed had nowhere to turn. Organized charities quickly exhausted their limited resources. Pessimism and despair were rampant, and many felt hopeless. Unemployment insurance was nonexistent, and no federal guarantees existed for monies lost in bank failures. The economic disaster resulted in a state of chaos never experienced before on American soil. As conditions worsened, homes were lost through foreclosed mortgages.

The New Deal

Although state and local governments attempted to respond to the fallout from the Great Depression to the extent that resources permitted, many of the poorer states lacked the resources to provide even temporary relief. In New York, an Emergency Relief Act passed, providing public employment, in-kind relief (food, clothing, and shelter), and limited cash benefits. This act later served as a model for federal relief programs.

Although he sympathized with those victimized by the Depression, President Herbert Hoover was convinced that the most effective solution to the Depression and its consequences would be to offer incentives for business to regain its footing, expand, and provide jobs for the jobless. In 1932, Hoover was swept from office by public discontent over his policies and was replaced by Franklin Delano Roosevelt, former governor of New York.

One of President Roosevelt's first actions was to institute emergency legislation that provided assistance for the jobless and poor. This legislation, coined the "**New Deal,**" marked the first time in history that the federal government became engaged directly in providing relief. It also provided an interpretation of the health and welfare provisions of the Constitution that established a historical precedent in mandating the federal government to assume health and welfare responsibility for its citizens. The statement was clear: Citizens were, first and foremost, citizens of the United States and, second, residents of specific states. This policy opened the door for later federal legislation in the areas of civil rights, fair employment practices, school busing, public assistance, and a variety of other social programs.

One of the first attempts to supply relief for depression victims was the Federal Emergency Relief Act (FERA). Modeled after New York's Emergency Relief Act, FERA provided food, clothing, and shelter allowances for the homeless and displaced. In a cooperative relationship with states, the federal government made monies available to states to administer the relief programs. States were responsible for establishing agencies for that purpose and also were required to contribute state funds, where possible, to broaden the resource base available to those in need. This established the precedent for "matching grants," which later became an integral requirement of public assistance programs.

Additional federal emergency legislation was enacted to provide public employment for those who were out of work. The Works Progress Administration (WPA), created in 1935 to provide public service jobs, ultimately employed approximately 8 million workers over the duration of the Depression. States and local governments identified needed projects and supplied necessary materials for laborers, who were paid by the WPA. Many public schools, streets, parks, post office buildings, state college buildings, and related public projects were constructed under the auspices of the WPA.

Youth programs also were established. Perhaps the most noteworthy was the Civilian Conservation Corps (CCC), designed to protect natural resources and to improve and develop public recreational areas. Primarily a forest camp activity, the CCC provided young men between the ages of 17 and 23 with jobs, food, clothing, and shelter. Wages were nominal (about $25 per month), and the major portion of the wages ($20 per month) was conscripted and sent home to help support families. CCC workers improved and developed many national parks. The National Youth Administration (NYA), also established under the WPA, gave work-study assistance to high school and college youth as an incentive to remain in school. In addition, the NYA provided part-time jobs for out-of-school students to learn job skills and increase their employability (Axinn & Stern, 2004). Also, FERA programs extended low-interest loans to farmers and small business operators. These programs enabled those activities to survive and become sources of employment for the jobless.

The New Deal legislation offered a temporary solution to the crisis generated by the Great Depression. The jobless found jobs, the hungry were fed, and the homeless received shelter. Perhaps of more importance, the nation felt the full impact of system changes. The issue of blaming poverty on idleness and laziness was put to rest—at least temporarily.

The Social Security Act

Congress passed, and President Roosevelt signed into law, the **Social Security Act** on August 4, 1935. This act remains the most significant piece of social legislation ever enacted in the United States. It also paved the way for greater federal involvement in health and welfare.

The act reflected a realization that our economic system was subject to vacillations that invariably would leave many people without resources because of unemployment. It also acknowledged that older adults needed income

security as an incentive to retire. This act was designed to be a permanent resource system administered by the federal government. Its provisions were outlined under three major categories (covered in more depth in chapter 7): social insurance, public assistance, and health and welfare services.

Social Insurance

Social insurance, commonly referred to as **Social Security,** is based on the premise that individuals and their families cannot always provide the financial resources necessary to meet their needs. Social insurance became the basis for financial support to the elderly, persons in poor health or with serious disabilities, individuals injured on the job, and dependents whose primary breadwinners were deceased. Funding for these social insurance programs comes from collective employees and government programs funded by taxes.

Social insurance under the Social Security Act initially included two important benefit programs:

1. Old Age, Survivors, and Disability Insurance (OASDI; see chapter 7); these three programs were based on taxes deducted from employees' wages and matched by employer contributions, and eligibility was based on participation earned through employment.
2. Unemployment insurance, in which employers contributed the funds, with the purpose of providing a source of income security for covered workers who had lost their jobs.

Benefits derived from these programs were considered to be a matter of right in that the recipients and their employers had paid "premiums" for the benefits they would receive. In many ways, social insurance was similar to private insurance, for which entitlement to benefits is directly related to beneficiary participation through contributions.

Public Assistance

The category of **public assistance** was based on "need" and was not established as a right earned through employment. It was administered by states with monies made available by states and matched by the federal government (matching grants). At the time, public assistance incorporated three components:

1. Old Age Assistance,
2. Aid to Dependent Children, and
3. Aid to the Blind.

In 1955, the Permanently and Totally Disabled component was added. Benefits under each of these programs were invariably limited and varied among the states according to each state's willingness to match federal funds.

Eligibility requirements were rigid and were enforced rigorously. Participation was based on a "means test," requiring applicants to demonstrate that they were hopelessly without resources. Recipients' private lives were opened to the scrutiny of welfare workers in an attempt to minimize fraud and to ensure that benefit levels did not exceed budgeted needs.

Perhaps the most controversial assistance program was Aid to Dependent Children (ADC). This program made limited funds available to mothers with dependent children when no man was present in the home. Because benefit levels were adjusted for family size (to a maximum of four children), concern arose that promiscuity and illegitimacy would be rewarded by increasing benefits as family size increased. Rigid cohabitation policies were instituted, mandating that mothers who were guilty of cohabitation would lose their grant funds entirely. Because most ADC recipients were able-bodied, there was added concern that welfare payments would be a disincentive for meeting financial needs through gainful employment. In many ways, ADC recipients were treated as the "unworthy" poor of the time and, as a consequence, often were dealt with in a punitive manner.

The public usually refers to public assistance as *welfare*. Because benefits are based on impoverishment and not earned through employment, participation in the program carries a stigma of personal imprudence, ineptness, or failure.

Health and Welfare Services

Programs authorized under **health and welfare services** provided for maternal and child care services, vocational rehabilitation, public health, and services for children with physical impairments. These services are discussed more fully in later chapters.

In the ensuing years, amendments to the Social Security Act extended each of these titles to cover more people. Social insurance later added health insurance (Medicare); and a health assistance program (Medicaid) was instituted for recipients of public assistance. The ADC assistance category was redefined as Aid to Families with Dependent Children (AFDC), and an AFDC–Unemployed Parent (AFDC-UP) provision was added so states could assist families under limited circumstances when an employable unemployed male was in the home. Only a few states opted to implement the AFDC-UP provisions. As requirements for participating in these programs became less stringent in the 1960s and 1970s, welfare rolls increased dramatically.

Social Welfare: The Post–Social Security and Welfare Reform Eras

The time since passage of the Social Security Act has been tumultuous, with three major wars, a longstanding cold war, followed by the fall of communism, periods of inflation and recession, the emergence of a global economy, an unprecedented terrorist attack on the United States, and increasing conflict throughout the world. Unemployment in the United States has varied from 12% of the workforce in 1979 to 4.7% (7.1 million individuals) in 2006. Nearly 40% of the marriages today end in divorce. Single-parent families, typically headed by females, have become a prominent family constellation. The population is aging at a rapid rate. Affordable housing is conspicuously absent throughout the country. The number of individuals with no health insurance is nearing 50 million. The cost of health care has escalated to a point of alarm.

All of these factors affect how the government responds to social needs. We now turn to a discussion of some of the more significant social welfare programs that have been instituted since the Social Security Act was passed in 1935.

The Great Society Programs

Attempts to broaden the activities of government in securing the rights of citizens and providing for personal, social, and economic development were introduced through social reform measures enacted during the Lyndon Johnson administration (1963–1968). This administration based many of its social programs on the premise that the environment in which an individual lives significantly influences personal outcomes. The so-called **Great Society** legislation promoted maximum opportunities for those in need, extending benefits of many existing programs and services designed to help the poor, the disabled, and the aged.

The Social Security Act was amended to provide for health care benefits to the aged under the Health Insurance Program (Medicare) and to public assistance recipients through the Health Assistance Program (Medicaid). Several pieces of new legislation designed to meet needs not specifically addressed through existing resources also were passed. The Older Americans Act (1965) established a legal base for developing senior luncheon programs, health screening, transportation, meals-on-wheels programs, and recreational activities. The Civil Rights Act (1964) sought to end discrimination in employment and in the use of public business facilities. It also was targeted toward nondiscriminatory extension of credit. Education bills were passed that sought to rectify many of the educational disadvantages experienced by children of the poor.

Perhaps the most significant—and controversial—effort to achieve social reform came through the Economic Opportunities Act of 1964, commonly called the War on Poverty. The objective of this act was to eliminate poverty through institutional change. Poverty traditionally was viewed as an individual matter, and its causes generally were thought to be the result of personal failure, lack of motivation, or personal choice. Those who designed the War on Poverty program came to a different conclusion. They considered poverty to be the result of inadequate social institutions that failed to provide opportunities for all citizens, and they concluded that traditional approaches to solving the problems of poverty were unsuccessful.

Changing the status of the poor would come not through working with them on an individual basis but, rather, through modifying institutions within a person's environment that produced the problems in the first place. Hence, programs under the Economic Opportunities Act were structured to offer the poor a greater likelihood of success by creating opportunities for their decision making and participation. Educational programs such as Head Start sought to extend relevant learning experiences to educationally disadvantaged children. Community Action Agencies encouraged the poor to become more vocal in community affairs and to organize efforts for community betterment.

Special employment incentives were generated to teach job skills. Youth Job Corps programs provided public service jobs contingent on youth remaining in school, thereby offering greater potential for employment upon graduation. Job Corps centers taught employment skills to teenage dropouts. Small-business loans were made to individuals with potential for developing businesses. Rural programs extended health and social services for the poor in rural areas.

In a nation boasting the highest standard of living in the world, it was believed that the scourge of poverty could be eliminated forever. The euphemism "war on poverty" was selected to rally the population to a full-scale commitment to overcome the enemy—poverty. Social action advocates found the climate produced by the Economic Opportunities Act favorable for their efforts. It was a heyday for the expansion of social programs, with spending often outstripping planning. But social legislation is invariably affected by the political climate. As government resources and attention were diverted to the Vietnam War, the domestic "war" soon was neglected and ultimately terminated.

Conservatism in the Mid-1960s and Early 1970s

The period from the mid-1960s through the mid-1970s was one of both domestic and foreign conflict. The anti-establishment movement in the United States was galvanized by the highly unpopular Vietnam War; rioting was occurring in the Watts section of Los Angeles; in Detroit, Martin Luther King was championing the cause of disenfranchised Americans; and inflation was depleting the buying power of those who were working.

In reaction to these disconcerting changes, a wave of conservatism emerged in the American public, leading to an effort to dismantle many of the social programs enacted during the New Deal and expanded through the Great Society programs. The welfare "establishment" was viewed as costly, ineffective, and counterproductive. The conservatives maintained that the federal government was much too large and cumbersome and that states could, and should, assume many functions.

Although federal involvement in public welfare programs had emerged largely because states lacked sufficient resources to provide needed supports, conservatives were convinced that states and localities were better suited to determine social welfare policies and administer social programs. One result was the reorganization—and

eventual termination—of the federal anti-poverty program. Several popular programs, such as Head Start and job training, were transferred to other government agencies. Under the Richard Nixon administration, a major welfare reform measure, the Family Assistance Program (FAP), was submitted for congressional approval. This measure, which was not enacted into law, would have eliminated the public assistance program and substituted a program designed to provide incentives for recipients to work without losing all of their government benefits. Often referred to as "workfare," proposed programs such as FAP require recipients to meet specific job-related requirements to continue to receive their welfare benefits. The expectation is that activities, such as job training, coaching, and work experience either as a volunteer or for limited pay, will improve job prospects and retention once a person is hired, leading to reductions in welfare rolls. Although many variations of "workfare" have been tried in recent years, few have worked well because full-time jobs that pay a living wage and health care benefits are few and far between, even if a recipient completes all of the required work-related programs. Although many congressional representatives and their constituents liked the proposed legislation, it did not pass because the level of defined need was far below the benefit levels already in place in the higher-paying states but higher than the benefits in more than half the states.

Countering this trend, public assistance programs for the aged, disabled, and blind were combined by enactment of the Supplemental Security Income (SSI) Act in 1974. SSI increased benefit levels for millions of recipients. AFDC continued to be funded and implemented under the federal-state arrangements already in effect.

Welfare Reform and the Late 1970s

Social welfare policymakers of the mid-1970s inherited a welfare system that had no positive constituency. Recipients, social workers, public officials, and tax-conscious groups agreed only on the inadequacy of the existing system. Each of the four constituencies had initiated a **welfare reform** effort, and each constituency had failed to achieve its reform, largely because of the others' opposition. The problems that had drawn such attention in earlier decades persisted. The rapidly expanding welfare costs in the years of Presidents Richard Nixon and Gerald Ford, in juxtaposition to the intractability of poverty, made welfare reform an urgent but unpleasant necessity.

Welfare reform continued to be an issue during the Carter administration, which proposed that $8.8 billion be appropriated to create as many as 1.4 million public service jobs. It was expected that 2 million persons would hold the jobs in a given year, as individuals were processed through these jobs on their way to regular employment. According to the proposal, most of the jobs would pay a minimum wage and be full-time, full-year jobs, yielding an annual income of $6,600.

In addition, families would receive an income supplement geared to family size. The jobs would not be eligible for the earned income tax credit (a refundable federal income tax credit for low income working individuals and families; if the tax credit exceeds the amount of taxes owed, those eligible persons who file an income tax claim receive a refund for the difference). A worker always would have an income incentive to move from the public job to regular employment in the public or private sector. Those eligible for the jobs would be adults—one per family—in the "expected to work" component of the second part of the program who could not find employment in the regular economy. These jobs were not to replace established public jobs, which removed labor unions' objections to the plan. Carter's proposal, however, was not adopted, and debate about the most effective way to overhaul the welfare system continued.

Cutbacks in the Reagan and Bush Years

The 1980s were characterized by a so-called **welfare devolution,** or relentless efforts to reduce and eliminate government social entitlement programs. Public expenditures for welfare were viewed as antithetical to economic progress. Mounting inflation was considered to be the result of federal domestic spending. The precarious state of the U.S. economy was thought to be the work of social progressives who had engineered the expansion of welfare programs and, as a result, caused the economy to falter. Many social support programs were either reduced dramatically or eliminated.

As part of his State of the Union message in 1982, President Reagan proposed his version of welfare reform, "New Federalism." The centerpiece was a plan whereby the states would assume financial and administrative responsibility for food stamps and AFDC while the federal government would assume responsibility for the Medicaid program. This reform was dubbed the "welfare swap." The plan went through a number of variations before the administration dropped it as politically infeasible.

Following his reelection in 1984, President Reagan again began to push for reshaping welfare responsibilities among the various layers of government. A presidential task force was appointed, which was to issue its report after the congressional elections in 1986. That election resulted in a Democratic landslide, and the responsibility for welfare reform shifted from the White House to Capitol Hill.

President George H. W. Bush's administration continued to be influenced by a conservative view of welfare. As the Cold War wound down, progressives hoped that monies appropriated for defense spending would be directed toward domestic programs. Meanwhile, welfare costs continued to escalate. In 1988, the Democratic Congress passed the **Family Support Act,** hailed by proponents of welfare reform as the most significant piece of domestic legislation enacted since the Social Security Act in 1935. The Family Support Act mandated that states provide job opportunities and basic skills (JOBS) programs for most AFDC recipients (some, such as those with very young children and those with health problems, were exempted from participation).

The act also provided as many as 12 months of Medicaid (health care) and child care after recipients found jobs, to ease the transition from welfare to work without loss of income. The act also mandated that states provide AFDC-UP benefits for a limited time to families with previously employed males who were unable to find employment. The act further required stronger enforcement of child support payments by absent parents. States were not required to implement some parts of the act until 1992.

The Family Support Act never materialized as a major piece of welfare reform legislation. The federal government took an inordinate amount of time to publish the regulations governing the act, and funding for its programs was inadequate. Jobs that paid a living wage for former welfare recipients failed to materialize. Attempts to mobilize the private sector to support the program proved more difficult than anticipated. In short, the program was doomed to failure before it even got off the ground.

The Clinton Years

By 1992, the political landscape of welfare reform had shifted again. Bill Clinton, the Democratic presidential candidate, was a "New Democrat" who had been instrumental, as governor of Arkansas, in support of the Family Support Act of 1988. Clinton sought a wider role for the states in the design of federal welfare programs. More significantly, as a "political centrist," he aimed to distance himself from "liberal Democratic reform" that also had been instrumental in passing the 1988 legislation. Clinton promised to "end welfare as we know it." The goal of the reform was to make welfare "a second chance, not a way of life" (Clinton, 1997). The cornerstones of Clinton's reform agenda were portrayed as employment readiness, parental responsibility, and state discretion.

Lawmakers at all levels of government and of both parties now were demanding that welfare recipients be required to take more responsibility for ending, or at least easing, their dependence on public support. The clamor for change was being driven by a significant shift to the right in public mood and a much-increased effort to reduce the federal deficit.

Republicans won both houses of Congress in the 1994 national elections. Various coalitions and individual members of Congress introduced many reform measures in the 104th congressional session. Nearly all reform measures proposed limiting the length of stays on welfare, restricting the right to welfare of unmarried mothers under the age of 18, and imposing far more stringent work requirements. Perhaps most disturbing to members of the social work community were the efforts to end AFDC as a national government entitlement program.

The landmark welfare reform legislation that passed in 1996 did precisely that. Under the Personal Responsibility and Work Opportunity Act of 1996, each state was charged with administering various assistance programs, including AFDC, with a change in name to Temporary Assistance for Needy Families (TANF), at the direction of state legislatures with minimal federal guidelines and reciprocal federal funding. The thrust of the reform measures was to move recipients off the welfare rolls and toward self-sufficiency by engaging in work, work-training, or education programs designed to enable them to develop skills essential for employment.

Many states, however, implemented "work first" programs, moving recipients into jobs without training. Although these programs reduced the welfare rolls because the economy was strong, most recipients who moved off TANF entered "dead-end," minimum-wage jobs without health care or other benefits. Recipients were allowed a maximum of 2 years to find employment. Those who failed to do so faced a significant reduction or termination of their benefits. This approach presumes that mandatory work requirements would reduce, if not eliminate, dependence on welfare benefits.

The George W. Bush Years

When he became President of the United States in 2000, George W. Bush ushered in a new era of social welfare policy. He argued that government cannot solve every problem, but it can encourage people and communities to help themselves and to help one another. He asserted that the truest kind of compassion is to help citizens build lives of their own and termed his philosophy and approach **compassionate conservatism:** It is compassionate to actively help fellow citizens in need, yet conservative to insist on responsibility and results.

Bush's campaign of compassionate conservatism resonated well with a broad range of Americans who were strongly influenced by the anti-welfare rhetoric of the late 1990s but who also believed in the need to reach out and help those less fortunate. In many ways, the principle of compassionate conservatism reflected the social welfare principles of colonial America: limited government intervention, personal responsibility, family values, and the role of the faith community and the private sector in addressing the social welfare needs of the citizenry.

Some opponents have argued that the notion of compassionate conservatism was a carefully disguised cover for a much more punitive approach to addressing the social welfare needs of the country—driven by a conservative religious element, a new Puritanism, and the interests of big business. The search for truth in this matter was interrupted abruptly by the terrorist attacks on America in September 2001, the ensuing global war on terrorism, dissension among world leaders about the war in Iraq, and the search for a solution to peace in the Middle East.

A more compelling question, perhaps, is not, "What are the Bush administration's motives in pursuing an agenda of compassionate conservatism?" but, rather, "How can the social work community operate within the framework of this agenda—which seems to be as strong today as it was when it was introduced—to ensure that the social welfare system in the United States is not dismantled to the point at which it no longer is responsive to the needs of the country's citizens

TABLE 1.1
Government Expenditures by Function

Function	Billions of Dollars		
	Federal	**State/Local**	**Total**
General public service	36.3	147.5	183.8
National defense	399.9	—	399.9
Public order and safety	26.3	192.4	218.7
Economic affairs	90.3	198.9	289.2
Housing and community services	1.3	28.2	29.5
Health	55.4	43.9	99.3
Recreation and culture	3.2	22.9	26.1
Education	6.8	537.2	544.0
Income security	8.6	58.8	67.4
Total	**628.1**	**1,229.8**	**1,857.9**

Source: *Government Consumption Expenditures and Gross Investment by Function* (Washington, DC: Bureau of Economic Analysis, 2006).

and incapable of being rebuilt without a huge investment in public funds?"

With the economic downturn in recent years and attention—and funds—devoted to the war in Iraq, priorities for spending at all levels of government have come under increasing debate. In 2007, the federal spending priority has become defense, the state priority has become the public education of school-age children, and the local priority has become public safety (see Table 1.1 and Figure 1.1).

Without question, the social welfare paradigm in the United States has shifted. Whether for better or for worse depends on one's perspective. As with any paradigm shift, the ways of the old paradigm are no longer relevant. The real challenge to the social work profession is how to acknowledge the change while sustaining the value system upon which the profession is based and ensuring that a basic system of services is available to

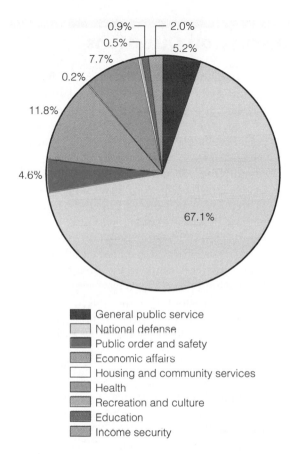

General public service

National defense

Public order and safety

Economic affairs

Housing and community services

Health

Recreation and culture

Education

Income security

FIGURE 1.1

Federal Government Expenditures, 2005

Source: Government Consumption Expenditures and Gross Investment by Function (Washington, DC: Bureau of Economic Analysis, 2006)

support those who are unable to care for themselves through no fault of their own.

The administrations of both Bill Clinton and George W. Bush concluded that the welfare reform legislation has been a resounding success because it achieved the intended outcomes—a reduction in the welfare rolls and expenditures for welfare programs. And this it has done. Nationwide, the drop in the welfare rolls is more than 50%; in some states, the drop is as much as 80% to 85%. Americans seem to be satisfied

with these results, and until discontent over the war in Iraq and issues other than welfare reform surfaced, they returned conservative politicians to office and increased their representation at all levels of government.

But there is another side to this story. A rapidly growing underclass of individuals in the United States, even though they work at one and often two jobs, are unable to lift themselves and their families out of poverty. These families no longer qualify for government assistance, yet they are unable to move out of poverty. Children born into these families are at high risk for repeating this pattern for themselves and their families. The long-term impacts of the latest round of welfare reform have been studied by many entities, including the federal government and private groups—foundations, think tanks, and universities. The Joint Center for Poverty Research, operated by Northwestern University and the University of Chicago (www.jcpr.org), and the Urban Institute (www.uran.org) offer comprehensive looks at the latest information on impacts of the 1996 welfare reform legislation.

Other controversial social welfare issues—such as ensuring the solvency of the country's social security system, a steadily growing homeless population, lack of affordable child care, and millions of families with no or inadequate health insurance—remain unresolved. Hurricanes Katrina and Rita, which destroyed New Orleans and other parts of the South in 2005, brought new attention to issues of poverty—and the relationship of poverty and race. But rather than resulting in coordinated assistance to impacted families and communities that could have produced long-term change, the aftermath of Hurricanes Katrina and Rita and other critical domestic social welfare issues have taken a back seat to increasingly volatile foreign policy issues, including waging a global war on terrorism and achieving peace in the Middle East. The longer these domestic social issues go unaddressed, the more difficult it will be to resolve them. The social work profession must put domestic social welfare issues at the center of attention of legislators, policymakers, and the general public.

Summary

Like all domestic policy, social welfare is in a constant state of evolution. Policies and practice historically have emerged from a set of choices— national or state, government or voluntary, expanding or restrictive. Social welfare in the United States will never be satisfactory to everyone. Some people will always believe we have made the wrong choices. Social welfare policy cannot escape the contradictions in its dual goals: to respond compassionately to those in need and at the same time to structure the compassion in such a way that the natural tendencies of people to work, save, and care for their own are not eroded.

Key Terms and InfoTrac® College Edition

The terms below are defined in the Glossary. To learn more about the key terms and topics in this chapter, enter the following search terms using InfoTrac or the World Wide Web:

Addams, Jane	indoor relief
compassionate	laissez-faire
conservatism	New Deal
Dix, Dorothea	outdoor relief
Elizabethan	public assistance
Poor Law	social insurance
Family Support Act	Social Security
Great Depression	Social Security Act
Great Society	social work
health and welfare	social welfare
services	values
Hull House	welfare devolution
humanitarianism	welfare reform

Discussion Questions

1. Compare the various values perspectives discussed in this chapter: institutional and residual, liberal and conservative. Give examples of how these different perspectives shape social welfare programs. What are your perspectives?
2. Identify the conditions that led to enactment of the Elizabethan Poor Law. Which aspects of that law can be found in the U.S. social welfare system today?
3. Discuss the differences between indoor relief and outdoor relief. Give an example of each. Which do you think is the better approach for assisting the poor? Why?
4. In what manner did the public assistance provisions of the Social Security Act differ from those of the Economic Opportunity Act (War on Poverty)?
5. What effect did passage of the Social Security Act have on the federal government's role in health and welfare? What components of the Social Security Act can be seen in today's social welfare programs?
6. In various forms, "workfare" has been attempted as a means of reducing welfare rolls. What is workfare? Why has it not been entirely effective in reducing welfare rolls? What approach do you suggest to reduce the number of individuals on public assistance? Why do you suggest that approach?
7. Do you think that political position (conservative, independent, liberal) should be a primary consideration in shaping social policy? Why?
8. Compare the values perspectives upon which the War on Poverty and compassionate conservatism are based. Does the point of time in history shape the values perspectives existing at that time and, in turn, the proposed outcomes to deal with social problems such as poverty?

On the Internet

www.aecf.org/

www.cbpp.org/

www.clasp.org/

www.financeprojectinfo.org/WIN/

www.jcpr.org

www.urban.org

References

Axinn, J., & Stern, M. (2004). *Social welfare: A history of the American response to need* (6th ed.). Boston: Allyn & Bacon.

Clinton, B. (1997). *Between hope and history: Meeting America's challenges for the 21st century.* New York: Random House.

Day, P. (2005). *A new history of social welfare* (5th ed.). Boston: Allyn & Bacon.

Karger, J., & Stoesz, D. (2004). *American social welfare policy: A pluralist approach* (5th ed.). Boston: Allyn & Bacon.

Kirst-Ashman, K. (2006). *Introduction to social work and social welfare: Critical thinking perspectives.* Belmont, CA: Wadsworth.

Marson, S. M., & MacLeod, E. (1996). The first social worker. *New Social Worker, 3*(1), 11.

Reid, P. N. (1995). *Encyclopedia of social work* (Vol. 3, pp. 2206–2225). Washington, DC: NASW Press.

U.S. Department of Commerce (2006). *Government consumption expenditures and gross investment by function.* Washington, D.C.: Bureau of Economic Analysis.

Suggested Further Readings

Albelda, R., & Withorn, A. (Eds.). (2002). *Lost ground: Welfare reform, poverty, and beyond.* Cambridge, MA: South End Press.

Chatterjee, P. (1996). *Approaches to the welfare state.* Washington, DC: NASW Press.

Danziger, S., & Gottschalk, P. (1995). *America unequal.* Cambridge, MA: Harvard University Press.

Dash, L. (1996). *Rosa Lee: A mother and her family in urban America.* New York: HarperCollins.

DiNitto, D., & Cummins, L. (2006). *Social welfare: Politics and public policy* (6th ed.). Boston: Allyn & Bacon.

Ehrenreich, B. (2002). *Nickel and dimed: On (not) getting by in America.* New York: Owl Press.

Jansson, B. (2001). *The reluctant welfare state: American social welfare policies—past, present, and future.* Belmont, CA: Wadsworth/Thomson Learning.

Schorr, A. (2001). *Welfare reform: Failure & remedies.* Westport, CT: Praeger.

Seccombe, K. (1999). *"So you think I drive a Cadillac?": Welfare recipients' perspectives on the system and its reform.* Boston: Allyn & Bacon.

Trattner, W. I. (1999). *From Poor Law to welfare state: A history of social welfare in America* (6th ed.). New York: Free Press.

CHAPTER 2

Social Work and Other Helping Professions

Consider the following scenarios:

- In a community drug abuse center, Jimmy Johnson is leading a group of teenage boys, helping them develop skills that will counter peer pressure from friends who are still using drugs.
- In another part of the city, Tony Gonzalez, a medical social worker, assists clients and their families in coping with the effects of illness and in developing resources that will provide support while family members are in the hospital or convalescing after a hospital stay.
- Just down the street, Charlotte Ray, a social worker, is working with a small group of pregnant teenagers on issues of health care, relationships, and decision making surrounding their pregnancies.
- Candace McNabb is a social worker employed by the local community council, where she assists the staff in identifying needed services and developing community resources to meet the identified needs.
- Maria Herrera, a social worker with the adult probation department, helps clients find employment and educational resources so they can choose a different life path that doesn't involve crime.

- Amy Lu, a social worker for a battered women's shelter, aids women and their children in locating safe havens while they develop coping skills that will enable them to live lives free from threatening attacks.
- In a rural area several hundred miles away, Jackson Lee is a social worker for the Department of Human Services. His generalist skills in social work are helpful in dealing with a wide variety of problems with few organized resources to address them.
- Peter Thacker and Jean Reeves, social workers at a senior activity center serving three counties, oversee a group of volunteers who are preparing lunches for the meals-on-wheels program that will be delivered to homebound elderly adults.
- At the large army base not too far away, social worker Lorenzo Vasquez visits a family struggling to care for three young children, including twin toddlers, while the children's mother is stationed in Iraq.
- Across the globe, Jason Stewart, a social worker with an international development group, finds his generalist social work skills helpful in aiding refugees from a war-torn village begin to rebuild their lives and homes.

These social workers are representative of the broad and diverse positions held by social workers throughout the world. Social workers are found in a wide variety of local, state, and federal agencies as professionals who engage individuals, families, groups, organizations, and communities in seeking solutions to unmet needs.

Social work practice demands from its practitioners the utmost in intellect, creativity, skill, and knowledge. It is an exciting, challenging profession. Students who have the aptitude and desire to prepare for a career in the helping professions may find social work well suited to their needs and interests. In this chapter we explore the professional culture, activities, knowledge base, and skills incorporated into social work practice. First, though, we examine why people have unresolved problems and why they need professional assistance in seeking solutions.

Why Do People Have Problems?

Social workers deal with problems that inhibit optimal functioning for individuals, families, groups, organizations, and communities. Among the many problems that professional social workers help people address are poverty, marital conflict, parent–child relationships, delinquency, abuse and neglect, substance abuse, and mental and emotional stress.

Why do individuals develop problems to the extent that they need outside assistance? No rational person deliberately plans to develop debilitating problems. No child plans to spend a life in poverty, nor does an adolescent choose a life of mental illness. What newly married couple, in love and looking forward to a joyful future together, plan for marital disharmony, family violence, or divorce? Why, then, do these problems emerge? Why do some couples have happy, satisfying marriages while others move from marriage to marriage without finding satisfaction? Why do some people prosper and climb the occupational and income ladders readily while others remain deeply enmeshed in poverty? Are these situations a matter of personal choice? Of course not! Problems in social functioning result from a mix of many factors. We will briefly examine the factors that contribute to adaptation.

Genetics and Heredity

From the biological standpoint, people are born with many of the physiological characteristics of our ancestors. Some individuals have a tendency to be tall, others short; some are lean, others heavy; some are physically attractive, others less attractive; and so on. Some presumably have greater intellectual potential than others; some are more agile, others less so. To an extent, these characteristics affect adaptation and, indeed, opportunities throughout life. For example, regardless of desire or ability, a 5-foot, 6-inch male would have extreme difficulty becoming a professional basketball player. Regardless of desire or skill, opportunity clearly is affected by physical characteristics. We encourage you to think of other examples in which genetic or hereditary factors might impose limitations on social behavior or opportunities.

Psychobiological approaches to behavioral dysfunctions focus on identifying anomalies in body chemistry and studying how environmental stress converges with those anomalies to produce maladaptive behavior. For example, conditions such as schizophrenia, depression, and chronic anxiety are widely believed to be genetically linked.

Socialization

Whatever limits heredity may impose, individuals develop as social beings through the process of **socialization.** Social behavior is learned behavior, acquired through interactions with other human beings. Parents are the primary source of early socialization experiences, and family culture has a significant impact on the development of values, priorities, and role prescriptions. Families are not the only source of social development, though. Neighbors, playmates, and acquaintances from school and other community institutions also play a part.

Lower-income parents and wealthy parents, for example, may socialize their children in different ways because the resources and problem-solving opportunities vary so much. Thus, as children develop, their behaviors are shaped by the learning opportunities available to them. Our thoughts and mental attitudes are as much a product of learning as the skills we develop. Children who grow up in at-risk families often learn inappropriate techniques of problem solving.

Cultural Differences

Behaviors that seem to conflict with broader societal norms and expectations may be attributed to cultural differences. Traditional customs and behaviors of some groups differ considerably from the expectations of the majority group and create dissonance, which results in behavior that is interpreted as maladaptive or dysfunctional. The United States takes pride in, and has been enriched by, immigrants from around the world. Many of our social institutions expect immigrants to adapt and assimilate to the dominant culture, but trying to meet these expectations may be difficult for them. Language differences and cultural traits often result in stereotyping, categorizing individuals as "out-group" members, and imposing barriers to social opportunities. How to balance celebrating and maintaining individual cultures with collective contributions to the common good of all requires further exploration of environmental factors.

Environmental Factors

Geography, climate, and resources all affect quality of life and opportunities available for satisfactory growth and development. These factors vary widely throughout the world. Added to the environmental factors are the economic and political forces that largely determine the availability of opportunities and resources around which people seek to organize their lives. Smog-infested, polluted areas contribute to various health problems. Unpredictable economic trends may result in loss of jobs for certain segments of the population. Discrimination limits opportunities for career development and impedes adequate employment.

The environment is a major element in the opportunity structure. It can serve as a stimulus for producing life's satisfactions or become a major source of the problems that people experience.

The Opportunity Structure

Clearly, genetics and heredity, socialization and cultural differences, and environmental factors are important in understanding why people have problems. All of these factors shape an individual's **opportunity structure**—the accessibility of opportunities for an individual within that individual's environment. For example, a person may have physical traits and characteristics that society values, a strong educational background, a stable and supportive family, work-oriented values and a desire to work, yet be without a job because of an economic recession or depression. In spite of suitable preparation, this person may remain unemployed for some time, with all of the problems associated with lack of income.

In another case, an individual may be born into a poor family, be abused as a child, lack encouragement or incentives from parents and teachers to complete school, and have limited social skills because of inadequate parenting. Even if jobs were plentiful, this person likely would be able to compete for only the lowest-paying positions, if at all.

Other illustrations relate to genetic traits. Gender, race, and ethnicity often result in discrimination and unequal treatment in job opportunities as well as the income a person will receive from the job. Women, African Americans, and Latinos, for example, are not afforded equal opportunity in the job market even when all other factors are equal.

Social Work Defined

In the minds of many, **social workers** are identified as "welfare" workers who are engaged in public assistance programs. This is a false and limited premise because social workers are involved in many different practice settings that offer a wide range of services. *Social welfare* literally means "social well-being," and in the United States this generally refers to providing institutional programs for the needy. To differentiate the profession of social work—the topic of this chapter—it is one of the professions that is instrumental in administering planned change activities prescribed by social welfare institutions.

The opportunity structure consists of more than what is available in the environment. It includes inner resources such as cognitive development and personality structure. Furthermore, many problems of individuals, families, groups, organizations, and communities result from the way society is organized and the limited choices available to some people.

Because social workers are actively involved in wide-ranging tasks, it is difficult to devise a specific, all-inclusive definition of social work. Unfortunately, this has resulted in definitions that are so general that they fail to identify appropriately all of the activities encompassed by the profession. Box 2.1 lists some of the roles of today's social workers. According to the National Association of Social Workers (NASW), the primary mission of **social work** is to

> . . . enhance human well-being and help meet the basic needs of all people, with particular attention to promoting social justice, addressing the needs

and empowerment of people who are vulnerable, oppressed, or living in poverty. . . . [Social workers help people] identify and manage the environmental forces that create, contribute to, and address problems in living. (NASW, 2006, p. 1)

Social work is an activity that seeks to help individuals, families, organizations, groups, and communities engage resources that will alleviate human problems. Social work is concerned, too, with enabling clients to develop capacities and strengths that will improve their social functioning. As the NASW definition indicates, social work is an active, "doing" profession that brings about positive change in problem situations through problem solving or prevention.

The social work profession is further committed to effecting changes in societal values and policies that limit or prohibit the free and full participation of individuals. Social workers have a professional responsibility to work for changes in discriminatory or otherwise restrictive practices that limit opportunities and prevent maximum social functioning.

The Early Years of Social Work

Professional social work developed slowly over the years as a result of efforts to refine and improve its knowledge and skill base. As discussed in chapter 1, early administration of relief to the needy was accomplished by a wide variety of individuals—overseers of the poor, friends and neighbors, church members, the clergy, philanthropists, and friendly visitors, among others. As early as 1814 in Scotland, the Reverend Thomas Chalmers expressed concern over the wasteful and inefficient approaches of relief programs and encouraged the development of a more humane and effective system for providing services and support.

Chalmers emphasized the need for more personalized involvement with the needy. He devised a system wherein his parish was divided into districts, with a deacon assigned to investigate each case to determine the causes of the

BOX 2.1
Roles Played by Generalist Social Workers

Enabler: a social worker who provides encouragement, offers hope, helps clients identify and focus on goals, and enables clients to make choices that improve their functioning.

Mediator: a trained professional who helps resolve conflicts between client systems at one or more levels of the environment while playing a neutral role.

Integrator or coordinator: a professional who is tasked with bringing together various components of a system into a unified whole to create positive change.

General manager: the professional who assumes administrative responsibility for a specific project, program, or agency.

Educator: a social worker whose main task is to convey information and knowledge with the goal of developing skills—a role that can be played in many situations in addition to a classroom.

Analyst or evaluator: a social worker whose role is to gather information to assess the effectiveness of work with clients or client systems and to make recommendations for change as needed.

Broker: a social worker who links client systems with existing resources, while ensuring that those resources treat client systems in a humane and effective way.

Facilitator: a social worker who facilitates change by bringing together groups of people and helping them use their own talents as well as other resources to create positive change.

Initiator: a social worker who calls attention to an unaddressed problem or need.

Negotiator: a social worker who advocates on behalf of a client system.

Mobilizer: a social worker who assembles, energizes, and organizes new or existing groups.

Advocate: a social worker who fights for the rights and dignity of people in need of help.

Outreach worker: a social worker who identifies specific client systems and reaches out to provide assistance.

Source: Adapted from *Generalist Practice with Organizations and Communities* (2nd ed.), by K. Kirst-Ashman and G. Hull (Pacific Grove, CA: Brooks Cole, 2001), pp. 22–27.

---

problems. If the resulting analysis indicated that self-sufficiency was not possible, an attempt was made to engage family, friends, neighbors, or wealthy citizens to provide the necessary assistance for the needy. As a last resort, the congregation was asked to provide assistance (Trattner, 1999).

Later, in the United States, the Association for Improving the Conditions of the Poor (New York City) and the Charity Organization Society (Buffalo, New York City, and Philadelphia) took similar approaches when organizing activities to help the poor. The **Charity Organization Society (COS)** had a profound effect on establishing social work as a specialized practice. It promoted "scientific philanthropy," emphasizing that charity was more than almsgiving. Furthermore, the COS stressed the importance of individual assessment and a coordinated plan of service.

The COS was the first relief organization to pay personnel to investigate requests for assistance and to refer eligible applicants to one or more existing agencies for intensive aid and supervision. Special emphasis was placed on "following up" on the recipients of assistance, and making efforts to secure someone to establish friendly relationships with them (Axinn & Stern, 2004).

Just as "friendly visiting" was encouraged, attention was directed to data collection and assessment. It was believed that a more structured, informed, and skillful approach would increase efficiency, discourage dependence on charity, lead to personal development and self-sufficiency, and reduce the practice of providing relief for chronic beggars.

As discussed in chapter 1, the **settlement house** movement emerged during the late 1800s as another viable means to provide a variety of community-based services and advocacy for the poor and disenfranchised. This movement contributed significantly to the beginning of the social work profession in the United States. Perhaps the most noteworthy of the settlements was Hull House, established in Chicago in 1889 by Jane Addams, a pioneer social worker. The success of this venture was immediate, and the programs offered by Hull House captured the imagination of philanthropic helpers and the needy alike. The settlements maintained a strong family focus, provided socialization experiences, and, through advocacy efforts, sought to influence the community to correct the dismal social conditions under which the poor were living.

This structured approach to managing charitable efforts quickly resulted in the need for trained workers. **Mary Richmond,** a major contributor to the COS movement who had a long-lasting impact on the profession, inaugurated the

Jane Addams, one of the first social workers in the United States and the founder of Hull House in Chicago, the first settlement house in the United States, advocated for social reforms to improve the lives of immigrants.

Photographer: Wallace W. Kirkland, Jane Addams Memorial Collection (JAMC neg. 613), Special Collections Department, University Library, University of Illinois at Chicago

first training program for social workers at the New York School of Applied Philanthropy, forerunner of schools of social work.

Richmond, considered by many to be the founder of the professional clinical social work movement, also formulated the concept and base for **social casework,** a practice method designed to "develop personality through adjustments consciously effected, individual by individual, between [persons] and their environment" (Richmond, 1922, p. 9).

In addition, Richmond maintained a keen interest in personality and family development, emphasizing the environmental influence within which interpersonal interactions transpire. Believing that environmental factors are significant contributors to personal as well as family problems, she maintained a strong interest in social reform that would promote a better quality of life for individuals (Axinn & Stern, 2004). Richmond was convinced that this task should be included in the social worker's sphere of responsibility. In her classic work *Social Diagnosis* in 1917, Richmond laid the framework for social casework practice. Under the impetus provided by Richmond, Jane Addams, and other early social work pioneers, a profession was born.

Schools of social work began to emerge along the eastern seaboard and in large cities of the Midwest, emphasizing direct social work practice (casework). Many were influenced by newly developing psychological perspectives, most notably those of Sigmund Freud and Otto Rank. Schools adopting Freudian psychology were more prevalent and became identified as "diagnostic" schools. Schools incorporating Rankian theory were known as "functional" schools. Shaping of curriculum around psychological theories increased the scientific knowledge base for social work practice.

By the late 1920s, **social group work** had gained visibility as a method of social intervention rather than "treatment" per se. Learning and social development were believed to be enhanced through structured group interactions. This technique soon was popularized in settlement houses and in work with street gangs, organized recreational clubs, and residents of institutions. Social group work became well entrenched as a viable helping method and later was adopted as a social work method.

Community organization had its roots in the New York Society for the Prevention of Pauperism, the Association for Improving the Conditions of the Poor, and the settlement house movement. By the late 1930s, community organization was prominent as a resource development method. Dealing largely with community development and emphasizing the importance of citizen participation and environmental change, community organizers plied their skills in identifying unmet human needs and working to develop community resources to meet those needs. Among the prerequisites for community organizers were skills in needs assessment, planning, public relations, organizing, influencing, and resource development.

By the 1950s, social casework, group work, and community organization all were considered methods of social work practice. In 1955, the various associations established to promote and develop each separate method merged and became known collectively as the **National Association of Social Workers (NASW).** NASW continues to serve as the main professional organization for social workers today, with 56 chapters throughout the world, and some 150,000 members. It seeks to promote quality in practice, stimulates political participation and social action, maintains standards of eligibility for membership in the association, and publishes several journals, including *Social Work.* Each state has a NASW chapter with a designated headquarters, and local membership units are active in all major cities. In addition, many college and university social work programs have student units of NASW.

Underpinnings of the Profession

Social work professional practice is based on values, ethics, a common body of knowledge that builds on a liberal arts base, and planned change. Each attribute is important to professional social workers. The **Council on Social Work Education (CSWE)** has incorporated these attributes into a curriculum policy statement and specific content areas that social work education programs must address at the bachelor's (BSW) and master's (MSW) levels (discussed later in the chapter).

Values

Social workers are committed to the dignity, worth, and value of all human beings regardless of social class, race, color, creed, gender, sexual orientation/gender identity, or age. The value of human life transcends all other values, and the best interest of human beings merits a humane and helpful response from society. People with problems, regardless of the nature of those problems, are not to be judged, condemned, or demeaned. Social workers emphasize that nonjudgmental attitudes are essential for maintaining clients' dignity and privacy and that clients must be accepted as they are, with no strings attached.

Furthermore, clients (or the **client system,** which may include more than one individual, such as a family or a group of adults with disabilities) have the right to autonomy—the right to determine courses of action that will affect their lives. Likewise, groups and communities hold these fundamental rights.

NASW has established a code of ethics (see Box 2.2) for its members, incorporating these values. A strong professional culture has developed and is expressed through the state and national associations of social work practitioners. Social work incorporates a strengths perspective, too, acknowledging that individuals, families, groups and communities are more likely to change when helping professionals build on their strengths rather than emphasize their deficiencies (see chapter 3).

Ethics

Ethics (moral duty) is a product of values. The concept of professional ethics, therefore, relates to the moral principles of practice. Social work values form the basis for social workers' beliefs about individuals and society, while ethics defines the framework for what should be done in specific situations. Both values and ethical dilemmas and conflicts are common.

Social workers, like their clients, have personal reference groups whose values frequently conflict with those of others. For example, a client may belong to a religious group that forbids and censures the use of professional medical intervention in cases of illness. The social worker may strongly favor medical intervention in those cases. Noting the value differences, what is the social worker's moral (ethical) duty in such cases? How can the client's best interests be served when value conflicts are present? Do clients have the right to self-determination in these cases?

As you ponder these questions, ask yourself what you would do. You will discover that responses to these types of situations are seldom achieved easily. Review the NASW ethics code summarized in Box 2.2 to see whether it helps you arrive at appropriate ethical behavior for cases such as the one suggested in the preceding paragraph.

Liberal Arts Base

Social workers at all levels must have a strong liberal arts base on which to build as they gain additional knowledge about human behavior,

BOX 2.2
NASW Code of Ethics

Preamble

The primary mission of the social work profession is to enhance human well-being and help meet the basic human needs of all people, with particular attention to the needs and empowerment of people who are vulnerable, oppressed, and living in poverty. A historic and defining feature of social work is the profession's focus on individual well-being in a social context and the well-being of society. Fundamental to social work is attention to the environmental forces that create, contribute to, and address problems in living.

Social workers promote social justice and social change with and on behalf of clients. "Clients" is used inclusively to refer to individuals, families, groups, organizations, and communities. Social workers are sensitive to cultural and ethnic diversity and strive to end discrimination, oppression, poverty, and other forms of social injustice. These activities may be in the form of direct practice, community organizing, supervision, consultation, administration, advocacy, social and political action, policy development and implementation, education, and research and evaluation. Social workers seek to enhance the capacity of people to address their own needs. Social workers also seek to promote the responsiveness of organizations, communities, and other social institutions to individuals' needs and social problems.

The mission of the social work profession is rooted in a set of core values. These core values, embraced by social workers throughout the profession's history, are the foundation of social work's unique purpose and perspective:

- service
- social justice
- dignity and worth of the person
- importance of human relationships
- integrity
- competence

This constellation of core values reflects what is unique to the social work profession. Core values, and the principles that flow from them, must be balanced within the context and complexity of the human experience.

Source: National Association of Social Workers (1999). Used with permission.

Note: The full Code of Ethics is available at www.socialworkers.org/pubs/code/code.asp

social welfare policy, research, and practice. Courses in English composition and literature; foreign language; government, history, and economics; sociology and psychology; mathematics and science; and culture and the fine arts—all provide students with connections to the past and a broad perspective on social and human conditions. These courses also strengthen critical thinking and problem-solving skills and foster a more holistic understanding of our world.

Knowledge That Builds on the Liberal Arts Base

Social work practice is derived from a common body of knowledge that encompasses theories of human behavior as well as experiential knowledge related to practice. Research is integrally important in understanding individual, family, group, organizational, and community behavior. Research also identifies more effective intervention techniques. Students of social work are expected to have knowledge of the life cycle, as well as personality development, social dysfunction, developmental processes, group dynamics, effects of discrimination, social policy formulation, research methods, and community environments.

Schools of social work encourage students to become familiar with a wide range of social and behavioral science theories that serve as a basis for knowing how client systems adapt and cope with client needs, and how theory guides planned social intervention. This knowledge undergirds the social worker's practice competence.

Practice Skills

Social workers are familiar with techniques related to direct practice with individuals (casework) and groups (group work), as well as communities (community organization). Organizing, planning,

and administration are included as areas of focus for many social work practitioners. Research skills are essential for evaluating practice effectiveness, too.

Planned Change

Professional social work intervention is based on a process of **planned change.** Change is indicated when clients present dysfunctional problems that are unresolved. Planned change is an orderly approach to addressing clients' needs and is based on assessment, knowledge of the client system's capacity for change, and focused intervention. The social worker functions as a change agent in this process.

Planned change is characterized by purpose and a greater likelihood of predictable outcomes derived from the change effort. Box 2.3 presents

---

BOX 2.3
Purposes of the Social Work Profession

The social work profession receives its sanction from public and private auspices and is the primary profession in the development, provision, and evaluation of social services. Professional social workers are leaders in a variety of organizational settings and service delivery systems within a global context.

The profession of social work is based on the values of service, social and economic justice, dignity and worth of the person, importance of human relationships, and integrity and competence in practice. With these values as defining principles, the purposes of social work are:

- To enhance human well-being and alleviate poverty, oppression, and other forms of social injustice.
- To enhance the social functioning and interactions of individuals, families, groups, organiza-

tions, and communities by involving them in accomplishing goals, developing resources, and preventing and alleviating distress.
- To formulate and implement social policies, services, and programs that meet basic human needs and support the development of human capacities.
- To pursue policies, services, and resources through advocacy and social or political actions that promote social and economic justice.
- To develop and use research, knowledge, and skills that advance social work practice.
- To develop and apply practice in the context of diverse cultures.

Source: *Council on Social Work Education Educational Policy and Accreditation Standards* (Washington, DC: Council on Social Work Education, 2004), p. 5.

a statement of the purpose of social work formulated by social workers. These underpinnings of the profession (values, knowledge, practice skills, and planned change) are discussed in more detail in later chapters.

Social Work Methods

Social workers are committed to the process of planned change. In their role, they become agents of change who attempt to improve the conditions that adversely affect the functioning of clients (or client systems). Change efforts may be geared toward assisting individuals, families, groups, organizations, or communities (or all five), and entail appropriate methods of intervention to achieve solutions to problems. Practice methods incorporate social work values, principles, and techniques in

- helping people obtain resources,
- conducting counseling and psychotherapy with individuals or groups,
- helping communities or groups provide or improve social and health services, and
- participating in relevant legislative processes that affect the quality of life for all citizens.

The variety of social work practice methods introduced next are discussed more extensively in Part Two of this text.

Social Work with Individuals and Families (Casework)

When the social worker's effort is aimed at working directly with individuals or families, the process is called **direct practice** (casework). This method is geared toward helping individuals and families identify solutions to personal or other problems related to difficulty with social functioning. In many instances, problems related to social inadequacy, emotional conflict, interpersonal loss, social stress, or the lack of familiarity

with resources produce dysfunction in individuals. Practitioners are skilled in assessment and know how to intervene strategically to ameliorate these problems. Direct practice often is considered to be therapeutic in nature.

Social Work with Groups (Group Work)

Group work techniques seek to enrich individuals' lives through planned group experiences. **Group work** stresses the value of self-development through structured interactions with other group members. This process, based on theories of group dynamics, encourages personal growth through active participation as a group member. Groups may be natural (already formed), such as street gangs, or formed purposefully at the group work setting, such as support groups. Whatever the composition, group work emphasizes the value of participation, democratic goal setting, freedom of expression, acceptance, and the development of positive attitudes through sharing.

Group work generally is not considered therapeutic, and it should not be confused with group therapy, which also uses group processes. Group therapy is designed to be therapeutic in that it seeks to alter or diminish dysfunctional behavior through the dynamic use of group interaction. Members of a therapeutic group often share emotionally distressing experiences in common (e.g., a group of recent divorcees) and develop options for more adaptive behaviors through focused discussion.

Community Organization

Social workers who practice at the community level draw on techniques of **community organization** to promote change. Recognizing that citizen awareness and support are vital to the development of resources in generating a more healthy and constructive environment for all citizens, community organizers work with established organizations within the community (such as Lions and Kiwanis Clubs, city governments, welfare organizations, the Junior League, political groups, social action groups, and other citizens' organizations) to gain support for needed services and secure funding to maintain them. Social workers who practice at this level typically are employed by city governments, planning agencies, councils of social agencies, or related community agencies.

Social Work Research

Although all social workers use research regularly, many social workers specialize in social work research. Research increases the knowledge base of practice as well as the effectiveness of intervention. In addition, it provides an empirical base on which to formulate more specific policy. Social research is essential in establishing a scientific framework for solving problems and refining social work practice methods. Evaluative research enables agencies and practitioners to better understand the effectiveness of efforts designed to meet the goals and objectives of their practice. Competent social work practitioners keep abreast of professional research and use research findings in their practice.

Social Work Administration and Planning

Administration and planning is a social work method that seeks to maximize the effective use of agency resources in problem solving. Administrators must be skilled in organizing, planning, and employing management techniques and be knowledgeable about social work practice. Many social agency administrators begin their careers as direct practitioners, subsequently become supervisors, and then move into administrative roles. Social planning also is seen as a social work role, which is discussed in chapter 6.

Professional Issues in Social Work

By now you have come to recognize that social work is a multifaceted profession wherein social workers are employed in a variety of roles and settings. With economic and technological changes erupting rapidly during the past century, the nature of problems experienced by the populace has mirrored those changes. At the same time, the knowledge base of the social and behavioral sciences has expanded and generated more insightful theories of human behavior.

In spite of the progress made over the past 100 years, a substantial number of people in the United States continue to be poor and disenfranchised. Some people argue that the social work profession has abandoned the poor, oppressed, and disenfranchised (Specht & Courtney, 1994) in favor of the more esoteric practices of counseling and psychotherapy. Proponents of this belief posit that the profession, once identified as a bulwark and vanguard for the oppressed, has turned its back on community action in favor of a case-by-case approach. The debate over the proper role of the social work profession is not likely to end soon. We invite you to review the definition of social work and its history and consider the stance you deem most appropriate for the profession in the future.

The Social Agency

Most social workers perform their professional functions through the auspices of a social agency. **Social agencies** are organizations that have been formed by states and communities to address social problems of their citizens. Agencies may be public (funded by taxes), voluntary (funded through contributions), or, in increasing numbers, proprietary (profit-oriented). The typical community social agency is headed by a board of directors of local citizens and meets regularly to review the agency's activities and establish policy that governs the agency's services. Many larger agencies have an administrator who has sole responsibility for supervising the agency's activities. In smaller agencies, the administrator may be involved in assisting clients with their needs as well.

Local agencies are community resources that stand ready to address needs that make day-by-day functioning difficult for a segment of people. Social workers are employed to carry out the agency's mission. Many agencies do not charge fees for the services they provide. In some instances, however, agencies have a "sliding-fee scale," adjusting the fee to the client's ability to pay. All clients, regardless of their economic resources, are afforded the same quality of service.

Typically, agencies cooperate with each other in meeting human needs. They readily make referrals when clients have needs that another agency can address more effectively. Interagency coordination is helpful, maximizing community resources to respond to unmet needs.

Education and Levels of Social Work Practice

Professional social workers assist clients with a wide variety of unmet needs. As a consequence, the nature and extent of skills necessary for addressing unmet needs vary with the complexities of the needs encountered. Recognizing that professional competence is a right of clients in seeking assistance, regardless of how difficult meeting their needs might be, the social work profession has developed three education levels of practice for meeting these differing needs. And the profession has established the Council on Social Work Education (CSWE), which, through

its division of standards and accreditation, serves as the accrediting body for professional educational programs at the bachelor's and master's levels. There are about 450 accredited undergraduate programs and 170 accredited master's programs in the United States, with a number of programs in candidacy to establish new programs (CSWE, 2006).

Bachelor of Social Work (BSW)

The entry level for professional social work practice is the BSW degree. Social work practitioners entering practice at this level must complete the education requirements for an undergraduate social work program accredited by the CSWE. Although professional social work education programs offered by colleges and universities vary, the CSWE mandates that, as a minimum requirement for meeting accreditation standards, each must build on a liberal arts foundation and provide basic education in human behavior and the social environment, social welfare policy and services, research, practice methods, social and economic justice, cultural diversity, populations at risk, and social work values and ethics.

All students who graduate from an accredited BSW program must complete 400 clock hours of field experience in a social work or related setting under the supervision of a social work practitioner. Typical field placements include senior citizens' centers, battered women's shelters, child welfare agencies, residential treatment centers, juvenile and adult probation programs, public schools, health clinics, hospitals, industries, and mental health agencies.

The education curriculum for baccalaureate-level practice is developed around the generalist method of practice. Typically, the generalist practitioner is knowledgeable about the systems/ecological approach (see chapter 3 for a complete discussion) to practice and is skillful in needs assessment, interviewing, resource development, case management, use of community resources, establishment of intervention objectives with clients, and problem solving.

The CSWE (2004) *Educational Policy and Accreditation Standards* outlines the **competencies,** or applied knowledge and skills, that undergird social work practice at the BSW level. Social work practitioners must:

1. apply critical thinking skills within the context of professional social work practice.
2. understand the value base of the profession and its ethical standards and principles, and practice accordingly.
3. practice without discrimination and with respect, knowledge, and skills related to clients' age, class, color, culture, disability, ethnicity, family structure, gender, marital status, national origin, race, religion, sex, and sexual orientation.
4. understand the forms and mechanisms of oppression and discrimination and apply strategies of advocacy and social change that advance social and economic justice.
5. understand the history of the social work profession and its contemporary structures and issues.
6. apply the knowledge and skills of generalist social work practice with systems of all sizes.
7. use theoretical frameworks supported by empirical evidence to understand individual development and behavior across the life span and the interactions among individuals and between individuals and families, groups, organizations, and communities.
8. analyze, formulate, and influence social policies.
9. evaluate research studies, apply research findings to practice, and evaluate their own practice interventions.
10. use communication skills differentially across client populations, colleagues, and communities.
11. use supervision and consultation appropriate to social work practice.

12. function within the structure of organizations and service delivery systems and seek necessary organizational change. (pp. 7–8)

Entry-level social workers are employed by agencies that offer a wide spectrum of services. As generalist social workers, they may perform professional activities as eligibility workers for state human services departments; work with children and families as protective services (protecting children from abuse and neglect) workers; serve as youth or adult probation workers; work in institutional care agencies that provide services for children or adults, especially the aged; engage in school social work; act as program workers or planners for area-wide agencies on aging; work in mental health outreach centers or institutions; serve as family assistance workers in industry; assist refugees in war torn countries; or perform their professional tasks in many other agencies providing human services. Baccalaureate-level professionals with experience and demonstrated competence frequently are promoted to supervisory and administrative positions.

Social work professionals at the BSW level are eligible for full membership in NASW. Their professional activities in helping clients are challenging and rewarding. Many social workers prefer to practice at this level throughout their careers. For others, an advanced degree in social work is desirable and opens up areas of practice that typically are not in the domain of BSW practitioners.

For those who have completed their undergraduate social work education from an accredited college or university, the school of social work to which they apply may grant advanced standing. Although not all graduate schools accept advanced-standing students, the CSWE provides a listing of those that do. When admitted to a graduate program, advanced-standing students are able to shorten the time required to secure the master's degree without diluting the quality of their educational experience. Advanced practice in social work is predicated upon receiving the master's degree in social work (MSW).

Master of Social Work: Advanced Practice

Students in master's degree programs in social work programs are engaged in an education curriculum that is more specialized than the BSW curriculum. Depending on how the curriculum is organized, students may specialize in direct services (clinical social work), community organization, administration, planning, research, or a field of practice (child welfare, medical social work, mental health, social work with the elderly, or school social work). All students master a common core of basic knowledge that builds on a liberal arts base, including human behavior and the social environment, social welfare policy and services, research, and practice methods related to their area of specialization.

The 2-year master's degree program is balanced between classroom learning and field practice. Graduates seek employment in specialized settings such as Veterans Administration hospitals, family and children's service agencies, counseling centers, and related settings that require specialized professional education.

Doctorate in Social Work (DSW and PhD)

Professional social workers who are interested in social work education, highly advanced clinical practice, research, planning, or administration often seek advanced study in doctor of social work (DSW) or doctor of philosophy in social work (PhD) programs. A number of graduate schools of social work offer education at this level. Students who are admitted tend to be seasoned social work practitioners, although this is not a prerequisite for admission to all schools.

Education at this level stresses research, advanced clinical practice, advanced theory, administration, and social welfare policy. Graduates usually seek employment on the faculty of schools of social work, in the administration of social welfare agencies, or, with increasing frequency, in private clinical practice.

Careers in Social Work

The number of employed social service workers grew rapidly from 95,000 in 1960 to more than 687,000 in 2004 (U.S. Bureau of Labor Statistics, 2006). Although federal and state funding for some social welfare programs has declined, social work is still one of the fastest-growing professions. New positions are being created in addition to the vacancies created through attrition. Areas that are experiencing growth include health care and aging.

Social work is an ideal profession for individuals who are interested in working with people and helping them address their needs. These broad interests are the heart of the social work profession. Positions in a wide variety of areas continue to attract social workers at all levels of practice, such as child welfare, health, corrections, developmental disabilities, family counseling, substance abuse, and public assistance programs (see Box 2.4). Wages in social work usually are adequate, and increases are based on skill and experience. According to the U.S. Bureau of Labor Statistics (2006), the median annual income of child, family, and school social workers in 2004 was $34,820, with social workers in nonprofit agencies and residential care facilities usually earning less ($30,5050) than those employed by local ($40,620) or state ($35,070) governments or elementary and secondary schools ($44,300). The median annual income of social workers in medical and health settings was $40,080, with hospitals generally paying more than home health care and nursing care facilities. The median annual income of social workers in other settings was $39,440.

BSW-level workers typically earn less than the more specialized MSW-degree workers. Median

BOX 2.4
The Power of Service

Everywhere, social workers provide practical and compassionate guidance to individuals confronting and resolving personal dilemmas. Every day, over half a million professional social workers bring hope, help, and opportunity for success into people's lives.

Community: To increase the capacity of individuals to address their own needs, social workers frequently connect people with critical community resources. They are skillful at providing the right tools to help their clients cope with and solve most severe challenges.

NASW members assist people of all ages in many different situations, and can be found working in a variety of settings:

Elementary, middle and high schools
Public health agencies
Family service agencies
Community action agencies
Child and adult care centers
Private clinical practices
Foundations
Armed Forces
Policy making organizations
Corporate employee assistance programs

Disaster relief organizations
Veterans services
Local, state, and national government
Hospitals
Domestic violence centers
Child welfare agencies
Psychiatric facilities
Rehabilitation facilities
Emergency assistance organizations
Drug treatment clinics
Home care agencies
Community mental health centers
Senior citizen centers
Developmental disabilities centers
Jails and prisons
Colleges and universities
Career centers
Legal service agencies
Homeless shelters
Hospices and nursing homes

Source: The Power of Service (Washington, DC: National Association of Social Workers, 2006). Retrieved from http://www.naswdc.org.

entry salaries vary, depending on experience, degree, location, and agency sponsorship. A few social workers earn upward of $100,000 after extensive experience.

Mobility often is a valuable asset to the social worker who is looking for an initial social work job. Rural areas have a shortage of social workers, whereas metropolitan areas tend to have a tighter employment market. Employment vacancies sometimes are listed with college placement services, state employment commissions,

professional associations, state agencies, or local newspapers.

In recent years, more social workers with advanced degrees in social work have engaged in **private practice.** Unlike more traditionally employed social workers, private practitioners must rely on fees from their clients to support their practice. Social workers often spend most of their time employed by a social agency and see clients in private practice on a part-time basis. Others practice full-time. Generally, private practice is directed to clients in need of counseling or group therapy. Private practitioners are governed by the NASW Code of Ethics and the social work value base. They extend their services to clients who may not seek assistance through traditional agency networks. Many private practitioners provide some services **pro bono** (meaning "for the public good" and at no cost) to clients who otherwise could not afford them.

Collaboration with Other Helping Professions

Social workers are not alone in assisting people who have problems. The unique skills of other helping professionals can be beneficial in addressing needs outside the realm of the social worker's skill and knowledge base or inappropriate for social work intervention. A key role of social workers is to refer clients to other resources. Thus, social workers have to be aware of the different types of helping professionals and the roles they typically play in working with people.

Frequently, social workers are part of a collaborative effort with other professionals who assist individuals, families, groups, or communities in finding solutions to problems or in establishing prevention programs. For example, a school social worker, school counselor, clinical psychologist, and school nurse might combine their professional expertise in developing a program to prevent teenage pregnancy. Or a social worker might work with a pastoral counselor and a psychiatrist to help a former client with emotional problems become reestablished into community life.

Social workers often facilitate or participate in case staffings as members of **multidisciplinary teams.** At these staffings, professionals and sometimes the client meet to determine what the

client's strengths and needs are, how best to maximize the strengths to address the identified needs, and who should be involved in addressing which needs. Multidisciplinary teams maximize the strengths and expertise of each professional on the team, to avoid duplication of effort, divergent interventions that might be at cross-purposes, and gaps in service to clients. Although professional teamwork in many instances enhances the opportunities for clients and furthers the opportunities for successful intervention, it is the social workers' responsibility to guard the integrity of the referral process when seeking the expertise of resources to which they refer their clients.

Other Professionals Likely to Collaborate with Social Workers

Other community professionals who practice in the area of human services include psychiatrists, psychologists, sociologists, pastoral counselors, school counselors, rehabilitation specialists, employment counselors, nurses, and attorneys.

PSYCHIATRISTS

Psychiatry is a field of medical practice that specializes in mental and emotional dysfunction. Psychiatrists are physicians with a concentration in mental and emotional disorders. Unlike other professionals who assist with psychological and emotional problems, as well as those of social dysfunction, psychiatrists can provide medications in cases when symptoms indicate the need for them. Because psychiatrists are physicians (with a medical degree), they have at their disposal a wide array of medical interventions as well as expertise in treating problems of a mental and emotional nature.

PSYCHOLOGISTS

Psychologists often work with social workers in assisting clients. Unlike psychiatrists, professional psychologists are not physicians. Psychologists who assist with clients' psychological and emotional problems generally are referred to as clinical or counseling psychologists. Many have skills in psychotherapy and psychoanalysis, and others prefer methodological approaches that reflect a behavior modification, cognitive therapy, Gestalt therapy, or related practice modality.

Some psychologists use **psychometric instruments** (testing) to help diagnose problems and provide helpful information to social workers and other professionals about clients and their functioning, which may not be readily observable during a client interview. Results of the tests provide a basis for establishing a personality profile for clients and to gain insights into a client's ability to handle stress and areas in which the client is vulnerable. Psychometric testing, however, is only one of many sources of evidence necessary to assess clients' problems. Psychologists who engage in psychometry are enlisted as consultants to test clients in social service agencies and educational institutions. This service frequently is helpful in gaining insights into clients and establishing appropriate treatment and intervention plans.

SOCIOLOGISTS

Sociologists engage in the study of society, its organization, and the phenomena arising out of group relations. As such, professionals in this area contribute much to the awareness of human interaction, including establishment of norms, values, social organization, patterns of behavior, and social institutions. Sociologists are skilled in research techniques and methodologies. Most are employed at institutions of higher education and related educational institutions, although a growing number of them are entering the field of clinical, or applied, sociology.

PASTORAL COUNSELORS

Perhaps no other single source of contact by people with problems is sought more often than religious leaders. Priests, pastors, ministers, rabbis, and others in positions of spiritual leadership are called on readily by members of their congregations and others in trouble. Pastoral counselors frequently serve as members of multidisciplinary teams with social workers. As spiritual leaders, they tend to be trusted by their congregations and are presumed to have an extraordinary understanding of human frailty and a special ability to communicate with spiritual powers. Professional **pastoral counselors** typically are educated at schools of theology that offer a specialization in counseling.

SCHOOL AND REHABILITATION COUNSELORS

School counselors and rehabilitation counselors are valuable allies of social workers. School counselors are vital on teams of professionals who work with school-age children and their families. If they are employed in public schools, school counselors may be required to have classroom teaching experience in addition to graduate education before they are eligible for certification as counselors by state education agencies. Counselors in school settings assist students with educationally related problems and in locating education resources that are best suited to their individual interests. Many students with behavioral problems, as well as those with academic difficulties, are referred to the school counselor for assistance.

Counselors also are employed in correctional systems, where they help inmates assess the attitudes and skills they need to obtain productive employment after they are released from prison. This type of intervention benefits from collaboration with other members of the correctional team, including social workers. Team members often network with the inmates' families as well as community social service agencies.

Social workers, especially those involved with individuals with disabilities and their families, often work with rehabilitation counselors. Most states have established agencies to help individuals with physical or mental disabilities identify competencies and secure academic or vocational training that will enable them to find employment. Counselors from these agencies also help clients obtain specialized medical treatment to enhance their physical, mental, and social capacities. By the nature of their specialization, rehabilitation counselors are heavily involved in teamwork and networking with social workers and other human and vocational service workers to secure resources for clients that will enable them to achieve their productive potential. If successful, clients' level of independence will increase along with their self-esteem and employability.

EMPLOYMENT COUNSELORS

Social workers also collaborate with employment counselors—professionals who assist clients in assessing their skill levels and providing educational courses to teach them the skills they will need for employment. Employment counselors must have knowledge of the employment market and be able to match clients who seek work with the needs of employers. The aim is to secure competence and job satisfaction for employer and employee alike.

Many employment counselors today work with employees who have lost their jobs because of an economic downturn or the continually shifting job market. Beyond helping their clients seek employment, these counselors help clients adjust to job loss and locate resources to assist them and their families while they are unemployed.

NURSE PRACTITIONERS

Social workers, particularly those who are employed in health and mental health settings, work closely with nurse practitioners on many occasions. In recent years, the role of nurses has changed dramatically, and they frequently have administrative roles in mental health programs that serve clients with substance abuse and mental health problems. Traditionally viewed as "doctors' helpers" or as pseudoprofessionals whose primary responsibility was to make sure that doctors' orders were dutifully carried out, contemporary nurses have emerged as professionals in their own right.

Schools of nursing now incorporate the psychosocial aspects of services to debilitated or hospitalized clients along with mastery of the basic skills related to patient care. Nurses specialize in a variety of areas such as pediatrics, gerontology, psychiatry and mental health, and oncology. The demand for well-trained nurses far exceeds their availability at this time, and the United States faces a serious shortage in this indispensable profession.

ATTORNEYS-AT-LAW

Social workers work with lawyers in criminal and civil matters with clients and as key members of state and local agencies, ensuring that the agency is meeting its legal mandate in serving clients. Lawyers engage in both criminal and civil matters to assist individuals in securing their rights under the law.

Many communities have established legal aid clinics that offer legal counsel to the poor or near-poor, addressing problems such as divorce, child custody, citizenship, and adequate defense in a court of law. These clinics are an invaluable resource for the poor. Many lawyers are employed as full-time legal counselors at the clinics, and others work part-time or volunteer their time. Legal aid clinics promote justice for the poor as well as those in better financial circumstances. Typically, law firms assign a portion of their staff time to pro bono efforts, representing indigent clients.

OTHER HELPING PROFESSIONALS

Social workers interact with a myriad of other helping professionals. Those who work in health care settings are likely to be involved with nutritionists, physical and occupational therapists, cardio-care specialists, and transplant specialists, depending on the nature of the health care area in which they work. Social workers in schools, juvenile and adult criminal justice programs, and child protective services programs are likely to work with law enforcement officers, judges, and others, besides attorneys, who are involved with the legal system. Social workers who are involved with young children are likely to work with child care providers and early childhood intervention specialists. Indeed, to serve clients effectively, social workers rely heavily on other professionals from various disciplines.

The Need for Professional Diversity

Although the brief discussion of selected professions involved with social workers is by no means complete, it does encompass the primary disciplinary areas in the human service field. Social workers and others in the helping professions must develop awareness of the expertise available in their practice area. The issues that many clients face require the attention of experts from diverse areas of practice to move toward resolution. If clients are to benefit maximally from those who assist them, professionals must develop an awareness of their limitations as well as strengths.

In our complex, highly technological society, specialization is necessary. With the explosion of knowledge and our understanding of human needs fostered by advances in technology, no one person can master it all. Just as society is complex, so are human beings. Values differ, as do the diverse groups with whom we hold an identity. In response to these diverse needs, specialty areas have emerged to understand and be able to apply the theoretical explanations of behavior. Life itself is a problem-solving journey, and our response to the problems we encounter involves our personality makeup as well as our knowledge, awareness, resources, and sensitivities. Invariably, all of us will encounter problems for which no ready solutions are apparent. Often, the friendly advice of a neighbor,

spouse, or confidant is sufficient to provide the perspective that will lead to an acceptable solution. At other times, professional assistance is essential.

One frequently asked question relates to how the professions are alike and different. With a specific client, for example, what does a psychiatrist do that is different from what a psychologist would do? Or a social worker? Or a pastoral counselor? And so on.

Several specialties might engage, for example, in marital counseling or assist a family struggling with the behavioral problems of an adolescent. To an uninformed observer, the professional response to those problems might seem to be about the same. The client sees the professional for an hour or so each week, the interaction consists primarily of verbal interaction, and the client typically is assigned specific tasks to work on before the next visit. The professional may contact other social systems, such as the school or the employment system, related to the client's functioning. What, then, constitutes the difference?

In part, although not exclusively, the difference may lie in the theoretical perspective that the professional brings to address the problem. The specialized emphasis on individual psychodynamics as reflected in psychiatry and psychology often varies with the emphasis of social work on the systems/ecological framework and the relationship between the person and the environment within which the person functions. Also, the emphasis of social work on using community resources is distinct from the approaches typically used in psychiatry and psychology.

Social work advocates a holistic approach with a goal of enhancing the client's strengths (see Box 2.5). Recognizing that stress may be generated by a lack of resources as well as intrapsychic conflict, social workers may offer their clients concrete resources, such as locating a job, adequate housing, health care services, child care, or other needed services. The different roles that

BOX 2.5
The Power of Relationships

Social workers are trained to make a positive impact in difficult situations. They do it because they want to improve lives. And they know that when social work succeeds, a lot of good things can happen:

Problems get solved
Prevention outweighs treatment
Families function
Children find parents
Sex becomes safer
Lights stay on
Stress is managed
Communities unite
Neighbors compromise
Life gets manageable
Homes stay heated
Homes are restored
Education is valued
Fears shrink
Sympathy becomes empathy
Prisoners don't go back
Exceptional people live normally
Battered people find shelter
Children are immunized
Doors are opened
Houses become homes
Teens come off the streets
Marriages are restored
Beliefs are respected
People learn to love
Children get adopted

Children play safely
Anxiety decreases
Homeless people find shelter
Immigrants are welcomed
Self-esteem increases
Friends are made
People help themselves
Families reunite
Barriers are hurdled
Emotions are healed
People die with dignity
Differences are valued
Violence stops
Hammers build houses
Health care is accessible
Disabilities are surmounted
Jobs get filled
Drugs aren't abused
Kids get clothes
Abuse is exposed
Goals are accomplished
Justice is served
Seniors find companions
Loneliness is lifted
People stay sober
Relationships work

Source: *The Power of Relationships* (Washington, DC: National Association of Social Workers, 2006). List provided by the University of Indianapolis School of Social Work. Retrieved from http://www.naswdc.org

the generalist social work practitioner plays, such as advocate, broker, enabler, case manager, and intervener, may be essential to creating an environment in which individual clients eventually can address their own needs.

Social workers may be the ones who provide the links to other professionals involved with a case and often are more attuned than other disciplines to the need for collaboration. Social work takes a systemic approach to intervention, and the importance of collaboration and case management is emphasized at all levels of professional training. One of the first questions social workers ask the client prior to developing an intervention strategy is: "Who else is involved?" followed by, "Who is not involved who should be?"

Some individuals are seen by a helping professional in isolation, and it is left to them to consider who else they might want to ask for help. Or they might receive a suggestion for a referral but are too overwhelmed, intimidated, or concerned about issues such as cost to follow up. Social workers play key roles in suggesting possible resources and linking clients to other helping professionals who can best meet their needs. In still other situations, clients may be working with multiple resources but those resources are unaware that others are involved. This could represent duplication of services and place undue strain on clients if they receive conflicting information or suggestions from different service providers.

One of the authors worked for an agency that received a referral about a family that had moved to the area. The family was about to be evicted from housing because of failure to adhere to housing policies. Also, the children were enrolled in multiple schools, and most were having difficulty. Some were in special education classes, two older children had come to the attention of the juvenile court, and a number of child neglect reports had been registered with the local child protection agency.

When the author called a meeting of the staffs from the six agencies she knew were involved with the family, 26 different personnel from 19 different agencies arrived at the meeting! The helping professionals present immediately realized how many personnel were involved and the different messages they had been giving the family, and they were not surprised when they were told that the family had resorted to keeping the shades drawn and refused to answer the door to any outsiders. Fortunately, with coordinated case

management from a social worker charged with overseeing the case and the agencies involved and fewer personnel working with the family, trust was established with the family and its members made significant gains.

Social workers frequently coordinate case staffings of those involved with a case, including the client(s), when appropriate. To address the needs of one family, a social worker might participate in a staffing that includes the client and extended family members and personnel from schools, hospitals, law enforcement, the court system, child protective services, and religious organizations.

An atmosphere of cooperation and respect among the helping professions is necessary to attain the optimum helping environment. Social workers have clients who need psychiatric treatment or the special services available from a clinical or counseling psychologist or pastoral counselor. Other clients are assisted by referral to an employment counselor. Students who are having difficulty in school can benefit from referral to a school counselor.

Professionals who work together and look at client situations from different lenses can achieve more positive outcomes for clients than if their services were provided independently. For example, a law enforcement officer involved in a situation of alleged child abuse would try to determine if a crime had been committed and what legal steps might be necessary to ensure the child's safety. A social worker in the same case would be interested in the child's safety but would not be involved directly in arresting a perpetrator. A medical professional would attend to the child's physical and mental health and would provide medical treatment. A social worker would be concerned about the child's physical and mental health but would not provide direct medical treatment. The social worker would focus on the holistic strengths and needs of the child and his or her family, working closely with both law enforcement officers and medical professionals.

Clearly, these professions overlap, but the specific characteristics of each ultimately should result in positive benefits to clients served. Positive interaction and collaboration among professionals enrich the service systems and improve intervention with clients in need. Each profession has its own distinct professional culture, and being aware of these differing cultures should promote more appropriate referrals.

The Baccalaureate Social Worker and Other Professions

Baccalaureate social workers (those holding the BSW degree) typically function as generalist practitioners and hold a unique position in the professional community. Their attention to a wide variety of human needs demands skills as counselors, resource finders, case managers, evaluators, advocates, brokers, enablers, and problem solvers. The BSW social worker's awareness of community resources and the ability to use them skillfully in problem solving are valuable tools in securing the needed assistance for clients. These social workers are employed in various social service agencies and community settings.

In a case that presents multiple problems and requires intervention by a number of different helping professionals, the BSW social worker may become engaged as a case manager, with primary responsibility for securing referrals to appropriate resources. The social worker, too, may become involved in providing the necessary supports to ensure that the client uses the services. In this role, the BSW social worker would continue to monitor and coordinate the intervention effort, with the cooperation of all components of the intervention system.

The BSW social worker may serve as a vital link among community professionals. The knowledge related to individual, family, group, organizational, and community functioning within the context of the systems/ecological framework helps this social worker identify the appropriate referral resources, engage them, and become an essential component in the helping process.

Summary

Social work is a complex profession, relying on a strong value base and clearly defined code of ethics. The social worker has to develop skills in direct practice, community organization, and research, as well as in administration and planning. All social work practice is based on knowledge of human behavior and social organizations.

Clients' problems and needs stem from factors including heredity and genetics, socialization, cultural differences, environmental factors, and deficiencies in the opportunity structure. Social workers use a holistic approach to address client problems and needs, gathering information about these factors that they then draw upon to determine appropriate intervention strategies.

Social work is the primary profession that is instrumental in administering planned change within the social welfare system. Change can occur with individual clients, their families, groups, organizations, and communities at the societal level. Social workers are engaged at all levels of the environment to address the social welfare needs identified in chapter 1, including poverty, mental health, and child welfare.

Social work as a profession draws on early work of the Charity Organization Societies and their emphases on individual assessment and coordinated plans of service, and the settlement house movement and its emphases on community-based services and advocacy for members of vulnerable populations. Three major practice methods of social work have emerged over the years: social case work, social group work, and community organization. In 1955, proponents of these three practice methods merged to form the National Association of Social Workers (NASW), the major professional organization for social workers, which promotes quality in practice and advocates for the profession and the members of society it serves. NASW maintains a Code of Ethics to which all members of the profession are expected to adhere.

The Council on Social Work Education is the national organization that oversees social work education. In collaboration with NASW, CSWE has worked to ensure that social work education incorporates the values and ethics of the profession, a common body of knowledge that builds on a liberal arts base, and planned change. Regardless of which social work program students attend, all receive coursework in social welfare policy, practice methods, research, human behavior, social justice, and working with vulnerable populations. Social work education has three levels: Bachelor of Social Work (BSW), Master of Social Work (MSW), and Doctorate in Social Work (DSW or PhD).

Social workers are known for their roles as collaborators and case managers. Using a holistic approach that focuses on the relationship between the client and the broader environment in which the client functions, social workers collaborate with other helping professionals, including psychiatrists, psychologists, sociologists, pastoral counselors, school and rehabilitation counselors, employment counselors, nurse practitioners, and attorneys. Social workers often facilitate case staffings as members of multidisciplinary teams, in which all professionals and often clients and their families participate to determine clients' strengths and needs and how best to maximize resources to address the identified needs. In our complex society, many professionals with specialized knowledge often are needed to best serve a client. An important role of social work is the case manager, who coordinates needed services to ensure that the client receives what is needed.

Key Terms and InfoTrac® College Edition

The terms below are included in the Glossary. To learn more about key terms and topics in this chapter, enter the following search terms using InfoTrac College Edition or the World Wide Web:

Charity Organization Society (COS)
client system
community organization
competencies
Council on Social Work Education (CSWE)
direct practice
ethics
group work
multidisciplinary teams
National Association of Social Workers (NASW)
opportunity structure

pastoral counselor
planned change
private practice
pro bono
psychiatry
psychobiology
psychologist
psychometric instruments
Richmond, Mary
settlement house
social agencies
social casework
social group work
social work
social worker
socialization
sociologist

Discussion Questions

1. What does the term *opportunity structure* mean? What are the characteristics of the opportunity structure? How might the individual's level of access to the opportunity structure shape outcomes for that individual?
2. What are social work values? How do values relate to ethics? Can you think of a values dilemma that a social worker might face when working with a client?
3. What constitutes direct practice? Community organization? Research? Administration and planning? How are they alike, and how are

they different? In which are you most interested? Why?

4. Compare and contrast the major contributions of the Charity Organization Society and the settlement house movement to social work practice.

5. What skills should the generalist-level (BSW) social worker have? How do these skills compare to those of the MSW social worker? The PhD social worker?

6. How important is a code of ethics for a profession? Why? Why would a code of ethics be particularly important for the profession of social work?

7. How does social work differ from other professions that also function in the human services arena? Compare how you think a social worker and another helping professional discussed in this chapter might differ in approach. Why do you think the differences would arise?

On the Internet

www.cswe.org/

www.naswdc.org/

www.sc.edu/swan/

www.uic.edu/jaddams/hull/hull_house.html

References

Axinn, C., & Stern, M. (2004). *Social welfare: A history of the American response to need* (6th ed.). Boston: Allyn & Bacon.

Council on Social Work Education. (2001/2004). *Educational policy and accreditation standards.* Washington, DC: Author.

Council on Social Work Education. (2006). *Directory of accredited social work degree programs.* Washington, DC: Author.

Kirst-Ashman, K., & Hull, G. (2001). *Generalist practice with organizations and communities.* Pacific Grove, CA: Brooks Cole.

National Association of Social Workers. (2006). *NASW code of ethics.* Washington, DC: Author.

National Association of Social Workers. (2006). *The power of social work.* Washington, DC: Author.

Richmond, M. (1917). *Social diagnosis.* New York: Russell Sage Foundation.

Richmond, M. (1922). *What is social casework?* New York: Russell Sage Foundation.

Specht, H., & Courtney, M. (1994). *Unfaithful angels.* New York: Free Press.

Trattner, W. (1999). *From Poor Law to welfare state: A history of social welfare in America* (6th ed.). New York: Free Press.

U.S. Bureau of Labor Statistics. (2005). *Employment and earnings, January, 2005 issue.* See http://www.bls.gov/cps/hom.htm

U.S. Bureau of Labor Statistics (2006). *Occupational outlook handbook, 2006–2007.* Retrieved from http://www.bls.gov/oco/ocos060.htm

Suggested Further Readings

Dolgoff, R., Lowenberg, F., & Harrington, D. (2005). *Ethical decisions for social work practice* (7th ed.). Belmont, CA: Wadsworth.

Dubois, B., & Miley, K. K. (2002). *Social work: An empowering profession* (4th ed.). Boston: Allyn & Bacon.

Ginsberg, L. (2001). *Careers in social work.* Boston: Allyn & Bacon.

Goldstein, H. (1990). The knowledge base of social work practice: Theory, wisdom, analogue, or art? *Families in Society, 71,* 32–43.

Grobman, B. (Ed.). (1999). *Days in the lives of social workers: 50 professionals tell real-life stories from social work practice* (2nd ed.). Harrisburg, PA: White Hat.

Grobman, B. (Ed.). (2005). *More days in the lives of social workers: 35 "real life" stories of advocacy, outreach and other intriguing roles in social work practice.* Harrisburg, PA: White Hat.

CHAPTER 3

The Systems/Ecological Perspective

Juan, a 12-year-old Mexican American male, is in the seventh grade in an urban school in California. His teachers are concerned about him and are recommending to Christina Herrera, the school social worker, that he be enrolled in the school's dropout-prevention program. Recently, Juan has been socializing during school with a group of much older students who are members of a local gang. He has been skipping classes, not completing class assignments, fighting with other students, and arguing with his teachers when they confront him about his behavior. During the past 2 weeks, he has been caught smoking marijuana and pulling a knife on a classmate.

Ms. Herrera has talked with both Juan and his mother. Ms. Herrera has suggested that Juan participate in a school support group and has referred Juan and his mother to the local teen–parent outreach center for counseling as soon as a counseling slot is available. Juan's mother is extremely concerned about him, but she also has indicated to Ms. Herrera that she is under a great deal of stress and is angry that Juan is adding to it.

Juan lives in a one-bedroom apartment with his mother and his younger brother, who is 5 years old. Juan's parents divorced 6 months ago, and his father moved to a neighboring state 300 miles away. Juan always had a fairly close relationship with both of his parents. Although he knew that they fought a lot and that his father drank and lost his job, he was surprised when his parents told him that they were getting a divorce.

When Juan's father moved out, his mother had to get an extra job to make ends meet, and the family had to move into a small apartment in another part of the city. Juan's mother's relatives and friends, all devout Catholics, were adamantly against the divorce and have not been supportive at all. When she is not working, Juan's mother spends much of her time crying or sleeping. At first, Juan tried hard to be supportive of his mother cooking meals, cleaning the house, and taking care of his little brother—but at times he doesn't cook or clean exactly the way his mother wants him to. When his brother is too noisy, Juan gets in trouble for not keeping him quiet. Lately, Juan's mother has begun yelling at or hitting Juan when this happens. Because she was abused as a child, Juan's mother feels guilty when she gets so angry at Juan, but she doesn't understand why he can't be more supportive when she is trying so hard to keep the family together.

Since the divorce, Juan has felt abandoned by everyone. His mother is usually angry at him, and his two longtime friends, who come from two-parent families, seem less friendly to him. When they do ask him to do things with them, he usually can't anyway because he has to take care of his younger brother or he doesn't have any money. Transportation is another problem, because Juan's friends live across town in his former neighborhood.

Although he used to do well in school, Juan has lost interest in his classes. He can't get used to the new school, and he doesn't know any of the teachers there. He does have several new friends who seem to accept him. They are older, and their interest in him makes him feel important. Juan is excited that they want him to be a member of their gang. As long as school is so boring, he can spend time with them during the day and still take care of his brother after school. But he is seriously considering running away from home and moving in with one of the gang members, who lives with an older brother. The friend's older brother recently got out of prison and has promised that Juan can make a lot of money as a drug runner for him.

Juan's case illustrates the many factors that influence how people react to what is going on in their lives. Juan's present situation is affected by

- his developmental needs as he enters adolescence;
- his relationships with his mother, father, younger brother, friends, and school personnel;
- his father's alcoholism and unemployment;
- his parents' divorce;
- his mother's abuse as a child;
- his family's tenuous economic situation;
- the lack of positive social support available to Juan's family from relatives, friends, the workplace, the school, the church, and the neighborhood;
- the lack of programs available to divorced parents and teens in Juan's community;
- Juan's cultural and ethnic background; and
- community and societal attitudes about divorce, female-headed households, and intervention in family matters.

From Juan's perspective, the family system, the economic system, the political system, the religious system, the education system, and the social welfare system have failed to meet his needs. Still, Juan is forced to interact continually with all of these individuals, groups, and social structures regularly and he depends on all of them in some way.

In this chapter we explore frameworks that social workers use to understand social problems and issues that individuals and families face in today's world. The **systems/ecological framework** is an umbrella framework used by generalist social work practitioners with a bachelor of social work (BSW) degree to understand both social welfare problems and individual needs and guide the various interventions that social workers use when helping clients.

The Impact of Theoretical Frameworks on Intervention

Everyone perceives what is going on in their lives and in the world somewhat differently. For example, an argument between a parent and a teenager over almost any topic usually is perceived quite differently by the parent and by the teenager. People view their environments and the forces that shape them differently, depending on many things: biological factors, such as their own heredity and intelligence; personal life experiences, including their childhood; ethnicity and culture; and level and type of education.

How people perceive their world determines to a large extent how involved they are in it and how they interact with it. For example, women who perceive themselves as unimportant and powerless may continue to let their partners beat them and may not believe that they can be successful if they leave their batterers. In contrast, women who perceive that they have some control over their lives and feel better about themselves may enter counseling programs and get jobs.

Professionals from different disciplines also view the world somewhat differently. A physicist, for example, will offer a different explanation than a philosopher or a minister about how the world began. A law enforcement officer and a social worker may disagree about how best to handle young teens who join gangs and harass elderly people. A physician may treat a patient who complains of headaches by meeting the patient's physical needs, whereas a psychologist may treat the person's emotional needs through individual counseling to ascertain how the individual can better cope. The way professionals who work with people perceive the world—their **worldview**—largely determines the type of intervention they choose in helping people.

Worldview is an important concept to social workers for two reasons. They must be continually aware of their own worldviews and how they affect their choices of intervention in helping people, and they also must be aware of the worldviews of others. Some worldviews have more influence than others on world, national, state, and local policies and the ways in which our society at all levels is structured. One key to being an effective social worker is to understand those influences, and how they have shaped current policies and systems and how those influences have affected at-risk and diverse populations. According to Joe Shriver (2004, pp. 15–16), an important aspect of social work is to help individuals find their voices to advocate for themselves and to be allies for them when they cannot. Shriver, a social work educator, suggests the following questions as criteria for analyzing worldviews, or ways of thinking:

1. Does this perspective contribute to preserving and restoring human dignity?

2. Does this perspective recognize the benefits of, and does it celebrate, human diversity?
3. Does this perspective assist us in transforming ourselves and our society so that we welcome the voices, the strengths, the ways of knowing, the energies of us all?
4. Does this perspective help us all (ourselves and the people with whom we work) to reach our fullest human potential?
5. Does the perspective reflect the participation and experiences of males and females, economically well-off and poor; white people and people of color; gay men, lesbians, bisexuals, transgender persons, and heterosexuals; old and young; temporarily able-bodied people and people with disabilities? (pp. 9–10)

Worldviews sometimes are called *paradigms* or *frameworks*. In our society, many individuals currently are rethinking ways to view critical social issues such as poverty and health care. The profession of social work requires a framework to understand how and why views are changing and how to work for social change during this shift.

The Difference Between Causal Relationships and Association

In the past, many professionals who dealt with human problems tended to look at those problems in terms of cause and effect. A **cause-and-effect relationship** suggests that if x causes y, then by eliminating x, we also eliminate y. For example, if we say that smoking is the sole cause of lung cancer, eliminating smoking would mean eliminating lung cancer. This limited worldview presents problems for many reasons. We know that smoking does not always cause lung cancer, and sometimes people who do not smoke get lung cancer.

Further, the relationship between smoking and developing lung cancer is not always one-dimensional. Other intervening variables or factors, such as living in a city with heavy pollution, also increase a person's chances of getting lung cancer. The chances of getting lung cancer are more than twice as great for a person who smokes and lives in a city with heavy smog than for someone who does neither. The causal-relationship viewpoint usually is not appropriate when examining social welfare problems.

Juan's case definitely cannot be discussed in terms of a cause-and-effect relationship. Are the situations he is experiencing caused by the abuse his mother suffered as a child, by the divorce, by his father's drinking too much, by his mother's worries about money, by Juan's use of marijuana, by his association with gang members, by the limited social support system available, or by discrimination because he and his family are Mexican American? It is unlikely that one of these factors caused Juan's current situation, but they all probably contributed to it in some way. In looking at factors related to social welfare problems, it is more appropriate to view them in **association** with the problem—meaning that all factors are connected to or relate to the problem, rather than saying that one isolated factor, or even several factors, directly causes a social problem.

A Conceptual Framework for Understanding Social Welfare Problems

Because many factors are associated with, or contribute to, social welfare problems, we need a broad theory or framework to understand them. First, it is useful to define *theory* and to discuss why theories are important.

A **theory** is a way of clearly and logically organizing a set of facts or ideas. All of us use theories daily. We continually are taking in facts, or information, from our environment and ordering them in some way to make sense of what is going on around us. Although some of our theories may be relatively unimportant to everyone else, they are useful to us in being able to describe, understand, and predict our environment.

Most important, theories are useful in helping us change either the environment or the ways in which we relate to it. For example, a college student has a roommate who always turns up the compact disc player to full volume whenever the student gets a phone call. During the year that they have shared a room, the student has gathered a great deal of information as to when this happens. She now is able to articulate a theory based on this information to describe the situation, to understand why it happens, and to be able to predict when her roommate will exhibit this behavior. Making sense of the facts in this situation has made it easier for her to deal with this trying behavior and attempt to change it. What theories might you suggest to understand why this roommate situation is happening? A theory can be relatively insignificant, such as the one just described, or it can have major importance to many people.

A theory can be used to describe something, such as Juan's family situation; to explain or to understand something, such as why a family in crisis would exhibit some of the behaviors of Juan's family; to predict something, such as what behaviors another family in a similar situation might experience; or to change something, such as Juan's ability to get his needs met from his environment in a healthier way.

The same set of facts can be ordered in different ways, depending on who is doing the ordering and the worldview of that person or group. If we think of facts as individual bricks and a theory as a way of ordering the bricks so they make sense, we can visualize several different theories from the same set of facts, just as we can visualize a number of different structures built from the same set of bricks.

If a theory is to be widely used, it must have three attributes:

1. A good theory must be **inclusive,** or able to explain consistently the same event in the same way. The more inclusive a theory is, the better able it is to explain facts in exactly

the same way each time an event occurs. For example, if the person in the roommate situation could describe, explain, or predict the roommate's behavior exactly the same way every single time the telephone would ring, she would have a highly inclusive theory.

2. A good theory must also be **generalizable,** which means that a general conclusion about what happens in one situation must be able to be transferred to other, similar situations. Even though the person may be able to explain the facts about her roommate in a highly inclusive way, the same situation would not likely occur with all roommates in the same university, much less in the same city, the United States, or the world. The more a theory can be generalized beyond the single situation it is describing or explaining, the better it is as theory.

3. A good theory must be **testable,** which means that we must be able to measure it in some way to ensure that it is accurate and valid. This is the major reason that theory in understanding and predicting social welfare problems and human behavior is somewhat limited. To develop accurate ways of measuring what goes on inside people's minds, their attitudes, and their behaviors is difficult. How do we measure, for example, behavior change such as child abuse, particularly when it happens most often behind closed doors? Can we administer psychological tests to measure attitudes that would lead to abuse, or can we measure community factors such as unemployment to predict child abuse?

Any time we try to measure human behavior or environmental influences, we have difficulty doing so. This does not mean we should stop doing research or trying to develop higher-level theories. Actually, this is an exciting area of social work, and the problems merely point out the need to develop skilled social work practitioners and researchers who can devote more attention to developing good social work theory.

Because social work draws its knowledge base from many disciplines, many theories are applicable to social work. These include psychological theories such as Freud's theory of psychoanalysis and its derivatives, economic and political theories, sociological theories such as Emile Durkheim's theory relating to suicide, and developmental theories such as Jean Piaget's. All of these theoretical perspectives are relevant to social work and an understanding of social welfare problems, but looking at only one of them limits understanding and, in turn, intervention. Thus, we are presenting a framework or perspective that allows us to view social problems and appropriate responses that incorporate a multitude of factors and a multitude of possible responses.

The Systems/Ecological Framework

Social workers, more than any other group of professionals, have directed their profession to the individual and beyond the individual to the broader environment, ever since the professional casework of the Charity Organization Societies and the settlement house reform movements of Jane Addams (Germain & Gitterman, 1996). Consider the definitions of *social work* presented in chapter 2. All emphasize enhancing social functioning of the individual or in some way addressing the relationships, interactions, and interdependence between people and their environments.

This perspective is exemplified by the many roles that social workers play within the social welfare system. True generalists, they advocate for changing living conditions of the mentally ill and obtaining welfare reform legislation that enables the poor to obtain employment and economic self-sufficiency; empower clients to advocate for themselves to reduce violence in their communities; lead groups of children who have experienced divorce; educate the community about parenting, AIDS, and child abuse; and provide individual, family, and group counseling to clients.

This broad framework allows for identifying all of the diverse, complex factors associated with a social welfare problem or an individual problem; understanding how all of the factors interact to contribute to the situation; and determining an intervention strategy or strategies, which can range from intervention with a single individual to an entire society and can incorporate a variety of roles. Such a framework must account for individual differences, cultural diversity, and growth and change at the individual, family, group, organizational, community, and societal levels.

The generalist foundation of social work is based on a systems framework that also incorporates an ecological perspective. We choose to use the term systems/ecological *framework* rather than *theory* because the systems/ecological perspective is much broader and more loosely constructed than a theory. This framework is most useful in understanding social welfare problems and situations and determining which specific theories are the basis for appropriate interventions.

In addition, although various systems (see, for example, works by Talcott Parsons, Max Siporin, Allen Pincus, and Anne Minahan) and ecological approaches (see, for example, works by Uri Bronfenbrenner, James Garbarino, Carel Germain, Alex Gitterman, and Carol Meyer) have been described extensively in the literature, they have not been tested or delineated with enough specificity to be considered theories. A number of advocates of the systems/ecological framework, in fact, refer to it as a *metatheory,* or an umbrella framework that can be used as a basis for incorporating additional theories.

For many years, a general systems framework has been discussed in the literature of many disciplines—medicine, biology, anthropology, psychology, economics, political science, sociology, and education—and it has been used somewhat differently in each discipline. Its principles, as well as similar principles associated with *social systems,* or systems associated with living things, have been incorporated into the social work literature since the beginning of social work.

Mary Richmond, the social work pioneer discussed in chapter 2, wrote in 1922, "The worker is no more occupied with abnormalities in the individual than in the environment, is no more able to neglect the one than the other" (pp. 98–99). Since then, many social work proponents (for example, Hearn, Pincus and Minahan, Siporin, Perlman, and Bartlett) have developed specific approaches or explored various aspects of social work from within the boundaries of the systems/ ecological framework.

More recently, other social work theorists including Germain, Gitterman, and Meyer have advocated an ecological perspective that incorporates many of the same concepts as the systems framework. Some social work theorists (Meyer, 1983) clearly separate the systems perspective and the ecological perspective, considering them as two distinct frameworks. These theorists view the systems framework as relating largely to the *structure,* or the systemic properties of cases, which helps us focus on how variables are related and to order systems within the environment according to complexity. They view the ecological perspective, in contrast, as directed more to *relationships* of person and environment, with more emphasis on interactions and transactions than on structure.

Others (Compton & Galaway, 2004) incorporate concepts that are similar in both perspectives and refer to one framework, the systems/ ecological framework. This is the approach taken in this text. Rather than getting confused over semantics, readers should attend to the broad definitions and principles of the various frameworks discussed and their commonalties rather than their differences. We emphasize these points in understanding a systems/ecological perspective and its significant contributions to social work.

The Perspective of Systems Theory

Systems theory was used initially to explain the functioning of the human body, which was seen as a major system incorporating a number of smaller systems: the skeletal system, the muscular system, the endocrine system, the circulatory system, and so on. Medical practitioners, even ones in ancient Greece, realized that when one component of the human body fails to function effectively, it affects the way that other systems within the body function and, in turn, affects the way the human body as a whole functions. This led to further exploration of the relationships among subparts of living organisms. (For example, Lewis Thomas's *The Lives of a Cell* (1974) clearly articulates the intricate interrelations among the many complex parts of a single cell that enable the cell to maintain itself and to reproduce.)

Systems theory has gained increased attention in fields in addition to social work. Consider the tenuous balance between the various ecosystems as our world becomes increasingly populated and resulting concerns about global climate change and the availability of resources such as water. Engineering and business are among the disciplines that employ various derivations of systems theory, specifically the interactions between complex technological and manufacturing components.

System

One early proponent of systems theory, Ludwig Von Bertalanffy (1968), defined a **system** as "a set of units with relationships among them" (p. 38). A system also can be defined as a whole, an entity composed of separate but interacting and interdependent parts. The early Greek physicians, for example, viewed the body as the larger system and the body's various smaller systems as interacting and interdependent parts.

Similarly, a family can be viewed as a system composed of separate but interdependent and interacting individual family members. From a global perspective, the world can be viewed as a system composed of separate but interdependent and interacting nations. One advantage of the systems/ecological framework is that it is a conceptual framework and can be applied in many different ways to many different situations.

Synergy

The contribution of biology to systems theory is its emphasis on the concept that the whole is greater than the sum of its parts; that is, when all of the smaller systems or subsystems of an organism function in tandem, they produce a larger system that is far more grand and significant than the combination of those smaller systems working independently. The larger system, when it functions optimally, is said to achieve **synergy,** the combined energy from the smaller parts that is greater than the total if those parts were to function separately.

Imagine for a moment that your instructor for this course will ask the class to take an exam on the chapters covered thus far in this text. Each student takes the exam separately, and the scores of each student are listed. The lowest score is 50; the highest is 85. Now suppose that your instructor decides to let the entire class take the exam together. Each person in the class now functions as part of the total group, together solving each exam question. As a class, your score on the exam is 100. The class has demonstrated the concept of the whole being greater than the sum of its parts, or synergy.

Boundaries

An important aspect of any system is the concept of **boundary.** A system can be almost anything, but, by its definition, has some sort of boundary, or point at which one system ends and another begins. The system's environment encompasses everything beyond this boundary. For example, the human body can be seen as a system, as discussed earlier, with the skin as a boundary and the various body subsystems as smaller components of the larger system. From a different perspective, the human mind can be seen as a system, with Freud's id, ego, and superego as components within that system interacting to form a whole that is greater than any of the three components alone—the human mind.

An individual, too, can be part of a larger system. For example, a family system might include one or two parents, a child, and the family dog. We might wish to expand the boundaries of the family system and include the grandparents, the aunts and uncles, and the cousins. We can establish larger systems, such as school systems, communities, cities, states, or nations, and study their interactions and interdependence with each other. We can look at a political system, an economic system, a religious system, and a social welfare system and the ways that those broader systems interact with one another.

When using a systems perspective, the important thing to remember is that the systems we define and the boundaries we confer on those systems are conceptual. We can define them in whatever ways make the most sense in looking at the broad social welfare or the narrower individual problem we are addressing.

For example, if we were to conceptualize Juan's family as a social system, we could include within its boundaries his mother, his younger brother, and Juan. We could choose to include Juan's father as part of his family system

The systems/ecological framework helps social workers and their clients determine who should be included in the family system when identifying potential strengths within the client's environment.

Yellow Dog Productions/Taxi/Getty Images

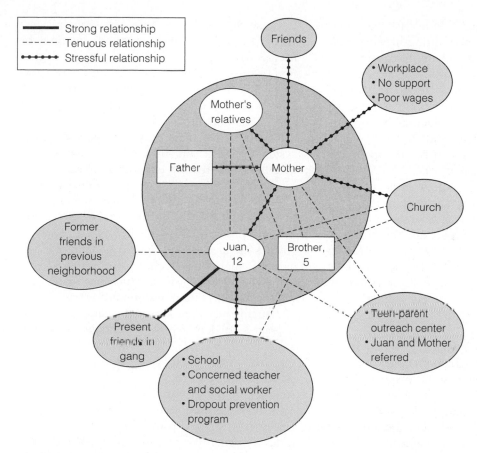

FIGURE 3.1

Using an Eco-Map to Understand Juan's Family Situation

(even though he is out of the home, he is still part of Juan's life, and his absence is a major emotional issue for Juan). We could include grandparents and other extended family members because, although they are not actively involved either physically or emotionally in supporting the family, they are a possible source of support because they have been heavily involved in the past (see Figure 3.1). If we were looking at another family system, however, we might well include more members. The systems/ecological framework is a useful way to organize data to help understand a situation, and its flexibility allows us to define systems and their boundaries in many ways.

OPEN AND CLOSED SYSTEMS

We can draw boundaries wherever it seems appropriate when using a systems/ecological framework, but we must be able to ascertain how permeable those boundaries are. Some systems have easily permeated boundaries between units (such as people) in the system and those outside. We call these **open systems.** Some families exemplify open systems, readily incorporating other people. When someone rings the doorbell at dinnertime, they add a plate. A cousin or a friend may live with the family temporarily or longer, so it may be difficult to know exactly who is a family member and who is not. Systems have internal boundaries as well, such as boundaries between parents and their children.

Sometimes boundaries can be *too* open. For example, in some families, members become overly involved in each others' lives. In other families, parents do not set consistent limits for their children, and no clear boundaries are established between the parents and the children. Unclear boundaries within systems can lead to family problems such as incest. But healthy open systems with clear boundaries are likely to achieve synergy because of their members' willingness to accept new energy from their interactions with the broader environment.

In contrast, some families represent **closed systems.** They have rigid boundaries and are tightly knit within. They may have special traditions for family members only. Although they might get along well with each other, they sometimes are isolated and rarely incorporate other individuals into their system. Sometimes boundaries can be too closed. For example, an abusive husband may not allow his wife to go anywhere unless he goes along.

Before Juan's father began drinking heavily, his family was a fairly open system. While his family engaged in many activities together just as a family, they also socialized a great deal with friends and relatives. If Juan's friends were playing at his house, they frequently were invited to have dinner or to participate in family activities. When Juan's father's drinking increased, his family system became more closed. Juan's mother tried to limit his father's drinking by limiting the family's social activities. When relatives became more critical of his drinking, Juan's family stopped socializing with them to avoid being confronted about the problem.

Because Juan's father lost his temper easily when he drank, Juan stopped inviting his friends to his home and began playing at their houses instead. The family became more isolated. The isolation continued, and the family system remained closed when Juan's father left and his parents divorced.

Organizations, too, may be open or closed systems. Some organizations welcome new members and readily expand their activities to meet new interests. Others are extremely closed and do not encourage new ideas or new members, making those who try to enter the organization feel unwelcome. Communities and other social structures can be viewed as open or closed as well. Juan's new school, for example, is a somewhat closed system, which has made making friends and fitting in difficult for him.

Usually, the more closed a system is, the less able it is to derive positive energy from other systems. Over time, closed systems tend to use up their own energy and develop **entropy,** which means that they tend to lose their ability to function and eventually can stagnate and die. The more isolated Juan's family becomes, the less energy it takes in from the environment, so it has less energy for family members and is less able to function. The family system becomes more and more lethargic and eventually will either change or die, with the family separating and its members becoming part of other family systems. If, for example, Juan's mother were to become extremely abusive and Juan were to become heavily involved in the gang and serious criminal activities, his brother might be placed in foster care, and Juan in a correctional facility for youth.

INTERACTIONS AND INTERRELATIONS

Boundaries and open and closed systems are structural aspects of systems. An additional feature of the systems/ecological framework is its emphasis on the *interactions* and *interrelations* between units rather than on the systems or subsystems themselves. This lends itself well to the need to identify associations among many factors rather than on cause-and-effect relationships between two factors. The interactions and interrelatedness between systems suggest constant motion, fluidity, and change.

The relatedness and interactions incorporate the concept that a change or movement in one part of the system, or in one system, will have an impact on the larger system, or on other systems. Imagine a room full of constantly moving ping-pong balls, each representing a system or a subsystem of a larger system. Hitting one ping-pong ball across the room will change the movement of the other balls.

Similarly, a change in the economic system (for example, inflation) will result in changes in other systems. The educational system could be affected because fewer students could afford to go to college; the social welfare system could be affected because more people would have financial difficulties and need public assistance and social services; the criminal justice system could be affected because more people might turn to crime; the political system could be affected because dissatisfied voters might not reelect the party in office.

The results of interactions and interrelatedness between systems can be seen when viewing Juan's family. Juan's father's drinking led to his job loss, which led to his increased drinking. Both of these factors affected Juan's parents' relationships with each other, or the marital system; the parents' relationships with Juan and his younger brother in the parent–child system; the communication patterns between the family as a system; and relationships between Juan's family system and other systems beyond the family, such as his father's workplace, his family's church, and Juan's school.

Interactions and interrelatedness occur continually, with a constant flow of energy within and across systems. This creates natural tensions that are viewed as healthy if communication is open, because the energy flow creates growth and change. Feedback among systems is important in the systems/ecological perspective, which emphasizes communication. Social workers and others who work within and across various systems must understand those systems' goals and communication patterns. In unhealthy systems, for example, the various members of the system may be communicating in certain ways and may have certain unspoken goals that maintain the system because its members are afraid to change the system or the system is productive for them in some way.

In a family such as Juan's, in which a parent is an alcoholic, the other parent or an older child may perpetuate the alcoholism and unconsciously try to keep the family system as it is because the nonalcoholic sees his or her role as one of caretaking—keeping the family together and protecting the younger children from the alcoholism. If the family system changes, the nonalcoholic parent or the older child no longer will be able to maintain that role and thus may try to force the system back to the way it once was.

Steady State

Another integral concept in the systems/ecological framework is **steady state,** in which systems are not static but are steadily moving. The system is adjusting constantly to move toward its goal while maintaining a certain amount of order and stability, giving and receiving energy in fairly equal amounts to maintain equilibrium. A healthy system, then, may be viewed as one that is not in upheaval but is always ebbing and flowing to achieve both stability and growth.

If Juan and his family receive counseling and other support from the broader environment, his family system might well achieve equilibrium. The system will not stop changing but, instead, will move toward its goals in a less disruptive manner.

Equifinality

A last concept in the systems/ecological framework is **equifinality,** the concept that the final state of a system can be achieved in many different ways. Because a given situation may be interpreted in many ways, many options usually are possible for dealing with it.

When working with Juan and his family, a number of alternatives can be considered to help them function better as individuals and as a family unit. Options might be individual and family counseling, support or therapeutic groups for Juan and his mother, a child-care program for his younger brother, increased interactions between Juan and his father, enrollment in a chemical-dependency program for Juan's father, enrollment in a job-training program for Juan's mother or father (or both), involvement in positive recreational programs for Juan, and membership in a supportive church. Although not all of these options might be realistic for Juan and his family, various combinations could lead to the same positive results. The concept of equifinality is especially important to social workers because their role is to help clients determine what is best for them, and clients' choices are as diverse as the clients themselves.

Critiques of the Systems/ Ecological Framework

One criticism of the systems/ecological framework in social work is that it encompasses the broad environment, yet ignores the psychosocial and the intrapsychic aspects of the individual. Proponents of the systems/ecological framework argue, however, that the individual is perceived as a highly valued system itself and that **intrapsychic** aspects and psychosocial aspects, which incorporate the individual's capacity and motivation for change, are parts of any system involving individuals that cannot and should not be ignored. The framework's inclusiveness encompasses the biological, psychological, sociological, and cultural aspects of developing individuals and their interactions with the broader environment. In fact, the systems/ecological framework often is referred to as a biopsychosocial-cultural framework.

Another criticism of the systems/ecological framework is that, because it incorporates everything, it is too complicated, so important aspects of a situation are easily overlooked. The ecological perspective articulated by social scientists Uri Bronfenbrenner and James Garbarino attempts to address this concern. While Bronfenbrenner and Garbarino incorporate individual developmental aspects into the systems perspective of the broader environment, they divide the system into different levels, or layers of the environment. Note that even though not all social work texts use the same terminology as this text in referring to layers of the environment, they all adhere to the same conceptual perspective that each layer impacts other layers.

Bronfenbrenner and Garbarino suggest that for all individuals, each of these environmental levels has both **risks** and **opportunities.** Opportunities within the environment encourage an individual to meet his or her needs and to develop as a healthy, well-functioning person. Risks are either direct threats to healthy development or the absence of opportunities that would facilitate healthy individual development. Social workers, then, assess risks and opportunities at each level of the environment, working with the client (or client system, such as a family) to achieve positive change by promoting or increasing the environmental opportunities and reducing or eliminating the environmental risks.

Levels of the Environment

Bronfenbrenner (1979) and Garbarino (1992) suggest that risks and opportunities can be found at all levels of the environment. They describe these levels as being like a series of Russian eggs, with a large egg cut in half that opens to reveal a smaller egg, which opens to reveal a still smaller egg, which opens to reveal a still smaller egg (see Figure 3.2 and Table 3.1). They suggest that we

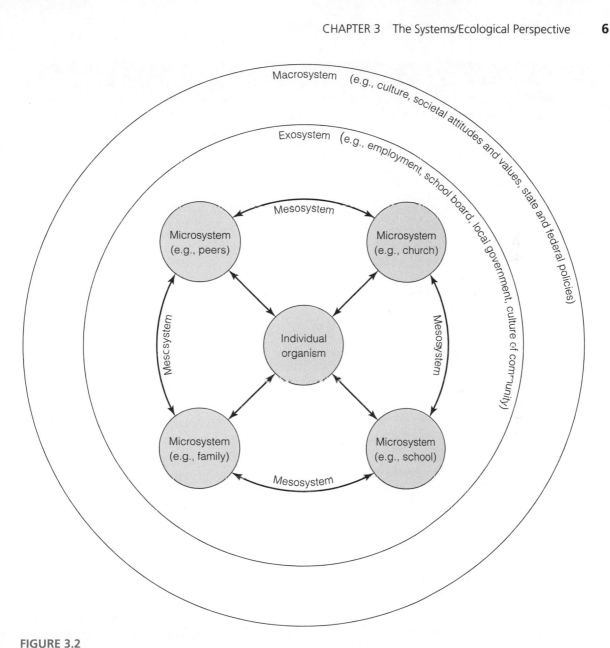

FIGURE 3.2

The Levels of the Ecological System

Source: Reprinted with permission from *Children and Families in the Social Environment*, 2nd ed., by James Garbarino, pp. 29–30. Copyright © 1992, Walter de Gruyter, Inc., New York. Published by Aldine de Gruyter, Hawthorne, NY.

TABLE 3.1
How Levels of the Environment Affect the Individual

Ecological Level	Definition	Examples	Issues Affecting Person
Microsystem	Situations in which the person has face-to-face contact with influential others	Family, school, workplace, peer group, church, or synagogue	Is the person regarded positively? Is the person accepted? Is the person reinforced for competent behavior? Is the person exposed to enough diversity in roles and relationships? Are the person's culture and ethnicity valued and positively affirmed? Is the person given an active role in reciprocal relationships?
Mesosystem	Relationships between microsystems; the connections between situations	Home-school, home-workplace, home-church/synagogue, school-neighborhood	Do settings respect each other? Are cultural factors respected between settings? Do settings present basic consistency in values?
Exosystem	Settings in which the person does not participate but in which significant decisions are made affecting the person or others who interact directly with the person	Place of employment of others in the person's microsystem, school board, local government, peer groups of others in the person's microsystem	Are decisions made with the interests of the person and the family in mind? How well do supports for families balance stresses for parents and children? Is diversity considered when decisions are made?
Macrosystem	"Blueprints" for defining and organizing the institutional life of the society	Ideology, social policy, shared assumptions about human nature, the "social contract"	Are some groups valued at expense of others? Are some groups oppressed (e.g., sexism, racism)? Is there an individualistic or a collectivistic orientation? Is violence a norm?

Source: Reprinted with permission from *Children and Families in the Social Environment.* 2nd ed., by James Garbarino, pp. 29–30. Copyright © 1992 Walter de Gruyter, Inc., Published by Aldine de Gruyter, Hawthorne, New York.

consider the tiniest egg to be the **microsystem** (individual) **level,** which includes the individual and all persons and groups that incorporate the individual's day-to-day environment. This level incorporates the individual's level of functioning, intellectual and emotional capacities, and motivation; the impact of life experiences; and the interactions and connections between that individual and others in the immediate environment.

The social worker's focus at this level also would be on whether the messages and regard for the individual are consistent across individuals and groups, and whether the individual is valued and respected. Juan's microsystem level incorporates all of his own personal characteristics, such as his biological makeup and intelligence; his culture and gender; and his interactions and connections with his mother, brother, father, teachers, and friends. His mother and his old friends, as well as the social worker, could be viewed as providing opportunity to Juan, and his new friends could be viewed as providing both opportunity through peer support and risk through drug use and skipping of school.

The next level of the system is termed the **mesosystem level.** A mesosystem involves the relationship between two microsystems that are linked by some person who is present in both microsystems. Because Juan is part of his family and his school, he provides the link between these two microsystems. The interactions in one microsystem influence the interactions of the others. For example, the conflicting messages to Juan from his school and family settings versus his peer setting had an influence on Juan and can be seen as environmental risks. While his mother and school personnel advocated against his skipping school and experimenting with marijuana, his new peers encouraged him to become involved in these activities. His mother's involvement with the school social worker, however, can be viewed as a mesosystem opportunity for Juan.

The third level, the **exosystem** (community) **level,** incorporates community-level factors that may not relate directly to the individual but affect the way the individual functions. This level includes factors such as the workplace policies of the parents (if they cannot take sick leave when the child is sick, for example, this policy has an impact on the child), school board and community policies, community attitudes and values, and economic and social factors within the neighborhood and community. For Juan's family, exosystem risk factors include the lack of jobs that pay well for employees with his mother's skill level, the unavailability of affordable child care for Juan's younger brother, and community attitudes toward divorce, Mexican Americans, and single parenting. The teen–family outreach center provides an exosystem opportunity for Juan, if it is not too overloaded with other clients.

The final level, the **macrosystem** (societal) **level,** consists of societal factors such as the cultural attitudes and values of the society (for example, attitudes toward women, people of color, the poor, and violence); the role of the media in addressing or promoting social problems (some suggest, for example, that the media promote violence and teen pregnancy); and federal legislation and other social policies that affect a given individual. Contributing to Juan's current life situation are a lack of governmental programs for single parents and potential school dropouts, societal attitudes toward divorce and single parents, discrimination toward Latinos, and the media's glamorizing of gangs and violence. These factors all can be viewed as environmental risks. In spite of these risks, however, opportunities for Juan include democracy, freedom of religion, and education, which might not be found within other macrosystems.

Many advocates of the ecological framework as conceptualized by Bronfenbrenner and Garbarino agree that it is a derivation of systems theory and another way of defining boundaries of systems. They suggest that its use is advantageous because it allows us to see the interdependence and interaction across levels from the microsystem level to the macrosystem level and also allows us to target intervention at a variety of levels to address social problems and individual needs. In Juan's case, we could do the following:

1. at the microsystem level, provide individual counseling to Juan, counsel his family, and help him develop a new network of friends;
2. at the mesosystem level, work with Juan's mother, teachers, and peers to help them become more consistent in the messages they are conveying to Juan;
3. at the exosystem level, advocate for the establishment of a community program to assist teens who are having family problems, as well as low-cost child care for working parents; and
4. at the macrosystem level, lobby for legislation to develop national media programs that educate the public about gangs, drugs, and the working poor.

Note that this framework is a guide to understand how systems interact with and are shaped by the broader environment. It may not always be clear at which level of the environment a factor fits, and some factors may fit at more than one level of the environment. In Juan's situation, religion and the church can fit all levels, depending on how they are conceptualized. If Juan has an individual relationship with a higher power or spiritual being, that relationship could be viewed as a microsystem relationship.

Juan's interactions with individual members of his church—his priest, for example—could be viewed as microsystem relationships as well. The church and Juan's family could be viewed as a mesosystem relationship because Juan is part of both of these microsystems. The church could be viewed at the exolevel of the environment, too, because its attitudes, values, and policies at the community level have a definite impact on how Juan and his family are perceived in the community, especially after the divorce. Likewise, the church plays a major role in shaping the norms, attitudes, and values about divorce and other issues at the societal level, and it can be a macrolevel factor that shapes Juan's development. Deciding where in the environment each factor

fits is not as important as the interdependence and interactions between and among the different levels of the environment and how they influence and are influenced by the developing system being viewed (Garbarino, 1992).

Problems in Living

Social workers Carel Germain and Alex Gitterman (1996) consider the ecological perspective somewhat differently in their approach, adding still another significant way of viewing individuals within their environments. They suggest that everyone has problems at some point—what they term "problems in living." They differentiate three common types of "problems in living" that may require social work intervention:

1. problems associated with life transitions, such as marriage/entering a long-term partnership, birth of a first child or movement of a child out of the family, or movement into middle age or retirement. Juan's family is experiencing the transitions of divorce and a child moving into adolescence.
2. problems associated with tasks in using and influencing elements of the environment. Juan's mother has had difficulty locating affordable child care for her youngest son, and Juan is having difficulty adjusting to a new school. The limited social networks available to Juan and his family suggest the need for intervention in this area.
3. interpersonal problems and needs in families and groups. Juan's family has developed some of the unproductive communication patterns typically found in families in which alcoholism is a problem. Even though these patterns maintained the family as an intact unit for many years, they will continue to stifle individual and family growth unless they change.

In summary, a systems/ecological framework emphasizes that our lives are shaped by the choices we make, that the environment shapes our choices, and that our choices in turn shape the way we interact with our environment. This continual interaction and cyclical perspective suggest that we cannot discuss the individual without including the environment, or the environment without considering the strong forces of individuals in its formulation. The individual and the environment are adapting to each other constantly. The social worker's primary role is to ensure that this adaptation is mutually supportive to both the individual and the environment.

Utility of the Systems/Ecological Framework

The systems/ecological framework is intended to be used as a mechanism to order facts about social welfare problems or individual needs in such a way that appropriate theories can be identified to explore the problems and needs further or to determine interventions. Box 3.1

BOX 3.1
Value of the Systems/Ecological Framework for Social Work Practice

The systems/ecological perspective makes a number of valuable contributions as an organizing framework for social work practice

1. The systems/ecological perspective allows one to deal with far more data than other models, and to bring order to these large amounts of data from a variety of disciplines.
2. The concepts relating to systems are equally applicable to the wide range of clients served by social workers, including individuals, families, groups, organizations, communities, and society.
3. The systems/ecological framework allows for identifying the wide range of factors that have an impact on social welfare problems, their interrelationships, and the ways that a change in one factor affects other factors.
4. The systems/ecological framework shifts attention from characteristics of individuals or the environment to the transactions between systems and their communication patterns.
5. The systems/ecological framework views individuals as actively involved with their environments, capable of adaptation and change.

6. The systems/ecological framework views systems as goal-oriented, supporting clients' self-determination and the clients' participation in the change process.
7. If systems require constant transactions with each other to survive, the social worker's purpose is to provide and maintain opportunities for transactions for all populations and to work to reduce isolation of individuals and systems.
8. Social workers need to work to ensure that change and tension are not resisted in systems and to remove the notions that change and conflict are pathological.
9. Social workers must be aware of the systems within which they work and how change within those systems affects the whole. This means that social workers must choose points of intervention with care.
10. Social workers are a social system and components of a social systems network.

Source: From *Social Work Processes,* by B. Compton and B. Galaway. Copyright © 1998 Wadsworth Publishing Company; The Dorsey Press. By permission of Wadsworth Publishing Company, Pacific Grove, CA 93950, a division of Thomson Learning.

presents some of the ways the framework aids social workers. This framework can be thought of as a way to "map the territory" or gather and fit together pieces of a puzzle to understand a situation.

When dealing with a problem such as poverty, for example (addressed in chapter 7), many individuals have one-dimensional ways of explaining the problem such as "because people are lazy" or "they are the victims of their own circumstance." A systems/ecological perspective would identify many factors—a large, complex territory and a puzzle with many pieces. Individual factors, family factors, community factors, and societal factors, such as the impact of the economic system and of unemployment, racism, sexism, and so forth—all contribute to poverty in some way. Table 3.2 lists some of the factors that shape the interactions between individuals and their environments.

Once the territory is mapped out or all of the puzzle pieces (or as many as possible) are obtained, the systems/ecological framework allows for further exploration of certain factors, parts of the terrain, or pieces of the puzzle. This perspective, too, allows for individualization and diversity, which means that cultural and gender differences are readily accounted for (see Table 3.2). After obtaining the larger picture, we can better ascertain where to direct our attention; whether more information is needed and in what areas; what aspects of the environment create risks or opportunities; and, if intervention is required, how risks can be minimized and opportunities promoted, and at what level and within which system or systems within the environment. One or more additional theories or frameworks can then be applied to obtain more information or to guide intervention. The advantage of the systems/ ecological perspective is that we are less likely to overlook a major aspect of a situation and, as a result, intervene inappropriately.

TABLE 3.2
Factors That Shape Individual Functioning and Relationship with the Environment

Factors	Examples
Personal	Level of prenatal care received
	Intellectual capacity or ability
	Emotional capacity or mental health
	Level of social functioning
	Physical health
	Age
	Ethnicity and culture
	Motivation
	Life stage or transitional period
	Crisis level
Family	Support systems and availability of significant others
	Family patterns, structure, and values
	Economic level and employment
	Level of functioning or family crisis
Community	Social class compared to rest of community
	Ethnic, cultural, and class diversity; attitudes and values
	Social roles available within community
	Community support
	Economic conditions
	Employment opportunities
	Educational opportunities
	Environmental stress
Societal	Societal attitudes and values
	Racism, sexism, poverty levels
	Supportive or lack of supportive legislation, programs, and policies
	Media role

The Utility of Other Theories and Frameworks

In their professional practice, social workers call upon other, more limiting theories and frameworks under the umbrella of the systems/ecological framework. Two useful types of frameworks are psychosocial frameworks and cognitive behavioral frameworks (Turner, 1996). These and other frameworks that social workers commonly use are discussed in greater depth in chapter 5.

Psychosocial Frameworks

Psychosocial frameworks include psychoanalytic theory, ego psychology, and life-span development frameworks. These frameworks often are used together and are not always viewed as mutually exclusive.

PSYCHOANALYTIC THEORY

Psychoanalytic theory, based largely on the works of Sigmund Freud, is built on the premise that children are born with biologically rooted functions, termed *drives,* that dictate individual functioning. These drives are related primarily to sexual expression and aggression. Psychoanalytic theory also is a stage or developmental framework because its premise is that individuals cope with different changes in biological, psychological, and social functioning at different stages of their lives. This framework includes both conscious and unconscious drives, and internal interactions within an individual among the id, ego, and superego.

The emphasis on interaction between the individual and the broader environment is more limited than it is in many other theories, although psychoanalytic theory does include attention to the impact of life experiences, primarily during early childhood, on later functioning; and on the development of internal defense mechanisms, such as denial and rationalization, to cope with the environment. If Juan's situation were to be viewed from this framework, his sexual drives during preadolescence and the impact of his father's leaving during this time would be major focal points.

This framework is complex and is based largely on individual psychopathology, or emotional illness. In applying this framework to individuals with problems, the suggested intervention is individual psychoanalysis to work through intrapsychic conflicts.

EGO PSYCHOLOGY AND LIFE-SPAN DEVELOPMENT FRAMEWORKS

Ego psychology stems from psychoanalytic theory, with a major concentration on the development of a strong ego as opposed to interactions among the id, ego, and superego. The ego psychology perspective also focuses more on the transactions between the person and the environment and the impact of the environment in shaping the development of a healthy ego (Erikson, 1959). From this perspective for Juan and his family, intervention would involve determining the impact of his family situation during his childhood and ways to help him feel better about himself and increase his self-esteem.

Psychoanalytic and ego psychology are both life-span development frameworks. They suggest that individuals interact with their environments in different ways to meet different needs at different points in the life cycle, and the ways that needs are met in previous stages shape individual functioning and later development. Like psychoanalytic theory, this approach emphasizes ways that early life experiences shape later behavior. The emphasis, however, is much more on the ways that the environment shapes the resolution of these issues.

For example, using a life-span development framework developed by Erik Erikson, an individual addresses issues of basic trust versus basic mistrust during the first year of life. If an infant is placed in an environment in which his or her basic needs (such as feeding or nurturing) are not met or are met inconsistently, the child does not develop a sense of trust. If trust is not developed later, the child is likely to have difficulty in other stages of life—for instance, in developing intimate relationships during young adulthood. Within this framework, Juan's developmental needs involve developing a sense of identity, primarily through peer relationships. Thus, for example, the gang members are filling a major developmental need for Juan that he does not feel can be met in other ways.

Although important and useful to social workers, these frameworks are more limiting than the systems/ecological framework. They place more emphasis on early life experiences than later experiences, and less emphasis on interactions and transactions among broader levels of the environment and the impact on the individual. Finally, they suggest intervention primarily at the individual level.

Cognitive Behavioral Frameworks

Cognitive behavioral frameworks place little emphasis on an individual's life experiences or biological factors. Their premise is that environment, and not heredity, is what largely determines behavior. These frameworks focus primarily on the present and on shaping individual thinking and behavior within the person's immediate environment. The goal is to shape behavior, not to change personality. In Juan's case, he may have developed a series of self-messages that suggest to him that he is not competent. These repeated messages have led to his poor schoolwork and his attempts to seek competence in other areas, such as drug use and illegal activities. If Juan is helped to change his self-messages to positive affirmations about himself, he will begin to see himself as competent and reengage in school.

The interventions within these frameworks are largely at the individual level, with much greater emphasis on the present and the environment. Cognitive behavioral frameworks are extremely useful to social workers. They can help individuals understand ways that unproductive thought patterns shape behaviors and, knowing this, help the person develop new thought patterns and behaviors leading to healthier functioning.

Political and Ideological Frameworks

Social workers often use political and ideological frameworks, as well as others, in a variety of ways and often in tandem with one other. In a political sense, people may adhere to perspectives that are considered liberal, conservative, libertarian, or radical. Although people often label themselves as fitting one category, their perspectives often fit more than one category, depending on the issue. Someone may be liberal in policies about child welfare and education and conservative about policies related to crime. Ideologies shape how we vote, our attitudes about social welfare programs and policies, and our beliefs about whether people are capable of change.

The systems/ecological framework can help us understand how environment shapes the development of a person's ideologies and political perspectives, as well as what might be likely to persuade someone to change a point of view. Understanding why someone holds a certain perspective is helpful for social work with clients and also in engaging in community action and legislative and political advocacy.

When addressing social welfare issues, an understanding of a person's worldview, as opposed to a more traditional approach based only on facts, has gained attention in recent years. Many social workers adhere to a constructivist perspective (Franklin & Nurius, 1998), which holds that each individual constructs his or her own reality based on his or her perceptions and belief systems. Social workers with this perspective try to see the world from their client's perspective rather than their own perspective, or employ a more global concept of reality. Because a social worker must understand the person's interactions with the environment to understand his or her reality, one can see how this perspective is consistent with the systems/ecological framework.

Although the systems/ecological perspective also can be used when intervening with an individual or the broader environment, social workers almost always use it as the major framework for understanding a given situation or problem. Once the problem is understood, however, and the broad terrain is mapped out using this framework, other frameworks may be added for further assessment as well as intervention.

The Systems/Ecological Framework in Professional Practice

Because the generalist model of social work incorporates all levels of the environment and the interactions and interdependence within and between levels, the systems/ecological framework is especially useful as an organizing framework for professional practice. Specifically, the framework

1. allows the social worker to deal with large amounts of information from many different areas and to bring order to that information;
2. includes concepts that are applicable to the full range of clients served by social workers, including individuals, couples, families, groups, organizations, communities, and broader societal systems;
3. incorporates not only the structures of the social units involved but also the interrelatedness and interactions within and between units;
4. shifts attention away from the characteristics of units to the transactions and interactions between them;
5. views individuals as active participants in their environments, capable of change and

adaptation, including shifting to new environments;
6. incorporates the concept of client self-determination and recognizes that multiple approaches can be effective in facilitating change;
7. focuses social workers on the need to provide and maintain continual transactions between people and their environments for all populations and to monitor social systems heading for isolation;
8. provides a constant reminder to social workers that change is healthy and necessary for systems to grow but that systems often resist change;
9. places both the social worker and the agency within the client's environment; and
10. reminds social workers that since a change at one level of the system creates changes at other levels, interventions must be thought through and chosen with care. (Compton & Galaway, 1998, pp. 130–131)

Applying the Systems/Ecological Framework

The systems/ecological framework is especially useful in understanding the complexities of large systems within our environment such as the social welfare system. The social welfare system in place at any given moment is the product of the interactions and interrelatedness of historical, economic, and political forces. As a large system, it is reshaped constantly by changes in societal values and events beyond its boundaries. Changes in societal values, for example, result in increased public acceptance of programs for battered women and child care for children of working mothers. An economic recession results in extensive cutbacks in social welfare services.

The scope of social welfare systems in the United States is neither as broad, comprehensive, and integrated as most social workers would like nor as constrained and limited as some contend.

In a sense, it is not a formal system at all but, rather, a collection of ad hoc programs developed in diverse and often unique political circumstances. Thus, although we have programs for the aged, individuals with physical disabilities, and dependent children, each program has its own political history and its own political constituency.

Target populations of social service agencies are groups that are not served adequately by the primary social systems in our society (the economic system, the political system, the family system, the religious system, the health system, and the educational system). Typically, the social welfare system comes into play as a result of family breakdown, problems in income distribution, and institutional failure in the religious, education, health, and/or business sectors.

Although each of us probably would offer a somewhat different mission statement for an ideal social welfare system, at a minimum we probably would agree that such a system should guarantee to each person a socially defined minimum standard of well-being. To attempt to meet this standard, the social welfare system interacts with primary social systems within our society: the family system, the economic system, and the political system. Each of these primary systems has a principal function, as illustrated in Table 3.3. The social welfare system is most often seen as a residual social system that comes into play when the primary system either fails in some way or generates undesirable consequences.

The organized social welfare system, composed of numerous and varied social services and institutions, is designed to help individuals and groups attain satisfactory standards of life and health. This view implies recurring failure in other social systems. It assumes that individuals sometimes need outside help in coping with a complex social order. Social welfare institutions that make up the social welfare system assist in meeting the needs of individuals when primary resources are not available or adequate to address them. A structured set of social agencies must stand ready to respond to personal crises

TABLE 3.3 **Social Systems and Their Functions**	
Systems	**Functions**
Primary	
Family	The primary personal care and mutual assistance system between parents and children and between adults and elderly
Political	The authoritative allocation of public social goals and values
Economic	The allocation and distribution of scarce resources to competing entities
Secondary	
Other goal-specific systems (e.g., education system, health care system, defense system)	The list and functions of secondary systems are dependent on individual choice. What would you include?
Social welfare system	To respond to failure or dysfunction in primary and secondary systems

and system failures—to overcome the crisis; to enhance problem-solving and coping skills of communities, groups, organizations, families, and individuals; and to empower these entities to create social change that will result in less frequent crises.

In this view, the social welfare system is seen as the structured set of responses developed to deal with the dysfunction of other systems. For example, the family system is intended to meet children's physical and emotional needs. But at times, the primary family system fails and is unable to serve this function. At that point, the social welfare system provides services such as respite child care, foster care, and counseling. When the social welfare system functions to assist or replace the family in its child care roles, this exemplifies a social welfare system response to a primary system failure. A second example of a social welfare system response to a primary system dysfunction can be seen in relation to the economic system. We know that in the economic system, income is uneven, leaving some people poor. Thus, we have generated an income-assistance system to provide various types of financial help to specific classes of people in need.

An overview of American social welfare institutions and social work practice reveals an incredible range of public and voluntary agencies seeking to respond to social problems. For some areas of need, the response is well conceptualized and generous. In other areas, the response is hasty and scanty. Still other social needs invoke no response at all. A major problem with our social welfare system is that each need usually is treated as a separate issue rather than an interactive and interdependent part of a larger issue. Seldom, for example, is attention given to how a response to need A is related to its impact on need B.

The federal welfare reform legislation enacted in 1996 serves as a good example. One of the highly publicized outcomes of passage of this legislation has been that more former welfare recipients have obtained jobs. In reality, most public-assistance recipients receive benefits for only a short time, but they often have to move back and forth between welfare and work because they cannot make ends meet with the low-paying jobs they are forced to take because of their limited education and training. Thus, while more former welfare recipients are employed now, the legislation has failed to address their other needs, such as child care, transportation, health-care benefits, and affordable housing. As a result, many of these individuals are in worse circumstances than when they were receiving the public assistance benefits.

These additional unmet needs are overloading local social service government agencies and private sector entities such as churches. Child advocates also are worried about the increase in cases of spouse abuse, child abuse, substance abuse, homelessness, malnutrition, and other problems that are likely to arise when the time limit ends

for individuals who are unable to make it without public assistance. The legislation unfortunately did not allow for the allocation of additional resources to meet these needs.

Health care also exemplifies the interrelatedness between systems and social problems. In recent years, state legislators, concerned about the high costs of health care for the poor, reduced the funds allocated for health care rather than raise taxes. In doing so, they ignored the fact that state dollars are matched by federal dollars to provide health care for the poor. For every dollar that a state contributes, the federal government matches the amount with federal money. The reduction in dollars by the states limits the amount of federal money coming into the states, which seriously reduces the number of clients who can be served by state public-assistance health programs. No longer served by these health programs, the states' poor do not seek health care until they are desperate, and when they do, they come to local hospitals as indigent (nonpaying) patients. This means that local hospitals have to foot these bills, which now are higher than they might have been if the poor had sought care earlier. It also means that the higher costs in these states are footed by local taxpayers who pay local taxes to support hospitals. Thus, what the legislators ultimately intended as a money-saving measure for their states' citizens has turned out to be far more costly in the long run.

The systems/ecological framework can be used to help understand issues at every level of the environment and across levels. The framework further can be used to determine types of intervention at all levels of the environment once the complex issues are understood.

The Generalist Model

As we discussed in chapter 2, the generalist model of social work practice taught at the BSW level suggests the use of multiple interventions in working with clients at the individual, family, group, organizational, community, or societal level. Generalist practice focuses on the interface between systems, with equal emphasis on the goals of social justice, humanizing systems, and improving the well-being of people. It uses a multilevel methodology that can be applied to varying levels of the environment, depending on the needs of the client system. Generalist practice incorporates a knowledge, value, and skills base that is transferable between and among diverse contexts and locations (Schatz, Jenkins, & Sheafor, 1990, p. 223).

The central theme of most generalist practice is the systems/ecological framework. Generalist practice is based on the need for congruency, or a positive fit, between the person and his or her environment, and the premise that the role of social work is to promote, strengthen, and restore—if necessary—that positive fit. **Person-environment fit** is the actual fit between the person's or group's needs, rights, goals, and capacities and the physical and social environment within which the person or group operates. The fit can be favorable, adequate, or unfavorable. When exchanges with the environment over time are inadequate, the individual's healthy development might be affected negatively, or the environment might be damaged (Germain & Gitterman, 1996, p. 817).

The Strengths Perspective

Generalist social work practice is aimed at identifying a system's strengths and using them to modify the environment with which that system interacts to increase the level of person–environment fit. Generalist practice requires knowledge of social work, as well as knowledge and skills in working with individuals, families, groups, organizations, and communities, including advocacy, to empower individuals to change their environments. In this view, the client is the expert, the one who is most knowledgeable about his or her needs, and the social worker builds on the strengths of individuals to facilitate

their ability to change their environment, or their coping mechanisms in interacting with it.

The generalist social work **strengths perspective** can be contrasted with what commonly is referred to as the "medical model," which considers the client as having some type of illness or weakness and the helper as the expert who determines and provides the treatment. Table 3.4 compares the generalist social work strengths perspective and the medical model.

All individuals have strengths, and they are much more likely to grow and change when these strengths, rather than the deficiencies, are emphasized. In his book *The Strengths Perspective in Social Work Practice,* Dennis Saleeby (2005), a social work educator at the University of Kansas, delineates six basic principles on which the strengths perspective is based:

1. *Respecting clients' strengths*—Social work practice is guided first and foremost by a profound awareness of, and respect for, clients' positive attributes and abilities, talents and resources, desires and aspirations. . . .
2. *Clients have many strengths*—Individuals and groups have vast, often untapped and frequently unappreciated reservoirs of physical, emotional, cognitive, interpersonal, social and spiritual energies, resources and competencies. . . .
3. *Client motivation is based on fostering client strengths*—Individuals and groups are more likely to continue autonomous development and growth when it is funded by the coin of their capacities, knowledge, and skills. . . .
4. *The social worker is a collaborator with the client*—The role of "expert" or "professional" may not provide the best vantage point from which to appreciate client strengths. . . .
5. *Avoiding the victim mindset*—Emphasizing and orienting the work of helping around clients' strengths can help to avoid "blaming the victim". . . .
6. *Any environment is full of resources*—In every environment there are individuals and institutions [that] have something to give, something

TABLE 3.4

Comparison of Generalist Social Work Strengths Perspective and Medical Model

Generalist Practice or Strengths Perspective	Medical Model
Lack of goodness of fit between person and environment; needs not being met	Problem with individual or weakness of individual; person is labeled as sick or deviant, given diagnosis
Client and environment present strengths or opportunities and barriers or risks; building on strengths can motivate clients to change themselves, their perceptions, or their environment.	Client has problems or needs; sick clients need help in changing their worldviews to fit the norm
Client is expert about his or her life and needs; social worker is facilitator to help client discover needs and identify possible resources to get them met.	Helper is expert who diagnoses client and prescribes treatment; expert is in charge of treatment; client is expected to cooperate.
Client can be empowered to get needs met/use or learn new skills and resources.	Client needs expert helper to help change; needs to be dependent on experts for help.

Source: Adapted from *The Integration of Social Work Practice,* by R. J. Parsons, J. D. Jorgensen, and S. H. Hernandez. Copyright © 1994. Brooks/Cole Publishing Company, Pacific Grove, CA 93950, a division of Thomson Learning. By permission of the publisher.

that others may desperately need . . . and for the most part, they are untapped and unsolicited. (pp. 9–13)

The systems/ecological framework enables the social worker and the client to identify strengths at all levels of the environment. This assessment includes the client's personal characteristics, individuals within the client's immediate environment who can be of support to the client, and neighborhood and community resources. The social worker can play a key role in helping the client and those within the client's environment reframe a quality so it can be seen as a strength and be used to address the client's needs.

A school social worker may reframe how school personnel view a mother who has been deemed overly persistent and someone to be avoided because she comes to the school every day to complain angrily about how school personnel are treating her children. The social worker can help school personnel see that this mother cares about her children deeply and

wants the best for them as a parent, pointing out the quality of persistence as a strength. The school social worker then can mediate with the mother and school personnel to help the parent use this strength in more appropriate ways so her concerns are heard.

Often, when strengths are identified and reinforced in positive ways, behaviors can go beyond change to even exceed expectations. For example, this mother could become an advocate for the school and use her persistence to obtain support for school bonds in the community. Contrast this approach with a deficit model, which would label the mother's persistence as negative, may anger the parent, and possibly eliminate the persistent behavior rather than help her learn how and when to use persistence effectively.

A goal of social work is to build on client and environmental strengths so clients can reduce barriers and increase opportunities. A strengths-based perspective supports the concept of **resilience,** the ability to recover or adapt successfully to adversity. Juan has many strengths that reveal his resilience. When he felt rejected by his family, he tried to find others in his environment for support. Although he initially found acceptance from gang members, his ability to establish relationships with peers and adults helped him reach out to receive the help he needed and ultimately end his relationship with those who erected barriers to his success. Instead he began to seek opportunities in his environment that would promote his success, building on his strengths as he saw the success that came with his new behaviors and relationships.

Social workers and other helping professionals are capitalizing on research that identifies characteristics of resilience, such as being more likely to seek out others (teachers, neighbors, parents of friends, grandparents if a child) in an environment for support when the usual resources (parents) are unavailable for some reason. Clients can learn resiliency skills, making them better able to capitalize on opportunities in their environments and to avoid or reduce risks.

School social workers such as Ms. Herrera are working with Juan and other students to build on their strengths and ultimately become more resilient when interacting with their environment. Box 3.2 identifies resiliency factors that she and other helping professionals can encourage in youth to help prevent juvenile delinquency and other problems.

Empowerment

Another key aspect of generalist social work practice is **empowerment,** the "process of increasing personal, interpersonal, or political power so individuals can take action to improve their life situation" (Gutierrez, 1990, p. 149). Many of the individuals with whom social workers interact are members of at-risk populations who face barriers at all levels of the environment, which often limits their functioning. They often lack the power and resources to change their environments, or they may be in situations where they perceive themselves as powerless, incompetent, or lacking in resources. Rather than "fixing" problems, which often reinforces such feelings, social workers help clients see that they can create change. People who are empowered can make changes at the individual, family, group, neighborhood, organizational, community, state, national, or international level.

Juan's situation illustrates how the strengths perspective and empowerment are used effectively. As Ms. Herrera continued to emphasize Juan's strengths, he realized that he had more power over his life than he had thought. He was able to talk with his mother and negotiate more time with friends. He also felt empowered to say no to his peers who were pressuring him to join the gang. Realizing that other teens were in situations similar to his, he became active in a school leadership program and a key member of a community group that helped to establish a youth center.

Empowering clients like Juan gives them hope and helps them see that they have a sense of control over their lives. Empowerment leads to continual growth and change and increased feelings of competence.

Social and Economic Justice

The systems/ecological framework is useful in committing the social work profession to promote **social and economic justice,** which includes fairness and equity in regard to basic civil and human rights, protections, resources and opportunities, and social benefits. How resources are distributed at every level of the environment, who has access to those resources and opportunities, and how policies at all levels of society affect human development shape social work practice and types and levels of intervention. Juan and his family, because they are Mexican American, poor, and in a family situation involving divorce, face social and economic injustice at all levels of the environment.

BOX 3.2
Resiliency Factors That Reduce Juvenile Delinquency and Other Problems Associated with Youth

- Competence—being able to do something well
- Usefulness—having something to contribute
- Belonging—being part of a community and having relationships with caring adults
- Power—having control over one's future
- Responsiveness—ability to elicit positive responses from others
- Communication—ability to assert oneself without violating others
- Empathy and caring—ability to know how another feels and understand another's perspective
- Compassion—desire and will to care for and alleviate another's suffering
- Altruism—doing for others what they need, not what you want to do for them
- Forgiveness—ability to cease to feel resentment against self and others, including one's abusers
- Problem solving—ability to plan and use identified resources effectively
- Positive identity—sense of one's internal, relatively stable self apart from others
- Internal locus of control and initiative—sense of being in charge, of having personal power; being motivated from within to direct attention and effort toward a challenging goal (initiative)

- Refusal to accept negative messages about one's gender, culture, or race (resistance)
- Goal direction, achievement motivation, and educational aspirations—relentless effort, persistent inner drive, or unshakable determination to survive
- Special interests, creativity, and imagination—interests and hobbies that bring a sense of task mastery (special interests); ability to create rather than imitate (creativity); ability to form a mental image of something not present to the senses or never before perceived in reality (imagination)
- Optimism and hope—choosing to see the glass half full and not half empty (optimism); confidence that the odds can be surmounted (hope)
- Faith, spirituality, and sense of meaning—having a belief system that allows you to attribute meaning to misfortune and illness (a form of reframing the situation)

Source: Adapted from *Four Pillars of the Positive Youth Development Model* (Washington, DC: U.S. Department of Health and Human Services Administration for Children and Families, Family and Youth Services Bureau, 2004); and *Risk and Protective Factors of Child Delinquency* (Washington, DC: U.S. Department of Justice, Office of Juvenile Justice and Delinquency Prevention, 2003).

Social workers advocate for social and economic justice by working to expand individual access to resources and opportunities at all levels of the environment, including adequate education; food, clothing, and shelter; employment; health care; and participation in local, state, and national political processes. Further, social workers have a commitment to alleviate social and economic injustice and its resulting oppression and discrimination. Some of the possible types of oppression that can result from social and economic injustice are shown in Table 3.5.

TABLE 3.5
Common Forms of Oppression

Institutional Oppression	Cultural Oppression
Housing	Values and norms
Employment	Language
Education	Standards of behavior
Media	Holidays
Religion	Roles
Health services	Logic system
Government	Societal expressions
Legal services	The arts
Transportation	
Recreation	

Source: *Interdependence: The Route to Community,* by A. Condeluci (Delray Beach, FL: St. Lucie, 1996), p. 18. Reprinted with permission of the publisher.

The Helping Process

The beginning generalist social work professional is seen as a "change agent" who can assist client systems in identifying needed change, developing strategies to make the change with those client systems, empowering and assisting client systems to implement those strategies, and monitoring and evaluating throughout the process to ensure that the desired change is happening. Note that the term *client system* is used rather than *client,* because social work intervention often is directed at a level of the environment beyond the individual. A **client system** can encompass individuals, families, groups, organizations, communities, or larger social entities at which intervention is directed.

Social workers with a bachelor of social work degree are trained to follow a generalist approach that can be applied to individual needs that are part of everyday life, as well as to larger client systems. No matter what level of the environment the social worker selects as an interven-

tion point, the generalist approach can be a useful tool in bringing about planned change.

Although many variations can be chosen when delineating the stages of the helping process from a generalist social work perspective, all have the systems/ecological framework as a base. In their identification of three stages, Miley, O'Melia, and DuBois (2003, p. 90) incorporate the framework with a strengths/empowerment perspective.

1. **Dialogue**
   a. Share and establish collaborative relationships with clients.
   b. Clarify client perspectives and social worker perspectives regarding strengths, challenges, and needs.

2. **Discovery**
   a. Search and explore resources and strengths that clients may not know they have.
   b. Assess and explore feelings and determine needs.
   c. Develop plans and frame solutions.

3. **Development**
   a. Strengthen and help clients get what they need.
   b. Activate resources, including clients' personal resources.
   c. Recognize successes and reinforce strengths.
   d. Build new resources and competencies.

Social work educators Compton and Galaway (1998) and others take a somewhat more traditional view, delineating what is referred to as a problem-solving approach, but they suggest similar stages when working with client systems:

1. **Contact or engagement**
   a. Develop a relationship with the client system.
   b. Define the problem(s) to be addressed.
   c. Identify preliminary goals.
   d. Obtain as much information as possible to develop intervention strategies.

2. Contract

   a. Assess and evaluate the strengths and needs of the client system.
   b. Formulate an action plan.
   c. Determine what resources are needed for the plan to be successful.

3. Action

   a. Carry out the plan.
   b. Monitor and adjust the plan as needed.
   c. Terminate.
   d. Evaluate.

Note the similarities between these stages and those with more emphasis on the strengths and empowerment of the client system. In moving through these stages with a client system, regardless of the specific model used, the social worker and the client address the following issues together:

- Who has the power?
- What connections does the client have?
- What connections are working?
- What connections are not working?
- What connections are missing?
- Is this the way things should be? What would the client like to see changed?
- What connections can be used as resources to facilitate the change?
- What about the big picture? How do all the pieces of the system fit together? (Miley, O'Melia, & Dubois, 2003, p. 293)

As you can see from the phases and issues addressed, the systems/ecological framework is the organizing framework, and intervention is from a generalist practice perspective, which incorporates the client's strengths and the broader environment, empowerment, and promotion of social and economic justice. A large part of generalist social work practice often involves mediating between systems to strengthen their connections to each other.

After reviewing the phases of the helping process, it is easy to see the "goodness of fit" between this process and the systems/ecological framework and the many ways in which the two are related. Ms. Herrera's involvement with Juan and his family illustrates how this framework can be applied to understand or to intervene at various levels of the environment.

Applications with Juan and His Family

During the *contact and engagement* or dialogue phase of the helping process, Ms. Herrera, the school social worker, applied all of the concepts of the systems/ecological framework. In developing an initial relationship with Juan and his mother, she called upon her preliminary knowledge about 12-year-old boys and their developmental needs during this preadolescence stage, single-parent women and their special needs, the Mexican American culture, and ways in which preadolescents and parents might view a professional from an authoritative organization such as a school. She empathized with Juan and his mother as she realized how they might view life in their day-to-day reality. As she continued to get to know Juan, Ms. Herrera allowed him to be the "expert," telling her what his life was like and what his needs were. She emphasized his strengths and helped him realize that he had many on which to draw.

As Juan and Ms. Herrera began the *contract* or discovery phase, Ms. Herrera gathered information about Juan from his mother, his teachers, his friends, and others within his environment who could help them obtain a holistic picture of Juan and his needs. Ms. Herrera and Juan looked at the characteristics of Juan, his mother, his teachers, and his friends and also at their interactions with Juan and with each other. They considered both needs and strengths. They realized that both Juan and his mother were motivated to change and that his teachers were committed to helping him.

Ms. Herrera incorporated information she learned about Juan's family with her knowledge about the dynamics of a family in which substance abuse had been a problem, about long-term effects of child maltreatment on parents, about gangs and peer relationships when adolescents feel lonely and isolated, and about Juan's family's church, Juan's mother's jobs, and the community and its attitudes toward Juan and his family. She was especially concerned about the lack of resources in the community and the lack of support for young adolescent males and single-parent mothers.

As she discovered more about Juan's situation, Ms. Herrera and Juan began to explore possible resources that would be available to help Juan get his needs met. Ms. Herrera set up a meeting with Juan and his mother to clarify their needs and to establish preliminary goals based on the information they had gathered. The three of them agreed that three initial needs were to (1) reduce Juan's responsibility at home, (2) address his sense of loss over his father's leaving and anger because he had left, and (3) help Juan create a positive peer support group.

They identified goals to reduce the pressure from Juan's mother for him to take care of his brother and do so much at home, to help Juan deal with his feelings about the divorce, and to help him develop a positive peer support group. The three of them agreed that, although the initial referral related to Juan's school behavior and performance, these underlying needs were more critical and would, in fact, most likely improve his school performance if they were addressed.

After these three goals were identified, Juan and Ms. Herrera began meeting, sometimes separately and sometimes with his mother. They considered all possible options regarding how these goals might be met, listing potential resources that might be helpful. Some resources, such as more financial help from Juan's father or Juan's mother quitting her job and going on public assistance, were rejected for various reasons. Finally, the three of them developed a contractual agreement specifying how Juan's needs would be addressed.

During the *action* or development phase, Ms. Herrera referred Juan's mother to the local human services agency, where she was able to qualify for low-income child care for her youngest child. Juan's mother also asked for information about a job-training program to upgrade her skills so she could obtain a higher-paying job and be able to have only one job instead of two. This would allow her to spend more time with Juan and his brother.

With Ms. Herrera's help, Juan and his mother negotiated specific tasks that Juan would do at home and agreed that he would have 2 hours after school every day to spend time with friends. They also agreed to rules regarding how he could spend his time with them. Juan and his mother also agreed that if Juan were to follow the rules and complete his chores, he could spend time weekly with his previous friends in his old neighborhood. In addition, Juan agreed to participate in a school support group for seventh-grade boys whose parents have divorced. Ms. Herrera believed that this approach would help Juan work through some of his feelings about the divorce and also develop a new set of peers with whom he could become socially involved.

Juan and his mother also began counseling at the local teen–parent center, and the counselor and Ms. Herrera conferred regularly about his progress there. Ms. Herrera, while maintaining confidentiality about Juan's specific family issues, communicated with Juan's teachers. They agreed to help Juan feel more accepted in his new school and to provide opportunities for him to get to know other students.

After 3 months, Juan's teachers reported that he was coming to class, participating in class discussions, handing in his homework, and no longer exhibiting behavior problems. His grades also improved significantly. Juan began to feel more empowered, and he dropped his friends who were gang members and formed several solid friendships with classmates at his new school. Two of his friends were from the support group. Although the group was terminated after

8 weeks, Ms. Herrera still met with Juan every 2 weeks or so to be sure that he was doing well.

Juan spent a great deal of time in the group talking about the divorce and his feelings about his father. He had visited his father twice and was looking forward to seeing him during spring vacation. Juan and his mother, and sometimes his younger brother, participated in family counseling sessions at the teen–parent center. Juan's mother developed a new set of friends and a support system through her youngest son's child care center, to which many other single parents brought their children. The mother enrolled in a computer-programming training course and was looking forward to the opportunity to upgrade her skills.

As positive changes in one system took place, they had a positive impact in other systems as well. The fact that Juan's mother was able to obtain child care, for example, reduced her stress and enabled her to interact more positively with Juan. Ms. Herrera's talking with Juan's teachers and helping them understand his needs for acceptance enabled them to view Juan more positively. This, in turn, reduced some of the pressure on him, increased his self-esteem, and gave him the needed confidence to seek new friendships and find more positive ways to gain acceptance. Juan became involved in a school leadership program and helped develop an outreach program for new students.

Although she believed that she was able to make a difference when helping Juan and his mother, Ms. Herrera was increasingly frustrated about many other of her students who were like Juan. She had referrals on her desk for 12 more students in similar situations. She decided that, as a more productive use of her time, she would develop additional resources at other levels of the environment rather than deal with each student on an individual basis. Ms. Herrera contacted the director of the counseling center and other individuals in the community who were concerned. A group of 15 community representatives, including Juan as the teen representative from the school, began to develop plans for a comprehensive program that would help teens and their families. The plan called for staff members from the counseling center to come to the school weekly to lead additional support groups, for outreach efforts to be made to local businesses to locate adult mentors to work one-to-one with teens in need of additional adult support, and for the development of a teen center with after-school, evening, and weekend recreational programs. Finally, the group decided to work with a state legislative group to advocate for additional funding for adolescent services and for single-parent families.

Summary

Social welfare needs involve many interrelated factors. These factors may be ordered in many ways to describe social welfare needs, to understand them, and to predict when they will occur and under what conditions. Because the needs are so complex and involve human behaviors and environmental influences that are difficult to measure, as well as a variety of disciplines, no one theory can address all social welfare or human needs. The systems/ecological framework, however, is a framework of choice for social workers because it incorporates the concept that an individual is part of a larger environment with which he or she continually interacts and is an interdependent part of that environment. This framework is useful in organizing information to determine what else is needed and to develop an appropriate intervention strategy.

The framework incorporates factors at the individual, family, group, organizational, community, and societal levels and allows for a variety of interventions at one or more levels. The framework is congruent with the generalist practice approach and its emphasis on client strengths, empowerment, and the promotion of social and economic justice.

Key Terms and InfoTrac® College Edition

The terms below are included in the Glossary. To learn more about key terms and topics in this chapter, enter the following search terms using InfoTrac College Edition or the World Wide Web:

association
boundary
cause-and-effect relationship
client system
closed system
empowerment
entropy
equifinality
exosystem level
generalizable
inclusive
intrapsychic
macrosystem level
mesosystem level
microsystem level

open system
opportunities
person-environment fit
resilience
risks
social and economic justice
steady state
strengths perspective
synergy
system
systems/ecological framework
testable
theory
worldview

Discussion Questions

1. Why is it difficult to develop good theory to address social welfare needs?
2. Briefly identify the key components of the systems/ecological perspective. Compare and contrast open and closed systems, and static and steady state systems, and offer examples to exemplify your discussion.
3. From a systems/ecological perspective, identify the social systems that currently affect Juan's life. Which aspects of each system you identified seem to be barriers and which are opportunities?

4. Using the systems/ecological perspective as conceptualized by Bronfenbrenner and Garbarino, identify at least one strategy you might use if you were a social worker to help Juan and his family at each of the four levels of the environment: microsystem, mesosystem, exosystem, and macrosystem.
5. What are at least four advantages of using the systems/ecological perspective to understand social welfare needs?
6. Briefly describe the helping process and its advantages to social workers within social welfare institutions. What type of intervention plan would you suggest if you were the school social worker assigned to work with Juan. Why?
7. How are the concepts of empowerment, client strengths, resilience, and social and economic justice congruent with the systems/ecological framework?

On the Internet

www.clasp.org/

www.sc.edu/swan/

www.jcpr.org/

www.who.int/violenceprevention/approach/ecology/en/index.html

References

Bronfenbrenner, U. (1979). *The ecology of human development.* Cambridge, MA: Harvard University Press.

Compton, B., & Galaway, B. (1998). *Social work processes* (6th ed.). Pacific Grove, CA: Wadsworth.

Condeluci, A. (1996). *Interdependence: The route to community.* Delray Beach, FL: St. Lucie.

Erikson, E. (1959). *Identity and the life cycle: Psychological issues.* (Monograph no. 1.) New York: International Universities Press.

Franklin, C., & Nurius, P. (Eds.). (1998). *Constructivism in practice: Methods and challenges*. Milwaukee, WI: Families International.

Garbarino, J. (1992). *Children and families in the social environment*. New York: Aldine de Gruyter.

Germain, C., & Gitterman, A. (1996). *The life model of social work practice: Advances in theory and practice* (2nd ed). New York: Columbia University Press.

Gutierrez, L. M. (1990). Working with a woman of color. *Social Work, 35*, 135-153.

Gutierrez, L. M., & Lewis, E. (1999). *Empowering women of color*. New York: Columbia University Press.

Meyer, C. (1983). *Clinical social work in the eco-systems perspective*. New York: Columbia University Press.

Miley, K., O'Melia, M., & DuBois, B. (2003). *Generalist social work practice: An empowering approach* (4th ed.). Boston: Allyn & Bacon.

Parsons, R., Jorgensen, J., & Hernandez, S. (1994). *The integration of social work practice*. Pacific Grove, CA: Wadsworth.

Richmond, M. (1922). *What is social casework?* New York: Russell Sage Foundation.

Saleeby, D. (2005). *The strengths perspective in social work practice* (4th ed.). Boston: Allyn & Bacon.

Schatz, M., Jenkins, L., & Sheafor, B. (1990). Milford redefined: A model of initial and advanced generalist social work. *Journal of Education for Social Work, 26*(3), 217–231.

Shriver, J. (2004). *Human behavior and the social environment: Shifting paradigms in essential knowledge for social work practice* (4th ed.). Boston: Allyn & Bacon.

Thomas, L. (1974). *The lives of a cell: Notes of a biology watcher*. New York: Viking.

Turner, F. (Ed.). (1996). *Social work treatment: Interlocking theoretical approaches* (4th ed.). New York: Free Press.

U.S. Department of Health and Human Services Administration for Children and Families, Family and Youth Services Bureau. (2004). *Four pillars of the Positive Youth Development Model*. Washington, DC: Author.

U.S. Department of Justice, Office of Juvenile Justice and Delinquency Prevention. (2003). *Risk and protective factors of child delinquency*. Washington, DC: Author.

Von Bertalanffy, L. (1968). *General system theory*. New York: Braziller.

Suggested Further Readings

Anderson, R., Carter, I., & Lowe, G. (1999). *Human behavior in the social environment: A social systems approach*. New York: Aldine de Gruyter.

Bloom, M., & Germain, C. (1999). *Human behavior and the social environment: An ecological view*. New York: Columbia University Press.

Buckley, W. (Ed.). (1968). *Modern systems research for the behavioral scientist*. Hawthorne, NY: Aldine de Gruyter.

Butts, J., Mayer, S., & Ruth, G. (2005). *Focusing juvenile justice on positive youth development*. Chicago: Chapin Hall Center for Children.

Catalano, R., Burglund, M., Ryan, J., Lonczak, H., & Hawkins, D. (1999). *Positive youth development in the United States: Research findings on evaluations of positive youth development programs*. Seattle, WA: U.S. Department of Health and Human Services.

Connard, C., & Novick, R. (1996). *The ecology of the family: A background paper for a family-centered approach to education and social service delivery*. Portland, OR: Northwest Regional Educational Laboratory.

Council on Social Work Education. (1999). *Curriculum policy statement for the master's degree and baccalaureate degree programs in social work education*. New York: Author.

Day, P. (2005). *A new history of social welfare* (3rd ed.). Boston: Allyn & Bacon.

Greene, R. (Ed.). (2001). *Resiliency: An integrated approach to practice, policy, and research*. Washington, DC: NASW Press.

Gutierrez, L., Parsons, R., & Cox, E. (1997). *Empowerment in social work practice: A sourcebook*. Pacific Grove, CA: Wadsworth.

Larson, R. (2000). Towards a psychology of positive youth development. *American Psychologist, 55*, 170–183.

McLaughlin, M. (2000). *Community counts: How youth organizations matter for youth development*. Washington, DC: Public Education Network.

Mullis, R., & Davis, M. (2005). An ecological model approach to childhood obesity. Retrieved from http://nasulgc.org/foodsociety/meeting05/Mullis.pdf

Networks for Youth Development. (1998). *The hand-book of positive youth outcomes*. New York: Fund for the City of New York.

Norman, E. (Ed.). (2001*). Resiliency enhancement: Putting the strength perspective into social work practice*. New York: Columbia University Press.

Pittman, K., Irby, M., & Ferber, T. (2000). Unfinished business: Further reflections on a decade of promoting youth development. In Public/Private Ventures (Ed.), *Youth development: Issues, challenges, and directions*. Philadelphia: Public/Private Ventures, pp. 17–64.

Roth, J. L., & Brooks-Gunn, J. (2000). What do adolescents need for healthy development?: Implications for youth policy. *Society for Research in Child Development Social Policy Report, 14*(1), 3–19.

Scales, P. C., & Leffert, N. (2004). *Developmental assets: A synthesis of the scientific research on adolescent development* (2nd ed.). Minneapolis, MN: Search Institute.

Schwartz, H. N. (2000). Juvenile justice and positive youth development. In *Youth development: Issues, challenges, and directions*. Philadelphia: Public/Private Ventures.

Tomison, A. M., & Wise, S. (1999, Autumn). Community-based approaches in preventing child maltreatment. *Issues in Child Prevention, 11*.

Villaruel, F. A., Perkins, D. F., Borden, L. M., & Keith, J. G. (Eds.). (2003). *Community youth development: Programs, policies, and practices*. Thousand Oaks, CA: Sage Publications.

Zastrow, C., & Kirst-Ashman, K. (2006). *Understanding human behavior in the social environment*. Pacific Grove, CA: Wadsworth.

CHAPTER 4

Diversity and Social Justice

Jackson Dupree, a 22-year-old African American male, is a student at a university in the Midwest. Growing up in a large city on the East Coast, he enjoyed a relatively easy childhood until he started high school. From the time Jackson and his friends began driving, the city police stopped them routinely for various reasons. They were told that they "look like suspects" in some recently-reported crime, or that they seemed to be "cruising" a neighborhood and were asked why they were there. On several occasions, Jackson and his friends were stopped by clerks or security guards at city malls and questioned about their activities. Jackson's parents had taught him to be respectful, especially when relating to police, so he always answered their questions politely. These events took a toll on Jackson, who was an honors student in school and active in his church. As a result of these experiences, he had trouble sleeping at night and became much more cautious around adults.

Hoping he would fit in better if he were to go to a university in an area that seemed more accepting of African Americans, he decided to attend college out of state. During his sophomore year, Jackson developed an intense relationship with another male and came out, declaring to his friends that he was gay. Jackson was a well-respected student leader on campus and his sexual orientation didn't seem to matter to those with whom he interacted on the small university campus. This past year, however, Jackson had two negative experiences indicating that sexual orientation clearly matters to some. At the suggestion of one of his professors, he applied for a summer job at a local youth center. After an interview, he did not hear back from the firm in spite of having phoned them several times. He later learned that he hadn't been hired because the center was worried about ruining its image and angering parents if it were to hire a gay person.

Later in the year, Jackson went to a local club with a group of friends, both gay and straight. When he decided to leave his friends early to study for an exam, he was attacked in the parking lot by two men, and beaten with a tire iron while his assailants called him names relating to his sexual orientation. Now physically recovered from the beating, Jackson wonders where he fits in a world that doesn't seem to support either his race or his sexual orientation.

Situations such as those experienced by Jackson are not rare. Many individuals seek fulfillment and opportunities only to find that social barriers hamper their ability to achieve these goals. Jackson represents only one case in millions of Americans who find that social and economic justice is not necessarily achieved through hard work, dedication, and quality performance. All too often, social mobility and opportunity are not equally available to all who seek to attain the American Dream. Women, people of color, gays and lesbians, and other members of diverse groups historically have been denied opportunities in business, religious, political, and social life, and the fair treatment that white males have come to expect and take for granted. Under the subtle guise of institutional sexism, racism, and homophobia, the right to free and full participation in our social and economic institutions is denied to those who fail to meet dominant-group criteria. In Jackson's case, the fear that he would influence young people at the recreation center to "become gay" was sufficient justification for denying him the opportunity for a job. And often, being a member of a marginalized group makes one an easy target for racial profiling or even the type of hate crime that Jackson experienced. Stereotypes, once institutionalized, are difficult to overcome.

In this chapter we will explore in some detail the concepts of social and economic justice and examine the characteristics of social injustice implicit in racism, classism, sexism, and gender orientation. The impact of social injustice is not always the same for people of color, women, or those who are gay, lesbian, bisexual, or transgender. It is somewhat ironic, for example, that white women, the targets of gender inequality, often discriminate against people of color, or that people of color discriminate against individuals because of their sexual orientation. To better understand the strengths of groups marginalized by society as well as the differential effects of institutional racism, sexism, classism, and homophobia, we review these separately. Keep in mind that social and economic injustices and their consequences lead to a life of second-class citizenship in our society for members of all groups who are impacted, and that being a member of more than one minority group may further marginalize an individual.

Social and Economic Justice

Although much has been written about the concepts of social and economic justice, many works talk more about social and economic *in*justice than justice. The term **social justice** was first used by a Sicilian priest in 1840, and then by philosophers in discussions about how society should be structured to best meet the needs of its citizens. The concept of social justice gained additional attention in 1861 in John Stuart Mill's essay *Utilitarianism*. Mill advocated that all resources and other benefits of living in a society should be distributed according to recognizable principles of justice. His writings were intended to appeal to the aristocracy in Europe to address the needs of uprooted peasants who had relocated to cities seeking jobs. Mill called for decision makers to attend to the "common good," whereby citizens would work collaboratively to build communities and programs that would contribute to the "good" of others.

Mill and other philosophers debated the question: What is a just society? Their writings covered a continuum of perspectives, from allowing members of society to create their own lives and use resources as they wished, as long as they didn't infringe on the rights of others, to the idea that resources generated by all members of society should be distributed to all, first meeting the needs of those members who were the worst off (Novak, 2000).

Today, social justice is viewed from both political and philosophical perspectives. This concept is imbedded in many religious teachings as well, including principles set forth in Judeo-Christian teachings. The goal of social justice is full participation of all groups in a society that is mutually shaped to meet their needs and ensures that all of its members are psychologically safe and secure (Adams, Bell, & Griffin, 1997). Social justice focuses on how individual rights are protected and supported in day-to-day interactions as well as within the fabric of society.

Advocates for social justice want all members of society, regardless of background or status, to have basic human rights and equal opportunities to access the benefits of the society. Although this concept sounds reasonable, particularly when talking about basic freedoms such as freedom of thought, the right to humane treatment, and other general principles, the concept of **economic justice,** which relates to fair allocation of resources, becomes more complicated. A basic problem with the perspective of economic justice is that few of us want to surrender our economic freedom if it means that ultimately we will have less so others can have more (Garcia & Van Soest, 2006; Rawls, 1971; Social Justice, 2006). The social work profession has as one of its core values the promotion of social and economic justice, in which social workers are called upon constantly to assess how their actions support these principles in all of their interactions and at all levels of the environment.

Prejudice and Discrimination

Social injustice and **social inequality** are generally considered to be products of prejudice and discrimination. **Prejudice** is a value learned through the process of socialization. Once internalized, prejudice becomes part of an individual's value system. People who are prejudiced rarely consider themselves to be so. Objects of prejudice are presumed to have behavioral characteristics that those who are prejudiced find objectionable. Through negative stereotyping, women, people of color, gays and lesbians, and members of other diverse groups are presumed to hold behavioral traits that justify their exclusion from free and full participation in the social roles of society.

Stereotypes are beliefs that members of certain groups behave in specific ways. Hence, some in our society hold beliefs that women are not as astute as men at decision making; that African Americans are less intelligent and prone to idleness and crime; that Latinos prefer the slower pace of agrarian life; and that gays and lesbians persist in encouraging heterosexuals to become homosexual. These are among the many negative stereotypes associated with each of these groups. In contrast, positive stereotypes—that women are nurturing and supportive; that African Americans gain strength from religion and their churches; and that Latinos place considerable value on their large, extended families—are just as liable as negative stereotypes to false presumptions. The notion that Caucasian males are endowed with intellectual prowess and creative skills that other groups lack is another example of a positive stereotype. To illustrate how prejudice affects decision making, consider the following:

> A conservative Caucasian couple had an older daughter who graduated from college and moved to Florida to work for a well-known national corporation. While there, she fell in love with an attorney who also worked for the corporation. At first her family was happy about the reported relationship, but became extremely upset when they learned that the attorney was Puerto Rican. In spite of family pressure, she married the attorney and joined the Catholic church. As a consequence, her parents, two of her four siblings, and one set of grandparents discontinued contact with her. Because there were also strong differences of opinion within the family about whether the marriage was desirable, in effect, intermarriage tore this family apart.

In this situation, the older daughter violated strong in-group values and traditions that had become institutionalized and affirmed as a matter of family beliefs and faith. There was little doubt that her husband was of impeccable character, a hard worker, an outstanding citizen, a man of faith, and a loving and caring husband. Those qualities from the family's perspective were necessary but not sufficient for their blessing and acceptance of the newlyweds. Indeed, from the parents' perspective, any male who was not Caucasian would have been unacceptable as a marriage partner for their daughter.

Although most people hold deep respect for traditions and strongly held values, one can readily understand how prejudgment can ensue. Like the family just described, dominant-group members in society have longstanding values, attitudes, customs, and beliefs related to women, poor people, gays and lesbians, and people of color. These beliefs often result in social barriers that preclude or limit women and people of color from living in a socially just society.

Social distance is invariably a mirror of prejudice, just as discrimination is a vehicle to ensure social distance. Prejudice is the presumption, without the benefit of facts, that certain behaviors are characteristic of all members of a specific group. As a consequence, members of the dominant group may demean members of a minority group by assuming that assigned behaviors are true, and by then relating to individual members of that group through the filter of prejudice.

Although the target of prejudice may vary, the paradox is that virtually no one is free from prejudice. For example, prejudice may not be directed toward gender, race, ethnicity, or creed. It may be directed toward people who themselves are prejudiced!

Prejudice is a psychological construct that may result in discrimination. Although prejudice can exist without discrimination (and discrimination without prejudice, for that matter), the two usually coexist. Prejudice fuels the fires and provides the justification for discrimination. If individuals hold the false belief (prejudice) that people of certain groups are less intelligent, incapable of equal participation, or would threaten traditional practices, they may practice differential treatment (discrimination), thereby placing the erroneously feared threat at some distance. Denying women, people of color, the poor, the elderly, gays and lesbians, and other social groups the right to equal social participation limits the opportunity structures through which the desired behavioral characteristics could be acquired. A vicious, self-perpetuating cycle then is set in motion.

Discrimination is the action that maintains and supports prejudice. Discrimination involves actions toward selected individuals or groups because of prejudicial beliefs: denying equal access to education, community services, employment opportunities, residential housing areas, membership in certain religious and social organizations, and access to community services. Although everyone has prejudices, the people most damaged by prejudice and discrimination are those who are not members of the dominant group. Individuals who are members of the group that has the most power are the least likely to suffer from the repercussions of prejudice and discrimination.

Over time, the impact of prejudice and discrimination becomes part of the everyday fabric of society. Members of both dominant and minority groups are not always aware that what they take for granted is discriminatory to some social groups.

Institutional discrimination is discrimination that results from accepted beliefs and behaviors and is codified in societal roles and policies. It is thereby "intrinsic" to the mores of a society. Institutional discrimination is reinforced through the social practices of dominant-group members, who may be oblivious to the effects of their actions. Examples of institutional discrimination include: lack of access to housing in specific geographic areas where ethnic groups have settled over time; the resulting ethnic composition of schools based on housing patterns; the location of freeways and storage units for dangerous chemicals; access and participation in higher education; access to certain types and levels of employment; and pay differentials among white males, women, and people of color who are doing the same type of job. Whereas institutional racism is based on a person's color, institutional sexism results in the denial of rights or opportunities for participation on the basis of gender. In both instances, free and full participation is denied on the basis of membership in some group.

Members of the dominant societal group with prejudices against other groups have the power to use their prejudices against those groups. These prejudices coupled with power result in

oppression, unjust uses of power against non-dominant groups by the dominant group. This power restricts the actions of the non-dominant groups and also allows the dominant group to exploit these groups to its advantage. Examples of oppression include the placement of tank farms and other dangerous environmental hazards in poor neighborhoods populated largely by people of color, and restricted access of certain groups to educational and employment opportunities.

Even if individuals who are members of the dominant social group do not demonstrate overt prejudice toward other groups, they have advantages that members of non-dominant groups are less likely to enjoy. Peggy McIntosh of the Wellesley College Center for Research on Women has written about "white privilege," noting that white males and females alike, regardless of whether they are personally prejudiced against non-white groups, have taken-for-granted privileges not always available to members of other groups. Her list includes privileges such as being fairly certain that one can rent or purchase a home in an area of choice if it's affordable; being exposed to educational materials that don't exclude their group; being assured that skin color won't be a barrier when making financial transactions with either checks or debit or credit cards; easily finding foods, music, and hair products that are part of one's culture; not having to educate one's children about physical safety, even from those who are supposed to protect them; not being expected to speak for all the members of one's group; and being fairly certain that mistakes made will not be attributed to one's racial group (McIntosh, 1988).

Groups that experience prejudice, discrimination, and oppression from the dominant group are considered to be **populations at risk.** Because of their treatment, both historically and presently, members of at-risk populations are more likely to experience serious health and mental health problems, live shorter lives, and be victims of hate or other serious crimes.

Before going into more detail in this chapter about commonly marginalized groups (women; gays, lesbians, bisexuals, and transgender persons; those who are in the bottom class economically; and members of non-white racial and ethnic groups), we point out that each group has many strengths as well as disadvantages because of marginalization and oppression. In addition, although large numbers of individuals within a group may have similarities (i.e., income level, education), members also show much diversity. Therefore, it is inappropriate to stereotype and assume that all members of a group exhibit the characteristics held by the majority of group members. Actually, there is more diversity *within* a group of individuals (e.g., a group of African Americans) than *between* groups (e.g., between African Americans and Caucasians or between African Americans and Asian Americans).

Social and Economic Justice for Women

In a grievance against her employer, a female staff member with a college degree charged that her male boss had touched her inappropriately on numerous occasions, pressured her to come to his hotel room while they were attending a conference, hired males for comparable positions at much higher salaries than hers, and told her when she applied for a transfer to a different division of the organization that she should either quit her job and stay at home with her children or go to work as a checker at a local grocery store.

Throughout recorded history, women have faced various forms of social inequality and discrimination. Invariably, inequality was—and is—justified on the basis of the biological superiority of men, despite no evidence to support that premise. Notwithstanding advances made during the past several decades, women in our society experience discrimination. Gender-biased discrimination is more visible in the occupational market and economic areas than in other aspects of social participation. Some progress has been made, but many male-dominated job positions have remained virtually unobtainable by qualified women. Males still primarily hold positions such as pilots, military officers, and construction supervisors.

Although many women have successfully entered and moved up in male-dominated careers, they tend to be concentrated in lower-paying, lower-status positions such as clerical workers, child-care workers, receptionists, nurses, hair stylists, bank tellers, and cashiers. Men tend to be concentrated in higher-paying positions including lawyers, judges, engineers, accountants, college instructors, physicians, and dentists, as examples. Management and administrative positions at the upper levels continue to be held mostly by men.

Income

From 1890 to 2004, the proportion of women in the labor force increased from 14.9% percent to just under 60% (U.S. Bureau of Labor Statistics, 2005b). This increase ushered in a number of conflicts and issues related to women's participation in the labor market. Chief among the issues is the concept of **comparable worth,** often best understood by the phrase "equal pay for equal work." Much of the income disparity between men and women, however, is attributable largely to differences in occupational positions, which have changed little over the past decade. Income differences exist primarily because men are employed in positions of leadership or in technical fields, whereas women are employed disproportionately in the lower-paying clerical and service fields. Even when women hold positions similar to those of men, their income is lower. Seniority or related factors do not always account for these differences, and employers generally concede that, for a given type of position, men receive a higher income than women (see Figure 4.1). In 2004, median weekly earnings for women who were full-time employees was $573, or 80% of the median weekly pay of $713 earned by men, up from 77.3% in 2000 (U.S. Bureau of Labor Statistics, 2005a).

Researchers note that this gap is closing because women are more likely to graduate from

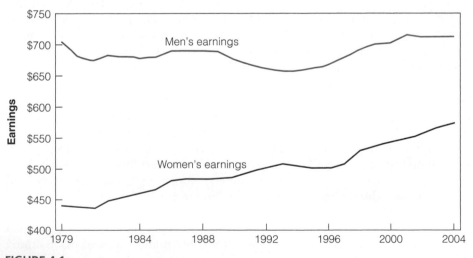

FIGURE 4.1

Median usual weekly earnings of full-time wage and salary workers in constant (2004) dollars by gender, 1979–2004 annual averages

Source: Highlights of Women's Earnings in 2004 (Washington, DC: U.S. Bureau of Labor Statistics, 2005), p. 3.

college and have more years of work experience than women in the past, rather than because of less discrimination in hiring and retaining women in the workforce. The discrepancy in pay between males and females, however, is increasing for one group—those with 4-year college degrees. In 2005, college-educated women between 36 and 45 years of age earned 74.7 cents for every dollar that their male counterparts earned, compared to 75.7 cents a decade earlier, in 1995 (Economic Policy Institute, 2007). Analysts note that this difference is most likely because of both gender discrimination and the fact that many women in this group are more likely to choose to stay at home with children rather than earn high salaries. Box 4.1 gives characteristics of women in the labor force. Not only are there discrepancies between what men and women earn, but women of color overall earn less than white women (see Figure 4.2).

The practice of channeling women into lower-level positions, with the resulting limited career choices and lower incomes, represents an institu-

tionalized policy of gender-based discrimination. Although efforts are being made to provide equal employment opportunities for women, social roles continue to be gender-typed and are passed down from generation to generation through the process of socialization. Women choose careers for many reasons, and there are interactive effects between careers chosen, salaries, and gender. For example, women traditionally have been socialized to be nurturers and find value in those roles. Because they also have been socialized to value relationships, they tend to enter careers that involve relating to people in some way, such as teaching, nursing, and social work. Even from a values standpoint, these careers should pay more than they do, but they remain at the lower end of the salary range because those positions historically have been filled by women.

Women continue to be less well represented in engineering and the sciences, law, transportation and utilities, mining, and construction, and

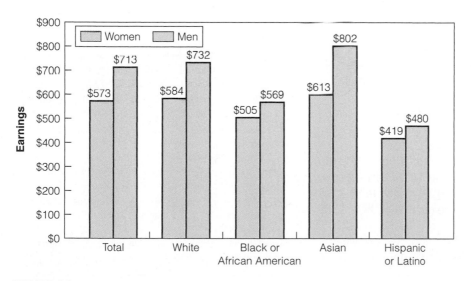

FIGURE 4.2

Median usual weekly earnings of full-time wage and salary workers by gender, race, and Hispanic or Latino ethnicity, 2004 annual averages

Source: Highlights of Women's Earnings in 2004, by U.S. Bureau of Labor Statistics. (Washington, DC: Author, 2005), p. 3.

BOX 4.1
Facts About Working Women and Gender Equity

- Percentage of women who participated in the labor force in 2004: 59.2%[1]
- Percentage of the workforce in 2004 who were women: 46%[1]
- Percentage of women working who worked full-time in 2004: 74%[1]
- Percentage of women who participated in the labor force in 2004 by ethnicity: 61.5% for Blacks; 58.9% for Whites; and 56.1% for Latinos[1]
- Difference in median weekly earnings for men and women by ethnic group in 2004: both Asian men and women had the highest earnings compared to members of other groups and Latinos had lowest earnings[2]
- Percentage of median income for full-time, year-round women workers compared to men in 2004: 80%[2]
- Amount of income working families in the U.S. lose annually because of the wage gap: $200 billion[3]
- Amount of income the average 25-year-old working woman will lose to equal pay during her work life: $455,000[3]
- Hourly salary college-educated women earned compared to college-educated men: $21.30 for women; $28.06 for men[4]
- Amount that incomes of single working mothers would increase if they earned comparable wages in 2002: 17% (and their poverty rates would be cut in half, from 25% to 12.6%)[3]
- Percentage of children under age 6 living in families headed by single-parent working mothers working full-time below the poverty level in 2002: 17.3%[5]
- Where largest percentage of employed women worked in 2004: management, professional, and related occupations (38%) and sales and office occupations (35%)[1]
- Occupations with the highest median weekly earnings among women who worked full-time in 2004: pharmacists ($1,432); chief executives ($1,310); lawyers ($1,255); computer and information systems ($1,288); computer software engineers ($1,149); computer programmers ($1,006); physicians and surgeons and human resource managers ($958)[1]
- Percentage of senior management positions held by women in Fortune 1000 and Fortune 500 companies in 2003: 3%[6]

---

[1]*Equal Pay for Working Families*, by American Federation of Labor–Congress of Industrial Organizations (Washington, DC: Author, 2007). See also www.aflcio.org.

[2]*The State of Working America 2006–2007*, by Economic Policy Institute (Ithaca, NY: Cornell University Press, 2007).

[3]*Fact Sheet: Why We Still Need Affirmative Action*, by National Employment Lawyers Association (San Francisco: Author, 2003). See also www.nela.org.

[4]*Highlights of Women's Earnings in 2004*, by U.S. Bureau of Labor Statistics (Washington, DC: Author, 2005).

[5]*Current Population Statistics, Annual Demographic Survey, March Supplement*, by U.S. Census Bureau (Washington, DC: Author, 2002).

[6]*Women in the Labor Force in 2004*, by Women's Bureau (Washington, DC: U.S. Department of Labor, 2006).

---

overrepresented in the fields of financial activities, education, health services, and leisure and hospitality. When women are excluded or limited from participating in these job arenas, educational preparation programs also are affected because women are forced to make career (and consequently educational) choices on the basis of opportunities for employment and advancement.

Education

Ironically, men hold leadership positions in professions that employ predominantly women, such as public education and social work. A career-oriented woman entering the education system usually has more difficulty than a similarly qualified man in securing promotion to an administrative position. Meanwhile, women are relegated to the lower-paying, less prestigious position of classroom teacher throughout their careers.

Even though nondiscrimination policies are in place, qualified women educators who seek promotion to administrative positions are confronted with the task of penetrating a gender-biased tradition of assigning men to those roles in the public school system. Some evidence points to changes in the numbers and percentages of women who hold administrative positions. Opening the opportunity structure to accommodate all qualified professionals, regardless of gender, is a slow process. The first step in widening the doors for women in these areas is higher education, and more women are pursuing degrees than in previous years. In fact, their participation in higher education overall is now greater than it is for men.

In 2004, women earned 58.2% of all college degrees awarded, receiving 57.5% of all bachelor's degrees and 58.9% of all master's degrees. Although the percentage of women earning graduate and professional degrees has increased slightly in recent years, women still earn slightly fewer degrees of this type than men do. In 2004, 49.4% of first professional degrees and 47.9% of academic doctoral degrees were awarded to women, as were 42.7% of the medical doctor degrees, 40.1% of the dental doctorates, and 29.2% of all theological degrees (U.S. Bureau of Labor Statistics, 2005b).

Social Work

Historically, most social work professionals have been women—in 2004, 76.1% of all social work practitioners. In a field that has championed equal rights for women (as well as a field that is predominantly female), median salaries, ironically, are higher for males (though at 95.8%, the gap is not as great as in many other job categories) and leadership roles are more often held by men. Men are represented disproportionately in administrative and managerial roles, and, as a group, receive slightly higher salaries than women (U.S. Bureau of Labor Statistics, 2005b). To that extent, the social work profession—despite its advocacy of women's rights—reflects the tendency of other professions as well as the business community.

Religion

In organized religion, in which women are more active participants than men, only 13.4% are in clergy roles, though this number has more than doubled over the last five years (U.S. Bureau of Labor Statistics, 2005b). Women seldom hold primary leadership positions in churches, and women are employed in religious associations even less often. Many religious groups base their male-biased pastoral leadership roles on the "holy writ," thereby effectively excluding women from appointments to significant leadership responsibilities in those bodies.

Politics

After the November 2006 elections, the majority of members of Congress are still men, but women have made gains in the House, the Senate, and governorships. Of the 435 U.S. representatives, 70 were women—a gain of 10 from 2002; and 16 of 100 U.S. senators were women, a gain of two from 2002. Only nine of the 50 governors were women, although this was an increase from six in 2002 (U.S. Department of Commerce, 2006). Although these figures reflect the subordinate role that women continue to play in the legislative process, major change may be indicated with the election of Nancy Pelosi (Democrat, California) as the first female Speaker of the House. Some progress has been made at the state level, where the percentage of women in office has been rising during the past 30 years.

In spite of the increase of women in politics, male bias often is present in legislative debates about proposed laws that directly affect women For example, recent federal legislation enacted by Congress relating to personal bankruptcy prohibits writing off credit card debt as part of bankruptcy proceedings. A secondary part of this legislation enables credit card companies to charge high interest charges and late fees for credit card holders. This legislation has a disproportionate impact on low-income people, particularly single-parent women, who often use credit cards to help pay for regular living expenses because they do not generate enough income to cover living costs. When these women get in over their heads financially and are forced to declare bankruptcy, they are left with extensive debt from which they may never recover.

Institutional Sexism

The discussion and examples just presented indicate the strong gender bias in our society. Women are treated differently in the professions, in business, and in other areas that impact their daily lives. Their status as women negatively influences their opportunities to survive economically and to move into prominent roles regardless of their competence or ability. In effect, women are discriminated against solely because they are women. This practice, called **sexism,** is a result of the values and practices embodied in our social institutions.

Most children are taught that boys are to be aggressive and dominant and that girls are to be nurturing and submissive. Parents often model these attributes in family interactions, in which the father assumes the roles of rule maker, disciplinarian, and decision maker and the mother assumes responsibility for the nurturing roles of caring for the children and the household. Even if parents try to rear their children in nonsexist ways, children are exposed to sexist views in interactions outside their families and via the media.

Performance differences between men and women invariably reflect societal attitudes and values far more than any inherent physical or psychological variances in maleness or femaleness. In modern society, few roles could not be performed by either men or women, although throughout the life cycle, gender-role distinctions are made and differences are emphasized. These distinctions become entrenched in societal values, hindering women from "crossing over" into roles considered masculine. Hence, an aggressive, goal-oriented, intelligent woman may be viewed as masculine and censured for departing from prescribed female role behavior.

Societal values and practices continue to result in a gender-segregated division of labor. Although some progress has been made in identifying roles as "asexual" (neither male nor female), roles in general are gender-typed. Women have great difficulty gaining access to roles identified as appropriate for men only. Gender differentiation, too, is observed in opportunities to secure credit, purchase homes, negotiate contracts, and obtain credit cards, in which men typically have the advantage.

Over the past decade, the issue of sexual harassment has received considerable attention as a problem that women must contend with in the workplace. **Sexual harassment** is a form of sex discrimination that violates Title VII of the Civil Rights Act of 1964. Unwelcome sexual advances, requests for sexual favors, and other verbal or physical conduct of a sexual nature constitute sexual harassment when submission to or rejection of this conduct explicitly or implicitly affects an individual's employment, unreasonably interferes with an individual's work performance, or creates an intimidating hostile or offensive work environment (U.S. Equal Opportunity Commission, 2006).

Sexual harassment includes graphic comments about a person's body, sexually suggestive pictures or other objects in the workplace, or threats that failing to submit sexually will affect adversely a person's job or salary. A person also may file charges of sexual harassment if he or she is affected by the behaviors of others (for example, a boss and a co-worker involved in a sexual relationship). It is highly likely that much sexually harassing behavior goes unreported by employees for fear that it might place their jobs in jeopardy. Although some progress has been made in reporting and eradicating these behaviors, it continues to pose a significant problem for working women.

Even common use of language conveys male dominance, albeit often unintentionally. Sexist language, whose use "creates, constitutes, promotes, or exploits an unfair or irrelevant distinction between the sexes" (Vetterling-Braggin, 1981, p. 3), shapes values, attitudes, and often behavior. Some argue that use of the pronouns "he/him" and the traditional term "man" are not sexist; however, studies show that they can influence our thinking. In an often-cited study, college students were asked to select photographs to illustrate a text. When chapters were titled "Society," "Industrial Life," and "Political Behavior," students selected photos of both men and women. When chapters were titled "Social Man," "Industrial Man," and "Political Man," however, both male and female students were likely to select pictures of men only (Miller & Swift, 1976, cited in Warren, 2000).

The American Psychological Association, which has published guidelines for writing that many university social work programs have adopted, includes specific guidelines for nonsexist language. Guidelines suggest using plural ("they" instead of "he") when possible, and being careful about examples that may appear sexist (e.g., women when talking about physical attractiveness, and men when talking about success) (2007). See the American Psychological Association website at www.apastyle.org/pubmanual. html for information about its style manual, or the American Philosophical Association website at www.apa.udel.edu for specific examples of nonsexist language.

Issues Relating to Reproductive Rights

One of the more emotionally charged issues that epitomizes conflicts in values for men and women alike is reproductive rights. Issues relating to reproductive rights can be discussed from legal, medical, and values perspectives. While early issues relating to reproductive rights focused on abortion, reproductive rights debates have included issues relating to contraception and other methods of family planning; sterilization; privacy issues involving pregnancy, such as whether minors should have to notify or receive permission from parents or legal guardians when making decisions that relate to reproduction; and who should be notified regarding sexually transmitted diseases. Advances in technology have resulted in issues relating to who has rights to embryos and decisions regarding embryos and births involving surrogate mothers.

Legal Issues

Early legal issues relating to reproduction centered on abortion, with the legal precedent for abortion established in 1973 by the *Roe v. Wade* decision. In effect, the U.S. Supreme Court maintained that a woman has the constitutional right to seek an abortion if she so desires. This decision defined abortion as a personal decision rather than one to be determined by government policy. Although the Court's interpretation was straightforward and clear, issues surrounding abortion are being revisited in many state courts, and policy attitudes have shifted considerably at the federal level. Much of the controversy involves philosophical and scientific issues about when life begins. Breakthroughs in biotechnology have escalated the debate, which is framed by some as a conflict between the status of the human embryo and a woman's right to privacy. These issues extend beyond the abortion debate to the use of stem cells and fetal tissue in research and whether the fetus should be protected legally before birth.

Who should obtain reproductive health services and under what conditions is also being debated in state legislatures across the United States. Legislation passed in a number of states limits the right of minors to obtain confidential health services, which many health providers fear will limit minors' access to health care to obtain family-planning information and contraceptives, to be tested and receive treatment for sexually transmitted diseases, and to receive pregnancy testing and prenatal care. A major change has been to limit federal funding for family planning for any agency that performs abortions or provides counseling or referrals to clients about abortions. This policy change has severely limited the services of programs such as Planned Parenthood, which does not perform abortions but does offer affordable family planning and gynecological services to low-income women and men who otherwise might not be able to afford them. Other proposed legislation would make it a federal crime for anyone other than a parent to help a minor travel out of state to obtain an abortion if the woman is not following the relevant laws regarding compliance in her own state.

As of July 2006, the Center for Reproductive Rights reports that 600 bills have been introduced in state legislatures, with 100 proposing increased access to family planning services and reproductive rights and the remaining bills increasing restrictions. Thirty-three bills have been enacted in 22 states, six of them increasing access and the remaining bills increasing restrictions. Many states have adopted laws limiting abortion. Some states prohibit third-trimester abortions for any reason, and others limit abortions to situations involving very young teens, rape, or cases in which a woman's health is severely jeopardized.

Since the U.S. Supreme Court upheld the use of what is commonly termed "partial birth" abortions in 2001 in *Stenberg v. Carhart,* two other cases that challenge the Partial Birth Abortion Ban Act of 2003 have been heard before the Court, and decisions are pending. Some states have passed laws that require counseling and waiting periods after receiving counseling before an abortion can be performed. Other states have laws requiring parental consent of minors prior to their obtaining an abortion. Both pro-choice and pro-life advocates expect the controversy over abortion and related issues to escalate in government policy and the courts over the next few years.

Medical Issues

From a medical perspective, abortion during the first trimester of a pregnancy is a relatively simple, uncomplicated procedure. Although any medical intervention entails risk, abortion generally is not considered a high-risk procedure, even during the second trimester. Most abortions are performed during the first trimester and few during the last trimester. Assessing women's psychological preparedness for an abortion can be difficult. Most medical facilities require a psychological assessment and counseling as prerequisites for an abortion. Few studies have attempted to assess post-abortion adaptation, and the results, for the most part, have provided limited insight.

Perhaps the most controversial medical abortion procedure—partial-birth (third-trimester) abortions—has been debated more heatedly by Congress because of the near-term development of the fetus and the more complicated medical processes involved. Theoretically, partial-birth procedures can be pursued only when either the life of the fetus or that of the pregnant female would be in jeopardy if the pregnancy is carried to full term. As indicated earlier, however, some states prohibit partial-birth procedures for any reason.

A related issue is the availability of drugs that can be taken to terminate a possible pregnancy, including mifepristone (RU-486), which was approved by the Federal Drug Administration in 2000. Another option is the so-called morning-after pill, such as Plan B, which can be taken within a limited time frame after intercourse to prevent pregnancy from occurring. Many women's health advocates would like to see morning-after pills become available without a prescription. Because these pills prevent conception, advocates hope they can be used to prevent unwanted pregnancies without some of the political controversy surrounding abortion.

The Alan Guttmacher Institute, a reproductive health policy and research organization, indicates that emergency contraception prevented 51,000 abortions in 2000 and could be responsible for almost half of the 11% decline in abortion rates between 1994 and 2000. In 2001, the Center for Reproductive Rights petitioned on behalf of 76 broad-based organizations to allow the FDA to approve emergency contraception as an over-the-counter medication, but no action has been taken as of 2006 (Center for Reproductive Rights, 2007).

Values Issues

Perhaps the most emotionally charged aspect of abortion involves values. On the one hand, members of the anti-abortion (right-to-life) movement base their resistance to abortion on the conviction that life begins at conception. Consequently, they view abortion as murder. Members of pro-choice groups, on the other hand, argue that life begins at birth, and they further insist that a woman has the constitutionally granted right to decide whether she wishes to continue her pregnancy or terminate it. Anti-abortion groups seek the government's protection of the life (and rights) of the fetus in the same sense that children and adults merit protection of the law from injury or injustice.

Within each of the groups is some variance in value positions. For example, while arguing that life begins at conception, some anti-abortion groups take the position that abortion is acceptable and justified in instances of rape or where the mother's health would be seriously jeopardized. Other anti-abortion groups oppose abortion under any circumstance, arguing that taking the life of the fetus is never acceptable.

Abortion is not solely a women's issue, but only women become pregnant and have the legal right to decide whether a pregnancy will be carried to full term or terminated. The law remains unusually silent concerning the role of men in matters of conception and pregnancy. Fathers are referred to as "alleged fathers," and they have no legal right to affect a woman's decision to terminate a pregnancy.

We have included this discussion to illustrate the differential treatment of women in our society. Although the topic of abortion is difficult to discuss, because of differing values issues, social work professionals must be willing to listen to different points of view and to remain informed about facts as well as values positions. Social workers, like everyone else, have differing personal values, and this is certainly true regarding reproductive rights.

Regardless of personal beliefs, social work professionals must follow the values of the profession in treating with dignity and respect those who have values and points of view that differ from their own. Social workers must be especially attuned to the impact of unplanned pregnancy and abortion on women and to the views surrounding abortion. If social workers have personal views that would preclude their participation in abortion counseling, they have a professional responsibility to work with clients in a nonjudgmental way that supports client self-determination and to make referrals to protect the rights of the client. The National Association of Social Workers (NASW) clearly outlines the profession's position (see Box 4.2).

BOX 4.2
Social Work Speaks

National Association of Social Workers Public Policy Statement on Family Planning and Reproductive Choice

Although a vocal minority has wielded undue influence on government policies and decisions regarding family planning, reproductive freedom, and individual choice, the social work profession's position on abortion, family planning, and other reproductive health services is based on the principle of self-determination. If an individual social worker chooses not to participate in the provision of abortion or other specific reproductive health services, it is his or her responsibility to provide appropriate referral services to ensure that this option is available to all clients.

Lack of funding for abortion for poor women, decreased availability of family planning services, and our current system of welfare reform with financial disincentives to pregnancy and childbearing, with no mention of family planning or abortion services or the responsibility of men in contraception and child rearing, clearly works to the disadvantage of women. Inequities in access to and funding for reproductive health services, including abortion services, must be eliminated to ensure that self-determination is a reality for all and that the nature of reproductive health care services a client receives is a matter of private, individual choice. Adequate financing is necessary to make family planning programs and professional services available to all, regardless of their ability to pay.

The use of contraception reduces but will never eliminate the need for access to emergency contraception and to abortion services. Therefore, women must have the right to decide for themselves, with the advice of qualified medical service providers, whether or not to carry a pregnancy to term. At the same time, the use of all reproductive health care services must be voluntary. Women of color, those in institutions, and those from other vulnerable groups should not be used in the testing and development of reproductive techniques and technologies.

Source: *Social Work Speaks*, by National Association of Social Workers, Washington, DC, 2003: Author.

Social Reform: The Feminist Movement

Ever since this nation's inception, women have pursued equal social treatment. Early leaders include

- Elizabeth Stanton (1815–1902), who petitioned for a property-rights law for women in New York (1845);

- Lucretia Mott (1793–1880), who organized the first women's rights convention in New York;
- Susan B. Anthony (1820–1906), who helped to form the National Women's Suffrage Association in 1869; and
- Lucy Stone (1818–1893), who formed the National American Women's Suffrage Association.

Carrie Catt (1859–1947), a political activist, founded the International Women's Suffrage Alliance and, later, following World War I, the League of Women Voters, an organization that today wields significant political influence. Catt's efforts were largely responsible for enactment of the 19th Amendment to the U.S. Constitution, which extended voting rights to women in 1920 (Axinn & Stern, 2005).

In more recent times, women's groups have intensified their efforts to secure equal rights. The **Civil Rights Act** of 1964 addressed the problems of discrimination in gender as well as race. A major attempt to secure women's rights was embodied in the **Equal Rights Amendment (ERA).** Bitterly opposed by organized labor, the John Birch Society, the Christian Crusade, and the Moral Majority, and over the protest of Senator Sam Ervin (D-North Carolina), who castigated the proposed amendment, the bill was passed by Congress in 1972 and remanded to the states for ratification.

Pro-ERA forces, including the National Organization for Women (NOW), the League of Women Voters, and the National Women's Political Caucus, lobbied the states to seek ratification of the amendment. Anti-ERA spokespersons lobbied the states against ratification, arguing that all women would be sent into combat, subjected to unisex public facilities, and required to secure jobs (Francis, 2003). The amendment passed. The Carter administration, favorable to passage of the ERA, had little influence on the states in encouraging its adoption. The Reagan administration opposed the measure. The amendment was never ratified and died in June 1982.

Since that time, efforts to achieve **gender equity** have met with some success. Active efforts by NOW and related women's rights groups and public sentiment have coalesced to remove some of the barriers that historically had subjugated women in their pursuit of social equality. During the Clinton administration a precedent was set in naming both women and people of color to key roles in government offices.

Although the profession of social work has advocated for the abolition of societal barriers that deny equal treatment of women, it has not been in the forefront in providing leadership for the more significant feminist movements. During the 1960s, however, women's equality was established as a major priority for the profession. Both the NASW and the Council on Social Work Education (CSWE) initiated policies committing the profession to promoting social and economic equality for women.

Social and Economic Justice: Sexual Orientation

Within the past decade, considerable attention has been directed to the prejudice and discrimination experienced by those who are gay, lesbian, bisexual, and transgender (often referred to as persons who are GLBT). Transgender individuals are those who either are born anatomically as one gender but have a psychological identity with the other or are born with a combination of male and female physiology (Nangeroni, 2006). Transsexuals, whether they have or have not had "sex-change surgery," are considered to be transgender persons. Transgender persons are particularly oppressed, sometimes by gays and lesbians.

Although a person's **sexual orientation** is considered to be a personal and private matter not related to free and full participation in our society, this has not been the case for those who are not heterosexual. The intense negative emotional reaction to homosexuals, a result of fear and hatred of homosexual lifestyles, is a state of psychological conditioning termed **homophobia.** Further promoting anxiety and fear toward homosexual relationships is acquired immunodeficiency syndrome (AIDS), despite the fact that the fastest growing groups of persons with AIDS now are heterosexual women and heterosexual people of color.

The rejection of homosexual practices, with the accompanying prejudice and discrimination, has been bolstered by fundamentalist religions as well as the more traditional psychologies. For example, the Moral Majority and the Christian

Coalition movements argue strongly that homosexual practices are sinful, and they condemn homosexuals along with deviants, pornographers, and atheists. In his classic work, *Homosexuality,* Irving Beiber (1962), a psychoanalyst, clearly describes the view of traditional psychoanalysts that homosexuality is abnormal and that it can be cured through psychotherapy. These and other "authoritative" sources reinforce the biases and prejudices that have long existed in the general population.

In 2003, 14 states had laws prohibiting sodomy. Ten states plus Puerto Rico had sodomy laws that applied to both heterosexuals and homosexuals. Four states—Kansas, Missouri, Oklahoma, and Texas—had sodomy laws that applied only to homosexuals. Penalties for violating sodomy laws in the United States ranged from $500 to life imprisonment.

In late June of 2003, in what some gay rights activists called a landmark legal victory, the U.S. Supreme Court reversed a previous ruling (1986) and ruled in a 6–3 vote that sodomy laws are unconstitutional. The 2003 decision, based on privacy rights, bans all states from "regulating private sexual expression between consenting adults regardless of whether the laws apply to homosexuals or both heterosexuals and homosexuals."

The majority opinion, authored by Justice Anthony Kennedy, states that homosexuals

> . . . are entitled to respect for their private lives. The State cannot demean their existence or control their destiny by making their private sexual conduct a crime. . . . When homosexual conduct is made criminal by the law of the state, that declaration in and of itself is an invitation to discrimination both in the public and in the private spheres. (U.S. Supreme Court, 2003b)

The ruling added private sexual expression to the list of constitutional protections under the 14th Amendment to the Constitution relating to privacy protections. The Supreme Court decision is viewed as a major step forward in legal protections for persons who are GLBT because sodomy laws had been used to prohibit persons who are GLBT from obtaining custody of or adopting children.

Although many states are introducing legislation to protect the rights of persons who are not heterosexual, these attempts have not always been successful. Ten states have passed legislation to protect the rights of gays and lesbians in the workplace. Although 44 states and the District of Columbia have enacted **hate crimes** legislation establishing penalties for crimes committed against individuals because of their race or ethnicity, only 31 states and the District of Columbia have legislation that includes sexual orientation (Center for Policy Alternatives, 2007). Hate crime legislation was introduced in Texas after the tragic death of James Byrd, an African American who was dragged behind a truck until his body became dismembered. The measure failed because the proposed statute included protection because of one's sexual orientation.

Increased attention was given to hate crimes with the release of the film *Boys Don't Cry,* based on the story of Brandon Teena, a transgender murdered at age 21 in Falls City, Nebraska, in 1993. Federal legislation, the Local Law Enforcement Hate Crimes Prevention Act, adds real or perceived sexual orientation, gender, gender identity, and disability to categories included in previous federal hate crimes laws.

Additional attention has been directed to hate crimes legislation since the September 11, 2001, terrorist attacks on the United States. A number of hate crimes have been committed against people of actual or perceived Middle Eastern origin throughout the nation. Hate crimes impact not only the targeted person and his or her targeted family but also send a threatening message to all members of a particular group.

Some gays and lesbians have become more vocal and have sought legal redress for discriminatory practices, whereas others, fearing loss of jobs, intimidation, and harassment, have opted to remain "in the closet." Although experts disagree as to whether sexual orientation is determined by genetics or is a product of socialization, many people continue to consider homosexuality as a matter of choice. In 1973, the American Psychiatric Association removed "functional homosexuality" from its list of behavior disorders. As a result, mental health professionals no longer view homosexuality as a form of mental illness. A large segment of the public, however, maintains that gay and lesbian relationships are a form of perversion and, further, that social contact with homosexuals should be avoided.

Although some progress has been made in securing legal rights for members of the gay community, discrimination and prejudice continue to characterize public responses to them. Ambivalence surrounding this issue is best expressed by the "don't ask, don't tell" policy for members of the military enacted by the Clinton administration in the mid-90s and still in place. Presumably this policy was designed to provide guarded protection to gay and lesbian military personnel (Lum, 2002).

More recent attention throughout the world has been on laws either allowing or prohibiting same-sex couples to marry. The first country to allow same-sex marriage was The Netherlands, in 2007. Since then, **same-sex marriage** has been recognized in Canada, Belgium, South Africa, and Spain. In the United States, previously passed laws allowing same-sex marriage have been overturned by higher courts and voters in a number of instances.

Proponents of same-sex marriages argue that gay and lesbian couples are denied access to health care, retirement and death benefits, inheritances, and other benefits that heterosexual married couples take for granted. Opponents argue that marriage is to be a religious union between a male and female for purposes of procreation. In 2004, a number of localities—including San Francisco and communities in New York and Oregon—passed laws allowing same-sex marriages. Hundreds of gay couples across the United States traveled to these communities to wed before state courts overturned local rulings. In response to outcries against same-sex marriages, members of the media compared the same-sex marriage of a well-known performer that lasted less than 24 hours to the many same-sex

couples who had been together for 25–50 years without being able to marry legally.

Debates continue throughout the nation about whether same-sex marriages should be allowed. The state of Massachusetts provides an example. The Massachusetts Supreme Court ruled in 2004 that gay and lesbian couples have a constitutional right to marry. Legislators and advocacy groups proposed a number of amendments to the state constitution forbidding same-sex marriage, incorporating language in several proposed amendments that would have allowed civil unions. An amendment in 2005 proposed that marriage be defined as a union between a man and a woman but did not disallow civil unions. This amendment received almost three times the number of signatures needed to be brought to state residents for a vote. The next step was scheduled to take place in the spring of 2007, when the state legislature was to approve putting the referendum before voters.

Gays and lesbians have had a number of strong advocates. One of the earlier groups to support the rights of gays and lesbians was the Chicago Society for Human Rights, established in 1924. In 1950, the Mattachine Society was founded to further rights for, and acceptance of, same-sex-oriented individuals. Currently, the Gay Liberation Front has established itself as a political organization promoting passage of legislation that would provide for nondiscriminatory practices against homosexuals, including recognition of same-sex marriages as well as adoption rights. NASW, too, is a strong advocate for GLBT rights. In 2006, NASW joined the Maryland Chapter of NASW in filing a brief in a suit brought by the American Civil Liberties Union. NASW's brief addressed issues relating to claims that same-sex couples should be prevented from marrying because they cannot be effective parents. The brief informs the court of "the extensive scientific evidence providing that children raised by lesbian and gay couples develop as well as children raised by heterosexual couples" (American Civil Liberties Union, 2006a; Stoesen, 2007).

Stereotypical thinking based on erroneous information guides most heterosexuals' reactions to those with non-heterosexual orientations. Thus, individuals who are gay, lesbian, bisexual, or transgender are often denied freedom of expression and access to the opportunity structure that is available for heterosexuals. In addition, members of these groups are subject to hate crimes committed against them. Anti-homosexual hostility runs especially high in certain parts of the United States. The senseless slaying of a young gay college student in Wyoming in 1998 is reflective of the extent to which angry individuals will go in expressing their derision for those whose sexual orientation differs from theirs.

Clearly, social work and related professions must address more forcefully the prejudices and biases toward homosexuality that remain pervasive within the professions. In spite of the acknowledged reticence, social work educators have made progress in preparing students to work effectively with clients who are gay, lesbian, bisexual, or transgender. Accreditation standards for schools of social work require that course content address the needs of divergent populations, including gays and lesbians. Advocacy on behalf of the homosexual population toward enforcing anti-discrimination legislation has become a priority of the profession. Until the fear and apprehension concerning homosexual behavior are dispelled through public enlightenment, however, prejudice and discrimination will continue to be barriers to social and economic justice for gay, lesbian, bisexual, and transgender people.

Social and Economic Justice: Class

Too often, when discussing social justice and equality, people ignore issues of class. Regardless of one's color, gender, or sexual orientation, people at the lower end of the economic structure in the United States are treated differentially by the dominant group. The stratification of individuals and groups according to their social and economic assets and power is termed **class.** Discrimination toward members of a group because of their economic status is termed **classism.** Labeling those who are poor as inferior gives justification to oppress this group.

Like other forms of discrimination, classism can be seen at the individual level, such as making disparaging comments or jokes about the poor or treating those who are poor in derogatory ways. At the institutional level, classism is shown by structuring policies and practices in ways that marginalize or exclude people at the bottom of the class structure from opportunities afforded to others. Examples of institutional classism are lack of access to safe neighborhoods and good schools, and the ability to influence politicians and government officials through political contributions (Classism, 2007).

Obviously, race, ethnicity, and gender play significant roles in determining the class to which one is likely to belong. Because of the oppression of these populations at risk, women and people of color are less likely to have access to superior educational opportunities, gainful employment that allows for upward mobility, adequate health care, and opportunities for their children to move into a higher economic class. Thus, members of these groups are likely to remain in the lower class for multiple generations. Interestingly, members of marginalized groups who are in higher-income groups advocating for changes for that group often fail to see how those in their group at the bottom of the class structure experience additional oppression because of classism.

Lahiri and Jensen (2002) provide a checklist to facilitate discussion about how we inadvertently may exhibit classist behavior:

- treatment of executives and managers in workplaces in comparison to lower-level clerical staff and custodians;
- recruiting personnel from Ivy League colleges instead of other universities;

- requiring personnel in lower levels of an organization to purchase uniforms at their own expense; and
- scheduling work hours without taking into consideration the availability of affordable transportation and child care.

Debate is increasing in the United States about the impact of class on individual and social well-being. African American scholar William Julius Wilson (1997) and others write about what they call the **underclass,** "oppressed people who have not been able, due to barriers and obstacles in society, to escape poverty" (Johnson, Schwartz, & Tate, 1996, p. 59). When talking about discrimination, class is discussed far less often than gender and race. Those with privilege often either feel guilty because they have advantage or believe that those who are less well off are in those circumstances by their own volition: If they would just work harder and be more motivated they, too, could be better off financially.

As skill in technology becomes a necessity for successful employment, the number of individuals with limited access to education left out of the U.S. economic structure will rise significantly (Wilson, 1997). This growth will impact not only the poor but those in other classes as well. For example, if an additional 630,000 Texans do not attend college between now and 2015 (330,000 more than projected if current trends in college participation continue), the average income of Texans in the year 2015 will be less than it was in 1991 because businesses are more likely to move to areas with educated workforces (Murdock, Hogue, Michael, White, & Pecote (1997); Texas Higher Education Coordinating Board, 2007).

Social and Economic Justice: Race and Ethnicity

Among other personal attributes that often result in social and economic injustices are race and ethnicity. People who are distinguished by specific physical or cultural traits are often singled out for differential or unequal treatment. In the United States, the dominant racial group is Caucasian, and people of color—African Americans, Latinos, Asian Americans, Iranians, Native Americans, and Vietnamese, among others—are considered by many members of the dominant (majority) group as having lower status.

The concept of race suggests the presence of marked, distinct genetic differences. The term actually is a social definition because few genetic differences are found among *Homo sapiens.* Race commonly is used to classify members of groups who have similar physical characteristics, such as skin color or facial features. Behavioral traits frequently are attributed incorrectly to physical differences rather than to socialization experiences. In contrast to racial groups, ethnic groups tend to be classified by language differences or cultural patterns that differ from those of the dominant group. Racial and ethnic groups are both viewed as "different" by the dominant group, and prejudice and discrimination are often the result.

Total integration of all groups in society would result in the loss of racial or ethnic identity. Many people of color find this prospect objectionable. In recent years, ethnic and racial pride have received considerable attention from groups of color. Although complete **assimilation** (the expectation that members of a non-dominant group adopt the values and behaviors of the dominant group) theoretically would result in the erosion of racial and ethnic discrimination patterns, it probably will not happen. Many people argue that the contributions of our divergent ethnic and racial groups enrich our culture.

An alternative to assimilation is **cultural pluralism,** or **cultural diversity,** the coexistence of various ethnic groups whose cultural differences are respected as equally valid. Cultural pluralism, however, is difficult to achieve within the matrix of prejudice, discrimination, and cultural differences. While people of color are creating and promoting cultural pride, less than equal coexistence continues to characterize their relationship with the dominant group.

Ironically, most immigrant populations have been subjected to prejudice and discrimination as each new group settled in the United States— the Irish, Italians, Swedes, Germans, French, and others. The irony is, of course, that, with the exception of Native Americans, all of us are descendants of immigrants. How quickly groups move from the role of the persecuted to that of persecutors!

Even more ironic, prejudices and discrimination persist and become institutionalized by members of a society that values its Judeo-Christian heritage and provides equal constitutional rights and privileges for all. Some progress is seen in opening up avenues for social and economic participation, but minority groups still must cope with differential treatment and limited opportunities.

In the following discussion, we identify some of the issues and problems that confront racial and ethnic groups and examine anti-discrimination efforts designed to neutralize racial, cultural, and ethnic prejudices. As we discuss these groups, keep in mind that although each group shares a common history and other characteristics, each group enjoys a rich diversity within itself.

The groups we will consider here are African Americans, Latinos, Asians and Pacific Islanders, and Native Americans.

African Americans

All non-Caucasian racial and ethnic groups have been subjected to discrimination, but perhaps none more visibly than the African American population. Emerging from slavery, in which they were considered chattel (property) and non-persons, African Americans continue to find that societally imposed constraints impede their progress toward achieving social equality.

During the "Jim Crow" days in the South, for example, African Americans could not dine at public restaurants used by Caucasians, could use only specially marked public restrooms and drinking fountains, had to ride in the rear of buses, were required to attend segregated schools, faced expectations of subservient behavior in the presence of Caucasians, and could get only lower-paying domestic or manual-labor jobs. Few could achieve justice before the law or gain acceptance as equals to even the lowest-class Caucasians. Although the prescribed behaviors that characterized "Jim Crowism" represent an extreme manifestation of discrimination, all minority groups have experienced social inequality, at least in its more subtle forms.

African Americans represent about 13% of the total U.S. population. Between 2000 and 2004, the African American population increased by 5% while the non-Hispanic white population decreased from 70% to 67% (U.S. Census Bureau, 2006). Just over 55% live in the South, and regardless of geographic region of the United States, slightly more than half live in inner-city metropolitan areas. They earn only 65% as much as Caucasians, are unemployed in greater numbers than their Caucasian counterparts, and are almost three times more likely than Caucasians to have incomes below the federal poverty line. Numerically, more Caucasians receive public assistance than African Americans; however, African Americans are proportionally overrepresented on welfare rolls (U.S. Census Bureau, 2003b).

Caucasians are more likely than African Americans to complete high school, and African Americans are underrepresented in the fields of law, medicine, dentistry, and business and overrepresented in occupations that require hard manual labor. There have been increases in high school graduation rates for African Americans (79% compared to 89% of Caucasians) and college participation (17% compared to 29% for Caucasians). These data reflect the differential opportunity structure available to the African American population in this country. While the middle-class and upper-middle-class African American population in the United States is increasing, income levels for African Americans overall are still lower than for Caucasians. More than half of African American married couples earn $50,000 or more annually, compared to 64% of Caucasians (U.S. Census Bureau, 2003b).

Latino Populations

People from Mexico, Puerto Rico, Cuba, and Central and South America are referred to as being of Hispanic or Latino origin. In 2004, more than 41 million Hispanics/Latinos lived in the United States, constituting 14% of the total population (U.S. Census Bureau, 2006). The Latino (the preferred term) population has come to the United States from 26 nations. Latinos constitute the fastest-growing population group in the United States, increasing 58% in the decade between 1990 and 2000, and 17% between 2000 and 2004 (U.S. Census Bureau, 2006). By 2010, Latinos are expected to become the majority group in some southwestern states and to compromise nearly 25% of the total U.S. population by 2050. By far the largest group is Mexican Americans (see Table 4.1), but increasing numbers of Latinos are coming to the United States from South and Central America, often replacing Mexican Americans and Puerto Ricans in some poverty neighborhoods and low-wage jobs as Mexican Americans and Puerto Ricans become more upwardly mobile.

People of Mexican descent constitute the second largest group of color in the United States. Although most live in major urban areas of the West and Southwest, many continue to reside in rural areas. The Mexican American population is

Immigration policy and the treatment of undocumented citizens are important social justice issues that many Latinos feel passionate about.

a diverse group. The urban Mexican American population tends to be better educated, and the effects of acculturation are more visible among them. Those living in rural areas are more apt to be less acculturated, continue to use Spanish as a primary language, and to work in lower-paying jobs often related to farming or ranching.

The population of Mexicans and Mexican Americans in the United States is growing rapidly as "undocumented immigrants" continue to flow across the border into the southwestern states and California. More vigilant surveillance at U.S.–Mexico borders since the September 11, 2001, terrorist attacks has resulted in increasing numbers of deaths of Mexicans trying to cross the border, either from suffocation (because of being hidden in close quarters without ventilation), drowning, or assault. (See chapter 16 for additional discussion on immigration issues.)

Cultural pride among Mexicans and Mexican Americans is best reflected in their retaining Spanish as a first language. Bilingual education programs are in place in some public school systems to enable Mexican American children to progress educationally, although dropout rates continue to be much higher for them than for the dominant-group population.

In general, people of Mexican ancestry have experienced the consequences of discrimination in that they hold lower-paying jobs, are

TABLE 4.1
Hispanic / Latino Populations in United States

Group	Percentage of Hispanic/Latino Population
Mexican	66.1%
Central and South American	14.5%
Puerto Rican	9%
Cuban	4%
Other Hispanic	6.4%

Source: *The Hispanic population in the United States: March 2002,* U.S. Census Bureau. (Washington, DC: Department of Commerce, 2003c).

David S. Holloway/Reportage/Getty Images

underrepresented in politics, live in *de facto* segregated neighborhoods, and are viewed as being "different" by the dominant group. Upward mobility has been painfully slow in coming. Ethnic organizations such as La Raza and LULAC (League of United Latin American Citizens) have sought to unite Spanish-speaking populations to promote favorable social change and to give more visibility to the issues and problems that impede their achievement of social equality.

Puerto Ricans and Cubans constitute the largest "other Latino" populations. Most of the Puerto Rican population in the United States resides in the metropolitan New York area or in eastern seaboard cities such as Newark, New Jersey, and New Haven, Connecticut. The Cuban population has settled primarily in the Miami area of Florida. The social and economic progress of these groups is similar to that of the Mexican American group. Housing often is inferior, jobs tend to be more menial and lower-paying, the school dropout rate is high, and access to services and support systems is difficult. Social progress has been considerably greater for the Cuban population due, in part, to the higher educational level of the first waves of Cuban immigrants to the United States.

As has been the case with newly migrated Mexicans, other Latinos came to the United States with the hope of being able to achieve a higher-quality life, only to find that prejudice and discrimination presented barriers to achieving that dream. Cultural and language barriers continue to make them "different," and more visible targets for differential treatment.

Asians and Pacific Islanders

Asian and Pacific Islander immigrants have distinct cultural traits and physical characteristics that separate them from the dominant group but represent one of the most diverse ethnic groups within the United States—Chinese, Japanese, Korean, Asian Indian, Vietnamese, and Pacific Islands descendents. "Asian" refers to those with origins in the Far East, Southeast Asia, or the subcontinent of India. These countries include

Cambodia, China, Japan, Korea, Malaysia, Pakistan, the Philippine Islands, Thailand, India, and Vietnam, among others. "Pacific Islander" refers to those with origins in Hawaii, Guam, Samoa, and other Pacific Islands. Although they represent less than 4% of the U.S. population, the number of Asian immigrants is increasing. The majority of Asians, Asian Americans, and Pacific Islanders live in the western United States, most often in urban areas (U.S. Census Bureau, 2006).

Chinese immigration dates back to the mid-19th century, and the Chinese represent the largest percentage of Asian immigrants (see Table 4.2). Japanese immigration began around the turn of the 20th century, the Korean population in the mid-20th century, and the Vietnamese population in the 1960s and 1970s. The aggregate total of all Asian Americans in the United States in 2004 was approximately 7.3 million, or 4.2% of the total U.S. population. In 2004, 42% of those living in Hawaii were Asian, and 12% of the California population was Asian. This group increased in population by 16% between 2000 and 2004 (U.S. Census Bureau, 2006).

The U.S. Census Bureau has begun distinguishing Asians from Pacific Islanders. Pacific Islanders comprise 9% of the population of Hawaii but less than 1% of the population in the remainder of

TABLE 4.2	
Asian Immigrant Population in the United States by Nationality	
Group	**Percentage of Asian Immigrants in United States**
Chinese	20.8%
Filipino	18.3%
Asian Indian	15.1%
Vietnamese	12.9%
Korean	10.5%
Japanese	7.7%
Other	14.6%

Source: Profile of the Foreign-Born Population in the United States: 2000 (Current Population Reports, Special Studies) (Washington, DC: U.S. Census Bureau 2001).

the U.S. states and the District of Columbia (U.S. Census Bureau, 2006).

Even though all of the nationalities constituting the Asian American population have experienced differential treatment, many have been able to achieve a relatively high standard of living despite the social barriers. The Chinese have been noted for their in-group living patterns. The "Chinatowns" in San Francisco, Los Angeles, New York, and other large cities encourage preservation of the Chinese cultural heritage. Still, prejudice and discrimination continue to impede significant social and economic progress. Because of their physical characteristics, language, and cultural heritage, they are viewed by many as "foreigners." Internment of the Japanese population in camps during World War II is one example of how the Japanese, many of whom were native-born, were viewed as foreigners with presumptive allegiance to Japan rather than the United States. Ironically, Germans and Italian Americans were not treated in this manner even though Germany and Italy, along with Japan, constituted the Axis powers.

More recently, the Vietnamese have been the target of discrimination, as reflected in their difficulty in securing housing, employment, and acceptance in American communities. In addition to physical characteristics, language barriers have intensified the "differences," resulting in closed avenues for social and economic participation for this group.

The number of Asian Indian immigrants has increased in recent years because of political turmoil in their countries, as well as the demand in the United States for computer programmers and other workers in technology fields. Despite the fact that many are highly educated, they experience discrimination.

Native Americans

Numerically the smallest group of color in the United States, Native Americans (American Indians) have experienced severe oppression over the years. Prior to colonization, they were free

to establish their villages and roam the countryside but lost all their rights and privileges once they were conquered. Settlers and the military considered them to be savages, and most were relegated to reservations, where they encountered oppressive limits on their behaviors and freedom of movement. The responsibility for overseeing these reservations was relegated to the Bureau of Indian Affairs (now the Administration for Native Americans), a government agency that more often

David H. Hamilton/The Image Bank/Getty Images

Valuing cultural traditions is an important part of one's identity. Too often, Native Americans and other groups have been given the message that they must reject their traditions to be accepted and viewed as successful. Fortunately, today many young people are learning to have pride in themselves and their heritage.

was a barrier rather than a help. Some Native American tribes have never lived on a reservation. This creates a unique set of social-justice issues about which social workers must be concerned.

The effects of differential treatment and limited opportunity are reflected in the limited average education for Native Americans age 25 and older—9.6 years, the lowest of any ethnic group in the United States. Nearly one-third are illiterate, and only one in five has a high school education (U.S. Census Bureau 2003a).

Although they were the first "Americans," Native Americans seldom have been able to experience free and full involvement in society. Many continue to live on reservations, which further segregates them from interacting with the dominant group and limits their opportunity structure. Reservations represent the most overt form of purposeful discrimination. Although the status of Native Americans has improved somewhat in recent years (with higher levels of education and commercial development on the reservations), many barriers remain to their free and full social participation.

During the decade between 1990 and 2000, the Native American populations increased by 26%, compared to an overall population growth of 13% in the United States. The Native American population increase, from 1.4% to 1.5% of the total population between 2000 and 2004, was much less than for other groups of color. In 2004, 40% of Native Americans reported living in the West (U.S. Census Bureau, 2006).

Like other racial and ethnic groups, not all Native Americans have the same values and traditions. Lifestyles, as well as opportunities, vary among the more than 300 tribes in the United States. Almost 75% of persons surveyed in the 2000 Census who indicated that they were Native American reported themselves as members of a tribe or tribal grouping, with the largest tribes being the Cherokee, Navajo, Latin American Indian groups, Choctaws, Sioux, and Chippewa. In the Alaska Native tribal grouping, the Eskimo was the largest group.

Many Native Americans have migrated to urban centers in search of employment and better resources. New York and Los Angeles have the largest urban populations of Native Americans, and large populations also are found in Chicago, Houston, Philadelphia, Phoenix, San Diego, Dallas, San Antonio, and Detroit. The migration of Native Americans to urban areas has created identity problems for many. Discriminated against, they don't always fit in well in city environments. Yet, because they left their reservation, they also have difficulty being accepted if they return to their homeland (McLemore & Romo, 2005).

Efforts to Produce Social Justice for Populations at Risk

Bringing an end to institutional racism and discrimination is not an easy task. Longstanding prejudices that have lingered over many generations are difficult to extinguish, despite efforts to enlighten the public about the consequences of maintaining false beliefs and practices. Little progress was made in dismantling segregation until the government decreed it. Before President Harry Truman ordered the integration of the armed forces in 1948, most government agencies supported separation of the races. Although racism and discrimination still are found in the armed forces, its desegregation has resulted in employment and educational opportunities for people of color that are inaccessible to them elsewhere in the United States. Many successful people of color attribute the opportunities afforded to them to their early military experiences.

School Desegregation

The catalyst for ending separate public school education was the Supreme Court decision *Brown v. Board of Education* in 1954, which mandated an end to segregation in public schools. Ruling that "separate is not equal," the Court ordered public schools to be integrated and opened to children of all races and ethnic groups. Because of *de facto* housing patterns, members of minority groups lived in segregated neighborhoods and their children attended neighborhood schools.

To implement the Court's decision, busing became necessary. Many communities required students of color to be bused to schools in predominantly white neighborhoods, which resulted in strong resistance by the dominant white population. White citizens' councils emerged in the South and Midwest to resist school integration.

Many state governments questioned the constitutionality of the Court's decision and resisted taking appropriate action to hasten the integration process. Evidence was sought to support the position that integration of schools would have catastrophic effects on the educational achievement of children of all races. In a 1962 report (*The Biology of the Race Problem*), Wesley C. George, a biologist commissioned by the governor of Alabama, attempted to offer scientific proof that blacks were innately inferior to whites and would not be able to compete with whites in the classroom. Other racist or supremacist groups, such as the Ku Klux Klan, joined in efforts to prevent school integration.

In time, school busing became common and school integration a technical reality. Universal public acceptance of desegregation through busing, however, was never achieved. In the 1980s and 1990s, the movement to return to neighborhood schools was strong. Charles Murray's (1994) book *The Bell Curve* was a rallying point for many, urging the elimination of busing and returning to neighborhood schools. Although advocates for neighborhood schools have argued that these schools could be more culturally relevant to students and their families, in many instances schools in non-white neighborhoods have seen a significant loss of resources when busing has been eliminated.

Civil Rights Legislation

During the 1960s, significant progress was made in eliminating segregationist policies and controlling the effects of discrimination. President Lyndon Johnson's Great Society programs sought to eradicate segregation entirely and to make discrimination an offense punishable under the law. In 1964, the **Civil Rights Act** was passed. Amended in 1965, this act sought to ban discrimination based on race, religion, color, or ethnicity in public facilities, government-operated programs, and employment. A similar act, passed in 1968, made illegal the practice of discrimination in advertising and the purchase, financing, or rental of residential property.

Under the new legal sanctions for desegregation, a groundswell of support mounted among disenfranchised people of color and sympathetic dominant-group members. The Reverend Martin Luther King, Jr. and organized freedom marchers sought to raise the consciousness of society regarding the obscenities of segregationist policies. King's nonviolent movement provided high visibility to the injustices of discrimination and served to stimulate and influence policies for change. During this period, other significant organizations, including the Southern Christian Leadership Conference (SCLC), the National Urban League, the National Association for the Advancement of Colored People (NAACP), La Raza, and the League of United Latin American Citizens (LULAC), actively pursued social and economic justice for people of color.

As the new civil rights legislation was implemented, an air of hope prevailed that discrimination would soon become a matter of history. School busing facilitated public school integration, public facilities were opened to people of color, and the employment market became more accepting of minority applicants. Further advances were made under the influence of the Economic Opportunities Act of 1964. Neighborhoods were organized, and their residents registered to vote. This movement was furthered by the Voting Rights Act of 1965, which prohibited the imposition of voting qualifications based on race, color, age, or minority status. The impact of the **civil rights movement** was far-reaching in the struggle for full and equal participation by minorities in the social and economic areas of our society.

Uneven Progress

The rapid pace of the change effort was short-lived. By the late 1970s, racial polarization had increased with a new wave of conservatism. Discussions of race, as they often are today, were centered most often on whites and blacks, ignoring other groups of color. Whites were much more prone to attribute the "lack of progress" among the black population to blacks themselves rather than to discrimination—thus supporting the position that discrimination was no longer a problem for "motivated" blacks. By the late 1970s, racial and minority issues were replaced by national defense, energy, and inflation as the top priorities for the white majority.

Although the *Brown v. Board of Education* court decision to end school desegregation was hailed as a major breakthrough in 1954, many public schools throughout the United States are segregated today, not because of laws prohibiting attendance but, rather, because of housing patterns, a result of institutional discrimination. Thus, much of the progress gained during desegregation has been lost. Central cities throughout the United States have become mostly non-white and economically poor, resulting in largely segregated schools.

Tax bases in rural and urban school districts alike in economically disadvantaged areas produce limited funding in comparison to wealthier districts. This raises issues in many states about the best way to fund public education so all students will receive a quality education. Funding is limited to provide resources to children who are less likely to speak English, more likely to have parents who work long hours and cannot be involved in their children's education as much as they would like, or are unfamiliar with the edu-

cation system and how to guide their children through it, and often need additional resources beyond the classroom to be successful.

The number of African American and Latino students in U.S. public schools has increased by almost 6 million students, while the number of Caucasian students has declined by almost that many (Orfield, 2001). Often, curricula, teaching methods, and ways to reach parents are not consistent with the diverse population of students in U.S. public schools today. Because demographers predict that U.S. schools will be the first major institutions to have non-white majorities, how schools fare in educating students will shape workforces and communities of the future. The fact that whites are by far the most segregated when it comes to school attendance also raises questions about the ability of future graduates to live and work effectively in a diverse environment.

Affirmative Action

Affirmative action programs, which once mandated the selection of qualified members of oppressed groups for publicly operated business and education, have been downgraded and, in many instances, dismantled. The concept of affirmative action was derived from the civil rights acts of the 1960s and was, in part, an attempt to initiate actions that would equalize the social and economic playing field for all people and ultimately break the barriers of discrimination for those who had long been oppressed by established values, policies, and practices.

Compensatory justice, an underlying axiom for affirmative action directives, provided the impetus for eliminating institutionalized barriers to employment, education, and social parity in general. It required that women and people of color be hired, or admitted to educational institutions and professional schools, on a basis equal to that of white males. Public reaction to what was considered a "quota system" resulted in cries of "reverse discrimination." Many of these cries have come from white women—the group that has benefited the most from affirmative action programs. In the late 1990s, the U.S. Supreme Court ruled on a number of cases that reversed parts of affirmative action.

Affirmative action programs clearly have opened up opportunities for the oppressed. Although "tokenism" has been a major concern, many women, African Americans, Latinos, and other members of non-majority groups have been able to achieve higher educational status, secure jobs, and achieve vertical mobility in the employment arena as a result of efforts to right historical wrongs. Critics of the downgrading of government efforts in the area of affirmative action argue that such actions will result in a return to past discriminatory practices. Proponents of downgrading these programs believe that they have not been effective, and, in the final analysis, all populations will be better served if positions are awarded on competency and merit rather than arbitrarily mandated by social legislation.

In this regard, one arena receiving more attention has been higher education. In the late 1990s, a court ruling in district federal courts prohibited Texas and other states in its region from using race as a criterion in admitting students or awarding scholarships. Many advocates for social justice viewed the ruling as discriminatory because it indicated that admissions decisions could be based on athletic or musical ability or legacy (meaning that a family member had attended the institution) but not race. Two subsequent lawsuits, *Grutter v. Bollinger* and *Gratz v. Bollinger,* filed against the University of Michigan regarding its admissions selection process for undergraduate and law students, were appealed to the U.S. Supreme Court. Many organizations, including the military and Fortune 500 companies, filed briefs in support of the university, concerned that limiting access to higher education would jeopardize diversity in the workplace and the military.

In a divided decision, the Court ruled in June 2003 that instituting racial quotas and assigning points based on one's race could not be used in admissions decisions, but that race could be considered as one of many factors. The Court noted that limited forms of affirmative action were reasonable because the value of diversity extends beyond the college campus. In the decision, Sandra Day O'Connor, stated that

> . . . the diffusion of knowledge and opportunity through public institutions of higher education must be accessible to all individuals regardless of race or ethnicity. Effective participation by members of all racial and ethnic groups in the civic life of our nation is essential if the dream of one nation is to be realized. (U.S. Supreme Court, 2003a)

The University of Michigan ruling was hailed as the most significant regarding affirmative action in some time. Opponents of the ruling, however, worked to organize the Michigan Civil Rights Initiative, also known as Proposal 2, a proposed amendment to the state constitution that would

> . . . prohibit state and local government from discriminating against or granting preferential treatment to any individual or group based on race, sex, color, ethnicity, or national origin in the areas of public employment, public contracting and public education.

In November, 2007, the amendment passed with 58% of voters supporting it. California already had adopted similar measures (Michigan Proposal 2, 2006). Following the passage of Proposal 2, the University of Michigan revised its admission policies to exclude race as a factor.

Universities and other institutions are working to develop other ways to try to ensure diversity in their populations. Approaches that universities have taken include recruitment efforts targeted at high schools with large numbers of students of color and including criteria associated with race or ethnicity, such as being a first-generation college student or a student from a disadvantaged background. Workplaces are recruiting at schools and other sites that reflect the populations of employees they hope to hire. Nevertheless, ways to ensure that members of marginalized groups have access to education and employment are becoming limited by court and voter decisions.

Law Enforcement and Profiling

Another area receiving increased attention has been the relationship between law enforcement and people of color. Several high-profile cases involving white law-enforcement officers beating or killing minority civilians have led to efforts to improve relationships between law enforcement agencies and minority communities. Some communities have implemented successful dialogue, training, and community-policing programs, involving law enforcement officers in activities at the neighborhood level, including citizens' efforts to strengthen their communities.

Although people of color have indicated for years that they have been stopped by police, arrested, and jailed more often than whites, documentation in many cities indicates that **racial profiling** (sometimes called "DWB"—"driving while black or brown"), the practice of law enforcement officers stopping and searching people not otherwise engaged in suspicious behavior but, because of their race, is practiced in many areas. Racial profiling also can involve stopping pedestrians, shoppers at malls, voters on their way to the polls, employees at sites where immigrants are likely to be working, and airport passengers (American Civil Liberties Union, 2006b) (see Box 4.3).

In many locations, African Americans and Latinos, particularly males, are stopped and searched at much higher rates than their Caucasian counterparts, and also are much more likely to be subjected to the use of force when being arrested. Many individuals, regardless of color, believe that racial profiling is a valid concern in the United States. A Gallup poll conducted in 2001 found that 55% of whites and 83% of blacks believed that racial profiling is widespread (American Civil Liberties Union, 2006b).

In 2001, the U.S. Congress introduced bipartisan legislation, the "End Racial Profiling Act," aimed at eliminating racial bias by law enforcement agencies (American Civil Liberties Union, 2006b). This legislation will prohibit the use of profiling based on race, religion, or national origin; establish programs to train and monitor incidents of racial profiling; withhold funds from law enforcement agencies that do not comply with the act and award additional funds to those that do; and require that an annual report be submitted to Congress (Amnesty International, 2006). The act was introduced prior to September 11, 2001, and although it has been reintroduced since that time, efforts to get it passed have not been successful to date.

The outlook for a well-articulated and implemented program to eliminate prejudice and discrimination is mixed. Efforts to creatively and forcefully address this issue have waned since the mid-70s, and race continues to be a sensitive topic that many individuals at all levels of society choose to avoid. Current efforts at both federal and state levels to balance the budget by scaling down government programs and services tend to overshadow concerted efforts to dismantle the institutional barriers that result in differential treatment for groups of color.

Even as efforts to achieve equality for oppressed groups continue, active government commitment has waned. Passage of welfare reform legislation in 1996 and the continual debate over affirmative action programs reflect the general public's ambivalence toward improving the opportunity structure for oppressed groups, which perpetuates the current power structure in the United States.

Social Work and the Civil Rights Movement

Inherent in the identity of social work is its commitment to social action directed toward eliminating barriers that deny equal rights and full

---

BOX 4.3
Reported Incidents of Racial Profiling in the United States

- *While driving:* A young African American schoolteacher reports being routinely pulled over in his suburban neighborhood in San Carlos, California, where only five other African American families live.

   Native Americans in Oklahoma report being stopped routinely by police because of the tribal tags displayed on their cars.

   In Texas, a Muslim student of South Asian ancestry is pulled over and asked by police if he is carrying any dead bodies or bombs.

- *While walking:* In Seattle, Washington, a group of Asian American youths are detained on a street corner by police for 45 minutes on an allegation of jaywalking. A sergeant ultimately ordered the officer in question to release them, but the young people say they saw whites repeatedly crossing the same street in an illegal manner without being stopped.

- *While traveling through airports*: An 8-year-old Muslim boy from Tulsa, Oklahoma, reportedly was separated from his family while airport security officials searched him and dismantled his Boy Scout pinewood derby car. He now is routinely stopped and searched at airports.

- *While shopping:* In New York City, an African American woman shopping for holiday presents was stopped by a security guard at a major department store. Even though she showed the guards her receipts, she was taken to a holding cell in the building where every other suspect she saw was a person of color. She was subjected to threats and a body search. Three hours later she was allowed to leave without being charged, but was not allowed to take her purchases with her.

- *While at home:* On the day after Father's Day, a Latino family in a Chicago suburb reportedly was awakened at 4:50 a.m. by nine building inspectors and police officers, who prohibited the family from getting dressed or moving about. The authorities reportedly proceeded to search the entire house to find evidence of overcrowding. Enforcement of the zoning ordinance, which was used to justify the search, reportedly was targeted at the rapidly growing Latino population.

- *While traveling to and from places of worship:* A Muslim imam from the Dallas area reports being stopped and arrested by police upon leaving a mosque after an outreach event. Officers stopped him, searched his vehicle, arrested him for expired vehicle tags, and confiscated his computer.

Source: Adapted from *Threat and Humiliation: Racial Profiling, National Security, and Human Rights in the United States.* (New York: Amnesty International, 2006). Available at www.amnestyusa.org/racial_profiling/index.do.

---

participation to all members of society. Since the early days, when social workers assisted in assimilating new immigrants into our culture and sought to improve social conditions for them, the profession has engaged the citizenry in working toward social equality and an equal opportunity structure. The National Association of Social Workers and the Council on Social Work Education have placed high priority on incorporating content about vulnerable populations—including women; gays, lesbians, bisexuals, and transgender persons; the poor; and people of color—into professional social work practice and social work education.

Social work practitioners strive to be familiar with the racial and cultural backgrounds of their clients, including strengths and the impact of oppression, when assisting them in achieving solutions to problems. Through social action, efforts are made to change community attitudes, policies, and practices that disadvantage members of at-risk populations. As advocates, social workers seek to modify rules and regulations that deny equal treatment to those accorded at-risk status. As organizers, they work with leaders from at-risk populations in identifying priorities, gaining community support, and facilitating change through the democratic process.

As citizens (as well as professionals), social workers are active in organized public efforts to abolish discriminatory practices. They support political candidates who are openly committed to working for social equality. They are involved in public education to dispel prejudice and to promote productive interactions among divergent racial and ethnic groups. In a public climate in which the pursuit of social and economic equality has lessened, social workers have a responsibility to maintain a vigilant pursuit of equality.

Social workers should view the concept of **social justice** as more than just rhetoric. Ever since the inception of the profession, social justice has been a basic axiom for practice. Social justice—achieving a society in which all members have access to the same rights and privileges without regard to gender, race, ethnic affiliation, creed, age, sexual orientation, or physical and mental capacities—is essential for the establishment of a nondiscriminatory society. Only when that goal is achieved can social and economic equality prevail.

A fundamental avenue through which social justice is achieved is by empowering disenfranchised and oppressed individuals and groups.

Empowerment is both a process and a goal, through which individuals and groups gain mastery over their lives, become active participants, and make decisions that will enable them to gain control over their lives and the environment in which they interact. Disempowered populations can only react to the norms and mandates of others, which can perpetuate discriminatory practices.

Summary

Few observers would deny that the United States has seen a major gender revolution during the past few decades. As part of the human rights movement, many advances have been made in reducing sexism in our society. Opportunities for economic and social participation of women are greater now than ever. Despite some reversals, such as the failure to ratify the ERA, societal pressures to assure equal treatment and opportunities for women continue.

Social inequality has characterized the treatment of racial and ethnic groups, the poor, and homosexuals in the United States. Although some progress has been made toward more favorable treatment, these groups have not achieved full participation rights. Discrimination and differential treatment of women, people of color, and those who are GLBT continue to restrict their achieving social and economic progress. Social work has a long tradition of promoting social equality, and the commitment of the profession to continue in this role this will increase as the societal thrust to do so declines.

Over the past decade the euphemism "politically correct" has gained popularity among those who question the validity of certain attitudes or practices directed toward oppressed or disenfranchised groups. Politically correct responses have become, for many, substitutes for "correct" responses. The concept of political correctness invokes negativism for positive actions taken. For example, a person may behave in a certain manner because it is the politically correct thing to do—not necessarily the right (or decent) thing to do. In reality, many politically correct responses are socially responsible ones. Prejudiced persons can behave in a socially responsible manner even though their intentions are simply to be politically correct.

Unfortunately, some may use the guise of political correctness out of fear that a true and honest response may place them in jeopardy of losing an advantage they treasure. Social workers should not be overly concerned with being politically correct. The value base of the profession and commitment of social work practitioners to genuineness always should be paramount when intervening with clients or serving as advocates on their behalf.

This chapter is intended to make you aware that prejudice, institutional discrimination, and oppression have long existed, and that the targets of these practices continue to suffer the consequences of differential treatment and limited opportunity. While advocacy groups have been able to bring about positive political changes and public attitudes have improved, much remains to be accomplished if we are to achieve social equality for all groups in the United States. Prejudice and discrimination are the products of social interaction. As social constructs, they can be replaced by values that respect the dignity and worth of all human beings and result in a society that promotes equal treatment for all.

Key Terms and InfoTrac® College Edition

The terms below are included in the Glossary. To learn more about key terms and topics in this chapter, enter the following search terms using the InfoTrac College Edition or the World Wide Web:

affirmative action
assimilation
Civil Rights Act
civil rights movement
class
classism
comparable worth
cultural diversity
cultural pluralism
discrimination
economic justice
empowerment
Equal Rights
   Amendment (ERA)
gender equality
hate crimes
homophobia

institutional
   discrimination
oppression
populations at risk
prejudice
racial profiling
same-sex marriage
sexism
sexual harassment
sexual orientation
social equality/social
   inequality
social justice/social
   injustice
stereotypes
underclass

Discussion Questions

1. How do you explain the presence of prejudice and discrimination in a society whose values are based in Judeo-Christian ideology?
2. Discuss early efforts to eradicate discriminatory practices against women, people of color, and gays, lesbians, bisexuals, and transgender individuals.
3. Why is social justice difficult to achieve in a society characterized by cultural pluralism?
4. Assume that you are a member of an oppressed group. What would your reaction be to the watering down of affirmative action programs? How would you react to so-called "reverse discrimination?"
5. What is the role of social work in breaking down institutional barriers of discrimination?
6. How do you explain that some white women, who historically have experienced gender

discrimination, discriminate against women of color?

7. What privileges in society are you afforded that you take for granted? What privileges are less available to you because of groups to which you belong?

8. What role, if any, do you think that race should play in deciding who should be admitted to colleges and universities and why? How important do you think diversity should be on a college campus?

On the Internet

www.vpcomm.umich.edu/diversityresources/
proposal2.html

www.affirmativeaction.org/

www.feminism.eserver.org

www.socialworkers.org

/www.dol.gov/dol/audience/
aud-women.htmwww.gendertalk.com

www.aflcio.org

www.antidefamationleague.org

www.pflag.org

www.amnestyusa.org

www.census.gov/

www.aclu.org

www.cesj.org/

www.nela.org

www.sjti.org/

References

Adams, M., Bell, L. A., & Griffin, P. (1997) *Teaching for diversity and social justice: A sourcebook.* Oxford, England: Routledge.

American Civil Liberties Union (2006a). *Lesbian gay rights.* Available: www.aclu.org/lgbt/index.html

American Civil Liberties Union (2006b). *Racial profiling: Old and new.* Available: www.aclu.org/racialjustice/racialprofiling/index.html

American Federation of Labor—Congress of Industrial Organizations (2007). *Equal pay for working families.* Washington, DC: Author. Available: www.aflcio.org.

American Psychological Association (APA). (2007). *APA Publication Manual.* Washington, DC: Author. Available: www.apastyle.org/pubmanual.html

Amnesty International (2006). *Threat and humiliation: racial profiling, national security, and human rights in the United States.* Available: www.amnestyusa.org/racial_profiling/index.do

Axinn, J., & Stern, M. (2005). *Social welfare: A history of the American response to need* (6th ed.). Boston: Allyn & Bacon.

Beiber, I. (Ed.). 1962. *Homosexuality.* New York: Basic Books.

Center for Policy Alternatives. (2007). *Hate crime prevention.* Washington, DC: Author. Available at www.stateaction.org/issues/issue.cfm/issue/HateCrimes.xml

Center for Reproductive Rights. (2007). *Emergency contraception.* Available: www.crlp.org

Classism. (2007). Available: at en.wikipedia.org/wiki/Classism

Economic Policy Institute (2007). *The state of working America: 2006–2007.* Ithaca, NY: Cornell University Press.

Francis, R. (2003). *Behind the Equal Rights Amendment.* Washington, DC: National Council of Women's Organizations. See also www.equalrightsamendment.org.

Garcia, B., & Van Soest, D. (2006). *Social work practice for social justice.* Alexandria, VA: Council on Social Work Education.

George, W. C. (1962). *The biology of the race problem.* Report prepared by Commission of the Governor of Alabama, Montgomery.

Guidelines for nonsexist language in APA [American Psychological Association] journals. *American Psychologist,* June 1977, pp. 487–494.

Johnson, L., Schwartz, C., & Tate, D. (1996) *Social welfare: A response to human need.* Boston: Allyn & Bacon.

Lahiri, I. & Jensen, K. (2002). *Uncovering classism: A checklist for organizations.* (The Gil Deane Group) Available at www.workforcedevelopmentgroup.com/

Lum, D. (2002). *Culturally competent practice: A framework for understanding diverse groups and justice issues.* Pacific Grove, CA: Brooks/Cole.

McIntosh, P. (1988). *White privilege: Unpacking the invisible knapsack.* Wellesley, MA: Wellesley College Center for Research on Women.

McLemore, S. D., & Romo, H. D. (2005). *Racial and ethnic relations in America* (6th ed.). Boston: Allyn & Bacon.

Michigan Proposal 2 (2006). *Voter guide to Proposal 2.* Available: www.michiganproposal2.org

Mill, J. S. (1861). Utilitarianism. In J. S. Mill, & J. Gray, (1998). *On liberty and other essays.* Oxford, England: Oxford Press.

Murdock, S., Hougue, N., Michael, M., White, S., & Pecote, B. (1997). *The Texas Challenge: Population change and the future of Texas.* College Station: Texas A & M University.

Murray, C. (1994) *The bell curve.* Washington, DC: New Republic.

NASW. (2003). *Social work speaks: Family planning and reproductive choice* (abstract). Washington, DC: Author.

Nangeroni, N. (2006). *Transgenderism: Transgressing gender norms.* GenderTalk. Available at www.gendertalk.com.

National Employment Lawyers Association, (2003). *Fact sheet: Why we still need affirmative action.* San Francisco: Author. See also www.nela.org

Novak, M. (2000). Defining social justice. *First Things.* Available: www.firstthings.com

Orfield, G. (2001). *Schools more separate: Consequences of a decade of resegregation.* Available: www.rethinkingschools.org/archive/16_01/Seg161

Rawls, J. (1971). *A theory of justice.* Cambridge, MA: Belknap Press of Harvard University Press.

Sirkin, M. (1994, July/August). Resisting cultural meltdown. *Family Therapy Networker, 18*(4),48–52.

Social Justice (2006). Wikipedia. Available at en.wikipedia.org/wiki/Social_justice

Stoesen, L. (2007, Jan.). Same-sex marriage, segregation, privacy briefs filed. Washington, DC: *NASW News, 1,* p. 9.

Texas Higher Education Coordinating Board (2007). *Participation and success.* Available: www.thecb.state.tx.us/

U.S. Bureau of Labor Statistics (2005a, Sept.). *Highlights of women's earnings in 2004* (Report 987). Washington, DC: U.S. Department of Labor.

U.S. Bureau of Labor Statistics (2005b, May). *Women in the labor force: A databook.* Washington, DC: U.S. Department of Labor.

U.S. Census Bureau (2001). Profile of the foreign-born population in the United States: 2000. *Current Population Reports, Special Studies.* Washington, DC: Author.

U.S. Census Bureau (2002a). *Current Population Statistics, Annual Demographic Survey, March Supplement.* Washington, DC: Author.

U.S. Census Bureau (2003a). *The American Indian and Alaska native population: 2000.* Washington, DC: Author.

U.S. Census Bureau (2003b). *The Black population in the United States: March 2002.* Washington, DC: Author.

U.S. Census Bureau (2003c). *The Hispanic population in the United States: March 2002.* Washington, DC: Author.

U.S. Census Bureau (2006). *Race and Hispanic origin in 2004.* Washington, DC: Author.

U.S. Department of Commerce. (2006). *Statistical abstract of the United States.* Washington, DC: Author.

U.S. Equal Employment Opportunity Commission. (2006). *Sexual harassment.* Washington, DC: Author. See also www.eeoc.gov

U.S. Supreme Court. (2003a). *Gratz et al. v Bollinger et al.* (June 23). Washington, DC: Author.

U.S. Supreme Court. (2003b). *Laurence v. Texas* (June 26). Washington, DC: Author.

Vetterling-Braggin, M. (ed.) (1981). *Sexist language, A modern philosophical analysis.* Totowa, NJ: Littlefield, Adams, & Co.

Warren, V. (2000). *Publications: Guidelines for nonsexist use of language.* Newark, DE: American Philosophical Association. Available: www.apa.udel.edu/apa/publications/texts/nonsexist.html

Wilson, W. J. (1997). *When work disappears: The world of the new urban poor.* New York: Vintage.

Women's Bureau (2006). *Women in the labor force in 2004.* Washington, DC: U.S. Department of Labor.

Suggested Further Readings

Carlton-LaNey, I. (Ed.). (2001). *African American leadership.* Washington, DC: NASW Press.

Davis, K., & Bent-Goodley, T. (Eds.). (2005). *The color of social policy*. Alexandria, VA: Council on Social Work Education.

DeAnda, D. (2004). *Social work with multicultural youth*. Binghamton, NY: Haworth Press.

Dhooper, S., & Moore, S. (2001). *Social practice with culturally diverse people*. Thousand Oaks, CA: Sage Publications.

Diller, Jerry. 2006. *Cultural diversity: A primer for the human services* (3rd ed.). Pacific Grove, CA: Brooks/Cole.

Fong, R. (Ed.) (2004). *Culturally competent practice with immigrant and refugee children and families*. New York: Guilford Press.

Gardella, L. G., & Haynes, K. (2004). *A dream and a plan: A woman's path to leadership in human services*. Washington, DC: NASW Press.

Heuberger, B. (2005). *Cultural diversity: Building skills for awareness, understanding, and application* (3rd ed). Dubuque, IA: Kendall Hunt.

hooks, b. (2000). *Feminism is for everybody: Passionate politics*. Cambridge, MA: South End Press.

hooks, b. (2000). *Where we stand: Class matters*. New York: Routledge.

Hunter, S., & Hickerson, J. (2003). *Affirmative practice: Understanding and working with lesbian, gay, bisexual, and transgender persons*. Washington, DC: NASW Press.

Hunter, S., Sundel, S., & Sundel, M. (2002). *Women at midlife: Life experiences and implications for the helping professions*. Washington, DC: NASW Press.

Igelhart, A., & Becerra, R., 2000. *Social services and the ethnic community*. New York: Waveland Press.

Institute on Inequality and Social Structure (part of the University of Washington School of Social Work). Available: depts..washington.edu/sswweb/ioe/iiss/

Journal of Ethnic and Cultural Diversity in Social Work (2001). Binghamton, NY: Haworth Social Work Press.

Journal of Gay and Lesbian Issues in Education. Binghamton, NY: Haworth Press.

Karger, H., & Stoesz, D. (2002). *American social welfare policy: A pluralist approach*. New York: Longman.

Kozol, J. (1991). *Savage inequalities: Children in America's schools*. NY: Harper Perennial.

Kozol, J. (2005). *The shame of the nation: The restoration of apartheid schooling in America*. NY: Three Rivers Press.

Logan, S. (2005). *Social work with people of African descent*. Alexandria, VA: Council on Social Work Education.

Martin, E., & Martin, J. (2003). *Spirituality and the Black helping tradition in social work*. Washington, DC: NASW Press.

Martin, J., & Hunter, S. (2005). *Lesbian, gay, bisexual, and transgender issues in social work*. Alexandria, VA: Council on Social Work Education.

Ortega, R., Gutierrez, L., & Yeakley, A. (2006). *Latinos and social work education*. Alexandria, VA: Council on Social Work Education. (bibliography)

Rose, F. (2000). *Coalitions across the class divide*. Ithaca, NY: Cornell University Press.

Sau-Fong, Siu, Lee, A., & Lu, Y. E. (2005). *Asians and Pacific Americans*. Alexandria, VA: Council on Social Work Education. (bibliography)

Social Justice Research. (2002.) Heidelberg, Germany & New York: Springer. (journal)

Sullivan, N., Mesbur, E., & Lang, N. (2003). *Social work with groups: Social justice through personal, community, and social change*. Binghamton, NY: Haworth Press.

Susser, I., & Patterson, T. (2001). *Cultural diversity in the United States: A critical reader*. Boston: Blackwell.

Van Wormer, K. (Ed.) (2004). *Confronting oppression, restoring justice*. Alexandria, VA: Council on Social Work Education.

Wing, Sue D., & McGoldrick, M. (2006). *Multicultural social work practice*. Hoboken, NJ: Wiley.

Social Work Practice:

Methods of Intervention

Andersen Ross/Digital Vision/Getty Images

Part Two of this text presents methods of intervention used by generalist social workers. Chapter 5, *Social Work Practice with Individuals, Families, and Groups*, explains the most prevalent method in professional social work practice—intervention with individuals and families who are having difficulty interacting within their environment. Included are theories and techniques that social workers use in helping individuals and families build on their strengths, along with strategies to meet their needs and improve their social functioning and the environment in which they function.

In chapter 5 we also examine methods used in working with clients in groups. Group work is an effective method of intervention that is receiving increasing attention, both because of its effectiveness with many populations and because it often is seen as more cost-effective than working with clients individually. The chapter reviews relevant theories related to working with groups and identifies a variety of groups in which individuals interact. Finally, the chapter brings up important factors to consider when social workers form groups, the importance of group process when working with groups, and various methods that social workers use when working with groups.

Chapter 6, *Generalist Practice with Agencies and the Community* points out the importance of the community and community agencies in working with clients and describes various methods of community organization and community intervention that social workers typically use to create individual and social change. Because the exosystem—or community—level of the environment has had such a large impact on individual and family functioning, one of the major ways in which social workers can address client needs is by working within the community to develop or strengthen programs and policies, advocate for client needs, and empower community members to advocate for themselves and develop interventions that address their needs.

In chapter 6 we also describe the relationships between social welfare policy and practice and approaches that social workers can take to evaluate proposed and existing social welfare policies. The chapter suggests administrative, leadership, and management strategies that social workers can use to gather resources and opportunities to create and maintain efficient and effective social services agencies. As social welfare needs continue to expand while resources to address these needs are shrinking, the management of social welfare programs is increasingly critical for an agency's survival.

Because sound practice and policy decisions should be based on research, this chapter also includes discussion of the interdependence of social work practice and research and the use of social research as integral in problem solving. The vital role of research in policy and practice is emphasized, to continually buttress practice with data from research findings. This role is essential so we can continue to conceive ways to address social welfare issues and work with client systems more effectively, and so we can demonstrate our effectiveness in garnering the resources to deal with the many social welfare needs of today.

As you learn about the methods of intervention used by social work generalist practitioners in Part Two, ask yourself the following questions that draw from what you learned in Part One:

- How do past and present social welfare perspectives and policies shape the ways people view individuals and families today, the types of needs that individuals and families might be likely to have, and the methods of intervention that might be used in working with individuals, families, and groups to deal with these needs?
- How can the systems/ecological framework help us understand issues relating to individuals and families and the impact of the broader environment on their functioning?
- How might these issues be addressed using the methods of intervention discussed in Part Two?
- What are the relationships among factors such as race and ethnicity, gender, age, and sexual orientation on individual and family functioning, and how would social workers consider these factors when working with individuals, families, and groups in practice settings?

CHAPTER 5

Social Work Practice with Individuals, Families, and Groups

At age 42, Patrice Dillon moved with her four children from Nebraska to Illinois. Later, she was joined by her mother, Susan. One of her children, Bill, age 18, is a school dropout who works sporadically at mechanical jobs. Laura, 19, completed high school and works at a clerical job while living at home. Robert, 11, has a physical disability and attends school now and then. Beatrice, 8, goes to school at times but often stays at home to help with family chores around the house. Patrice's mother, who is functionally illiterate, tries to manage the household while Patrice works.

In Nebraska, Patrice had a job as a waitress and also received TANF (public assistance) benefits. After moving to Illinois, she found a job she liked but was laid off recently because she began to have health problems. She went to the county health center, but her diagnosis remained a mystery.

Patrice has come to the local social services agency seeking help with her "down feelings." She says she is "about ready to give up" because she never seems to be able to "get on top of my problems." Even though she feels reasonably strong now, she has not heard from her most recent employer, who told her, according to Patrice, "You can have your job back as soon as you're well enough to handle it." She has considered applying for food stamps and TANF benefits but

would prefer to work, and with all the changes in welfare reform, she's not sure she is eligible any more.

Because Beatrice has missed so much school, Patrice is concerned that child welfare officials might remove her daughter from her home. Patrice is too depressed to get Beatrice up and ready in the morning and to do the laundry, so the girl has no clean clothes to wear. Patrice says she needs money for food and rent and has come to the agency as a last resort.

Patrice's family is best classified as one having multiple needs. She and the social worker she sees at the agency identify some immediate objectives to work on together. First, the social worker will help Patrice contact the food bank to arrange for food for the family. After being reassured that child welfare workers will not remove Beatrice from the home for not going to school, unless there are other problems of abuse or neglect, Patrice agrees to go with the social worker to the school to discuss how to help Beatrice get caught up in her schoolwork.

The social worker also agrees to help Patrice contact her landlord and arrange for rent support until Patrice can find a job or reestablish her eligibility for TANF. In addition, Patrice and the social worker agree to meet weekly and develop options to deal with her needs, and Patrice agrees to join a group to gain emotional support and strengthen her employment skills. The social worker also gets Patrice to agree to enroll Robert in a program at the local rehabilitation center. This program provides physical therapy and also group socialization experiences and skill building that will help Robert learn self-care and self-sufficiency skills. As Patrice builds her relationship with the social worker and gains self-confidence, her health problems diminish and she finds a job with the local hospital food service.

Patrice's problems are neither rare nor unusual. Thousands of people like her are coping with a variety of problems and are turning to social agencies for help. Generalist social workers often represent the only hope that many people have in finding avenues to resolve their problems.

In this chapter we identify the components and characteristics of generalist practice methods that are used with individuals, families, and groups. Chapter 6 continues the topic with generalist practice in the community and policy, administration, and research. These chapters will acquaint you with social work processes and methods, as well as with the theories that undergird generalist practice. As you progress through the social work curriculum, you will examine methods, processes, and theories in more depth.

Generalist Practice: Background

The society and world in which we live are characterized by rapid transition, change, and uncertainty. The technological revolution and globalization have contributed to sweeping modifications in lifestyle, increased mobility, and changing values. Along with the growing capacity to create new products, the shifting job market is requiring new skills and more adaptable employees. Relationships among individuals have become more tenuous and short-lived.

As a result, people have difficulty achieving a sense of roots in the community. Social and job-related pressures and upward mobility have affected family life. The pursuit of success has clashed with long-cherished, family-first values. These changes, which began in the 1960s, have given rise to an emphasis on individuation and happiness, in contrast to strong family commitments. Broken families have become commonplace as marriages are being terminated with ever-increasing frequency.

Children with special needs, the illicit use of drugs by both adults and children alike, an increasing burden of caring for older adults, higher costs of housing and other necessities, and two-career marriages—all have placed demands on individuals and families that too often leave them disrupted, confused, tense, and frustrated.

At one time or another, virtually all of us have experienced these and many other social pressures generated by our rapidly changing society. To seek professional help with alleviating stress and its **dysfunctional** consequences is neither an unusual response nor a sign of weakness for individuals and families in stressful situations. All of us have needed the steady guidance of a respected friend or professional at some time. When problems become stressful and self-help efforts fail to produce desired solutions, professional assistance may be needed. **Generalist** social work practice offers that assistance.

As described in chapter 2, generalist practice with individuals and families, traditionally called **casework,** is the oldest social work practice. Another form of generalist practice is **group**

work, a method that fosters personal development through the mechanism of group process.

Generalist Practice: A Definition

A social work generalist practitioner assists clients in attaining a higher level of social functioning. **Generalist practice** is both a process and a method. As a process, it involves a more or less orderly sequence of progressive stages in engaging the client (or client system, such as a family) in activities and actions that promote agreed-on goals. As a method, generalist practice entails the creative use of techniques and knowledge that guide intervention activities designed by the social work practitioner. Generalist practice, too, is an art that applies scientific knowledge about human behavior and the skillful use of relationships to enable the client to activate or develop interpersonal and, if necessary, community resources to achieve a more positive balance with his or her environment. Generalist social work

practice seeks to improve, restore, maintain, or enhance the client's social functioning.

The most significant converging elements in social work practice are that it

- is an art—involving a skill that results from experience or training;
- applies knowledge about human behavior;
- is based on client involvement in developing options to resolve problems;
- emphasizes using the client's resources (psychological and physical), as well as those available in the community, to meet client needs;
- is based on an orderly helping process;
- is based on planned change efforts; and
- focuses on solutions.

Social work generalist practice with individuals and families is grounded in the philosophy and wisdom of early social work pioneers such as Mary Richmond, Gordon Hamilton, Helen Harris Perlman, Florence Hollis, and others, but practice has seen significant changes over the years. With emerging knowledge of human development, ecology, economics, organizational behavior,

Generalist social workers practice in many settings. Here, a social worker in a university counseling center talks with a student to determine how to best meet her needs.

© Heinle/Index Stock

stress management, social change, and more effective intervention techniques, social work practice with individuals, families, and groups has been enriched and offers a more scientifically buttressed model for intervention.

The face-to-face relationship between the social worker and the client has maintained its integrity as a fundamental prerequisite for intervention, as has the emphasis on process (study, assessment, intervention objectives, intervention, evaluation, and follow-up). Democratic decision making and belief in the dignity, worth, and value of the client system continue to undergird the philosophy of social work practice. The client's right to self-determination and confidentiality are fundamental practice values in the helping process. These values and practice principles form the fundamental concepts and practice techniques identified with generalist practice with individuals, families, and groups.

Preparation for Generalist Practice with Individuals, Families, and Groups

As we indicated earlier, a requisite for generalist social work practice with individuals, families, and groups is knowledge of factors that affect human behavior. The practitioner must be armed with an understanding of personality theory and knowledge of the life cycle, and also must be able to assess the effects of the social systems context within which behavior occurs. Factors such as race, gender, ethnicity, religion, social class, sexual orientation, physical condition, occupation, family structure, health, age, income, and educational achievement are among many contributing variables that converge to account for behavior within different social contexts. Although practitioners obviously cannot master all knowledge related to behavior, theories allow us to make guided assumptions about behavior from which

we can infer possible factors associated with the client's unmet needs. The generalist social work practitioner is able to arrive at probable causes of problems and to establish theoretically plausible interventions that will assist client systems in addressing needs.

Generalist practice at all levels is based on social work values, which are at the core of the profession. Interventions incorporate the dignity and strengths of the client/client system and emphasize self-determination and empowerment. The orderly process of social work generalist practice consists of social study, assessment, goal setting, contracting, intervention, and evaluation. Each step in this process is guided by the application of theory and knowledge of human behavior.

Social Study

The process begins with the **social study,** which consists of obtaining relevant information about the client system and perceived needs. Important to the social study is the client's perception of his or her needs and problems, antecedents, ways these are affecting life satisfaction and performance, attempts at life management, and outcome goals. The practitioner also obtains information regarding the client's ability to function in a variety of roles and collects data that enhance the practitioner's ability to form initial judgments about probable causes and potential actions that might lead to resolution.

The social study responds to questions such as these (Dubois & Miley, 2002):

- Who is the client?
- What is the nature of the needs and problems as the client sees and experiences them?
- What has the client done to alleviate these needs and problems?
- How effective were the efforts?
- What other individuals or groups are affected by the needs and problems, and how is the client related to or associated with them?

- What are the client's strengths and weaknesses?
- How motivated is the client to work toward solutions to address these needs and problems?

Assessment

Assessment is the process of making tentative judgments about how the information derived from the social study affects the client system in its behaviors, as well as in the meaning of those behaviors. As Dubois and Miley (2002) suggest, "The purpose of assessment is to understand the problem and determine how to reduce its impact" (p. 252). As such, assessment provides the basis for initiating and establishing intervention objectives and formally engaging the client system in the intervention process. This is the stage of the generalist practice process at which the perceived reality of client behaviors is filtered through the matrix of practice theory and a basic understanding of human behavior to arrive at potential sources of the problem(s).

Accurate assessment is the catalyst for establishing goals and objectives with the client and is an essential precursor to focused intervention. For that reason, assessment is a dynamic process that is modified and updated as the practitioner gains more insight, information, and experience in working with the client system, including estimates of how the client is using the helping process to address identified needs. In addition, a meaningful assessment reflects the ethnic, gender, racial, and cultural context of the client system.

At the most rudimentary level, assessment seeks to answer questions such as:

- What factors are contributing to the client's unmet needs?
- What systems are involved?
- What is the effect of the client's behavior on interacting systems (and vice versa)?
- What is the potential for initiating a successful change effort?

Goal Setting

In **goal setting,** the client and the practitioner ascertain intervention options that have the potential to address identified needs based on the client's abilities and capacities. After reviewing all options and determining which are most appropriate for the client, need, and situation, short- and long-term goals are developed.

The responsibility for goal setting evolves as a product of mutual exploration between the social worker and the client. Effective goal setting can serve as a therapeutic "jump-start" for the client as an initial commitment to engage in the change process. Goals should be realistically achievable, organized around specific targets for change, and related to the client's capacity to engage in behaviors that will move in the direction of positive change. As a practical matter, the least emotionally charged goals should be addressed first because they are more likely to be achieved. As a consequence of successfully achieving goals, the client's confidence is bolstered and he or she will likely be more enthusiastic about the change effort.

Contracting

In **contracting,** the practitioner and the client (or client system, as in a family or a group) agree to work toward the identified intervention goals. To facilitate and clarify the commitment implied by the contract, the practitioner's role is identified explicitly and the client agrees to perform tasks that address identified needs and problems. The contract makes visible the agreement both parties have reached and serves as a framework from which they may assess intervention progress periodically. During the course of intervention, contracts may be renegotiated or altered as more viable goals become apparent. Contracts also help maintain the focus of intervention.

Intervention

Generalist practice **intervention** with individuals, families, and groups is derived from the social study and assessment and is sanctioned by the contract between the practitioner and the client. The implementation phase of intervention is directed to meeting established goals and may involve activities such as

- counseling;
- role playing;
- engaging other community resources;
- establishing support groups;
- developing resources;
- finding alternative-care resources;
- encouraging family involvement;
- offering play therapy; or
- employing related strategies.

The goal of intervention is to assist clients toward acceptable resolution of their problems and to address their unmet needs. The practitioner must skillfully involve the client throughout the intervention process by providing regular feedback and support, and also an honest appraisal of the problem-solving efforts.

Evaluation

Clients are not likely to remain in the intervention process unless they perceive some positive movement toward meeting their needs. **Evaluation** is an ongoing process in which the practitioner and client review intervention activities and assess the impact on the client's problem situation. Both the practitioner and the client must intensively examine their behavior, with the goal of understanding the impact on intervention goals.

- What has changed?
- What has not changed? Why?
- How does the client view identified needs and problems at this time?
- Has social functioning improved?
- Has become less functional?
- What is the overall level of progress?
- Are different interventions needed?

Evaluation within this context becomes both a self-assessment and a joint assessment process. Based on the evaluation, intervention may continue along the same lines or be modified as implied by the evaluative process (Dubois & Miley, 2002).

The Social Worker–Client Relationship

The relationship between the social worker and the client (or client system) is the conduit through which assistance is extended by the social worker and received and acted on by the client. The principles and values underpinning the relationship are much more than a mere catechism for the social worker to learn. The client must experience them in interacting with the social worker. The practitioner must be genuine and approachable if the client is to feel enabled to share his or her problems and to develop confidence and trust in the social worker and the helping process. As the client invests time and energy in the problem-solving process, trust (an underlying axiom for an effective helping relationship) will be established only if the relationship principles and values are a distinctive aspect of client–social worker interaction.

The principles of social work practice are derived from the profession's value base and reflected in its code of ethics. Historically, professional social workers have been committed to the following principles as the basis for establishing a helping relationship with client systems:

- *Self-determination:* Social work practitioners respect their clients' rights to make choices that affect their lives. On occasion, when those choices do not seem to be in the client's best interests, the practitioner's role is to point out the potentially negative or dysfunctional aspects of the choices. Of course, this does not preclude or limit the practitioner's effort to assist the client in making more appropriate choices, but it does indicate that exerting undue influence or belittling the client is unacceptable in "bringing the client around" to more appropriate choices. Social work is based on a democratic process in which self-determination is fundamental.

- *Confidentiality:* The client's right to privacy is guarded by the principle of confidentiality, the notion that information shared between the client and practitioner is privileged. The practitioner must not compromise the client by making public the content of information disclosed during the intervention process. Confidentiality assures that the client's feelings, attitudes, and statements expressed during intervention sessions will not be misused. This principle also commits the practitioner to using client information only for professional purposes in working with the client.
- *Individualization and acceptance:* Regardless of the nature of the client's problems, each client has the right to be treated as an individual with needs, desires, strengths, and weaknesses that are different from those of anyone else. Acceptance means the ability to recognize the dignity and value inherent in all clients, in spite of the complex array of problems and needs that characterize their behavior.
- *Nonjudgmental attitude:* Recognizing that all human beings have strengths and weaknesses, experience difficult problems, make improper choices, become angry and frustrated, and often act inappropriately, the practitioner maintains a neutral attitude toward the client's behavior. To judge clients and their behaviors is to implicitly erect a barrier that may block communication with them. The client may view a social worker who is judgmental as just another person who is making negative judgments about him or her. The social worker does have a responsibility to confront the client about his or her inappropriate behaviors but must not condemn the client because of those behaviors.

- *Freedom of expression:* The practitioner encourages clients' need to express their feelings and emotions. Often, pent-up emotions become disabling to the client, resulting in more problematic behaviors. The client is encouraged to engage in free and unfettered self-expression within the safety of the social worker–client relationship.

The Development of Practice Skills

Social workers can develop competency in the generalist practice method with individuals, families, and groups through study, role playing, and supervised practice. Because generalist practice involves the application of knowledge, it is an effective method of problem solving only if it is employed skillfully.

As in other applied professions, the application of skill is an "art" that is enriched and refined continually through controlled and thoughtful interaction with clients. Just as you might expect the skills of a surgeon to increase with time and experience, that same principle applies to the development of social work practice skills. We now examine some of the more significant skill areas that are essential for effective social work practice with individuals, families, and groups.

Conceptual Skills

The ability to understand the interrelationships of various dimensions of the client's life experiences and behaviors and to place them within an appropriate perspective provides a framework within which to establish intervention goals. Conceptual skills enable the worker to view the client's many incidents and interactions not as discrete entities within themselves but, rather, as interacting parts of the client's behavioral repertoire. Without conceptual skills, social study data have little meaning and assessment may become less accurate. Conceptual skills also involve an ability to place the client's needs within a theoretical framework and to arrive at appropriate intervention strategies to address those needs.

Interviewing Skills

The interview is more than just a conversation with the client. It is a focused, goal-directed activity to assist clients with their problems. Communication skills are essential in assuring that the interview will be productive. The practitioner must assume the responsibility for maintaining the professional purposes of the interview. Sensitivity to both the client's statements and feelings is necessary. Putting the client at ease, asking questions that enable the client to share observations and experiences, and being a sensitive listener enhance the productivity of the interview. The social worker's sensitivity to the client's feelings and ability to communicate an awareness of those feelings strengthen the helping relationship and encourage and support the client.

Empathy, the ability to "put oneself in the client's shoes," is a benchmark quality of the helping relationship. Clients who conclude that the social worker really understands their needs are more relaxed and hopeful that they will be able to work together and find ways to address their needs.

Interviews are conducted for different purposes. Zastrow, Gebo, and Concilla (2003) have identified three types of interviews that facilitate the helping process in social work:

1. *Informational interviews* are used primarily to obtain a client history that relates to the client's current needs and problems. The history-collecting process should not be concerned with all of the client's life experiences but, instead, only with selected information that may be influencing his or her current social functioning.
2. *The diagnostic (assessment) interview* has a more clinical focus in that it elicits responses

that clarify the client's reactions to his or her needs and problems and establishes some sequential ordering of events that enables the practitioner to make initial judgments about events that affect the client's behaviors.
3. *Therapeutic interviews* are designed to help clients make changes in their life situations that will enable them to function more effectively. The client shares his or her feelings and emotions in these interviews. Also, problem-solving options are developed and efforts at change are reviewed.

Recording

Maintaining case records that provide insightful information into the client's background (social study data), judgments about the nature of needs and problems (assessment), and client–social worker activity are essential. Practitioners typically carry a large caseload with many clients over a long time. Properly maintained records enable the social worker to review the nature of the situation, objectives, and progress in each case prior to appointments with clients. In many instances, cases are transferred both inside and outside the agency, or an individual or family may participate in more than one activity within the same agency—e.g., individual counseling and a therapy group. The case record facilitates coordination by giving everyone involved an up-to-date accounting of the client's problems and activities directed toward their resolution. Case records also are useful for research purposes. Properly maintained records strengthen the process of social work practice. If viewed within this context, record keeping becomes less of an irrelevant chore and more of a vital tool for effective service delivery.

Beginning social workers should be informed that not all client systems are equally motivated to engage in a process designed to help them resolve their problems. Even voluntary clients (those who take the initial steps to seek help) are not always strongly committed, although they are motivated to some extent. Involuntary clients (those who are mandated to seek help, such as criminal offenders) may or may not be motivated to engage in the change effort. Practitioners must be aware that even if they cannot motivate their clients (motivation comes from within), they may provide the incentives that will cause the client to become motivated to work on his or her problems.

Practice Theories and Skills: Individuals and Families

Over the years, social workers have adopted a number of theoretical approaches in their work with individuals and families. Some theories are used primarily to understand human behavior, and others are used primarily for intervention. Many practitioners take an eclectic approach— integrating elements of several theories as a framework for understanding human behavior and for practice. They may find that a specific model is viable in one type of situation and another model may have greater utility in other situations. For example, a social worker may use behavior therapy with children and ego psychology with adults. The point is that many different approaches to social work practice are possible, each offering the practitioner a theoretical framework for intervention. Following are brief synopses of the theories that generalist practitioners typically use.

Systems/Ecological Framework

The systems/ecological framework is based on the perspective that individuals and their environment are continually interacting and that problematic behavior is the result of disequilibrium between these entities (the individual and the environment). The systems/ecological framework, discussed extensively in chapter 3, is the overriding framework that generalist practitioners use to understand human behavior and how it is impacted by the environment, although this framework also is used as a practice model. Most other practice models can be incorporated within this broad framework.

Because people live in a constantly changing environment, adaptive skills are necessary to maintain coping abilities that are consonant with environmental demands. Adequate coping skills are predicated on the abilities of individuals, families, and groups to integrate the consequences of environmental forces into their adaptive response repertoires and to influence (and change) the environmental factors that are producing dysfunctional stress. The individual and the environment shape each other. Styles of coping with the demands of the environment emerge based on the person's perceptions of those demands and his or her capacity to respond.

The systems/ecological framework directs the social worker's attention to the interacting systems within which the client system lives, and it provides a theoretical basis for understanding the rationale underlying the system's adaptive responses. As an assessment tool, this framework enables the social worker to identify both functional and dysfunctional responses to environmental demands and stresses. Once these have been identified, the social worker can focus on the processes of social work intervention and goal setting with the client system.

Ego Psychology

Often referred to as *psychosocial treatment theory,* **ego psychology** stresses the interplay between the individual's internal state and the external environment. The individual's developmental experiences, fears, hostilities, failures, successes, and feelings of love and acceptance all converge to form an estimate of self through which life experiences are filtered and responded to. A main feature of this theory is that it deals with the individual's ability to cope with external pressures and to respond in such a way as to produce satisfaction and feelings of security and self-worth. Often, internal stress results from the inability to solve problems of a mental or physical nature. Inappropriate or underdeveloped coping skills aggravate and intensify the problems, causing the person to become apprehensive, insecure, unwilling to risk, anxious, or, in extreme cases, mentally ill.

Ego psychology also is concerned with environmental factors that affect the individual's adaptive abilities. Among many potentially stressful conditions that may overextend coping capacities are job loss, immobility, death, divorce, poverty, discrimination, and child management. Because stress is experienced individually, practitioners must give individualized consideration to the client and his or her specific situation. Knowledge of stress management, personality organization, and effective coping mechanisms is essential in the assessment process. Ego psychology is an "insight" therapy. Thus, clients are helped by developing an awareness of their unmet needs and problems and their reactions to them, then developing more adaptive coping skills.

Perhaps the key principle associated with ego psychology as a treatment therapy is that it can enable the individual to develop more adaptive coping skills. The result should be reduction of internal stress, more satisfactory role performance, and greater life satisfaction.

Problem-Solving Approach

One of the more widely used approaches in social work practice with individuals and families is the **problem-solving approach.** Developed by Perlman (1959), this approach holds that successful intervention is based on the motivation, capacity, and opportunity of the client systems for change. Recognizing that problems often immobilize the client, that the client's abilities then are neutralized or applied inappropriately, and that opportunities for problem solutions are not engaged, this approach emphasizes the need to "free up" the client system so the client can work toward solving the problem.

The problem-solving approach requires that the client do more than just identify and talk about problems—although both are necessary. The client must move toward taking action (within his or her capacity to do so) to resolve or alleviate the discomfort produced by those problems. Often,

this requires that resources (the opportunity structure) be tapped to achieve these goals. Generally, opportunity resources include those of the client, the client's family, and the agency involved in the helping process, although they may extend to other community resources as well.

MOTIVATION

Conceptually, the problem-solving approach is based on the premise that without *motivation* (the will or desire to change), the client can make only limited progress. Motivation frequently is stymied as a result of stress experienced through dysfunctional or unresolved problems. Social workers often hear the client's doubts through statements such as, "I know it won't do any good to try," "It hasn't worked out in the past," or "Nothing ever turns out right for me." In such instances, the social worker must provide inducements, such as encouragement, that will motivate the client to risk taking steps toward resolution of the problem, with the social worker's assistance. Groups can be a powerful tool in motivating clients because the same messages conveyed by the social worker can be conveyed by other group members. Successful problem solving likely will be accompanied by increased motivation.

CAPACITY

In the problem-solving process, the social worker must be aware of other issues, too. *Capacity* addresses the client's limits (or ability) to change, and includes physical as well as psychological characteristics. For example, a client functioning at a sixth-grade level probably could not become an electrical engineer, but he or she might attend a vocational training program and thereby develop skills to enhance job opportunities.

OPPORTUNITY

Opportunity relates to possibilities within the environmental milieu in which the client interacts daily. A client might attend a vocational school if one is available within the client's locale. If the client has to travel 50 miles, however, transportation and finances might well serve as deterrents, and the client thus might not have the opportunity

BOX 5.1
Behavior Modification

Shortly after Fred and Mary Chapman accepted 3-year-old Tonya into their home for foster care, their 6-year-old son, Frank, became enuretic. Neither Fred nor Mary could identify the reason(s) for Frank's bedwetting behavior, as his last episode had been more than 3 years ago. In an effort to help Frank control this behavior, Fred and Mary reduced his liquid intake before bedtime, withheld privileges, and, in their frustration, scolded him—all to no avail.

They discussed the problem with the foster care social worker, who suggested that Frank's behavior may have resulted from Tonya's placement in their home: Frank felt displaced! Fred and Mary agreed that they had been overly solicitous of Tonya in their attempt to make her feel safe, wanted, and secure. Following the

social worker's cue, they began spending more time with Frank alone and included him as an important family member in helping Tonya feel more secure. Within 2 weeks, Frank's enuretic episodes had ended.

Dramatic family changes such as the one described here can be threatening to a child, as Frank's behavior demonstrated. His involuntary enuresis was a reflection of insecurity prompted by the arrival and attention given to Tonya. As a 6-year-old child, Frank lacked the insight and maturity to verbalize his feelings. As a consequence, regressive behavior took the form of enuresis. When his parents directed more attention to him and included him in planning for Tonya, his fears of displacement were abated and the consequent enuresis ceased.

to participate. Optimal problem solving can be achieved only if the three components—motivation, capacity, and opportunity—are engaged in the process.

Cognitive-Behavioral Approaches

Cognitive-behavioral theories fall into the general category of behavioral intervention, which emphasizes the client's responsibility to actively engage in behaviors that should reduce or eliminate problems. These include behavior modification and reality therapy.

BEHAVIOR MODIFICATION

Social learning theory undergirds behavior modification therapy. Based on the assumption that all behavior (adaptive as well as maladaptive) is learned, **behavior modification** is an "action" therapy (see Box 5.1). Developmental processes that contribute to the acquisition of positive

human responses also are responsible for the development of inappropriate or dysfunctional responses. Because behavior is learned, the client possibly can be assisted in discarding faulty behaviors and acquiring new and more appropriate response patterns.

Recognizing that external events and internal processing result in specific behaviors, change is effected by modifying one's actions, which will result in changing thought patterns. Any attempt to change the internal process (that is, helping the client develop insight into the problem apart from addressing behavior changes directly) is considered largely ineffective.

Based on these general principles, the practitioner using behavior modification approaches intervention with the following organizing framework:

- In a social study, only information that is related directly to the current problem is essential for intervention, not past life experiences. Antecedent factors are pertinent, such as when the problem began, the circumstances that contribute to the problem behavior, and the client's efforts at problem resolution.

- Intervention must focus on specific problems, not the entire range of problems, that the client experiences. The practitioner assists clients in resolving each problem in an independent manner rather than treating them in total.
- Although the client's "feelings" are considered an important factor, the behavioral act is the target, not intrapsychic dynamics. The practitioner assists the client in developing specific techniques and learning more appropriate behavioral responses, as opposed to altering thought processes related to the problem and its effect. Thought processes are considered to be the results, not causes, of behaviors.

Behavior modification treats the objective, definable dimensions of human response patterns. To facilitate the intervention process, the practitioner and the client must agree on the problem to be addressed, contract to work on that problem, agree on the responsibility that each will assume in the change effort, specify goals and objectives, discuss the techniques to be employed, and commit themselves to the treatment effort. As with other therapies, monitoring and evaluation are important. As more functional and acceptable behavior evolves, it is reinforced by more adaptive functioning. Dysfunctional responses are discarded as they become less functional and rewarding for the client.

REALITY THERAPY

Reality therapy is based on the assumption that individuals are responsible for their behavior. Maladaptive behavior is viewed as the product of an identity deficiency. Identity—a basic psychological need of all human beings—is achieved by experiencing love and a sense of self-worth. Individuals who have been deprived of love fail to gain a sense of worth and, as a consequence, develop a poor self-concept. Change is effected by confronting clients with their irresponsible behaviors and encouraging them to accept responsibility for their behavior. It is assumed that clients cannot develop a sense of self-worth while they are engaging in irresponsible behaviors.

Because **self-concept** is a person's internal reaction to the perception of how others see him or her, the practitioner's role in establishing a warm, friendly, accepting relationship becomes an important factor in the intervention process. As with behavior modification, the focus of intervention is on the client's actions rather than feelings. Reality therapy emphasizes confrontation with inappropriate behaviors, along with rejection of rationalizations (excuses). Many practitioners elect reality therapy as an intervention framework because of its straightforward application and the therapist's more informal, relaxed role. Reality therapy also is used effectively with groups, particularly youth groups and groups involved with the criminal justice system.

Task-Centered Social Work

The **task-centered method,** which builds on the problem-solving approach, exemplifies a short-term therapeutic approach (Reid & Epstein, 1972). It stresses the selection and establishment of specific tasks to be worked on within a limited time. Although different models of intervention may be used (such as the ones discussed previously), the emphasis on setting brief time limits for problem solutions is an integral therapeutic ingredient. By "compacting" the agreed-on time limits to work on problems, the client must concentrate his or her attention and energy on the problem and quickly adopt tasks to achieve resolution. The task-centered approach is an action model designed to engage the client quickly and meaningfully in identifying, confronting, and acting on problems.

Social Work Intervention with Families

Social workers long have recognized that the family unit provides physical and emotional support for its members and shapes their identity. Socialization of the young is a basic task of the family, and when problems arise, all family members are affected. As an example, when a husband/ father loses his job, the income available for food, clothing, shelter, and family recreation becomes limited, which alters the family's daily patterns. He may become depressed, which affects relationships with his wife and children. Or a teenager may develop emotional problems, have difficulty with schoolwork, and in turn resist completing home-maintenance responsibilities. Again, this problem affects all family members. We can all identify with family problems of some sort, recalling when our family life has been disrupted and the resulting stress and tension.

Social workers often focus on the family as a unit of intervention. Recognizing that all members of a family are affected by the problems of any one member, intervention is directed to treating the family system. This approach recognizes that the attitudes and emotions of each family member are significant components in moving the family toward healthier functioning. Family therapy (or intervention) does not preclude any individual member from specialized treatment. Ideally, however, all members agree to be included in the intervention process because all family members both contribute to and are affected by ongoing problems within the unit. If one family member is left out of the intervention process, he or she can, consciously or unconsciously, sabotage the progress of other family members and the family as a whole.

Other Approaches

In addition to the theoretical approaches identified, social work practitioners may elect to use other approaches. *Rational emotive therapy* emphasizes "self-talk" as a target for change. *Role therapy* examines both prescriptive and descriptive roles played by clients and identifies incongruities in role expectations as well as dysfunctional role behaviors. Its purpose is to guide the client toward more functional and appropriate role performance. Other approaches are briefly described below.

- **Client-centered therapy,** based on the perspective that clients know most about their problems and needs, seeks to provide an accepting emotional climate in which clients can work out their own solutions with support and reflection from the therapist.
- **Feminist therapy,** which many also view as client-centered, empowers individuals who have been members of an oppressed group to find their own voices and view themselves as equals as they make decisions about their lives.
- **Solution-focused therapy** takes a more cognitive-behavioral approach, often consisting of only a few sessions, during which the therapist guides the client through a series of questions such as: "When does this problem you are talking about *not* occur?" "If you could wave a magic wand and make this problem go away during the night, when you wake up in the morning, how will things be different?" "On a scale of 1 to 10, how serious is this problem for you now?" "What would it take for you to move from where you are on the scale now up one notch?" Clients are assigned "homework" between sessions, and report back on their success during the next session.

Some of these approaches sound fairly simplistic, but any of them requires a highly skilled practitioner to know when and how to use the approach. In working with individuals and families, many additional methods of intervention can be used. The more advanced methods require additional training and are studied in MSW (master of social work) programs with a clinical specialization. Throughout their careers, social workers develop deeper and more complete awareness of intervention theories. As new knowledge and understanding of human behavior evolve, social workers must remain vigilant and open to incorporating new theoretical concepts into their practice modalities.

Practice Theories and Skills: Groups

Many of the problems that clients or client systems encounter can be addressed and resolved more effectively through the group work process. As a generalist practitioner, the BSW (bachelor of social work) social worker recognizes, first, the importance of groups in achieving intervention goals and, second, the utility of group methods in effective problem solving. We will examine group work as a social work method that assists individuals and groups in problem solving.

Social groups are formed for many purposes. The most common is the **natural group,** in which members participate as a result of common interests, shared experiences, similar backgrounds and values, and personal satisfactions derived from interacting with other group members. A street gang or a group of neighbors who hang out together is a natural group. Members of natural groups are characterized further by face-to-face interactions, and they share an emotional investment in the group. Natural groups seldom are formed purposefully to meet specific objectives.

All of us are members of natural groups, and seldom is our membership in those groups the result of a planned effort to become involved. In natural groups, a leader often emerges without premeditation or election by group members but, rather, because one member possesses behavioral attributes or resources that the other group members highly

value. Like all groups, natural groups tend to be transitory, with old members exiting and new ones entering throughout the group's life cycle.

Some of the most effective interventions that social workers undertake are with groups. Members of indigenous groups—such as street gangs, runaway youth, homeless persons, or single-parent women living in the same apartment complex—can begin to trust the efforts of a social worker who interacts and listens nonjudgmentally to their stories and concerns. Once trust develops, the social worker may be able to provide assistance and convince group members to go to a local agency to receive services and other types of assistance (see Box 5.2).

Other groups are formed purposefully for a specific reason. As examples, apartment residents organize to seek building repairs and better living conditions, and a church or synagogue organizes a softball team. Established agencies, such as the YMCA and YWCA, organize recreational groups within the city. A common characteristic of each of these groups is that they are developed to fulfill a specific purpose.

Before attempting to understand the components and process of generalist practice with groups, a basic understanding of what is meant by **group** will be helpful. Chess and Norlin (1996) defined a group as a form of social organization whose members identify and interact with one another on a personal basis and also have a shared sense of the group as a social entity. The type of group with which the generalist practitioner works is called a *primary group*—a group with face-to-face interaction among group members. Regardless of the reasons for forming a group (a natural group or a planned group), the group work method may be used to assist group members in achieving personal growth through the democratic process.

Group work is a process and an activity that seeks to stimulate and support more adaptive personal functioning and social skills of individuals through structured group interaction. The goal of the group work experience is to

BOX 5.2
The Impact of Group Work

Harry, Charlie, John, Manuel, Frank, and Oscar were all teenagers who grew up in a lower-income area of a large city. Although they were not related, from very early in their lives they had played with each other, gone to school together and now "hung out" together. None of them did very well in school. Three were from single-parent families, two had fathers who were alcoholics, and one had a father in the state penitentiary.

Often considered to be a "gang," this small group had several brushes with the law for theft, fighting, and malicious mischief. They spent most of their hours after school roaming the streets, often late into the night. Although, as individuals, each of the boys appeared to be somewhat compliant (if not shy), as a group they represented a threat to be reckoned with. None of the boys had developed adaptable social skills, and they all had difficulty coping with peers who had.

Aaron Stein, a social worker at a nearby settlement house, had, on occasion, discussed with his supervisor and the nearby high school the possibility of enrolling these boys in a socialization group at the agency. Initially it was decided that Aaron would work with the six boys as a small group. Aaron met with the boys as a group (and later, individually), identified the group leader (Oscar), and was able to enlist Oscar's

interest in settlement-house activities. Aaron identified the strengths that each of these individuals brought to the group, as well as the dynamics guiding their group activities. Using this knowledge and the strengths of each group member, he was able to assist group members in developing more adaptive social skills. As the group engaged in activities through the center, including a neighborhood cleanup project, a summer camping trip, and weekly group sessions during which they discussed a wide range of topics, the boys became motivated to achieve goals that were more socially productive and less threatening to the community.

As Aaron worked with the group, he also became involved in a community network on working effectively with at-risk youth. Aaron and the other members of the network developed close ties with school, law enforcement, and juvenile probation personnel and secured state funding for a community-wide prevention program. Aaron and two of the boys in his group served as members of the task force and its committees, and this past year one of the boys was honored for his work in preventing youth gangs. In an interview with the press when he received the award, he said he wanted to be a social worker like Aaron and work to help other kids see that there are other ways than gangs to meet important needs.

---

develop effective skills in communication, coping skills, and effective problem-solving techniques (Toseland & Rivas, 2006). Group work techniques can be used more effectively when goals and objectives are related to the needs of group members. Effective group work capitalizes on the dynamics of interaction among members of the group. Members are encouraged to participate

in making decisions, questioning, sharing, and contributing toward achievement of the agreed-upon goals and objectives.

Group Focus

Social workers engage in practice with groups to accomplish a variety of tasks. Generally, groups may be classified in terms of a specific purpose. Several of the more common types of groups are identified and discussed in Box 5.3.

Effective Group Development

Achieving the desired outcomes of the group process depends on several key considerations—purposefulness, leadership, selection of group members, and size.

PURPOSEFULNESS

Purposefulness, an essential characteristic for maximum effectiveness of the group work process, involves establishing specific goals and objectives and access to their achievement by the group. It provides the direction or intent for each group session and a framework for monitoring and evaluating the group's progress.

LEADERSHIP

Leadership is essential in helping the group maintain its focus and in encouraging maximum participation. The group worker may play an active or a passive role in the group, depending on the needs of the group as it moves toward the established goals and objectives. The leader must be skilled in group processes and able to fill a variety of roles in supporting the accomplishment of tasks necessary to maintain group integrity and continuing progress. A wide range of role responses may be required of a group leader—director, policymaker, planner, expert, external group representative, facilitator, nurturer, disciplinarian, cheerleader, mediator, scapegoat (Zastrow, Gebo, & Concilla, 2003).

Effective leadership is essential to achieve the group's purposes. The methods a leader may use to accomplish group goals should be consistent with the values and purposes of social work practice. Although leaders of groups have diverse leadership styles, the style most compatible with social work encourages empowerment of group members, helping members assume responsibility for the life of the group, including planning, developing skills and values, and making their own decisions about the group's goals and activities. The empowerment method fully embraces the principles of democratic process and encourages individual responsibility and risk sharing as products of group interaction and decision making. The success of group process and goal attainment is related, to a large extent, to effective group leadership. Needless to say, the group leader is accountable for group maintenance and the success (or failure) of the group in achieving its purposes.

SELECTION OF GROUP MEMBERS

The selection of group members is an important factor in achieving group cohesion. In composing groups, the group worker must accurately assess each individual's needs, capacity for social functioning, interests, and willingness to assume an active role as a group member. Although diversity of background and experience may enhance the alternatives for achieving the group's purposes, homogeneous (similar) motives are essential to formation of the group and identification as a group member.

Members with few interests in common often have more difficulty in becoming involved in group activities. Age, ethnicity, and/or gender may be critical factors, depending on the group's purposes and the activities designed to achieve those purposes. Individuals with severe emotional problems or behavior disorders may be disruptive to the group process; therefore, careful consideration should be given to including them as group members.

Members should have the ability to attend to group tasks. Systematic disruptive behavior is disconcerting and even may cause group disintegration. The type of group being formed (for example, recreational, educational) will determine the criteria for selecting members. In all instances, selection should be based on the "principle of maximum profit" (individuals with specific needs who would be most likely to achieve the greatest benefit from the group). Assessment of individuals for group membership is enhanced by a personal interview prior to their being included in the group.

BOX 5.3
Different Types of Groups, Their Focus, and Membership

- **Recreation group** Purpose: to provide for participants' entertainment, enjoyment, and experience, and allow opportunities for shared interaction, interdependence, and social exchange; also can serve as constructive outlets for individuals in a monitored environment. Examples: Community centers, YMCAs and YWCAs, settlement houses, senior centers for older adults organizing sports teams and table games.
- **Recreation-skill groups** Purpose: to promote development of a skill within a recreational context. Skills are often taught by a resource person with expertise; participants develop competency in a craft, game, or sport. Task development is emphasized, and mutual interaction is encouraged in the learning process. Examples: School district and college extension programs, settlement houses, YMCAs, YWCAs, senior centers offering sessions on sewing, pottery-making, learning a sport, or creative writing.
- **Educational groups** Purpose: To transmit knowledge and enable participants

to acquire more complex skills; to provide opportunities for interaction. Leaders have professional expertise in the area of interest. Examples: Can range from learning about the aging process and coping with aging parents, to parenting skills, to substance abuse or other health or mental health issues, to English as a second-language.

- **Socialization groups** Purpose: to help participants strengthen their social skills and develop socially acceptable behavior; to stimulate behavior change and increase self-confidence; focusing on cooperation, personal decision making. Examples: Anger management group for youth, groups for youth that include games and other activities fostering socialization through democratic participation and personal decision making.
- **Self-help groups** Purpose: To provide support and reassurance to group members in dealing with specific issues, with the goal of facilitating behavior change. Participation may be either voluntary or involuntary

---

SIZE

The size of a group is determined largely by its purposes. To determine in advance that 4, 6, or 15 members is the "ideal" size of a group has little validity. Examining the goals and purposes of the proposed group is more effective in determining group size. If, for example, anonymity (the ability to "lose" oneself) is a desirable end, a larger membership may be indicated, to assure more limited interaction and group fragmentation (through the emergence of subgroups). Smaller groups, by definition, demand more intimate interaction, so group pressures typically are intensified. Absenteeism affects group process and

task accomplishment more in small groups than large ones. Small groups may function more informally than larger ones, which usually require a structured format.

The role of the group leader also varies with the size of the group. The democratic process can be achieved in both large and small groups, although it is more difficult in the former. The principles and techniques of social group work are effective with large and small groups alike.

The number of members selected for the group depends on the desired effect on its individual members, their needs, and their capacity (abusive parents or persons charged with driving while intoxicated may be required by the court to participate in groups). Groups emphasize mutual aid and interdependence and playing an active role in responding to the needs of other group members. Members often select their own convener, or the group is facilitated by a person that has personal experience with the issue being addressed. Professional group workers often do not facilitate these groups, although they may serve as a resource to the group. Examples: Alcoholics Anonymous; Parents Anonymous.

- **Therapeutic groups** Purpose: To facilitate behavior change in individuals with intensive personal or emotional problems such as interpersonal loss (death, divorce, or abandonment), physically disabling injuries, terminal illness, marital or family conflict, or mental illness. Therapeutic groups require skilled professional leadership from a well-trained professional such as an MSW social worker or a clinical psychologist. Groups

may be supplemented by individual counseling. Examples: Therapeutic groups for individuals who have difficulty dealing with emotional problems associated with divorce, interpersonal loss, alcohol and drug-related problems, mental health problems, parent–child relationships, or other areas in which dysfunctional behavior results. Typically, emotional problems are related significantly to the problems in day-to-day living of group members.

- **Encounter groups** Purpose: To assist individuals in developing more self-awareness and interpersonal skills in an atmosphere that encourages trust, open expression, candid feedback, and sensitivity to one's own and others' emotions (sometimes called sensitivity or personal-growth groups). Examples: group organized by local service agency to help young women who lack assertiveness, are self-deprecating, and feel inadequate; groups facilitated by professionals to encourage self-exploration and personal growth.

to participate in and support group purposes. Generally, a small group is composed of 4 to 9 members, whereas a large group may consist of 10 to 20 members.

Theory for Group Work Practice

Group work is a direct social work practice method requiring the social worker to be familiar with theories related to group behavior. Group theory provides a framework for promoting

guided change through group interaction. The discipline of social psychology has contributed much to our understanding of group formation, roles, norms, values, group dynamics, and cohesion (Baron & Byrne, 2002). Early social group work pioneers also contributed valuable experiential and theoretical insights that added to the knowledge base from which an informed approach to working with groups can be employed (Toseland & Rivas, 2006).

Social group work can be distinguished as a professional social work method by the informed application of theory in helping groups achieve their objectives and goals. Because groups vary extensively in composition, types, and purposes, the practitioner also must have a broad-based understanding of the life cycle, emotional reactions to stress, and maladaptive behavior. Group workers must be skilled in working with the group and sensitive in helping the group move toward achieving its goals.

Group Work as a Practice

As indicated previously, group work is directed toward the enrichment of an individual's life through a group. Although group members are unlikely to derive equal benefit from the group experience, all can be expected to show some measure of growth. Positive group work is a planned change effort in which change is predicated on benefits derived from group process and interaction. The social worker is responsible for incorporating these principles governing social work practice in the process (National Association of Social Workers [NASW], 1999):

- ensuring the dignity and worth of all members;
- developing an articulated understanding of the group's purpose and the roles that group members agree to follow (for example, exercising confidentiality; treating each other with respect);
- assessing the problems and needs of individual group members and the group as a whole and offering support as needed;
- helping the group develop its own identity, which reflects its unique character, relationships within the group, and needs;
- facilitating the development of communication among group members, which permits the expression of feelings and emotions;
- facilitating the planning and implementation of relevant group activities that promote

constructive interaction, assessment of group process, and the advancement of the group's purpose; and
- preparing for termination.

Each group also has its own life cycle, characterized by developmental stages. Within this context, the stages of a group's development often follow this pattern:

1. *Beginning:* basic orientation and getting acquainted; "honeymoon period"
2. *Norm development:* establishing ground rules for operation; beginning level of trust among members
3. *Conflict phase:* members asserting individual ideas; as members get to know each other better, the resulting conflict often leads to members questioning the group's purpose and suggesting that they leave the group or that the entire group disband
4. *Relationship phase:* replacing initial conflicts with acceptance of others; members working through the conflict and deepening their relationship with each other; sharing of leadership, tasks, and trust; appreciation for the group and a strong sense of group identity; flexibility, consensus, and decision making
5. *Termination:* ending of the group, with recognition of the loss that the group experience is ending, along with acknowledgement of personal growth.

Awareness of these stages is helpful in monitoring the group's progress as it moves toward greater cohesion and effectiveness. Dysfunctional "blocking" at any stage, once identified, can be addressed and resolved by the group, and the developmental progress can continue. If allowed to continue unchecked, the unresolved blockage may result in dissolution of the group.

Groups involve both cyclical and progressive processes. While groups navigate the stages of development from beginning to end, they also come back to revisit or address certain basic process issues in a cyclical stage (Toseland & Rivas, 2006). Skill in working with groups is an important aspect of social work practice. The efficiency and effectiveness of the group work process may result in personal enhancement, skill development, and reduction of problems.

Group Settings

Traditionally, social group work was practiced in recreational settings, such as the YWCA or YMCA, settlement houses, and community centers. With the growing popularity of group work, along with redefinition of the scope of social work practice, group work has become a valuable practice method within most social service agencies. For example, a family service agency might form a group of prospective adoptive parents to orient them to the adoptive process. A treatment center might organize a group of adolescent substance abusers to assist them in identifying and eliminating these undesirable behaviors and to manage their stress and interpersonal problems. A recreational center might sponsor athletic teams for middle-school youth. Older adults living in a long-term care facility could constitute a "re-motivation" group.

Working with groups promotes growth and change through interactions of the members and also enables the agency and workers to serve more clients. Although some group members may need individual counseling in addition to the group experience, in most instances the group activity is sufficient for personal change. When the agency offering the group does not work individually with clients, it makes referrals to an appropriate agency, and a cooperative relationship between the service providers assures the client of maximum assistance with problems.

Group Termination

Groups are terminated when the purposes for which they were established are achieved. Although many groups are initiated with a predetermined expiration period, termination usually is related to meeting group goals and members' personal goals. Occasionally a group is aborted when it becomes obvious that its goals are unattainable or when dysfunctional behavior of one or more group members continually disrupt the group's activities. Most often, however, conflict within the group is typical in group development, and how conflicts are addressed is an important contributor to individual and group growth and how well the group handles termination.

The practitioner must be sensitive to the needs of group members at the time of termination, and assist them in phasing out their attachment to the group. Often, resistance to termination becomes highly emotional and vocal. Among the more common reactions to the loss of the close ties that have developed among members throughout the life of the group are frustration, anger, withdrawal, and grief. By helping the group assess its accomplishments and plan alternatives, the practitioner can assist members in a more adaptive transition.

Practice Effectiveness with Individuals, Families, and Groups

Like all professionals who are engaged with clients in efforts to strengthen their ability to function, social workers have a profound interest in assessing the effectiveness of their work. In social work practice with individuals, families, and groups, the concept of accountability relates to the social workers' ongoing monitoring, feedback, and evaluation of their efforts in assisting clients and client systems toward the resolution of issues and problems for which they sought professional help.

Professional practice with individuals, families, and groups must include an evaluative process. Evaluation is done to determine the extent to which the client or client system is achieving its objectives. This may be an ongoing process as well as an assessment of the total intervention process upon termination of the social worker or group. The social worker continually monitors the intervention process to enable the client or client system to concentrate on its goals. Monitoring also may help redefine its purpose and goals if it becomes evident that the original goals are unachievable. Monitoring consists of critical assessment of the client's output.

Evaluation involves assessing all activities and behaviors related to the client system's performance. Factors including attendance and participation in individual or group sessions, resources, changes in behavior, and agency support, among others, are all reviewed in relation to achievement of the goals and objectives. Evaluation has the potential of providing a basis for answering questions such as:

- What could have increased clients' growth and change?
- What were the positive achievements of the clients or client systems?
- What implications for change are suggested?

Efficiency and better quality of service are likely when rigorous evaluative standards are maintained. Various methods have been developed (see chapter 6) to provide an empirical framework for making this assessment. Practice evaluation is essential for viewing movement in cases, and it also provides a basis for reviewing the effectiveness of various techniques the social worker employs to address specific problems, as well as provide an impetus for updating skills. On the broader scene, social work researchers have been engaged continually in reviewing practice effectiveness, using differing intervention modalities, and found that outcomes vary, given the nature of the problem, the individuals or groups involved, and projected outcome goals.

Issues related to the practitioner's technique and/or personality, in terms of positive outcomes, are generally considered to be invalid. Like all professions, some social workers are more personable, highly skilled, engaging, and effective than others, and provide good role models for all who desire to become helping professionals.

Research on the whole has been encouraging with respect to the effectiveness of social work practice with individuals, families, and groups. As techniques are refined through practice and as knowledge accrues through research, social workers are expected to become even more effective in helping individuals and families meet their needs.

Supervision of Generalist Practitioners

Supervision typically is thought of as a management function—that of overseeing and ensuring that employees are fulfilling the purpose and goals of an agency or organization. Although this function may be one of the responsibilities of social work supervisors, they must do much more. They provide enrichment to practitioners by helping them develop practice skills through periodic feedback and discussion of cases. They regulate the flow of cases assigned to social workers and use their unique skills through selective case assignment. They are at different times educators, listeners, enablers, and resources for identifying alternative techniques for addressing problems.

In their management functions, supervisors present the need for resources to agency executives and maintain standards for excellence in the performance of the social workers they supervise. Supervisors play a vital role in helping an agency achieve its purposes.

Social Work Practice and the MSW Social Worker

Most social workers interact directly with individuals, families, or groups, although contemporary practice requires that the social worker become involved in other aspects of social work practice as well. MSW practitioners may specialize in community organization, social policy, research, social planning, or social administration, as well as practice with individuals, families, and groups. At the master's level, the **specialization** builds on generalist practice knowledge and skills. Many MSW workers are employed in highly clinical environments such as psychiatric or family service settings, in criminal justice settings, in centers serving AIDS patients, and in related fields of practice requiring specialized knowledge and skill. Others work in agencies such as a department of human resources, serving people with less specialized problems.

Competence in all social work methods enhances the social worker's effectiveness in helping client systems seek solutions to problems at all levels of the environment. As discussed in chapter 2, private practice has increased in recent years. This kind of practice typically calls for competence in psychotherapeutic and intensive counseling skills. Practitioners continue to develop resources that will enable clients to attain a more satisfactory level of adaptation, regardless of the setting in which social work is practiced.

The BSW Social Worker in Practice with Individuals, Families, and Groups

Education for social work at the BSW (bachelor of social work) level is geared toward enabling the student to become skilled in generalist social work practice. Guidelines for curricula content are established by the Council on Social Work Education, which also serves as the accrediting body for undergraduate social work programs.

As generalist social workers, practitioners at the baccalaureate level typically find employment in social agencies specializing in direct practice with individuals, families, and groups. Appreciation of the nature of client needs and problems in these settings is enhanced by a generalist background and focus.

Direct practice with individuals, families, and groups does not always demand in-depth psychotherapeutic treatment. Although interviewing and assessment skills are essential in establishing intervention goals, the BSW social worker need not be concerned with skills required for intensive psychotherapy. Social work practice with individuals, families, and groups extends far beyond psychotherapeutic involvement.

The case presented at the opening of this chapter is a good example. The BSW social worker could be involved as a **case manager** in helping identify needed resources for reducing stress and linking with other appropriate resources to ensure that needs are being addressed. His or her interviewing and counseling skills would be useful in providing opportunities to identify needs and problems and explore resources necessary for resolving them. The BSW social worker also could facilitate the support group in which Patrice was involved or the skills group in which her son participated.

The skill of the BSW practitioner in articulating community resources in the problem-solving process must not be underestimated. Knowledge of resources and preparation of clients to use those resources are paramount in resolving problems.

BSW practitioners are employed in a variety of direct practice settings that offer services to individuals, families, and groups. Among the many opportunities are agencies such as state departments of human resources (or public welfare), mental health and substance abuse programs, programs that serve children and adults with disabilities, children's service agencies (child welfare and child care institutions), halfway houses, nursing homes and other long-term care facilities, area-wide agencies on aging, agencies serving battered women, rape crisis centers, schools, and child care centers.

Summary

Social work is a multifaceted profession requiring its practitioners to be familiar with theories of human behavior and social intervention. Social workers also must understand the logic of the social work process.

Professional values serve as the underpinning for the relationship that social workers establish with their client systems. These values also are the catalyst for promoting societal change designed to enrich the lives of the populace. The goal of generalist social work practice with individuals, families, and groups is to empower client systems to take charge of their lives and to act on their environment so as to produce positive change for themselves and those with whom they interact.

To be an effective change agent, a social work practitioner must have far more than counseling skills. Generalist social workers engage a variety of social systems to facilitate positive change for their clients. This requires interpersonal skills as well as conceptual, planning, and evaluative skills. To become effective, social work practice requires the skillful application (an art) of scientific knowledge in the problem-solving process.

Key Terms and InfoTrac® College Edition

The terms below are included in the Glossary. To learn more about key terms and topics in this chapter, enter the following search terms using InfoTrac College Edition or the World Wide Web:

assessment
behavior modification
casework
case manager
client-centered therapy

contracting
dysfunctional
ego psychology
evaluation
feminist therapy

generalist
generalist practice
goal setting
group
group work
intervention
natural group
problem-solving
  approach

reality therapy
self-concept
social study
socialization group
therapeutic group
solution-focused
  therapy
specialization
task-centered method

Discussion Questions

1. Define generalist social work practice. What components are essential in generalist practice intervention?
2. What skills are necessary to become a generalist practitioner? How do the skills used by generalist practitioners differ from those used by advanced specialist social workers?
3. What is the importance of theory in social work intervention?
4. What is the relationship between social work values and effective social work intervention?
5. Identify the components of the problem-solving process used in social work practice. Using a case example, show how these would be used in working with a client/client system.
6. Review the vignette at the beginning of the chapter. Which practice approaches discussed in this chapter would be effective in working with the family members? How might the outcomes differ depending on the approach used?
7. What are some of the primary considerations that a social worker must consider when forming groups?
8. What are the basic principles governing group work practice? Explain how those principles would be applied to the different types of groups delineated in Box 5.3.
9. Why is it important for social workers to evaluate their practice with clients and client systems?

On the Internet

http://eserver.org/feminism/

http://www.planet-therapy.com/

http://www.nyu.edu/socialwork/wwwrsw/

www.asgw.org/

www.socialworkers.org/

References

Baron, R. A., & Byrne, D. (2002). *Social psychology* (8th ed). Boston: Allyn & Bacon.

Chess, W. A., & Norlin, J. M. (1996). *Human behavior and the social environment* (3rd ed.). Boston: Allyn & Bacon.

Dubois, B., & Miley, K. K. (2002). *Social work: An empowering profession*. Boston: Allyn & Bacon.

National Association of Social Workers (1999). *NASW Code of ethics*. Washington, DC: Author.

Perlman, H. H. (1959). *Social casework: The problem solving process*. Chicago: University of Chicago Press.

Reid, W. J., & Epstein, L. (1972). *Task-centered casework*. New York: Columbia University Press.

Toseland, R., & Rivas, R. (2006). *An introduction to group work practice*. Boston: Allyn & Bacon.

Zastrow, C., Gebo, L., & Concilla, C. (2003). *The practice of social work*. Pacific Grove, CA: Wadsworth.

Suggested Further Readings

Compton, B. R., Galaway, B., & Counoyer, B. R. (2005). *Social work processes* (7th ed.). Pacific Grove, CA: Brooks/Cole.

Congress, E., & Gonzales, M. (Eds.). *Multicultural perspectives in working with families*. New York: Springer.

Constable, R., & Less, D. (2004). *Social work with families: Content and process*. Chicago: Lyceum Press.

Cooper, M., & Lesser, J. (2005). *Clinical social work practice: An integrated approach*. Boston: Allyn & Bacon.

Corcoran, J. (2000). *Evidence-based social work practice with families: A lifespan approach*. New York: Springer Press.

Garvin, C., Gutierrez, L., & Galinsky, M. (2004). *Handbook of social work with groups*. New York: Guilford Press.

Hepworth, D. H., Rooney, R., & Larsen, J. A. (2002). *Direct social work practice*. Pacific Grove, CA: Brooks/Cole.

Lowenberg, F., Dolgoff, R., & Harrington, D. (2005). *Ethical decisions for social work practice* (7th ed.). Itasca, IL: Peacock.

Malekoff, A. (2007). *Group work with adolescents: Principles and practice*. New York: Guilford.

Mattaini, M., Lowery, C., & Meyer, C. (2002). (Eds.). *Foundations of social work practice*. Washington, DC: NASW Press.

Zastrow, C. (2006). *Social work with groups: A comprehensive workbook*. Pacific Grove, CA: Wadsworth.

CHAPTER 6

Social Work Practice with Agencies and the Community

Leticia Fontenot is an administrator for a county social services program in a large northern city. A licensed social worker, she worked her way up through the agency ranks from a child abuse and neglect investigator to her current position. Daily, she is faced with a variety of critical issues that impact the lives of children throughout the county. Despite a number of prevention programs, the rates of child maltreatment continue to rise. Staff caseloads are increasing, and worker turnover is alarmingly high.

A highly respected administrator within the community, Leticia has been asked to convene a task force to develop strategies that will address these issues before they result in the tragic deaths of children. The task force will propose recommendations for changes in agency administration, including staffing patterns and agency structure, as well as policy initiatives that will garner more resources for the agency. As Leticia thinks about the problems, she realizes that a first step is to determine what research has been conducted that can help her and the task force members better understand the issues. Although she no longer works directly with clients, her role as an agency administrator has a major impact on children and families in the community and the state.

This chapter addresses the roles of social workers in generalist practice at the *exo-* (community) and *macro-* (societal) levels of the environment, including agency administration, community organization, policy development, and research. Often, assistance to individuals and families is more effective if changes are made at the community or societal level rather than trying to assist people on a case-by-case basis. Sound plans for community change, social welfare policies, and agency administration must be based on empirical research; and funding sources, including legislative bodies, are increasingly demanding agency accountability for any funding they provide.

In addition, because social welfare issues are complex and not always easily understood, agency administrators must have good data to support their recommendations for effective programs to community, state, and federal leaders. Leticia, for example, knows that research has demonstrated that, in the long run, preventive programs will reduce the incidence of child maltreatment and result in healthier children and families. She also knows that government funding sources often allocate limited funding to social welfare-related problems, and that funding is insufficient for the staff to deal with actual situations of child maltreatment, let alone prevention programs.

One of the dilemmas faced by social agency administrators such as Leticia is how to develop collaborative relationships with key policymakers and advocates within their states and communities to support programs that will result in positive change for the children and families that their agencies serve. Although the politics and administration of social welfare laws have a clear and direct relevance for planners, administrators, and policymakers, state and federal laws often are made without input from programs at the community level, where social workers and clients interact directly.

After graduation, most BSW students obtain entry-level jobs in direct practice—delivering social services in direct interactions with clients. Social workers in direct practice at the local level are the first to hear what clients think about these laws and the related policies put in place to comply with the laws. Thus, the flow of information from client to policymaker and the sensitivity of policymakers to clients' circumstances are best accomplished when social workers appreciate and understand both the opportunities and the limitations of the American policymaking process.

Social Work with Communities

Social work with communities is a generalist practice method that enables individuals and groups to achieve greater life satisfaction, as well as more effective levels of adaptation. Community social work may take a variety of forms (see Box 6.1 for an example).

Successful social work intervention, as in the case of Brenda, often requires the social worker to engage community agencies and organizations

BOX 6.1
Making a Difference at the Community Level

Norma Carlson, a BSW social worker, has been working with Brenda Bostwick for several months. Brenda, age 16, is a single parent who aspires to complete her high school education with the hope that she can find a good job and better provide for her child. She has had difficulty concentrating on her schoolwork because she often had to miss school to care for her baby. On several occasions school officials suspended her for absences, and she was becoming more discouraged every day.

With Brenda's consent, Norma visited with the school officials to engage them in working out an educational program for Brenda so she would not fall behind in her studies. Norma contacted a local child care center and helped Brenda arrange for her child to be cared for while she was in class. Norma helped Brenda secure reduced-rate transportation with the local bus company so she could get to and from school as well as to her child's child care center.

After being assigned to work with other teen parents, Norma realized that the community had no resources for working specifically with teen parents. She helped organize a network of interested social workers and school officials. Together, network members secured reduced child care and transportation rates for all teen parents in the community so they could attend school regularly. Norma and other network members wrote a grant and received funding to establish a program to work exclusively with pregnant and parenting teens.

in the process. Without Norma's knowledge and skill, Brenda probably could not have made the arrangements that resulted in a positive solution to her need to complete her high school education. Clients frequently are unaware of available resources or the process through which successful solutions can be achieved. In some instances, clients do not have the self-confidence to pursue alternatives that would result in goal achievement. Also, needed resources may not be available in their communities. Thus, social workers in direct practice often find that work with the community is essential in the problem-solving process.

Community: Definition and Social Work Roles

Community is a descriptive term with many meanings. Communities are said to be groups of people who live within certain incorporated limits, such as Philadelphia, Pennsylvania; Boise, Idaho; or Mena, Arkansas. Others speak of a "religious community," which refers to a group of people with religious values in common. A community also may be a subunit of a larger metropolitan area, such as Watts in Los Angeles or Shadyside in Pittsburgh. Members of an ethnic group who live in a specific geographic area, too, are often referred to as a community. The illustrations are endless, and the purpose here is to call attention to the ambiguity of the concept.

As a workable definition, **communities** may be defined as spaces, interactions, and identifications that people share with others in place-specific and non-place-specific locations. Of the many types of communities, those in which social work professionals are most likely to be involved are classified as geographical or territorial communities, communities of identification and interest, traditional communities, and communities of diversity.

- **Geographic or territorial communities** (sometimes referred to as modern communities) include neighborhoods, cities, towns, villages, and boroughs that have clearly defined geopolitical boundaries.

- **Communities of identification and interest** (also referred to as functional communities, relational/associational communities, communities of affiliation or affinity, or communities of the mind) are formed around shared concerns and deeply held beliefs and values that often bring community members into conflict with other communities Examples are communities based on ethnicity, race, religion, lifestyle, sexual orientation, or profession.

- **Traditional communities** exist side by side with modern communities. For the most part, these community members attempt to maintain their separateness, uniqueness, cultural integrity, and historical identify. Traditional communities are distinguished from modern communities by their emphasis on mutual relationships, commonality, tradition, ritual, and social bonds. Examples of traditional communities are the Amish, Native Americans, Hasidic Jews, and aborigines.

- **Communities of diversity** constitute a subset of modern communities whose community members often engage in a struggle to navigate a hostile world. Examples of these communities are barrios, ghettos, and Indian reservations.

Roles of Social Workers in Communities

The same basic skills necessary to work effectively with people are used in community practice. Generalist social work practitioners engaged in community practice play many of the same professional roles as those who work with individuals, families, and groups (see Box 2.1 in chapter 2). Social work with the community may encompass a wide range of problems and issues, of which the case illustration with which we initiated this chapter is only one example.

Social workers who practice at the community level use a number of approaches to improve the well-being of community members.

Rober E. Daemmrich/Stone/Getty Images

A social worker may serve as a **broker** (linking clients with resources and services) with several agencies to obtain sources necessary to achieve treatment goals. In the broker role, the social worker helps clients navigate the maze of agencies to locate resources that are most appropriate to problem resolution. In addition to the active role of **negotiator** (an intermediary to resolve conflicts) with agencies, the social worker gathers and transmits information between client systems and the broader environment (Kirst-Ashman & Hull, 2005).

Sometimes the social worker in community practice serves as an **enabler** in helping people identify and clarify their problems (assessment) and in supporting and stimulating the group to unite in its efforts to secure change. For example, a group of tenants in a rat-infested apartment might be encouraged to unite and confront the owners or landlords with the problem and seek redress for those conditions.

At other times the social worker in community practice functions in the role of **advocate** (promoting fair and equitable treatment of clients and working to obtain needed resources) for a client system in confronting unresponsive representatives of community institutions. In the advocate role, the social worker clearly is aligned with the client system in urging unresponsive institutions to take action. A social worker may, for example, represent the client system in trying to increase police protection in high-risk neighborhoods.

Social workers at the community level also might serve in the **educator** role (providing information/teaching skills to facilitate change), for example, by organizing an effort to educate non-English-speaking women in the community about the importance of obtaining mammograms. Other roles that social workers in the community typically take on, according to Kirst-Ashman & Hull (2005, pp. 21–26), are

- **analyst/evaluator** (determining the effectiveness of programs or agencies),
- **facilitator** (bringing participants together to promote change through improved communication),

- **general manager** (assuming administrative responsibility for an agency at some level),
- **initiator/coordinator** (bringing people together and helping organize for change),
- **mediator** (helping factions work out their differences), and
- **mobilizer** (identifying and convening resources to address unmet community needs)

As indicated, generalist social work practitioners are constantly engaged in community practice as they work with various organizations to address specific needs of their clients or the populace in general. In Brenda's case, the social worker had to engage the school system, a child care center, and the local transportation company to establish an effective solution for Brenda's dilemma, as well as other teen parents in similar situations.

Community Practice Models and Approaches

Social workers engage in a variety of **community practice** approaches (Netting, Kettner, & McMurtry, 2004):

- neighborhood and community organizing;
- organizing functional communities;
- community, social, and economic development;
- social planning;
- program development and community liaison;
- political and social action;
- coalition building; and
- social movements

The desired outcome of **neighborhood and community organizing** is to develop the capacity of community members to organize around quality-of-life issues in the community (e.g., air quality, noise pollution, activities for children to participate in after school, planning for controlled neighborhood development, affordable housing). Systems targeted for change include municipal government, developers, and community members. Social justice directed to advocacy and changing behaviors is the desired outcome of **organizing functional communities.** The system targeted for change is the general public and government institutions. The scope of concern is advocacy for a specific issue or population (e.g., marriage rights for gays and lesbians, a living wage, resources for the homeless, legal rights of immigrants).

The desired outcome of **community social and economic development** is to prepare citizens to make use of social and economic investments (e.g., Earned Income Tax Credit, child care tax credit, low-interest housing loans, weatherization programs). The system targeted for change includes banks, foundations, developers, and the general public. The scope of concern is income, resource, and social support development.

The desired outcomes of **social planning** are proposals for action by elected bodies or human services planning councils. The system targeted for change consists of community and human services leaders. The scope of concern is the integration of social needs into planning in the public arena. Social planning strategies include working behind the scenes with others to bring to the table a specific proposal for action, direct participation in the planning, and influencing people who participate in the planning.

The desired outcome of **program development and community liaison** is expansion or redirection of agency programs (e.g., school-based services for pregnant or parenting teens, safe havens for the community's children). The system targeted for change consists of agency funding sources and beneficiaries of agency services.

The desired outcome of **political and social action** is social justice focusing on changing policy or policymakers. The system targeted for change includes the voting public, elected officials, and potential participants. The scope of concern is to build political power and institutional change (get the message to those who can do something about the issue or problem).

The desired outcome of **coalition building** is to create a multiorganizational power base large enough to influence program direction or draw down resources. The system targeted for change consists of elected officials, foundations, and government entities. The scope of concern is a specified issue related to a social need or concern (e.g., eliminating open-air drug markets, creating a safe place in which community members can live).

The desired outcome of **social movements** is action for social justice (social reform) that provides a new paradigm for an identified population or issue. The system targeted for change is the general public or political systems. The scope of concern is social justice within society. Historical examples of social movements include the settlement house movement, welfare rights movement, civil rights movement, anti-Vietnam war movement, farm worker movement, and feminist movement.

Profile of an Effective Community Organizer

Social work practitioners, with their use of the systems/ecological framework to understand the interactions between the larger community and its members, can be effective community organizers. The profile of an effective community organizer includes the following elements:

- familiarity with community customs and traditions, social networks, and values (sometimes referred to as "settling in")
- leadership capability
- knowledge of political systems with their access and leverage points
- knowledge of past organizing strategies, their strengths, and their limitations
- skill in developing critical consciousness and empowerment
- skill in evaluative and participatory research
- skill in program planning and development
- awareness of self and personal strengths and limitations

- an understanding of power
- a sense of curiosity
- the ability to imagine and dream

Macro social workers are obligated to seek opportunities to develop or expand skills in these areas, work with others who have these skills, and learn by example (and, conversely, to reach out and help others gain these skills after mastering them), put the skills into practice once gained, and embrace a "lifetime learning" approach to skills development.

Policy Practice

DiNitto (2005) defines **social welfare policy** as "anything a government chooses to do, or not to do, that affects the quality of life of its people" (p. 2). Social welfare policies are influenced by the prevailing social values.

The Development of Social Welfare Policy

Day (2006, pp. 5–12) identifies the following social values that have the potential for influencing the development of social welfare policies:

- *Judeo-Christian charity values:* Those requiring assistance have a right to help, and society has an obligation to respond.
- *Democratic egalitarianism:* No one has privileges based on class, heritage, wealth, or other factors not related to basic citizenship.
- *Individualism* (also referred to as the "bootstrap mentality" or "frontier mentality"): Failure to achieve is the fault of the individual, not society.
- *Protestant work ethic and capitalism:* The emphases are on work as a means of achieving religious salvation; individualism; personal achievement; and the morality of wealth.

- *Social Darwinism:* The lives of the "economically unfit" should not be saved by giving them public assistance; the poor are morally degenerate and should perish; any society aiding the poor will be destroyed by its immorality.
- *Patriarchy:* Power and authority are vested in men.
- *New Puritanism:* Society must return to patriarchy and the Puritan values of the past—chastity, particularly for women; honesty in dealing with others; abstinence from things defined by religion and custom as immoral; and behavior that will not offend others.
- *Marriage and the nuclear family:* The traditional marriage system—husband, wife, and one or more children—should be preserved.
- *"American Ideal":* The "ideal" consists of looking and acting a certain way, coupled with race and gender stereotypes.

Taken alone or in combination, these values can have a powerful influence on the social welfare policies that guide the work of the social work profession.

Gilbert and Terrell (2006) view social welfare policy as an explicit course of action, stressing decisions and choices that help determine the outcomes of that course of action. They believe that social welfare policies can be interpreted as choices among principles determining what benefits are offered and to whom, how the benefits are provided, and how they are financed. They express these dimensions of choice in the following four questions.

1. What are the bases of social allocations? (the "who" of social welfare policy—recipients or beneficiaries)
2. What are the types of social provisions to be allocated? (the "what" of social welfare policy—financial support or goods and services)
3. How will these provisions be delivered? (the organizational arrangements made for delivering benefits to clients)
4. What are the ways these provisions will be financed? (identifying the necessary funds to deliver the agreed-upon services to the agreed-upon clients or beneficiaries). (p. 60)

According to Gilbert and Terrell, the choices that are made in determining who gets what, how services are delivered, and how services are financed are influenced by the range of available alternatives, the social values that support the alternatives, and the theories or assumptions that underlie them (p. 60). Each choice is subject to tradeoffs between what is desirable, what the circumstances necessitate, and what the public will support.

Models of Policy Analysis

Haynes and Mickelson (2006, pp. 69–74) argue that understanding policy models (patterns of something to be made) is central to simplifying and clarifying our understanding of social welfare policy. They offer the following models as a framework for determining how social welfare policy is developed and implemented:

1. *Institutional model:* The focus is on social welfare policy as the output of governmental institutions such as Congress, state legislatures, the courts, and political parties.
2. *Process model:* The focus is on gaining an appreciation for and an understanding of how social welfare policy decisions are made.
3. *Group theory model:* The focus is on the interaction between political interest groups such as advocacy groups, policy institutes or "think tanks," political action committees or PACs, or lobbying organizations.
4. *Elite theory model:* The focus is on the preferences, values, and behaviors of a "governing elite," usually at the expense of other members of society.
5. *Rational model:* The focus is on efficiency, positive outcomes, costs–benefits, long-term

results, and the common good (rational poli-cymaking is comprehensive, objective, and free from the influence of special-interest groups).

6. *Incremental model:* The focus is on using ex-isting policies as a baseline for change; atten-tion is concentrated on how new or proposed policies affect (increase, decrease, or modify) that base (this approach typically involves limited change, political expediency, or fine-tuning rather than dramatic change, result-ing in something for everyone and minimal conflict).

Understanding the framework from which social welfare policy is developed enables social work-ers to be more effective in influencing the policy development process.

The Practitioner's Role in Social Welfare Policy

Social work professionals of all kinds—direct ser-vice workers, planners, administrators, advocates, and researchers—are affected by and have the potential for affecting social welfare policy. Refer-ring to our previous discussion, social welfare policy provides the basis for determining who (clients or beneficiaries) is eligible for services as well as the extent of services provided. Social wel-fare policy is the blueprint upon which social welfare programs are planned, designed, and operated. Social welfare program administrators must follow the rules and regulations that are used to translate social welfare policy into subsequent action. Social work researchers are charged with determining the relative effectiveness of various social welfare policies in achieving their intended outcomes—moving clients from welfare to self-sufficiency, keeping children safe, helping the elderly to live with respect and dignity.

Formulation and developing social welfare policy are not one-way undertakings. Social work professionals have a significant role in defining and shaping social welfare policy as well. Direct

service workers have first-hand knowledge of the impact of social welfare policies on their clients—what works, what doesn't work, and what has to be changed.

Program planners know which policies lead to trouble-free, straightforward implementation and which do not. Social welfare advocates provide important information to policymakers about the needs and concerns of the client groups they rep-resent, and also monitor policy development to ensure that those needs and concerns are not neglected. Social welfare researchers develop the evidence base for deciding which policies are best suited for which client and under what conditions. Good social welfare policy simply cannot be developed without the input and involvement of the social work profession.

Administration and Delivery of Social Welfare Services

Most social welfare services are delivered by some type of agency. Today, there are almost as many types of agencies as the problems they ad-dress. The social welfare agency is many things to many people. It is a place where people go for help when problems arise and a place that soci-ety holds responsible for addressing specific problems. It also is a place of employment for some and a setting for voluntary action by others. With the multiple motives of multiple actors, the social welfare agency has no single purpose but, rather, a myriad of purposes.

Meeting the Challenge

Above all, the major task of the social welfare agency's administrator is to bring resources, opportunities, and goals together to accomplish a variety of social missions. Management activities are not the sole responsibility of agency adminis-trators. All staff members of the agency, members of the board of directors or other governance oversight body, and the agency's clients play vital roles in the administrative process.

The administrator of any social welfare agency is faced with the following questions in operating the agency:

- How should I organize the agency?
- Who should I hire, and what is the best way to organize and support them?
- What role(s) can volunteers play in the work of the agency, and what is the best way to recruit and support them?
- Which programs should be offered, and how should they be delivered?
- How do I keep track of critical client-related and other information?
- How can I be accountable to the agency's board, funding sources, and accrediting organizations?
- How do I develop the necessary funding to provide services and enable the agency to grow and thrive?
- How do I know that agency programs and services are achieving their intended outcomes?

The social work literature offers a wide variety of tools and techniques for answering these and related questions (see, for example, Kettner, 2002; Netting, Kettner, & McMurtry, 2004; and Clegg, Hardy, & Nord 1999).

Weighing the Client's Best Interests

Social service agencies that represent clients with little or no political power have unique problems. Too much concern with the needs and desires of clients served can erode the economic and political support necessary for the agency's very existence. But too little concern can result in exploitation of the clients the agency purports to serve.

Another concern that social service administrators face is the question of who makes what choices. Children, individuals with mental illness, those with developmental disabilities, and others may not know what is in their best interest. Often,

the agency is left to make such decisions. The complexity of the situation and the number of available options influence these decisions.

The professional social worker in the social service agency has to steer between two dangers. On the one hand, rigid adherence to the rules that govern the agency or the wishes of those who fund the agency can result in a subtle but debilitating form of tyranny. On the other hand, overinvolvement of clients in decisions that affect the structure and nature of the services being offered can result in a limited agency perspective. Of course, the best course of action is to involve clients in a meaningful way while maintaining the integrity of the agency's overall decision-making process.

Social Welfare Agencies

Social welfare has its roots in the 1700s, as detailed in chapter 1. Today's structures, while maintaining the integrity of their roots, have evolved to meet today's conditions.

A Historical Perspective

Organized social welfare in colonial America was essentially nonexistent. Times were tough, and resources were scarce. All able-bodied adults were expected to work to support themselves and their families. Movement between cities and towns was restricted. Families were accountable for taking care of their own. Children in families who could not support them were apprenticed out to others, where they earned their keep through forced labor.

Adults who could not support themselves through no fault of their own (those with disabilities and the elderly) were cared for in the homes of others or were relegated to almshouses, where they received minimal care. Able-bodied individuals who refused to work or were unable to find work were placed in workhouses, where they lived in squalid conditions, sometimes with their children, in return for forced work. Some charitable associations existed, but their resources were limited and the number of people they were able to serve was small in comparison to the need.

In the 1700s, the **private voluntary sector** began to grow in response to the public disgrace surrounding the living conditions in the alms-houses, where children lived with the adults in the same quarters. Limited government involvement in providing social welfare services continued throughout the 18th century and well into the 19th century. Care for the poor and the needy was almost exclusively the purview of religious institutions and private charitable organizations.

Successive waves of immigration throughout the 1800s, coupled with the aftermath of the Civil War, brought about a rapid expansion of private voluntary agencies (charity organization societies and **settlement houses**), particularly in urban areas along the eastern seaboard and in large Midwest cities such as Chicago. Advocacy efforts of early social workers during the so-called Progressive Era (1875–1925) forced the federal government to at least take notice of the problems, as well as to begin developing policies and programs addressing the plight of the poor and the needy.

Not until the stock market crash of 1929 and the ensuing Great Depression did the federal government assume a major role in the American social welfare system. Local governments, religious institutions, and private voluntary organizations were unable to meet the demand for services created by the Depression. Like it or not, the federal government had no choice but to get involved. Passage of the Social Security Act in 1935 marked the formal entry of the federal government into the public social service arena. The age of large-scale, public social services had begun.

Growth of federal government involvement in public social welfare programs continued through the first half of the 20th century. This growth peaked with the War on Poverty and the Great Society programs of the Johnson administration and has been on the decline since that time. Successive Republican presidential administrations since the 1970s have emphasized a "new

federalism" characterized by limited government involvement, transfer of responsibility for social welfare programs to the states through block grants, renewed emphasis on personal and family responsibility, privatization of public social services, reliance on religious institutions and faith-based organizations and the private voluntary sector to pick up the slack, and strict accountability requirements. As a result, even though many more resources are available, the contemporary social welfare system in the United States is similar in some ways to the one in colonial America. For a detailed discussion of the evolution of the American social welfare system, see Axinn and Stern (2005), Day (2006), and Jansson (2006).

Contemporary Structures

Today, organized social service activities are provided directly by local, state, and federal governments, by sectarian or faith-based organizations, and by private nonprofit agencies. **Private non-profit agencies** provide a host of services to individuals, groups, neighborhoods, and communities. They also serve as an organizing entity and conduit for charitable funds and voluntary efforts.

Three interdependent parts make up the social service portion of private nonprofit agencies, of which a specific agency can represent one or all three:

1. agencies that serve public and charitable purposes principally for fund raising and planning, such as United Way agencies;
2. advocacy organizations, which bring together a group of like-minded people who seek to generate government funding or promote public understanding of and support for a specific social problem or a specific class of individuals;
3. direct service agencies that deal with clients who have specific or multiple problems of social functioning.

Voluntary agencies are bounded on one side by the private, profit-oriented approach of the free market and, on the other side, by a politically driven public sector. They are free to be creative and innovative but, at the same time, vulnerable to their own excesses. Thus, any agency may exist only briefly. Much like businesses, few private voluntary agencies have existed for a hundred years or more, a small number of agencies are in the middle years, and there are a plethora of new agencies (those less than 10 years old).

Will private voluntary agencies survive as a significant provider of social welfare services? Probably so, but they will look quite different in the future than today. Shifts in private charitable giving brought about by a flagging economy and the aftermath of the terrorist attacks on the United States in September 2001 and the subsequent War on Terrorism waged in Iraq, Afghanistan, and elsewhere around the world forced private voluntary agencies to look at the benefits of social entrepreneurship, to engage in strategic alliances and partnerships with business and industry, and to entertain the thought of merging with other agencies to secure their future. Increasingly, the distinction between public and private social service agencies is blurring as public agencies are entering into purchase of service and other arrangements to fulfill their statutory mandates.

Research Practice

Given the increased demand for accountability by those who fund social welfare programs, research is playing an ever-increasing role in determining how resources are allocated. Social work as a profession is committed to empirical research to generate new knowledge and evaluate practice methods that will ensure that client systems at all levels are adequately served.

Social workers incorporate three types of research in their interventions at all levels of the environment: disciplinary research, policy research, and evaluative research. All three types are scientific (they depend on the scientific method),

objective (the investigator is required to conform to established canons of logical reasoning and formal rules of evidence), and ethically neutral (the investigator does not take sides on issues of moral or ethical significance). Although the three types are similar in their demand for objectivity, each type has its own specific purposes.

Disciplinary Research

Disciplinary research is the term that denotes investigations to expand the body of knowledge of a discipline. The intent is explanation for its own sake. Disciplinary research begins with a **paradigm** or perspective that structures the research, the research goals, and the research methods. The paradigm directs the investigator to where and how to seek evidence.

Paradigms or perspectives allow researchers within a discipline to build on the work of others in their field. Social workers also must make use of these paradigms to identify pragmatic methods of intervention with clients, families, and communities. The social investigator is interested in providing an explanation of *why* something happened.

The first step in this inquiry is to identify a dependent or outcome variable (the phenomenon we wish to explain) and show how it is related to one or more independent variables (factors that produce changes in the dependent variable). For example, with changes in economic and social circumstances (independent variables), observable changes in employment opportunities (dependent variable) follow. Careful selection of independent and dependent variables, use of both inductive and deductive reasoning, and precise application of the established rules of evidence are required to produce correct inferences about relationships.

The "glue" that holds together any disciplinary investigation is theory. A **theory** is a set of logically related, empirically verifiable generalizations that intend to explain relationships clearly. A theory is derived from a set of generalizations.

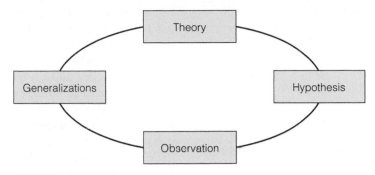

FIGURE 6.1
The Investigation Process

No one theory is right or wrong, but some are more useful than others in directing practice. Theory can be used to generate one or more **hypotheses,** which can direct attention to certain observations, which in turn can be used to formulate certain empirical generalizations (see Figure 6.1). Because of the cyclical nature of the research process, the process can begin at any one of the four points shown in Figure 6.1 (theory, hypothesis, observation, and generalizations).

Policy Research

Policy research is a specialized form of inquiry whose purpose is to provide reliable, valid, and relevant knowledge for public officials, agency managers, and others, to support the decision-making processes of government. Although it is used (or misused) at all levels of government, scientific research does not always guide or control policy choices. History is replete with examples of public officials' rejecting the advice of the research community. Deciding on the contribution to, and limits of, research findings to public decision making is a complex undertaking (DeParle, 2005). For example, raising welfare benefits while broadening eligibility standards will have certain consequences. These consequences may be in general agreement, but the value placed on that information can be enormously different.

Reducing the uncertainty surrounding policy formulation and evaluating the consequences of policy implementation are central tasks of policy research. How a society uses the products or outcomes of policy research is a political issue. Politicians often select the research finding that best fits the ends or goals they seek. Just as expert medical testimony is used (or misused) by both prosecution and defense attorneys in the same case, so, too, the results of policy research can be used (or misused) for political purposes.

Problems arise in the design, execution, and interpretation of research for specific policy choices that are not encountered in disciplinary research. Policy analysis frequently is expected to produce specific kinds of information in a short time within a limited budget. Both policy research and disciplinary research are governed by the canons of scientific methodology. They differ in that disciplinary research is structured to develop theoretically relevant explanations of social phenomena, while policy research is structured to identify, assess, and evaluate public strategies used to produce public ends.

The importance of policy research cannot be underestimated. All too often, social policies are formulated with no empirical basis. These policies are doomed to fail at some point because they do not reflect the realities of the situation(s) they address.

Evaluative Research

Evaluative research is used to assess the efficacy of a given policy or set of policies or to measure the impact of a specific treatment modality. The typical starting point of evaluative research is to conduct a review of relevant literature. This task is made easier today because of search tools available through the Internet. Once the literature search has been conducted, the researcher can examine the information for trends and unique differences.

In evaluative research, the scientific method is the basic analytic tool used to determine the impact of the program. Because social work research rarely takes place under controlled laboratory conditions, specific research designs have been developed to accommodate research in the field (Rubin & Babbie, 2007; Royse, Thyer, Padgett, & Logan, 2005). The principal task of the policy evaluator is not just to show success or failure but also to indicate the range of certainty with which that judgment is made.

In addition to evaluating the effectiveness of social work programs, social workers evaluate the effectiveness of their direct work with clients. **Single-subject designs** or **single-case designs** (Rubin & Babbie, 2007; Scruggs & Mastropieri, 2006) are used to evaluate the impact of interventions or policy changes on a single client or case. These designs typically are used by social workers and other professionals in clinical settings.

Demonstrating a Causal Connection

To report that a favorable outcome occurred while a program was in place is not sufficient. The evaluator must demonstrate that the outcome reasonably can be attributed to the policy action or program and not to some other explanation. For example, if an intervention is developed to help children adjust to their parents' divorce, we have to be able to demonstrate that the children were better adjusted because of the intervention, not because of time spent with sympathetic teachers or relatives, or merely because the children grew older or more mature.

In the classical research design, the evaluator uses both theory and probability to increase the likelihood that the observed relationship is truly a causal relationship. Because theory is used to select the observations to be made, theories guide observations and bring investigators closer to a realistic understanding of the relationship between observed outcome and the program or policy action. The real understanding depends on adequacy of the theory.

Social work researchers have to be keenly aware of chance as an alternative explanation for observed results. Statistical tools are available that allow the researcher to calculate the probability that the observation would occur by chance versus the specific intervention under study (see, for example, Weinbach & Grinnell, 2006).

Regardless of the researcher's level of sophistication or the statistical tools available to analyze results, the researcher cannot prove that "A" caused "B." The best he or she can do is to conclude that there is a strong relationship between the two. Thus, social science evaluation can be used to help decision makers reject bad policy, but it cannot help them select with certainty the "best policy."

The Status of Social Work in Communities, Policy, Administration, and Research

In shaping communities and social welfare agencies, the social work profession shares key roles with a number of other groups, including politicians, economists, psychologists, educators, attorneys, and, increasingly, lobbyists for various constituent groups. Social work researchers have played a key role in shaping practice and policies at local, state, and federal levels. To strengthen its relationship with these other entities and its role as a key shaper of social welfare policies and programs, the profession has continued to seek new ways to maintain credibility in an increasingly technological and politicized society. One way the profession has increased its status is through state and national licensing and certification programs.

Social workers' status as professionals depends on two conditions: (a) a recognized body of knowledge that can be transmitted, and (b) a defined and legitimized area of activity. Certification as a professional by the state protects the public from unwarranted claims by individual purveyors of a service and also protects the intellectual property rights of a person who is trained and educated to perform the service.

Whether the real purpose behind the certification of a professional group is to protect an unsuspecting public or to protect the practice rights of a politically powerful professional group is often difficult to discern. Through certification, each professional group seeks to enlarge its own domain of practice, make more restrictive the rights to operate within that domain, and justify its expansive and protective stance with the ethic of client interest. Social work professionals are not exempt from this generalization.

Increasingly, social workers are saying that their practice wisdom is highly relevant to policy development. To date, however, this policy–practice perspective has not been highly developed. A clear challenge for the future is to find ways to make the practice knowledge—the local-level knowledge about effective interventions—a central part of policy development.

Signs of a new professional commitment to the development of policy perspectives are emerging across national lines (see for example, Alcock and Craig, 2001; Klare, 2002; Kunstler, 2005; Perkins, 2004). Sometimes referred to as **comparative social research,** this approach enables one nation to build on the policy design initiatives of others, thereby avoiding the need to start afresh.

Making social welfare policy is the result of a political process. In the main, the social work literature has neglected a methodology for intervention in that process, relying instead on teaching policy development from a case or historical perspective. Traditionally, policy analysis has used frames of reference to answer questions about who is covered by the policy, what benefits are provided, the form of delivery, and the financial source (e.g., Gilbert and Terrell, 2004). This is changing. Analyses of the dynamics of policy—legislative, judicial, and administrative processes—are finding their way increasingly into social work writings.

During the coming decade, hard choices have to be made. Should state or national governments play the leading role in the delivery and funding of social welfare programs? Should unmarried mothers under age 18 be eligible for direct income support? To what extent, if at all, should the right to a publicly supported abortion be abridged? To what extent can a cultural group deviate from the general standards of child welfare? These are tough questions, and they involve technical, political, and value considerations. Regardless of the auspices of the social agencies in which they work, social workers must maintain a strong professional presence in both the policy and practice arenas at community, state, and national levels.

Career Opportunities in Agency Administration, Community Social Work, Policy, and Research

An almost infinite number of career opportunities is available for social workers in the areas of agency administration, community social work, policy, and research. The baccalaureate (BSW) social worker develops beginning competency in working within agencies and the community as part of the BSW educational program. Accredited

BSW programs require coursework in both theory and practice in working within the community, and many opportunities are available for work with communities at the BSW level.

Family service agencies, state departments of human services, hospitals, correctional centers, mental health agencies, programs for individuals with disabilities, school social services, youth organizations, and a variety of related service delivery organizations—all use community practice methodologies. Social workers with an MSW degree also are often employed as community organization workers, sometimes specializing in that area as a field of practice. At this level, they may serve as administrators of state or federal programs, department heads in a city's human services division, or directors of agencies.

Many state and local government agencies employ social workers as policy analysts, including agencies that oversee programs providing public assistance, services to abused and neglected children and their families, services for individuals and their families who have problems with substance abuse, and services that address the myriad other social welfare problems discussed in this text. Policy analysts work with state and federal legislators to initiate legislation, provide interpretations regarding the impact of proposed legislation, and oversee the implementation of legislation once it is passed. These individuals play a key role in interpreting policy to direct service practitioners in their agencies. Policy analysts, too, are employed by social action agencies such as the Children's Defense Fund and the Child Welfare League of America, which provide their constituents and allies with information about the impact of existing and proposed policies.

Social workers also are employed as policy advocates, working for activist organizations. And many social workers are employed in policy-related jobs in the offices of state and federal elected officials, as well as congressional and state legislative committees, in areas such as health and human services. A social worker in this role might draft bills, meet with client advocates, and attend countless meetings and legislative sessions relating to bills on topics such as homelessness, child care, welfare reform, hate crimes, health care, child abuse and neglect, domestic violence, long-term care and nursing homes, and criminal justice, among others.

More and more social workers are being elected to local, state, and national office and are playing important roles in strengthening our social welfare system. Other social workers serve as agency administrators for public, private nonprofit, and private for-profit organizations that address the wide range of issues discussed in this text.

Social workers serve as branch or division administrators or commissioners for large state agencies, heads of local government agencies, and heads of private agencies of all sizes. Some social workers, frustrated with the lack of services available in an area in which they work or have an interest, have successfully started their own agencies. One enterprising woman, for example, had difficulty getting existing agencies that served persons with AIDS—and overwhelmed by the number of gay male clients served—to address the needs of the Mexican American women with AIDS with whom she worked. She began a small outreach program to several women, and it has grown into a nationally recognized program serving Latino women and their families.

Other social workers are engaged in a variety of research-related jobs. State social welfare agencies; federal, state and local governments; United Way and other agencies that distribute funds for human services programs; and local agencies, both public and private, employ social workers in research roles to determine the needs of the clients they serve and evaluate the success of their programs. The emphasis on outcome measures for social services provided at all levels of society has increased the demand for social work researchers. As new knowledge is generated relating to bio-psycho-social relationships between social problems, social workers' knowledge of the systems/ecological framework and their emphasis on an interdisciplinary approach make them excellent candidates for research positions.

Summary

Social work in the community, in policy, in agency administration, and in research is a key component of generalist social work practice. To be effective, social workers involved in generalist practice with individuals, families, and groups must rely heavily on, and collaborate with, their colleagues at exo-levels and macro-levels of generalist practice.

Social work within the community enhances the capacity of that community to better serve the needs of its diverse members (community practice). Community change efforts are facilitated through social action, social planning, and community development approaches. In all of these, members of the community establish goals and objectives and the facilitator helps the members achieve their goals. Democratic decision making is important to the process. Monitoring and evaluation are major activities that help the community achieve its goals and enrich practice methods.

Social welfare policy determines the way resources are allocated and how they are delivered. Who becomes a client with need, how clients are served, and the likelihood that they will get their needs addressed are primarily the result of social welfare policies. How and which social service agencies are funded and what roles the staff, including social workers, play in those agencies are also determined largely by social welfare policy. Social workers play critical roles in developing and shaping policy at all government levels. Increasingly, social workers are being elected to political office. Social work as a profession is gaining credibility in policy arenas at local, state, national, and international levels.

Policy has shaped the historical development and current status of social welfare agencies. The first social welfare agencies were primarily nonprofit agencies. The Depression gave rise to public nonprofit agencies' producing a variety of services, including public assistance and child welfare. Since the 1980s, under Republican presidential administrations, the trend has been toward privatization of social welfare services to for-profit agencies and heightened emphasis on volunteerism. Because many social services and volunteer efforts by private nonprofit and profit-oriented agencies are funded by various public entities, however, roles and responsibilities are blurring as partnerships and alliances are increasing. At the beginning of the 21st century, public, private nonprofit, and even profit-oriented agencies are becoming more similar to one another, with administrators facing similar issues regardless of the type of agency they oversee. Social workers in administrative roles bring critical profession-based knowledge, values, and skills that are needed to be effective in dealing with increasingly complex funding, political, and service delivery situations.

The wide range of activities that constitute social work research are paramount to effective social welfare policy and agency administration. Social workers are committed to empirical research to generate new knowledge and evaluate practice methods. Three types of research are commonly used: (1) disciplinary research, which is designed to expand the body of knowledge of a particular discipline and to test theory with a set of hypotheses; (2) policy research, used to provide knowledge for public officials and others to support the decision-making processes of government; and (3) evaluative research, used to assess the efficacy of a particular policy or to measure the impact of a specific intervention. Single-subject designs are used to evaluate the impact of policy changes or interventions on a single client or case.

If this chapter has one message, it is that policy, administration, research, and practice at individual, family, group and community levels are not separate spheres but, rather, are interrelated domains, each fundamentally dependent on the other. All social workers have to be involved in evaluating their efforts and continuing to generate new knowledge that will strengthen social welfare policies and services.

Key Terms and InfoTrac® College Edition

The terms below are defined in the Glossary. To learn more about key terms and topics in this chapter, enter the following search terms using the InfoTrac College Edition or the World Wide Web:

advocate
analyst/evaluator
broker
coalition building
communities
communities of
    diversity
communities of
    identification and
    interest
community practice
community social
    and economic
    development
comparative social
    research
disciplinary research
educator
enabler
evaluative research
facilitator
general manager
geographic or
    territorial
    communities
hypothesis
initiator/coordinator

mediator
mobilizer
neighborhood and
    community
    organizing
negotiator
organizing functional
    communities
paradigm
policy research
political and social
    action
private nonprofit
    agencies
private voluntary sector
program development
    and community
    liaison
settlement house
single-case designs
single-subject designs
social movements
social planning
social welfare policy
    theory
traditional
    communities

Discussion Questions

1. Review the definition of *communities,* and discuss the characteristics identified in the definition in terms of their importance for community social work practice. How might a social worker's role differ when working with the following types of communities?

   a. a geographically-defined neighborhood of recent immigrants;
   b. the deaf (persons with hearing impairments) community in a large city;
   c. a group of first-generation Italians living within a neighborhood with many other ethnic groups;
   d. a small, rural community of fewer than 1,000 residents.

2. Identify and discuss the community practice approaches discussed in this chapter. Compare and contrast those approaches. Identify three issues of concern in your community. Which community practice approach(es) described in this chapter would work best to address each of these issues?
3. What are some of the factors to be considered when shaping the direction an agency takes in developing and implementing new programs?
4. How many social services agencies in your community are public? How many are voluntary? Are there ones about which you are unsure? Discuss the differences between voluntary and public social service agencies in your community.
5. Which of the local agencies do you think ought to be voluntary, and which ought to be public? Why?
6. What principle of separation into public and voluntary would you use as an ideal for social services agencies in the United States? What principle of separation seems to operate in practice?

7. What roles should the social work profession play in developing and administering social welfare programs? Why do you think so?

8. To what extent do you think the practice of social work research helps efforts to assist a client? Give examples.

9. Can you think of an example in which the research process and the practice process actually reinforce one another?

10. Select a social work-related topic of interest to you. What are some research questions you might address at each of the three levels of research discussed in this chapter?

On the Internet

http://www.aa.org/econtent.html

http://www.cfpa.org/

http://www.clasp.org

http://www.communityleadership.org/

http://www.danenet.wicip.org/snpo/

http://www.indeppsec.org/

http://www.libertynet.org/kwru/

http://www.mdrc.org/

http://www.urban.org/

http://www.utedas.edu/research/cshr/

References

Alcock, P., & Craig, G. (2001). *International social policy: Welfare regimes in the developed world.* New York: Palgrave Macmillan.

Axinn, J., & Stern, M. J. (2005). *Social welfare: A history of the American response to need* (6th ed.). Boston: Allyn & Bacon.

Christopher, H. (2005). *Single-subject designs for school psychologists.* Binghamton, NY: Haworth Press.

Clegg, S. R., Hardy, C., & Nord, W. (Eds.) (1999). *Managing organizations: Current issues.* Thousand Oaks, CA: Sage Publications.

Day, P. J. (2006). *A new history of social welfare* (6th ed.). Boston: Allyn & Bacon.

DeParle, J. (2005). *American dream: Ten kids, and a nation's drive to end welfare.* New York: Penguin Press.

DiNitto, D. M. (2005). *Social welfare: Politics and public policy* (6th ed.). Boston: Allyn & Bacon.

Dolgoff, R. (2006). *Understanding social welfare* (6th ed.) Boston: Allyn & Bacon.

Gilbert, N., & Terrell, P. (2004). *Dimensions of social welfare policy* (6th ed.). Boston: Allyn & Bacon.

Grinnell, R. M. (2000). *Social work research and evaluation: Quantitative and qualitative approaches.* Belmont, CA: Wadsworth/Thomson Learning.

Haynes, K. S., & Mickelson, J. S. (2006). *Affecting change: Social workers in the political arena* (5th ed.). Boston: Allyn & Bacon.

Homan, M. S. (2007). *Promoting community change: Making it happen in the real world.* Belmont, CA: Wadsworth/Thomson Learning.

Horwitt, S. D. (1992). *Let them call me rebel. Saul Alinsky: His life and legacy.* Visalia, CA: Vintage.

Janssen, B. S. (2007). *The reluctant welfare state.* Belmont, CA: Wadsworth/Thomson Learning.

Kettner, P. M. (2002). *Achieving excellence in the management of human service organizations.* Boston: Allyn & Bacon.

Kirst-Ashman, K. K., & Hull, G. (2005). *Generalist practice with organizations and communities* (2nd ed.) Chicago: Nelson-Hall.

Klare, M. T. (2002). *Resource wars: The new landscape of global conflict.* New York: Owl Books.

Kunstler, J. H. (2005). *The long emergency: Surviving the converging catastrophes of the twenty-first century.* New York: Grove/Atlantic, Inc.

Netting, F. E., Kettner, P., & McMurtry, S. (2004). *Social work macro practice* (3rd ed.). Boston: Allyn & Bacon/Longman.

Perkins, J. (2004). *Confessions of an economic hit man.* San Francisco: Berett-Koehler Publishers.

Reynolds, D. B. (2002). *Taking the high road: Communities organize for economic change.* Armonk, NY: M.E. Sharpe.

Royse, D., Thyer, B. A., Padgett, D. K., & Logan, T. K. (2005). *Program evaluation: An introduction* (4th ed.). Belmont, CA: Wadsworth/Thomson Learning.

Rubin, A., & Babbie, E. R. (2007). *Essential research methods for social work* (6th ed.). Belmont, CA: Wadsworth/Thomson Learning.

Scruggs, T. E., & Mastropieri, M. (2006). *Applications of research methodology: Vol. 19. Advances in learning and behavioral disabilities.* Los Angeles: JAI Press.

Sen, R. (2003). *Stir it up: Lessons in community organizing and advocacy.* San Francisco: Jossey-Bass.

Weinbach, R. W., & Grinnell, R. M. (2006). *Statistics for social workers* (7th ed.). Boston: Allyn & Bacon.

Suggested Further Readings

Edwards, R. L., & Yankey, J. A. (Eds.) (2006). *Effectively managing nonprofit organizations.* Washington, DC: NASW Press.

Ellis, R. A. (2003). *Impacting social policy: A practitioner's guide to analysis and action.* Belmont, CA: Wadsworth/Thomson Learning.

Gardella, L. G., & Haynes, K. S. (2004). *A dream and a plan: A woman's path to leadership in human services.* Washington, DC: NASW Press.

Janssen, B. (2003). *Becoming an effective policy advocate: From policy practice to social justice.* Belmont, CA: Wadsworth/Thomson Learning.

Lewis, J. A., et al. (2001). *Management of human service programs.* Belmont, CA: Wadsworth/Thomson Learning.

Martinez-Brawley, E. E. (2000). *Perspectives on the small community* (2nd ed.). Washington, DC: NASW Press.

Meenaghan, T., & Gibbons, W. E. (2000). *Generalist practice in larger systems.* Chicago: Lyceum.

Meenaghan, T., & Kilty, K. (2000). *Policy analysis and research technology.* Chicago: Lyceum.

Nagel, S. S. (Ed.). (2002). *Handbook of public policy evaluation.* Thousand Oaks, CA: Sage Publications.

Unrau, Y. A., et al. (2001). *Evaluation in the human services.* Belmont, CA: Wadsworth/Thomson Learning.

Fields of Practice and Populations Served by Social Workers

© Heinle/Index Stock

Part Three explores many of the settings in which social workers practice and the special populations served. Each chapter presents, from a systems/ecological perspective, the issues that social work practitioners face in their work with specific populations. This information will help you make career decisions based on what social work jobs are available in the various fields of practice and what each entails.

Chapter 7, *Poverty, Income Assistance, and Homelessness,* defines poverty and explores why people are poor, who is poor in the United States, and what types of policies and programs are available to help reduce poverty in the United States. The chapter concludes with a discussion of the roles social workers play in the fight to eradicate poverty.

Chapter 8, *Mental Health, Substance Abuse, and Developmental Disabilities,* covers definitional issues concerning mental health, mental illness, and developmental disabilities. The discussion includes historical and contemporary events that have shaped the way mental health problems are viewed and the types of mental health services available. Among the critical current mental health issues discussed are substance abuse and suicide, along with the roles of social workers in alleviating these social problems.

Chapter 9, *Health Care,* offers an explanation of the current health-care system in the United States, the problems it faces, and the types of health-care policies and programs that guide and shape the health-care delivery system in the United States. Health issues include, among others, increased costs of care, ethical decisions when balancing available technology with costs and needs, and HIV/AIDS. Health care is the fastest-growing area of employment for social workers today, and we describe career opportunities for social workers in health-care settings.

Chapter 10, *The Needs of Children, Youth, and Families,* presents an overview of the diverse types of families today and the many issues that even the healthiest families face in contemporary society. The chapter explores factors that contribute to healthy families, as well as factors that place families at risk for social problems, including divorce, alcoholism and other forms of substance abuse, child abuse and neglect, and family violence. Issues that are more likely to be associated with at-risk adolescents include teenage pregnancy, gang membership, and youth crime.

Chapter 11, *Services to Children, Youth, and Families,* addresses current policies and programs that attempt to prevent or alleviate the needs discussed in Chapter 10. The present child welfare service-delivery system focuses on family preservation and other programs and policies, with the goal of keeping families together. The chapter concludes with a discussion of the wide variety of activities that social workers provide in serving children, youth, and families, including child protective services and school social work.

Chapter 12, *Older Adulthood: Needs and Services,* highlights a special population that increasingly is requiring attention from the social welfare system and social work practitioners—older adults. This chapter describes physical and social support systems to meet their specific needs. As more people are fitting this age category and as the field of social work is growing rapidly to respond to their needs, so, too, are activities and roles of social workers who assist this population.

Chapter 13, *Criminal Justice,* is directed to another specific group—youth. The chapter covers the nature of crime and the criminal justice system, including the roles of law enforcement, the courts, and the prison system. A special section explains the juvenile justice system and differences in treatment of adult and juvenile offenders. Again, the roles of social workers in providing services are described

Chapter 14, *Social Work in Rural Settings,* speaks to an important segment of social work that often is neglected—rural America. The chapter differentiates rural and urban life and the unique issues facing rural populations. The discussion leads to implications for social workers who choose to practice in rural settings.

Chapter 15, *Social Work in the Workplace,* investigates a field of social work that is increasingly important because of changes in workplace demographics. Interaction between the family setting and the work setting is important in understanding how the individual functions at work and what social workers can do to promote better functioning in the workplace and beyond.

Chapter 16, *The Globalization of Social Work: What Does the Future Hold?* concludes the book with this exciting and expanding area of social work. A number of global issues relate to economic development and social injustice and the many roles that social workers can play in a variety of international settings. This last chapter reviews the history of changes that characterize the social work profession and the field of social welfare, emphasizing the impact of global, technological, and economic changes on the individual, the family, and the community.

What lies ahead for the social work profession and social welfare as they are influenced by future changes at the global level? This chapter offers opportunities to reflect on what you have learned about our social welfare system, the profession of social work, the diversity of our society, and the many challenging issues we face at all levels of our environment.

CHAPTER 7

Poverty, Income Assistance, and Homelessness

Robert and Robin Warren, both age 65, have just retired from satisfying jobs. Their three grown children are well established, with families and jobs. By any standard, the Warrens are financially well off. They planned their retirement around their employers' pension plans and social insurance, commonly known as Social Security. Their annual retirement income amounts to slightly more than $60,000. Along with the income derived from their savings, their retirement income is actually larger than their income during their working years.

Neither Robert nor Robin thinks of these benefits or their Medicare benefits as a form of welfare because, in their view, they paid for these through taxes while they were employed. Robert wrote to his congressional representative to complain about the health-care reform package being proposed by Congress because he and his wife already are covered by a private plan, and both believe that such drastic changes would hurt them. In their working years, Unemployment Insurance provided the Warrens with much-needed cash during brief periods of unemployment. Now Social Security is providing them with both security and income. Although they are pleased with their income, both worry about the future of Medicare funding, on which they also are dependent. Their children worry about the future of the Social Security program, but the senior Warrens do not.

Mary Smith, a 72-year-old widow, is another recipient of social insurance. Her $684-a-month Social Security check provides 80% of her income. The remaining amount is from the income she invested from the sale of her house 6 years ago. Now she lives in a pleasant apartment and is covered by Medicare for major illness and hospitalization. She is not covered for the more immediate threat of a long stay in a nursing home. Her investment income and Social Security payments would not be sufficient to cover the costs of living in those facilities.

Maria and Joe Saldana live in the central part of a large city. Both in their early 30s, they have five children, ranging in age from 2 to 14. Joe works on construction projects and has received three promotions in 3 months. Maria was employed in the housekeeping department at a local hotel when she could find child care for her younger children. When Joe's work picked up, she quit the hotel job. Joe and Maria have a combined annual income of $32,000—just above the poverty level for a family of seven. The rent for their two-bedroom house is $450 a month. Money spent for bus fare, utilities, and other necessities often leaves the Saldanas short on cash at the end of the month.

Neither of the Saldanas works at a job that provides health insurance, which means that the family usually goes without medical care when someone is sick. Both grew up in poverty, and both quit school before graduation to earn money to help their parents provide for their brothers and sisters. Although they have a strong value system and are hard workers, only recently is their hard work paying off. Before Joe found his construction job, he was unemployed more than a year when the local economy took a downturn and he was laid off. He and his family had to rely on public benefits (Temporary Assistance for Needy Families or TANF, food stamps, and Medicaid). However, because of new welfare reform legislation, benefits were extremely limited since Joe is an able-bodied male. To continue to receive the much-needed benefits, Maria had to look for a job or participate in a community work experience, even though once she returned to work at the hotel housekeeping job she had held previously, the child care needed for her three young children cost more than her wages. Because the child care bills were so high, the family was forced to rely on local charities for food and other necessities. In desperation, it was decided that the Saldana's 14-year-old daughter would drop out of school to care for the younger children since they could not pay for child care and still make ends meet.

Now that Joe has the construction job, things are slightly better. Maria has gotten a promotion at her hotel job, and between both jobs the Saldanas can pay for child care for their younger children, which has enabled their oldest daughter to return to school. Though they are often short on cash at the end of the month and neither Joe nor Maria has health insurance, the children are covered by the Children's Health Insurance Plan (CHIP). In spite of the precariousness of their economic situation, both Saldanas think their income future is the best it has ever been, though they worry about the recent changes in the welfare system and are fearful that if they have another job setback they will lose what they have.

Maria's sister, Alice, is not so well off. She is a single mother of three and has not seen the father of her children since 6 months before her youngest child was born. For a while, with TANF, food stamps, Medicaid, and subsidized public housing, Alice was better off than Maria. Because of changes in the state welfare program, however, her cash benefits and food stamp benefits have declined by more than 25%. Now she hears that her public housing assistance also may be threatened. Her monthly TANF allotment is scheduled to end in 3 months unless her caseworker grants her a rare exemption.

Although Alice wants to work and dreams of becoming a nurse, she quit school at age 15 to help support her younger siblings. Because of her limited job skills, finding a job that allows her to meet her financial needs, including affordable child care, is almost impossible.

From the preceding stories, it seems as if the better off people are, the better the country's social welfare system helps them. Our social welfare system is structured to provide temporary help when income from work is disrupted. The social welfare system provides a tenuous safety net, as it is structured to encourage quick reentry into the labor force, except for those who have left the labor force to retire. The way current welfare reform theory goes, gainful employment is supposed to keep people from a life of poverty and welfare dependence. In practice, it does not always work that way.

In this chapter we look at the poverty debate from colonial times to the present. As a society, we have been uncertain about the relative importance to place on explanations of poverty linked to the person and explanations of poverty linked to the social and economic system. Even when we agree that individual responsibility should be enhanced, we vacillate between a strategy of deterrence versus a strategy of compassion. The fundamental purpose of anti-poverty programs is at the heart of the debate.

To some people, the simple goal of the social welfare system is to help the truly needy, but in a way that discourages dependency. To other people, the social welfare system should provide real opportunity to all citizens. Ideally, we would like to have a society with a guarantee against poverty but with the caveat that the family must do all it can to help itself.

Views on Poverty and How to Help

Before you were born, suppose you were given the following "opportunities":

- You are endowed with a native intelligence (whatever that is) above the normal range.
- Your parents are married, and they love both you and each other.
- At least one of your parents has a marketable job skill.

To be born with these three "opportunities" is to be born to economic advantage. If one, two, or three of these opportunities is absent, you are at risk of being poor for part or all of your life. Anti-poverty programs are designed to overcome or compensate for people who do not have these "opportunities." In our society, intellectual endowment, family, and employment opportunities influence most fundamentally our efforts to avoid poverty and also the stigma of being on welfare. In reality, social welfare policy can do little with respect to any of these three variables.

We do not know how much of a person's intellectual endowment is genetic and how much is influenced by the environment. Furthermore, we do not know how much is immutable and how much is changeable. Few people doubt, however, that skills in science, technology, math, and verbal communication are the strongest individual anti-poverty weapons. Poverty is concentrated among those who lack these skills.

Intellectual endowment by itself, however, is not enough. Having hopes and dreams about the future, coupled with a strong sense of self and an unwavering determination to rise above one's situation, are necessary to rise above the poverty line. All of these characteristics must be nurtured. In our society, nurturing traditionally has

been the primary role of the family. If a child from birth to age 18 lives in a family in which the parent(s) enjoys continuous employment in a job that pays enough for food, housing, and other necessities, chances are that the child will not experience involuntary poverty at any time in his or her life. Assuming that one is paid at least a living wage, employment seems to be a strong deterrent to poverty at any time during one's life.

Discussions about how to promote factors that are most likely to result in gainful employment, what type of safety net should be available for those who are not gainfully employed, and who should be supported by that net have become increasingly emotional in recent years. Virtually no one is indifferent to poverty in the United States, but very different ideas prevail about how to help the poorest in our society.

The average citizen wants successful and efficient anti-poverty programs, even if he or she is against "welfare." Some believe that public social welfare programs should be the responsibility of state governments, and others believe that the federal government should bear this responsibility. Some prefer giving cash to the poor; others want to provide aid as in-kind goods. Still others want to offer service and job training. Most people believe that a proper policy includes some mix of cash, in-kind benefits, service, and training.

Some people want to limit the duration of federal assistance; others disparage that approach. Some are concerned about the increases in nonmarital births. Some prefer a "tough love" approach that would limit assistance to very young single mothers. Others think this idea is out of touch with the *real* causes of poverty, dependency, and the rise in number of births to unmarried women.

Poverty and dependency are linked in the public mind. One thing is clear: Resolving the poverty problem in a democratic society requires a healthy respect for those who have distinct and different ideas about how best to conceptualize the problem.

Conceptualizations of Poverty

DiNitto (2005) has defined five different approaches to the conceptualization of poverty in the United States: poverty as deprivation, poverty as inequality, poverty as culture, poverty as exploitation, and poverty as structure.

POVERTY AS DEPRIVATION

Those who view poverty as deprivation conceptualize poverty as having insufficient food, housing, clothing, medical care, and other items required to sustain a decent standard of living. This definition assumes a standard of living (poverty level) below which individuals and families can be considered "deprived." Each year, the federal government computes the amount of income—**federal poverty income limit,** or **FPIL**)—required for individuals and families to satisfy their minimum living needs. These figures are published every January in the *Federal Register,* a government document that includes a wide range of information about the legislative and policy development activities of the federal government.

The 2007 FPIL for the 48 contiguous states and the District of Columbia was $10,200 for one person and $20,650 for a family of four (U.S. Department of Health and Human Services, 2007). Separate figures are given for Alaska and Hawaii because the cost of living in these states is higher than that of the remaining states and the District of Columbia. FPIL figures are adjusted annually to reflect changes in the **Consumer Price Index (CPI),** which adjusts the prices of goods and services for inflation.

POVERTY AS INEQUALITY IN
THE DISTRIBUTION OF INCOME

In this view, some people perceive that they have less income than most Americans (relative deprivation) and believe they are entitled to more. One way to look at poverty as inequality in the United States is to measure the distribution of total personal income across various classes or groups of families.

The most common method of achieving this is to divide American families into five groups, from the lowest one-fifth in personal income to the highest one-fifth. If each fifth of U.S. families were to receive 20% of all family personal income, income equality would be achieved. This is not the case (*Statistical Abstract,* 2006) Rather, the Census indicates that the poorest fifth of U.S. families received slightly less than 4% of all family income. Conversely, the wealthiest fifth of U.S. families received nearly 50% of all family income.

POVERTY AS CULTURE

In viewing poverty as culture, poverty is seen as a way of life passed on from generation to generation. This conceptualization encompasses more than low income to also include attitudes of hopelessness, indifference, alienation, apathy, lack of incentives and self-respect. Proponents of this view argue the futility of providing opportunities for upward mobility for the poor, as they would be unlikely to take advantage of them. This view of poverty is perhaps the most controversial—and the position that has generated the most debate among scholars and policymakers.

POVERTY AS EXPLOITATION
BY THE RULING CLASS

In the view of poverty as exploitation, more government assistance is seen as going to the middle and upper classes than to the poor. For example, the middle classes receive government assistance in the form of home mortgage loans and associated tax deductions. The wealthy receive government assistance through various income tax deductions, government contracts, and subsidies to business. Whatever this assistance, the middle class and the wealthy receive more than their poor and near-poor counterparts. If this view of poverty were to prevail, the only way to resolve the issue would be to radically restructure society to eliminate class differences.

POVERTY AS STRUCTURE

Those who view poverty as structure see the continuation of poverty as being fostered by institutional and structural discrimination. For example, poorer school districts typically receive fewer resources than schools in wealthier districts to purchase the latest technologies in support of their educational programs. This results in deepening of what has come to be known as the **digital divide**—the economic and social gaps between those with computer skills and access to technology and those without these skills and access.

Definitions of Poverty

Regardless of how poverty is conceptualized, the definition of poverty is elusive. **Poverty** generally means that household income is inadequate as judged by a specific standard. Translating this concept into practical terms produces ideological debate as well as technical problems. Even defining the term *household* for a census count is not simple. Is the unit to be composed of only the nuclear family, or do we count elders, boarders, roommates, foster children, and others who share the dwelling? Similarly, *income* is elusive. Should income include gifts or in-kind benefits provided by the employer or the government? What about goods and services traded in barter? What should the time frame be? How do we address wealth as opposed to income? Does choice enter into the notion? Should a Jesuit priest or Carmelite nun be considered poor? After all, they have vowed to be poor.

What should the standard be? As each question is confronted, the challenge of definition becomes more complex. As each question is given a specific answer, the numbers of persons who are considered poor changes. Several methods to define poverty are used today.

THE STANDARD

When the federal government began measuring poverty in the early 1960s, the continued existence of poor people in an affluent society was considered an anomaly. One way to explain this anomaly is to look at the distribution of income and make adjustments in terms of **relative poverty.** By this definition, after adjusting for family size, the lowest one-third, one-fourth, or one-fifth would be considered poor. One problem with this definition is that the proportion of the population of poor would remain constant, regardless of whether the economy were to worsen or improve or anti-poverty programs were to help large numbers of individuals improve their standard of living.

Another way to measure poverty is to consider the relative income of the lowest income class. Measured in this way, our progress against poverty is not good. After adjusting for family size, the lowest fifth's share continues to decrease while the share of income to the richest fifth continues to increase (Ziliak, 2006).

A third way—the one used in the United States—is to measure poverty by the number of households with incomes below some fixed official standard. How the fixed standard is determined is one reason that different poverty rates are reported by various sources.

THE MARKET BASKET

To counter the problem of standards, public officials use a definition of poverty based on a **market basket concept.** Mollie Orshansky (1965) developed this concept based on some relatively simple calculations. She used a survey that determined the cost of a minimum adequate nutritional diet for families of different sizes. She used another survey to determine that families generally spend one-third of their income on food. Orshansky then multiplied the diet figure for a household of a given size by 3 so a family could purchase the minimum diet and still have twice that amount left over for housing and all other purchases.

Since 1969, poverty thresholds based on this definition have been adjusted by taking into account the changes in the CPI. Poverty guidelines represent a simplification of poverty thresholds.

TABLE 7.1
Federal Poverty Guidelines for Differing Family Sizes, 2000–2006

Size of Family	2000	2001	2002	2003	2004	2005	2006
1	$ 8,350	$8,590	$8,860	$8,980	$9,310	$9,570	$9,800
2	$11,250	$11,610	$11,940	$12,120	$12,490	$12,830	$13,200
3	$14,150	$14,630	$15,020	$15,260	$15,670	$16,090	$16,600
4	$17,050	$17,650	$18,100	$18,400	$18,850	$19,350	$20,000
5	$19,950	$20,670	$21,180	$21,540	$22,030	$22,610	$23,400
6	$22,850	$23,690	$24,260	$24,680	$25,210	$25,870	$26,800
7	$25,750	$26,710	$27,340	$27,820	$28,390	$29,130	$30,200
8	$28,650	$29,730	$30,420	$30,960	$31,570	$32,390	$33,600

Note: Figures are for the 48 contiguous states and the District of Columbia. Separate figures are available for Alaska and Hawaii.

Source: *Prior HHS Poverty Guidelines and Federal Register References* (Washington, DC: U.S. Department of Health and Human Services, 2006a). Available: http://aspe.hhs.gov/poverty/figures-fed-reg.htm

The federal government uses these for administrative purposes to determine who is eligible for federal poverty programs. The poverty guidelines for various sized families for 2000 to 2006 are shown in Table 7.1.

The "official" measures of poverty based on Orshansky's model and used by the federal government count income from wages, salaries, and self-employed income plus interest, dividends, and cash grants from the government. The measures do not estimate or consider the value of food stamps, Medicaid, or public housing subsidies. To include these benefits would lower the numbers of those who are considered poor. The poverty line is calculated before taxes are paid or tax credits are calculated. The wealth available to the household is counted for the real interest it produces, not for its purchasing potential. A *household* is defined as a group of individuals who are not necessarily related but share a domicile and share income and responsibilities for those in that domicile.

No economist's line in the sand could account for the real dynamics of family incomes. Nonetheless, this line and the proportion of the population under this line are used in calculating the proportion of the United States that is poor. Regardless of how poverty is measured, the important issues to address are who is poor and why they are poor so anti-poverty programs relevant to these groups and their need can be developed.

Who Are America's Poor?

Many factors interact to determine who is poor in the United States. Four factors, however, predominate in affecting poverty demographics:

1. overall performance of the economy,
2. composition of households within the nation (for example, more single-parent households headed by women) and their access to the economic system,
3. levels of expenditure of social programs, and
4. types of programs implemented and the effectiveness of those programs.

The first factor significantly influences the others. If the free-market economy cannot provide jobs that keep everyone above the poverty line, certain groups of individuals will be locked out of the opportunity structure that enables them to be self-sufficient.

Although the stereotype of a poor family in the United States is an African American single mother on welfare with three or more children living in an inner-city ghetto, the poor actually comprise a diverse group. Most individuals on "welfare" in the United States are children, and many people who are poor live in two-parent families in which one or both parents work full-time, often with a second job. Table 7.1 shows, for example, that a single parent with one child who is employed in a minimum wage job at $5.15 per hour ($10,712 annually) would be living in poverty regardless of gender, ethnicity, or place of residence. See Box 7.1 for a description of one poor person's experience.

Table 7.2 reveals a great deal about who is poor in the United States. Overall, approximately 12% of the population is living in poverty. About one in 10 adults 65 years and older lives in poverty. More women than men live in poverty. This difference is particularly pronounced for the almost 27% of heads of households who are women. The poverty rates for Blacks (24.1%) and Latinos (21.8%) are more than twice the rate for Whites (10.2%).

A similar pattern is revealed when comparing the poverty rate of the nation's children under 18 years of age. Many individuals are surprised to learn that nearly one in six children in the United States (16.3%) lives in poverty when the country is portrayed as being so wealthy. This figure is nearly double for children who are Black (32.1%) and Latino (28.2%); in contrast, just over 13% of their White counterparts are growing up in poverty. The poverty rate for non-naturalized citizens (20.7%) is nearly twice that for native-born individuals (11.5%).

Interestingly, the poverty rate for naturalized citizens (10.0%) is slightly lower than that of native-born persons (11.5%). Poverty rates also vary considerably depending on where one lives. For example, the poverty rate for central cities of large metropolitan areas (16.3%) is nearly double the rate for persons who live outside central cities of large metropolitan areas (presumably in suburban neighborhoods).

Finally, many people assume that all poor people are on welfare. With increasingly limited access to education and the subsequent inability of those who are not well-educated to obtain

TABLE 7.2 U.S. Poverty Rates for Selected Population Groups, 2002	
Population Group	**Percentage Below Poverty**
All persons	12.1
Children under 18	16.7
Persons 65 years and older	10.4
Female householder, no husband present	26.5
Ethnicity (all persons)	
White	10.2
Black	24.1
Latino	21.8
Ethnicity (children under 18)	
White	13.1
Black	32.1
Latino	28.2
Nativity	
Native	11.5
Foreign born	16.6
Naturalized citizen	10.0
Not a citizen	20.7
Residence	
Inside metropolitan areas, inside central cities	16.3
Inside metropolitan areas, outside central cities	8.9
Outside metropolitan areas	14.2

Source: *Statistical Abstract of the United States* (Washington, DC: U.S. Bureau of the Census, 2006).

well-paying jobs, many individuals in the United States who fall below the poverty line work at least one, and often two, full-time jobs. The working poor constitute approximately 20% of families who fall below the poverty line (U.S. Bureau of Labor Statistics, 2003).

Although significant sums have been spent on anti-poverty programs in the United States, these

BOX 7.1
Working Out of Welfare

Terri Lynn is employed as a night cashier at a bowling alley across town. She continues to receive a partial welfare payment because the hours are sporadic and, at minimum wage, her income does not lift her above the eligibility of limits for aid. "But I wish I wasn't getting none of it," she told me. She's tried to get off welfare by taking computer classes at a for-profit business school in town. But after graduation, without experience, and without their help in finding employment, she could not find anyone to hire her. Instead, she found the job at the bowling alley and slowly works to pay off her tuition debts.

Luckily for Terri Lynn, her mother or sister babysit her daughter for free, a savings of several hundred dollars per month. On her income and her small welfare grant, Terri Lynn would not be able to pay them or anyone else to take care of her child. She does not own a car, and neither does her mother or sister, so she relies on the bus to get to work. For Terri Lynn, transportation logistics are a nightmare. The bus ride takes over an hour and a half each way.

Thus, between working and commuting, her daughter often spends 11 hours a day with her child-care provider, in this case Terri Lynn's mother or sister. She is thankful she does not have to leave her with a stranger, and in an unfamiliar place, for such long periods of time. When she works late into the night and the bus has stopped running, she usually takes a taxi cab back to her mom's house, where her daughter is sleeping. The cab costs her $6.00, and cuts into a sizable portion of her minimum wage earnings. She cannot afford to take the cab all the way back to her own house on the other side of town.

I leave here at 3:45, and get downtown at 4:15. Then I wait until 4:30 to catch the #7 bus. And then by the time I get there, it's 5:05. And then I have to walk on down there, and I get there at 5:30 on the dot. But after work at 1:00 in the morning, I have to catch a cab because the bus has stopped running. So I catch a cab to my mom's house where she [the daughter] is sleeping. I sleep there too, and then I get up real early so that we can catch the early bus back to my house so I can get her [the daughter] ready for school. See, and by then I have to take her to school because she'd done missed the school bus.

expenditures have not been targeted at specific groups of the poor and increasingly are meeting only a small fraction of the total need. Therefore, the number of poor people in this country has continued to rise, particularly for vulnerable populations such as people of color and female-headed households with children. Tracing how the needs of the poor have been addressed historically will help us see how we have arrived at the current provision of services and why these services are not working.

Welfare Reform—An End to Welfare as We Knew It

Structures and systems of aid for the needy are derived from the dominant social values of the historical period in which they are formulated. Prevailing social values have a significant impact on the attitudes toward, and delivery of, economic assistance to the poor. Chapter 1 provides a detailed

After that I go back home and try to get some rest, and then, after school, I go back and pick her up. We take the bus back to my mom's house so she can watch her, and then I go to work again. So I be running back and forth all day long.

Sometimes her brother is able to pick her up from work late at night, and take her and her daughter directly home, which makes their morning routine considerably easier. She told me, in no uncertain terms, that this assistance from her family was invaluable to her. Without it, she would not be able to work. Her daughter's father, in contrast, provides no emotional or financial support.

Terri Lynn has received welfare since her daughter was born 6 years ago. Is she "dependent" on the system? By traditional definitions of welfare dependency, yes. However, a cogent argument can be made that Terri Lynn's family provides at least as much assistance to her, if not more, than does the state. A closer look reveals a portrait of a hard-working young woman who is doing her best to improve the life conditions for herself and her daughter.

Yet, despite working hard, what are Terri Lynn's chances of beating poverty? Unless her income nearly doubles from her current minimum wage, her chances of pulling herself and her daughter out of poverty are slim at best. This is not because of her own laziness, personal inadequacy, or lack of family support, but because of structural features of the social system that snowball against poor women. Given the largely grim statistics of women's under-employment in general, what are the odds that a 24-year-old woman with a high school diploma, who is without reliable transportation, who needs child care, and whose only work experience is in the service sector, will soon land the $8.00 to $10.00 per hour job needed to lift her out of poverty? Moreover, why does her daughter's father not contribute to her support? Can we really expect Terri Lynn, alone, to provide for all her daughter's emotional and financial needs without any help from the government?

Source: From *So You Think I Drive a Cadillac? Welfare recipients' perspectives on the system and its reform* by Karen Seccombe. Copyright © 1999 by Allyn & Bacon. Reprinted with permission.

discussion of the history of assistance to the needy in the United States. As pointed out there, decisions about who should receive assistance, the type and amount of assistance to be provided, and the mechanism for providing that assistance are all affected by dominant social values of the time.

Relevant Legislation

The Social Security Act of 1935 established a "right to welfare" (entitlement) under conditions established by federal law. That act instituted the Aid to Dependent Children program, later retitled **Aid to Families with Dependent Children (AFDC).** This program—a broader version of mothers' pension programs established earlier for war widows—was intended to support children of single, and most often widowed, mothers.

In more recent times, the Personal Responsibility and Work Opportunity Budget Reconciliation Act (Public Law 104-93), signed into law by President Bill Clinton in 1996, is considered to be the most significant social welfare legislation since the Social Security Act. This 1996 law ended the AFDC entitlement program and featured deep cuts (nearly $55 billion over a 6-year period) in basic programs for low-income children, families, the elderly, and persons with disabilities, as well as fundamental structural changes in the AFDC program.

The act converted the AFDC program to **Temporary Assistance to Needy Families (TANF),** a block grant program. Under this arrangement, states received a fixed level of resources for income support and work programs based on what they spent on these programs in 1994, without regard to subsequent changes in the level of need in the state. Ironically, by using 1994 as the base funding year for the TANF grant, the federal government actually created the opportunity for large state surpluses in unexpended TANF block grant funds, as welfare rolls were substantially higher in 1994 than they were in 1996 and subsequent years.

The 1996 act did provide some additional "contingency funds" if the need were to increase in the states, but the contingency funds were widely believed to be insufficient to cover a sustained downturn in the economy. States are allowed to withdraw or divert substantial amounts of state resources (approximately $40 billion between 1997 and 2002) from basic income support and work programs for poor families with children from federal TANF block grant funds to other uses without affecting the level of federal block grant funds they receive.

This legislation also allows states to deny aid to any poor family or category of poor families. In addition, with some exceptions, the legislation prohibits states from using block grant funding to provide aid to families that have received assistance for at least 5 years (the so-called federal lifetime limit), with a 20% "hardship" exemption (20% of the state's clients can be exempted from the lifetime limit if they live in economically depressed areas where opportunities for employment are minimal or nonexistent) (Urban Institute, 2006a). The act also included an almost 20% reduction in food stamp program expenditures.

These reductions affect all food stamp recipients, including the working poor, the elderly, and people with disabilities (Laprest & Zedlewski, 2006).

The legislation includes a particularly harsh food stamp provision that affects poor, unemployed individuals between the ages of 18 and 50 who are not raising children. Under the act, these individuals are generally limited to 3 months of food stamp benefits while being unemployed in any 3-year period. Many of these individuals qualify for no government benefits other than food stamps, leaving them with an extremely limited safety net.

The legislation made most poor legal immigrants ineligible for almost all forms of assistance. Of the net savings in the act, 40% was achieved by denying a wide range of benefits to immigrants, including poor immigrant children and poor immigrants who are very old or who have incurred disabilities after entering the United States and are no longer able to work. Immigrants in the United States illegally already were ineligible for most major means-tested entitlement benefits at the time the law was passed. Many states, in anticipation of the federal **welfare reform** legislation, applied for and were granted "welfare waivers" that allowed them to implement their own, and often more punitive, version of welfare reform. These waivers, which typically have a 5-year life cycle, allowed states even more flexibility in using federal funds for welfare reform.

Revisions to the Law

Some of the initial provisions of the federal welfare reform law have been relaxed, as the provisions were recognized as actually creating the reverse of the intended effect. For example, in 1998, as part of reenactment of the federal food stamp legislation, food stamp benefits were restored to the elderly, people with disabilities, and children of legal immigrants. Although welfare caseloads throughout the country have dropped dramatically since Public Law 104-93 was enacted, the decrease in percentage of people who are poor has lagged far behind those declines (see Table 7.3).

TABLE 7.3
TANF Caseloads and Percentage of Persons Living in Poverty: Comparisons since Passage of Public·Law 104-193

State	TANF Caseload, Aug. 1996	TANF Caseload, Mar. 2003	Caseload Reduction (%)	1996 Poverty Rate (%)	2001–2002 Poverty Rate (%)	Poverty Rate Reduction
Alabama	100,662	44,646	56	17.1	15.2	1.9
Alaska	35,544	15,927	55	7.7	8.7	1.0*
Arizona	169,442	111,334	34	18.3	14.1	4.2
Arkansas	56,343	25,382	55	16.1	18.8	2.7*
California	2,581,948	1,085,627	58	16.8	12.8	4.0
Colorado	95,788	34,862	64	9.7	9.2	0.5
Connecticut	159,246	43,292	73	10.7	7.8	2.9
Delaware	23,654	12,351	48	9.5	7.9	1.6
District of Columbia	69,292	43,136	23	23.2	17.6	5.6
Florida	533,801	119,080	78	15.2	12.6	2.6
Georgia	330,302	132,003	60	13.5	12.1	1.4
Hawaii	66,482	25,409	62	11.2	11.4	0.2*
Idaho	21,780	3,204	85	13.2	11.4	1.8
Illinois	642,644	99,952	84	12.3	11.5	0.8
Indiana	142,604	140,571	1	8.6	8.8	0.2*
Iowa	86,146	51,713	40	10.9	8.3	2.6
Kansas	63,783	39,093	39	11.0	10.1	0.0
Kentucky	172,193	76,688	55	15.9	13.4	2.5
Louisiana	228,115	56,157	75	20.1	16.9	3.2
Maine	53,873	37,562	30	11.2	11.9	0.7*
Maryland	194,127	62,066	68	10.2	7.3	2.9
Massachusetts	226,030	108,469	52	10.6	9.5	1.1
Michigan	502,354	202,469	60	11.7	10.5	1.2
Minnesota	169,744	93,665	45	9.5	6.9	2.6
Mississippi	123,828	45,191	64	22.1	18.9	3.2
Missouri	222,820	108,561	51	9.5	9.8	0.3*
Montana	29,130	18,074	38	16.2	13.4	2.8
Nebraska	38,592	27,079	30	9.9	8.0	1.9*
Nevada	34,261	25,832	25	9.6	6.1	3.5
New Hampshire	22,937	15,061	34	5.9	6.1	0.2*
New Jersey	275,637	101,854	63	8.5	8.0	0.5
New Mexico	99,661	42,999	57	25.4	17.9	7.5
New York	1,143,962	341,004	70	16.6	14.0	2.6
North Carolina	267,327	83,906	69	12.4	13.4	1.0*

(continued)

TABLE 7.3—continued

TANF Caseloads and Percentage of Persons Living in Poverty: Comparisons since Passage of Public Law 104-193

State	TANF Caseload, Aug. 1996	TANF Caseload, Mar. 2003	Caseload Reduction (%)	1996 Poverty Rate (%)	2001–2002 Poverty Rate (%)	Poverty Rate Reduction
North Dakota	13,146	8,602	34	11.5	12.7	1.2*
Ohio	549,312	188,108	66	12.1	10.1	2.0
Oklahoma	96,201	35,974	63	16.9	14.6	2.3
Oregon	78,419	43,591	44	11.5	11.3	0.2
Pennsylvania	531,059	207,429	61	11.9	9.5	2.4
Rhode Island	56,560	35,714	37	10.8	10.3	0.5
South Carolina	114,273	48,028	58	16.5	14.7	1.8
South Dakota	15,896	6,143	61	13.2	10.0	3.2
Tennessee	254,818	180,466	29	15.7	14.5	1.2
Texas	649,018	333,435	49	17.0	15.3	1.7
Utah	39,073	21,800	44	8.1	10.2	2.1*
Vermont	24,331	12,737	48	11.5	10.2	1.3
Virginia	152,845	70,199	54	11.3	9.8	1.5
Washington	268,927	140,721	48	12.2	10.8	1.4
West Virginia	88,039	41,478	53	17.6	16.6	1.0
Wisconsin	148,888	47,712	68	8.7	8.2	0.5
Wyoming	11,398	729	94	12.1	8.8	3.3
U.S. Total	12,241,489	4,963,771	59	13.8	11.9	1.9

*Denotes an *increase* in poverty rate since passage of Public Law 104-93.

Sources: *Change in welfare caseloads since enactment of new welfare law,* by Administration for Children and Families (Washington, DC: U.S. Department of Health and Human Services, 2003): Author. Available: http://www.acf.dhhs.gov/news/stats/aug-sept.htm.

Statistical Abstract of the United States, by U.S. Bureau of the Census (Washington, DC: author, 2006).

Over time, the country's primary public assistance program has shifted from concern with cash benefits (1935–1961), to providing a number of services to those who wanted help to become self-sufficient (1962–1981), to requiring behavioral changes as a condition of future assistance (1982–present). The real purchasing value of government cash assistance benefits has declined over the years because of inflation.

An examination of state welfare reform initiatives reveals that states with the greatest decline in caseload also have implemented the most aggressive or punitive welfare reform initiatives.

One can't help but wonder about the fate of all the women, children, and families who once populated the U.S. welfare caseload.

Without question, the "work first" (emphasis on clients taking any job, regardless of wages and benefits rather than on job training and education to move off welfare) initiatives throughout the country have resulted in many clients becoming employed. With some notable exceptions, however, most of these clients have been able to find jobs that pay only between $5.50 and $7.00 per hour ($10,712 and $14,560 per annum, respectively), with little opportunity for advancement, and well below the living wage needed to achieve self-sufficiency. These jobs typically do not include employee benefits, particularly benefits related to health care. These jobs also are less likely to have flexible work arrangements (e.g. schedules that do not include evening and weekend work, and schedules that allow for time off when children are sick or need heath checkups or for parent–teacher conferences) that support the child-care needs of former recipients.

The most recent round of welfare reform initiatives has reduced dramatically the welfare roles in the United States, but to consider this a victory would be short-sighted. Although many advocates for the poor agree that the previous welfare system created dependency for many recipients, they also believe that the 1996 legislation and its reauthorization will not reduce poverty in the long term because, like previous efforts, it fails to address the root causes of poverty (Albelda & Withorn, 2002; Ehrenreich, 2002; Iceland, 2006; Lens, 2002). (See Table 7.4)

In contrast, welfare reform advocates argue that local resources such as faith-based organizations, food banks, voluntary agencies, and the like should take up the slack in addressing the unmet needs of former welfare recipients. This private or voluntary infrastructure, however, may not be robust enough to accomplish the job. As a result, increasing numbers of former welfare recipients are becoming mired more deeply in poverty (Biggerstaff, McHarth, & Nichols-Casebolt, 2002; DeParle, 2005; Duncan & Chase-Landsdale, 2004; Grogger & Karoly, 2005; Kilty & Segal, 2006); Urban Institute, 2006b).

Although the White House and Congress herald their accomplishments in "ending welfare as we knew it," welfare rolls would not have decreased as significantly without the strong economy of the late-1990s. The real test of the recent welfare reform policies will come with a serious economic downturn and a resulting rise in unemployment. And the private and faith-based infrastructure for helping people in need is becoming quickly saturated (U.S. General Accounting Office, 2002). The rush to dismantle the public welfare infrastructure in this country marks the disappearance of a safety net for those who need temporary assistance in difficult times (Anderson, Halter, & Grzylak, 2002; Currie, 2006; Ehrenreich, 2002).

Current Strategies for Addressing Poverty

Current strategies for addressing poverty include a strong market and family system, social insurance programs (Social Security), public assistance programs, and in-kind benefits and tax credits, among others.

A Strong Market and Family System

The first defense against poverty is a market and family system structured to provide full employment at wages sufficient to bring workers and their families out of poverty. Within the family, work and child care are to be integrated in a way that children are cared for and jobs are done.

It is increasingly difficult for families to earn enough to pay for housing, food, and other necessities needed to maintain a minimum standard of living. Even though regulations require workplaces to pay a minimum wage, this amount in many geographic areas falls far short of the amount needed to make a **living wage,** defined as three times the amount of money needed in a given location for fair market rent, established by the U.S. Department of Housing and Urban Development (Universal Living Wage Campaign, 2006). Affordable housing has become increasingly difficult to obtain in the United States, and costs for child care, health care, and other basic necessities have become a luxury for many families.

Social Insurance Programs

The second line of defense against poverty is a social insurance system that provides retirement income to supplement private pensions and savings of the elderly and persons with disabilities

TABLE 7.4

Some Key Differences Between AFDC/EA/JOBS and Proposed TANF Reauthorization

	AFDC/EA/JOBS (Old Law)	TANF (New Law)
Federal Funding	• Unlimited for AFDC and EA. • Capped entitlement for JOBS (federal share of AFDC and JOBS costs varied inversely with state per capita income)	• Fixed grant ($16.6B per year) • Extra funding ($319M over 5 years) for population growth and historically low federal spending per poor person • Contingency funds to states to offset high growing levels of unemployment or increasing food stamp caseloads ($2B) • States allowed to designate some or all of their current or previous TANF for placement in a "rainy day" fund, supporting prudent state efforts to plan for periods of economic downturn • Restore full state transfer authority to the social services block grant (capped at 10% of state TANF allocation) • Increase state flexibility to carry over unexpended TANF funds from previous years to be spent on any benefit, service, or activity otherwise allowed under TANF
State Funding	• Dollar-for-dollar matching required for each federal dollar spent	• States must spend 80% of "historic" level (100% for contingency funds) and must provide matching for contingency fund
Categories of Families Eligible to Receive Benefits	• Children with one parent or with an incapacitated or unemployed second parent	• Set by state
Income Limits	• Set by state	• Set by state
Benefit Levels	• Set by state	• Set by state
Entitlement	• States required to aid all families eligible under state income standards	• TANF expressly denies entitlement to individuals
Work Requirement	• JOBS program had participation requirements, but participation did not require work	• By 2007, states must have 70% of their caseload in work and other activities that lead to self-sufficiency as quickly as possible • Within 60 days of opening an ongoing TANF case, each family must have an individualized plan for pursuing their maximum degree of self-sufficiency • Families must be involved in constructive activities averaging 40 hours per week in order to count toward state participation rate • Families must also average at least 24 hours per week in a variety of work-related activities • Work credit offered to families engaged in short-term substance abuse treatment, rehabilitation, and work-related training • No distinction between single- and two-parent participation rates

TABLE 7.4 (Continued)

	AFDC/EA/JOBS (Old Law)	TANF (New Law)
		• Current credit for caseload reduction to be phased out as it reduces states' minimum required work participation rates • States may exempt up to 20% of their caseload from time to time without penalty
Exemptions from Work Requirement	• Parents (chiefly mothers) with child under 3 (under age 1, at state option)	• States have flexibility in establishing sanctioning policies, except that states must continue assistance for single, custodial parents who have a child under age 6 but who cannot obtain child care
Work Trigger	• None	• Work (as defined by state) required after maximum of 24 months of benefits
Time Limit for Benefits	• None	• 5-year lifetime limit on benefits received (20% hardship exceptions allowed)
Child Well-Being and Healthy Marriages	• None	• Greater emphasis on strengthening families and improving the well-being of children • Enhanced funding made available for research, demonstrations, technical assistance, and matching grants to states • Increased focus on marriage and child well-being added to both the purposes of the program and the state plan requirements
Encourage Abstinence and Prevent Teen Pregnancy	• None	• Authorizes funding for state programs that emphasize abstinence as the only certain way to avoid both unintended pregnancies and sexually transmitted diseases (STDs)
Enhance Child Support Enforcement	• Limited state initiatives with mixed results	• Rigorous enforcement of child support obligations while targeting child support obligations to families with greatest need • Financial incentives to states to increase the amount of collections on overdue child support given to families, especially those that left welfare
Food Stamp Program Reform	• Limited state and federal initiatives with mixed results	• Variety of initiatives and funding that make it easier for states to fashion a food stamp program that is friendlier to working families
Food Benefits for Legal Immigrants	• Limited state-initiated efforts	• New waiver authority that will allow states to build stronger, more integrated and effective service systems across a broad range of public assistance and training programs • States will be able to deliver more seamless services tied to stated program goals and self-sufficiency and employment outcomes

Note: EA = employment assistance
JOBS = Job Opportunities and Basic Skills (training and education program)

and their survivors. The social insurance system is structured to provide income security for all income classes, not just the poor. The most extensive social insurance program in the United States is **Old Age and Survivors Disability Insurance (OASDI),** commonly referred to as **Social Security.** This program operates much like a private insurance program; employees and their employers contribute funding to federally operated trust funds.

When retirement, disability, or death ends continuous employment, members or their dependents draw income from the trust funds. Greater numbers of senior citizens and higher costs of living have raised questions about whether social security trust funds will be able to continue to provide adequately for those who are now paying into the system when they need to draw income from the funds. In addition, because Social Security provides a fixed income that is limited, even though there are provisions for periodic cost of living increases, many retired persons cannot afford to live on just this income, particularly because increased costs of housing and health care are not covered by Medicare, the health-care program for the elderly.

Another type of social insurance is **unemployment compensation,** a program that operates much like OASDI. The federal government requires employers to contribute to state-operated unemployment trust funds. These monies are used to provide assistance to employees who have been laid off involuntarily. Unemployment compensation has some problems: Benefits are not paid to persons who are fired, and employers sometimes fire rather than lay off employees so they will not qualify for benefits. Other employees do not meet guidelines to qualify or they live in economically depressed areas and are unable to locate other jobs before the benefit time period runs out.

Workers' compensation, another type of social insurance program, provides medical assistance and cash benefits to employees who are injured on the job and those who develop job-related illnesses. This program is not mandatory in all states, nor are all employers required to participate, although most employers do provide some sort of workers' compensation program.

Public Assistance Programs

The third line of defense against poverty is a system of public assistance to those whose family system has fallen apart and to those who have limited or no income from wages. Simply put, these people do not have enough money to maintain an adequate standard of living. They are helped by cash assistance programs (cash grants determined by category of need) such as Temporary Assistance for Needy Families (TANF), general assistance, and Supplemental Security Income (SSI).

These benefits are funded from general tax revenues (local, state, and federal) and are provided on the basis of applicants' ability to prove need and their eligibility for assistance. The benefit amount is not enough to bring a person above the poverty line, only up to a standard that is established for the specific benefit program and the level of funds that a state is willing to put up to match federal funds for this purpose.

General assistance is a state and local public assistance initiative. No federal funds are used to support general assistance programs. This aid may be furnished to needy people and to those with disabilities who are ineligible for federal categorical programs. Eligibility criteria and benefit levels vary by state and often within states. Payments generally are limited and for a short duration. Benefits range from cash payments to groceries and shelter.

As part of the Social Security Act of 1935, federal–state programs were enacted for old-age assistance and aid to the blind. Aid to individuals with permanent and total disabilities was added in 1950. In 1974, the means-tested, federally administered **Supplemental Security Income (SSI)** replaced these state-administered programs. SSI provides minimum national monthly cash payments indexed to the CPI with uniform, nationwide eligibility requirements to needy persons who are aged, blind or disabled. People with disabilities have become the primary recipients of SSI, viewed as the "deserving poor." In 2004, the latest year for which national statistics are available, disability benefits were paid to nearly 7.2 million people, totaling some $70 billion. The average SSI benefit paid to eligible recipients was $894.10 monthly (U.S. Social Security Administration, 2006).

In-Kind Benefits and Tax Credits

The final line of defense against poverty is a complex system of in-kind benefits and tax credits, the most significant of which is the **Earned Income Tax Credit (EITC)** program. From its passage in 1975 until its dramatic expansion in 1996, EITC has grown from a small program to one that provides more Americans with more cash than any other public welfare program. EITC has become the largest public assistance program in the United States (Karger & Stoesz, 2006).

Basically, EITC supplements the income of all working poor up to income just under $30,000. Taxpayers with one child can claim a credit of 34% of earnings, not to exceed $6,330. This amount of the credit is constant up to $11,600 in earnings; after that, the amount is at a rate of 16% of earnings until it falls to zero at roughly $26,000. Because it is an earned income tax credit, poor people outside the labor force receive no benefit. The idea is to encourage work and to reduce the regressive impact of the Social Security tax.

Other types of in-kind benefits designed to assist the poor include food stamps, subsidized housing, and Medicaid. Administered and funded by the U.S. Department of Agriculture and states, food stamps are redeemable for certain food items, primarily at retail food stores.

Diapers, paper products such as toilet tissue, soap and shampoo, light bulbs, and other household necessities cannot be purchased with food stamps because of the historical connection of the food stamp program to the agricultural industry, which still has a strong influence on the program. Most states have replaced paper food stamps with an online debit card or an off-line "smart card" (card with an embedded computer chip). Other in-kind benefits, including subsidized housing and **Medicaid** (health care for the poor), are discussed elsewhere in this text.

Other forms of in-kind benefits include health care benefits through the workplace, vouchers given by some employers for child care, and employee retirement plans. Most employers, however, do not offer these benefits to individuals who are employed in lower-level jobs or they require a substantial employee share of the cost of these benefits, thereby making them inaccessible to a large portion of the nation's poor.

Other Anti-Poverty Programs

Five types of programs exist to combat poverty that occurs despite our best efforts to prevent it through sound macroeconomic policies:

1. cash support;
2. direct provision of basic necessities such as food, shelter, and medical care;
3. efforts to help the poor learn new behaviors that will empower them to feel more in control of their own lives;
4. job-training and job-searching help; and
5. restructuring of existing institutions to produce a better quality of economic opportunity.

Basic Political Perspectives

Considerable efforts have been expended on behalf of the poor over the years. Billions of state and federal dollars have been spent since the Social Security Act was passed in 1935 to eradicate poverty in the United States and to ameliorate the negative effects of a market (capitalist) economy on those who were unable to reap its benefits.

Gilbert and Terrell (2004) propose two basic political perspectives on American social welfare policy: the individualist perspective and the collectivist perspective. The market economy favors the **individualist perspective,** which holds that individual problems are the result of bad choices, personal dysfunction, and a culture of poverty. In essence, this perspective "blames the victims" for the situation they are in, even though they may have had no choice in the matter, such as when children are born into poverty. The individualist perspective also supports markets with few or no government controls. The primary social policy agenda of the individualist perspective is to minimize government intervention and provide a minimum safety net for the poor.

The alternative to the individualist perspective, the **collectivist perspective,** holds that social problems reflect fundamental socioeconomic circumstances, barriers to access, and lack of opportunity. In a collectivist's view of markets, "unregulated markets create risky economic cycles, unemployment, urban blight, poverty, and inequality" (Gilbert & Terrell, 2004, p. 18). The primary social policy agenda is to ensure full opportunity and economic security. The market economy does not support the collectivist perspective.

Looking back to the passage of the Social Security Act of 1935, one might ask what went wrong. Given the expenditure of billions of state and federal dollars, why hasn't the problem of poverty been resolved in the United States? Where did all that money go? Why didn't the expenditures have the intended effects?

The question has many possible answers. One is that money itself rarely solves a problem; it must be accompanied by a carefully crafted and well-implemented plan as to how the money will be spent and accounted for. It takes time to solve

serious problems that have deep roots and a long history. To help solve the problem, the United States must invest in human capital and pay less attention to the immediate functioning of the marketplace. Although many individuals may be able to survive at some minimum level in a healthy economy, ignoring human capital places those in poverty at considerable risk and also makes it increasingly difficult for the United States to continue to compete in a global economy. Society must embrace the notion of social and economic justice, and that belief should be reflected in all of the social welfare programs provided to its citizens (Albert & Skolnik, 2005; Stretch, 2003).

The United States has the necessary tools to solve contemporary social welfare problems. There is no "silver bullet" here. To the contrary, the solution is well within our reach if we are willing to embrace diversity, opportunity, and prosperity for all citizens. The concepts of social justice and economic justice are easy to comprehend but difficult to achieve unless members of society are committed to spread the wealth and power held by so few. Creating a just world is not about taking something away from one person or group and giving it to another. It is about sharing the wealth of society with all members of society rather than a select few.

You might ask yourself how, then, do we reach consensus or agreement on these issues? Most social welfare professionals agree that all five strategies noted earlier have their place in a comprehensive program to combat poverty in the United States. Most also acknowledge that all five strategies can be, and have been, misused, which results in making things worse for the individual, for society, or both.

The poverty debate in this country is not about the appropriate mix of strategies to address the problem. When all the rhetoric is cast aside, the debate is really about equality of opportunity and sharing the wealth. One thing is painfully clear: Despite a long history of efforts to eradicate poverty in this country, poverty is still one of the most significant social problems and at the core of a host of other social problems in the United States today.

The New Millennium: 2000 and Beyond

State and federal welfare reform efforts continue to achieve success in reducing the public assistance rolls throughout the United States. This success was buoyed initially by a robust economy, a plentiful supply of low-paying service-sector jobs, and a strong public anti-welfare sentiment. Long-term effects of the 1996 welfare reform legislation, however, will not be known for some time, as most clients did not begin to exhaust the 5-year lifetime benefit limit until 2002. The following are some observations to date.

WAGES

Research on the short-term impacts of the legislation has not been promising. Despite the large reduction in caseload that followed implementation of the welfare reform law, the national poverty rate remains about the same. Many who left the welfare rolls as a result of sanctions because they failed to meet program requirements or because they had exhausted their 5-year lifetime limit to receive benefits remain poor but do not receive the food stamp and Medicaid benefits.

In addition, former and current welfare recipients have limited earning potential in a labor market that demands higher skills than they possess. A study by the Urban Institute (2006b) revealed that on average, welfare leavers earn $6.53 per hour, or $13,582 per year. These wages are well below the living wage of the cities in which the clients live, and they are forced to live in substandard housing, take an additional job, or both. The long-term prospects for escaping poverty for both those who stay on or leave welfare are at best uncertain (Bavier, 2003; Danziger, 2000).

DISPOSABLE INCOME

Although the earned income of those who have left welfare as a result of the new law has increased, their disposable income has remained the same or declined. Newly employed former and current welfare recipients may have new work-related expenses that lower their disposable incomes. Many are forced to sacrifice formerly unreported income when they enter the regular labor force (Winship & Jencks, 2001).

WORK PERFORMANCE

With regard to work performance, Holzer, Stoll, and Wissoker (2001) found that most welfare recipients perform as well as or better than employees in comparable jobs, and that their turnover rates seem to be fairly low. Absenteeism, however, was found to be pervasive and often linked to child-care or transportation problems (Fletcher, Garasky, & Jensen, 2002). Poor attitudes toward work and problems in getting along with co-workers also were cited as a contributor to low job retention for some individuals.

RISK OF INVOLVEMENT WITH THE CHILD WELFARE SYSTEM

The results of several studies regarding the impact of loss of welfare benefits on involvement with the child welfare system conclude that the impact has been minor or nonexistent (Duncan & Chase-Lansdale, 2001; Frame & Berrick, 2001; Geen, Fender, Leos-Urbel, & Markowitz, 2001; Kauff, Fowler, Fraker, & Milliner-Waddell, 2001; Slack, 1999; and Taylor, 2002). In a related study, Dunifon, Kalil, and Danziger (2002) found that moving from welfare-reliance to combining welfare and work was associated with a decrease in harsh parenting, an increase in positive parenting, and decreases in both internalizing and externalizing behavior problems in children. These findings suggest that policies that allow women to combine welfare and work may be most beneficial for children.

Children who grow up in poverty often have limited opportunities for health care, education, and other programs that promote success in later life, resulting in long-term poverty that persists across generations.

DOMESTIC VIOLENCE

Tolman, Danziger, and Rosen (2002) found that women who experienced physical aggression during the first 12 months of post-welfare employment had about one-third the odds of working at least 30 hours per week for 6 months or more during the following years as did women who had not experienced such aggression. This supports the concern that domestic violence may interfere with some women's ability to work and may lead to loss of welfare benefits, unemployment, or employment stability.

FAMILY FORMATION

The architects of welfare reform stressed the importance of mothers of children who received TANF benefits being gainfully employed, as well as the putative fathers of these children being increasingly involved. Although most people might conclude that this argument has merit, early research in this area (see, for example, Garfinkle, McLanahan, & Harknett, 1999) found no scientific evidence to support the contention that poor children would be better off if their mothers were to work and their fathers were more involved in their upbringing, both financially and otherwise.

MENTAL HEALTH ISSUES

Jayakody and Stauffer (2000) found that low-income single mothers and those receiving cash assistance have higher rates of psychiatric disorders than mothers earning more than $20,000 per year. Rates of depression in low-income families are approximately twice those of higher-income families. Poor women who have been exposed to childhood trauma, such as child abuse, domestic violence, rape, and other criminal behaviors, are at even greater risk for mental health problems.

BARRIERS TO EMPLOYMENT

Rural mothers, especially poor, single mothers, face formidable barriers to employment. In a study of welfare reform in rural areas, Lichter and Jensen (2000) confirmed the persistent rural–urban inequality. They found that more than 40% of rural, female-headed families were poor and about half of these had an income less than half of the poverty income threshold (the definition of those considered to be living in *extreme poverty*).

FOOD SECURITY

In a study of the impact of welfare reform on the long-term stability of food security (ready availability of nutritionally adequate and safe foods) among children of immigrants, Van Hook (2004) found that food security was higher for children of non-citizens who did not become naturalized immediately following welfare reform, but food insecurity levels declined and evened out across all groups by 2001. The conclusion was that reductions in allotments rather than reductions in receipt of food stamps explained the higher food insecurity levels of children of non-citizen parents.

OTHER FINDINGS

In a meta-analysis of findings of eight random assignment studies representing 16 welfare and work programs, Gennetian et al. (2004) concluded that welfare and work programs have a clearly detrimental effect on the schooling outcomes of teen parents. Mandated work programs, those that imposed time limits, and those that supplemented wages all resulted in similar negative results. Additional research conducted on the short-term impacts of welfare reform legislation is available through the Joint Center for Poverty Research (http://www.jcpr.org).

The RAND Corporation (2002), under contract to the U.S. Department of Health and Human Services' Administration for Children and Families, has produced the most comprehensive analysis to date of the consequences of the TANF program created by the 1996 welfare reform legislation. The report contains a synthesis of the current state of knowledge (research literature) about the effects of the TANF legislation and the TANF programs of individual states.

The analysis encompasses a wide range of outcomes of the TANF program, including the welfare caseload, employment and earnings, use of other government programs, fertility and marriage, household income and poverty, food security and housing, and child well-being. The primary focus of the report was on the net effects of TANF, taking into account the impact of other factors such as the economy, specific policy changes (benefit structures, time limits, work requirements, and sanction policies), and the effect of the TANF reform as a whole.

Key findings of the RAND study are the following:

- Many of the effects of welfare reform on welfare use have been well-studied; all but a few indicate that reform has substantially reduced the welfare caseload.
- Most of the reforms introduced in the 1990s had a positive effect on employment and earnings (former recipients were able to find jobs and eliminate their dependence on welfare benefits), but most of the jobs found by clients exiting the welfare system were low-paying, had few or no benefits, and offered little opportunity for advancement.
- Little information exists about the effects of welfare reform and the use of other government programs, with the exception of the food stamp program, in which the research is generally consistent with the belief that welfare reform has led to part of the recent decline in the use of food stamps. The existing evidence fails to support a general conclusion about whether welfare reform caused part of the initial decline in Medicaid enrollment following implementation of TANF.

- The evidence is insufficient or inconsistent to draw any firm conclusions about the effects of welfare reform on marriage and fertility. For example, evidence from the Minnesota Family Investment Program (MFIP) suggests that providing generous financial work incentives, either alone or with work requirements, is associated with marriage or keeping existing marriages intact. But mixed results from other projects cautions against interpreting the MFIP results.
- Some welfare-reform components can result in higher incomes and reduced poverty, although this result is not associated with all policy components and there is reason to believe that some of the initially favorable effects will not persist over time.
- There is evidence of both positive and negative effects (socio-emotional behavior, academic performance, and health) of various components of welfare reform on the well-being of children.

The authors of the RAND study conclude that, although the extent of knowledge about the effects of welfare reform measures is better today than at any other time in the past, a concerted effort with financial backing from the federal government is needed to produce findings that can guide future policy development in the public welfare arena.

The work of other authors has made one thing clear: The latest efforts to reform welfare have swelled the ranks of the American underclass (Albelda & Withorn, 2002; Albert & Skolnik, 2005; Besharov, 2003; Duncan & Chase-Lansdale, 2001; Grogger & Karoly, 2005; Hays, 2003; Kilty & Segal, 2006; Sawhill et al., 2002; Weil & Finegold, 2002). Karger and Stoesz (2006) define the **underclass** as "the lowest socioeconomic group in society, characterized by chronic poverty; that is, its members are poor regardless of the economic circumstances of the society at large" (p. 519). Thus, these individuals are

unable to rise above their situation even if the society in which they live enjoys a sustained level of prosperity such as that witnessed by the United States in the late 1990s.

Consider, for example, the plight of children who live in poverty in the United States. About 12 million children are living at or below the official poverty level. Child poverty is most prevalent among the very young (those under age 6) and among populations at risk, such as African American and Latino youth. More than 11% of all children living in the United States in 2005 were without health insurance coverage of any kind. That figure jumped to 19% for children living in poverty (U.S. Bureau of the Census, 2006). The United States has the worst record among industrialized nations in reducing the poverty of children (UN Development Programme, 2005).

Researchers agree that the following factors related to poverty have a detrimental effect on children (Brooks, 2004; Downer, 2000; Fraser, 2004; Kozol, 2006; National Center for Children in Poverty, 2002; Scott & Ward, 2005; Shapiro, 2005; Solley, 2005):

- Stress and conflict related to low income can undermine the strength of the family.
- Learning opportunities at home are limited.
- Child care is of lower quality.
- Nutrition is poor.
- Housing is inadequate.
- There is increased homelessness.
- Transportation options are fewer.
- The family is more isolated.
- Elevated levels of stress hormones in the brain may interfere with early brain development in some children.

After a series of six-month temporary resolutions that authorized funding to continue the original TANF program, the Personal Responsibility and Work Opportunity Budget Reconciliation Act of 1996 (PRWOA) was finally re-authorized by Congress as part of the Deficit Reduction Act of

2005 and signed into law by President George Bush on February 8, 2006.

In the signing ceremony, President Bush touted the success of welfare reform over the past decade, citing the importance of having welfare programs that insist on work and self-sufficiency in return for federal aid. The Budget Reduction Act of 2005 builds on the success of the original act in reducing the country's welfare caseloads by requiring states to move even more families from welfare to work. The Budget Reduction Act of 2005 reauthorizes the original welfare reform legislation for 5 additional years.

Key aspects of the reauthorization include the following:

- Maintains the original law's requirement that 50% of states' welfare caseloads meet statutory work requirements (recipients must participate for 20 hours per week—30 hours in cases where the youngest child is 6 years or older—in one or more of the 12 work activities cited in the statute);
- Updates the incentive for states to reduce welfare caseloads;
- Broadens the pool of families subject to the work requirements; and
- Creates a new penalty for failing to comply with work verification procedures.

In addition to tightening the focus on work, the reauthorization also strengthens state accountability:

- Requires that all work activities be supervised in order to count toward the state's work participation rate;
- Uses federal reviews and the single state audit to monitor state compliance with federal regulations;
- Implements a penalty for non-compliance with the work verification plan—a 1% to 5% reduction in the state's TANF block grant; and

- Requires states to justify the basis for the state's "good cause" exemptions for recipients that are sanctioned for violating a program requirement (good cause is granted on a case-by-case basis, is temporary, and does not exempt a person from complying with program requirements in the future).

Homelessness

Increases in the poverty rate in the United States, coupled with marked increases in the costs of housing and the precipitous decline in availability of public assistance benefits, have resulted in large numbers of homeless individuals and families (U.S. Department of Health and Human Services, 2006). Demographic groups that are more likely to experience poverty also are more likely to be homeless. According to the Stewart B. McKinney Act (42 U.S.C. Section 11301, et seq., 1994), a person who is considered **homeless**

> . . . lacks a fixed, regular, and adequate night-time residence; and . . . has a primary night-time residency that is: (A) a supervised publicly or privately operated shelter designed to provide temporary living accommodations . . . (B) an institution that provides a temporary residence for individuals intended to be institutionalized, or (C) a public or private place not designed for, or ordinarily used as, a regular sleeping accommodation for human beings.

The term *homeless individual* does not include any individual imprisoned or otherwise detained because of an act of Congress or a state law.

Homelessness is not a recent phenomenon in the Untied States (Blau, 2002; Day, 2006; Depastino, 2005; Feldman, 2006; Hopper, 2003; Kyle, 2005; Levinson, 2004). During colonial times, individuals who were poor and had nowhere to live were housed in poorhouses (also called *almshouses*) and orphanages. The conditions within these institutions were, at best, dismal. Following the tradition of the English Poor Laws of 1601, colonial America had little tolerance for able-bodied men and women who were not gainfully employed (Axinn & Stern, 2005). Thus, the most meager of accommodations were provided for them. This early tradition of treating homeless individuals as second-class citizens carried forward through the growth and development of this country to present times.

During the Great Depression, a nationwide census conducted by the National Committee on Care of Transient and Homeless suggested that some 1.2 million persons, about 1% of the country's population, were homeless (Axinn & Stern, 2005; Day, 2006). These people were not vagrants and vagabonds, tramps, or thieves but, instead, were responsible members of society who had lost their jobs and their homes as a result of economic chaos in the country.

The classic stereotype of the homeless individual in America is a white male alcoholic who has lost his job and his family to his addiction and is forced to live on the streets. Another stereotype is that homeless people have chosen homelessness as a lifestyle and have an aversion to working and following the rules of society. Although some among the homeless might fit these stereotypes, for the most part they have been forced to live on the streets because of a wide array of problems and issues, many of which are not of their doing or are beyond their control.

Composition of the Homeless Population

The homeless population is composed of homeless youth, homeless elderly, families with children, ethnic homeless, survivors of domestic violence, veterans, people with mental illness, those with addiction disorders, the unemployed and underemployed, individuals in ill health including HIV/AIDS, and the rural homeless. Compounding the situation, isolation tends to accompany homelessness.

HOMELESS YOUTH

Homeless youth (sometimes referred to as "unaccompanied minors" or "unaccompanied youth") are individuals under the age of 18 who lack parental, foster, or institutional care. The homeless youth population has been estimated at between 500,000 and 1.3 million young people each year (Center for Law and Social Policy, 2003). According to the U.S. Conference of Mayors (2006), homeless youth comprise some 3% of the urban homeless population.

Causes of homelessness in youth fall into three interrelated categories: family problems, economic problems, and residential instability (National Coalition for the Homeless, 2006). Many homeless youth leave home after years of physical and sexual abuse, strained relationships, addiction of a family member, and parental neglect. Disruptive family conditions (their parents told them to leave or knew they were leaving and did not care) represent the main reasons for young people leaving home (Finkelstein, 2004; Meyer, 2006; Slesnick, 2004).

Some youth become homeless when their families incur financial crises resulting from lack of affordable housing, limited employment opportunities, insufficient wages, no medical insurance, or inadequate welfare benefits. These youth become homeless as part of their families but later are separated from them by shelter, transitional housing, or child welfare policies.

Residential instability also contributes to homelessness among youth. A history of foster care has been shown to be correlated with becoming homeless at an earlier age and remaining homeless for a longer time. Some youth living in residential or institutional placements become homeless upon discharge (National Coalition for the Homeless, 2006; Shirk, Stangler, & Carter, 2004).

Homeless youth face many challenges on the streets. Because of their age, they have few legal means by which to earn enough money to meet their basic needs. Homeless adolescents often suffer from severe anxiety and depression, poor health and nutrition, and low self-esteem. Homeless youth face difficulties attending school because of legal guardianship requirements, residency requirements, lack of proper records, and lack of transportation.

HOMELESS ELDERLY

About 30% of homeless persons are older than age 45. While the proportion of older persons in the homeless population has declined over the past two decades, their absolute number has grown (National Coalition for the Homeless, 2006).

Increased homelessness among the elderly is largely the result of the declining availability of affordable housing and poverty in certain segments of the elderly population (Joint Center for Housing Studies, 2006; National Low Income Housing Coalition, 2004, 2005b, 2006). Of the 12.5 million in households identified as having the "worst case housing needs," 1.5 million were elderly people (U.S. Department of Housing and Urban Development, 2003). Of very low-income elderly people, 37% were receiving housing assistance.

Although people 65 years and older have a lower poverty rate than the general population (10.4% compared to 12.1% for all people), they are more likely than the non-elderly to have incomes just above the poverty level threshold (U.S. Bureau of the Census, 2006). With less income for other necessities such as food, medicine, and health care, the elderly population is particularly vulnerable to homelessness (National Low Income Housing Coalition, 2004). In addition, overall economic growth will not alleviate the income and housing needs of elderly poor people, as they are unlikely to continue or return to work, or to gain income through marriage.

Once on the street, elderly homeless persons often have difficulty getting around and, distrusting the crowds at shelters and clinics, they are more likely to sleep on the streets. Some studies indicate that elderly homeless persons are prone to victimization and more likely to be ignored by law enforcement (National Coalition for the Homeless, 2006). Elderly homeless people also are more likely than other homeless people to have a variety of health problems, including chronic disease, functional disabilities, and high blood pressure (National Low Income Housing Coalition, 2004).

To prevent older Americans from becoming homeless, they must be able to sustain independent living, through access to low-income housing, income supports, and health-care services. For those who have lost their homes already, comprehensive outreach health and social services must be made available, as well as special assistance to access existing public assistance programs (National Coalition for the Homeless, 2006; National Low Income Housing Coalition, 2006).

HOMELESS FAMILIES WITH CHILDREN

Families with children represent the fastest-growing segment of the homeless population; approximately 40% of people who become homeless today represent this group (U.S. Conference of Mayors, 2006). Families, single mothers, and children constitute the largest group of people who are homeless in rural areas (Friedman, 2003; Housing Assistance Council, 2006).

Stagnating wages and changes in welfare programs account for increasing poverty in families (National Low Income Housing Coalition, 2005a). Housing rarely is affordable for families leaving welfare for low wages, yet subsidized housing is so limited that fewer than one in four TANF families nationwide lives in public housing or receives a housing voucher to help rent a private

Bushnell/Soifer/Stone/Getty Images

Homeless families represent the fastest-growing segment of the homeless population. Here a mother and her daughter, both homeless, share time together.

unit (Center for Budget and Policy Priorities, 2002.

According to the National Low Income Housing Coalition (2005a), some 80% of American renter families live in counties where a two-bedroom apartment at the Fair Market Rent is unaffordable to a family with two full-time minimum-wage earners. In 2005, the *housing wage*—the hourly wage necessary to pay the Fair Market Rent for a two-bedroom home while spending no more than 30% of income on housing costs—was $15.78 nationally, equivalent to an annual income of $32,882 (National Low Income Housing Coalition, 2005a).

For most families leaving the welfare rolls, housing subsidies are not an option (Center for Budget and Policy Priorities, 2002). Extensive waiting lists for public housing mean that families must remain in shelters or inadequate housing arrangements longer. Homeless families that live in shelters are not allowed to live there indefinitely. Living with friends or family members is almost always short-lived as well. Thus, many homeless families are forced to live in abandoned buildings or in their cars, and when that fails, they have no choice but to live on the streets.

Homelessness impacts the health and well-being of all family members, particularly children. Compared to housed poor children, homeless children have worse health; more developmental delays; more anxiety, depression, and behavioral problems; and lower educational achievement (National Coalition for the Homeless, 2006). Moreover, many homeless children do not receive their proper immunizations and they have asthma and middle-ear infections at rates much higher than the national average (National Coalition for the Homeless, 2006).

ETHNIC HOMELESS

The homeless population is made up of about 40% African American, 40% Caucasian, 11% Hispanic, 8% Native American, and 1% Asian (National Law Center on Homelessness and Poverty, 2004). Homeless people in rural areas are more likely to be Caucasian, and homelessness among Native Americans and migrant workers is largely a rural phenomenon (National Coalition for the Homeless, 2006; Friedman, 2003). Oppression and subsequent lack of access to quality education, good jobs, and other opportunities account for the large numbers of people of color living in poverty, compounded by the lack of informal or formal networks that can help provide affordable housing.

HOMELESS SURVIVORS OF DOMESTIC VIOLENCE

The homeless population in the United States includes survivors of domestic violence (American Civil Liberties Union, 2006; National Coalition for the Homeless, 2006; National Law Center on Homelessness and Poverty, 2005; National Network to End Domestic Violence, 2004; National Resource Center on Domestic Violence, 2005). Of the cities surveyed by the U.S. Conference of Mayors (2006), 50% of respondents identified domestic violence as a primary cause of homelessness. The American Civil Liberties Union (2006) reported that 25% of homeless mothers in 10 locations around the country had been physically abused within the last year. A substantial number of welfare recipients have been subjected to violence from a current or former male partner (Lyon, 2002; National Institute of Justice, 2006; Tolman & Raphael, 2000).

When a woman leaves an abusive relationship, she often has no place to go. Lack of affordable housing and long waiting lists for assisted housing force many women to choose between abuse and homelessness. Shelters provide immediate safety to battered women and their children and help women gain control over their lives. The provision of safe emergency shelter, therefore, is a necessary first step in meeting the needs of women who are fleeing domestic violence (American Civil Liberties Union, 2006).

HOMELESS VETERANS

It has been estimated that nearly 200,000 veterans are homeless on any given night. More than 500,000 are homeless over the course of a year. The National Coalition for Homeless Veterans (2006) indicates that

- most homeless veterans are single males (only 2% are female) from poor, disadvantaged communities;
- nearly half suffer from some type of mental illness;
- of homeless veterans, 47% served in the Vietnam War,
- nearly two-thirds served in the military at least 3 years; and
- a third of homeless veterans were stationed in a war zone.

A large number of displaced veterans or veterans at risk of homelessness live with the lingering effects of post-traumatic stress disorder (PTSD) and substance abuse, both of which are exacerbated by a lack of family and social support. Homelessness among veterans is not clearly related to combat military experience. Veterans at greatest risk of homelessness are those who served during the late Vietnam and post-Vietnam era.

The U.S. Department of Veterans Affairs administers two special programs for homeless veterans: the Domiciliary Care for Homeless Veterans program and the Health Care for Homeless Veterans program. Both provide outreach, psychosocial assessments, referrals, residential treatment, and follow-up case management to homeless veterans. The U.S. Department of

BOX 7.2
"Street Crazy—America's Mental Health Tragedy"

The bus doors whooshed open, and the driver finally spoke. "Ask for Big John," he said, without turning. "And God help you."

I don't recall thanking him because the instant I stepped off the bus I was surrounded. "Spare change?" said a man with a "ZZ Top" beard and shoulder-to-shoulder tattoos, gruffly thrusting a hand toward me.

"Nice shirt," an even stragglier fellow lisped, fingering the cloth of my left sleeve. He had no teeth.

"Got money for food?" demanded a third person, reeking of gin. He was swaying two inches from my face.

It was time to scream and run. Turning to hail the bus, its exhaust trail was just fading around the corner. Certain the three men were going to stab me, I almost wet my pants. Then, like Daniel in the lion's den, I was saved. The front doors of the mission exploded open and Goliath himself stood in the maw. "Dinner!" he shouted, and with that, my tormentors were gone, scrambling to join an instantly assembled line of people forming at the entrance.

They came from alleyways, behind dumpsters, and out of rusting, tireless cars slumped at the curb. They sprang, it seemed, from the very refuse that lay rotting in the gutter. Watching this, I was filled with the strangest sense of nauseating familiarity. There were men in that queue so filthy their skin was no longer visible and women so rank with accumulated secretions even the dirt-stained men turned away. Children were gaunt from malnutrition. Nearly everyone had open sores, poorly healed fractures or caked blood. I could see the lice and vermin. They were a symphony of coughs and wheezes.

So went the first (and possibly the last) visit by Doctor Stephen Saeger to the Safe Haven Rescue Mission located in the skid row area of downtown Los Angeles. Dr. Saeger was looking for someone who could tell him about the next of kin of a patient named "John Doe," who he had been seeing who was found dead, face down in the pool spa at the apartment complex where Dr. Saeger and his wife lived.

Dr. Saeger spent the first nine years of his medical career as an emergency room physician at a level-one trauma center in a large southwestern city. The defining event that signaled his departure from emergency medical work was the night that the ER team had to resuscitate four shooting victims, all of whom were bleeding to death at the same time. There were only three breathing tubes available to use, so one of the victims had to go. The man died quietly, alone.

After considerable soul searching, Dr. Saeger decided that he would become a psychiatrist as this would afford him a quiet respite from the constant chaos of the ER— or so he thought. He applied for and was accepted into a psychiatric residency training program at a Southern California county hospital, which he completed four years later. After completing his residency Dr. Seager became employed as a psychiatrist at another large county hospital in Los Angeles, the Benjamin H. Miller Medical Center (referred to on the street as the "Mill"). The Mill is a collection of outpatient clinics, research buildings, and machinery that supplied heating and cooling to the complex. The Mill is also home to numerous cafeterias, laboratories, a helicopter landing pad, waiting rooms, parking lots, and gift shops—overall, it encompassed four city blocks. Doctor Saeger had two jobs at the Mill—he was one of the doctors responsible for what happens to patients that are hospitalized, and he also ran the psych ER on specified days where he saw people as they come in off the street.

John Doe was a young white male with eighty-four admissions to the Mill in four years. No one knew much about him. He was found by the police wandering down the 91 freeway covered in feces and flies. In an agitated state when he was admitted, he was required to be placed in restraints twice—once for threatening to punch the night nurse and the other for calling another patient a "Nazi faggot." He was administered Haldol, one of a powerful group of anti-psychotic drugs. He was characterized by the staff as "still crazy but doing better." John suffered from untreated severe chronic schizophrenia.

People who contract severe chronic schizophrenia make up the bulk of the homeless mentally ill. As pointed out in the book, they are usually relegated to a miserable life and an early death. "Street Crazy" is about how the mental health system fails people like John Doe. Dr. Saeger asserts that physicians (including psychiatrists) fail to see the connection between mental illness and homelessness because it is not something that is taught in medical school. He argues further that few judges and lawyers who deal with the homeless mentally ill or politicians or policymakers are conversant with the facts either. Often, the only help that the mentally ill homeless get is a three-day emergency stay at a facility like the Mill where they are cleaned up, detoxified, and fed a few decent meals before being released back into the streets.

The district attorney, representing the hospital, stood. "Do you think living under a car is appropriate shelter?" he asked.

"Shit, yes," Mr. Smith said.

"And eating garbage gives you enough nutrition?"

"I've been sick some but ain't died so far. No maggots in me." He grinned crookedly.

"No further questions," the D.A. said.

The courtroom fell silent as the judge pondered his decision.

"It's dry underneath the car?" he finally asked Mr. Smith.

"No maggots, no rain. Dry as a bone," Mr. Smith answered. "And food with maggots is bad."

"You know that?" the judge continued.

"All maggots are bad," Mr. Smith replied confidently.

"Thank you, Mr. Smith."

After another pause, the judge began speaking again. "Mr. Smith has demonstrated that he can provide himself with shelter and food. He's not dangerous. The writ is granted. The hospital's hold is released. You're free to go, Mr. Smith."

Mr. Smith rose, mumbling something over his shoulder, hobbled past the spectators, and out the door. Back to the streets.

My jaw dropped. I had thought the decision to keep Mr. Smith hospitalized had been so obvious. Watching that ragged man limp away, I could no longer contain myself. "He'll die out there," I blurted as the psychiatrist

Continued

BOX 7.2—*Continued*
Street Crazy—America's Mental Health Tragedy"

sitting next to me, a middle-aged woman was preparing to testify in the next mental health hearing. She didn't look over.

"Probably so," she said.

"I don't get this."

"No one does," she replied.

What can you do as an aspiring social worker to help address the problem of mentally ill homeless individuals? You can become aware and involved. Many of you have brain-diseased relatives or friends, some of them on the streets. Inform others about the problem. Provide them literature about the problem and available services. Find ways to use the media to help make everyone aware of the problem. Finally, help make treatment for the chronically brain diseased a national priority.

Source: Street Crazy: America's Mental Health Tragedy, by Stephen Saeger, M.D. Copyright © 2000 by Westcom Press. Reprinted with permission.

Veterans Affairs has initiated several programs for homeless veterans and has expanded partnerships with public, private, and nonprofit organizations to increase the range of services for this group (National Coalition for the Homeless, 2006).

HOMELESS PEOPLE WITH MENTAL ILLNESS

Serious mental illness is overrepresented in the homeless population. Only 4% of the U.S. population overall has a serious mental illness, in contrast to 20%–25% of the homeless population with serious mental illness. Their diagnoses include severe, chronic depression; bipolar disorder; schizoaffective disorders; and severe personality disorder (National Resource and Training Center on Homelessness and Mental Illness [NRTCHM], 2006). Although many people become homeless because their mental illness impairs their ability to function, some individuals experience severe emotional problems *after* becoming homeless (see chapter 8).

People with serious mental illness have more difficulty than other people in exiting homelessness. They are homeless more frequently and longer than other homeless subgroups. Many have been on the streets for years (NRTCHM, 2006). Upwards of half of homeless persons with severe mental illness have both mental health disorders and substance-use disorders. Their symptoms often are active and untreated, making it difficult for them to negotiate basic needs for food, shelter, and safety. Many are not receiving benefits for which they may be eligible (NRTCHM, 2006).

The majority of homeless individuals with severe mental illness have had prior contact with the mental health system. They may have been hospitalized involuntarily or received treatment and medications of little or no benefit to them. The symptoms exhibited by homeless persons with severe mental illness, as well as poor hygiene, tend to result in many untreated physical health problems such as respiratory infections, dermatologic problems, as well as risk of exposure to HIV and tuberculosis (see Box 7.2).

Homeless persons typically are citizens of the communities in which they are homeless; however, their social support and family networks usually are nonexistent (family members often have lost regular contact with their homeless relatives or are no longer equipped to be the primary caregivers). Homeless persons with severe mental illness are twice as likely as other people who are homeless to be arrested or jailed, primarily for misdemeanor offenses (NRTCHM, 2006).

HOMELESS WITH ADDICTION DISORDERS

Untreated addictive disorders contribute to homelessness. The onset or exacerbation of an addictive disorder for individuals with below living-wage incomes and just one step away from homelessness can plunge them into residential instability. Many homeless people with addictive disorders desire to overcome their addiction, but the combination of being homeless and a service system that is ill-equipped to respond to these circumstances essentially prevents their access to treatment services and recovery supports.

There is no generally accepted number with respect to the prevalence of addiction disorders among homeless adults. The destruction of single-room occupancy (SRO) housing is a major factor in the growth of homelessness, particularly among people with addiction disorders (National Coalition for the Homeless, 2006).

UNEMPLOYED AND UNDEREMPLOYED HOMELESS

Inadequate income and lack of affordable rental housing leave many people homeless (Chasanov, 2004). The U.S. Conference of Mayors (2006) survey of 24 major U.S. cities found that 20% of the urban homeless population was employed. About 15% of homeless people have jobs, yet they are unable to escape homelessness because those with limited skills or experience have difficulty finding jobs that pay a living wage (National Coalition for the Homeless, 2006). The declining value of wages as a result of increases in cost of living has put housing out of reach for an ever-growing number of people in society, including homeless individuals.

The homeless often are employed in nonstandard jobs (contracting, working for a temporary help agency, day labor, and regular part-time

work). These kinds of work arrangements typically offer lower wages, fewer benefits, and less job security (National Coalition for the Homeless, 2006). Homeless individuals who do work tend to be underemployed. They may want to work full-time but are able to secure only part-time work (Economic Policy Institute, 2005).

HOMELESS PEOPLE IN ILL HEALTH

Poor health is closely associated with being homeless. The rates of both chronic and acute health problems are extremely high in the homeless population. Conditions requiring regular, uninterrupted treatment, such as tuberculosis, HIV/AIDS, diabetes, hypertension, addictive disorders, and mental disorders, are difficult to treat or control in those who do not have adequate housing (National Center for the Homeless, 2006; National Health Care for the Homeless Council, 2005, 2006).

Many homeless people have multiple health problems and also are at greater risk of trauma resulting from muggings, beatings, and rapes. Homelessness precludes good nutrition, personal hygiene, and basic first-aid. Some homeless people with mental disorders use drugs or alcohol to self-medicate, and those with addictive disorders are more at risk of contracting HIV and other communicable diseases.

People who are homeless are overwhelmingly uninsured and often lack access to the most basic health care services for their health care needs (NHCHC, 2006). Access to affordable, high-quality, comprehensive health care is essential in the fight to end homelessness. A universal health care system could reduce the current homeless population as well as prevent future episodes of homelessness. It also could prevent unnecessary deaths on the streets and reduce the fiscal impact and social cost of communicable diseases and other illnesses.

One resource that is available to provide heath-care resources to the homeless is the Health Care for the Homeless (HCH) program included as part of the Stewart B. McKinney

Homeless Assistance Act of 1987 (as amended) and operated by the Health Resources and Services Administration (HRSA), a division of the U.S. Department of Health and Human Services. HCH is a competitive grant program that provides funds for primary health care and addiction services to homeless people. HCH programs are initiated and managed at the community level. Any local public or private nonprofit entity— freestanding nonprofit organizations, community health centers, local health departments, homeless shelters, and homeless coalitions—is eligible to apply for HCH funds.

HRSA currently funds 182 HCH projects in all 50 states, the District of Columbia and Puerto Rico. In 2004, HCH projects served more than 600,000 men, women, and children who lived in poverty and/or had no financial resources. Congress appropriates funds annually for the HCH program. In fiscal year 2006 (October 2005–September 2006) $155 million was authorized for the HCH program (National Health Care for the Homeless Council, 2006).

The prevalence of HIV among homeless people is between 3% and 20% (National Coalition for the Homeless, 2006). Homeless adolescents are particularly vulnerable to contracting HIV because they may find that exchanging sex for food, clothing, and shelter is their only chance for survival on the streets. HIV-infected homeless persons are believed to be sicker than their housed counterparts. For example, they tend to have higher rates and more advanced forms of tuberculosis and higher incidences of other opportunistic diseases. Homeless people with HIV face many barriers to optimal care. Injection drug use and lack of insurance have been shown to negatively affect utilization of health care, level of medical care, and health status.

Homeless persons with HIV/AIDS need safe, affordable housing and supportive, appropriate health care. Those who are about to lose their homes would benefit greatly from emergency housing grants, and those who are already on the streets would welcome housing assistance. The federal government could play a key role by providing adequate funding for targeted housing and health programs for homeless people with health problems.

RURAL HOMELESS

Although homelessness often is assumed to be an urban phenomenon, small towns and rural areas have many homeless people (Cloke, Milbourne, & Widdowfield, 2002). Because rural areas have far fewer shelters, homeless people in these areas are more likely to live in a car or camper or with relatives in overcrowded or substandard housing. Homeless people in rural areas are likely to be white, female, married, currently working, homeless for the first time, and homeless for a shorter time. Families, single mothers, and children make up the largest group of people who are homeless in rural areas (Cloke et al., 2002; Fisher, 2005; Hopper, 2003; Housing Assistance Council, 2006; Rollinson & Pardeck, 2006).

Rural homelessness, like urban homelessness, is the result of poverty and lack of affordable housing. It is most prevalent in regions that are primarily agricultural; regions whose economies are based on declining extractive industries such as mining, timber, and fishing; and regions with economic problems.

Housing costs are lower in rural areas than in urban areas, but so are rural incomes. Homelessness in rural areas is often precipitated by a structural or physical housing problem that jeopardizes safety. When families have to relocate to safer housing, housing is less available, which leads to higher rents. If the rent is often too much to handle, they become homeless again.

Efforts to end rural homelessness are often hampered by isolation, lack of awareness, and insufficient resources. Ending homelessness in rural areas requires jobs that pay a living wage, adequate income supports for those who cannot work, affordable housing, access to health care, and transportation.

ISOLATED HOMELESS

Homeless people increasingly detach from traditional social roles, such as being a family member or an employee. They reaffiliate with new groups of people in the same situation. In doing so, they become more comfortable with this new group because of the shared stigma and discrimination. As time goes on, the homeless become more isolated from others, more entrenched with other homeless persons, and they lose touch with social support systems that might alleviate their situation, such as locating employment or housing.

Policies and Programs That Address Homelessness

In the early 1980s, the initial responses to homelessness were primarily local. In the years that followed, advocates from around the country demanded that the federal government acknowledge homelessness as a national problem requiring a national response.

THE STEWART B. MCKINNEY HOMELESS ASSISTANCE ACT

In late-1986, legislation containing emergency relief provisions for shelter, food, mobile health care, and transitional housing for homeless persons was introduced as the Urgent Relief for the Homeless Act. After the death of its chief sponsor, Representative Stewart B. McKinney of Connecticut, the act was renamed the Stewart B. McKinney-Vento Homeless Assistance Act and was signed into law by President Ronald Reagan in 1987.

The McKinney Act originally consisted of 15 programs that provided a range of services to homeless people, including emergency shelter, transitional housing, job training, primary health care, education, and some permanent housing. Since then, the act has been amended four times—in 1988, 1990, 1992, and 1994—and, for the most part, expanded the scope and strengthened the provisions of the original legislation.

Support for McKinney-Vento Act programs has declined by nearly 30% since 1995, when homeless plans were consolidated (National Coalition for the Homeless, 2006; National Law Center on Homelessness and Poverty, 2005). Funding for some of these programs has been restored, but not to 1995 funding levels. The Bush administration proposed a 36% decline in federal housing assistance by fiscal year 2010 (National Coalition for the Homeless, 2006; NLCHP, 2005).

While inadequate funding impedes the effectiveness of the McKinney programs, the act's greatest weakness is its emphasis on emergency measures: It responds to the symptoms of homelessness and not its causes. The McKinney Act remains landmark legislation for the homeless, but after more than a decade of an emergency response to a long-term crisis, only by addressing the **root causes** of homelessness—lack of jobs that pay a living wage, inadequate benefits for those who cannot work, lack of affordable housing, and lack of access to health care—will homelessness be ended.

OTHER PROGRAMS

In addition to the programs authorized under the McKinney Act, many national programs provide assistance to the homeless in some way (National Resource Center on Homelessness and Mental Health, 2004; U.S. Department of Health and Human Services, 2006b; U.S. Interagency Council on Homelessness, 2006). As with the McKinney programs, most of these programs concentrate on emergency assistance and do not address underlying causes.

Besides affordable housing for low-income families, needs include increased employment, education, and job-training opportunities, allowing the homeless to accumulate assets, comprehensive physical and mental health services and substance-abuse treatment, discharge planning for individuals from institutions, child care and education for homeless children, and attention to public laws prohibiting the criminalization of sleeping and panhandling in public places.

A number of innovative programs to address problems of homelessness have been developed throughout the United States. Several utilize street outreach workers to link individuals with resources such as health care, immunizations, dental care, employment and job training, family planning, tuberculosis outreach, health education, substance abuse treatment, and housing assistance (U.S. Interagency Council on Homelessness, 2006). For example, Dade County, Florida, has established a trust fund that serves as a dedicated source of funding for programs for the homeless. This program is funded by a one-cent tax on all food and beverages sold in restaurants that have a liquor license. The fund is overseen by representatives from the civic, business, and religious communities; homeless service providers; former homeless persons; and homeless advocates.

A number of child welfare service programs offer special transition programs to help youth in the foster care system make the transition to independent living. Economic development and small-business programs for the homeless involve homeless clients in business efforts such as producing and selling artwork, newspapers, and other printed media; contracting services such as housekeeping and home repair; and furniture refinishing and repair. One innovative program builds low-income housing and trains homeless and disenfranchised youth for jobs in the construction industry.

The common theme among these programs is an emphasis on community-based initiatives that include the homeless and homeless service providers in program design and development and empowerment. These efforts capitalize on the strengths perspective of social work by recognizing that homeless people have the desire, motivation, and skills to better their situation.

The Roles of Social Workers in the Fight against Poverty

Social work, more than any other profession, maintains a strong commitment to fighting poverty at all levels. Social workers provide direct services to individuals and families living in poverty; advocate for programs and policies that improve the lives of the poor and reduce poverty at the community, state, and federal levels; and develop and administer policies and programs that serve America's poor.

Some BSW graduates become public-assistance workers in state and local human services agencies. They help individuals apply for TANF, food stamps, Medicaid, and general assistance benefits. They also help individuals apply for social insurance programs such as Social Security and Medicare and oversee public assistance and social insurance benefit programs.

Many public assistance programs have furthered the roles of social workers in the fight against poverty by mandating that all TANF clients receiving employment services be assigned a case manager to help them become self-sufficient. Applying a generalist practice approach, these social workers assess client strengths and needs; work with clients to develop appropriate goals to achieve self-sufficiency; create appropriate service plans; assist clients in accessing needed resources; and terminate with their clients when the plans have been completed. Case managers also assist clients in developing skills in areas such as interviewing, assertiveness, and handling stress on the job; help them enroll in job-training and education programs; and assist them in locating appropriate resources such as transportation, housing, child care, health care, and family counseling.

In an effort to serve adults, children, youth, and families who live in poverty, social workers also are employed by faith-based organizations such as the Salvation Army; housing programs; child development programs such as Head Start; teen pregnancy and parenting programs; school dropout-prevention programs; settlement houses; and health clinics and hospitals. In addition, social workers work with federal, state, and local agencies and governments; state legislatures and the U.S. Congress; and advocacy organizations in developing, lobbying for, and administering anti-poverty programs.

Urban housing authorities employ social workers to work with individuals and families living in public housing to help break the cycle of poverty and homelessness. Because many individuals have difficulty making the transition from public housing to paying for housing themselves when they become employed and no longer meet income guidelines for public housing, social workers link families with resources that can help them make this transition.

Social workers also are outreach workers to serve the homeless in many areas. In a number of cities, roving workers provide services to homeless youth, helping them access health care, safe shelter, counseling, education, and employment. In some areas, programs for battered women have worked with programs serving the homeless, such as the Salvation Army, to establish transitional living programs for women and their families until they can locate employment and save enough money to locate housing independently.

In advocacy and administrative roles, social workers are employed in programs that aim to alleviate homelessness, such as Habitat for Humanity, an international program in which volunteers and future homeowners work together to build low-income housing. In one city, a dropout-recovery agency for young adults operates a highly successful construction program that trains individuals in a variety of construction jobs while building affordable housing. In another program, a social worker is the director of a private foundation that leverages funding from corporate and private donors to create affordable housing.

The values base of the social work profession mandates that social workers treat all clients, including those living in poverty, with dignity and respect and work to empower them to be in charge of their own lives. Much of the debate in the years ahead will be about the place of faith-based organizations in supplementing publicly funded efforts to combat poverty and dependency.

Summary

Poverty in America has a long history that begins with the austere times of colonial America. Although numerous public programs to eradicate poverty have been implemented over time, none has been successful in eliminating the problem. Why these programs have failed to reach their mark is a matter of speculation tempered by one's personal and political ideology, as well as the prevailing social values of the time. The one reality is of the growing underclass in America composed of a diverse mix of people who are not likely to fight their way out of poverty despite their desire and efforts to do so.

Lack of affordable housing, low-wage jobs, and the impact of welfare reform have contributed to a growing homeless population—the fastest growing segment of which consists of women with children. Poverty is a complex problem with no easy solutions, and efforts continue to solve the myriad of issues involved.

Key Terms and InfoTrac® College Edition

The terms below are defined in the Glossary at the end of this text. To learn more about key terms and topics in this chapter, enter the following search terms using the InfoTrac College Edition or the World Wide Web:

Aid to Families
  with Dependent
  Children
  (AFDC)
collectivist
  perspective
Consumer Price
  Index (CPI)
digital divide
Earned Income
  Tax Credit
  (EITC)
Federal Poverty
  Income Limit
  (FPIL)
general assistance
homeless
individualist
  perspective
living wage
market basket
  concept

Medicaid
Old Age Survivors
  and Disability
  Insurance
  (OASDI)
poverty
relative poverty
root causes
Social Security
Supplemental
  Security Income
  (SSI)
Temporary Assistance
  to Needy Families
  (TANF)
underclass
unemployment
  compensation
welfare reform
workers'
  compensation

On the Internet

http://www.urban.org

http://www.nlihc.org

http://www.nrchmi.samsha.gov

http://www.aspe.hhs.gov

http://www.nlchp.org

http://www.rand.org

http://www.huduser.org

http://www.ich.gov

http://www.universallivingwage.org

http://www.bls.gov

http://www.census.gov

http://www.nccp.org

http://www.jcpr.org

http://www.cbpp.org

http:/www.aclu.org

http://www.nami.org/

http://www.mentalhealth.gov/

http://samhsa.gov/

http://www.naswdc.org/

http://www.nationalhomeless.org

Discussion Questions

1. Do you believe that a preference for living on welfare keeps TANF recipients out of the workforce?
2. How does the changing shape of the American economy change the shape of American poverty?
3. To what extent is the number (or percentage) of poor people a good measure of a society's commitment to social welfare?
4. Which level of government, local, state or national, do you think is best equipped to deal with poverty? Why?
5. Identify at least five factors associated with homelessness, and suggest at least one possible intervention strategy for each.

References

Albelda, R., & Withorn, A. (Eds.). (2002). *Lost ground: Welfare reform, poverty, and beyond.* Cambridge, MA: South End Press.

Albert, R., & Skolnik, L. (2005). *Social welfare programs: Narrative from hard times.* Belmont, CA: Thomson Wadsworth.

American Civil Liberties Union Foundation, Women's Rights Project (2006). *Domestic violence and homelessness.* New York: Author.

Anderson, S. G., Halter, A. P., & Grzylak, B. M. (2002). Changing safety net of last resort: Downsizing general assistance for employable adults. *Social Work,* 47(3), 249–258.

Axinn, J., & Stern, M. J. (2005). *Social welfare: A history of the American response to need* (6th ed.). Boston: Allyn & Bacon.

Bavier, R. (2003). *Non-economic factors in early welfare caseload declines*. Chicago: Joint Center for Poverty Research Working Paper 335.

Besharov, D. (Ed.). (2003). *Family well-being after welfare reform*. Somerset, NJ: Transaction Publishers.

Biggerstaff. M. A., McHarth, P., & Nichols-Casebolt, A. (2002). Living on the edge: Examination of people attending food pantries and soup kitchens. *Social Work, 47*(3), 267–277.

Blau, J. (2002). *The visible poor: Homelessness in the United States*. Surrey, United Kingdom: Replica Books.

Brooks, S. (2004). *Poverty and schooling in the U.S.: Contexts and consequences*. Mahway, NJ: LEA Publishers.

Center for Budget and Policy Priorities (2002). *Improving TANF program outcomes for families with barriers to employment*. Washington, DC: Author.

Center for Law and Social Policy. (2003). *Leave no youth behind: Opportunities for Congress to reach disconnected youth*. Washington, DC: Author.

Chasanov, A. (2004). *No longer getting by: An increase in the minimum wage is long overdue*. Economic Policy Institute. Available: http.www.epinet.org

Cloke, P. J., Milbourne, P., & Widdowfield, R. (2002). *Rural homelessness: Issues, experiences and policy responses*. Bristol, England: Policy Press.

Currie, J. M. (2006). *The invisible safety net: Protecting the nation's poor children and families*. Princeton, NJ: Princeton University Press.

Danziger, S. (2000). *Approaching the limit: Early lessons from welfare reform*. Ann Arbor, MI: University of Michigan Poverty Research and Training Center.

Day, P. (2006). *A new history of social welfare* (5th ed.). Boston: Allyn & Bacon.

DeParle, J. (2005). *American dream: Three women, ten kids, and a nation's drive to end welfare*. New York: Penguin Press.

Depastino, T. (2005). *Citizen hobo: How a century of homelessness shaped America*. Chicago: University of Chicago Press.

DiNitto, D. M. (2005). *Social welfare: Politics and public policy* (6th ed.). Boston: Allyn & Bacon.

Downer, R. (2000). *Homelessness and its impact on children's psychological well-being and family functioning that reaches far beyond financial costs*. Abbington, Oxford: United Kingdom.

Duncan, G. J., & Chase-Lansdale, P. L. (Eds.). (2004). *For better and for worse: Welfare reform and the well-being of children and families*. New York: Russell Sage Foundation.

Duncan, G. J., & Chase-Landsale, P. L. (2001). *Welfare reform and child well-being*. Chicago: Joint Center for Poverty Research Working Paper 217.

Dunifon, R., Kalil, A., & Danziger, S. K. (2002). *Maternal work behavior under welfare reform: How does the transition from welfare to work affect child development?* Chicago: Joint Center for Poverty Research Working Paper 293.

Economic Policy Institute. (2005). *Datazone 2005*. Available: http://www.epinet.org

Ehrenreich, B. (2002). *Nickel and dimed: On (not) getting by in America*. New York: Metropolitan Books.

Feldman, L. C. (2006). *Citizens without shelter: Homelessness, democracy, and political exclusion*. Ithaca, NY: Cornell University Press.

Finkelstein, M. (2004). *With no direction home: Homeless youth on the road and in the streets*. Belmont, CA: Thomson Wadsworth.

Fisher, M. (2005). *Why is U.S. poverty higher in nonmetropolitan than metropolitan areas?* Columbia, MO: Rural Poverty Research Center. Available: http://www.rpronline.org

Fletcher, C. N., Garasky, S., & Jensen, H. J. (2002). *Transitioning from welfare to work: No bus, no car, no way*. Chicago: Joint Center for Poverty Research Working Paper 303.

Frame, L., & Berrick, J. D. (2001). *Longitudinal, ethnographic study of 10 families from Alameda County, California recycling on TANF as a primary source of income*. Washington, D.C: U.S. Children's Bureau. Available: http://childwelfare.com/impact_of_welfare_reform.htm.

Fraser, M. W. (Ed.) (2004). *Risk and resilience in childhood: An ecological perspective* (2nd ed.). Washington, DC: NASW Press.

Friedman, P. (2003). *Current issues in rural housing and homelessness*. Columbia, MO: Rural Policy Research Institute.

Garfinkle, I., McLanahan, S., & Harknett, K. (1999). *Fragile families and welfare reform*. Chicago: Joint Center for Poverty Research Working Paper 113.

Geen, R., Fender, L., Leos-Urbel, J., & Markowitz, T. (2001). *Influence of welfare reform on child welfare experts' expectations regarding the potential impact of welfare reform on child welfare caseloads in 12 states.* Washington, D.C.: U.S. Children's Bureau. Available: http://www.childwelfare.com/impact _of_welfare_ reform.htm.

General Accounting Office (2002*). Charitable choice: Overview of research findings and implementation.* Washington, DC: Author. Available: http://www.gao. gov/new.items/d02337.pdf\

Gennetian, L. A., Duncan, G., Knox, V., Vargas, W., Clark-Kauffman, E., & London, A. S. (2004). How welfare policies affect adolescents' school outcomes: A synthesis of evidence from experimental studies. *Journal of Research on Adolescents, 14*(4), 399–423.

Gilbert, N., & Terrell, P. (2004). *Dimensions of social welfare policy* (6th ed.). Boston: Allyn & Bacon.

Grogger, J., & Karoly, L. A. (2005). *Welfare reform: Effects of a decade of change.* Cambridge, MA: Harvard University Press.

Hays, S. (2003). *Flat broke with children: Women in the age of welfare reform.* New York: Oxford University Press.

Holzer, H. J., Stoll, M. A., & Wissoker, D. (2001). *Job performance and retention among welfare recipients.* Chicago: Joint Center for Poverty Research Working Paper 231.

Hopper, K. (2003). *Reckoning with homelessness.* Ithaca, NY: Cornell University Press.

Housing Assistance Council. (2006). *Poverty in rural America.* Washington, DC: Author.

Iceland, J. (2006). *Poverty in America: A handbook.* Berkeley: University of California Press.

Jayakody, R., & Stauffer, D. (2000). Mental health problems among single mothers: Implications for welfare reform. *Journal of Social Issues, 56*, 617–634.

Joint Center for Housing Studies. (2006). *The state of the nation's housing 2006.* Cambridge, MA: Author.

Karger, J., & Stoesz, D. (2006). *American social welfare policy: A pluralistic approach* (4th ed.). New York: Longman.

Kauff, J., Fowler, L., Fraker, T., & Milliner-Waddell, J. (2001). *Differences in Iowa families' rates of child welfare involvement before and after exiting TANF.* Washington, D.C.: U.S. Children's Bureau. Available: www.childwelfare.com/impact_of_welfare_reform. htm.

Kilty, K. M., & Segal, E. A. (Eds.) (2006). *The promise of welfare reform: Political rhetoric and the reality of poverty in the twenty-first century.* New York: Haworth Press.

Kozol, J. (2006). *The shame of the nation: Restoration of apartheid schooling in America.* New York: Three Rivers Press.

Kyle, K. (2005). *Contexualizing homelessness: Critical theory, homelessness, and federal policy addressing the homeless.* Florence, KY: Routledge Press.

Laprest, P. J., & Zedlewski, S. R. (2006). *The changing role of welfare in the lives of low-income families.* Washington, DC: Urban Institute.

Lens, V. (2002). TANF: What went wrong and what to do next. *Social Work, 47*(3), 279–290).

Levinson, D. (Ed.) (2004). *Encyclopedia of homelessness* (Vol. 2). Thousand Oaks, CA: Sage Publications.

Lichter, D., & Jensen, L. (2000). *Rural America in transition: Poverty and welfare at the turn of the 21st century.* Chicago: Joint Center for Poverty Research Working Paper 187.

Lyon, E. (2002). *Welfare and domestic violence against women: Lessons from research.* Hamsburg, PA: National Resource Center on Domestic Violence.

Meyer, N. (2006). *Psychosocial factors associated with the working alliance between shelter workers and homeless youth.* Ann Arbor, MI: Proquest/UMI.

National Center for Children in Poverty. (2002). *Early childhood poverty: A statistical profile.* New York: Author.

National Coalition for the Homeless. (2006). *NCH fact sheet series.* Washington, DC: Author.

National Coalition for Homeless Veterans. (2006). *Background and statistics.* Washington, DC: Author.

National Health Care for the Homeless Council. (2005). *Comprehensive services to meet complex needs.* Washington, DC: Author.

National Health Care for the Homeless Council. (2006). *Health care for the homeless (HCH) program.* Nashville, TN: Author.

National Institute of Justice. (2006). *Compendium of research on violence against women: 1993–2005.* Washington, DC: Author.

National Law Center on Homelessness and Poverty. (2004). *Key data concerning homeless persons in America.* Washington, DC: Author.

National Law Center on Homelessness and Poverty. (2005). *What's the impact of the Violence Against Women Act 2005: Re-authorization on the housing rights and options of domestic violence victims.* Washington, DC: Author.

National Low Income Housing Coalition (2004). *America's neighbors: The affordable housing crisis and the people it affects.* Washington, DC: Author.

National Low Income Housing Coalition. (2005a). *Out of reach 2005.* Washington, DC: Author.

National Low Income Housing Coalition. (2005b). *Who's bearing the burden? Severely unaffordable housing: An examination of national and state affordable housing needs from the 2003 American Community Survey.* Washington, DC: Author.

National Low Income Housing Coalition. (2006). *Housing crisis fact sheet: NLIHC housing action agenda.* Available: http://www.nihc.org/news/090606.html

National Network to End Domestic Violence. (2004). *Housing, homelessness, and domestic violence.* Washington, DC: Author.

National Resource Center on Domestic Violence. (2005). *Categorical annotated resource guide for housing and domestic violence.* Washington, DC: Author.

National Resource and Training Center on Homelessness and Mental Illness. (2006). *Get the facts.* Washington, DC: Author.

National Resource Center on Homelessness and Mental Illness. (2004). *Homelessness and mental illness among older Americans.* Bethesda, MD: Author.

Orshansky, M. (1965, January). Counting the poor. *Social Security Bulletin,* pp. 3–29.

RAND Corporation. (2002). *Consequences of welfare reform* (Labor and Population Program Report DRU-2676-DHHS). Santa Monica, CA: Author.

Rollinson, P. A., & Pardeck, J. T. (2006). *Homelessness in rural America: Policy and practices.* New York: Haworth Press.

Sawhill, I. V., Dawhill, B., Weaver, K., Kane, A., & Haskins, R. (Eds.). (2002). *Welfare reform and beyond: The future of the safety net.* Washington, DC: Brookings Institution.

Schram, S. F., & Beer, S. H. (Eds.). (2000). *Welfare reform: A race to the bottom.* Baltimore: Johns Hopkins University Press.

Scott, J., & Ward, H. (Eds.) (2005). *Safeguarding and promoting the well-being of children, families, and communities (child welfare program).* Philadelphia: Jessica Kingsley Publishers.

Secombe, K. (1999). *So you think I drive a Cadillac? Welfare recipients' perspectives on the system and its reform.* Boston: Allyn & Bacon.

Shapiro, T. M. (2005). *The hidden costs of being African American: How wealth perpetuates inequality.* New York: Oxford Press.

Shirk, M., Stangler, G., & Carter, J. (2004). *On their own: What happens when they are out of the foster care system?* Boulder, CO: Westview Press.

Slack, K. S. (1999). *Does the loss of welfare income increase the risk of involvement with the child welfare system?* Chicago: Joint Center for Poverty Research Working Paper 65.

Slesnick, N. (2004). *Our runaway and homeless youth: A guide to understanding.* New York: Praeger.

Social Security Bulletin. (2000). *Annual statistical supplement (2000).* Available: http://www.ssa.gov/policy/docs/statecomps/supplement/2000/sup00/pdf

Solley, B. A. (2005). *When poverty's children write: Celebrating strengths, transforming lives.* Portsmouth, NH: Heinemann Publishers.

Stretch, J. J. (Ed.) (2003). *Practicing social justice.* New York: Haworth Press.

Taylor, L. (2002). *Differences in child welfare involvement for Kentucky families exiting TANF and families remaining on TANF.* Washington, D.C: U.S. Children's Bureau. Available: http://www.childwelfare.com/ impact_ of_welfare_reform.htm.

Tolman, R. M., Danziger, S. K., & Rosen, D. (2002). *Domestic violence and economic well-being of current and former welfare recipients.* Chicago: Joint Center on Poverty Research Working Paper 304.

Tolman, R., & Raphael, J. (2000). *A review of the research on welfare and domestic violence.* Ann Arbor: University of Michigan, School of Social Work.

Universal Living Wage Campaign. (2006). *Universal living wage formula.* Austin, TX: Author.

Urban Institute. (2006a). *The changing role of welfare in the lives of low-income families with children.* Washington, DC: Author.

Urban Institute (2006b). *Welfare reform: Ten years later.* Washington, DC: Author.

U.S. Bureau of the Census. (2002). *Poverty in the United States: 2001.* Washington, DC: U.S. Bureau of the Census, Income Statistics Branch.

U.S. Bureau of the Census. (2006). *Statistical Abstract of the United States.* Washington, DC: Author.

U.S. Conference of Mayors. (2006). *A status report on hunger and homelessness in America's cities.* Washington, DC: Author.

U.S. Department of Health and Human Services. (2007). 2007 HHS *poverty guidelines*. Washington, DC: Author. Available: http://aspe.hhs.gov/poverty/07poverty.htm

U.S. Department of Health and Human Services. (2006a). *Prior HHS poverty guidelines and Federal Register references*. Washington, DC: Author. Available: http://aspe.hhs.gov/poverty/figures-fed-reg.htm.

U.S. Department of Health and Human Services. (2006b). *Homelessness*. Washington, DC: Author. Washington, DC: Author. Available: http://aspe.hhs.gov/homeless/index.shtml

U.S. Department of Health and Human Services, Administration for Children and Families (2003). *Change in welfare caseloads since enactment of new welfare law*. Washington, DC: Author. Available: http://www.acf.dhhs.gov/news/stats/aug-sept.htm.

U.S. Department of Housing and Urban Development. (2003). *Trends in worst case housing, 1978–1999: A report to Congress on worst case housing needs—plus update on work case housing needs in 2001*. Washington, D.C: Author.

U.S. White House (2006) *Toward independence*. Washington, DC: Author. Available: http://www.whitehouse.gov

U.S. General Accounting Office. (2002). *Charitable choice: Overview of research findings and implementation*. Washington, DC: Author. Available: http:www.gao.gov/new.items/d02337.pdf

U.S. Interagency Council on Homelessness. (2006). *Innovations*. Washington, DC: Author. Available: http:www.ich.gov

U.S. Social Security Administration. (2006). *Annual statistical report on the Social Security Disability Insurance Program, 2004*. Washington, DC: Author. Available: http://www.ssa.gov/policy/docs/statcomps/di_asr/2004/index.htm.

Van Hook, J. (2004). *Welfare reform and long-term stability in food security among children of immigrants*. Chicago: Joint Center for Poverty Research Working Paper 352.

Weil, A., & Finegold, K. (Eds.). (2002). *Welfare reform: The next act*. Washington, DC: Urban Institute Press.

Winship, S., & Jencks, C. (2001). The well-being of single mothers after welfare reform, as measured by changes in food security. Chicago: Joint Center for Poverty Research, Working Paper 286.

Ziliak, J. (2006). *Understanding poverty rates and gaps*. Boston: Now Publishers.

Zorza, J. (1991). Women battering: A major cause of homelessness. *Clearinghouse Review, 25*(4).

Suggested Further Readings

Anderson, L. P., Sundet, P. A., & Harrington, I. (2000). *The social welfare system in the United States: A social worker's guide to public benefits programs*. Boston: Allyn & Bacon.

Burt, M., Aron, L., Lee, E., & Valente, J. (2001). *Helping America's homeless: Emergency shelter or affordable housing*. Washington, DC: Urban Institute Press.

Da Costa Nunez, R. (2004). *A shelter is not a home . . . Or is it?: Lessons from homelessness in New York City*. New York: White Tiger Press.

Dolgoff, R., & Feldstein, D. (2007). *Understanding social welfare* (7th ed.). Boston: Allyn & Bacon.

Failer, J. L. (2002). *Who qualifies for rights: Homelessness, mental illness, and civil commitment*. Ithaca, NY: Cornell University Press.

Gittins, A. J. (2006). *Where there's hope there's life: Stories of homelessness and survival*. Liguori, MO: Liguori Publications.

Harrell, R. (2000). *American poverty in a new era of reform*. Armonk, NY: M.E. Sharpe.

Hopper, K. (2003). *Reckoning with homelessness (the anthropology of contemporary issues)*. Ithaca, NY: Cornell University Press.

Jacobson, N. (2000). State low-income tax relief: Recent trends. *National Tax Journal, 53*(3, Part 1), 403–417.

Karger, H. J., Midgeley, J., & Brown, C. B. (Eds.). (2003).*Controversial issues in social policy*. (2nd ed.). Boston: Allyn & Bacon.

Kraimer-Rickaby, L. (2006). *A case study of the state of Connecticut Department of Children and Families' one-on-one mentor program for youth aging out of foster care*. Ann Arbor, MI: ProQuest/UMI.

Layton, J. (2000). *Homelessness: The making and unmaking of a crisis*. New York: Penguin Books.

Levine, D. P., & Rizvi, A. T. (2005). *Poverty, work, and freedom: Political economy and the moral order*. New York: Cambridge University Press.

Linhorst, D. M. (2002). Federalism and social justice: Implications for social work. *Social Work, 47*(3), 201–208.

Mary, J. D. (2003). *Social Welfare: The American Partnership.* Boston: Allyn & Bacon.

Nilan, D. D. (2006). *Crossing the line: Taking steps to end homelessness.* Bangor, Maine: Available: Booklocker.com.

Orr, C. (2006). *Homelessness: A challenge to African American males.* Mustang, OK: Tate Publishing & Enterprises.

Scholz, J. K., & Levine, K. (2000). The evolution of income support policy in recent decades. In S. H. Danziger & R. H. Haveman (Eds.), *Understanding poverty* (pp. 193–228). Cambridge, MA: Harvard University Press.

Stoesz, D. (2005). *Quixote's ghost: The right, the liberati, and the future of social policy.* New York: Oxford University Press.

Urban Institute. (2006). *Getting on, staying on, and getting off welfare: The complexity of state-by-state policy choices.* Washington, DC: Author.

Withorn, A. (Eds.). (2002). *Lost ground: Welfare reform, poverty, and beyond.* Cambridge MA: South End Press.

Yankowski, M. (2005). *Under the overpass: A journey of faith on the streets of America.* London, United Kingdom: Multnomah Publishers.

Zucchino, D. (1997). *Myth of the welfare queen.* New York: Scribner.

CHAPTER 8

Mental Health, Substance Abuse, and Developmental Disabilities

For 3 months, Lindsey Andrews, age 24, has been living in a halfway house in the inner-city area of a large northern city. This came on the heels of her 14th stay at a state mental hospital since the age of 16. Lindsey and her roommates earn money for food and part of the rent by working for an industrial cleaning company. They are supervised by a social worker from the local mental health outreach center that meets with them as a group twice a week and is available on-call whenever they need support. With her social worker's help, Lindsey is planning to enroll in a job-training program next month and to move into her own apartment with one of the other residents of the halfway house within the next 6 months. She is excited at the prospect of living on her own.

Lindsey enjoyed a relatively stable childhood, growing up in a rural area of the South with her middle-class parents and four brothers. During junior high school she began to experience severe headaches and what she terms "anxiety attacks." Her parents took her to several doctors, who could find no physical reasons for these problems. At about age 15, Lindsey's behavior changed from being calm and stable to becoming erratic—ranging from screaming rages to long periods of crying to fun-loving, carefree behavior.

She began to experiment with drugs, ran away from home a number of times, and got into several physical altercations with other girls at school. Her family had difficulty coping with her behavior. After one serious incident when Lindsey threatened her mother and her younger brother with a knife, she was hospitalized in a local private psychiatric hospital for 30 days. She was placed on medication to help stabilize her erratic behavior, and she and her family received therapy.

After her release from the hospital, Lindsey functioned better for several months. But she soon reported feeling overwhelmed and pressured and told her family that "I can't stop the frightening thoughts that keep running through my head." Her psychiatrist wanted to rehospitalize her, but her family's insurance benefits had been exhausted during her first hospitalization and Lindsey did not want to admit herself to the state mental hospital nearby.

After continual arguments with her family and school personnel and several minor run-ins with the law, Lindsey quit school and moved with a boyfriend to California, where she held a series of temporary jobs. When the boyfriend left her because of her mood swings, her behavior became even more erratic. Finally, after she was found asleep in a dumpster and unable to remember who or where she was, the police picked her up and took her to the state hospital.

For the next 6 years, Lindsey repeated a pattern of holding a menial job for a short time, losing the job, living on the streets, entering the state hospital, and being released in a more stable condition. When Lindsey was released from her last hospital stay, the local mental health center in Lindsey's area finally had space available at the halfway house where she is living now. She has developed a real bond with her social worker and hopes to be living independently in the near future. Lindsey is quick to say that without her social worker, she would not be ready to make this move toward independence.

The World Health Organization has determined that mental disorders account for 8 of the 10 leading causes of disability (including death) in established market economies worldwide. The National Institute of Mental Health (2004) ranks the leading causes of disability as:

1. major depressive disorders,
2. alcohol use,
3. roadway traffic accidents, and
4. schizophrenia.

For the age group 15–44, mental disorders are the leading cause of disability in the United States.

More than one-fourth of the adult population in the United States is estimated to be affected by some type of diagnosable mental disorder in a given year (see Table 8.1). Nearly two-thirds of all people with mental illness do not seek treatment, although about half of all adults with some type of mental illness report that it impairs their ability to function (National Institute of Mental Health, 2006c).

Major depression is the leading cause of mental disability in the United States, afflicting almost 15 million people over 18 years of age at any given time. In 2004, the President's New Freedom Commission on Mental Health estimated the costs of mental illness, including treatment, disability benefits, and lost productivity, to exceed $175 billion annually (National Institute of Mental Health, 2004). Mental health services in the United States are available to only one in every eight individuals who need them, and they are available to far fewer individuals worldwide. Because of increased individual stresses, financial pressures, divorce and marital problems, and work-related pressures, most individuals are expected to experience emotional problems at some point in their lives.

Emotional problems are highly correlated with substance abuse, a related field of practice in which large numbers of social workers are employed. The systems/ecological framework can be used to understand the relationships among environmental factors that contribute to emotional problems and substance abuse. Problems in one area, such as mental illness, are not automatically accompanied by substance abuse. But researchers find that about half of individuals with severe mental disorders also are affected by substance abuse, and that 37% of individuals who abuse alcohol and 53% of individuals who abuse other drugs have at least one serious mental illness (National Alliance on Mental Illness, 2006b).

In addition, many people in the United States have some type of developmental disability, either

TABLE 8.1
Estimated Persons with Mental Disorders in the United States in a Given Year

Mood disorders	**20.9 million (9.5%) of adults 18 and older**
Major depressive disorder	14.8 million (6.7%) of adults 18 and older
Dysthymic disorders (chronic, mild depression)	3.3 million (1.5%) of adults 18 and older
Bipolar disorder	5.7 million (2.6%) of adults 18 and older
Suicide	31,655 died in 2002 (90% had diagnosable mental disorder)
Schizophrenia	**2.4 million (1.1%) of adults 18 and older**
Anxiety disorders	**40 million (18.1%) of adults 18 and older**
Panic disorder	6 million (2.7%) of adults 18 and older
Obsessive-compulsive disorder (OCD)	2.2 million (1%) of adults 18 and older
Post-traumatic stress disorder (PTSD)	7.7 million (3.5%) of adults 18 and older
Generalized anxiety disorder	6.8 million (3.1%) of adults 18 and older
Social phobia	15 million (6.8%) of adults 18 and older
Agoraphobia	1.8 million (.8%) of adults 18 and older
Specific phobia	19.2 million (8.7%) of adults 18 and older
Eating disorders	**.5%–3.7% of all females** (5–35% of persons with anorexia or bulimia and 35% of persons with binge-eating disorders are male)
Attention deficit disorder	**4.1% of adults 18 and older**
Autism	**3.4 cases per 1000 children ages 3–10**
Alzheimer's disease	**4.5 million; 1:10 over 65 and nearly half over 85 are affected**

Source: The Numbers Count, by National Institute of Mental Health (Washington, DC: NIMH, 2006). http://www.nimh.nih.gov/healthinformation/statisticsmenu.fcm

physical or mental. Often, individuals with physical developmental disabilities abuse alcohol or other drugs as a way to cope with their disabilities. Some types of developmental disabilities are a result of drug abuse by mothers during pregnancy. The relationship between developmental disabilities and substance abuse is dramatized by legislation prohibiting discrimination against individuals with disabilities in which the definition of disability includes both substance abusers and persons with emotional problems.

The topics of this chapter are mental health and mental illness, the abuse of alcohol and other drugs, and developmental disabilities. First we provide definitions and characteristics related to mental health and mental illness, substance use and abuse, and developmental disabilities. The later part of the chapter focuses on policies, services and programs, current breakthroughs that are likely to change how these issues are addressed, and roles that social workers play in addressing these issues.

Students should keep in mind that the three issues do not always overlap. Different histories, policies, and issues surround each. Nevertheless, they have many similarities, particularly in the stigma, oppression, and discrimination that persons with mental illness, substance abuse, and developmental disabilities experience. Social workers can play many important roles at all levels of the environment in working with individuals, families, and communities to address these problems. Key roles include recognizing the strengths of individuals, families, cultural groups, and communities and empowering them to use their strengths to develop a healthier environment in which to live.

Mental Health

How do we determine what mental health is and who should receive mental health services? The stigma placed on individuals with mental health problems and the stereotypes about the services offered to them cause many individuals with mental health problems to avoid seeking services. People think of mental health services and those who receive them as portrayed in popular movies and books, such as the classic novel *One Flew over the Cuckoo's Nest* (Kesey, 1962) and the films *Silence of the Lambs* (Harris, 1991) and *Monster* (Jenkins, 2003). For this reason, many communities are passing zoning or other ordinances to disallow individuals with mental health problems from moving into their areas.

The rights of people with mental health problems also are receiving more attention. Should they be forced to be hospitalized, receive electric shock treatments, or get drug therapy against their wishes? Or, like Lindsey, when they desperately need treatment that is not available because of scarce resources, do they or their advocates have a right to demand services, especially if it means that they will be less likely to need more intensive services, such as institutionalization, in the future? Does someone who currently is in an institution but could function in a less restrictive environment have the right to demand such a placement?

From another perspective, what about protections for those in our society who may encounter individuals with serious mental health problems? What should happen if they become dangerous to themselves or others?

This issue was exemplified by court cases involving Andrea Yates, a mother from Texas who drowned her five young children in a bathtub in 2001. At her initial trial, her attorneys argued that she should be found not guilty by reason of insanity. A number of mental health professionals testified that she had post-partum depression and other mental illness, which raised the issue of whether she knew right from wrong at the time of the deaths. Jurors found Yates guilty and sentenced her to life in prison. Because of a procedural error, however, the case was retried 4 years later and a second jury found her not guilty by reason of insanity. She was committed to a high-security mental health facility.

In a contrasting case, a young adult who killed a number of women over several years, and was diagnosed by several psychiatrists as having severe psychological problems, was sentenced to death in a Florida court and executed. And a young adult with mental retardation who aided in a murder at the age of 17—when his mental age was about 6—was put to death.

Individuals who have been found guilty in courts of killing their children, killing their partners, committing serial murders across the country, or killing large numbers of people at one site have received disparate sentences. The mental health status of all of those charged has been introduced in these cases. Are these individuals less accountable to society for their actions because of their diminished mental capacity? Who is responsible for looking after them to ensure that they do not harm themselves or others? What legal protections should be guaranteed?

Studies also show a strong relationship between mental health problems and physical health problems. When people do not get help for their mental health problems, they are much more likely to become physically ill. For example, researchers found that half of those going to company physicians with health-related problems had mental health problems. A number of studies have found that those who receive mental health services for a specific psychological problem experience a significant drop in subsequent medical costs (National Alliance on Mental Illness, 2006a). Although these studies show that the high costs of health care could be reduced if more attention were directed to the mental health needs of individuals, mental health funds have been cut significantly because of federal and state budget constraints.

If left untreated, mental health problems increase the financial costs to taxpayers and decrease productivity in the workplace. Disruptions to the individual with the problem and family members take financial and emotional tolls, although it is difficult to obtain accurate data on actual expenditures for mental health services and other related costs to individuals with mental health problems, as well as the costs to their families, workplaces, and communities.

According to the National Association of Social Workers (2006), 60% of those providing mental health services today are social workers, and almost 40% of licensed social workers recently surveyed by NASW reported being employed in mental health-related jobs. They work in state mental hospitals, private psychiatric treatment facilities, community outreach facilities, child guidance clinics and family service agencies, emergency hotlines, crisis centers, and private offices. The area of mental health services offers many vital roles for social workers.

Mental Health and Mental Illness: Definitions

Societies throughout history have developed their own systems for labeling acceptable and unacceptable behavior. What is tolerated in one society may be unacceptable in another. For each society there is a continuum, with certain definitely unacceptable behaviors at one end and definitely acceptable and appropriate behaviors at the other end. Members of a society agree almost uniformly on the behaviors at either end of the continuum, while the behaviors in the middle of the continuum are often the subject of extensive disagreement and debate. For example, most would consider murder as a definitely unacceptable behavior, but where on the continuum would they place continually talking aloud to oneself?

Some societies tolerate little deviance from acceptable behavior. For a brief period during colonial times in Salem, Massachusetts, for example, some individuals whose behaviors were considered "deviant" were labeled as witches and were tortured and burned at the stake. Other individuals with mental illness in colonial times were locked in attics or cellars or warehoused in "lunatic" asylums. Later research (Mechanic, 1999) suggested that many of these individuals had severe psychological problems, and others were women in nontraditional roles who refused to give them up.

By contrast, in certain other societies, those whose behavior deviates from the norm are given special roles and, in some instances, elevated to status positions. For example, in many Native American tribes, nonconforming individuals often became shamans, or medicine men, assuming high-status positions within the tribes.

More often, historically, those labeled as mentally ill or "retarded" have been isolated or punished. Although society has advanced, there is carryover ambivalence about how they should be regarded and treated. Attempts at integrating individuals with emotional disturbance and mental illness into classrooms and communities are often met with much resistance. David Mechanic (1999), a prominent social policy analyst in the mental health field, has argued that the stigma attached to the labels "mentally ill" and "disabled" further damages those already stigmatized and increases their problems. Some advances have been made in the current preference for referring to the condition instead of the individual, as in "individuals with mental illness" rather than "the mentally ill," for example.

Informal definitions have their genesis in groups within which the person operates, usually family members or co-workers. The definitions depend on the norms of the specific group and what is tolerated, as well as the position the person occupies within the group. A boss's behavior, for example, may be defined as outside the group norms much less quickly than a file clerk's behavior. Informal definitions also depend on whether the other members of the group can empathize. Can they fit that behavior into their own frame of reference? In an example by Mechanic (1999), a person who continually carries on an imaginary conversation with his mother while on the job is more likely to be tolerated if the group is aware that the mother recently died and the son is still grieving her death. But if there is no apparent context for the behavior or if the behavior persists, the individual is likely to be labeled as strange or odd.

Definitions of so-called abnormal behaviors typically are based on visible symptoms—such as talking to people who are not present—rather than the severity of the actual problems. Attempting to define a condition based on invisible factors, such as what is going on inside an individual's mind, is difficult. Only those who in some way enter the mental health system are likely to be defined specifically as having some type of emotional or mental problem.

Despite its problems, the mental health system is likely to accept—at least for short periods of time—almost all individuals who seek its services, including the unwanted, the aged, the indigent, the lonely, and those with nowhere else to go. At times, this results in overestimates of the number of individuals defined as having emotional problems and underestimates of those who should enter the system.

Categorizing Mental Illness

Formal definitions of mental illness traditionally have followed the **medical model,** which considers those with emotional problems as sick and thus not responsible for their behavior. This model also assumes that sick people are entitled to be helped, and that help or treatment should be guided by the medical profession in medical settings or settings such as psychiatric facilities directed by medical professionals. The medical model conceptualizes **mental illness** as severe emotional problems caused by brain dysfunction or intrapsychic causes, with little attention to systems or environmental influences. (See chapter 3 for a comparison of the medical model and the systems/ecological perspective.) Traditionally, mental illness also has been viewed from a genetic or physiological perspective as a disease of the mind or a disturbance in the individual's functioning.

DSM CLASSIFICATION SYSTEM

The American Psychiatric Association has attempted to monitor the categorization and definition of various types of emotional disorders through a classification system termed the ***Diagnostic and Statistical Manual of Mental Disorders (DSM).*** This classification system is currently in its fourth revision and is referred to informally as the *DSM-IV-TR*. It uses a multiaxial system for evaluation, which focuses on the psychological, biological, and social aspects of an individual's functioning. The system incorporates information from five axes in diagnosing an individual (Williams, 1995):

Axes I and II	incorporate all of the mental disorders, such as schizophrenic and psychotic disorders
Axis III	incorporates physical disorders and conditions

Axes IV and V rate the severity of the psychosocial stressors that have contributed to the development or maintenance of the disorder and the highest level of adaptive functioning that the individual has maintained during the previous year

Some social work professionals believe that the *DSM* classification system is consistent with a systems/ecological perspective in assessing an individual, allowing a focus on either organic factors or environmental factors, or both, that affect an individual's condition. They believe when completing an assessment that the *DSM* allows for incorporating the individual's strengths as well as problems. This classification system has been used increasingly for third-party insurance reimbursement when mental health services are provided (Williams & Spitzer, 1995).

Although many social workers find the *DSM-IV-TR* helpful, its use by social workers and other professionals to label conditions of clients in order to obtain third-party insurance reimbursements has raised questions about whether such labels really are beneficial in improving services. Critics argue that a diagnostic process of this nature actually may be more detrimental to clients, because labels such as "schizophrenia" and "conduct disorder" can negatively affect clients and the way others treat them, particularly if the label included in a client's records is obtained and misused.

Other criticism of the *DSM* by social workers is in its reduced emphasis on environmental factors that affect a person's mental health and increased attention to disorders and deficits—more consistent with the medical model. In their book *Making Us Crazy: DSM: The Psychiatric Bible and the Creation of Mental Disorders,* Herb Kutchins and Stuart Kirk (1997), suggested that decisions surrounding what is considered a mental disorder are significantly shaped by societal prejudices and special interests. They noted, for example, that the *DSM* included homosexuality as a mental disorder until 1973. And these authors pointed out the manual's insensitivity to cultural factors that may shape a person's behavior. Still other mental health professionals have criticized the *DSM* for its lack of clarity in defining disorders and for not basing its definitions on empirical evidence (Beutler & Malik, 2002).

PIE CLASSIFICATION SYSTEM

The National Association of Social Workers (Karls & Wandrei, 1994) published an alternative classification system, the person-in-environment (PIE) system, which offers a more holistic approach based on the systems/ecological framework. Like the *DSM,* this system can be used to describe, classify, and code the emotional, mental, and social problems of adults. The PIE system assesses clients according to four major factors:

1. *social functioning* (the social role in which each problem is identified: type of problem, severity of problem, duration of problem, and client's ability to cope with the problem);
2. *environmental problems* (the social system in which each problem is identified, specific type of problem within each social system, severity of the problem, duration of the problem);
3. *mental health problems* (clinical syndrome and personality and developmental disorders); and
4. *physical health problems* (diseases diagnosed by a physician and other health problems reported by the client and others).

A major difference between the PIE and the *DSM* is that the PIE system emphasizes the interrelationship of the person and the environment. The PIE system also "seeks to balance problems and strengths; it delineates problems pertinent to both the person and the environment and qualifies them according to their duration, severity, and the client's ability to solve or cope with them" (Karls & Wandrei, 1994, p. 3). PIE cannot be used as a basis for securing third-party payment as the *DSM* can.

Mental Health: A Matter of Viewpoint

The traditional view of mental health and mental illness is that they are found at opposite ends of a continuum. Other viewpoints, like that of psychiatrist Thomas Szasz (1998), have suggested that mental health and emotional problems defy specific boundaries. Szasz objects to labeling the mentally ill, arguing that there is no such thing as mental illness. He agrees that some mental illnesses are the result of neurological impairment, but he believes that these illnesses are "brain diseases" rather than mental illnesses. Although he acknowledges the existence of emotional problems, Szasz contends that labeling nonorganic emotional problems implies a deviation from some clearly specified norm. Szasz thinks such labeling not only stigmatizes individuals but also may actually cause them to assume those behaviors.

Szasz argues that instead of talking about definitions of mental illness, we should talk about problems of living—the individual's struggle with how to live in our world. He and others believe that positive **mental health** is promoted by our competence in dealing with our environment and our confidence of being able, when necessary, to cause desired effects. He advocates a systems/ecological perspective for viewing mental health. Within his framework, problems in living can be viewed as stemming from biological/physiological, economic, political, psychological, or sociological constraints. Promoting positive interactions between individuals and their environments is viewed as congruent with promoting optimal mental health and social functioning for individuals. A longtime activist in the mental health

arena, Szasz (1998) pioneered a classification system with three categories of mental health problems:

1. *personal disabilities,* such as depression, fears, inadequacy, and excessive anxiety;
2. *antisocial acts,* such as violent and criminal behaviors; and
3. *deterioration of the brain,* such as Alzheimer's disease, alcoholism, and brain damage.

Many mental health experts prefer this system and its emphasis on healthy functioning rather than a system that emphasizes mental illness. Szasz's system assumes that at some point all individuals have difficulties in negotiating their complex environments. It assumes that mental health services are available to and needed by all individuals at some time during their lives instead of something to be avoided. This perspective is much more consistent with the systems/ecological perspective and the PIE classification system than the medical model and the *DSM-IV.*

The Development of Mental Health Problems

Considerable debate surrounds the question of how mental health problems arise. To say that one specific factor causes a mental health problem is difficult, if not impossible. More likely, mental health problems are the result of a variety of factors. Research suggests a number of possible explanations.

HEREDITY, BIOLOGICAL, AND GENETIC FACTORS

The most significant breakthroughs in understanding mental health problems are based on biological and genetic factors as more continues to be learned about DNA markers and their consequences. The Human Brain Project, launched in 1993 by the National Institute of Mental Health, and worldwide efforts to map the human genome, are expected to result in new strategies to prevent and treat mental health disorders and promote positive mental health (National Institute of Mental Health, 2006b). Modern brain-imaging technologies have contributed significantly to understanding and treating mental health and mental disorders. For example, researchers indicate that in depression, neural circuits responsible for regulating moods, thinking, sleep, appetite, and behavior do not function properly and critical neurotransmitters (chemicals used by nerve cells to communicate) are imbalanced.

Researchers also have identified genes and their interactions that seem to impact other conditions such as Alzheimer's disease and alcoholism and drug addiction. Imaging techniques that allow "real time" viewing of the tiniest components of a cell make it possible to determine the impact of various stressors in the environment on a living organism, as well as to introduce various drugs into an organism and determine not only the impact of a drug, but also the reasons why the organism reacts as it does. Scientists indicate that before long a scan of an individual can be conducted, followed by computer-generated determinations tailored specifically to that individual, identifying appropriate medication or other interventions to address identified problems.

Many researchers, however, caution that the impact of the environment cannot be disregarded. Genetics research indicates that vulnerability to mental disorders such as depression results from the influence of multiple genes acting together with environmental factors (National Institute of Mental Health, 2003). One study found that individuals who were more likely to experience depression after life stressors had a different serotonin transporter gene variant than others (see Figure 8.1).

Research also suggests that schizophrenia, like heart disease and diabetes, results from the complex interaction of genetic, biological, developmental, and environmental factors. Mental illnesses are viewed increasingly as chemical imbalances in the brain. "Just as diabetes is a disorder of the pancreas, mental illnesses are brain disorders that often result in a diminished capacity for coping with the ordinary demands of life" (National Alliance on Mental Illness, 2006b).

Research exemplified by genetic studies on depression and life stressors suggests that genetic factors alone do not cause mental health disorders. Many research findings indicate that individuals are predisposed to certain problems through heredity, and certain environmental conditions trigger this predisposition, resulting in the emotional problem. A variation of this position is that, because of genetic traits or physiological characteristics, some individuals are biologically less capable of coping with environmental stress.

PSYCHOSOCIAL DEVELOPMENTAL FACTORS

Based on the work of developmental theorist Erik Erikson and others, the psychosocial developmental perspective suggests that mental health problems result from environmental experiences during childhood. Research shows that individuals who experience severe trauma during childhood—such as physical or sexual abuse, separation from a close family member, or alcoholism or drug abuse by family members—are much more likely to develop mental health problems later in life. Post-traumatic stress disorder, common in combat veterans, also is often experienced by survivors of child sexual and physical abuse and individuals who have witnessed violent attacks on others, particularly family members. Research indicates that exposure to such trauma also changes a person's brain chemistry, suggesting an interactive effect between physiological and developmental factors.

SOCIAL LEARNING

The social learning perspective proposes that mental health problems are the result of learned behaviors. The behaviors may be learned by observing parents or other role models, or used as survival mechanisms to cope with difficult life experiences.

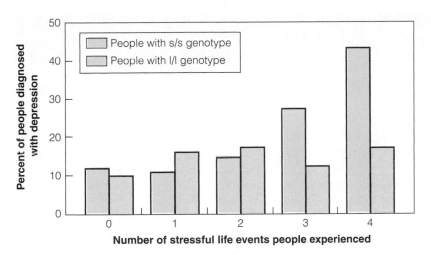

FIGURE 8.1

Rates of Depression by Persons Experiencing Stressful Life Events According to Gene Type

Note: Among people who had inherited two copies of the stress-sensitive short version of the serotonin transporter gene (s/s), 45% developed depression following four stressful life events in their early 20s, compared to 17% among people with two copies of the stress-protective long version (l/l). About 17% of the 847 subjects carried two copies of the short version, 31% two copies of the long version, and 51% one copy of each version.

Source: Avshalom Caspi, University of Wisconsin, from National Institute of Mental Health, *Gene More Than Doubles Risk of Depression Following Life Stresses,* July, 2003.

SOCIAL STRESS

The social stress perspective, based on the work of Szasz (1998), emphasizes the relationship between environmental stress and mental health. This perspective suggests that individuals who are under duress—including the poor, people of color, and women—are more likely to develop mental health problems.

SOCIETAL REACTIONS AND LABELING

This perspective suggests that society creates individuals with mental health problems through a societal reaction process. By establishing social norms and treating as deviant those who do not subscribe to the norms, a society identifies individuals with mental health problems. In addition, individuals who are identified or labeled as somehow different will assume the role prescribed to them; that is, individuals labeled as having mental health problems will behave as they would be expected to if they had the problem. Individuals labeled as having mental health problems, even though they do not behave any differently than those without problems, also may also be perceived as behaving differently because of how they are labeled (see Box 8.1).

COLLECTIVE MOBILIZATION

The collective mobilization perspective proposes that mental health problems are "as much the product of social expectations, social stigma, and exclusion from opportunities as they are a direct

BOX 8.1
Does Labeling Shape Our Expectations of How People Will Function?

The identification of individuals with mental health problems and the ways those problems are defined are hotly debated issues by mental health professionals. A number of years ago, psychologist David Rosenhan* and his associates conducted a study that exemplifies this concern. Rosenhan and his seven colleagues went separately to the admissions offices of 12 psychiatric hospitals in five different states, all claiming that they were hearing voices. In every instance, they were admitted to the hospitals as patients. Immediately upon admission, they all assumed normal behavior. At least one of the researchers did not try to hide his role as a researcher. He sat on the ward and took copious notes on legal pads of all of the events going on around him.

Even though the researchers all behaved normally while hospitalized, hospital professionals were unable to distinguish them from other patients. In a number of instances, however, the other patients were able to determine that they were not mentally ill.

Rosenhan and his associates remained at the hospitals as patients from 7 to 52 days, with an average stay of 19 days, before they were discharged. The diagnosis at discharge for each of them was "schizophrenia in remission."

---

*"On Being Sane in Insane Places," by David Rosenhan, *Science* (1973), *179*, 250–257.

---

function of mental or physical impairments" (Mechanic, 1999, p. 85). Organizations representing persons with mental disabilities have mobilized to advocate for their inclusion in educational opportunities, employment, and access to social participation. These collective mobilization efforts have changed social definitions and viewpoints toward these groups, which in turn have changed individual behavior (Mechanic, 1999).

THE SYSTEMS/ECOLOGICAL PERSPECTIVE ON MENTAL HEALTH ISSUES

The systems/ecological perspective suggests that mental health problems are the result of a variety of factors that interact in a complex fashion and vary according to the uniqueness of the individual and the environment within which he or she interacts. Research on brain chemistry elevates the importance of physiological factors

but also lends support to the systems/ecological perspective.

Although the environment cannot completely control whether a person develops an emotional disorder, it can exacerbate the problem or, in some instances, facilitate an individual's ability to cope more effectively. Within the systems/ecological framework, many factors that shape a person's self-concept, competence, and behaviors can be addressed. These factors include the person's biological characteristics; ethnicity; gender; place within the broader environment, including family, peer groups, and the neighborhood and community in which the person functions; and cultural and societal expectations.

In addressing mental health problems, the systems/ecological perspective allows us to consider all of the factors within an individual's past and present environment, as well as the individual's physiological characteristics. For example, a person may be predisposed biologically toward mental health problems, may have suffered from sexual abuse as a child, may have had a parent who had mental health problems, and currently may be in an extremely stressful living situation (for example, an unhappy marriage, a stressful job, or financial problems). If we know which factors are most important, we are more able to intervene successfully to alleviate the problems.

This emphasis on both the individual and the individual's environment allows the social worker and the client to "map out" the factors that are most likely to account for the problems and then to develop an intervention plan to specifically address those factors. How and when an individual's emotional problems are identified and defined depend on a number of factors (Mechanic, 1999, p. 114):

1. the visibility, recognizability, or persistence of inappropriate/deviant behaviors and symptoms;
2. the extent to which the person perceives the symptoms as serious;
3. the extent to which the symptoms disrupt family, work, and other activities;
4. the frequency of the appearance of the signs and symptoms, or their persistence;
5. the tolerance threshold of those who are exposed to and evaluate the signs and symptoms;
6. the information available to, the knowledge of, and the cultural assumptions and understandings of the evaluator;
7. the degree to which processes that distort reality are present;
8. the presence of needs within the family/environment that conflict with the recognition of problems or the assumption of the sick role;
9. the possibility that competing interpretations can be assigned to the behaviors/signs once they are recognized; and

10. the availability of treatment/intervention resources, their physical proximity and psychological and monetary costs of taking action, including money, time, and effort as well as costs of stigmatization and humiliation.

Types of Mental Health Problems

Although people with mental disorders are still stigmatized, increasing openness by many individuals with various diagnoses has resulted in more public awareness about them. The most common types of mental disorders are major depression, bipolar disorder, schizophrenia, anxiety disorders, attention deficit hyperactivity disorder, and autism. The following data are from the National Institute of Mental Health (2006c) unless indicated otherwise. Attention deficit hyperactivity disorder and autism are discussed later in the chapter.

Depression

Depression is the leading cause of disability worldwide, with many individuals incapacitated for weeks or months if untreated. Almost 10% of the U.S. population age 18 and older have a depressive disorder. Breakthroughs in effective medication have allowed many of them to lead typical lives. Still, people in general often do not realize how debilitating depression can be, and even make fun of those who cannot function without medication. Depression is more than having a few bad days or sad moments. It is an overwhelming feeling of incapacitation that, in the extreme, may result in a person not being able to get out of bed and go to work or school or function.

Nearly twice as many women (12%) as men (7%) are affected by depression each year, leading some researchers to suggest a relationship between hormonal imbalance and neurotransmitters in the brain. This argument is bolstered in that most women diagnosed with depression are of childbearing age. Many women—as many as 50% to 90%—develop depression after the birth of a child. This depression has been linked to the abrupt post-childbirth hormonal changes (National Alliance on Mental Illness, 2006b).

With improved clinical skills and increasing attention directed to mental health issues in children and adolescents, more young people also are being diagnosed with depression. Estimates by the National Institute of Mental Health (2003) indicate that 2.5% of children and 8.5% of adolescents have severe and persistent depression. Depressive disorders often occur concurrently with anxiety disorders and substance abuse. Approximately 80% of individuals with depression respond positively to treatment, which often combines medication, counseling, exercise, and diet (National Alliance on Mental Illness, 2006b).

Bipolar Disorder

According to the National Alliance on Mental Illness (2006b), about 2.3 million people in the United States have bipolar disorder, characterized as mood cycles alternating between depression and mania. Those with mild disorder have rapid swings between depression and anxiety, and sometimes panic disorder. Those with more serious bipolar disorder alternate between episodes of major depression and mania. In the manic condition, the individual has periods of abnormally and persistently elevated mood or irritability, often accompanied by overly inflated self-esteem, less need for sleep, talkativeness, racing thoughts, distractibility, increased goal-directed activity or physical agitation, and excessive involvement in pleasurable activities that have a high potential for painful consequences. A combination of medications and holistic approaches have been successful in treating many individuals with bipolar disorder.

Schizophrenia

More than 2 million adults in the United States are affected by schizophrenia—the most chronic and disabling of the mental disorders (National Alliance on Mental Illness, 2000b). Increasingly thought to be a chemical disorder, schizophrenia usually first appears in women in their 20s or early 30s and in men in their late teens or early 20s. It is manifested in impaired ability to manage emotions, interact with others, and think clearly. Symptoms include hallucinations, delusions, disordered thinking, and social withdrawal.

Although medication has helped many individuals with schizophrenia, this disease is particularly debilitating and often results in periodic hospitalizations. More than half of individuals with schizophrenia receive inadequate care. They may spend time in a mental hospital, where they are put on medication and then released. Without appropriate community mental health facilities and outreach, many of them run out of medication or have undesirable side-effects and stop taking their medication.

Anxiety Disorders

According to NIMH (2006c) statistics, more than 40 million adults in the United States suffer from anxiety disorders, which include panic disorder, obsessive-compulsive disorder, post-traumatic stress disorder (PTSD), phobias, and generalized anxiety disorder. Symptoms of each are as follows:

- *panic disorder:* feelings of extreme fear and anxiety that strike for no apparent reason, resulting in an overpowering shortness of breath, feelings of being out of control, and other intense physical symptoms.
- *obsessive-compulsive disorder:* repetitive, intrusive thoughts or behaviors, such as washing the hands excessively or checking to see whether lights are turned off when leaving a room.
- *post-traumatic stress disorder (PTSD):* a reaction to previously experienced terrifying

trauma that results in frightening memories or intense body reactions.

- *anxiety disorder:* excessive worry over everyday events and decisions.
- *phobia:* the fear of specific or generalized objects or events.

Women are more likely than men to have anxiety disorders, which often occur concurrently with depression, eating disorders, and substance abuse.

Anxiety disorders may occur because of a chemical imbalance in the brain, an emotional trauma, or a learned response to specific situations. Anxiety disorders are increasingly treatable with medication and therapy, and cognitive behavioral and desensitization therapies have been found to be especially effective in treating anxiety disorders.

Suicide

Suicide is a serious mental health problem in the United States, which has a higher suicide rate than many other Western countries. In 2004, 32,439 people committed suicide in the United States. In that year, suicide was the eleventh leading cause of death in the United States, but the third leading cause for young adults age 15–24 and the third leading cause for children ages 10–14 (American Association of Suicidology, 2006).

People with manic-depressive illness, schizophrenia, and other mental health disorders are much more likely than others to attempt suicide. Also, there is a strong relationship between substance abuse and suicide. Research by the National Institute of Mental Health (2006c) indicates that 90% of people who commit suicide have some type of diagnosable mental or substance-abuse disorder. Alterations in neurotransmitters such as serotonin are not only associated with depression, impulsive disorders, and substance abuse but also with suicide (National Institute of Mental Health, 2003).

Determining which groups are most at-risk to commit suicide is difficult, as risk factors associated with suicide vary by ethnicity, gender, and age and often occur in combination. The highest rate of suicide in the United States is found in white males over age 85. The suicide rate is highest for white males and lowest for black females. It is the eighth leading cause of death for Native Americans and Asians/Pacific Islanders. Men choose more lethal methods and are more than four times as likely as women to commit suicide, while women are two to three times more likely as men to attempt suicide (National Institute of Mental Health, 2005).

The suicide rate for children and adolescents has increased significantly in recent years. In general, attempts at suicide also are increasing. An estimated 811,000 persons in the United States attempted suicide in 2004, and more than 5 million living Americans have tried to kill themselves at some point in their lifetime (American Association of Suicidology, 2006). The greatest risk factors associated with suicide attempts for adults are depression, alcohol abuse, cocaine use, and separation or divorce. Risk factors for youth include depression, alcohol or other drug use, and aggressive or disruptive behaviors. Other risk factors include a prior suicide attempt, family history of mental or substance-abuse disorder or suicide, family violence, firearms in the home, incarceration, and exposure to the suicidal behavior of others, including family, peers, and the media in news or fiction stories (National Institute of Mental Health, 2006d).

People who attempt suicide are likely to have experienced one or more significant losses in their lives—the death of a close family member or friend, loss of a job, or failing health. They feel so helpless and hopeless that they do not see any options other than ending their pain. Other significant factors associated with persons who attempt suicide are loneliness and isolation, coupled with the lack of a stable support system.

Individuals at risk to attempt suicide also often abuse alcohol and other drugs as a means of reducing their emotional pain. Because alcohol and some other types of drugs are depressants, though, these substances tend to make a depressed person even more depressed, as well as impairing the person's ability to think rationally. Also contributing to suicide, particularly among elderly people, is poor health, especially when they see no hope of getting better and do not want to be an emotional or financial burden to anyone.

Signals that a person may have decided to commit suicide include a sudden change from a depressed state and a hopeless perspective to seeming to get better, and giving away possessions. Most suicide threats are not just attempts to get attention but are outcries for help. Therefore, suicide threats should be taken seriously. In such situations, individuals should not be left alone, and immediate mental health intervention should be sought. According to the American Association of Suicidology (2006), 52% of suicides are committed with firearms, and firearms are used to commit suicide far more often than to commit homicide.

Because the reasons for attempting suicide are so complex and variable, multiple prevention efforts are needed. Community- and school-based prevention programs, therefore, should be directed to reducing stress, instilling coping skills, preventing and reducing substance abuse, and working toward early identification and treatment of emotional problems, as well as limiting access to firearms.

Impacts of Mental Health Status on At-Risk Populations

A host of studies show that women, people of color, the elderly, the poor, individuals who are gay, lesbian, bisexual, or transgender, and individuals living in rural areas are more likely to have mental health problems. Members of marginalized groups who receive messages from the broader society that they are somehow "different" and do not have ready access to basic resources such as food, clothing, shelter, and employment are more at risk to have their mental health impacted by their circumstances than are those

in more positive circumstances. In addition, when members of marginalized groups begin to experience symptoms of mental health problems, they are much less likely to have access to needed services than are those in society who are not marginalized.

It has been estimated that nearly 5%, or 2.7 million U.S. children, have moderate or severe emotional or behavioral problems that are likely to interfere with their ability to learn and their relationships with families and peers. A report, *America's Children: Key National Indicators of Well-Being 2005* (National Institute of Mental Health, 2006a), discusses the short- and long-term implications for children's development and future if more attention is not paid to their needs when they are young.

SURVIVORS OF DISASTER AND TRAUMA

Other populations at-risk for mental health problems include survivors of disaster and trauma. Among these are individuals who experience or observe trauma, such as rape, serious injury or death of another person, combat, or a natural disaster such as a hurricane or earthquake. Although strong reactions to trauma are expected, some individuals have long-term impacts and are diagnosed with post-traumatic stress disorder. This condition is characterized by signs of intense fear, nightmares and flashbacks to the event; problems with sleeping, concentrating, eating, and focusing on common tasks; increased use of alcohol and other drugs; and physiological symptoms.

Those who work with individuals who have experienced trauma—emergency-room personnel, rescue squad workers, police officers, firefighters, and emergency medical service personnel—also can experience PTSD (U.S. Department of Veterans Affairs National Center for PTSD, 2006). Reports from many soldiers who had been in Vietnam, their families, and those who provided care for them observed serious mental health issues upon their return, but not until much later did the U.S. Departments of Defense and Veterans Affairs acknowledge and give serious attention to their concerns. An estimated 30% of those who have spent time in war zones experience PTSD, and the illness creates problems for the soldiers, and for their families, upon their return (American Psychological Association, 2006). Statistics reported by the Pentagon are similar for troops returning from the Iraq war (MentalhealthAmerica, 2006).

The Department of Veterans Affairs hosts a National Center for Post-Traumatic Stress Disorder (see www.ncpsd.va.gov/), which provides information and training for military personnel and their families, and also for those who work with survivors of natural disasters such as Hurricanes Katrina and Rita. Reports after these two devastating hurricanes indicate that many survivors have PTSD, and that suicide rates also are higher than national averages for this group. Many social workers are trained to deal specifically with PTSD and are members of emergency-response teams that work with survivors after traumatic experiences. Despite increased attention to PTSD, there are still major gaps in awareness of the problem, acknowledgement of its extent and impact, and availability of services among both providers and consumers.

HOMELESS PERSONS

Homelessness was discussed in chapter 7, but we note here the relationship between homelessness and mental health and substance-abuse problems. The release of individuals with mental illness, developmental disabilities, and chemical dependency from institutional care and the lack of community services have resulted in a significant risk of their becoming mentally ill or chemically dependent. According to the National Resource and Training Center on Homelessness and Mental Illness (2006), approximately 40% of the homeless report some type of mental health problem and 20%–25% meet the criteria for serious mental illnesses. Almost 40% report problems with alcohol use, and 26% report problems with other drug use.

The characteristics of mental illness make it difficult for homeless persons to negotiate street

life and meet basic needs for food, safety, and shelter. They also are at greater risk for developing serious health problems such as tuberculosis, HIV, and severe upper respiratory infections. Because they lack a permanent address and often are unaware of or unable to apply for benefits, many do not receive funds and services for which they might be eligible (National Resource and Training Center on Homelessness and Mental Illness, 2006). Other homeless people develop mental health problems *after* becoming homeless, as a result of the stress of survival and the associated stigma. Their problems often are serious enough to require hospitalization.

Many homeless mentally ill have serious cognitive disturbances, like Lindsey (at the beginning of this chapter) and are out of touch with reality, unaware of where they are going or where they have been. Their most frequent contacts with community resources are with the police and emergency psychiatric facilities. Typically, they remain on the streets, extremely vulnerable, until they are unable to function and are rehospitalized. For many, their lives become a pattern of homelessness and hospitalization (Liebow, 1993).

Alcoholism and Substance Abuse

In addition to the relationship between alcohol/ chemical dependency and mental illness, problems of alcoholism and substance abuse can be related to developmental disabilities, child and family issues, poverty, criminal justice, and the workplace. And vulnerable populations, including women, the elderly, people of color, and gays and lesbians, are at higher risk than other groups for serious problems with alcoholism and chemical dependency.

Until recently, alcohol abuse and alcoholism were considered to be moral issues. The general societal perception was that people drank too much because they were weak and they could stop drinking if they wanted to. Although many people still hold this view, attention began to be directed during the 1940s and 1950s to the concept that alcoholism is a disease and must be treated as a person with diabetes or another chronic illness is treated. The prevalent contemporary view considers alcoholism as a chronic condition (is treatable but incurable), progressive (becomes worse if the drinking does not stop), and fatal (can result in death if untreated).

Although the debate continues on whether alcoholism should be considered as an individual disease, a family or societal disease, or an individual, family, or societal problem, the disease model of alcoholism offers the advantages that

1. individuals and their families are more likely to accept the alcoholism and become involved in an intervention program if they view the alcoholism as a disease rather than as a moral weakness or a social problem.
2. conceptualizing alcoholism as a disease allows for insurance coverage for treatment and hospitalization and coverage for public health-care programs.

The laws in many states also allow the serious abuse of other drugs to be treated as a disease, but because use of drugs other than alcohol more often involves illegal and/or counterculture activities, there has been much more reluctance to consider as a disease the abuse of drugs other than alcohol.

Many substance abusers and their families deny that alcoholism and the abuse of other drugs is a problem that affects them. To absolve themselves, they define a substance abuser in many ways—as someone who takes one more drink or drug than they or their family member takes; as someone who drinks excessive amounts of only hard liquor and not beer or wine as they do; as someone who uses more dangerous drugs and not marijuana, which they use; or as someone who drinks and uses the substance every morning or every day, not just evenings or weekends as they do.

Contemporary definitions of alcoholism emphasize the personal implications of the drinking or drug use rather than the amount or frequency. The National Institute on Alcohol Abuse and Alcoholism (2006b) has defined **alcoholism** as a disease with four symptoms:

1. craving, or a strong need or urge to drink;
2. loss of control, or not being able to stop once drinking has begun;
3. physical dependence, or withdrawal symptoms that occur when one has stopped drinking, such as nausea, sweating, shakiness, and anxiety; and
4. tolerance, or the need to drink greater amounts of alcohol to get "high."

Alcoholism also has been defined as any use of alcohol that results or interferes with personal life—including school, jobs, family, friends, health, or the law—or spiritual life (Royce & Scratchley, 1996).

Definitions of **substance abuse** are similar. Although the abuse of alcohol is considered more socially acceptable than the abuse of other drugs, it is increasingly difficult to separate the two. Alcohol is still the most widely misused drug, and it has serious individual and societal costs, but the majority of individuals under age 40 abuse more than one substance (National Institute on Drug Abuse, 2003).

Research on addiction reveals further that many individuals treated for one type of substance abuse stop using that substance and "cross-addict" to another drug. Thus, some professionals in the field refer to the substance a person has abused as his or her "drug of choice" and those who abuse more than one drug as "polyaddicts." Other professionals view substance abuse and chemical dependency as a problem of **addiction,** which can be defined as physical and/or psychological dependence on mood-altering substances or experiences including, but not limited to, alcohol, drugs, pills, food, sex, pornography, gambling, shopping/spending, or exercise. This conceptualization supports an intervention focus on eliminating addictive behaviors in all areas of a person's life, including food, work, and relationships, as well as drugs.

Commonly Abused Substances

Alcohol, the oldest and most commonly abused substance in the world, is most often viewed as a depressant, although it also can be a stimulant and, for some individuals, a hallucinogen. According to the Substance Abuse and Mental Health Services Administration (2006a), nearly half of people over age 12 in the United States use alcohol, and about 23% report being binge drinkers. Of the 16 million persons in the United States who are considered alcoholics or problem drinkers, an estimated 4.2 million are adolescents. In a household survey on drug abuse that SAMSA conducted in 2005, 4.2% of 12–13-year-olds, 15.1% of 14–15-year-olds, 30.1% of 16–17-year-olds, and 51.1% of 18–20-year-olds reported

Alcoholism and other types of substance abuse often lead to other problems such as domestic violence and child abuse.

Ingram Publishing/Getty Images

being current users of alcohol. About 10% of youths reported binge drinking. The leading cause of death for U.S. teens ages 15 to 24 is alcohol-related auto accidents. Medical problems stemming from alcohol abuse include neurological, cardiological, and respiratory problems; liver disease; damage to the gastrointestinal system, pancreas, and kidneys; malnutrition; suppression of the immune system; and psychological problems.

In addition to alcohol, **depressants** include sedatives, such as sleeping pills, tranquilizers, and pain killers. Two groups more at risk to abuse depressants than other groups are women and those who have experienced or are experiencing chronic pain. **Narcotics** such as opium and its derivatives, morphine and heroin, are also highly addictive. Legally, cocaine is considered a narcotic, but it often acts more like a stimulant, creating a high in its users.

Recreational use of cocaine declined in the late 1980s and early 1990s, but its use has increased since the mid-1990s, particularly by adolescents. According to the National Institute on Drug Abuse (2003), just over 11% of individuals age 12 and older reported using cocaine at least once, and .5% indicated that they were current users. In another study, only 2.4% of youth ages 12–17 reported using cocaine at least once, and .6% reported being current users.

Cocaine is the most powerful central nervous system stimulant known. The use of crack—the smokable, rapidly reacting form of cocaine—has become extremely popular in recent years because of its lower cost, easy availability, and highly addictive nature. Use of crack and cocaine often results in high rates of addiction and also can produce delusional and paranoid behavior, acute toxic psychosis, cardiovascular problems including strokes and heart attacks, depression, neurological problems, lung problems including respiratory failure, increased injury from accidents, aggressive and violent behavior, and risks of hepatitis, HIV infection, and endocarditis (heart inflammation) (Phoenix House, 2006). Crack use also has been associated

with increases in crime, overdoses, prostitution, AIDS, and homelessness. Publicity also has been drawn to "crack babies," who are born addicted and at risk to die during the their first year or to survive with serious physical and emotional problems.

Heroin, which in the past was more likely to be used by people living in poverty in inner-city areas, more recently has become a drug of choice by middle-class youth and currently is the most commonly abused of all narcotics. A morphine derivative, heroin use affects the autonomic nervous system and often causes euphoria, which results in dangerous and often violent behaviors, life-threatening cardiorespiratory problems, hepatitis, AIDS and other infections, and addiction. Most habitual users are incapable of clear thought, holding a job, or maintaining relationships (Phoenix House, 2006).

Stimulants are drugs that stimulate the central nervous system, creating a sense of heightened euphoria. Common stimulants include caffeine, amphetamines such as speed, ecstasy, and Ritalin, an often-abused legal drug prescribed to individuals with attention deficit disorder. Amphetamines are highly addictive, particularly because users often plunge into extreme depression when they are coming down from the euphoric high as the drug begins to wear off.

Use of the stimulant methamphetamine—commonly called "meth"—is increasing at an alarming rate. This highly addictive drug produces a strong reaction even when taken in small doses, and it has serious side-effects. Use of meth increases the risks of contracting HIV/AIDS and hepatitis because of impaired decision making when on the drug. Methamphetamines are especially dangerous to children born to pregnant women who use the drug. Prolonged high-dose use leads to psychotic behavior, delusions, paranoid episodes, seizures, and permanent brain damage. Methamphetamine use has had significant impacts in many areas of the United States, including rural areas, where meth labs are more easily located to avoid arrest. Entire families can become addicted to methamphetamines, resulting in loss of jobs (and thus family income), child abuse and neglect, domestic violence, and criminal behavior. In efforts to reduce manufacturing of methamphetamine, many businesses are restricting the purchase of common cold medications, which contain a key ingredient in meth, and possession of common laboratory equipment outside of a lab is now a felony.

Illicit drugs also include the **hallucinogens** such as LSD as well as marijuana, the most commonly used. One group of substances that is abused and often overlooked consists of **inhalants.** Use of inhalants is especially prevalent among Latino youth and often results in retardation or death. The wide variety of inhalants includes, among others, petroleum products such as gasoline, freon, aerosol products, paint, and glue. Amyl nitrate and butyl nitrate, commonly called "poppers," are also inhalants. Use of inhalants can result in irresponsible, dangerous behavior; permanent brain damage; cardiorespiratory problems; and sudden death (Phoenix House, 2006).

A drug that has received recent attention is rohypnol, commonly called the "date rape" drug. Prescribed as a sleeping pill outside of the United States, rohypnol is a sedative hypnotic drug that is 10 times more potent than valium. When rohypnol is dissolved in a drink, it is undetectable. Teens often use it in combination with alcohol or other drugs to create a dramatic high, or to incapacitate a victim of intended rape. Rophynol induces blackouts and memory loss, but it is addictive and also can result in death, especially when combined with other drugs.

Marijuana is by far the world's most commonly used illegal drug. Almost 35% of individuals age 12 and older, 18% of individuals ages 12–17, and 46% of individuals ages 18–25 report using marijuana at least once (Substance Abuse and Mental Health Services Administration, 2006a). The largest group of current users is 18–25, in which 13.6% report that they are current users. About 7% of youth ages 12–17 report being current users. Although, like alcohol, many do not consider marijuana use to be dangerous, the effects last for several days after its use. The drug inhibits the ability to learn and retain information and also produces respiratory and hormonal problems. Further, impairment of judgment and perception results in more accidents and violence and casual sex, linked to sexually transmitted diseases and pregnancy.

In addition to its addictive nature, marijuana is considered to be a "gateway drug." In one report, teens who used marijuana were 85 times more likely to use cocaine than those who did not use the drug, and of those who used marijuana before they turned 15, 60% went on to use cocaine later (Phoenix House, 2006).

Social and Economic Costs of Substance Abuse

Substance abuse is said to be the most serious public health problem in the United States, resulting in more deaths and disabilities each year than any other cause. Highly correlated with substance abuse are child abuse and neglect, domestic violence, homicide and other violent crimes, and serious traffic accidents. Most of the media attention highlights the use of drugs other than alcohol—cocaine/crack, heroin, and methamphetamine. Yet, alcohol remains the drug of choice for most substance abusers in the United States. Estimates are that 17.6 million alcoholics reside in the United States, and that more than 50 million Americans are affected directly by alcohol abuse by a family member (National Institute on Alcohol and Alcoholism, 2006b).

The typical image of an alcoholic is an older male, unkempt, unemployed, and living on the streets. In reality, only 3% of alcoholics can be characterized this way. About 45% of alcoholics hold professional or managerial positions, 25% are white-collar workers, and 30% are manual laborers. Physicians, air traffic controllers, airline pilots, law-enforcement officers, attorneys, and members of the clergy—all have high rates of alcoholism (Royce & Scratchley, 1996).

Children who grow up in families where substance abuse is a problem are at risk for becoming substance abusers. Studies have found that 25% of males and 10% of females who grow up in families in which their parents abuse either alcohol or other drugs become substance abusers themselves. Even those who do not develop substance-abuse problems themselves often develop other addictive behaviors or emotional problems. Fewer women than men repeat the pattern of substance abuse, but they are much more likely to select a mate who is a substance abuser.

According to the Substance Abuse and Mental Health Services Administration (2006a), substance-abusing parents are almost three times more likely than parents who are not substance abusers to abuse their children, and more than four times as likely to neglect them; three-fourths of survivors of domestic violence by a spouse report that the perpetrator had been drinking, and alcohol was a major contributing factor in 32% of all homicide cases, 31% of all deaths from unintentional injury, 23% of all suicides, and 32% of all fatal accidents involving an intoxicated driver or pedestrian. Alcohol is also reported to be a factor in the majority of sexual assaults.

As substance abuse becomes more widespread, the implications are becoming more obvious, more costly, and of greater concern. Costs go beyond intervention for the substance abuser to also include lost productivity, motor-vehicle losses from accidents, and property losses from violent crimes. And cost estimates typically do not include personal costs such as physical and emotional injury and loss of life. The most recent comprehensive estimates of drug-abuse-related costs in the United States were developed in 1992, but using extrapolation techniques, the economic costs of alcoholism and alcohol abuse in the United States in 2004 were estimated to be $345.5 billion (National Institute on Alcohol Abuse and Alcoholism, 2006a).

At-Risk Populations and Substance Abuse

Even though substance abuse can affect anyone, some groups of people are more at risk than others. These groups include adolescents, the elderly, people of color, women, and children.

ADOLESCENTS

The increasing use of alcohol and other drugs by adolescents is cause for concern. Studies by the National Institute on Alcohol Abuse and Alcoholism (2006a) show that approximately 12% of eighth graders, 22% of tenth graders, and 28% of high school seniors were engaged in heavy episodic drinking, with about 60% of seniors, 40% of tenth graders, and 20% of eighth graders reporting that they have been drunk. Other NIAA (2006a) surveys show that approximately 10% of 9–10 year-olds had started drinking already, and nearly a third of youth before age 13. Alcohol consumption in childhood or early adolescence is a strong predictor of later problems, including substance abuse.

While the death rate for other age groups has declined, the death rate for adolescents has increased significantly in recent years. Most of these deaths are attributed to traffic accidents and suicides in which alcohol or other drug abuse was a factor. Use of alcohol and other drugs by adolescents often is viewed as a way to be an adult—a "rite of passage" from childhood to adulthood—and is part of the risk-taking behavior common among adolescents.

Many adolescents believe that using drugs is not harmful (National Institute on Drug Abuse, 2003). And heavy substance abuse and addiction among adolescents are more often found among those who are faced with other problems, such as survivors of childhood sexual abuse, gay and lesbian teens subjected to discrimination and oppression, and individuals with depression. These adolescents turn to drinking and drugging to deaden their pain, as a form of self-medication so they will feel better, or as a way to relate to peers more comfortably.

THE ELDERLY

Substance abuse, particularly alcoholism, is a problem in the elderly population. This age group, like adolescents and young adults, has a high death rate from alcoholism. Among the elderly, primary contributors to death are chronic alcohol-related diseases such as cirrhosis of the liver, digestive diseases, and hepatitis. Factors associated with substance abuse by this group include loneliness and isolation, in which older adults use substances as a coping mechanism to deaden the emotional or physical pain, present or past.

PEOPLE OF COLOR

Some ethnic groups are more at risk to abuse alcohol and drugs and to experience serious problems because of the abuse. African Americans, for example, are three times more likely to die as a result of alcoholism than are whites, even though their actual rates of alcohol use are less than for whites, because of the interactive effects of oppression on access to healthy food and health care (Jones-Webb, 1998). The situation is similar for Latinos. Some Native American tribes contribute to this ethnic group having the highest incidence of alcoholism of any ethnic group in the United States. Overall, this group has high rates of alcohol-related homicide, suicide, and serious car accidents. An estimated half of Native American children are born with either fetal alcohol syndrome or fetal alcohol effect—medical conditions at birth usually resulting in serious developmental disabilities—caused by the mother's consumption of alcohol during pregnancy.

Members of marginalized groups outside the mainstream of society also are more at risk to abuse substances because they are more likely to be unemployed and living in poverty. Many of them turn to alcohol and other drugs as coping mechanisms to overcome feelings of despair and hopelessness and the added burden of discrimination. In addition, in some communities drug pushers easily tempt children, often from impoverished families, to become drug runners so they can make a lot of money quickly. Still too young to realize the consequences of using drugs, they begin experimenting with the drugs they are delivering and become addicted themselves. The heightened risk of some ethnic groups for suffering the personal, emotional, and economic consequences of substance abuse raises a number of issues, as non-members of these groups are most often those who oversee large-scale production and sale of drugs and reap the economic profits.

To be effective, interventions for people of color must be culturally relevant and sensitive. For example, participation in Alcoholics Anonymous groups may be highly effective for some, but if group membership consists largely of whites, people of color may not feel comfortable participating. In addition, some cultures are reluctant to divulge any personal information outside of their families. Many Asians, for example, have been socialized to believe that their personal problems, such as substance abuse, bring shame to their families and should not be discussed with people outside the family. From a macro perspective, opportunity and access to economic success are important ways to reduce substance abuse.

WOMEN

The National Institute on Alcohol Abuse and Alcoholism (2006a) estimates that one-third of all alcoholics in the United States are women, and that 6 million women are addicted to substances other than alcohol; the largest increases are among younger women. Women who abuse substances have different issues than men do. They are more likely than male drug abusers to abuse legal drugs such as tranquilizers and sedatives. Also, they are more likely to become addicted to multiple drugs and to use drugs in isolation rather than in combination with other drugs. They also are more likely to be in a family in which another member is a substance abuser, and to have experienced rape, incest, or other sexual assault.

According to the Institute on Women and Substance Abuse (2000), women are much less likely than men to seek treatment, even though they develop more health problems related to their substance abuse and their lives often are more disrupted. Female substance abusers, too, are subjected to greater stigma than males. Many women receive opposition from friends and family when they enter substance-abuse treatment programs (Institute on Women and Substance Abuse, 2003).

Women also are less likely than men to have support from family members during treatment. In families in which alcoholism is a problem for male spouses, women remain in the relationship in 90% of situations; in families in which alcoholism is a problem for female spouses, however, men remain in the relationship only 10% of the time (Royce & Scratchley, 1996). Substance abuse has been accompanied by increases in AIDS, prostitution, and homelessness among women.

Few substance-abuse intervention programs have been designed specifically for women, who face different issues than men. Women are more likely to experience depression and to abuse substances as a way to cope with it. They, too, are more likely to have been sexually abused, and repressed memories of sexual abuse sometimes surface after they have been sober for a period of time. Recovery programs for women must include recognition of clients' strengths, encouragement to set healthy boundaries and establish positive and healthy relationships, with a focus on increasing self-esteem. As they recover from substance abuse, women often need assistance with child care, transportation, support in parenting, housing, education, and employment (Institute on Women and Substance Abuse, 2003).

CHILDREN

Alcoholism and chemical dependency have serious effects on children (see chapters 10 and 11). The number of abused and neglected children in the United States has more than doubled over the past decade as a result of substance abuse, and increased use of methamphetamine has escalated these numbers in some areas of the United States. In one survey, 85% of states reported that substance abuse was one of the two major problems in families in which child abuse or neglect was suspected (Child Welfare Information Gateway, 2003).

More attention is being directed to infants born addicted or impaired because of their mothers' addiction or misuse of alcohol or other drugs during pregnancy. Fetal alcohol syndrome (FA), one of the three leading causes of mental retardation and birth defects, is the most serious of fetal alcohol spectrum disorders (FASD), prenatal alcohol-related conditions experienced by infants born to mothers who drank alcohol during pregnancy (Centers for Disease Control and Prevention, 2006). Child welfare advocates suggest that the United States has not yet begun to see the long-term effects of so many children being born to women who are drug addicts.

OTHER FACTORS ASSOCIATED WITH SUBSTANCE ABUSE

Research suggests that genetic/hereditary factors may be associated with substance abuse. Some researchers believe that substances are metabolized or broken down differently for certain individuals, resulting in an inability of the body to eliminate some chemicals, which then build up in the body and also serve as stimulants for even greater use when the addictive substance is used again. Studies linking differences in serotonin levels in the brain to both substance abuse and depression support the idea that some individuals may "self-medicate" with alcohol or other drugs to try to deal with the chemical imbalance impacted by the serotonin.

Other researchers suggest that for some individuals, substance abuse is a form of self-medication to attempt to regulate their emotions or dampen their emotional pain (see Box 8.2).

BOX 8.2
A Young Adult's Story

Three years of drinking pushed a seemingly out-going, good student to the depths of depression and despair. This is her story:

I began ninth grade excited about starting high school. I was like most other teenagers—I wanted to make good grades and be accepted by my teachers and peers. The peers I sought out were popular—cheerleaders, and on the student council—and they seemed to know everyone. I liked being included in their parties and other activities.

My mom asked me questions about my friends and the rules their parents had for them, but she usually let me go with them if I was waiting for her when she picked me up. At games and the other teen hangouts there was lots of drinking, and it looked like people drinking were having a good time.

One night I stayed over at a friend's house and we went to a party. When I was offered a beer, I drank it. When the alcohol hit my body, I found I wanted more. That night I drank seven beers. I was 14 years old.

After that, I drank almost every weekend. I drank to be accepted, escape day-to-day pressures of my home and school life, and forget the pain from some experiences I had while growing up. When I drank, I usually laughed and clowned around a lot. People told me how much fun I was and what a great sense of humor I had. I felt relaxed and accepted when I drank.

I continued to drink on weekends, and my activities with my friends usually centered on sneaking beer or other alcohol from our parents' pantries or having older friends buy it for us. We drank it at games, parties, or at each others' houses after the parents were asleep. Soon we went to the mall to meet older guys. We had no

sense of risk. Our parents dropped us off at the mall, then we hopped in some guy's car to go to a party where everyone was drunk. Then we were dropped back at the mall in time for our parents to pick us up. We sprayed ourselves with perfume, chewed gum, and somehow managed to hide our drinking from our parents most of the time.

I often felt guilty about my drinking and worried about what my parents would do if they found out, but I also enjoyed it. I felt grown up, and my friends enjoyed telling me how hilarious I had been with all of my antics. Boys paid a lot of attention to me, and I discovered that it was much easier to relate to them when I had been drinking.

I became more popular and was elected to the student council. I rationalized that drinking even helped my grades, since the few times I decided that I was drinking too much and stopped for a week or two, I became depressed and my grades went down. I became more involved in school activities, got a part-time job at the mall, and partied even more. When my parents confronted me with their suspicions about my drinking, I either managed to convince them that everyone else was drinking except me or to tell them that I had a little bit now and then, but didn't every teenager?

During my junior year I made the dance team. I thought all my feelings of insecurity and my drive to fit in would be over and that I could slow my drinking. To my surprise, being on the dance team meant even more pressure. I had to maintain my popularity, be more involved in school activities, and work even harder to be sure that I wasn't surpassed by the many girls who I thought were almost all smarter, prettier, and had more personality than I did. Soon I was drinking in the locker room in the morning

Continued

BOX 8.2—*Continued*
A Young Adult's Story

before dance practice "just to wake me up and help me stretch better," in the parking lot or the bathroom after lunch "just to make it through the afternoon," or at my job "just to make it until closing," and always on the weekends.

I still could hide my drinking from teachers and my parents. I sat in the back of the classroom, answered questions, and did my homework and handed it in on time. I always gave my parents a plausible explanation what I would be doing when I went out and I was lucky enough to be where I said I would be when they checked up on me. When I didn't drink a lot, I came home at or before my curfew. When I did drink a lot, I stayed overnight at friends' homes. I began blacking out at parties and waking up at a friend's house and not remembering how I got there. I rode with drivers who were drunk and I would drive when I was drunk too. I also began to get involved with a lot of guys who I never would have gotten involved with if I had been sober. I got really scared about getting pregnant, since I knew someone could take advantage of me during my blackouts.

At that point, my drinking wasn't fun anymore, but I couldn't stop. In fact, I began drinking more and more. It was nothing for me to drink 16 or 17 cans of beer all by myself in one night. All of my friends could still drink and

enjoy it, but it started getting me in trouble. My grades went down and I started skipping school. I became edgy and worried about everything. I started having fights with my friends and my family over little things. The drinking was controlling me. The more I drank, the worse I felt, and the worse I felt, the more I needed to drink to ease my pain. What had started out to be fun was now completely out of my control.

During the summer my parents suspected something was really wrong. I started seeing a psychologist, and both she and my parents tried to convince me that my drinking was a problem and that I was using it to escape the pain I had about some of the things that had happened in my life. I got angry at them and refused to see the psychologist. I began to rebel more and more. One night a party I was at turned into a brawl. I got knocked out when I tried to break up a fight. I left with a friend and a guy I barely knew. I woke up the next morning in the guy's apartment and couldn't remember what had happened. Driving home, I was still so drunk that I had to stop and get out of the car to read the street signs, and I was only a half mile from home. I told my parents we'd stayed up all night talking at my girlfriend's house and I slept the whole next day.

Gradually I stopped caring what everyone thought of me and trying to hide my drinking

---

These include, among others, individuals who have been sexually abused, have had a significant personal loss or series of losses, or are depressed. Other substance-abuse experts suggest that people use drugs for excitement, to fit in with peers, to alleviate pressure, or to improve their performance along one or more dimensions. Still other experts propose that it is behavior learned from family members.

Developmental Disabilities

Developmental disability, as the term suggests, refers to problems, such as mental retardation and cerebral palsy, that become apparent before adulthood. In the past these persons were termed "mentally retarded" or "handicapped." Now the preferred terminology emphasizes the from my parents. Finally one weekend I stayed out all night when I had a midnight curfew. When I came home and got grounded, I ran away and stayed with a friend for three days, mostly drinking. When my friend went to work, I got a six-pack of beer and drank it alone. When I came home, my parents grounded me for a month and took away my car. They told me I had to see the psychologist. I was going to leave home for good, but I knew that I had reached a dead end and that my life was out of control. I didn't care about myself, my parents, or anything any more. Life had no purpose.

When I was confronted with my drinking again, I decided to enter a treatment program. I was tired of fighting, and at that time I thought that anything, even treatment, would be better than living at home and being nagged about my behavior. I now realize that entering treatment was the most important risk I have ever taken. The six weeks that I spent there were some of the hardest days of my life, but they were also some of the best. I was able to get rid of some of the pain, hurt, and anger that I had stored up for so many years. I learned new ways to communicate, share my feelings, and how to have fun while I was sober instead of drunk. I realized not only had I hurt myself, but also my family and other people who cared about me. My whole family took part in my treatment, and we all grew together. They began going to Alanon while I went to Alcoholics Anonymous.

After I got out of treatment, I continued to attend AA regularly. I had found a place where I fit in. AA members understood how I felt and where I was coming from. Each day got better for me. I became more content and gained self-confidence. I also found the peace I had never had before. I got in touch with myself and met many wonderful people in the process. Today I'm a recovering alcoholic and have now been sober for two years.

Finding sobriety at 17 has meant a whole new world for me. I have fallen in love with a wonderful person who understands my need for sobriety, and we are building our life together. My family and I enjoy being together. I am a college sophomore and plan to attend graduate school and work with children. I have goals and a sense of purpose I didn't have before. Although life is still difficult, I have learned to take things as they come, one day at a time. I am grateful that I had the courage to change myself.

Source: Journal entry by an anonymous student, University of Texas at Austin.

person, not the disability—for example, "individuals with developmental disabilities." Because individuals with disabilities may have preferences about which term to use for their specific condition, it is best to ask them how they would like to be addressed. Box 8.3 gives a first-hand account of disability.

In 1984, Congress passed the Developmental Disabilities Assistance and Bill of Rights Act (PL 98-527), which defined developmental disability as follows:

A severe, chronic disability of a person 5 years of age or older which

(a) is attributable to a mental or physical impairment or combination of mental and physical impairments;

(b) is manifested before the person attains age 22;

BOX 8.3
The Me in the Mirror

Do you know what people with disabilities want? Nothing special, nothing unusual. We want to be able to attend our neighborhood school, to use the public library, to go to the movies, to get on a bus to go shopping downtown or to visit friends and family across town or across the country. We want to be able to get into our neighborhood polling place to vote with everyone else on election day. We want to be able to get married.

We want to be able to work. We want to be able to provide for our children. We want high quality, affordable medical care.*

We want to be seen as real people, as part of society, not someone to be hidden away, or pitied, or given charity. We reject media portrayals that show us as evil, or pitiful, or super-cripples. We just want to be seen as what we are—regular people.

There are 49 million of us. Our disabilities vary. We cut across all designations of race, religion, politics, income, sexual orientation—you name it—whatever labels we use to describe and divide people, some people in each of those groups are disabled. I have read that most people will at some point in their lives experience a temporary or permanent disability and that virtually all families will be touched by the disability of one or more of its members. This makes me ask, what could be more *normal* than disability?

———————————————

*Do you have time for another horror story? This highlights the kind of attitude that leads to discrimination. My family doctor recommended that I see a gynecologist and gave me a doctor's name. I called to check accessibility and the receptionist told me that I probably could get in okay with the wheelchair but she really didn't think it was a good idea for me in a wheelchair to sit in a waiting room full of pregnant women. What did she think? That they'd look at me and give birth to monsters?

Source: "The Me in the Mirror" by Connie Panzzarino, in *The Disability Rights Activist: Why Disability Rights?* at http://www.disrights.org/dr-whydr.html. April 10, 1996. Reprinted with permission of Adrienne Rubin Barhydt.

(c) is likely to continue indefinitely;

(d) results in substantial functional limitations in three or more of the following areas of major life activity: (i) self-care, (ii) receptive and expressive language, (iii) learning, (iv) mobility, (v) self-direction, (vi) capacity, for independent living, and (vii) economic self-sufficiency; and

(e) reflects the person's need for a combination and sequence of special, interdisciplinary, or generic services, supports, or other assistance that is of lifelong or extended duration and is individually planned and coordinated, except that such term, when applied to infants and young children means individuals from birth to age 5, inclusive, who have substantial developmental delay or specific congenital or acquired conditions with a high probability of resulting in developmental disabilities if services are not provided. (PL 98-527, Title V, 1984)

This definition was expanded in the **Americans with Disabilities Act (ADA),** passed in 1990, to include persons with AIDS, substance abusers, and individuals with mental disorders.

More than three-fourths of those classified as having a developmental disability have a mental impairment. Others may be so classified as having cerebral palsy; epilepsy; autism; spina bifida; or speech, hearing, vision, or orthopedic disabilities. Still others have learning disabilities such as dyslexia (a reading disability in which symbols are perceived differently than they are) or attention deficit disorder (an inability to pay attention for a reasonable amount of time (which may also include hyperactivity), so as to impede learning).

Of individuals classified as having a mental disability according to the DSM-IV, about 80% are considered "mild," with an IQ between 50 or 55 and 70, and can be educated to function fairly independently or with some supervision. About 10% are in the "moderate" classification, with IQs generally between 35 and 50; persons with this classification usually progress to about a second-grade level academically but can take care of themselves as adults with supervision and perform unskilled or semi-skilled work. Only 3%–4% of persons classified as having mental retardation have "profound" disabilities that necessitate constant care and supervision (Encyclopedia of Childhood and Adolescence, 1997).

Attention is turning to early identification of children with developmental delays, to try to prevent more serious disabilities in later life. **Developmental delay** is defined as the slowed or impaired development of a child under 5 years of age who is at risk for having a developmental disability because of one or more of the following (Developmental Disabilities Center, 2000, p. 1):

- chromosomal conditions associated with intellectual disability;
- congenital syndromes and conditions associated with delay in development;
- metabolic disorders;
- prenatal and perinatal infections and significant medical problems;
- low-birth-weight infants weighing less than 1200 grams;
- postnatal acquired problems known to result in significant developmental delays;

- a child younger than 5 years old who is delayed in development in one or more of the following areas: communication, self-help, social-emotional, motor skills, sensory development or cognition;
- a child less than 3 years old who lives with one or both parents who have a developmental disability.

Factors Associated with Developmental Disabilities

The types of disabilities vary as much as the factors associated with them, and researchers still are uncertain why some types of disabilities occur. Among the factors associated with developmental disabilities, based on current knowledge and research, are the following (ARC, 2007):

- *Hereditary and fetal development factors:* Metabolic disorders, brain malfunctions, or chromosomal abnormalities can result in disabilities such as Tay-Sachs disease and Down syndrome. Fragile X syndrome, a genetic disorder, is the leading cause of mental retardation.
- *Prenatal factors:* Chemical and alcohol addiction, radiation, infections such as rubella (a form of measles), syphilis, and HIV, or exposure to environmental contaminants during pregnancy can result in disabilities, as can fetal malnutrition if mothers do not receive adequate prenatal care. Smoking also increases the risk of developmental delays, including mental retardation.
- *Perinatal factors:* Premature birth, trauma at birth, and infections transmitted during birth, such as herpes, can result in developmental disabilities.
- *Postnatal factors:* Infections after birth, such as meningitis, trauma from accidents or child abuse, lack of oxygen during illness or an accident, and nutritional deficiencies can result in developmental disabilities.

Environmental factors, such as lead poisoning, parents with severe emotional problems, or parental deprivation, are additional environmental factors that can precipitate developmental disabilities. Children who do not receive proper nurturing, especially during their early years, often show developmental delay, and if intervention does not come soon enough, mental retardation, learning disabilities, or other problems can result and may be permanent.

Specific causes of developmental disabilities often cannot be identified. Many parents who have children with these problems spend a great deal of time—sometimes their entire lives—blaming themselves for their children's disabilities. Research has enabled the early identification of many types of disabilities, such as phenylketonuria (PKU), which causes retardation. A simple test at birth can allow for immediate treatment, and this has virtually eliminated the condition in most Western countries.

Changing Views Toward Mental Health Problems, Substance Abuse and Developmental Disabilities

Interventions for individuals with mental health and substance-abuse problems and developmental disabilities have undergone considerable change. Historically, the fate of substance abusers and individuals with mental illness or other disability depended on their families. In most cases they remained at home. In some cases they were treated humanely, but many people with mental illness and retardation were chained in attics and cellars, and sometimes they were killed. When no family members could provide for them, they often were transported to the next town and abandoned.

Later, almshouses were established (see chapter 1). Individuals with mental illness or developmental disabilities sometimes were jailed if they were deemed too dangerous for the almshouse. Alcoholics also were jailed, and their remaining family members, unable to care for themselves, were sent to almshouses.

The Pennsylvania colony's hospital, established in 1751 for the sick poor and "the reception and care of lunatics" was the first hospital in the United States that provided care for individuals with mental illness, although treatment of these patients was little better than it had been in jails and almshouses. Individuals who were deemed "mentally ill" were assigned to hospital cellars and were placed in bolted cells, where they were watched over by attendants carrying whips, which they used freely. Sightseers paid admission fees to watch the cellar activities.

The First Revolution: From Inhumane to Moral Treatment

During the late 1700s, people throughout the world began to seek better approaches to address the needs of those with mental illness. The first revolution in caring for those with mental illness began in France rather than the United States, with a shift from inhumane to moral treatment. Phillippe Pinel, director of two hospitals in Paris, ordered "striking off the chains" of the patients in 1793, first at the Bicetre Hospital for the Insane in Paris. He espoused a philosophy of **moral treatment,** which meant offering patients hope, guidance, support, and treatment with respect in small, family-like institutions.

The moral-treatment movement soon spread to America. Benjamin Rush, a signer of the Declaration of Independence, wrote the first American text on psychiatry, advocating that people with mental illness have a moral right to humane treatment. But not until the 1840s, through the efforts of Dorothea Dix, a schoolteacher, did people with mental illness in the United States actually begin to receive more humane treatment (see chapter 1). As a Sunday school teacher for a group of patients in a Massachusetts hospital,

Dix became aware of the plight of individuals with mental illness. Appalled by what she saw, she gave speeches, wrote newspaper articles, and met with government officials to bring attention to the inhumane and abusive treatment she observed in the many facilities she visited.

As a result of her efforts, a bill was introduced in Congress to use the proceeds from the sale of western land to purchase land for use in caring for people with mental illness. This bill was vetoed by President Franklin Pierce, which set a precedent for the federal government's refusal to be involved in state social services programs, which remained unchanged until the New Deal era (see chapter 7).

Refusing to give up, Dix turned her efforts to the individual states, and by 1900, 32 states had established state mental hospitals. But Dix and other advocates for the humane treatment of persons with mental illness soon had additional cause for concern. What had begun in many hospitals as humane treatment changed as hospitals became overused and overcrowded, admitting all who could not be cared for elsewhere. State insane asylums became warehouses, called "snake pits."

Dix and her group of reformers demanded that strict guidelines be established for the treatment of patients in mental hospitals. Again the states responded, by expanding facilities and adopting detailed but often burdensome operating procedures. Although abuse and neglect of patients decreased dramatically, the guidelines left little room for innovation, and until the 1960s, patients in state mental hospitals received little more than custodial care.

In the years immediately following the Dix reform, nearly half of patients who had been admitted were released, often for the sole reason of making room for new admissions and alleviating overcrowding. Once the overcrowding stabilized somewhat, however, long stays in mental hospitals became the norm and discharge rates fell to as low as 5% annually. Although these state institutions had been intended to house a transitory

patient population, the absence of effective treatment technologies forced the retention of many patients until their death. The desire for single state facilities to house large populations of patients with mental illness resulted in their being located in rural areas, where land was less expensive, expansion of facilities was possible, and the safety of the community was protected. Thus, the state mental hospitals became—and, in many instances, still are—the principal industries in the areas where they are located.

Although much less attention was given to the population with developmental disabilities, institutionalization became prevalent for this group as well. During the 1850s, many states established state training schools for individuals with mental retardation, which housed persons ranging from those with profound to mild retardation. Many individuals with retardation were mistakenly labeled as having mental illness and placed in state hospitals for the mentally ill.

In spite of the efforts of Dorothea Dix and others, overcrowded conditions and neglect of residents with mental illness and developmental disabilities continued in many state facilities, which also housed many immigrants. Some staff members who provided moral support, love, and respect to certain residents had difficulty transferring this attitude to foreigners. Also, it was increasingly difficult to find competent medical personnel who were willing to work in state mental institutions. Graduates from medical schools often were repelled by the alcoholics, severely disturbed individuals, and foreigners who populated the institutions.

A second effort to reform conditions in state mental hospitals was undertaken in the early 1900s by Clifford Beers, a Yale graduate from a wealthy family who had been hospitalized in a Connecticut mental hospital for 3 years. After his release, Beers almost immediately suffered a relapse and was hospitalized for a second time. During this stay, he began to formulate plans for more effective treatment of those deemed to be mentally ill. He kept careful notes of the maltreatment he received from physicians and the well-intended but ineffective care he received from caregivers.

After his release in 1908, Beers wrote a book, *A Mind That Found Itself,* which exposed the horrendous conditions in mental hospitals. This book led to the formation of state mental health advocacy organizations, such as the Connecticut Society for Mental Health. Later, state organizations formed the National Association for Mental Hygiene, which became a lobbying force for the continual reform of state hospitals and the development of alternative systems of care.

The Second Revolution: The Introduction of Psychoanalysis

What has been described as the second revolution in the mental health field occurred in the early 1900s with the writings of Sigmund Freud and the introduction of **psychoanalysis** in the United States. Professional mental health workers who were trained in Freud's techniques attempted to gain cooperation and insight through verbal or nonverbal communication with patients, seeing them at regular intervals over long periods of time.

The first social workers working in state mental hospitals actually were hired before Freud's teachings were introduced into the United States. Their primary role was to provide therapy to clients, but it was based on limited knowledge about what the therapy should entail. As psychoanalysis gained popularity in the United States, psychiatric social workers, like others working with individuals with mental illness, quickly adopted a system of therapy that reportedly was much more effective than the often haphazard treatment they had been using.

In 1905, Massachusetts General Hospital in Boston and Bellevue Hospital in New York City hired psychiatric social workers to provide therapy to patients. Because of staff shortages and the large numbers of patients, however, few patients actually received psychotherapy—which requires highly trained therapists, fairly verbal patients who speak the same language as the therapist, and long hours of treatment. Psychotherapy as a treatment approach for dealing with mental health problems was more likely to be used in outpatient facilities—either private practices established by psychiatrists or child guidance centers—which were established in the United States in the 1920s primarily to promote healthy relationships between middle-class children and their parents.

The Third Revolution: A Shift to Community Mental Health Programs

The third revolution in mental health, a shift in the care of individuals with mental health and substance-abuse problems and developmental disabilities from institutions to local communities, began in the 1940s and continues today. Public interest in mental health issues and treatment of those with mental illness was stimulated by the onset of World War II.

The military draft brought mental health problems to the attention of Congress. Military statistics showed that 12% of all men drafted into the Armed Forces were rejected for psychiatric reasons. Of the total number rejected for any reason, 40% were rejected for psychiatric reasons (Felix, 1967). Serious questions began to be raised about the magnitude of mental health problems within the entire U.S. population.

INITIAL POST-WAR DEVELOPMENTS

After the war ended, mental health concerns, which had been neglected during the war, began to receive attention again. In 1946, Congress passed the National Mental Health Act, which enabled states to establish **community mental health programs** aimed at preventing and treating mental health problems. The act also provided for research and educational programs and mandated that each state establish a single state entity to receive and allocate federal funds provided for by the act.

Attention also began to turn toward state facilities for the mentally ill. Albert Deutsch (1949) wrote a series of exposés on state mental hospitals, later published as *Shame of the States*. This stimulated a series of similar books, one of which was made into a film, *The Snake Pit*. All of this attention resulted in widespread public outcry and furthered the climate for reform.

In 1949, Congress created the **National Institute of Mental Health (NIMH),** the first federal entity to address mental health concerns. In 1955, with impetus from a working coalition of leadership from the National Institute of Mental Health and the **National Association of Mental Health (NAMH),** university medical schools and schools of social work, and organizations of former mental patients and their families, the National Mental Health Study Act was passed. This act verified the belief among mental health professionals and government officials alike that large custodial institutions could not deal with mental illness effectively. The act authorized an appropriation to the Joint Commission on Mental Illness and Health to study and make recommendations for mental health policy.

In the late 1950s and early 1960s, the commission published a series of documents calling for major reform. The commission sought a substantial increase in mental health expenditures to be used for comprehensive community mental health facilities, increased recruitment and training programs for staff, and long-term mental health research. The commission also called for an expansion of treatment programs for the acutely mentally ill in all facilities while limiting the numbers of patients at each hospital to no more than a thousand inpatients.

The commission further recommended a major emphasis on community programs, including preventive, outpatient treatment, and aftercare services that could reduce the numbers of institutionalized patients and allow for their successful treatment within their local communities. The group recommended that the states play a smaller role in providing services and that the federal role be increased in addressing mental health needs. At this time, President John Kennedy made mental health issues a high priority and strongly supported the commission's efforts, becoming the first U.S. President to address mental health concerns publicly. Furthermore, the public was beginning to see the effectiveness of **psychotropic drugs** in treating individuals with mental illness, and consequently became more receptive to the idea of community care.

COMMUNITY MENTAL HEALTH INITIATIVES

Congress passed the Mentally Retarded Facilities and Community Mental Health Center Construction Act in 1963. This act provided major funding to build community mental health centers and community facilities for people with developmental disabilities. The act mandated that centers built with federal funds be located in areas accessible to the populations they serve, and that they provide the basic service components: inpatient services, outpatient services, partial hospitalization (day, night, or weekend care), emergency services, consultation, and educational services. By 1980, more than 700 community mental health centers had been established in the United States, partially funded with federal funds.

The intent of the community mental healthcare legislation was to replace the custodial care provided in large-scale institutions with therapeutic care in the community. The emphasis was to be on **deinstitutionalization**—keeping individuals from being placed in hospitals whenever possible—and on the **least restrictive environment**—a setting as much like one for nondisabled individuals as possible. The Presidential Commission on Mental Health (1978) defined the purpose of providing a least restrictive environment as

> . . . maintaining the greatest degree of freedom, self-determination, autonomy, dignity, and integrity of body, mind, and spirit for the individual while he or she participates in treatment or receives services. (p. 44)

These programs were deemed cost-effective because many individuals could work at paid jobs and live in situations that were less expensive than in an institution, and they also were seen as encouraging individuals' self-esteem and feelings by their contributing to society. (A discussion of the impact of deinstitutionalization on current services is included later in this chapter.)

The community health center legislation, coupled with the use of psychotropic drugs, significantly reduced the numbers of individuals housed in mental institutions. In 1955, 77.4% of all patients received inpatient services and 22.6% received outpatient services. By 1980, the numbers had virtually reversed themselves, with only 28% receiving inpatient services and 72% receiving outpatient services (Mechanic, 1999). The treatment emphases had shifted from custodial care, shock treatment, and long-term psychotherapy to short-term treatment, group therapy, helping individuals cope with their environments, and drug treatment. The number of outpatient clients visiting community mental health centers continues to increase.

The Fourth Revolution: Legal Rights of Clients and Consumer Advocacy

Mental health and developmental disabilities professionals have identified clients' rights as the fourth revolution in the mental health/disabilities arena. The legal advocacy movement, which began in the 1960s, was part of the civil rights movement of the 1960s. It received further impetus in 1971 in the landmark case *Wyatt v. Stickney,* in which a federal judge restricted "extraordinary or potentially hazardous modes of treatment" (Lin, 1995, p. 1706) with patients in state mental hospitals in Alabama. In a landmark 1975 decision, the U.S. Supreme Court ruled that being mentally ill and in need of treatment was not sufficient grounds for involuntary confinement.

The increasing options available to individuals with developmental disabilities and mental health problems, including placement in less restrictive facilities, new counseling techniques, and drug treatment, have spawned a number of legal issues that merit serious deliberation. On the one hand, do individuals have the right to refuse treatment? On the other hand, if treatment technology or knowledge about more appropriate types of treatment exists but such treatment is not available, do individuals have the right to demand treatment? In some states, class-action lawsuits have been brought on behalf of persons in institutions demanding that they be placed in less restrictive settings where they can receive treatment that is unavailable to them in the institutions.

The National Association of Mental Health and other advocacy organizations have forced the court system to establish a series of patients'/clients' rights, including the right to treatment, the rights to privacy and dignity, and the right to the least restrictive condition necessary to achieve the purpose of commitment (see Box 8.4 for NASW's Mental Health Bill of Rights). The courts also have determined that individuals cannot be deemed incompetent to manage their affairs; to hold professional, occupational, or vehicular licenses; to marry and obtain divorces; to register to vote; or to make wills solely because of their admission or commitment to a hospital.

Patients in mental institutions have the same rights to visitation and telephone communication as do patients in other hospitals, along with the right to send sealed mail. They also have the right to freedom from excessive medication or physical restraint and experiments and the rights to wear their own clothes and worship within the dictates of their own religion. And patients have the right to receive needed treatment outside a hospital environment (Mechanic, 1999).

Most states make it difficult to commit a person to an institution involuntarily. In many states, however, law-enforcement agencies can order that persons be detained in state institutions for a limited time without a court hearing. At the end of that time, a court hearing must be held, and involuntary commitments can be ordered only if

BOX 8.4

Mental Health Bill of Rights Project: Principles for the Provision of Mental Health and Substance Abuse Treatment Services

Our commitment is to provide quality mental health and substance abuse services to all individuals without regard to race, color, religion, national origin, gender, age, sexual orientation, or disabilities.

Right-to-Know Benefits

Individuals have the right to be provided information from the purchasing entity (such as employer or union or public purchaser) and the insurance/third party payer describing the nature and extent of their mental health and substance abuse treatment benefits. This information should include details on procedures to obtain access to services, on utilization management procedures, and on appeal rights. The information should be presented clearly in writing with language that the individual can understand.

Professional Expertise

Individuals have the right to receive full information from the potential treating professional about that professional's knowledge, skills, preparation, experience, and credentials. Individuals have the right to be informed about the options available for treatment interventions and the effectiveness of the recommended treatment.

Contractual Limitations

Individuals have the right to be informed by the treating professional of any arrangements, restrictions, and/or covenants established between third party payer and the treating professional that could interfere with or influence treatment recommendations. Individuals have the right to be informed of the nature of information that may be disclosed for the purposes of paying benefits.

Appeals and Grievances

Individuals have the right to receive information about the methods they can use to submit complaints or grievances regarding provision of care by the treating professional to that profession's regulatory board and to the professional association. Individuals have the right to be provided information about the procedures they can use to appeal benefit utilization decisions to the third party payer systems, to the employer or purchasing entity, and to external regulatory entities.

Confidentiality

Individuals have the right to be guaranteed the protection of the confidentiality of their relationship with their mental health and substance abuse professional, except when laws or ethics dictate otherwise. Any disclosure to another party will be time limited and made with the full written, informed consent of the individuals. Individuals shall not be required to disclose confidential, privileged or other information other than: diagnosis, prognosis, type of treatment, time and length of treatment, and cost.

Entities receiving information for the purposes of benefits determination, public agencies receiving information for health care planning, or any other organization with legitimate right to information will maintain clinical information in confidence with the same rigor and be subject to the same penalties for violation as is the direct provider of care.

Information technology will be used for transmission, storage, or data management only with methodologies that remove individual identifying information and assure the protection of the

Continued

BOX 8.4—*Continued*
Mental Health Bill of Rights Project: Principles for the Provision of Mental Health and Substance Abuse Treatment Services

individual's privacy. Information should not be transferred, sold, or otherwise utilized.

Choice

Individuals have the right to choose any duly licensed/certified professional for mental health and substance abuse services.

Individuals have the right to receive full information regarding the education and training of professionals, treatment options (including risks and benefits), and cost implications to make an informed choice regarding the selection of care deemed appropriate by individual and professional.

Determination of Treatment

Recommendations regarding mental health and substance abuse treatment shall be made only by a duly licensed/certified professional in conjunction with the individual and his or her family as appropriate. Treatment decisions should not be made by third party payers. The individual has the right to make final decisions regarding treatment.

Parity

Individuals have the right to receive benefits for mental health and substance abuse treatment on the same basis as they do for any other illnesses, with the same provisions, co-payments, lifetime benefits, and catastrophic coverage in both insurance and self-funded/self-insured health plans.

Discrimination

Individuals who use mental health and substance abuse benefits shall not be penalized when seeking other health insurance or disability, life or any other insurance benefit.

Benefit Usage

The individual is entitled to the entire scope of the benefits within the benefit plan that will address his or her clinical needs.

Benefit Design

Whenever both federal and state law and/or regulations are applicable, the professional and all payers shall use whichever affords the individual the greatest level of protection and access.

Treatment Review

To assure that treatment review processes are fair and valid, individuals have the right to be guaranteed that any review of their mental health and substance abuse treatment shall involve a professional having the training, credentials, and licensure required to provide the treatment in the jurisdiction in which it will be provided. The reviewer should have no financial interest in the decision and is subject to the section on confidentiality.

Accountability

Treating professionals may be held accountable and liable to individuals for any injury caused by gross incompetence or negligence on the part of the professional. The treating professional has the obligation to advocate for and document necessity of care and to advise the individual of options if payment authorization is denied.

Payers and other third parties may be held accountable and liable to individuals for any injury caused by gross incompetence or negligence or by their clinically unjustified decisions.

Source: National Association of Social Workers. Available: http://www.naswdc.org/practice/behavioral-health/mental.asp, November 21, 1999. Used with permission.

persons are found to be dangerous to themselves or others.

Often, individuals who are not really capable of functioning on their own but who are not found to be dangerous to themselves or others are released to be on their own. As a result, many individuals receive what some mental health professionals have termed "the revolving door approach to treatment." Individuals who are too incapacitated to function on their own are picked up on the streets, admitted to the hospital, given medication, food, and rest, then released quickly because they legally cannot be held against their wishes any longer.

An issue that has received even less attention is the right of children to refuse or to demand mental health treatment. In many instances, parents commit children to institutions because they do not want or are unable to care for them. In other instances, the child's problems stem from family problems that the parents do not want to deal with. The rights of individuals to avoid treatment and to receive treatment are unclear and await clarification by the U.S. Supreme Court.

Consumers of services and their families, like social work professionals, are becoming more concerned about these issues. Advocacy groups for people with mental health problems have stepped up their efforts to include individuals with mental health problems and their family members in treatment planning, and in many instances also have involved them as employees, board members, and spokespersons for their organizations. The consumer movement emphasizes empowerment and self-sufficiency. Many social workers work closely with consumer groups and have become strong allies of the consumer movement and the changes they advocate.

Neurobiology and Implications for Mental Health, Substance Abuse, and Developmental Disabilities

The wave of the future in mental health, substance abuse, and developmental disabilities may well come from discoveries in neurobiology and related technology. We have entered this wave already. Genetic and genome research, computer modeling, and other technologies offer tremendous hope for individuals with mental-health and substance-abuse problems and developmental disabilities as well as for their families.

Specific genes have been identified, for example, that cause diseases associated with developmental disabilities such as cystic fibrosis, and identify those who are at more risk for depression. Although schizophrenia previously was thought to be more environmentally than biologically related, research now is showing that factors associated with this serious illness are more likely related to genetic makeup or chemical functioning within the brain. Research suggests that similar factors are associated with Alzheimer's and other forms of dementia and neurodegenerative diseases.

Understanding the genetic and biochemical abnormalities associated with these diseases, possibly related to complex involvement with how the body uses proteins, will likely lead to early detection of such diseases as well as possible gene therapy treatment. Research relating to regenerative medicine suggests possible breakthroughs in combating many brain and spinal cord injuries, as well as diseases such as Parkinson's and Alzheimer's.

These discoveries represent tremendous advances, because they pave the way for interventions such as gene therapy and medication to change the course of, or even prevent, these illnesses. A new drug also is being tested that alters an individual's craving for alcohol and has the potential to significantly reduce problems associated with alcoholism.

The National Institutes of Health and the National Institute on Mental Health have funded a number of research efforts on mapping human genomes and studying the impact of various illnesses, addictions, and trauma on brain development and brain chemistry. Researchers can observe features of neuron ensembles and signaling mechanisms that help to determine how the brain responds to addictive substances. For example, they can document cellular and molecular adaptations during the use of addictive drugs, as well the depressive state that follows the use of many substances. These adaptations in the brain's system indicate why individuals increase the use of a drug to maintain brain stability (Koob & Le Moal, 2006).

Innovations in social neuroscience through neuroimaginging of how the brain interacts with the social world show that the brain is activated differently when making judgments about people versus judgments about inanimate objects. Brain functioning and discoveries about the role it plays in moral reasoning, too, have implications in understanding some types of deviant behavior.

Although these are exciting advances, they raise new issues for social workers. First, what are the ethical implications of such knowledge? If early detection is possible—for example, before birth—what are the choices, and who should make them? No matter when problems are identified in individuals, should all individuals have affordable access to these interventions, even if they are expensive? Who should pay for the interventions? What if an individual decides not to take advantage of the interventions? The issues of right to treatment and client empowerment will surface in new areas that have important implications for social workers.

Availability of Resources and Responsibility for Care

Perhaps the most overriding issue in the arenas of mental health, substance abuse, and developmental disabilities is how to manage limited resources to best address the needs of those who require services. More than 10% of national health-care resources are spent on public and private mental health care. Medicaid is the largest funding source of seriously ill people, and mental-health costs continue to increase. Mental health

delivery systems also are changing with the trend toward community-based programs. Many state mental hospitals have either closed or offer non-hospital care as part of their services.

The 1970s and 1980s witnessed a dramatic growth in private psychiatric hospitals and residential treatment centers for children and youth with emotional disturbances. This trend was curtailed by the emergence of managed care, an overriding theme in the delivery of mental health services today. When patients are hospitalized, the stays are much shorter than in the past. The predominant pattern of mental health care today consists of brief hospital stays to stabilize symptoms, and often initial monitoring of prescribed medication, followed by outpatient care at a community facility (Mechanic, 1999). Many individuals, like Lindsey in the opening vignette, are caught in a lifelong cycle of numerous short-term hospitalizations, discharge to the community, escalation of symptoms, and rehospitalizations.

Individuals with mental illness and developmental disabilities, often unable to advocate for themselves, do not always receive their just share of funding. Public attitudes that persist in viewing alcoholism and substance abuse as moral issues have an influence on, and can limit funding for, substance-abuse programs. Many of the gains in mental health and developmental disabilities programs established in the 1960s have been eroded as governments battle over who should have the responsibility for individuals with mental illness or developmental disabilities and what constitutes appropriate levels of service for these groups. Although attitudes have changed significantly since colonial times, ongoing change is required to achieve normalization of these populations. We will explore a number of issues relating to current resources.

Deinstitutionalization

The field of mental health has been subjected to considerable shock since the movement toward deinstitutionalization. Some have argued that deinstitutionalization has resulted in the "ghettoization" of those with mental illness and other disabilities. In many instances, communities have neither the funding nor the commitment to provide care for individuals released from institutions, forcing them to subsist in subhuman conditions in poverty areas.

In 1976, two social workers from the Mental Health Law Project visited Mr. Dixon, who had won his right to freedom in a class action lawsuit several months after being transferred from the hospital to a boarding care facility. The workers described their observations in testimony before a Senate subcommittee:

> The conditions in which we found Mr. Dixon were unconscionable. Mr. Dixon's sleeping room was about halfway below ground level. The only windows in the room were closed and a plate in front of them made it impossible for Mr. Dixon to open them. There was no fan or air conditioner in the room. The room had no phone or buzzer. There would be no capacity for Mr. Dixon to contact someone in case of fire or emergency and this is significant in the face of the fact that Mr. Dixon is physically incapacitated. Mr. Dixon had not been served breakfast by 10 a.m. He stated that meals were highly irregular and he would sometimes get so hungry waiting for lunch that he would ask a roomer to buy him sandwiches. He can remember having only one glass of milk during his entire stay at his new home. (U.S. Senate Subcommittee on Long-Term Care, 1976, p. 715)

Shortly after this testimony, Mr. Dixon returned to St. Elizabeth Hospital and was placed in a more suitable home. Twenty years later, in 1996, a series of articles by an investigative reporter for an urban newspaper in a large southwestern state found similar or worse conditions for people throughout the state who had been released from state hospitals. In one setting, many men were found living in an unheated, un-air-conditioned metal building with no indoor plumbing. They were malnourished and stayed indoors most of the time, watching programs on a small television set. Although states

have begun to establish regulations, including licensing or certification systems for group and boarding homes for clients of the mental health system, monitoring and sanctioning are difficult. Even if facilities are forced to close, often no other facilities are available to house the displaced residents.

Many states and local communities have successfully reduced the number of individuals with developmental disabilities or mental illness who are living in institutions, but some are reluctant to do so because of inadequate local resources and the economic disruption caused by shutting down institutions in areas where they are a major source of employment.

Deinstitutionalization also has resulted in some unintended consequences. Many people who could function well within an institutional setting do not do as well in a community setting, particularly if they have little day-to-day supervision. And deinstitutionalization carries with it the potential for failure to meet established standards of care as well as failure to provide follow-up services to clients. Decentralization of care requires a case-management system in which social workers or other mental health professionals are responsible for a specific number of clients, ensuring that their living conditions are appropriate, that they are maintaining health care and taking medication, and that their other needs are being met.

Some community-based mental health programs have been extremely successful. For example, George Fairweather, a noted mental-health professional, has established a series of community programs for individuals who were institutionalized previously. Called Fairweather Lodges, these facilities provide supervised living for individuals in small groups, and residents share housekeeping chores. Residents also work in the community, and a lodge coordinator ensures that residents are successful in the workplace. The coordinator facilitates support group meetings for residents' families as well as for lodge members. The rate of reinstitutionalization for this program has been extremely low. Some communities that initially were reluctant to establish lodge programs now view the lodges and their residents as important to the community.

Much remains to be done to develop adequate community-based mental health programs for people of all ages. Many previously deinstitutionalized individuals have difficulty adjusting to community living, particularly when adequate support programs are not available. As one former state hospital resident stated:

> At the hospital, I had hot coffee every morning, three meals a day and a warm bed every night, and people to talk to if I wanted to talk. Here, I have the street and that's about it. No food on a regular basis, no bed, and no one to talk to. I didn't have a bad life at the hospital. (Iscoe, 1990, personal communication)

To date, the most significant problem with deinstitutionalization has been the inability of communities to develop the necessary infrastructure to support these individuals.

Wide-Ranging Program Alternatives

Consumer groups and experts in mental health care suggest that quality mental health programs should have the following characteristics (National Alliance on Mental Illness, 2006a):

- comprehensive services and supports;
- an integrated service delivery system;
- sufficient funding;
- consumer and family-driven systems;
- safe and respectful treatment environments;
- accessible information for consumers and family members;
- access to acute care and long-term treatment;
- cultural competence;
- an emphasis on health promotion and morality reduction; and
- an adequate mental health workforce.

Beneficial community programs that have been established for people with mental illness, substance-abuse problems, or developmental disabilities include

- partial hospitalization, through which individuals attend hospital day programs and receive treatment, leave the hospital to sometimes work in the community and to return to their homes at night, returning to the hospital for treatment and monitoring the next day;
- day programs for persons with developmental disabilities that provide education, supervision, and in some instances employment opportunities; and
- halfway houses and refurbished apartment complexes, with resident supervisors who oversee and lend support to residents with mental illness and developmental disabilities and recovering substance abusers.

Many former residents have been able to return to their own homes. Some go to adult or special children's day-care centers during the day while their family members work and return home at night. Respite-care programs established in some communities, using trained volunteers, make it possible for family members to find substitute caregivers so they can have some time away from the person on occasion to regain their energies.

Community-based alternatives for the elderly also have received increased attention as the general population continues to age. Prior to deinstitutionalization, many residents of state mental hospitals and state schools for people with developmental disabilities were elderly people who could function in a less restrictive environment if they were to have someone to care for them. A number of elderly individuals have been successfully placed in nursing homes, often in integrated facilities that accept residents with and without mental illness or disability. But with our increasingly aging population, mental health advocates are concerned about the availability of mental health services for the elderly. It has been estimated that about 20% of individuals over age 55 have mental disorders that are not a normal part of aging, such as depression, substance abuse, Alzheimer's disease, anxiety disorders, and late-onset schizophrenia (U.S. Surgeon General, 1999).

Interventions for Substance Abusers and Their Families

Early efforts to eliminate problems of alcoholism and substance abuse were aimed at moral rehabilitation, prohibition, and temperance. The most significant breakthrough in the area of alcohol abuse came in 1935 with the founding of **Alcoholics Anonymous (AA),** a self-help group for alcoholics. AA was established by Bill W., a New York stockbroker, and Dr. Bob, a physician, who discovered that they could maintain sobriety by supporting one another and following a formal program of gradual recovery, which since has been incorporated into the 12 steps for which AA is known. AA continued to grow in numbers and in popularity, and, over time, intervention efforts shifted from the moral concept of alcoholism to the disease concept. Education and advocacy groups such as the National Council on Alcoholism, founded in 1944, drew further attention to alcoholics' problems.

Federal attention to the problem of alcoholism did not come about until 1970, when Senator Harold Hughes of Iowa (a recovering alcoholic at the time of his election) advocated for passage of the Comprehensive Alcohol Abuse and Alcoholism Prevention, Treatment, and Rehabilitation Act. This act provided financial assistance to states and communities to embark on treatment, education, research, and training programs and established the National Institute on Alcohol Abuse and Alcoholism. The act also provided for withdrawing federal funding from any hospital that refused to treat alcoholics.

Programs have expanded significantly since that act was passed. Early intervention models were based on inpatient hospitalization and participation in Alcoholics Anonymous; however, research has shown that these programs are not effective with all substance abusers. Different types of clients require different intervention approaches. Some clients are so entrenched in substance abuse that they require hospitalization, and they often undergo detoxification before they can effectively begin treatment. Most hospitalization programs range in duration from 30 to 60 days.

Many substance-abuse professionals argue that 30 days is not long enough for those receiving treatment to recover enough to stay sober after being released from the hospital. Complicating the situation is that some insurance companies are refusing to pay for even short-term inpatient treatment. Proponents of outpatient and partial hospitalization programs argue that clients should be made to deal with the pressures of day-to-day living while receiving support from the program, rather than being placed in a sheltered therapeutic environment away from the previous pressures and individuals with whom they abused substances.

Whether treatment is inpatient or outpatient, treatment programs usually incorporate community-based self-help groups such as Alcoholics Anonymous or Narcotics Anonymous (NA). Individuals released from treatment programs typically are encouraged to continue attending NA or AA meetings as well as aftercare programs, usually held on evenings and weekends, for up to a year after leaving the more intensive intervention program.

Many addiction specialists view a family systems model as the most effective approach to treat substance abuse, because family members reinforce, often unconsciously, the abuser's drug use and learn individual patterns of coping that frequently result in intergenerational substance abuse in families (Black, 1987; Freeman, 2002). Therefore, many chemical-dependence programs in which social workers are employed incorporate a family systems model and provide psychoeducational experiences for family members in addition to the client. These experiences involve educational and therapy sessions with other clients and their families, as well as individual, group, and family therapy.

Some chemical-dependence programs take a more cognitive/behavioral approach, particularly with adolescents and individuals in the criminal-justice system. These programs emphasize consequences for abusing substances and other inappropriate behaviors and reinforcers for appropriate actions. Some juvenile and adult corrections programs, including jails and prisons, incorporate substance-abuse treatment. But services often are limited in both duration and numbers served, in spite of the large numbers of inmates who are incarcerated for crimes involving substance abuse. Without treatment, these individuals are likely to be incarcerated again, often for more serious crimes.

Agencies that serve clients with a wide range of problems are incorporating special programs that target substance abuse. Child protective services agencies that work with abusive and neglectful parents are reporting that the bulk of the increased reports are related to substance abuse. In response, these agencies have developed substance-abuse treatment programs for their clients. The programs not only deal with the substance abuse but also provide parenting programs that address the impacts of substance abuse on children.

Of the inpatient or residential programs available for women with children, few provide care for the children. Those that do provide this care emphasize modeling of parenting skills, working through communication problems and other family dynamics, and providing a safe, supportive environment for the mothers and their children with others who are in similar circumstances so they do not have to face the added stress of reuniting with their children when the treatment is concluded. Increasingly, substance-abuse programs also are addressing the needs of clients who have emotional problems in addition to substance abuse, called **dual diagnosis.** Frequently, an individual will go through treatment for chemical dependence and, after maintaining sobriety for a long time, return to the mental-health system for help in dealing with other emotional problems such as depression or family-of-origin issues, including sexual abuse.

Interventions for Persons with Developmental Disabilities and Their Families

Early efforts to improve conditions for people with developmental disabilities focused primarily on institutionalization, usually in large state schools for the blind, deaf, and individuals with retardation. In the 1950s, parent advocates formed the Association for Retarded Children, which later became the Association for Retarded Citizens and, now, simply The ARC. This group has been instrumental in advocating for national and state legislation and improved conditions for those with developmental disabilities.

Additional attention to their needs came during President John Kennedy's administration. His sister, Rosemary, had a developmental disability, for which she received extensive publicity. The Community Mental Health Centers Act, passed during the Kennedy administration, included funding for research and facilities for those with developmental disabilities. Kennedy established the Presidential Panel on Mental Retardation, which called for additional research and a system that would provide continuity in caring for people with disabilities. In 2003, President George W. Bush changed the name of this group to the President's Committee for People with Intellectual Disabilities after advocates requested this change to help mainstream persons with intellectual disabilities and to recognize their strengths.

The Americans with Disabilities Act

In 1986, the National Council on the Handicapped published its report, *Toward Independence,* which

Although changes are still needed to better address their needs, The Americans with Disabilities Act and advocates have paved the way to provide opportunities not available to persons with disabilities in the past.

© Heine/Index Stock

provided a comprehensive national approach for addressing problems of individuals with disabilities. The Americans with Disabilities Act (ADA) (PL 101-336) passed both the House and Senate with little opposition and was signed into law. Prior to passage of ADA, people with disabilities could be discriminated against readily. A major problem for many persons with mental illness or developmental disability has been the denial of basic rights that others take for granted.

ADA bans discrimination based on disabilities by private employers with a workforce of more than 15, mandating public accommodations, public services, transportation, and telecommunications. This act also extends protections provided by the 1964 Civil Rights Act to an estimated 43 million individuals with physical and mental disabilities including heart disease, diabetes, emotional illnesses, drug addiction, alcoholism, and persons with AIDS. The act requires public places—including non-government entities such

as restaurants, hotels and motels, business places, and other facilities used by the general public— to provide "reasonable accommodations" to persons with disabilities, in terms of both service and employment. In short, the act mandates the elimination of discrimination and establishes standards and mechanisms for enforcement.

This law significantly changed the way that individuals with disabilities historically have been treated. Ever since the Elizabethan Poor Laws, people with disabilities have been considered to need public assistance, and definitions of who has a disability have been used primarily for determining eligibility for public assistance. The intent of ADA is to reduce the stigma toward individuals with disabilities and remove barriers that resulted in their forced isolation. The law has empowered many persons with disabilities to take charge of their lives and has helped to reduce the stigmatization. Under ADA, individuals with disabilities and their family members can insist on reasonable accommodations. For example, a person with a disability who can perform a job with reasonable accommodations cannot be passed over for that job, nor can the primary caregiver of a child with a disability.

States and local communities now have to establish special transportation systems, place elevators and ramps in buildings, and install special telephones for individuals with hearing impairments, as well as for those in wheelchairs. Additional public education is needed, though. One disabilities advocate gave the following report about her trip to check accessibility at a large mall, which the mall manager claimed met ADA guidelines:

> There were numerous parking spaces for people with disabilities. However, they were in an area of the parking lot which was poorly lighted, and the closest entrance, some distance away, had heavy doors that could only be used by someone on crutches or in a wheelchair if someone came along to open them for you. There also was an elevator to go from the first to the second floor; however, it was located on the opposite side of the mall from this entrance. The one restroom that had been remodeled to meet ADA guidelines was not close to either this entrance or the elevator.
>
> The telephone that had been installed was in still another direction from all of the other facilities. The elevator and restrooms were marked in Braille, but the signs were made so poorly that it was impossible to distinguish the markings from each other. The manager had not considered the implications of these upgrades and has agreed to make changes so they are more accessible to persons with disabilities. (Barrera, 1995, p. 6)

Ten years later, when a social-work advocate visited the same mall, the doors were electronic and the restrooms were accessible, but the locations of the elevator, telephones, and lighting had not changed. And the recently renovated food court was difficult to navigate, especially when carrying food.

ADA also advocated for supported employment of individuals with disabilities, including employment for wages and benefits in workplaces that integrate persons with and without disabilities, and continuous on-the-job training to reinforce job skills. Community-based programs in many areas have obtained employment for clients with disabilities in recycling centers, mail centers, offices, food-service settings, grocery stores, and landscaping and park programs. Some programs have placed clients as aides in schools and centers that mainstream children with disabilities, giving them a chance to work—and to be successful role models for the children.

Despite the ADA mandates, stereotypes still raise significant barriers for individuals with disabilities. The Special Olympics commissioned an international study, conducted in 10 countries. It found that while 46% of the respondents believed that persons with intellectual disabilities could play on a team with others with similar disabilities, only 14% believed they would be capable of playing on a team with players without intellectual disabilities. In addition, 79% believed that children with intellectual disabilities should be educated in segregated settings, either at home or in special schools, and 54% thought that including people with intellectual disabilities in the workplace would increase the risk of accidents (Special Olympics, 2003).

Individuals with physical disabilities face similar discrimination. A student at the university where one of the authors teaches arrived on campus wheelchair-bound and connected to a breathing tube so he could receive oxygen. Modest and quiet, the student did not disclose that he had received a perfect SAT score. At first, peers and faculty treated him as if he were both physically and intellectually challenged. Three years later, however, with a straight-A average, he has changed many attitudes about persons with disabilities.

In 2005, the U.S. Surgeon General, in collaboration with the federal government's Health and Human Services Office on Disability, released a call to action to improve the health and wellness of individuals with disabilities (U.S. Department of Health and Human Services, 2005). This report, issued on the 15th Anniversary of the Americans with Disabilities Act, included four priorities (see www.surgeongeneral.gov):

1. Increasing understanding that people with disabilities can lead long, healthy, and productive lives
2. Increasing knowledge among health-care professionals and providing them with tools to screen, diagnose, and treat the whole person with a disability with dignity
3. Increasing awareness by people with disabilities of the steps they can take to develop and maintain a healthy lifestyle
4. Increasing accessible health care and support services to promote independence for people with disabilities.

Among the many implications of ADA for social service providers and social workers, services must be accessible and individuals cannot be denied participation in a program because of their disability, nor can they be required to participate. Clients with disabilities who participate in social services programs report that many social services providers play a significant role in disempowering rather than empowering them to meet their own needs. In one study, the majority of clients interviewed said the biggest obstacle they faced regarding employment was discouragement from their social service providers regarding seeking jobs (Rapp, Shera, & Kisthardt, 1993).

Social workers should ensure that clients have access to people who can meet their needs. For example, clients with hearing problems need social workers who can sign or interpreters to help them communicate. Further, social service agencies must be able to lead persons with disabilities to employment opportunities (and not just in agencies that work with individuals with disabilities). Jobs can be structured with special equipment and accommodations such as part-time work and job-sharing. Table 8.2 suggests appropriate employment interventions for individuals with developmental disabilities, based on

TABLE 8.2
Sample Employment Interventions at Multiple Levels for People with Severe Mental Illness

Level	Sample Interventions
Individual	Career counseling Volunteer work opportunities Job placement Supported work
Group	Fairweather Lodge Job clubs Consumer-owned and consumer-operated businesses Consumer self-help groups
Organization	Make employment the number one agency priority Include considerations of work in all case reviews Set rewards for staff members who get the most people employed Convert day treatment program to prevocational program Provide vocationally oriented staff training Put aside agency funds for transportation and clothing for work
Service system	Assign vocational rehabilitation counselors to treatment teams Increase funding for supported work programs Liberalize vocational rehabilitation eligibility criteria Include vocational content in core discipline degree programs
Community	Public educational campaign to reduce stigma in employment (for example, media exposure to consumer achievement) Chamber of commerce-initiated jobs program for clients

Source: Research Strategies for Consumer Empowerment of People with Severe Mental Illness, by C. Rapp, W. Shera, and W. Kisthardt, *Social Work* (1993), *38*(6), 731. Copyright 1993, NASW, Inc.

the systems/ecological framework, at levels of the environment ranging from the individual to the community. Successful programs for individuals with disabilities require consistent advocacy and community support if they are to receive the services they need.

Other Disabilities Legislation

Federal and state legislation and funding have decreased markedly since the 1980s. The previous pattern of categorical funding for mental health programs tied to specific client groups has been replaced by block grants to states, giving each state considerable latitude in how it spends its funds. This change means that advocacy groups have to ensure that resources are allocated to these groups.

In 1998, Congress passed several pieces of legislation aimed at providing services to individuals with disabilities:

- The Rehabilitation Act provides funding for education and rehabilitative services for individuals with disabilities.
- The Assistive Technology Act offers resources for adaptive technology to assist individuals with disabilities in leading more typical lives.
- The Crime Victims with Disabilities Awareness Act provides specific services for individuals with disabilities who are the victims of crime.

Legislation proposed in the first decade of the new millennium includes protection against discrimination in seeking housing, consumer protections in Medicaid-managed care, adding individuals with disabilities to the federal Hate Crimes Prevention Act, and funding and regulation of attendant services for individuals with disabilities who need someone to assist them with daily care.

Advocates for individuals with disabilities are calling for additional resources for children with special needs. Those diagnosed with autism, at-

tention deficit disorder, and other disabilities can make significant gains with early intervention. Advocates are concerned that the Leave No Child Behind Act and other policies emphasizing accountability in education may result in less attention to children with special needs, particularly adolescents who are likely to score poorly on standardized tests. Some school districts across the nation have developed model programs for children as young as 3, providing a holistic array of services to the children and their parents.

The United States has the capacity to support children and adults with mental health problems and developmental disabilities in community-based settings. With adaptive equipment and facilities, and in some instances a personal-care attendant, many individuals with disabilities can function well in their own homes or in a residential, apartment-like facility with some assistance. Many can drive themselves to and from a workplace or use public transportation if it is disability-accessible, allowing them to attend public schools, hold jobs, and make a living.

Individuals with Disabilities Education Act

The **Individuals with Disabilities Education Act (IDEA)** replaced previous legislation providing special education resources for children and youth with disabilities and included funding for early intervention programs for infants and toddlers with disabilities and their families. The legislation emphasizes the development of comprehensive, coordinated, multidisciplinary, interagency programs that include public school systems, health agencies, and social services agencies.

This law mandates that public school systems provide educational and social services for children with a range of disabilities, including emotional disturbance, mental retardation, and speech, vision, hearing, and learning disabilities. Parents and educators are required to develop jointly an individualized educational plan (IEP) for each child. The law also requires that each child be placed in the least restrictive setting possible, with the intent of including as many children with disabilities and emotional problems as possible in general classrooms; special education classes are to be a last alternative.

Preschool early intervention programs are required to develop an individualized family intervention plan to ensure that families of these children receive the services they need. Services usually include counseling, as parents often believe there is a "cure" somewhere for their child's disability and may succumb to denial, self-blame, anger, and grief and loss. Parents also need help in navigating the myriad of available services that often are confusing and difficult to access, as well as respite care so they can take time for themselves and their other children.

Many communities have preschool programs, funded with state and federal monies to assist children with disabilities, that combine early childhood education with physical and speech therapy and other needed services. Working and non-working parents alike can bring their children to the centers, where trained staff members work with the children individually and in small groups to help them progress developmentally. Some preschool programs include children both with and without disabilities so both groups can learn to value each other and discover and grow together.

Other children have disabilities that prohibit them from remaining in their own homes, and still others have parents who are overwhelmed by their own needs and the added stress from having a child with a disability and being unable to provide adequate care. Advances in technology have enabled children with serious disabilities, who formerly would not have lived, to remain alive. How best can these children be cared for? The costs to keep such children in hospitals are prohibitive, and a hospital setting does not provide the nurturing that a child needs to develop to his or her maximum potential.

Many state schools for individuals with intellectual and developmental disabilities have closed, and attention is turning to how to care for the children who previously were housed there. In some instances, they have been placed in nursing homes with elderly residents, and these facilities are not likely to be equipped to meet the special needs of children.

Prevention versus Treatment

Mental health professionals address prevention issues at three levels:

1. **primary prevention**—prevention targeted at an entire population (for example, prenatal care for all women to avoid developmental disabilities in their infants; parenting classes to decrease mental health problems among children)
2. **secondary prevention**—prevention for at-risk populations, groups more likely to develop mental health problems than others (such as individual and group counseling for families with members having schizophrenia or alcoholism)
3. **tertiary prevention**—prevention targeted at individuals who already have problems, to prevent the problems from recurring (for example, treatment groups for alcoholics or mental health programs for individuals who have attempted suicide)

Numerous studies show that prevention programs are cost-effective in reducing substance abuse, mental illness, and developmental disabilities. Still, policymakers often develop only short-term solutions to these problems. For example, although substance-abuse prevention programs can be expensive, the costs are greater for residential or other more extensive treatment programs later or for imprisonment and services to victims if substance abuse leads to crime.

Other problems involving mental health, such as homelessness and family and youth violence, while not new, are having significant negative impacts on the individuals with these problems and on the entire family. The emphasis on intergenerational, cyclical problems has refocused attention on the need to provide resources not just to the children and families experiencing these problems but also to adults who grew up in such families (see chapters 10 and 11).

Cultural and gender differences must also be taken into account when discussing mental health, mental illness, substance abuse, and developmental disabilities. The importance of these differences, including the impact of oppression and social injustice, must be considered in relation to theories used to understand human behavior and to identify "normal" and pathological behavior. These differences, too, must be considered when using diagnostic classification systems such as the *DSM-IV*, identifying the ways that practitioners view and relate to individuals with whom they interact, and determining the ways by which mental health and developmental disabilities services are organized and delivered (Munson, 2001).

Trends in Services and Treatment

Chief among the current issues in mental health is managed care. Also, legislation is affecting how mental health programs and services are conceived and administered.

Managed Care

Managed care is at the core of the current debate surrounding mental health services. Many of the pros and cons are similar to those discussed in chapter 9, addressing health care. Managed health care has raised a number of ethical dilemmas for social workers and other mental-health professionals. With insurance company personnel rather than mental-health treatment providers increasingly making treatment decisions, concern has been raised about whether adequate services are being provided. Managed care emphasizes accountability and ensuring that services are provided only if they are needed. Many mental health services are paid for by third-party insurers or, if the client meets eligibility requirements, by Medicaid (see chapter 9).

Third-party insurers also restrict the choice of service providers available, often to a list of professionals and specific hospitals who have agreed to the managed-care terms and conditions for that insurance company. Hospital stays, particularly for substance abuse, have been limited, and more insurance providers are mandating outpatient treatment first to determine whether that approach is successful.

Managed-care initiatives, too, have changed the types of outpatient services provided. More agencies are seeing clients in groups and limiting the number of group and individual counseling sessions in which a client can participate. The trend is toward case management, with a case manager, sometimes from the insurance company, sometimes from the agency, monitoring the services received to ensure that they are appropriate.

Insurance Legislation

Insurance coverage for mental health and substance abuse is generally much more restricted than for other types of health care. In 1996, Congress passed the Domenici-Wellstone Amendment to require parity for lifetime and annual dollar limits between mental health services and services for other medical conditions. In 2001, the Senate passed the Mental Health Equitable Treatment Act, comprehensive legislation that would require private group health insurance plans to cover mental health services in the same way that they cover health services. The House rejected the Senate provision and passed a one-year extension of the 1996 Act. The same legislation has been extended each year since that time.

In response to the high costs of medication for a number of mental health problems, such as schizophrenia, legislation passed in 2003 provides senior adults and persons with disabilities covered by Medicare with prescription drug benefits. However, mandatory co-payment and refill policies vary by state, making it difficult for some individuals to maintain the medications needed to keep them healthy.

Deficit Reduction Act

In 2006, President George W. Bush signed the Deficit Reduction Act, which is seen as both an asset and a liability for persons with mental health, disability, or substance abuse needs and their families. A significant change involving persons with mental health needs and their families is a shift away from the federal government to the states. The act allows states to offer packages of benefits to Medicaid recipients that actually can be less than what states were offering prior to the legislation.

An important piece of the legislation relates to immigrants. Prior to the legislation, states could allow individuals to declare in writing that they were citizens without providing documentation. Most states followed this process. As of July 1, 2006, citizens applying for, or being recertified to receive, Medicaid benefits must provide documentation of citizenship with limited exceptions. The legislation states that individuals who are either physically or mentally incapacitated and have no one to assist them can be declared exempt.

The Deficit Reduction Act also calls for two programs to expand access to mental health services for children: Medicaid waivers and demonstration programs for community alternatives to psychiatric residential treatment. Medicaid waivers are available for individuals with mental illness that will enable them to receive community-based services rather than hospitalization (previously

these waivers in most states had been available for health problems that did not include mental health). The legislation requires states requesting waivers to show "budget neutrality," or that the average cost of serving a child under the waiver will be the same or less than that average cost of serving a child in a hospital. Because most states do not hospitalize children for long periods of time, instead releasing them to communities with minimal follow-up services, it will be difficult for some states to show that it is less or equally expensive to keep children in their own homes and receive community-based services.

It is hoped that, over time, states will apply for waivers and develop community-based programs that will provide the kinds of supports that are most effective in helping children with serious mental illnesses and their families, including parent support and training, respite care services, social workers and other staff members who can provide crisis intervention and prevent hospitalization, transportation, and adaptive equipment (National Alliance on Mental Illness, 2006c). These programs also may reduce fragmentation, as schools, juvenile justice programs, social service providers, and hospitals collaborate to provide referrals and coordinated "wrap-around" services to meet individual needs.

The Deficit Reduction Act has ramifications for people with mental illness and disabilities. Because of deinstitutionalization and the closing of state schools for persons with disabilities and state hospitals for persons with mental illness, the only available care for many individuals requiring intensive services has been nursing homes. Young adults, and in some instances children, have been housed in facilities with primarily elderly adults, which are poorly equipped to meet their specific needs.

Another program authorized by the DRA is The Money Follows the Person Rebalancing Demonstration, designed to move individuals to the community from long-term care facilities such as nursing homes. States will receive funding to pay for designated home and community-based services during the first year that someone lives in the community.

Evolving Therapies

The Commission on Mental Health, established by President Jimmy Carter in 1978, found that people of color, children, adolescents, and the elderly were underserved, as were residents of rural and poor urban areas. The commission also found that many of the services provided were inappropriate, particularly for those with differing cultural backgrounds and lifestyles. In many instances when mental health centers were first established, they were directed by psychiatrists trained in psychotherapy or influenced by educational psychologists who were accustomed to testing and working with students. As a result, the staff members often were inexperienced at dealing with involuntary clients, who did not want to be seen, failed to keep appointments, and were unfamiliar with the concept of one-hour therapy sessions. Staff members often were also unequipped to deal with problems such as family violence, child abuse, and sexual abuse.

As programs developed, many centers became skilled at reaching special populations and developing more effective ways of addressing client needs. In the 1970s, centers were required to establish special children's mental health programs. Currently, many centers provide programs that address special populations such as abused children, individuals with substance abuse problems, and Vietnam veterans. Mental health professionals also assist in establishing self-help groups, such as Alcoholics Anonymous, Adult Children of Alcoholics, Alateen, Parents Without Partners, and Parents Anonymous (a child abuse self-help and mutual assistance program).

Today, social workers in mental health settings provide crisis intervention, operate telephone hotlines, conduct suicide-prevention programs,

and provide alcoholism and drug abuse services. Mental health services increasingly are provided in settings other than mental health centers—churches, nursing homes, police departments, schools, child-care centers, the workplace, and health and medical settings. Problems addressed by mental health professionals have expanded to include loneliness and isolation, finances, spousal and child abuse, male–female relationships, housing, drugs, and alcohol. Mental health staff members have become more multidisciplinary, using teams of professionals as well as volunteers.

SHORT-TERM THERAPY

Intervention approaches based on "brief" or "short-term" therapy, often taking a cognitive-behavioral approach, are being used to stabilize clients and help them cope more quickly. One short-term intervention approach is solution-focused therapy (deJong & Berg, 2002), which emphasizes the strengths of clients and empowers them to come up with effective solutions. Questions such as, "What worked for you before?" and comments such as, "How have you managed to do as well as you have with all this going on?" take clients' own ideas and affirm their abilities to cope. This intervention approach is effective for some types of mental health problems but not for others, such as sexual abuse and substance abuse.

PSYCHOEDUCATIONAL APPROACHES

Research and current thinking support a systems/ecological approach for dealing with mental health, substance abuse, and developmental disabilities issues and, in particular, a family systems perspective. Treatment interventions that involve the entire family are more likely to reduce recidivism (recurrence of the problem) or prevent the problem from getting worse.

A psychoeducational approach is highly successful in many situations. Individuals and their families receive education that helps them understand the problem their family member is experiencing, the roles they have played in trying to cope with the problem, and possibly more effective ways of coping, as well as family therapy to address the dynamics within their own families.

COMMUNITY EMPHASIS

Community-level services are expected to continue to expand, with local communities determining the level and type of services needed. Pressure from the federal government for community mental health centers to become financially independent will continue. Although some individuals with mental health or substance-abuse problems still will require hospitalization in state or private psychiatric facilities, more and more individuals will be treated in community-based programs. Numerous studies have found that the vast majority of people in psychiatric hospitals can be treated successfully in local communities at significantly reduced costs, and with more effective outcomes than hospitalization.

In the future, community-based treatment models will include "one-stop mental health centers" that incorporate individual and group counseling services, expanded day and partial day treatment programs, social skills training, and recreation programs, as well as assistance with housing and employment. Social workers in therapist or case-management positions will be sent into clients' homes to provide services there, further reducing the need for outpatient and inpatient care. Intensive case management and therapy services provided in the home on a short-term basis often can stabilize situations and get the entire family to work together with the client before problems escalate, requiring hospitalization or other out-of-home services.

NIH REPORT

In late 2004, the National Institute of Mental Health convened a panel of mental health consumers, providers, researchers and academicians, advocates, and government officials at all levels to determine how mental health care should be strengthened to better meet client and family needs. The report, *Transforming Mental Health Care in America, Action Agenda: First Steps* (Substance Abuse and Mental Health Services Administration, 2006b), cited recovery as the single, most important goal, noting that

> . . . mental health recovery is a journey of healing and transformation enabling a person with a mental health problem to live a meaningful life in a community of his or her choice while striving to achieve his or her full potential.

The report calls for

- sending a message that mental illnesses are treatable and recovery is possible;
- reducing suicides by developing a national strategy for suicide prevention;
- helping the mental health workforce become more culturally competent;
- increasing employment of persons with psychiatric disabilities;
- enhancing technology to protect privacy and confidentiality of consumer health information;
- expanding services that are based on evidence-based practice;
- improving coordination between health and mental health services; and
- increasing the focus on the mental health needs of children and early intervention to meet their needs.

The report indicates that recovery should be a primary first goal and advocates the following 10 components of recovery:

1. self-direction;
2. individualized and person-centered;
3. empowerment;
4. holistic;
5. non-linear (based on growth, setbacks, and learning);
6. strengths-based;
7. peer support;
8. respect;
9. responsibility; and
10. hope.

These components overlap with social work values and the focus on the client. NASW is partnering with other advocacy groups to promote the concept that mental health is a national priority for the public and private sectors alike. Social workers are involved in political action efforts at national, state, and local levels to increase funding for prevention, treatment, and research in mental health and for passing legislation that requires adequate mental health benefits for all citizens as part of any health reform. They also are working to ensure that social workers are included as providers of mental health services under such legislation. Finally, they advocate for policies that clients be placed in least restrictive environments and for a mental health service delivery system that allows for a continuum of care, including community-based prevention programs.

Roles and Opportunities for Social Workers

Social workers today are involved in the total continuum of mental health and developmental disabilities services. They provide these services in a variety of settings, including traditional social services agencies—such as community mental health centers, child guidance centers, and public social services departments—as well as nontraditional settings—the courts, public schools and colleges and universities, hospitals and health clinics, child-care centers, workplaces, and the military. While they fulfill a variety of roles, social workers presently form the largest group of psychotherapists in the United States.

Historical Background

The first social workers credited with providing mental health services were the psychiatric social workers hired in New York and Boston mental hospitals in the early 1900s. They were responsible primarily for providing individual therapy to hospitalized mental patients and overseeing the care of discharged patients in foster homes. The mental health field expanded during the 1920s with the establishment of child guidance centers.

With the influence of psychoanalysis and the child-guidance movement, social workers in mental health moved increasingly into the role of psychotherapist, in which the individual is the unit of attention. The unique perspective of social work on the person-in-environment and intervention at levels of the environment beyond the individual waned during the 1930s, 1940s, and 1950s. But the civil rights movement and Vietnam war in the 1960s prompted activism in the social work profession as a whole, redirected again to community organization, advocacy, and a return to the roots of the profession.

Emphasis on the systems/ecological perspective since the late 1960s has broadened the roles of social workers in all fields, including mental health. While psychiatrists traditionally have played a more technical role in the mental health system, stressing medication and biopsychological perspectives, social workers have tried to maintain leadership in the mental health arena:

> As the largest group of mental health care providers in the country, . . . social workers are in a unique position to address the social context of clients' problems. (NASW, 1995, p. 4)

For instance, social workers might consider the following questions:

- Why do some communities and geographic areas have higher incidences than others of mental illness, substance abuse, people with disabilities, and homelessness?
- What factors constitute a healthy community—or society—that promotes mental health and values diversity?

Quality of life for individuals and families can be improved by eliminating environmental racism, oppression, and discrimination; creating adequate housing and employment; and maintaining an environment that values diversity and difference, children and families, and the elderly. Regardless of their field or the environment in which they practice, social workers have important roles to play.

Career Opportunities in Mental Health, Substance Abuse, and Disability Services

CLINICAL SOCIAL WORKERS

Many social workers in mental health settings provide individual counseling, including psychotherapy, to clients. Instead of being referred to as psychiatric social workers, though, most are called **clinical social workers.** Most agencies that hire clinical social workers require that they meet the qualifications of the National Association of Social Workers Academy of Certified Social Workers (ACSW) certification or obtain appropriate state certification or licensing.

ACSW certification requires a master of social work (MSW) degree from an accredited graduate school of social work, two years of social work experience under the direct supervision of an ACSW social worker, and a satisfactory score on a competency examination administered by the NASW. State licensing and certification programs have similar requirements, but they vary by state.

CRISIS INTERVENTION AND CHILD AND FAMILY SERVICES

Many social work jobs are available in the field of mental health and developmental disabilities for social workers with a bachelor of social work (BSW) degree. BSW social workers provide services such as crisis intervention for women and their children at battered women's centers, and they operate suicide, runaway youth, child abuse, and other types of crisis hotlines (see chapter 2).

They also counsel adolescents and their families at youth-serving agencies and are employed as social workers in state hospitals and community living programs for individuals with mental illness and state schools and community programs for individuals with developmental disabilities. In these settings, they counsel residents and serve as the primary professional involved with the individual's family.

SCHOOL-BASED SERVICES AND DRUG TREATMENT PROGRAMS

Social workers work in schools with troubled students and their families, providing individual counseling, family counseling, and family outreach, and they lead groups for children and their families on topics such as divorce, child maltreatment, anger management, techniques for getting along with adults, and substance abuse. Legislation establishing services for children with disabilities requires social workers among the professionals who are authorized to provide services.

PUBLIC MENTAL HEALTH SERVICES

Social workers currently comprise the largest professional group in public mental health services. More than half of the labor force employed in mental health-related jobs are social workers, and in more than a third of the federally funded community mental health centers, a social worker is the executive director.

SOCIAL WORKERS IN MULTIDISCIPLINARY TEAMS

Many mental health programs take a multidisciplinary team approach, in which social workers, psychiatrists, physicians, psychologists, psychiatric nurses, child development specialists, and community aides work together to provide a multitude of services. Although social workers on multidisciplinary teams are involved in all aspects of treatment, most often they are given the responsibility of working with the client's family and the community in which the client resides.

Because of their training from a systems/ecological perspective, they help other team members understand the many competing factors that can support or impede a client intervention plan. If resources from another agency are needed, the social worker usually is the one who obtains them and ensures that they are provided.

SOCIAL WORKERS AS CASE MANAGERS

Even if they are not employed in agencies that use multidisciplinary teams, social workers in mental health settings often provide case management services. Case managers are responsible for monitoring cases to ensure that clients receive the needed services. A case manager does not necessarily provide all services directly but manages the case, coordinating others who provide the services.

BSW social workers who work with people who have mental illnesses, developmental disabilities, or are substance abusers often serve as case managers. Assigned a group of clients, they ensure that their clients are following intervention plans and are functioning adequately. Case managers empower clients to become as self-sufficient as possible by promoting their strengths and providing support and affirmation. They also serve as the liaison with the client and other service providers when necessary, monitoring the provision of services and advocating for changes in services including additional services when necessary. Individuals frequently can function fairly well with a case manager to lend support, ensure that they are taking medication if needed, advocate with an employer if there is a problem, help them access health care if they get sick, and keep them from becoming isolated from their environment.

Many states are employing case managers at community mental health centers to oversee clients who are living in the local community, including those previously in institutions, who can function independently with supervision and support. The case manager meets regularly with the client and contacts family members, employers, and other appropriate individuals to ensure that the client is functioning adequately.

SOCIAL WORKERS AS ADVOCATES

Still other social workers involved in the mental health field serve as advocates. Organizations such as The Arc (formerly ARC—the Association for Retarded Citizens) advocate for persons with disabilities on an individual basis, ensuring that they receive needed services. For example, a 14-year-old girl with mental disabilities in a junior high school in an urban area was not receiving special education services and had been suspended several times for behavior problems. An advocate assigned to her arranged for the school district to provide the needed testing, saw that she was placed in a special education program that reduced her anxiety level and allowed her to function in a setting where she felt better about herself, and arranged for her to receive counseling.

Advocates also work to ensure that groups of citizens are provided for, such as being involved in a community to ensure that housing is available to individuals with mental health problems and developmental disabilities. Advocates work within an empowerment framework, urging the targeted population to advocate for themselves for individual and social change.

SOCIAL WORKERS AS POLICYMAKERS

Social workers function in the mental health arena as administrators and policymakers. Many direct mental health programs, and others work for government bodies at local, state, and federal levels. They develop and advocate for legislation, develop policies and procedures to meet the needs of individuals with mental health problems and disabilities, and oversee governing bodies that monitor programs. Increasingly, social workers are being elected to local, state, and national office. Social workers at all governmental levels have played key roles in getting legislation passed to improve services for individuals who have mental illness, chemical dependencies, and/or developmental disabilities.

Summary

Services for individuals with mental health needs and developmental disabilities have changed significantly since colonial times. Mental health services have seen four major revolutions since that time: the shift from inhumane to moral treatment, the introduction of psychoanalytic therapy, the move from institutions to community programs and the development of psychotropic drugs to effectively treat many types of mental health problems, and a new emphasis on the rights of clients and patients.

Current issues in the mental health field encompass the legal rights of clients and whether they should be able to refuse or demand treatment; scarce resources and conflict over the roles of federal, state, and local governments in providing services; attention to substance abuse and the expansion of substance-abuse treatment facilities; the need for more effective services for women, people of color, the homeless, and individuals in rural settings; and the special needs of rural and ethnic populations.

Social workers play a critical role in providing mental health services, serving as therapists, advocates, case managers, administrators, and policymakers. Rapid changes in society brought about by technology and globalization are expected to further expand the roles of social workers in meeting mental health needs.

Key Terms and InfoTrac® College Edition

The terms below are defined in Glossary at the end of this text. To learn more about key terms and topics in this chapter, enter the following search terms using InfoTrac or the World Wide Web:

addiction
Alcoholics
    Anonymous (AA)
alcohol
alcoholism
Americans with
    Disabilities
    Act (ADA)
clinical social
    workers
community mental
    health programs
deinstitutionalization
depressants
depression
developmental
    delay
developmental
    disability
*Diagnostic and
    Statistical Manual
    (DSM* or *DSM-IV)*
dual diagnosis
hallucinogens
Individuals
    with Disabilities
    Education
    Act (IDEA)

inhalants
least restrictive
    environment
managed care
medical model
mental health
mental health
    services
mental illness
moral treatment
narcotics
National Association
    of Mental
    Health (NAMH)
National Institute
    of Mental
    Health (NIMH)
primary prevention
psychoanalysis
psychotropic drugs
secondary prevention
stimulants
substance abuse
suicide
tertiary prevention

Discussion Questions

1. Discuss the problems in defining mental illness. Give a recent example from the media that exemplifies the complexity of how mental illness is defined.
2. Identify and briefly describe at least four frameworks that can be used to understand mental health problems.
3. Do you agree with Szasz's concept of mental health? Discuss your rationale for either agreeing or disagreeing.

4. Identify the four major revolutions in the field of mental health. What do you predict will be the next revolution?

5. Identify at least three different ways by which substance abuse may be conceptualized. Which conceptualization do you think is best? Why?

6. Identify at least four ways in which substance abuse is costly to society. How can these costs be reduced?

7. What is your definition of a substance abuser? Identify at least three factors at each level of the environment that can place an individual at risk to become an alcoholic.

8. What is the meaning of the term *developmental disabilities?* How does this term contrast with previously used terminology to identify those within this category?

9. Discuss the advantages and disadvantages of deinstitutionalization. What are your thoughts about hospitalization versus community-based care?

10. How have the media portrayed people with emotional problems, substance abuse, and developmental disabilities? Compare the portrayals in two popular films. What messages do these portrayals send to individuals with similar characteristics? To the general public about individuals with these characteristics?

11. Identify at least five areas in which social workers in mental health settings might work. What are some of the roles in which they might function? Which of these career opportunities interest you most, and why? The least?

12. What are the advantages and disadvantages of managed care in addressing mental health issues? From a client perspective? From the perspective of a social worker employed in a mental health agency?

13. How do you think scientific breakthroughs will shape the future of services for persons with mental illness, disabilities, and addictions? How do you think the roles of social workers might change as a result?

On the Internet

http://www.nami.org/

http://www.cms.gov

http://www.apa.org/

http://www.mentalhealth.gov/

http://samhsa.gov/

http://www.naswdc.org/

http://www.ddrcco.com/

http://www.nrchmi.com/

References

American Association of Suicidology. (2006). *Suicide statistics*. Washington, D.C: AAS. Available: www.suicidology.org

American Psychological Association (2006). *What is PTSD?* Washington, D.C: APA. Available: www.apahelpcenter.org/articles/article.p;hp?id=122

ARC. (2005). *Developmental disabilities*. Silver Spring, MD: ARC. Available: www.thearc.org.

Barhydt, Adrienne Rubin. (April 10, 1996). *The disability rights activist: Why disability rights?* Minneapolis, MN: disrights.org. Available: http://www.disrights.org/dr-whydr.html

Barrera, M. (1995). *Implementing the Americans with Disabilities Act: Issues for social workers*. Unpublished paper, School of Social Work, University of Texas, Austin.

Beutler, L. E., & Malik, M. L. (2002). The emergence of dissatisfaction with the DSM. In L. E. Beutler & M. L. Malik (Eds), *Rethinking the DSM* (pp. 3–16). Washington, DC: American Psychological Association.

Black, C. (1987). *It will never happen here*. New York: Ballantine.

Caspi, Avshalom. (2003, July). *Gene more than doubles risk of depression following life stresses*. Washington, DC: National Institute of Mental Health.

Centers for Disease Control and Prevention. (2006). *Fetal alcohol spectrum disorders*. Washington, D.C: Author. Available: cdc.gov/ncbddd/fas/faqs.htm

Child Welfare Information Gateway (2003). *Substance abuse and child maltreatment.* Available: http://www.childwelfare.gov/pubs/factsheets/subabuse_childmal.cfm

DeJong, P., & Berg, I. K. (2002). *Interviewing for solutions.* Pacific Grove, CA: Brooks/Cole.

Deutsch, A. (1949). *Shame of the states.* New York: Columbia University Press.

Developmental Disabilities Center. (2000). *What is a developmental disability?* Boulder, CO: Author. Available: http://www.dbcboulder.com/whatsdd.htm

Encyclopedia of Childhood and Adolescence. (1977). *Mental retardation.* Farmington Hills, MI: Thomson Gale.

Felix, R. (1967). *Mental illness: Progress and prospects.* New York: Columbia University Press.

Freeman, E. (2002). *Substance abuse intervention, prevention, rehabilitation, and systems change.* New York: Columbia University Press.

Harris, T. (1991). *The silence of the lambs.* New York: St. Martin's Press.

Institute on Women and Substance Abuse. (2000). *Women and substance abuse.* Lexington: University of Kentucky Center on Drug and Alcohol Research. Available: http://www.uky.edu/RGS/CDAR/IOWASA/abuse

Jenkins, P. (2003). *Monster.* Los Angeles: Media 8 Entertainment.

Jones-Webb, R. (1998). Drinking patterns and problems among African Americans: Recent findings. *Alcohol Health and Research World,* 22 (4), 260–264. Washington, D.C: U.S. National Institute on Alcohol Abuse and Alcoholism.

Karls, J. M., & Wandrei, K. E. (1994). *Person-in-environment system: The PIE classification system for social functioning problems.* Washington, DC: NASW Press.

Kesey, K. (1962). *One flew over the cuckoo's nest.* New York: Basic Books.

Koob, G., & Le Moal, M. (2006). *Neurobiology of addiction.* London: Academic Press.

Kutchins, H., & Kirk, S. (1997). *Making us crazy: DSM: The psychiatric bible and the creation of mental disorders.* New York: Free Press.

Liebow, E. (1993). *Tell them who I am: The lives of homeless women.* New York: Free Press.

Lin, A. (1995). Mental health overview. In *Encyclopedia of social work* (19th ed., Vol. 2): Silver Spring, MD: NASW Press, pp. 1705–1711.

Mechanic, D. (1999). *Mental health and social policy: The emergence of managed care* (4th ed.). Boston: Allyn & Bacon.

MentalhealthAmerica (2006). *Operation healthy reunions.* Alexandria, VA: Author. Available: http://www.mentalhealthamerica.net/reunions

Munson, C. (2001). *The mental health diagnostic desk reference: Visual guides and more for learning to use the diagnostic and statistical manual (DSM-IV-TR)* (2nd ed.). Binghamton, NY: Haworth Press.

National Alliance on Mental Illness (2003). *Dual diagnosis and integrated treatment of mental illness and substance abuse disorder.* Arlington, VA: NAMI. http://www.nami.org/Template.cfm?Section=By_Illness&Template=TaggedPage/Tagg

National Alliance on Mental Illness. (2006a). *Grading the states: A report on America's health care system for serious mental illness.* Arlington, VA: NAMI.

National Alliance on Mental Illness. (2006b). *What is mental illness? Mental illness facts.* Arlington, VA: NAMI. Available: http://www.nami.org/Content/NavigationMenu/Inform_Yourself/About_Mental_Illness/About_Mental_Illness.htm

National Alliance on Mental Illness. (2006c). *What you need to know about the deficit reduction act.* Arlington, VA: NAMI. Available: http://www.nami.org/

National Association of Social Workers. (1995, January). Community mental health centers grow. *NASW News,* p. 4.

National Association of Social Workers. (1999). *Mental health bill of rights project: Principles for the provision of mental health and substance abuse treatment services.* Washington, DC: NASW. Available: http://www.naswdc.org/practice/behavioral-health/mental.asp

National Association of Social Workers. (2006). *National study of licensed social workers.* Washington, DC: NASW.

National Institute on Alcohol Abuse and Alcoholism. (2003). *The economic costs of alcohol and drug abuse in the United States—1992.* Bethesda, MD: NIAAA. Available: http://www.health.org/govstudy/bkd265/

National Institute on Alcohol Abuse and Alcoholism. (2006a). *The scope of the problem.* Bethesda, MD: NIAAA. Available: http://www.pubs.niaa.nih.gov/publications/arh283/111-120.htm

National Institute on Alcohol Abuse and Alcoholism. (2006b). *What is alcoholism?* Bethesda, MD: NIAAA. Available: http://www.niaa.nih.gov/FAQs/General-English/FAQ1.htm

National Institute on Drug Abuse. (2003). *InfoFacts* (summaries of NIDA research studies). Bethesda, MD: NIDA. Available: http://nida.nih.gov/Infofax/

National Institute of Mental Health. (1999). *Research fact sheets.* Washington, DC: NIMH. Available: http://www.nimh.nih.gov/publicat/resfacts.cfm

National Institute of Mental Health. (2003). *Depression.* Washington, DC: NIMH. Available: http://www.nimh.nih.gov/

National Institute of Mental Health (2004). *Burden of mental illness.* Washington, DC: NIMH. Available: http://www.nimh.nih.gov/about/2005budget.pdf-04-12-2004

National Institute of Mental Health (2005). *U.S. suicide rates by age, gender, and racial group.* Washington, DC: NIMH. Available: http://www.nimh.nih.gov/suicideresearch

National Institute of Mental Health (2006a). *America's children: Key national indicators of well-being 2005.* Washington, DC: NIMH. Available: http://childstats.gov/americaschildren/spe3.asp

National Institute of Mental Health (2006b). *Neuroinformatics: The human brain project.* Washington, DC: NIMH. Available: http://www.nimh.nih.gov/neuroinformatics/

National Institute of Mental Health (2006c). *The numbers count.* Washington, DC: NIMH. Available: http://www.nimh.nih.gov/healthinformation/statisticsmenu.fcm

National Institute of Mental Health (2006d). *Suicide in the U.S.: Statistics and prevention.* Washington, DC: NIMH. Available: http://www.nimh.gov/publicat/harmsway.cfm

National Resource and Training Center on Homelessness and Mental Illness. *Get the facts.* Washington, D.C: Author. Available: http://www.nrchmi.com/facts

Phoenix House (2006). *Drug facts.* New York: Author. Available: http://www.phoenixhouse.org/National/DrugFacts/drugfacts_

Presidential Commission on Mental Health. (1978). *Report of the Presidential Commission on Mental Health.* Washington, DC: Government Printing Office.

Rapp, C., Shera, W., & Kisthardt, W. (1993). Research strategies for consumer empowerment of people with severe mental illness. *Social Work, 38*(6), 727–733.

Rosenhan, D. (1973). On being sane in insane places. *Science, 179,* 250–257.

Royce, J., & Scratchley, D. (1996). *Alcohol problems and alcoholism: A comprehensive survey.* New York: Free Press.

Special Olympics. (2003). *Multinational study of attitudes: Groundbreaking international study reveals stereotypical views greatest barriers to better quality of life for individuals with intellectual disabilities.* Washington, DC: Author. Available: http://www.specialolympics.org/Special+Olympics+Public+Website/English/Press.

Substance Abuse and Mental Health Services Administration. (2006a). *Prevention pathways: Substance use, crime and violence.* Rockville, MD: Author. Available: http://www.preventionpathways.samhsa.gov/res_fact_drugs.htm

Substance Abuse and Mental Health Services Administration (2006b). *Transforming mental health care in America.* Rockville, MD: Author. Available: http://www.samhsa.gov/Federalactionagenda/NFC_execsum.sapx

Szasz, T. (1998). Myth of mental illness. In *Encyclopedia of mental health* (Vol. 2). New York: Academic Press.

U.S. Department of Health and Human Services (2005). *U.S. Surgeon General issues first call to action on disability.* Washington, DC: U.S. Government Printing Office. Available: http://www.surgeon-general.gov

U.S. Department of Veterans Affairs National Center for PTSD (2006). *Mental health reactions after disaster: A fact sheet for providers.* Washington, DC: Author. Available: http://www.ncptsd.va.gov/

U.S. Senate Subcommittee on Long-Term Care. (1976). *Hearings on long-term care.* Washington, DC: U.S. Department of Health, Education, and Welfare.

U.S. Surgeon General. (1999). *Mental health: A report of the Surgeon General.* Rockville, MD: U.S. Department of Health and Human Services, Substance and Mental Health Services Administration, National Institutes of Mental Health.

Williams, J. (1995). Diagnostic and statistical manual of mental disorders. In *Encyclopedia of social work* (Vol. 1, pp. 729–739). Washington, DC: NASW Press.

Williams, J., & Spitzer, R. (1995). Should *DSM* be the basis for teaching social work practice in mental health? Yes! *Social Work Education, 31*(2), 148–153.

Suggested Further Readings

Abbott, A. (2000). (ed.). *Alcohol, tobacco and other drugs: Challenging myths, assessing theories, individualizing interventions.* Washington, DC: NASW Press.

Allen, S., & Mor, V. (1998). *Living in the community with disability: Service needs, use and systems.* New York: Springer.

Barry, P. D. (2002). (ed.). *Mental health and mental illness.* (7th ed.). Philadelphia: Lippincott Williams & Wilkins.

Benshoff, J., & Janikowski, T. (2000). *The rehabilitation model of substance abuse counseling.* Pacific Grove, CA: Brooks/Cole.

Bentley, K. (2002). *Social work practice in mental health—Contemporary roles, tasks, and techniques.* Pacific Grove, CA: Thomson/Wadsworth.

Bentley, K. J., & Walsh, J. M. (2000). *The social worker and psychotropic medication: Toward effective collaboration with mental health clients, families, and providers* (2nd ed.). Pacific Grove: CA: Brooks/Cole.

Brink, T. L. (Ed.). (1994). *The forgotten aged: Ethnic, psychiatric and societal minorities.* Binghamton, NY: Haworth.

Dodes, L. (2003). *The heart of addiction: A new approach to understanding and managing alcoholism and other addictive behaviors.* New York: Harper Collins.

Farber, S., & Szasz, T. (1993). *Madness, heresy, and the rumor of angels: The revolt against the mental health system.* Chicago: Open Court.

Goffman, E. (1961). *Asylums: Essays on the social situation of mental patients and other inmates.* Garden City, NY: Doubleday.

Goodwin, D. (2000). *Alcoholism: The facts.* Oxford, England: Oxford University Press.

Green, H. (1964). *I never promised you a rose garden.* New York: Holt, Rinehart, & Winston.

Johnson, J. (2004). *Fundamentals of substance abuse practice.* Pacific Grove, CA: Thomson/Wadsworth.

Lewis, J., Dana, R., & Blevins, G. (2002). *Substance abuse counseling.* Pacific Grove, CA: Thomson/Wadsworth.

Luby, J. L. (2006). *Handbook of preschool mental health development, disorders, and treatment.* New York: Guiford Press.

National Institute on Alcohol and Alcohol Abuse (2006). *The cool spot.* Bethesda, MD: Author. Available: http://www.thecoolspot.gov/

Perlin, M. (2000). *The hidden prejudice: Mental disability on trial.* Washington, DC: American Psychological Association.

Rapp, C. (1997). *The strengths model: Case management with people suffering from severe and persistent mental illness.* New York: Oxford University Press.

Sales, B., & Shuman, D. (1996). *Law, mental health, and mental disorder.* Pacific Grove, CA: Thomson/Wadsworth.

Scheff, T. (1966). *Being mentally ill.* Chicago: Aldine.

Schwartz, D. (1994). *Crossing the river: Creating a conceptual revolution in a community and disability.* Cambridge, MA: Brookline.

Szasz, T. (1997). *Insanity: The idea and its consequences.* Syracuse, NY: Syracuse University Press.

CHAPTER 9

Health Care

Arturo and Alicia Hernandez and their 2-year-old daughter Alejandra live in a rural community in the Southwest. Until 2 years ago, Arturo and Alicia owned a family restaurant. Because of a downturn in the economy, however, they were forced to declare bankruptcy. Then Arturo began to work seasonally as a farm worker and as a construction worker and Alicia got a waitressing job in a neighboring town.

Three years ago Alicia became pregnant. Because she and Arturo did not have health insurance, Alicia waited until she was 5 months pregnant to see a doctor. Two months later she gave birth prematurely to a daughter. Shortly after the birth, the baby developed severe respiratory and cardiac problems, and the doctors decided to fly her to the regional neonatal center 300 miles away. The baby remained at the neonatal center for 3 months and required heart and lung surgery, as well as an extended period of intensive care.

When Alejandra finally was allowed to return home, she required extensive care, and Alicia was unable to return to work. Already financially strapped, the Hernandez family now faced a $75,000 medical bill for Alejandra's delivery and care. A visit to the local human services department to seek Medicaid was unsuccessful. Even though Alicia and Arturo's combined income was low, they still earned too much to qualify for medical assistance. Alicia's boss and friends held a dance to raise money for the family, which netted $4,000.

At this point, Alicia and Arturo are overwhelmed with medical bills and unsure whether they ever will be able to pay them all. Doctors say that Alejandra has developmental delays and is likely to require extensive physical therapy and possibly more surgery later. Arturo and Alicia had hoped to have a larger family, but they have decided they cannot afford any more children. Over the last 6 months, Arturo has developed kidney problems and has missed 5 days of work already, but he can't bring himself to see a doctor, considering the already extensive medical bills. He hopes that whatever is wrong will clear up by itself.

In this chapter we give an overview of our country's current health-care system, the problems it faces, and the types of health-care policies and programs available. We trace the relevant legislation and discuss the roles that social workers play in making those policies and programs possible.

The State of Health in the United States

Currently, **health care**—care provided to individuals to prevent or promote recovery from illness or disease—is in a crisis state in America. Many citizens, like Arturo and Alicia Hernandez, are facing huge medical bills that they can ill afford. More than 46 million Americans—about 17% of the total population—had no health insurance at all in 2003, the latest year for which national statistics are available (National Coalition on Health Care, 2006). Nearly 82 million people below the age of 65 spent a portion of either 2002 or 2003 without health coverage (U.S. Census Bureau, 2005).

Most employees formerly relied on their employers to pick up their health-care costs, or at least to pay for some of those costs. The percentage of people with employment-based health insurance, however, has dropped from 70% in 1987 to less than 60% in 2004, the lowest level of employment-based insurance coverage in more than a decade (Center for Budget and Policy Priorities, 2005). Employers also are covering fewer benefits, and often at more cost to the employee. Because many individuals either are not attached to workplaces that offer health-care benefits or cannot afford to purchase them when they are offered, the number of uninsured children in 2004 was 8.3 million, or 11.2% of all children in the United States (U.S. Census Bureau, 2005).

The problem of being medically uninsured in the United States is a result of these and other factors (Kaiser Family Foundation, 2005):

- Only about a third of small businesses now offer health-care benefits to their employees. More than 265,000 companies dropped their health coverage between 2000 and 2005, and 90% of those firms have fewer than 25 employees.

- The main reason that small firms do not offer coverage is the rapidly rising cost of health insurance premiums.

- Even if employees are offered health-care coverage, they are not always able to afford their share of the premium.

- A person's link to employer-sponsored coverage can be reduced or even terminated by a life-changing event (e.g., change from full-time to part-time work, self-employment, retirement, divorce).

Not having health insurance coverage has serious consequences for individuals and families (Kaiser Commission on Medicaid and the Uninsured, 2006b):

- Individuals who are uninsured receive less preventive care, are diagnosed at more advanced disease stages, and, once diagnosed, tend to receive less therapeutic care and have higher mortality rates than insured individuals.

- Uninsured adults often are unable to fill a drug prescription or to go forward with a recommended treatment because of the cost.

- Patients who are unable to pay up front in cash for the full medical bill may be turned away from receiving care.

- Individuals without health-insurance coverage sometimes turn to the emergency room to get their health-care needs met, and this is one of the costliest options.

- Uninsured individuals frequently have problems paying medical bills, and many are forced to change their life significantly to pay medical bills.

- Uninsured individuals at times require hospitalization for problems that could have been prevented had they received appropriate and timely outpatient care.

Having insurance negates some of these problems, results in improved health overall, and could reduce mortality rates for the uninsured by 10%–15%. Having health insurance lowers the

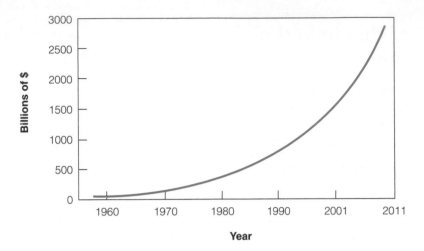

FIGURE 9.1

National Health Expenditures—1960–2001 and Projections to 2011

Source: U.S. Department of Commerce. (2002). *Statistical abstract of the United States.* 2002. (122 ed.).

debt that individuals and families face because of medical bills. And having health insurance makes a difference in a person's credit history.

As noted, employers cite dramatic increases in the cost of health care as the reason for dropping health-care benefits for employees or requiring employees to pick up a hefty portion of the costs of insurance premiums. National expenses for health care have increased exponentially over the past 30 years—from $73.2 billion in 1970 to an estimated $1.7 trillion in 2003, the last year for which official statistics are available (National Center for Health Statistics, 2006a, 2006b). Health-care expenses currently make up about 15% of the U.S. gross domestic product, or a per-capita cost (cost per person) of $5,313 (Centers for Disease Control and Prevention, 2005a). The United States spends nearly $100 billion annually to provide health services to uninsured persons for preventable diseases and those who could be treated more efficiently with earlier diagnosis, with hospitals covering about one-third of that amount (Institute of Medicine, 2003).

Health-care expenditures in the United States are expected to increase to $3.1 trillion by 2012

(see Figure 9.1). Not having health insurance is a significant impediment to achieving one's full potential. From a social justice perspective, all Americans should have health-care coverage, participation should be mandatory, and everyone should have basic benefits (National Coalition on Health Care, 2006).

Moral and Ethical Issues

Debates over national health-care issues focus on two primary concerns—the proportion of the country's resources that should be allocated to health care and how those resources should be allocated. As our knowledge and technology in the health-care arena continue to expand, health-care decisions will become increasingly moral and ethical. Given scarce resources, for example, should a premature baby who requires tens of thousands of dollars to be kept alive be given maximum treatment to save his or her life, particularly when the child may live a life continually fraught with health problems? And what about organ transplants and kidney dialysis? Should these costly procedures be available to everyone? If not, who should receive them?

Given the growing numbers of persons with life-threatening diseases such as AIDS and cancer, how many dollars should be allocated to research, education, and treatment, and who should pay what costs? Does the government have the right to mandate good health practices for women drug users who are pregnant or to impose penalties on individuals with AIDS who do not practice safe sex? With more U.S. citizens living longer, to what extent should resources be allocated toward health care for older persons? And to what extent should attention be given to environmental concerns, such as nuclear power, poor sanitation, and pollution, and their impacts on personal health? Finally, given the high costs of health care, who should pay for health care for the indigent—the federal government, states, local communities, or individuals and their families themselves? If individuals cannot afford health care, should it be denied to them?

Increasingly, social workers are playing a central role in helping policymakers, medical practitioners, and family members make these critical decisions. Social workers provide services in a variety of health-related settings, ranging from basic care and specialty hospitals to family-planning clinics, rape crisis centers, home health-care programs, and hospice programs. The area of health care, particularly as it relates to the elderly, is one of the fastest-growing areas of employment today (U.S. Department of Health and Human Services, 2003).

A Systems/Ecological Approach to Health Care

Because the systems/ecological perspective was first introduced as a mechanism to explain the functioning of the human body, this perspective has a longer history within the health-care arena than other arenas in which social workers

function. As early as the Greek and Roman eras of civilization, many health problems were observed to be precipitated by changes in the environment. An ancient Greek medical text entitled *Airs, Waters, and Places,* said to be authored by Hippocrates, explained health problems in terms of person–environment relationships. This work attributed human functioning to four body fluids: blood, phlegm, and black and yellow bile. As long as these body fluids were in equilibrium, the individual was considered to be healthy. But Hippocrates attributed changes in the balance of these fluids to ecological variations in temperature, ventilation, and an individual's lifestyle in relation to eating, drinking, and working. Negative influences in the environment caused these fluids to become unbalanced, which in turn resulted in illness (Catalano, 1979).

Other early works subscribed to germ theory, based on the premise that illness is a function of the interactions among an organism's adaptive capacities in an environment full of infectious agents, toxins, and safety hazards. The Greeks and Romans also were cognizant of the relationship between sanitation and illness. Early Roman writings suggested that people could predict and control their health through the environment and prevent epidemic diseases by avoiding marshes, standing water, winds, and high temperatures. Public baths, sewers, and free medical care were ways by which early civilizations promoted health and reduced disease (Catalano, 1979).

The focus on the relationship between individual health and the environment continued during later centuries. Johann Peter Frank's medical treatise, *System of a Complete Medical Policy* (written in 1774–1821), advocated education of midwives and new mothers, a healthy school environment, personal hygiene, nutrition, sewers and sanitation, accident prevention, collection of vital statistics such as births and deaths, and efficient administration of hospitals to care for the sick.

Numerous studies throughout the years have attributed the incidence of infant mortality, heart disease, and cancer to environmental influences. A number of early studies (see for example,

Dohrenwend & Dohrenwend, 1974) show strong relationships between stressful life events and the subsequent development of physical disorders, supporting Hippocrates' earlier theories of the ways that a negative lifestyle can affect health. Brenner (1973) demonstrated the relationships between health problems—heart disease, infant and adult mortality rates, and other health indicators—and national employment rates between 1915 and 1967. When employment rates were high, health problems were low and low employment rates were associated with higher incidences of health problems.

Interactions between environmental factors, such as unemployment, and mental health significantly affect individual health (National Association of Chronic Disease Directors, 2005; U.S. Department of Health and Human Services, 2001). The relationship between health problems and mental health problems began to receive more attention in the late 1970s with the release of the U.S. Surgeon General's national health report, *Healthy People,* which emphasized the link between physical and mental health and noted the significance of strong family ties, supportive friends, and informal and formal support systems in promoting healthy individuals.

Israel, Eng, Schulz, Parker, and Satcher (2005) take a somewhat different systems perspective. They present research showing that people who perceive their environments as stressful, such as those living in highly urban or highly rural areas, place their psychological systems in jeopardy and develop ways to cope that are tied to their perception of the situation. For example, an elderly man living in a rural area who perceives himself as being extremely isolated and without the resources to get him to a hospital quickly if he becomes ill is more likely to incur health problems than an elderly man who perceives that he is living in an area where health care is more readily available. As can be seen in Table 9.1, the greatest contributions to premature death are not individual hereditary factors but, rather, environmental and lifestyle factors.

Factors Affecting Health

Studies show that the leading factors affecting health are related to income, ethnicity, gender, age, disability, and where one lives (National Center for Health Statistics, 2005c; U.S. Department of Health and Human Services, 2006a). Note that all of these factors interact with environmental and lifestyle factors to either increase or decrease the likelihood of good health. These factors are further explained below.

INCOME

The higher the income, the more likely a person is to be in good health. The poor are much more likely to have health problems. This is because people with higher incomes are more likely to have health insurance, seek medical care earlier and more often, buy and eat more nutritious foods, and have less mental stress. The poor also are more likely to live in environmentally unhealthy places, such as areas with poor sanitation or close to hazardous wastes (Campbell-White, Merrick, & Yazbeck, 2006; Herd, House, & Schoeni, 2006; Knab, Garfinkel, & McLanahan, 2006; Williams & Mohammed, 2006).

Even families in which all adult members are employed have difficulty affording health insurance and health care. Eight in 10 uninsured Americans come from "working families." Of those, 70% are not offered employer-based health insurance. While 90% of workers who earn $15 an hour or more are offered coverage, less than half earning $7 or less are offered coverage (Families USA, 2003b).

According to the National Center for Chronic Disease Prevention and Health Promotion (2006b), most Americans report themselves to be in good health. In a national survey conducted by the Centers for Disease Control and Prevention (2003a), Americans reported feeling physically or mentally unhealthy about 5 days a month and "healthy and full of energy" about 19 days a month. Adults with the lowest income, however, reported feeling unhealthy more days than those with higher income. Studies show that the impact

TABLE 9.1

Major Factors Contributing to Death: Estimated Percentage Contribution of Cause for 15 Leading Causes of Death in 2001

Leading Causes of Death	Age-Adjusted Rate*	Lifestyle (%)	Environment (%)	Inadequacy of Health Care Services (%)	Genetic/ Hereditary Factors (%)
Heart diseases	247.7	54	9	12	25
Cancer	195.8	37	24	10	29
Strokes	57.49	50	20	10	22
Pulmonary diseases	44.0	50	22	7	21
Diabetes	25.2	50	0	6	60
Influenza/Pneumonia	22	34	20	18	2
Non-motor vehicle accidents	19.6	23	31	4	4
Motor vehicle accidents	14.7	69	18	12	1
Alzheimer's disease	19.0	NA	NA	NA	NA
Kidney diseases	14.0	NA	NA	NA	NA
Septicemia	11.4	NA	NA	NA	NA
Suicide	10.3	60	35	3	18
Liver diseases	9.4	NA	NA	NA	NA
Homicide	6.9	63	35	0	2
Hypertension	6.7	NA	NA	NA	NA
Pneumonitis	6.2	NA	NA	NA	NA
All causes listed	855.0	51	19	10	20

*Per 100,000 population

NA = Data not available.

Notes:

1. Accidents in this chart are delineated by motor vehicular and non-motor vehicular.
2. Rates for diseases of the heart, cancer, strokes, and influenza and pneumonia decreased slightly; increases were seen in Alzheimer's disease, kidney disease, and hypertension.
3. Homicide rate increased due to the 2001 terrorist attack against the United States.
4. The death rate for HIV declined by 3.8% and is no longer one of the leading causes of death for all ages, although it is the sixth leading cause of death for those 25–44 years of age.

Source: Data compiled from *National Vital Statistics Reports, 51*(5) (March, 2003), National Center for Health Statistics, Centers for Disease Control and Prevention, U.S. Department of Health and Human Services, 2003a.

of low income on health is especially damaging to infants and children. The chances of death or serious illness at birth can be linked directly to whether the mothers have health insurance. Uninsured babies are 30% more likely than insured babies to die or to have serious medical problems at birth, and the infant mortality rate of births to women living in poverty is more than 50% higher than for women above the poverty line who are giving birth (Annie E. Casey Foundation, 2006).

Almost 30% of children living in low-income families had no health insurance in 2003. This figure is even higher for pockets of deep poverty in the country such as Appalachia and the area along the Texas–Mexico Border. In 2003, 5.8 million uninsured children were living in families below the poverty line (Families USA, 2003b). Some of these children may have been eligible for programs such as Medicaid (the federal medical care plan for the poor) or the Children's Health Insurance Program (CHIP). Because of state and federal budget deficits, however, many states passed legislation that significantly reduced the numbers of children and adults eligible for these programs, as well as available services. Increasing numbers of children and adults likely will continue to lose either work-related healthcare benefits or Medicaid or CHIP benefits in the future because of the cost of these benefits and the lack of political will to do something about it.

ETHNICITY

Primarily because of higher income, whites as a group enjoy better health than people of color. Native Americans report the most unhealthy days, and nearly twice as many African Americans as Caucasians report that they are in fair or poor health. Chronic disease has a devastating impact on minority populations. For example, the prevalence of diabetes among African Americans is about 70% higher than among Caucasians, and the prevalence among Latinos and Native Americans is considerably higher than it is for Caucasians (National Center for Health Statistics, 2006b).

Although life expectancy is increasing for all groups, the expectancy rates for groups of color are still lower than for whites. **Infant mortality rate**—the number of infant deaths compared to total infant births during a given time period—is twice as high for people of color as for whites. Infants born to uninsured African American mothers are twice as likely as babies born to insured mothers to die or to have serious medical problems (Children's Defense Fund, 2006).

Further, people of color are less likely to seek health care for themselves and their children. Although special outreach programs and mandatory vaccination programs associated with preschool programs have increased the number of all preschoolers receiving immunizations, fewer African American, Latino, and Native American children than Caucasian children are fully immunized. African American preschoolers, for example, are apt not to be fully immunized, and 40% of all African American women, compared to 20% of Caucasian women, do not receive any prenatal care during their first trimester of pregnancy (Health Resources and Services Administration, 2004b).

People of color also are at higher risk to develop heart disease, diabetes, and cancer. African American males are 85% more likely than Caucasian males to experience strokes, and African American females are 80% more likely than Caucasian females to experience strokes. High blood pressure—a major cause of kidney failure, strokes, and heart disease—affects African Americans one-third more than Caucasians. Research indicates that low socioeconomic status (SES) is the link between high blood pressure and ethnicity. The high blood pressure could be attributed to environmental stress caused by oppression and limited access to social and economic resources (National Center for Health Statistics, 2005). And African Americans are twice as likely as Caucasians to have a disability, often because of high blood pressure and related problems.

Health practitioners are concerned about the growing number of individuals in the United States who are diagnosed with diabetes. Many states and local communities are conducting special outreach efforts in African American, Native American, and Latino communities, as the incidence is much higher in these groups than for Causacians. Serious concern also has been raised about the increased numbers of African American children developing asthma, which has serious life-threatening implications if not properly addressed. Diabetes has been linked to lower income, resulting in poor diet; and asthma is associated with unsafe environmental living conditions including excessive rodent and insect debris (Children's Defense Fund, 2006).

Health conditions that should not be major problems in a wealthy industrialized country such as the United States are increasing among all groups, but particularly in people of color. Studies of health care along the United States–Mexico border, for example, show high rates of tuberculosis, hepatitis, and malaria (Office of Rural Health Policy, 2006). Life expectancies for people of color also are much shorter than for whites: 75.3 years for white men compared to 69.0 years for non-white men, and 80.5 years for white women compared to 76.1 for non-white women (National Center for Health Statistics, 2006b). Common causes of death also differ by ethnicity (see Table 9.2).

Latino immigrants are less likely than members of other groups of color to be insured, although immigrants and their U.S.-born children make up two-thirds of the Latino population. Many immigrants who are eligible for coverage are afraid to apply because they think it will jeopardize their citizenship status. Many also are unaware that their children may be eligible for benefits if they are born in the United States (Flores, Abreu, & Tomany-Korman, 2006; Rehm, 2003).

Increasing attention is being given to how to cover health-care costs for immigrants. Initially, the Welfare Reform Act of 1996 restricted immigrant access to health care. In 2003, in every state except Wyoming, to be eligible for Medicaid or the State Children's Health Insurance Program, immigrants who arrived in the United States after August 22, 1996, must wait 5 years after arriving and meet other criteria (Borjas, 2003).

TABLE 9.2
Top Causes of Death in the United States by Ethnicity, 2000

Cause	All Groups	White	Black	Hispanic	American Indian	Asian or Pacific Islander
Heart disease	1	1	1	1	1	2
Cancer	2	2	2	2	2	1
Strokes	3	3	3	4	5	3
Pulmonary disease	4	4	8	8	7	5
Accidents	5	5	4	3	3	4
Diabetes	6	7	5	5	4	7
Influenza/pneumonia	7	6	10	9	9	6
Alzheimer's disease	8	8			4	
Kidney disease	9	9	9		10	9
Septicemia	10					
Suicide		10			8	8
Liver diseases				6	6	
Perinatal conditions						10
Homicide			6	7		
HIV			7	10		

Source: National Center for Health Statistics (2002, Sept. 16). *Deaths and Percent of Total Deaths for the Top 10 Leading Causes of Death,* Tables C, E and F, *National Vital Statistics Report, 50*(16).

GENDER

The average life expectancy continues to increase for men and women alike. Since 1950, it has increased 9.3 years for men and 9.1 years for women. In 2003, the life expectancy was 74.8 years for men and 80.1 years for women (National Center for Health Statistics, 2006b). Although the longer average life expectancy for women might be viewed as an advantage for women, it also is a disadvantage for them. Because of the difference in life expectancy and because women have less built up in Social Security as a result of staying home and rearing children, more elderly women who become widowed have little or no health insurance coverage and limited Social Security benefits. Thus, these women are more likely to spend their last years in poverty, which in turn places them at more risk for poor health.

AGE

Our country's oldest and youngest citizens are at the highest risk for poor health. The elderly are at risk as a result of aging and because many live in poverty. One-third of today's elderly are poor and do not seek health care as needed because the high costs are prohibitive. One group of at-risk elderly is the more than 1.5 million persons in the United States with Alzheimer's disease, 80%–90% are age 65 and older. The incidence is increasing partly as a result of better diagnostic ability, and now is the eighth leading cause of death in the United States (National Center for Health Statistics, 2006a).

The aging factor will be of even greater significance as the U.S. population continues to age: About 12% of the population is over age 65, and by 2050, nearly one in every five persons in the United States will be over 65 (U.S. Census Bureau, 2006c). The nursing-home population is expected to at least double by 2030 for persons ages 65, and perhaps triple for those ages 85 and older (Administration on Aging, 2005).

One of the wealthiest countries in the world, the United States nevertheless continues to have a higher infant mortality rate (6.6 deaths per 1,000 live births) than any Western country (U.S. Census Bureau, 2006c). As the number of children growing up in poverty continues to increase and health care options for them are reduced because of funding, U.S. children will be at more risk for serious health problems.

The major causes of death vary significantly by age. Although tremendous gains have been made in preventing some major causes of death, many deaths are not related to major physical illness, particularly in youth. Accidents are still the leading cause of death for individuals under 25 years of age. Homicide is one of the three leading causes of death for persons ages 5 to 25. Although HIV/AIDS is no longer one of the 15 leading causes of death for the general population, it is sixth for individuals 25–44 years of age (National Center for Health Statistics, 2004a).

DISABILITY

People with both permanent and temporary disabilities are much more at risk than nondisabled people to have serious health problems. People with a severe disability are more likely to have Medicaid or Medicare coverage, to live below the poverty level, to report their health status as "fair or poor," and to receive public assistance (U.S. Census Bureau, 2006a). Their lesser resilience as a result of their disability often is compounded by the lack of affordable, accessible, appropriate health care that would allow them to maintain good preventive health practices.

RURAL AND URBAN AREAS

People who live in either rural or highly populated urban areas are more at risk to have health problems. In a highly populated urban area, this can be attributed to more environmental hazards such as pollution and increased stress. In sparsely populated rural areas, poorer health can be attributed to a lack of medical facilities for prevention and early medical care. More than half of all people at the poverty level live in rural areas, and they also are more likely than persons in urban areas to have emotional disorders (see chapter 14).

Applying a Systems/Ecological Perspective

A systems/ecological perspective focuses on the interaction and interdependence between person and environment in understanding **health risk factors**—the factors that affect individuals' health and place them at risk for serious health problems and health conditions (see Table 9.1). The current emphasis on **holistic health care** stems from a systems/ecological approach. This perspective views all aspects of an individual's health in relation to how that individual interacts with family members, the workplace, and the community, and also to how the environment, including community quality of life, as well as legislation and funding available to support quality of life, affects a person's health.

This perspective gradually is replacing the more traditional medical model used by health practitioners, which is concerned with symptoms and malfunctions of only one part of the body to the exclusion of other body systems or the environment within which the individual interacts. The World Health Organization (2003) has defined **health** as "a state of complete physical, mental, and social well-being and not merely the absence of disease or infirmity." This definition reflects the systems/ecological perspective in viewing health as clearly dependent on a combination of environmental, physiological, sociological, and psychological factors.

U.S. health experts are directing more attention to indicators of health. The U.S. Department of Health and Human Services has established indicators to measure the health of Americans, with anticipated gains targeted to be met by 2010 (see Table 9.3).

The Evolution of Health Care in America

The early emphasis for health care in the United States was on keeping people alive. Those born in the United States 200 years ago had only a 50% chance of surviving long enough to celebrate their 21st birthday. One-third of all deaths were children younger than 5 years old. Even then, people of color had higher death rates. In the late 18th century, the death rate was 30 per thousand for whites and 70 per thousand for slaves (U.S. Public Health Service, 1977). Health practitioners at that time were limited in number and training, and they faced great difficulty in keeping their patients alive because of environmental constraints such as poor sanitation and extreme poverty.

Many illnesses resulted in catastrophic epidemics, which claimed the lives of entire families. In 1793, during a yellow fever epidemic in Philadelphia, three physicians were available to care for 6,000 patients stricken with the disease. Thus, early attempts to improve health care in the United States included national and state legislation relating to control of communicable diseases, sanitation measures such as pasteurization of milk, and education for midwives, physicians, and young mothers (U.S. Public Health Service, 1977).

Although more recent legislation and programs have been directed to controlling chronic, degenerative diseases such as heart disease and cancer, self-inflicted illnesses such as cirrhosis of the liver, and other health problems such as accidents and violence, most efforts are still directed to restoring health *after* illness has occurred. The health-care system in the United States still allows many U.S. citizens to remain unserved or underserved, and mortality rates remain higher than in many developed countries (U.S. Census Bureau, 2006a).

TABLE 9.3
Healthy People 2010 Leading Indicators with Established Targets for 2010

Leading Health Indicator	1990	2000	2010 Target
% of adolescents in grades 9–12 who engaged in 20 minutes or more of vigorous activity 3 or more days per week	—	65	85
% of adults over 18 who engaged in moderate or vigorous activity at least 20 minutes 3 days a week	—	32	50
% of overweight youth ages 6–19	11	15	5
% of obese adults over 20 years of age	23	31	15
% of adolescents in grades 9–12 who smoked cigarettes one or more days in past 30 days	—	28	16
% of adults 18 or over who smoked more than 100 cigarettes in their lifetime and now report smoking on some days or every day	25	23	12
% of adolescents 12–17 who reported no use of alcohol or illicit drug use in past 30 days	—	80	89
% of adults 18 and over who reported illicit drug use in past 30 days	—	5.9	2
% of adults 18 and over who reported binge drinking in past 30 days	—	22	6
% of adolescents in grades 9–12 not sexually active or sexually active and using condoms	—	86	95
% of sexually active unmarried women 18–44 who report condom use by partners		23 (1995)	50
New cases of gonorrhea per 100,000 population	277	129	19
% of adults 18 and over with recognized depression who received treatment		23 (1997)	50
Age-adjusted suicide rate per 100,000 population	12.5	10.6	5
Age-adjusted death rate for motor vehicle traffic-related injuries per 100,000 population	18.0	15.2	9.2
Age-adjusted homicide rate per 100,000 standard population	9.4	6.1	3
% of population exposed to ozone above EPA standard	—	43	0
% of persons age 4 and over exposed to environmental tobacco smoke	65	—	45
Hospital admissions for asthma of persons under 18 per 10,000 population	18	21.4 (2001)	17.3
% of children 19–35 months who received all recommended immunizations	—	73	80
% of adults over 65 who received influenza vaccine	—	65	90
% of persons under 65 with health insurance	—	84	100
% of persons with specific source of on-going primary care	—	88	96
% of pregnant women who receive prenatal care in first trimester	76	83	90

Source: *Healthy People 2010 Leading Health Indicators, Table 52. Health, United States, 2002* (Washington, DC: Centers for Disease Control and Prevention. U.S. Department of Health and Human Services, 2003a).

Critical Issues in Current Health-Care Delivery

Many domestic-policy professionals believe that the United States is in the midst of a crisis in health care. While health-care costs are increasing significantly, more and more Americans are finding that health care is inaccessible to them. More infants are dying at birth, and other people are developing serious health problems that go untreated.

Funding and Costs of Health Care

The rapidly increasing cost of health care at all levels in the United States—for consumers, local health-care practitioners, community hospitals, local governments, and state and federal programs—is considered to be one of the most critical issues facing our country today. In 2003, the latest year for which national statistics are available, national spending on health care reached $1.7 trillion (National Center for Health Statistics, 2005b). According to Heffler et al. (2005), the United States spent $5.5 billion a day on health care alone in 2005, and this amount was predicted to increase to $10.2 billion a day by 2014, or about $3.2 trillion per year (see Figures 9.2 and 9.3). Most of the increased expenditures funded prescription drugs—the fastest-growing health-care expense—as well as hospitals, nursing homes, and home health care (Heffler et al., 2005).

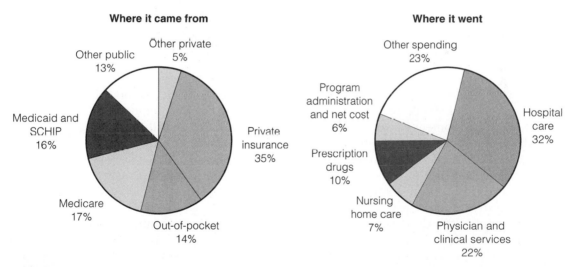

Where it came from

Other private 5%
Other public 13%
Medicaid and SCHIP 16%
Medicare 17%
Out-of-pocket 14%
Private insurance 35%

Where it went

Other spending 23%
Program administration and net cost 6%
Prescription drugs 10%
Nursing home care 7%
Physician and clinical services 22%
Hospital care 32%

FIGURE 9.2

The Nation's Health Dollar: 2001

"Other Public" includes programs such as workers' compensation, public health activity, Department of Defense, Department of Veterans Affairs, Indian Health Service, and state and local hospital subsidies and health.

"Other Private" includes industrial in-plant, privately funded construction, and non-patient revenues, including philanthropy.

"Other Spending" includes dental services, other professional services, home health care, durable medical products, over-the-counter medicines and sundries, public health activities, research, and construction.

Source: Centers for Medicare and Medicaid Services. *Where the Nation's Health Dollar Came From and Where It Went* (Washington, DC: Office of the Actuary, National Health Statistics Group, 2003b).

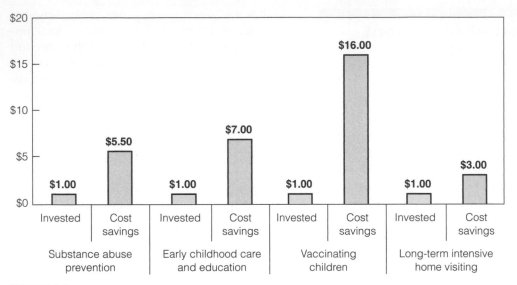

FIGURE 9.3

Look What a Dollar Can Do!

Source: Prevention Pays Work Group (Seattle: Children's Alliance Work Group, 2002).
Available: http://www.childrensalliance.org/whatwedo/preventionpays.htm

One of the major issues being debated at all government levels is who should pay for what. In 2005, the federal government paid $627.2 billion for health care, state and local governments paid $264.3 billion, and private expenditures totaled $1,045.3 billion. Nearly 54% of health care expenditures are paid by private sources (individuals and third-party insurance payments), and about 46% with public funds (Heffler et al., 2005). Governments at all levels are trying to find ways to reduce health-care costs at the same time that more and more individuals and families currently paying health costs themselves are struggling to afford the rising costs.

Individuals like Arturo and Alicia Hernandez, introduced at the beginning of this chapter, are not the only ones facing financial bankruptcy because of health-care costs. Physicians are leaving independently owned practices or have stopped taking reimbursements from third parties such as Medicaid, Medicare, and private health insurance, particularly in rural and poverty areas; hospitals are closing; insurance companies are going out of business; communities and states are in the red because of increased costs of indigent health care; and the federal government's Medicaid and Medicare systems are in danger of not having enough money to meet the needs of eligible clients. Major changes are being proposed in both Medicaid and Medicare (discussed later in the chapter).

The emphasis during the 1950s and 1960s was on providing the best possible health care to all Americans and improving health personnel, services, and research. As costs for health care have skyrocketed, though, attention has shifted to ways to control costs and to determine who should pay for what expenditures. In 2003, the most recent year for which national statistics are available, the U.S. health-care system accommodated more than 1 billion ambulatory care visits to physicians' offices and hospital outpatient and emergency departments; admitted and treated more than 36 million persons in 6,600 hospitals; provided care to almost 1.8 million persons, mostly elderly, in more than 16,000 nursing homes; provided more than 500 million outpatient visits to hospitals; and offered home health and hospice care to more than 8 million people. While hospital emergency room and outpatient visits have increased, hospital inpatient numbers have decreased, from almost 38 million in 1980, and the average stay has decreased from 7.3 days to 4.9 (National Center for Health Statistics, 2004b).

Health Insurance Plans and Managed Care

In 2002, almost 70% of the U.S. population under 65 years of age had some form of **private health insurance** (purchased by individuals or employers from companies such as Blue Cross/Blue Shield). The major source of insurance coverage for this group is private employer-sponsored group health insurance obtained through a current or former employer or union. Until recently, the standard practice among employers was to provide health insurance coverage (employer-sponsored insurance) at no cost to their employees.

As health-care costs skyrocketed, employers began to charge employees for a portion of the premiums for health-care insurance (a practice called *premium sharing*), or they restricted coverage to only the employee and not the employee's spouse or children, or they stopped providing coverage at all. Between 2001 and 2005, employer-sponsored health insurance premiums rose by about 9% to 14% annually for premiums for a family of four, and an average family's health insurance premium was $10,880 in 2005. While the average share of a family premium that employees were required to pay themselves remained about 27% between 2001 and 2005, that share, given the large increases in premiums, amounted to an increase of nearly $1,000 over this period, from $1,788 a year in 2001 to $2,712 by 2005 (Kaiser Family Foundation, 2005).

Here, we point out that employees' earnings grew more slowly than the percentage increase in health-care premiums, making health care even less affordable. As a result, employees are either dropping coverage or, if their coverage

is provided, not paying for the far more expensive coverage for their families. The intersecting issues of who should get employee- or government-sponsored health-care benefits, how much those benefits should be, and what types of illness are covered are increasingly becoming issues of social justice as large segments of society (predominately low-wage workers) are being relegated to a life of low-income or even poverty, for which there is no way out.

One factor that has contributed to the higher costs for private and public health care alike has been the shift from retrospective to prospective payment systems. In the past, with the exception of insurance for hospitalization, most health care was paid for after it was used. People went to the doctor and paid the full amount after the visit. Today, most health care is paid in advance through premiums to private insurance companies or federal programs such as Medicaid, because the health-care industry is trying to contain costs and promote preventive health care.

Most current health-care plans are based on a **managed care system,** in which health-care delivery limits the use and cost of services and measures performance through a program of careful monitoring and control. Under managed care, "health-care professionals" hired by health insurance companies and large employers systematically review specific health-care needs and determine the most cost-effective ways to provide for them. After review, limited options are presented to consumers. Some plans include preferred provider organizations (PPOs), which offer health care through a network of specific providers. An individual who chooses providers other than those in the pre-approved network usually must get specific permission from the health-care plan to do so, pay additional costs to use other providers, or not have those health-care costs covered by the plan at all.

Another group in the health care industry consists of **health maintenance organizations (HMOs),** prepaid medical group practices to which individuals pay monthly fees and receive specific types of health care at no cost or minimum costs per visit. The five HMO models are (National Center for Health Statistics, 2006d):

1. *group model*—an HMO that contracts with a single multi-specialty medical group to provide care for the HMO's membership,
2. *staff model*—a system through which patients receive services from only a limited number of providers, and physicians are employees of the HMO,
3. *network model*—an HMO that contracts with multiple physician groups to provide services to HMO members,
4. *individual practice association* (IPA)—a type of health-care provider organization composed of a group of independent practicing physicians who maintain their own offices and band together for the purpose of contracting their services to HMOs, and
5. *mixed model*—an HMO that combines features of more than one HMO.

In 2003, almost 23% of individuals in the United States were enrolled in HMOs (National Center for Health Statistics, 2005c). HMO enrollment increased steadily during the 1990s but declined by nearly 3 million between 2003 and 2004, reflecting a shake-out in the industry, reduction in the number and variety of plans available for selection, and consumers' growing dissatisfaction with the quality of services delivered. The number of available HMO plans also decreased by 27% between 2000 and 2004, with 412 plans available in 2004 (National Center for Health Statistics, 2005c).

More children than adults are covered through HMOs, and both Medicare and Medicaid have developed HMO plans to manage care and costs. Payment of a monthly amount to a health insurance company or an HMO entitles a person—and, if insured, the person's family—to needed health care on demand at either no additional cost or a limited cost (for example, 15% of the cost) with the insurance or health-care company paying the additional 85%. HMOs offer less choice. The insured must see someone from the HMO or receive a referral from the HMO, but the co-pays usually are lower and are advantageous for some families with children requiring frequent visits.

Managed-care plans emphasize more preventive services, reduced hospital stays, and fewer expensive medical tests, but some have expressed concern about managed-care efforts. For example, what happens when managed-care organizations override the recommendations of physicians and limit or deny coverage for medical care or treatment? State and federal policymakers have responded to these issues by introducing legislation and enacting laws. Virtually all states have adopted one or more laws addressing specific consumer concerns. These laws are aimed at increasing consumer access to services (for example, emergency care, prescription drugs, specialists), prohibiting the use of incentives that encourage physicians to deny care, and assuring consumer rights in the case of disputes.

Although these laws provide health-care consumers some reassurance, managed-care consumers cannot count on basic protections. The states have little consistency in their protections for consumers. Some states have enacted only one or two protections for example, prohibiting provider "gag rules" (which prevent physicians and health providers from fully disclosing treatment options to patients) or the guarantee of women to direct access to obstetricians and gynecologists. Few states have established comprehensive protections for managed care enrollees.

In its report *Hit and Miss: State Managed Care Laws,* Families USA (1998) suggested managed health-care protections, including:

- the right to go to an emergency room and have the managed-care plan pay for resulting care, if a person reasonably believes that he or she is in an emergency situation;
- the right to receive health care from an out-of-network provider when the health plan's network of providers is inadequate;

- the right of a person with a serious illness or disability to use a specialist as a primary care provider;
- the right of a seriously ill person to receive standing referrals to health specialists;
- a woman's right to gain direct access to an obstetrician or gynecologist;
- the right of a seriously ill patient or a pregnant woman to continue receiving health care for a specified period of time from a physician who has been dropped by the health plan;
- establishment of a procedure that enables a patient to obtain specific prescription drugs that are not on a health plan's drug formulary;
- the right to appeal denial of care through a review process that is external to, and independent of, health plans;
- establishment of consumer assistance, or ombudsman, programs;
- prohibitions against plans' use of "gag rules" (rules that prevent physicians and health providers from fully disclosing treatment options to patients);
- prohibitions against plans' reliance on inappropriate financial incentives to deny or reduce necessary health care;
- establishment of state laws that prevent plans from prohibiting participation in clinical trials; and
- creation of state laws enabling enrollees to sue their health plans when they improperly deny care.

A survey of state consumer protection laws as of March 2001 revealed the following (Families USA, 2003c).

- No state had passed a series of laws addressing all of the protections listed above.
- Vermont had enacted the greatest number of those protections (11 total), and Mississippi and Wyoming the fewest (one each).
- 36 states and the District of Columbia had enacted between five and nine of these protections.

- Approximately one-third of Americans with employer-provided health care (about 51 million persons) had "self-insured" plans and were preempted from patient protections established by state laws.
- Of those with health insurance provided by their employer, 83% (approximately 124 million Americans) were preempted, under the Employee Retirement Income Security Act (ERISA) of 1974, from seeking state-prescribed remedies for wrongful denials of care, and federal remedies for these individuals were unavailable as well.

As can be seen, the unevenness in state consumer protection legislation is compounded by ERISA, which exempts many millions of Americans from the state protections that do exist. As a result, even within the same state, protections vary. One set of rules applies to those who purchase their own insurance; another set of rules applies to those in employer-paid, self-insured plans; and yet another set of rules applies to those in employer-paid plans who are not self-insured. This variability is an enormous source of confusion for consumers, leaving them uncertain about their health-care coverage and concerned about whether they will get the care they need. In 2002, the U.S. Supreme Court upheld state laws allowing consumers the right to an independent medical review of decisions made by HMOs.

Several bills have been introduced at the federal level, expanding patients' rights. One bill that met with success was the Health Insurance Portability and Accountability Act of 1996 (HIPPA). This legislation, which took effect in April of 2003, establishes federal privacy standards to protect patients' medical records, giving individuals access to medical records and more control over how personal health information is shared, including electronic protections. Health and mental health facilities are required to follow HIPPA standards (Office of Civil Rights—HIPPA, 2003).

Managed plans have had mixed success in meeting the twin goals of cost-containment and ensuring accessible, quality health care. If anything, the pendulum has swung to the cost-containment side at the expense of ensuring accessible, quality health-care services. A number of prominent physician groups around the country have raised concerns about managed care plans and are supporting managed-care reform. Chief among them is the American Academy of Family Physicians, which published the following list of provisions that it believes are essential for Congress to include in any comprehensive managed care legislation (American Academy of Family Physicians, 2001, p. 1):

- a requirement that basic information about covered and excluded benefits, financial obligations, plan providers, experimental benefits, and other important plan provisions be available to all plan enrollees;
- a requirement that plans have an internal and external appeals process enabling meaningful and prompt access for patients and the physicians;
- a requirement that plans have a "prudent layperson standard" enabling patients to secure emergency care out of the plan without prior authorization;
- a requirement that plans honor the right of each physician and other health-care providers to communicate freely with all patients;
- a requirement that plans have a policy that protects physicians who advocate on behalf of their patients for needed medical benefits;
- an assurance that "medical necessity" decisions on clinically appropriate care will be made by physicians;
- a requirement that self-funded ERISA plans are held responsible for medical outcomes, as are other plans, within any given state;
- a requirement that self-funded ERISA plans allow injured patients to seek recovery in federal court for improper denials of coverage, and that meaningful liability caps in federal

court will ensure that doctors recognize their responsibility to ensure that patients have timely access to needed medical care;
- a requirement that plans have a process to enable use of non-formulary drugs when they are medically indicated;
- the inclusion of family physicians in any definitions of women's and children's health-care providers to ensure access to all qualified physicians;
- an accurate definition of primary care (care provided by family physicians, general internists, and general pediatricians);
- a requirement that managed-care entities must update their list of participating providers every 30 days and make it available to physicians and patients; and
- a requirement that managed-care entities furnish physicians with a fee schedule showing what they will be paid for services that will be provided by that physician under the plan when negotiating with the physician to become or continue as a healthcare provider under the managed care plan.

Because the health-care system is part of the free-market system in the United States, there always will be tensions between those who wish to maximize profit and return on investment and those who demand accessible, quality health care for all Americans. Thus, social work professionals must advocate for a health-care system that is accessible to everyone, regardless of their ability to pay for services.

In short, attempts have been made to promote early preventive health care to create a nation that is physically healthier, and to reduce costs. Neither task has been successful. Administrative costs alone to manage such a complex system have escalated over the years. Health-care costs continue to rise rapidly in spite of efforts at cost-containment. Increases can be seen at every level, and the average cost of health care per person per year in the United States is the highest rate of any industrialized country. Employees' share of health insurance of health-care benefits

TABLE 9.4
Comparisons of Health-Care Costs, Life Expectancy, and Infant Mortality Rates for 20 Industrialized Countries

Country	% of GDP Allocated to Health Care/Rank	Infant Mortality Rate per 1,000 2001/Rank	Average Life Expectancy (Years) 2001/Rank
United States	12.9/1	6.8/13	77.3/12
Germany	10.3/2	4.7/4	77.6/11
Canada	9.3/3	5.0/7	79.6/5
France	9.3/3	4.5/3	78.9/3
Belgium	8.8/5	4.7/4	78.0/9
Netherlands	8.7/6	4.4/2	78.4/8
Australia	8.6/7	5.0/7	79.9/2
Greece	8.4/8	6.4/12	78.6/7
Italy	7.9/9	5.8/10	79.1/6
Japan	7.5/11	3.9/1	80.8/1
Czech Republic	7.4/12	7.4/15	74.7/17
Spain	7.0/13	4.9/6	78.9/3
United Kingdom	6.9/14	5.5/9	77.8/10
Hungary	6.8/15	9.0/18	71.6/20
Poland	6.2/16	9.4/19	73.4/19
Portugal	7.7/10	5.9/11	75.9/15
South Korea	5.4/17	7.7/17	74.7/17
Cuba	NA	7.4/15	76.4/14
Taiwan	NA	6.9/14	76.5/13
Chile	NA	9.4/19	75.9/15
*Turkey	2.7	47.3	71.2

Note: Shows only top 20 countries re infant death rates and longevity with populations of 10 million or more in 2001.
*Turkey is included for comparison purposes only; it is not ranked in the top 20 of any category
NA = Data not available.
Source: Data compiled from U.S. National Center for Health Statistics, Hyattsville, MD, 2002.

borne by employers remains high, and these costs are passed on to consumers through higher prices for products and services.

Comparing Health-Care Costs to Outcomes

While the United States spends more on health care than any other country, its health-care system does not produce superior outcomes in comparison to other countries (see Table 9.4). In 2001, the United States ranked 12th in life expectancy and 13th in infant mortality among 20 industrialized countries with populations of 10 million or more (U.S. Census Bureau, 2005).

In 2004, according to the U.S. Census Bureau (2006c), infant mortality rates in countries with 12 million or more people ranged from 3.9 per 1,000 live births in Japan to 166.0 in Afghanistan. The U.S. rate was 6.6 deaths per 1,000 live births.

Twelve countries had infant mortality rates lower than that of the United States. Life expectancy in 2004 ranged from 80.8 in Japan to 39.0 in Zimbabwe. The U.S. average life expectancy was 77.3, twelfth among the countries cited. It is understandable that Afghanistan's infant mortality rate is high and Zimbabwe's life expectancy rates so low, as life in these countries is more challenging than in many countries. It is more difficult to understand why the infant mortality rate in the United States is higher than most Western countries and why the life expectancy for both males and females is much lower, because the United States spends more than any other country on health care as a percent of **Gross Domestic Product (GDP)** (U.S. Census Bureau, 2006c). When comparing significant health-care indicators, the U.S. investment in health care has failed to achieve its intended outcomes. Of all children in the United States, nearly one in five is born to mothers who received no prenatal care during the first 3 months of pregnancy (Children's Defense Fund, 2006).

Reasons for Rising Health-Care Costs

Although costs of health care, like costs in other areas, have risen because of inflation, other reasons for rising health expenditures must be considered, too. Some attribute the increased costs to more extensive use of medical resources by a more educated population interested in preventive health care. They argue that accessibility to group insurance plans through the workplace and the increase in HMOs and other health programs aimed at reducing health costs actually increase costs because of more extensive use. Statistics show, however, that many Americans, particularly poor people—people of color, single-parent females, and the elderly—work for employers that do not offer health insurance or are paid such low wages that they cannot afford the health insurance offered. Thus, they are less apt to use health-care resources, and when they do, they are more likely to need more costly services because they have not sought preventive care.

Even with today's emphasis on wellness and public awareness about the potential damages of smoking, use of alcohol and other drugs, and lack of exercise, private citizens and all levels of U.S. government spend relatively few dollars (see Figure 9.3). This trend continues even though studies show that dollars spent for prevention more than pay for themselves in the long run (Children's Alliance Work Group, 2002).

AN INCREASING ELDERLY POPULATION

Because of greater access to health care, improved knowledge and technology, and a better quality of life, people are living longer, which results in greater needs for medical care for people age 65 and older. Comprising approximately 12% of the population and more likely to be poor and unable to pay for health care than other groups, people over age 65 have three times more health problems and needs than people in younger age groups. Between 2005 and 2050, the population over age 65 is projected to increase from 36.7 million to 86.7 million in the United States, a nearly 67% increase (U.S. Census Bureau, 2006c).

As this population continues to grow, the accompanying costs will increase. Few insurance premiums cover the costs of long-term (nursing home) care, and those that do are rapidly raising the premiums for this coverage. The insurance system, particularly care for the elderly, also is fragmented, with separate systems paying for home health care, medical equipment, nursing home care, and medical transportation to and from health-care facilities. By the year 2040, people age 65 and older are expected to account for more than half of the total personal health-care expenditures in the United States.

Concurrently, Medicare and Medicaid costs are expected to increase significantly. Medicare costs in 2003 were $283.1 billion, and they are expected to have an annual growth rate of 10%. Medicaid costs, which were $279 billion in 2003, are expected to increase significantly as the elderly population increases. Although only 8% of the Medicaid population in 2002 was 65 years and older, this group accounted for more than 24% of Medicaid expenditures. In comparison, Temporary Assistance for Needy Families (TANF) recipients and their families made up 45% of the Medicaid population but accounted for only 14.6% of expenditures, while individuals with disabilities made up 15% of the population and accounted for 43% of expenditures (U.S. Census Bureau, 2006a).

INCREASED KNOWLEDGE AND AVAILABILITY OF TECHNOLOGY

A second explanation for the increased costs of health care is the wider availability of knowledge and technology for saving lives—neonatal procedures for infants born prematurely; heart, lung, and other organ transplants; heart surgery to restore circulation and reduce the incidence of heart attacks and other cardiac problems; and sophisticated combinations of medications for a variety of conditions that would have resulted in death in earlier years.

Currently, the extent of and knowledge about technology exceed the dollars necessary to support such sophisticated systems and make them available to everyone in need. In many instances, heroic procedures are covered by health-care policies but preventive care, such as long-term care, rehabilitative services, and health education, are not. Recognizing that values issues are inherent when discussing health care, our current health technologies have become costly. Current studies suggest, for example, that individuals who receive heart transplants live an average of 4 years longer than persons who do not receive transplants, at a cost of $148,000 per transplant, or $37,000 for every additional year of life.

In addition, with more private hospitals and the difficulties faced by public medical facilities in remaining solvent, health care has become increasingly competitive. Many private hospitals now are owned by large corporations with real estate subsidiaries and their own insurance divisions. In many instances, the heightened competition has resulted in duplicative purchases of expensive equipment by hospitals in close proximity.

While hospitals struggle to compete with each other for paying clients, the number of people who are unable to pay hospital bills continues to increase. The limits on **public health insurance** (Medicare and Medicaid) reimbursements to hospitals also have resulted in serious financial problems for hospitals that are unable to provide services at reimbursement levels. The number of hospitals in the United States has been declining steadily in recent years, from 6,965 in 1980 to fewer than 5,764 in 2003. In addition, hospitals are losing large sums of money as a result of uncompensated care. Today, nearly one in 10 patients is indigent and unable to pay for medical costs at all.

EMPHASIS ON THIRD-PARTY PAYMENTS

A third reason suggested for escalated health-care costs is the use of third-party billing by many medical practitioners (billing an insurance company directly rather than billing the patient). Many physicians and hospitals charge the maximum amount allowable under an insurance system, whereas they might be reluctant to charge individual clients the same amount if they knew the clients would be paying for the services directly.

Faced with rapidly increasing costs, private insurance companies in the United States, which cover about half of the population, are minimizing their risks by reducing the benefits covered, requiring second opinions in many instances, increasing co-payments from consumers, and excluding the chronically ill. At the same time, insurance premiums continue to rise, with high costs to employers who pay a portion of employees' premiums, as well as to employees themselves. As a result, many employers, particularly smaller ones, now no longer cover employees or their families or they cover a smaller percentage of premiums, which means that employees are paying much larger shares. More and more people who carry health insurance on an individual basis rather than an employee policy are being forced to cancel their policies because they cannot afford them, requiring local communities to pick up the rising costs of their health care if these individuals become ill and cannot pay their bills.

INCREASED COSTS OF HEALTH CARE FOR THE POOR

A fourth reason for the higher costs of health care is the number of poor people who need health care and cannot afford to pay for it. As this number continues to increase, federal and state governments struggle with the high costs of health care. But efforts to reduce Medicaid and Medicare expenditures by setting ceilings for reimbursable costs have led some physicians and nursing homes to refuse to accept clients under these health-care assistance plans, claiming that they lose too much money because the actual costs are much higher than the ceilings allowed. For those physicians who do continue to see Medicare and Medicaid clients, low reimbursement rates have led some to inflate their billings so they can be paid the prevailing market rate for their services. Ironically, if this practice goes undetected (which, in many cases, it does), the government's desire to drive down the cost of health care is reversed.

One of our country's highest priorities is how to pay for health care while addressing the needs of those who cannot afford it. **Medicaid,** the federal–state partnership program that assists states in providing medical services to eligible low-income individuals, is the single largest source of funding for health services for low-income people. In 2003, Medicaid and Medicare cost states and the federal government $279 billion and $283 billion, respectively, accounting for one-third of national health-care expenditures.

Though eligibility requirements vary by state, all states must provide coverage for children under age 6 and pregnant women in families with incomes at or below 133% of the poverty level ($26,600 for a family of four). Many states cover children under age 1 and pregnant women whose family income is at or below 185% of the poverty level ($37,000 for a family of four). States

are required to provide early and periodic screening, diagnosis, and treatment (EPSDT) services to children, as well as physicians' services and inpatient and outpatient hospital care. States are reimbursed a certain portion of funds they spend for Medicaid, depending on what they cover and whom they serve. In 2003, if a state paid its own funds to expand coverage or to improve services, the federal government reimbursed the state 50%–77% of costs, depending on the rate negotiated between the federal government and the state (Park, Mann, Alker, & Nathanson, 2003).

In 2002, the most recent year for which national statistics are available, Medicaid provided health coverage to more than 50 million people—more than 25 million children, 8 million persons with disabilities, almost 5 million senior adults, and 13 million other low-income adults. Medicaid also covered the costs of approximately 40% of all births and the majority of nursing home care (U.S. Census Bureau, 2006c).

As the U.S. population continues to age, costs of **Medicare**—the medical care coverage program for older adults established as one of the pillars of the War on Poverty programs of the mid-1960s—continue to increase. One major source of concern among senior adults and their families has been the high cost of prescription drugs (see discussion later in this chapter). Compounding the situation, health-care services are fragmented, inaccessible, and unattainable for many U.S. residents, and when they are provided, are not well-matched to the needs of those receiving them. The health-care system in the United States is an unfortunate example of how lack of planning and funding has created an ineffective, narrowly focused, fragmented, and expensive approach to a major social welfare problem.

Even though the Medicaid system of health care for the poor and group insurance programs have problems, of greater concern are the many persons who have no health coverage at all. More than half of the poor in the United States either are not covered by Medicaid or do not use the system. Those who have neither Medicaid nor other health insurance coverage can become destitute immediately when they or members of their family incur catastrophic health problems. Few poor families can afford several thousand dollars in health-care costs, and this amount is not a rarity for serious health problems that require hospitalization. When individuals have no way to pay for their health care, local communities are left to pick up the costs. For many poor people, the emergency room—one of the most expensive forms of health care—is the only choice they have to receive primary health care services. And by the time they do seek health care, their problems are more advanced, further escalating the cost of their care.

Many local public hospitals that are obligated to accept medically indigent patients (referred to by the federal government as *disproportionate share hospitals*) are operating at a deficit. As an example, one local hospital spent more than $2 million on a young child with serious health problems because the girl was not covered by any type of private or public health care plan. Thus, the hospital—and the local taxpayers—absorbed the costs of her care. The story had a happy ending: The child was adopted and moved to a home with parents who were able to provide for her special needs at a cost significantly lower than the $1,500-per-day cost for her hospital care.

In any case, the costs of indigent health care to local communities are increasing. Many state legislators and citizens do not understand the complicated reimbursement system for government programs such as Medicare and Medicaid. Although the proportion of reimbursement to states varies by category of service, for every dollar of Medicaid money spent, the state contribution usually is between 50 and 65 cents. Some state legislatures limit dollars allocated for state health care, not always understanding that limiting state costs reduces the number of federal dollars available to the state and ultimately results in more money, not less, paid by that state's citizens as a result of non-reimbursed costs that are passed on to consumers who are able to pay for services.

An example is provided by one large state that consistently limits its legislative authorization of state dollars for health-care coverage for the poor. As a result, less federal matching money comes into that state and more goes to other states. This means that many of the dollars paid by citizens and businesses of that state in federal income and other taxes go to other states. In one recent year, for example, for every $3.00 that a citizen of the state paid in federal income taxes, only $1.89 was returned to the state. The other $1.11 went to other states for their programs. Yet, because the state authorized only a limited Medicaid program, many women and children were not eligible to receive Medicaid benefits. When they became ill, they went to public hospitals, funded by local tax dollars, while the hospitals and the communities in which they were located had to absorb the costs of their unpaid care. As noted, these nonreimbursed costs ultimately are borne by those who can afford to pay for their health services, creating a vicious cycle with no apparent end in sight.

INCREASING MALPRACTICE SUITS

The propensity to instigate lawsuits is another cost-raising factor in the United States. Medical practitioners fear the increasing number of malpractice suits being filed. One study found that all practitioners face at least one lawsuit during their careers, no matter how competent they are (Baicker & Chandra, 2004). This development has resulted in extremely high costs for malpractice insurance and practitioners' feeling compelled to order numerous tests, exploratory surgery, and other medical procedures when they are not sure what is wrong with an individual, to eliminate the risk of a lawsuit for a wrong decision. Although legislation has been introduced in many states to limit malpractice suits and the amount of settlements allowable under the broad category of tort reform, these efforts have not progressed far in the legislative process.

Current Major Health Problems

Many health problems that faced Americans in the past have been all but eliminated, but new ones have arisen to take their place. Current major health problems facing the United States and its citizens include heart disease, cancer, stroke, pulmonary disease, diabetes, kidney disease, and liver disease. Taken together, these diseases constituted nearly 62% of the total deaths in the country in 2003 (National Center for Health Statistics, 2006a).

The three leading causes of death in the United States are heart disease, strokes, and cancer. Nearly 30% of the total deaths in the United States in 2003 were caused by diseases of the heart. Cancer rates continue to rise and are increasingly associated with environmental factors. Cancer is projected to be the cause of death for one in three persons in the United States. Though new technology and medications have made treatment of these diseases more effective, they remain major causes of death.

HIV and AIDS

Acquired immunodeficiency syndrome (AIDS) has affected all of the social institutions and most communities in the United States. With recently discovered medication regimens, the life spans of many persons diagnosed with HIV (human immunodeficiency virus) infection have been extended considerably. Over time, however, the majority of individuals with HIV develop AIDS, which has a high fatality rate associated with the opportunistic diseases from a weakened immune system. HIV continues to spread to all segments of the population. Because the method of transmission of the virus is tied to culturally sensitive topics, including illegal drugs, sex, and sexual orientation, HIV and AIDS often are viewed in political, cultural, and moral contexts rather than as a serious public health issue.

AIDS first came to the attention of health authorities in the early 1980s. For the 5-year period 2000–2004, the number of AIDS cases in the United States totaled 944,306 cases, including 9,443 cases in children under age 13. During the same time period, 529,113 persons, including 5,094 children under the age of 13 years, died of the disease (Centers for Disease Control and Prevention, 2004b). The Joint United Nations Programme on HIV/AIDS (2006) estimates that worldwide, 38.6 million people were living with HIV/AIDS at the end of 2005. Of this number, some 2 million were young people between ages 15 and 24. About 4.1 million became newly infected, and 2.8 million lost their lives to the disease.

Women are becoming increasingly affected by HIV. Approximately half, or 19.2 million, of the 38.6 million adults living with HIV or AIDS worldwide are women. More than 95% of all HIV-infected people now live in least-developed parts of the world. For example, in parts of Africa, 30% of all adults ages 15–49 are infected (Joint United Nations Programme on HIV/AIDS, 2006).

DEFINITIONS

A new definition adopted by the Centers for Disease Control and Prevention (2005b) broadened conditions from those previously associated with the virus. This definition has resulted in earlier detection of individuals infected with the virus, doubled the numbers of persons known to have it, and lengthened their survival time. A person referred to as being **HIV-positive** has tested positively for the HIV virus, is infected with the virus, and has HIV antibodies present in his or her blood. HIV is an intracellular parasite that binds to molecules in the body. Unless the spread of HIV is interrupted by treatment, the infection spreads throughout the body, causing the destruction of cells that help maintain the immune system and leading to a gradual but progressive destruction of the entire immune system (Gandhi, Bartlett, & Linkinhoker, 1999).

During the primary HIV-infection period, 50% to 90% of individuals develop a mononucleosis-like infection that begins 1 to 3 weeks after infection and continues for 1 to 2 weeks. Most individuals do not recognize HIV-related symptoms at this point, and many of them do not receive HIV testing until much later, when their health is more at risk and they are more likely to have infected others. An estimated third of those infected with the virus are unaware that they have it (Centers for Disease Control and Prevention, 2004b). Many persons with the HIV virus are living longer, healthier lives because of the development of antiviral and other effective medications that can slow the rate at which HIV weakens the immune system.

If the immune system becomes seriously damaged, AIDS is more likely to develop. As medications have improved the health of persons with HIV, definitions of what constitutes AIDS have changed. Currently, certain "markers"—including the number and ratio of "T-helper" cells to other cells, and the presence of opportunistic diseases—determine a diagnosis of AIDS. Opportunistic diseases common among persons diagnosed with AIDS include PCP (pneumocystis carinii pneumonia, a lung infection), KS (Kaposi's sarcoma, a skin cancer), CMV (Cytomegalovirus, an infection that usually affects the eyes), and Candida, a fungal infection. Other AIDs-related illnesses include brain tumors and serious weight loss (aids.org, 2006). As more women are diagnosed with HIV and AIDS, cervical cancer and chronic yeast infections have been added to the list of conditions associated with these conditions.

More and more is becoming known about how the disease can be treated, and with new medications and medical treatment, the death rate from AIDS-related diseases has declined. Many individuals infected with HIV are living 10 years or longer before being diagnosed with AIDS. Still, research efforts have yet to find a cure or a vaccine to prevent its spread.

PREVALENCE AND POPULATIONS AFFECTED

Although AIDS originally hit the populations of gay men and substance abusers hardest, young adults under 25 are the most at-risk group; half of new HIV cases in 2002 were from this age group (Centers for Disease Control and Prevention (2005b). In 2002, half of new cases were men who reported having sex with other men. The rates for newly infected individuals also are high among women through heterosexual transmission of the virus or intravenous drug use. AIDS specialists have suggested that because AIDS symptoms do not show up for several years, we should look at the numbers of individuals who have the HIV virus in their blood instead of data relating to the numbers of persons with AIDS.

Results of blood-testing of persons with AIDS reported to the Centers for Disease Control and Prevention (2005b) confirm that whereas rates among homosexual and bisexual men have stabilized, rates in the heterosexual population, particularly intravenous drug users, women, and children, are increasing. Of the adolescents and adults reported with HIV in the United States through December 2004, 26.9% were women and 72.9% were men; 49.5% African American, 28.3% Caucasian, 20.4% Latino, .4% Native American, and 1.2% Asian/Pacific Islander. Of the HIV/AIDS cases reported for 2004, 56.5% were acquired through male-to-male sexual contact, 19.0% were acquired through injection drug use, 6.1% were acquired through male-to-male sexual contact coupled with injection drug use, and 16.4% were acquired through heterosexual contact (Centers for Disease Control and Prevention, 2005b).

AIDS, which first appeared in the United States among urban middle-class adults, has now spread to rural communities and to poorer and younger population groups (Centers for Disease Control and Prevention, 2004b). The brunt of the epidemic is being felt most by groups whose access to services and information is limited by low income.

TREATMENT

About half of persons with HIV are not receiving any treatment. The costs of medications to delay onset of AIDS and treat AIDS once it occurs are exorbitant, and coverage of prescriptions is becoming a problem for affected individuals, as well as the insurance companies that cover the costs of their care. Although the issues that those with AIDS and their families face are similar to those of others with life-threatening illnesses, persons with AIDS and their families also face discrimination in communities where they live and the places they work. Too, they have difficulty obtaining health-care insurance, a place to live, housing, employment, needed social services, and emotional support. The Americans with Disabilities Act (see chapter 8) specifically mentions persons with AIDS in its listing of disabilities covered under the act, but oppression and discrimination remain major issues for individuals with AIDS and their families (see Box 9.1 for the NASW policy statement on AIDS).

To complicate matters further, more than 100,000 children in the United States have lost one or both of their parents to AIDS. Developing permanent plans for their children is a difficult issue that confronts persons with AIDS who are parents. Many of these children go to live with relatives, but increasing numbers are placed in foster care or become candidates for adoption (Save the Children, 2006).

Other Illnesses and Health Problems

Other illnesses receiving more attention are diabetes, musculoskeletal diseases such as arthritis and osteoporosis, and respiratory diseases. These conditions are much more prevalent among the poor, people of color, and the elderly, who are unable to afford either preventive or rehabilitative health care. Some life-threatening diseases, such as Huntington's disease and cystic fibrosis, are genetically linked. Prenatal genetic screening currently is available to detect the presence of Down syndrome, Tay Sachs disease, cystic fibrosis, and sickle-cell anemia. Researchers believe that it is

just a matter of time before prenatal genetic testing will be able to identify those who are predisposed to hypertension, dyslexia, cancer, manic depression, schizophrenia, type 1 diabetes, familial Alzheimer's disease, multiple sclerosis, myotonic muscular dystrophy, and alcohol and other drug abuse.

These discoveries have raised the level of debate regarding moral and ethical choices in relation to birth, fetal and parental rights, abortion, and the associated emotional and financial costs to individuals and society. If a child will be born with multiple sclerosis, HIV antibodies, or cancer, who should decide the outcome? If the child is born with one of these diseases, who should pay the costs for care?

Present pregnancy-termination rates for women who have undergone genetic screening are nearly 100% for muscular dystrophy and cystic fibrosis, 60% for hemophilia, and 50% for sickle cell anemia. But what if the disease is one that occurs much later in life, such as Huntington's disease; is not fatal, such as Down syndrome; or reveals a predisposition to a disease, such as cancer, heart disease, or schizophrenia? And how do these issues relate to decision making to terminate a pregnancy? The field of **bioethics** is a fast-growing one in which social workers can play a major role.

Another health concern is the increasing numbers of persons with serious head or spinal injuries who have permanent brain injuries or multiple disabilities. Many require years of rehabilitation, and some, institutional care for the remainder of their lives. As technology enables many more people with such injuries to remain alive more often than in the past, costs for their care also increase. Because many individuals have received head and spinal injuries from motorcycle accidents when they were not wearing helmets or had alcohol- or drug-related accidents or car accidents when they were not wearing seat belts, additional concerns are raised about who should pay for health costs and how much should be paid.

A growing number of individuals with these injuries involves those in the military who have

BOX 9.1

Humane Treatment for Persons with AIDS: National Association of Social Workers Policy Statement on AIDS

Because of the complex biopsychosocial issues presented by AIDS, ARC, and HIV infection, social workers, with their special knowledge, skills, and sensitivity, can make a unique contribution to the management of this crisis by pursuing action in eight areas:

1. **Research:** Basic research, including epidemiological, clinical, and psychosocial studies, is imperative. Social workers, particularly in the area of psychosocial research, have a special contribution to make. They have been at the forefront of issues relating to AIDS and have demonstrated significant leadership in identifying critical issues and needs and have a responsibility to continue in these research efforts.

2. **Public Education and Dissemination of Information:** Accurate information about AIDS; HIV infection control measures; prevention; treatment; and medical, financial, and psychosocial resources available should be widely distributed. The fears of caregivers and the general public must be addressed with appropriate education and interventions. Adequate public funds must be authorized for educational efforts among the general public to reduce the fear of AIDS, ARC, and HIV infection and the stigmatization of persons assumed to be at risk for infection.

    Adequately funded public education programs should encourage prevention, early treatment, and formulation of new behaviors to reduce the risks of HIV infection. Professional health care organizations, training programs, and continuing education programs should incorporate the latest information and address especially the needs of minority groups, adolescents, women, infants and children, the developmentally and physically disabled, and the chronically mentally ill. Education and training programs must accommodate differences in culture and ethnicity among people. Program materials must be clear and explicit and targeted to individuals of all sexual orientations.

    Social workers should work cooperatively with existing AIDS-related educational, treatment, and research organizations. Especially important, social workers should be educated and updated on all AIDS-related issues, including prevention strategies, and should play major roles in reducing public hysteria and prejudice.

3. **Psychological and Social Support:** Comprehensive psychological and social support is necessary to help persons with AIDS, ARC, and HIV infection and all individuals close to them.

    Extended families, including domestic partners and significant others, represent rich resources of emotional and social support, just as they represent a network of persons likely to be affected by the disease-related changes, including death, of persons with AIDS and HIV infections. All care providers should respect the individuality of people with AIDS, ARC, and HIV infection and the importance of the individual's relationships with family, domestic partners, and close friends.

    The diversity of interpersonal relationships and support systems should be recognized, nurtured, and strengthened. Supplemental

Continued

BOX 9.1—*Continued*

Humane Treatment for Persons with AIDS: National Association of Social Workers Policy Statement on AIDS

services, including support groups, counseling, and therapy, should be made available to people with AIDS and AIDS-related conditions and their loved ones as well as to others who feel vulnerable. In addition, all providers of care should have access to support groups and related services to alleviate the stress inherent in assisting persons with AIDS-related conditions. All AIDS-related service organizations should provide for support, supervision, respite, and recognition of social workers engaged in the emotionally demanding work of serving people with AIDS.

4. **Service Delivery and Resource Development:** A comprehensive service delivery system to respond to AIDS based on a case management model must include suitable housing; adult-child foster care; home health and hospice care; appropriate; affordable health care; access to legal services; and transportation services. Children needing foster care should be provided care at the least restrictive level in nonsegregated settings. Traditional health and social welfare agencies including income maintenance programs must become responsive; eligibility

requirements and coverage by health insurance and income maintenance should be adapted to meet the rapid onset and catastrophic effects of AIDS. The health status of people with AIDS-related disorders may vary daily. Currently, service delivery systems do not take health care needs and work requirements into consideration. Systems should be more flexible in providing services for individuals with AIDS-related disorders.

Adequate funding both from public and private sources should be provided to assist alternative health and social services that deal with AIDS and AIDS-related conditions in various communities. Such services, many of which are complementary to and cooperative with mainstream services, help broaden and strengthen the range of traditional supports available to persons with AIDS and AIDS-related conditions. Social workers should be encouraged to be involved in the initiation of—and serve as membership on—local, statewide, regional, and national AIDS task forces.

5. **Civil Rights:** No person should be deprived of civil rights or rights to confidentiality

---

seen combat in recent conflicts such as the war in Iraq. Advances in field medicine in war zones have made it possible to save the lives of many soldiers who receive traumatic injuries and would have died in previous wars. Accurate statistics regarding the number of these individuals have been difficult to obtain, but they are projected to be in the thousands. The American public bears the cost of caring for these

soldiers, which for many extends for their entire lifetime.

Catastrophic Illness

National attention also is being directed to the problems of catastrophic illness. A **catastrophic illness** is a chronic and severely debilitating condition that results in long-term dependence because he or she has been diagnosed as having contracted AIDS, is infected with HIV, or is assumed to be at risk for infection. Nondiscrimination laws should be extended and existing legal protection should be vigorously enforced to protect individuals with AIDS, ARC, and HIV infections from being presumptively deprived of health care, employment, housing, and immigration rights.

6. **HIV Testing:** Social workers should be concerned particularly with the violation of human rights and the psychosocial consequences to people taking HIV antibody tests. Given the potential for serious discrimination, all testing should be voluntary, anonymous, and conducted with informed consent. Social workers should make certain that the limits of the predictive value of such testing are known in advance by clients. Appropriate pre- and post-test counseling must be offered by social workers or other skilled professionals. Social workers are mandated to protect client confidentiality.

7. **Professional Accountability:** The helping professions and appropriate licensing authorities should use their full range of persuasive and regulatory powers to assure that people with AIDS, ARC, and HIV infection and their significant others are not discriminated against in their eligibility for or receipt of services because of their illness or lack of financial or social resources.

8. **Political Action:** Social workers, individually and organizationally, should participate with other groups to lobby actively at local, state, and federal levels on behalf of people with AIDS in order to improve their quality of life; protect their civil liberties; and advocate for increased funding for appropriate education, prevention, interventions, treatment, services, and research.

The National Association of Social Workers (NASW), as the organizational arm of the profession, must help coordinate a response to AIDS, ARC, and HIV infection by pursuing the multifaceted strategy outlined in this policy statement.

Source: *Social Work Speaks: NASW Policy Statements* (3rd ed.), by the National Association of Social Workers (Washington, DC: NASW Press). Copyright © 1994, National Association of Social Workers, Inc.

---

on the health-care system. Although many families can provide health care for themselves during typical, less serious bouts of illness, a catastrophic illness can wipe out family savings and force some to declare personal bankruptcy or relinquish their care to the already overloaded public health-care system.

To date, no legislation has been passed to address this serious issue. The debate centers on who should be covered, how much care should be provided and at what cost, and how long the care should be provided. These questions have no ready answers. One bill passed by Congress in 1988, the Catastrophic Health Care Act, provided coverage for families and the elderly who experienced catastrophic illness or disability. This law was repealed in 1989 after a strong lobby effort by well-to-do elderly persons protested against increased Medicare premiums resulting from the legislation. The law also did not cover long-term nursing home care.

Many national groups and health-care lobbyists continue to advocate a national health-insurance program that provides some type of health-care coverage for everyone in the United States. So far, coverage limited only to catastrophic health care is a compromise measure that is more likely to be approved.

Teen Pregnancy

In recent years, one of the most publicized at-risk groups has been teenage parents. Pregnancy, birth, and abortion rates among U.S. teens declined during the past decade, but this is still a major public health issue. The United States has the highest adolescent pregnancy rate of industrialized countries. While African American and Caucasian teen pregnancy rates declined, with African Americans showing the greatest decline, the decrease among Latina teens was not as significant (Sexuality Information and Education Council of the United States [SIECUS], 2006). Birth rates of teens 15–19 years of age declined from 62.1 live births per 1,000 women in 1991 to 41.2 per 1,000 in 2004. Overall, the rates for Caucasian women declined from 43.4 to 26.8; rates for African American women from 118.8 to 62.7; for Latina women from 106.7 to 82.6; for Native American women from 85 to 52.5; and for Asian or Pacific Islander women from 27.4 to 17.4 (National Center for Health Statistics, 2005a).

Pregnant teens receive little or no prenatal care, poor nutrition during pregnancy, and limited services (Bavier, 2004). As a result, they are at more risk of having miscarriages and of giving birth to premature and low-birthweight infants, and infants with congenital problems.

Prenatal services and nutritional assistance such as the Supplemental Nutrition Program for Women, Infants, and Children (WIC) are cost-effective and result in healthy infants who are better able to grow up to become healthy adults. Premature

births declined and birthweight of infants increased among low-income pregnant women who participated in a food and nutrition education program (U.S. Department of Agriculture, 2004).

Environmental Factors

In recent years increasing attention is being directed to environmental factors and their impact on people. These factors include hazardous household substances and other poisons, as well as household building materials, such as lead-based paints and formaldehyde in insulation. Workplaces also present risks to health, resulting in environmental protections for employees from dangerous chemicals, pollutants in the air, and hazardous jobs. In 2005, 8% percent of fatal work injuries were caused by exposure to harmful substances or environments (U.S. Department of Labor, 2006). An estimated one-fifth of all deaths from cancer are associated with occupational hazards.

One of the more publicized environmental hazards associated with increased incidence of cancer and respiratory diseases was the discovery of harmful asbestos in many older buildings. In spite of the known health risk, workers hired to remove asbestos in many instances have not received the needed protection to avoid being exposed to the substance. Of those with long-term exposure to asbestos, half die and the remainder suffer long-term debilitation from respiratory complications such as asbestosis (National Cancer Institute, 2004).

Other occupational risks are garnering little attention. For everyone living in the United States, regardless of occupation, the environment is an increasing health hazard (National Cancer Institute, 2004). Increasing pollutants in the air and in food products are associated with significant increases in heart disease, cancer, and respiratory diseases in the United States in comparison to other countries. Other environmental risks include:

- road and traffic safety;
- unsafe housing;

- contaminated food, meat, and dairy products;
- pest and animal control;
- biomedical and consumer product safety;
- inappropriate disposal of chemical and human wastes;
- storage and treatment of water; and
- control of nuclear energy plants.

Tobacco use is the single most preventable cause of premature death in the United States, and smoking is recognized as an environmental hazard to smokers and those who inhale their smoke. According to the Centers for Disease Control and Prevention (2005a), an estimated 44.5 million adults in the United States smoke cigarettes, even though this single behavior will result in death or disability for half of all continuing smokers. Each year, more than 440,000 Americans die from smoking or other tobacco use. More than 8.6 million people in the United States have at least one serious illness caused by smoking.

Annual medical costs related to tobacco use are more than $75 billion; and another $92 billion per year results from lost productivity. Each year, 3,000 nonsmoking Americans die of lung cancer and an estimated 150,000 to 300,000 children younger than 18 months of age have lower respiratory tract infections because of exposure to secondhand smoke.

Concern has risen because of the increasing number of young people who smoke. Every day almost 4,000 youth under 18 try their first cigarette (Centers for Disease Control and Prevention, 2003a). Approximately 80% of adults who smoke began smoking before they were 18. One of the prevention priorities of the Healthy People 2010 federal initiative is to reduce tobacco use (Centers for Disease Control and Prevention, 2005a).

Federal and state legislation, local community ordinances, and workplace policies are limiting smoking to designated areas or prohibiting it completely from public areas. Smoking has not been allowed on airline flights for some time. The $206 billion tobacco settlement with more than 40 states, reached in November 1998, poured billions of dollars into state treasuries and provided about $1.5 billion for research and advertising against underage tobacco use.

Prevention and Wellness Programs

The preventive aspects of health care are receiving more attention, although prevention is still secondary to taking action after a health problem has developed. Some businesses have established wellness programs—exercise and fitness programs, nutrition and weight-control programs, smoking-cessation workshops, and other health and prevention efforts. A number of employers are working with insurance companies to offer incentives, such as salary bonuses or reduced insurance rates, to employees who are considered low-risk. Problems in the workplace and the broader society from substance abuse have led employers and insurance companies to establish substance-abuse prevention programs in the workplace.

Most recently, obesity in youth and its relation to major health problems such as diabetes have become a concern. Many public schools are removing unhealthy snacks from school buildings or limiting their access, and introducing fitness and physical education programs.

Ethical Issues

As health-care costs continue to escalate, more people need health care, and new technology and knowledge make it possible to keep people alive who previously could not have been helped. These changes have given rise to ethical dilemmas in the area of health care, and many of

Preventive health care is far more cost-effective than medical problems that arise when preventive services are not provided. This father was able to access early medical care for his daughter, who was born with a serious medical condition, that will allow her to live a full life; doctors told him she would have died before age three if her medical problems had not been identified and addressed.

© Heinle/Index Stock

these issues are before our courts. Examples of these pressing questions are:

- When infants born 3 and 4 months premature can be saved, at what point, if at all, should abortion be prohibited?
- When infants require extensive neonatal care to survive, should such care be made available even if the parents cannot afford the costs?
- Should the circumstances change to provide care if the infant can survive but with serious mental and/or physical disabilities?
- If technology for heart and lung transplants is available, should everyone of all ages and income groups have equal access to these procedures?
- If genetics testing reveals that a fetus has a serious illness or disability, what choices should be considered, and who should be involved?

- If individuals can survive with medical care or special procedures, should they have a right to decide whether to receive the care or to be allowed to die?
- Do people have the right to choose unsafe behaviors, such as riding motorcycles without helmets, not using seat belts, or using drugs or alcohol heavily, when injuries or other health problems may result in high costs to others—taxpayers, state and local governments, and other individuals in the same insurance group?
- Does a pregnant woman have the right to drink alcoholic beverages, use other drugs, or smoke if it can compromise the survival or health of her child?

Related questions are:

- Who should make such decisions?
- What are the rights of the individual?

- . . . of the parents if the person is a child?
- . . . of the state or local governments faced with paying for the care?
- . . . of our society at large?

There is no neutral ground from which to make these decisions, as they all involve values based on cultural, social, and religious beliefs (Meilaender, 2003).

Baby Doe Cases

A number of court cases have attempted to address some of the issues listed above. In the early 1980s, the so-called Baby Doe case received national attention. This case involved an infant born with serious health problems who would have been seriously disabled—physically and mentally—with surgery and who would have died immediately without surgery. The parents did not want the child to have surgery or to suffer but, instead, to die a peaceful death. Some members of the hospital staff wanted the child to have the surgery; others wanted the child to die. In 1986, the U.S. Supreme Court invalidated government regulations ("Baby Doe" rules) based on Section 504 of the Rehabilitation Act of 1973 that required life-prolonging medical treatment for newborn infants with severe disabilities, citing that there was no basis for federal intervention in such sensitive decisions. This action resulted in new amendments to the rules that govern the Child Abuse Prevention and Treatment Act (CAPTA), signed into law in 1974. Concern has been raised in similar situations throughout the country. In some instances, infants were reported to have been starved to death or had experienced great pain when life supports were removed from them.

Federal legislation was introduced requiring local child welfare agencies to handle this type of situation as child protective services cases and to conduct investigations before reaching medical decisions, to ensure that children are being protected. The legislation was changed before it passed, but it did mandate that hospitals establish special review boards to deal with such cases.

Some states, too, have made legislative decisions addressing serious ethical issues. In 1987, the state of Oregon voted to stop using its Medicaid funds to pay for liver, heart, bone marrow, and pancreas transplants, and to use the $2.3 million saved to provide prenatal care for women in poverty. Many states have set limits on what they will pay for organ transplants. Citizens groups are being formed throughout the United States to address ethical decisions like these. One of the first, Oregon Health Decisions, formed in 1983, held meetings throughout the state to determine and then advocate for priorities for health funding.

Right-to-Die Cases

Another major ethical issue relates to decisions surrounding what is called "the right to die." Cases involving people who are kept alive by life-support systems but are in what the medical community refers to as a *vegetative state* have generated much debate. Other situations involving persons who have serious health problems and decide themselves that they wish to die are receiving attention, too.

Ethical issues also are raised regarding the role of others in aiding those who decide they want to die. For example, the state of Oregon passed the Death with Dignity Act in 1994, which allows dying patients to control their own end-of-life care. Oregon became, and remains, the only state allowing legal **physician-assisted suicide** (Oregon Department of Human Services, 2005).

The Death with Dignity Act allows terminally ill Oregon residents to obtain and use prescriptions from their physicians for self-administered, lethal medications. Under this law, ending one's life in accordance with the law does not constitute suicide. The law allows for physician-assisted suicide but specifically prohibits euthanasia, in which a physician or other person directly administers a medication to end one's life. The term "physician-assisted suicide" is used in the medical literature to describe ending one's life through the voluntary self-administration of lethal medications prescribed by a physician for that purpose.

To request a prescription for lethal medications, the Death with Dignity Act requires that a patient be 18 years of age or older, a resident of Oregon, able to make and communicate healthcare decisions, and diagnosed with a terminal illness that will lead to death within 6 months. Patients meeting these criteria then are eligible to request a prescription for lethal medication from a physician licensed by the state of Oregon. To receive a prescription for lethal medication (Oregon Department of Human Services, 2005):

- The patient must make two oral requests to his or her physician, separated by at least 15 days.
- The patient must provide a written request to his or her physician, signed in the presence of two witnesses.
- The prescribing physician and a consulting physician must confirm the diagnosis and prognosis.
- The prescribing physician and a consulting physician must determine whether the patient is capable of making the decision to end his or her life. If either physician believes that the patient's judgment is impaired by a psychiatric or psychological disorder, the patient must be referred for a psychological evaluation.
- The prescribing physician must inform the patient of feasible alternatives to assisted suicide, including comfort care, hospice care, and pain control.
- The prescribing physician must request, but may not require, the patient to notify his or her next-of-kin of the prescription request. (p. 8)

Physicians are required to report to the Oregon Department of Human Services, within 7 working days of prescribing the medication, all prescriptions for lethal injection. The Oregon Legislature added a requirement in 1999 that pharmacists must be informed of the ultimate use for the prescribed medication. Physicians and patients who adhere to requirements of the law are protected from criminal prosecution, and the choice of legal physician-assisted suicide cannot affect the status of a patient's health or life insurance policies.

A total of 37 Oregonians used physician-assisted suicide in 2005, with about an equal split between males and females requesting lethal medication. All of the patients were white. The age range of individuals requesting lethal medication was 34 to 89. More than half were widowed, divorced, or never married. Slightly more than half had earned a baccalaureate degree or higher. The major underlying illness was malignant neoplasms (Oregon Department of Human Services, 2005). A Death with Dignity National Center can be accessed at www.deathwithdignity.org.

Opponents of physician-assisted suicide object that physicians' participation in assisting people to die violates the basic moral obligations of physicians to do no harm. The debate about legalizing euthanasia (painless termination of life to end a terminally ill patient's suffering) raises ethical and legal questions such as: How does one assess the competency of those requesting death? Is the involvement of a physician or nurse necessary and, if so, to what extent, for those seeking to end their lives?

In 1997, the U.S. Supreme Court unanimously upheld Washington state and New York state laws banning assisted suicide (*Compassion in Dying v. Washington; Quill, Klagsbrun and Grossman v. New York*). The Court ruled that the Constitution does not guarantee citizens the right to end their lives with a doctor's help, but it left individual states the option of legalizing the practice. In 2003, 35 states had laws making assisted suicide a criminal act, and three states—North

Carolina, Utah, and Wyoming—had abolished laws relating to assisted suicide. In Ohio, the state supreme court ruled in 1996 that assisted suicide is not a crime.

The American Medical Association has estimated that 70% of the 6,000 U.S. deaths that occur each day involve some sort of negotiation regarding life or death. In many instances, ethical dilemmas can be avoided, and dollars saved, by providing accessible and affordable health care before the problem arises. For example, pregnant women who do not receive care during the first 3 months of pregnancy are 30% more likely to deliver infants with low birthweight and the attendant problems. Every dollar spent on prenatal care is estimated to result in a savings of between $1.70 and $3.38 by reducing neonatal complications. Savings increase dramatically when the long-term costs of caring for newborns with physical and developmental disabilities are factored in (National Conference of State Legislatures, 2006a).

Bioethics

New genetic technologies promise to make medical ethics an even more central part of social decision making. For example, the Human Genome Project, a 15-year, federally funded $3 billion effort to code the entire human genetic map, already has resulted in the discovery of a number of genes that lead to specific diseases or traits. This project will enable individuals to receive more information about their own genetic makeup. Medical ethicists are debating whether this genetic information is the exclusive property of patients or is properly the concern of insurers, employers, and society at large. This information has the potential to enhance individual health.

New computational tools will allow knowledge that can impact specific populations. For example, researchers have learned that one reason African Americans die from heart attacks more than members of other ethnic groups is that a drug commonly given to heart-attack patients is less effective in people of African ancestry. Because much of the current biological research focuses on DNA, it is expected that in the years to come, unique medication regimens will be developed that are tailored to a specific individual, not just to an age or ethnic group.

Further, gene therapies are being developed using genetically engineered viruses to manipulate patients' cells. Some people wonder about whether the manipulation of human cells through genetic engineering is somehow contrary to the laws of nature or religion. Others have proposed that it will lead to the manipulation of human sperm or eggs for purposes of improving the hereditary qualities of a race. Still others applaud the therapies and see them as a way to improve the quality and longevity of life.

Cloning—the production of organisms genetically identical to a parent—has become another controversial topic in medical ethics. In 1997, Scottish scientist Ian Wilmut and his colleagues announced the birth of a sheep named Dolly that was produced from a cell of an adult female sheep. This event and other attempts at cloning mammals have led many people to believe that cloning humans may be possible one day. This possibility has touched off a debate about the ethics of creating human clones, the circumstances under which human cloning might be used, and the possibility of using the technique to manipulate the traits of children. This issue remains unresolved and will continue to challenge medical ethicists well into the 21st century.

Another major issue being debated by state legislatures, Congress, and ethicists relates to the use of stem cell tissue. Stem cells from adult stem cells have effectively saved the lives of individuals who would have died otherwise. Issues that will be addressed in state and federal courts in the coming years include what kind of tissue can be used to obtain stem cells, and under what conditions.

Bioethicist Scott Gottlieb (2003) suggests that some of these issues may become less controversial. Knowledge, he says, is shifting to computer-generated therapies based on individual DNA profiles, "making targeted drugs and diagnosis a reality and drug development faster, cheaper, and better" and tissue, organ, and stem cell therapies obsolete (p. 9).

Alternative Medicine

Finally, debate and advertising have focused attention on the role of alternative medicine in health care, and bioethicists are debating the rights of patients to insurance reimbursement for alternative therapies and the need for standards for their use. Examples of research include the potential use of psychoactive alternative medicines, including St. John's wort and gingko biloba, to treat depression, memory loss, and Alzheimer's disease. The lack of standards for their use has prompted concern that healthy Americans will engage in unsafe experiments with life enhancement drugs. Several other alternative therapies, including acupuncture and crystal healing, have been formally included in managed-care plans around the United States.

Health Planning

To eliminate problems in costs of health care, duplication of care in some areas and gaps in others, and the interface of public- and private-sector health-care delivery, several important pieces of legislation have been enacted.

Hill-Burton Act

Passed in 1946, the Hill-Burton Act was funded for the purpose of constructing rural hospitals. Amendments in 1964 authorized the development of area-wide hospital planning councils and the concept of area-wide hospital planning. The law also specifies that hospitals that receive funding through this legislation cannot refuse to serve clients who are unable to pay for services. Later legislation authorized hospitals that provide more than their fair share of health care to medically indigent patients (disproportionate share hospitals) to receive additional funding from Medicare and Medicaid to cover costs (Centers for Medicare and Medicaid Services, 2006).

Medicare and Medicaid

National legislation in 1965 established Medicare and Medicaid programs, which provide the majority of federal financing for health care. Both programs have undergone significant changes over the years and are far more costly and cover far more Americans than anticipated.

MEDICAID

In recent years, Congress attempted to increase Medicaid to cover more of the nation's poor. The 1988 Family Support Act extended Medicaid coverage to AFDC (now Temporary Assistance for Needy Families, or TANF) recipients for up to 1 year after they became employed. Although more expensive initially, it was hoped that this plan actually would reduce government health-care costs because large numbers of recipients who leave the TANF rolls have been forced to return when they or their children have health problems and they have not been able to become financially stable enough to afford health insurance. Thus, it was hoped that the extension of Medicaid as a transitional benefit would help recipients remain off TANF once they obtained employment.

With passage of the 1996 welfare reform legislation, however, eligibility-services workers discouraged the poor from continuing to receive Medicaid benefits, even though their coverage for cash assistance under the TANF program had ended. Many individuals continue to leave TANF rolls because they have obtained jobs, but these often are low-level jobs that do not cover health insurance benefits or offer opportunities for promotion into jobs that do offer these benefits. Even though both federal and state governments are concerned about the increasing costs of Medicaid, more than half of the nation's poor do not qualify for coverage.

Even with provisions to expand Medicaid to children and their parents in the late 1990s, the bulk of increase in Medicaid expenditures has funded health care for the elderly. Medicare was intended to provide the bulk of health care for the elderly, and Medicaid was intended to serve children and families, but Medicaid dollars are increasingly being used to pay for nursing-home care that is not provided under Medicare. In 1999, for example, nearly 60% of all nursing-home residents in the United States were covered by Medicaid (National Conference of State Legislatures, 2006b). State and federal budget crises in Medicaid have resulted not from higher costs to serve families but, rather, from the need to cover nursing home and other extensive health-care costs for the increased numbers of elderly persons who cannot afford to pay for health care that is not provided by Medicare.

In 2002 and 2003, Congress and the states were spending considerable time debating proposals to reduce Medicaid costs. The Bush administration proposed capping federal Medicaid payments to states for services they are not required to provide by federal law, which in 2003 accounted for two-thirds of all Medicaid expenditures. Because about 17% of all health-care spending is covered by Medicaid, changes in Medicaid would also impact hospitals, physicians, clinics, pharmacies, and other health-care providers, including social workers (National Conference of State Legislatures, 2006b).

To make the cap more palatable to states, the Bush administration also proposed giving states block grants of funds so they could be more flexible in deciding how to spend the monies. States are concerned, however, that even with more spending flexibility, block Medicaid grants will require them to absorb the bulk of the additional costs. Medicaid matching rates set by the federal government for fiscal year 2002 reduced rates for 29 states, or a total of $565 million, requiring states to increase their state funds by that amount (GFOA Federal Liaison Center, 2002).

Rising costs in health care and lower state revenues have jeopardized the availability of Medicaid funding across the nation. Besides cutting or reducing services that are not required by federal law, many states plan to pass on, or are already passing on, some of the costs to Medicaid recipients, requiring them to make co-payments for services received (Kaiser Commission on Medicaid and the Uninsured, 2004). One Southwest state, for example, reduced home care for frail and elderly persons; health care for pregnant women; payments to nursing homes and physicians; coverage for eyeglasses, hearing aids, and mental health services except by psychiatrists for adults; and community and home care for the mentally ill, also eliminating social workers as Medicaid providers in the process (Center for Public Policy Priorities, 2006).

One proposal to address the Medicaid funding crisis calls for the federal government to fully fund Medicaid costs for prescription drugs, long-term care, and other services to individuals already receiving Medicaid benefits. Health-care analysts say, however, that the plan might work well during a strong economic period but would not work during an economic downturn, leaving states to shoulder the burden or pass it on to those who can least afford it. In short, the plan would be too risky for states to agree to, as it has the potential to adversely impact those from the most vulnerable populations—those with disabilities and the elderly (Kaiser Commission on Medicaid and the Uninsured, 2004; National Association of Community Health Centers, 2005).

A study conducted by Goldman et al. (2004) for the Rand Corporation found that low-income adults and children reduced their health-care services and medications by as much as 44% when they were required to make co-payments, which led to poorer health in this population overall. Other studies show that low-income individuals already use expensive emergency-room services much more often than those with higher incomes, leading to the need for more critical care because they have delayed seeking medical attention (Artiga, Rousseau, Lyons, Smith, & Gaylin, 2006; Center on Budget and Policy Priorities, 2005).

MEDICARE

Although Medicare pays many health-care costs for people over age 65, it does not provide long-term care for chronic needs, particularly nursing-home care, or pay for other costs such as special wheelchairs that might enable more elderly persons to be cared for in their own homes. Because of increases in Medicare premiums, Medicare currently pays less than half of the total costs of health care for senior citizens (Federal Interagency Forum on Aging Related Statistics, 2004).

As costs of medications and the number of seniors needing them have both increased, how to pay for them has become an issue. The Medicare Prescription Drug, Improvement, and Modernization Act of 2003 created a federally subsidized benefit, which may vary from plan to plan, subject to certain constraints. Beneficiaries who choose to sign up pay a monthly premium, estimated as $25 per month in 2006. Beneficiaries are responsible for the first $250 in drug expenses, then will pay, on average, 25% co-insurance until they reach the benefit limit ($2,250 in 2006). Once they reach the benefit limit, they will face a gap in coverage in which they will pay 100% of their drug costs up to $5,100 in total drug spending (equal to $3,600 in out-of-pocket spending). Medicare then will pay 95% of drug costs above that amount. These benefit levels are indexed to rise annually with the growth in per-capita drug expenditures for the Medicare population. Plans are required to provide drugs in each therapeutic class and category but have flexibility to modify cost-sharing (other than the out-of-pocket limit) and also can modify formularies and preferred drug lists (Kaiser EDU.org. 2006, p. 1).

As of June 2005, 22.5 million Medicare beneficiaries had prescription drug coverage from the voluntary Medicare Part D plan. Another 10.4 million had creditable drug coverage from an employer plan. The Medicare drug benefit is voluntary; individuals may choose whether to enroll in a Part D plan. The U.S. Department of Health and Human Services estimated that 5.4 million beneficiaries had creditable drug coverage from an alternative source, such as the Veterans Administration. Overall, about 90% of the 43 million people on Medicare have creditable prescription drug coverage (Kaiser Family Foundation, 2006a). By January 1, 2006, all 43 million people on Medicare had access to the Medicare Part D prescription drug benefit offered by stand-alone prescription drug plans (PDPs) or Medicare Advantage prescription drug plans. Among the many questions associated with the effort to privatize drug-care benefits to Medicare beneficiaries are:

- Will private plans choose to participate and offer drug coverage?
- What share of beneficiaries will be covered under a fall-back plan if at least two plans do not agree to accept the risk to provide drug coverage for beneficiaries in their areas?
- How much variation will there be in drug coverage across prescription drug plans and the Medicare Advantage plans?
- Will employers elect to take the subsidy and maintain retiree health coverage for Medicare-eligibles?
- Will Medicare-endorsed discount cards provide higher discounts than those currently available through existing arrangements?
- What share of low-income Medicare beneficiaries will apply for and receive subsidies?
- How will plans work for Medicare beneficiaries residing in nursing homes and other residential care facilities?
- What will be the impact of the legislation on prescription drug expenditures for Medicare beneficiaries?
- Will new legislation affect prescribing practices of physicians?
- Will plans allow beneficiaries to obtain only generic drugs, or allow some flexibility if physicians prescribe a non-generic brand that may work better for the person?

Two organizations that advocate for accessible and affordable health care for the elderly have raised yet other concerns. The Medicare Rights Center estimates that about 9 million people will see their drug coverage cut. The Center also is concerned about the benefit's monthly premium. Because this type of program has no precedent, the monthly premium for the drug benefit remains unknown. In addition, after one year, Medicare beneficiaries would see their $250 deductible and the $2,850 so-called "doughnut hole", for which there is no coverage, increase by 10% by 2013. The deductible and coverage gap are both projected to grow by nearly 80% (Havrda, Omundsen, Bender, & Kirkpatrick, 2005).

Finally, under the legislation, 6.4 million Medicare and Medicaid beneficiaries will lose their Medicaid drug coverage and get help with the Medicare drug premiums, deductibles, and co-insurance; however, no new savings are likely and the new drug benefit is not guaranteed to cover all the drugs this population needs. Much remains to be seen in the years following implementation of this legislation.

Maternal and Child Health Act

Title V of the Social Security Act of 1935 (as amended) through the Supplemental Food Program for Women, Infants, and Children (WIC), provides screening, counseling, and food supplements for pregnant women and children up to 5 years of age who are at nutritional risk because of low income. Studies show that WIC reduces infant deaths, low birthweight, and premature births and increases good health and cognitive development in preschoolers (see, for example, Koweleski-Jones & Duncan, 2002).

After funding for the program was reduced in the 1980s during the Reagan administration, some states have been able to document that an increase in low birthweight and premature births can be tied directly to the reduction in WIC programs. In addition, because states have the option of offering the program, only half of eligible women and children in the country receive WIC services.

Healthy Steps for Young Children Program

Healthy Steps is a holistic approach to pediatric health care for all children from birth to age 3, encompassing their physical, psychological, emotional, and intellectual growth and development. This program encourages strong relationships between pediatric practices and parents. By focusing on families with very young children, the Healthy Steps approach helps ensure that children are nurtured at a critical time in their development, with the expected outcomes that they will grow and develop into well-adapted, healthy children who are confident young learners.

Among the several agencies and organizations involved in the Healthy Steps initiative are: the Commonwealth Fund; community and regional foundations and local health-care providers; the American Academy of Pediatrics; Boston University School of Medicine, Department of Population and Family Health Sciences; and the Johns Hopkins University School of Public Health. In 2006, 15 national evaluation sites and nine affiliate sites were implementing the Healthy Steps approach in 14 states across the country (Healthy Steps, 2006).

Children's Health Insurance Program (CHIP)

In August 1997, Congress enacted the **Children's Health Insurance Program** to expand health insurance coverage for low-income children up to age 19. Established as Title XXI of the Social Security Act, CHIP is a voluntary program that entitles states to approximately $40 billion through 2007 ($20.3 billion over the first five years of the program and an additional $19.4 billion over the second four years of the budget period). States must supply matching funds, but the required matching rates are lower than Medicaid rates.

The Balanced Budget Act of 1997 provides states with three options for increasing coverage under CHIP: (a) expand Medicaid, (b) establish a new insurance program separate from Medicaid, or (c) implement a combination of both. Of the 51 CHIP plans set forth by each state and the District of Columbia, 18 expand Medicaid, 17 create programs separate from Medicaid, and 16 do both.

States receive federal block-grant payments on a matching basis, up to a limit established for each state based on the allocation formula in the law. The law limits the extent to which states can impose premiums or cost-sharing (deductibles, co-insurance, and co-payments) for health care provided to children who are enrolled in separate state programs financed with child health block-grant funds.

In general, states cannot adopt cost-sharing or premium policies that favor higher-income families over lower-income families. States also are prohibited from imposing cost-sharing for well-baby and well-child care, including immunizations. Finally, states cannot count money raised through premiums or cost-sharing as state dollars for purposes of meeting the block grant's matching requirements.

As noted, the CHIP program requires state matching funds as a requirement to draw down federal funds to operate the state's CHIP program. These matching rates are lower than those of any other federal program having a matching requirement and are designed to maximize state participation in the program. Despite this incentive, some states have elected to restrict their investment in the state's CHIP program. As a result, many eligible children are prevented from receiving benefits from the program.

In one large, high-growth state in the Southwest, the state's reluctance to invest general revenue in the CHIP program has resulted in nearly 700,000 eligible children who have yet to receive program benefits. Since implementation of the program in 1998, the state has failed to take advantage of some $832 million in federal matching funds that could have been applied to operating the state's CHIP program. Other states that have maximized federal financial participation for their CHIP program are pleased to ask the federal government to apply these unexpended funds to expanding their CHIP program.

Other Child Health Provisions under the Balanced Budget Act of 1997

In addition to the child health block grant, the Balanced Budget Act of 1997 included a number of provisions designed to increase children's health-care coverage through the Medicaid program. These provisions are largely independent of the child health block grant and apply regardless of whether a state elects to use its block grant funds to expand Medicaid or establish a separate state program. Despite the large amount of federal funds invested in the CHIP initiative, only about 4 million of the 8.3 million uninsured children in the United States actually received health-care coverage in 2005 (Economic Policy Institute, 2006; Kaiser Family Foundation (2006c).

Comprehensive Health Planning Act

Passed in 1966, the Comprehensive Health Planning Act expanded on the concept of local health-planning districts to coordinate services and requires review of other factors affecting the health of area residents, such as lifestyle and environmental conditions. The National Health Planning and Resources Development Act of 1974 further mandated the establishment of health systems agencies and statewide health-coordinating councils to prevent the overbuilding of medical facilities such as obstetric and neonatal special care units and to monitor the availability of pediatric beds, open-heart surgery, and expensive technological equipment such as megavoltage radiation equipment. The intent of this legislation was to increase the availability of services in rural and other underserved areas and to eliminate duplication in other areas, as well as to provide high-quality care at reduced costs by requiring rate-review panels and professional standards of care.

Health Maintenance Organization Legislation

The Health Maintenance Organization Act of 1972 enabled the development of health maintenance organizations (HMOs) to reduce health-care costs for individuals. Most HMOs require a monthly fee, which allows free or low-cost visits to a special facility or group of facilities for health care. HMOs are intended to reduce health costs and encourage preventive health care. Nevertheless, because of increased concerns raised by HMO clients and physicians about limited access to needed health care, a number of states have passed legislation specifying the rights of clients served by HMOs. (HMOs were discussed in more depth earlier in this chapter.)

CARE Act

The Ryan White Comprehensive AIDS Resources Emergency (CARE) Act of 1989, named in honor of 18-year-old Ryan White (who died of AIDS in 1989) authorizes emergency funds to metropolitan areas hardest hit by AIDS, grants to states for comprehensive planning and service delivery, early intervention with HIV-infected infants, and the development of individual pilot projects to serve children with AIDS and to provide AIDS services in rural areas. The Act has five titles:

Title I:	provides grants to eligible metropolitan areas based on case rates
Title II:	provides grants to states for health care and support services for persons with HIV/AIDS
Title III:	provides support to primary care providers through local health departments' homeless programs, community and

migrant health centers, hemophilia centers, and family planning centers

Title IV:	provides health and support services for children, adolescents, and women and families utilizing comprehensive, community-based services
Title V:	provides funding for the education and training of service providers

Part F of the law provides funding for Special Projects of National Significance, awarded on a competitive procurement basis to support the development of innovative models of HIV/AIDS care with special emphasis on hard-to-reach populations including Native Americans and other minorities. Areas targeted for this funding include managed care, infrastructure development, training, comprehensive primary care, and access to care.

The law also provides funding to support the provision of dental and oral health services for HIV-positive individuals (the Dental Reimbursement Program and the Community-based Dental Partnership Program). Signed into law in 1990, the act was reauthorized by Congress in 1996. In fiscal year 2006, Congress authorized approximately $2 billion for CARE programs and initiatives (Health Resources and Services Administration, 2006c).

Future Legislation: Health-Care Reform

The absence of universal access to health care is creating a dual system of health care in the United States. Health care is readily available for those who are employed in organizations that offer adequate health-care coverage for individuals, are healthy enough to be covered, and can afford to pay health care premiums. Other people are either receiving government health-care benefits—most likely Medicaid and/or Medicare—or have no options for health care because they are unemployed, underemployed, or employed by businesses that are too small to provide adequate benefits or offer benefits that are too expensive for the average employee to purchase.

Many individuals are caught in the middle as health-care providers and employers grapple with ways to reduce the rapidly escalating health-care costs. For example, some health-care plans restrict benefits that cover previous health problems, which often denies benefits to those who need them most. Thus, if an individual changes jobs or an employer changes benefit plans, new rules may force reduced coverage or no coverage at all. These individuals then may not obtain preventive health care or may end up with health-care problems so serious that they are forced to leave the workforce, possibly becoming eligible for Medicaid or other government health care.

HEALTH SAVINGS ACCOUNTS (HSAs)

Health Savings Accounts (HSAs) were part of Medicare legislation signed into law by President Bush in December 8, 2003. An HSA is used in conjunction with a high-deductible health plan (HDHP), in which insurance does not cover "first-dollar" medical expenses except for preventive care. First-dollar medical benefits include those provided through Medicare, Tricare (health care benefits for the military), flexible spending arrangements, and health-reimbursement arrangements. The HDHP plan has a minimum deductible of $1,050 for self-only coverage and $2,100 for family coverage. Annual out-of-pocket expenses (including deductibles and co-pays) cannot exceed $5,250 for self-only coverage and $10,500 for family coverage. These amounts are indexed annually to accommodate the effects of inflation.

Eligible participants in an HSA include anyone who is covered by an HDHP, is not covered by other health insurance, and is not enrolled in Medicare. In addition, the individual cannot be claimed as a dependent on someone else's tax return. There are no income limits on who may contribute to an HSA, and no requirement of having earned income to contribute to an HSA. HSA contributions are tax-deductible (U.S. Treasury Department, 2005). The underlying aim of HSAs is to increase the market discipline of the health-care industry and to allow individuals to control more of their health-care spending directly.

Critics of HSAs contend that they are a tax shelter for the rich—that most uninsured people do not face high enough marginal tax rates to benefit substantially from the tax deductibility of HSA contributions. Another criticism is that HSAs are geared to healthy people to the exclusion of those who need health-care benefits the most (removing healthy people from the insurance pool results in higher premiums for everyone else). Still another criticism is that medical costs typically rise faster than the inflation rate.

Not as many people have signed up for HSAs as originally expected. Some people who are used to conventional health-care plans find the new plans confusing. Also, most health-care consumers currently are not involved in financing their health-care plans and would rather have the government and the insurance industry make those decisions for them. Still others might be waiting to see the outcome of national health insurance legislation that is expected to be taken up in Congress in the near future.

HEALTH CARE REFORM

Currently, the United States and South Africa are the only two industrialized countries that do not have some type of government-funded **universal health-care system.** Because of the complex reasons for high health-care costs and the many groups concerned about health care in the United States, tackling health-care reform is difficult. President Bill Clinton made health-care reform the single most important issue when he first took office, but his administration's efforts to oversee the overhaul of the health-care system met with resistance from a wide range of sources. Efforts by the Bush administration to tackle health care reform likewise have been largely stymied (with the exceptions mentioned above). Although most individuals and constituency groups agree that reform is needed, a great deal of controversy persists regarding the types of reforms that should be adopted.

Many advocates of a universal health care system in the United States are calling for a national health insurance program for all types of health care, not just catastrophic illness. Those in favor of such a program base their support on the following arguments:

- Costs for health insurance are too high for large numbers of individuals to afford.
- Many local hospitals are going into debt because they are having to pay health-care costs for the increasing numbers of indigent persons.
- Health costs are higher because people are not seeking preventive health care, which would be more likely if there were a national health insurance program with such an emphasis.

Those who are against such a program pose the following arguments:

- Such a program would mean going to a system of socialized medicine.
- The costs would be too high.
- Individuals would lose their freedom of choice regarding which health-care provider they want.
- People would clog the health-care delivery system with trivial health problems that do not require medical attention.

Proponents of government-funded health care programs have proposed a variety of alternatives. Many, including NASW, call for a universal-access, single-payer system with national standards. They want to eliminate the relationship between health care and employment so those who are jobless, or employed by employers without available or affordable health care, or not covered because of prior health conditions can still receive health coverage. Some plans call for

the federal government to collect funds for a national health-care program from various taxes, with the program administered by private insurance companies instead of by a single government system.

Others advocate for a "pay-or-play" proposal, in which employers would provide health care to their employees, contributing to a public fund to pay for those without insurance or underinsured. Critics of this plan say it is a punitive system that does not guarantee universal coverage and still creates a dual health-care system. Still other proposals call for having persons claim a tax credit on their income tax form if they use health care and provide health coverage for only catastrophic illnesses.

Current proposals to change health-care funding call for eliminating federal bureaucracy and channeling health funds to the states to administer directly. Many state leaders, including a number of governors, are concerned that these efforts will merely pass the burden of complex issues and astronomical costs to them. Some states that had begun to implement health-care reforms had to cut their programs significantly when the economy slowed and they incurred serious deficits in state budgets. States also are passing health-care legislation to limit the amounts that can be collected in malpractice suits in an attempt to lower medical costs, mandating the availability of health care for indigent persons and reducing the burden on local hospitals in poor areas of states, and establishing procedures for decision making about organ transplants and life-threatening situations.

Proposals will continue to be made and debated at all levels of government. The U.S. Government Accountability Office (GAO, 2006) offers the following criteria for evaluating **health-care systems reforms:**

- The reform should allow for a balance between societal needs and individual wants.
- The reform should include consumers, employers, and governments in planning efforts and funding decisions.

- The reform should include provisions to control spending.
- Funding of the reform should be sustainable over time.
- The reform should help providers and consumers make prudent choices about health-insurance coverage and the use of medical services.
- The reform should be transparent with respect to the value and costs of care.
- The reform should include accountability from health plans and providers to meet standards for appropriate use and quality.

Other critical issues for the coming decades include reducing the fragmentation of care, developing private and/or government insurance for long-term health care for the elderly, and increasing the availability of funding for home health and respite care. More resources will be devoted to outpatient community-based care and case management. And more attention also will be directed to prevention, including teen pregnancy and violence as well as AIDS education, and to the promotion of lifestyle changes such as improved diet and the elimination of substance abuse and smoking.

Social Work Roles in the Delivery of Health Services

Today, social workers have many roles in providing health care in a variety of settings. Social work in health care, particularly in working with the elderly, is one of the fastest-growing occupational areas today. Overall, health care is the third largest field of social work practice, and 14% of social workers are employed in health-care settings.

Federal legislation relating to nursing homes requires that all nursing homes in the United States with 120 or more beds must have a social worker with a BSW or an MSW degree. Changes in legislation relating to Medicare now mandate that social workers with an MSW degree who also have professional social work certification be reimbursed for providing outpatient mental health services to the elderly. (Previously, only psychiatrists or psychologists could be reimbursed under Medicare for these services.)

As the number of home health-care agencies increases, the role of social workers in assessing mental health needs and providing intervention and case-management services will expand as well. Social workers will have to direct more attention to fostering the strengths of family members as they face greater demands as caregivers of family members with health needs (Dziegielewski, 2003; Meleis, 2001; Mental Health Resource Foundation, 2005; Moniz & Gorin, 2002; Germain, 2002). Too, as individuals with serious physical and mental injuries continue to live longer because of technological advances, the role of social workers in rehabilitation hospitals will become more important. Federal legislation provides training monies for those who are interested in health care including social workers along with nurses and physicians.

Historical Background

Roles and settings have changed significantly since social workers first became involved in health care. As early as 1888, social workers were advocating for some sort of insurance coverage for all U.S. citizens. Jane Addams and other social workers advocated prevention of illness and community action relating to concerns such as poor sanitation, malnutrition, unsafe housing, and poverty, among others (Axinn & Stern, 2005).

The first known hospital social worker was employed at Massachusetts General Hospital in Boston in 1905. At that time, hospitals and general physicians were the major sources of health care. The social worker worked with the physician, other hospital staff members, and the patient's family to ensure that high-quality care and attention would continue after the patient returned home.

Contemporary Roles in Health-Care Settings

Although responsibility for care after a patient leaves the hospital is still a major focus for many social workers in health-care settings, social workers in these settings today provide a variety of other tasks as well. Social workers often serve as a liaison between the patient's family and health-care staff. They assist the staff in understanding family concerns and how family constraints and other environmental factors may affect a patient's ability to recover. They explain to patients and their families the implications of illness and issues relating to recovery and care. In many instances, the social worker provides support to the family in cases of death or if a patient's condition worsens.

Among the functions of social workers in health-care settings, they

- conduct screening and assessments to determine health risk factors, particularly those involving the family and the broader environment;
- offer social services to patients and their families, such as individual counseling to help a patient deal with a major illness or loss of previous capabilities following an accident or illness, support family members who are grieving a dying individual, or reinforce a teenage mother's decision to place her child for adoption;
- provide case-management services, including working with other social and health-services agencies regarding patient needs, such as helping to arrange for financial assistance to pay hospital bills, nursing home or home health care for patients when they leave the hospital, or emergency child care for a single parent who is hospitalized;
- serve as a member of a health-care team and help others understand a patient's emotional needs and home or family situation;

- advocate for the patient's needs at all levels of the environment, including the patient's family, hospital and other health-care settings, social-services agencies, school, workplace, and community;
- represent the hospital and provide consultation to other community agencies, such as child protective services agencies in child abuse cases;
- provide preventive education and counseling to individuals, including family planning, nutrition, prenatal care, and human growth and development; and
- make health planning and policy recommendations to local communities, states, and the federal government in areas such as hospital care, community health care, environmental protection, and control of contagious diseases.

Many social workers function in agencies administered by and hiring primarily social workers, called **primary settings.** In comparison, health-care settings are considered **secondary settings** because they are administered and staffed largely by health-care professionals who are not social workers. Social workers in health-care settings must be comfortable with their roles and able to articulate their roles and functions clearly to other health-care professionals.

A strong professional identity is important for **medical social workers.** In addition, social workers in health-care settings must be able to work comfortably within a medical model. Knowledge and understanding of the medical profession and health care are important for these social workers, as is the ability to function as a team member with representatives from a variety of disciplines. Social workers in health-care settings, particularly hospital settings, must be able to handle crisis intervention, and they typically prefer short-term social work services rather than long-term client relationships. They must be able to work well under pressure and high stress and be comfortable with death and dying.

Hospital Settings

The American Hospital Association requires that a hospital maintain a social services department as a condition of accreditation. Social workers in hospitals may provide services to all patients who need them, or they may provide specialized services. Larger hospitals employ emergency-room social workers, pediatric social workers, intensive-care social workers, and social workers who work primarily on cardiac, cancer, or other specialized wards.

Some hospitals have added social workers who provide social services primarily to HIV/AIDS patients. Other hospitals employ social workers in preventive efforts, providing outreach services, including home visits to mothers identified during their hospital stay as potentially at-risk to abuse or neglect their children. Still other hospitals employ social workers to coordinate rehabilitative services, serving as case managers to ensure that occupational, physical, recreational, speech, and vocational therapy services are provided.

Social workers work in public and private hospitals alike, providing both inpatient and outpatient care. Many are employed by Veterans Administration (VA) hospitals, which have a longstanding tradition of using social workers to work with persons who have served in the armed forces. Many VA social workers provide specialized counseling relating to physical disabilities and alcohol and drug abuse. A number of VA social workers now specialize in post-traumatic stress disorder (PTSD), providing services to military veterans and their families.

Because of accreditation standards, most medical social workers must have a master's of social work (MSW). Many graduate schools of social work offer specializations in medical or health care.

Long-Term Care Facilities and Nursing Homes

Many people with illness or disability do not need the intensive services of a hospital, but they cannot care for themselves in their own homes without assistance. Particularly for the frail elderly, **long-term care facilities,** such as nursing homes, are most appropriate. These facilities provide medical care and other services to individuals including the elderly and people with disabilities.

Licensing and accreditation requirements vary depending on the levels and types of care facilities. From 1965 to 1972, social work services were mandated for all nursing homes that cared for residents covered by Medicare. Beginning in 1990, all nursing homes with 120 or more beds must employ a social worker. Social workers in these settings help residents adjust to the nursing home environment, help families deal with their guilt and feelings of loss after such placements, serve as liaisons to other social services and health-care agencies, provide individual and group counseling and other social services for nursing home residents and their families, network with others who are involved with and interested in services for the elderly at local and state levels, and advocate for improved services for the clients they serve.

Provision of social work services to the elderly in health-care settings is probably the fastest-growing area of social work. Many schools of social work are offering specializations at the MSW level in health and gerontology, and special courses at the BSW level in these areas to meet the demand.

Community-Based Health Care Programs

Many social workers, at both the BSW and MSW levels, are employed in local community-based health-care programs. Most state health departments operate local health clinics, which offer a variety of health services to low-income residents, as well as community-education programs for all residents. The topics of these programs include immunizations, family planning services, prenatal care, well-baby and pediatric services, nutrition and other types of education programs, and basic health care.

Health clinics frequently employ social workers to work with patients and their families in the context of other health-care services. For example, some clinics operate high-risk infant programs, which include social services for parents of infants at-risk for abuse, neglect, or other serious health problems and children who already have serious health problems and whose parents need monitoring and support. Social workers also work with local community groups and schools, providing outreach programs to publicize and prevent problems such as sexually transmitted diseases and teen pregnancy.

Social workers are employed, too, in family-planning clinics such as Planned Parenthood, providing counseling and help in reaching decisions regarding pregnancy prevention or intervention, such as planning for adoptive services in the case of an unwanted pregnancy. With new technology that can diagnose problems in embryos in the uterus, many health providers are employing social workers to offer genetic counseling that will help clients understand the possibility of giving birth to infants with potential problems and make appropriate decisions regarding whether to become pregnant or to terminate a pregnancy.

Many social workers are employed in community health-care settings that provide services to persons with AIDS and their families. Social workers perform individual, family, and group counseling; serve as case managers assisting clients and their families in accessing community resources; advocate for clients and their families; and offer community-education programs.

Increasingly, health-care settings are recognizing the impact of environmental factors, such as unemployment, on mental and physical health. To help address this concern, traditional health-care settings increasingly are employing social workers. For example, local physicians' clinics—usually operated by a small group of physicians who share a practice—are hiring social workers to provide counseling to patients in an effort to improve their mental health and reduce stress. HMOs are hiring social workers to perform similar functions.

Home Health Care

Many states and communities are recognizing the need for **home health care**—services that enable persons with health problems to remain in their own homes. Home health-care services strive to preserve self-esteem and longevity for the individual and are far less costly than hospital or nursing home care. Trained nurses and home-health aides, as well as social workers, make home visits to perform health care in a person's home. Social workers provide counseling to the client and family, help clients cope emotionally, and serve as case managers, ensuring that appropriate resources are accessed to deal with client needs.

Home health care allows the elderly, persons with AIDS, and other people who do not have to be hospitalized to have greater control over their lives. Home care affords them dignity and the emotional support they might not receive in a hospital or other institutional setting. Because home health-care programs are more cost-effective than hospitalization or other institutional care, these programs will be expanded during the next several decades, and more social workers will be needed to work in them.

State Department of Health and Health-Planning Agencies

Many social workers at both the BSW and MSW levels are employed in health-care policy and planning jobs. They have input into critical decisions regarding funding, policies, and programs for state legislatures, federal officials, and state and local health departments and planning agencies. A social worker might determine, for example, how many more elderly persons could be served if Medicaid income eligibility requirements were to change from 130% to 150% above the poverty line. Or a social worker might develop plans to implement a community-wide HIV/AIDS education program, or suggest ways that a local hospital can be more responsive to the needs of the primarily African American and Latino population it serves.

In one state, for example, planners in the state health department recommended that the agency solicit bids for infant formula for infants served by the WIC program instead of contracting with the same company the agency had used over the years. The bids received were much lower than the amount the department had been paying for the formula, which enabled the department to serve many more clients while saving money.

Other programs in which social workers become involved include those related to the impact of environmental changes on individuals, disease prevention and control, monitoring of solid waste and water facilities, and emergency and disaster planning. State health departments provide services involving dental health, family planning, nutrition, and teenage pregnancy; nutrition programs for pregnant women and young children; periodic health screening of infants and young children; substance-abuse programs; and teen parent services. Health departments and other federal, state, and local agencies also develop policies and implement plans for the provision of emergency and disaster services. Social workers from a number of federal, state, and local public and private agencies from around the United States were involved in planning and overseeing emergency services after the September 11, 2001, terrorist attack, and many others provided assistance after Hurricanes Katrina and Rita in 2005.

The U.S. Public Health Service provides health and health-related services to indigent populations in areas with few medical practitioners, such as American Indian reservations and migrant areas. The Service also monitors communicable diseases and provides research in a variety of health areas. Many students who receive federal funds to attend college or professional schools in health-related areas, including social work, are required to devote a set number of years of service to the Public Health Service after graduation.

Other federal programs, such as the National Institutes of Health (NIH), also provide research and policy alternatives. Both the Public Health Service and the NIH employ social workers at the BSW and MSW levels. The NIH, for example, employs social workers in direct-care settings established to develop new techniques in health care, such as its pediatric AIDS program in Washington, DC.

Other Health-Care Settings

Among the numerous other health-related programs in which social workers are involved is the American Red Cross, which provides emergency services to families when disaster strikes. Social workers also are employed in women's clinics that provide reproductive, gynecological, and primary care using a holistic health approach; genetic counseling centers; and rape crisis centers. Many emergency medical service (EMS) programs in large cities are employing social workers to assist in crisis intervention as a result of family violence, child maltreatment, rape, and homicide.

Increasingly, social workers are being employed in military hospitals and at military installations around the world to help individuals and families cope with the medical and mental health causalities of wars in which the United States is involved around the globe. State-of-the-art mobile medical care units have saved the lives of military personnel in combat situations. Many injuries involve the amputation of limbs, severe damage to the brain and central nervous system, spinal-cord injuries, and loss of hearing and/or sight. Helping military members with disabilities and their families deal with the realities of these injuries is a natural role for social work professionals, and military social work represents a growing field of endeavor for social workers worldwide.

Hospices are multiplying throughout the country. With their inception in England, hospice programs allow terminally ill persons to die at home or in a homelike setting surrounded by family members rather than in an often-alien hospital environment. Applying the stages of grief described by Elizabeth Kübler-Ross (1969/1997) as a framework, many hospices employ social workers to work with families and the dying person or to supervise a cadre of volunteers who provide similar services. As more elderly individuals and persons with HIV/AIDS continue to live longer, the need for hospice programs will increase. Similarly, as critical issues in health care continue to be identified, the functions of social workers in health-care settings will continue to expand.

Summary

Social work in health-care settings is one of the fastest-growing areas of social work today. Issues relating to health care continue to be controversial and complex. Along with new technical and medical discoveries, health-care costs continue to rise. This reality brings up ethical issues in health care—who should receive services at what cost, who should be allowed to make decisions about the right to refuse medical care, and who should be held accountable when a person's health is jeopardized by that person or another individual.

Because cultures shape one's views about health, wellness, and illness, understanding and addressing issues of diversity in health care are essential. Social workers must be able to convey individuals' own roles in preventing and dealing with health-related concerns and to communicate this understanding to others involved in their care.

Recent legislation in the health-care arena, while aimed at streamlining and reducing the costs of the health-care services in the United States through cost controls and privatization, has failed to accomplish the intended effect. To the contrary, such legislation has left millions of low-income Americans or those on fixed incomes with a limited health-care safety net, forcing them to forgo preventive health care and to use more expensive forms of health care such as hospital-based emergency services. Social workers can play a key role in working with members of federal and state legislative bodies to educate them about the long-term effects of current efforts to cut health-care costs through managed care, increased deductibles and co-pay costs, and a host of privatization schemes.

With people living longer, concerns about health care will become increasingly evident. The relationships between environmental factors and health require additional exploration. Finally, the large numbers of Americans, particularly children and the poor, who receive inadequate health care, if any, and the long-term implications for these individuals in all areas of their lives and for our country as a whole must be addressed. Whatever is in store, social workers will play an ever-increasing role in both the planning and the delivery of health-care services.

 ## Key Terms and InfoTrac® College Edition

The terms below are defined in the Glossary at the end of this text. To learn more about key terms and topics in this chapter, enter the following search terms using InfoTrac or the World Wide Web:

acquired immunodeficiency syndrome (AIDS)
bioethics
catastrophic illness
Children's Health Insurance Program (CHIP)
Gross Domestic Product (GDP)
health
health care

health maintenance organizations (HMOs)
health risk factors
health savings accounts (HSAs)
health-care systems reforms
HIV-positive
holistic health care
home health care
hospices

infant mortality rate
long-term care facilities
managed care system
Medicaid
Medicare
medical social workers
physician-assisted
   suicide

primary settings
private health
   insurance
public health
   insurance
secondary settings
universal health care
   system

On the Internet

http://www.cms.hhs.gov/

http://www.cdc.gov/

http://www.nga.org/

Discussion Questions

1. What changes in health care have taken place in the United States since colonial times? What are the reasons for these changes?

2. What are at least three reasons that health-care costs have increased over the last decade?

3. Which groups of persons in the United States are most at-risk for problems with their health? Why?

4. What are some of the ethical issues faced by health-care providers and policymakers? Whom do you think should receive priority in access to health care if costs prevent it being available to everyone?

5. Select one of the recent proposals for health-care reform. Using the criteria proposed by the U.S. General Accountability Office (GAO), evaluate the proposals. Which do you think have the most merit? Why?

6. What are some preventive programs that social workers can implement to reduce the need for health care in the United States?

7. Identify at least three roles social workers might play at various levels of the environment in dealing with pollution and other external conditions that compromise health.

8. What are at least five roles that social workers can play in the delivery of health-care services? How do careers for social workers in health care compare to careers in other areas in terms of availability and opportunity? Why?

References

Administration on Aging. (2005). *A profile of older Americans: 2005*. Washington, DC: Author.

Aids.org. (2006). *What is AIDS?* Los Angeles, CA: Available: http://www.aids/org/factSheets

American Academy of Family Physicians. (2001). *Managed care reform*. Leawood, KS: Author. Available: http://www.aafp.org/online/en/home/policy/policies/m/managedcarereform.printview.html

American Academy of Pediatrics. (1999). Planning for children whose parents are dying of HIV/AIDS. *Pediatrics, 103*(2), 509–511.

Annie E. Casey Foundation. (2006). *KIDS COUNT data book*. Washington, DC: Author.

Artiga, S., Rousseau, D., Lyons, B., Smith, S., & Gaylin, D. (2006). Can states stretch the Medicaid dollar without passing the buck? Lessons from Utah. *Health Affairs, 25*(2), 532–540.

Axinn, J., & Stern, M. (2005). *Social welfare: A history of the American response to need* (6th ed.). Boston: Allyn & Bacon.

Baicker, K., & Chandra, A. (2004). *The effect of malpractice liability on the delivery of health care*. Cambridge, MA: National Bureau of Economic Research.

Bavier, K. (2004). *The impact of barriers to prenatal care in rural and urban teenage pregnancies*. Durham, NC: Duke University School of Nursing.

Borjas, G. (2003). *Welfare reform, labor suply, and health insurance in the immigrant population*. Ann Arbor: University of Michigan, Economic Research Initiative on the Uninsured.

Brenner, M. H. (1973). Fetal, infant and maternal mortality during periods of economic stress. *International Journal of Health Sciences, 3*, 145–159.

Brown, E. R., Ojeda, V. D., Wyn, R., & Levan, R. (2000). *Racial and ethnic disparities in access to health insurance and health care.* Los Angeles: UCLA Center for Health Policy Research; and Menlo Park, CA: Henry Kaiser Family Foundation.

Campbell-White, A., Merrick, T., & Yazbeck, A. (2006). *Reproductive health: The missing millennium development goal—poverty, health, and development in a changing world.* New York: World Bank Publications.

Catalano, R. (1979). *Health behavior and the community: An ecological perspective.* New York: Pergamon.

Center on Budget and Policy Priorities. (2005). *The effect of increased cost-sharing in Medicaid: A summary of research findings.* Washington, DC: Author.

Center for Public Policy Priorities. (2006). *Texas Medicaid and CHIP enrollment update.* Austin, TX: Author.

Centers for Disease Control and Prevention. (2002). *Annual smoking-attributable mortality, years of potential life lost, and economic costs—United States, 1995–1999.* Atlanta: Author. Available: http://www.cdc.gov

Centers for Disease Control and Prevention. (2003a). Healthy people 2010 leading health indicators, Table 52. *Health, United States, 2002.* Atlanta: Author.

Centers for Disease Control and Prevention. (2003b). *Chronic disease and their risk factors.* Atlanta: Author. Available: http://www.cdc.gov/nccdphg/statbook.htm

Centers for Disease Control and Prevention. (2004a). *HIV/AIDS surveillance report: Cases of HIV/AIDS, by area of residence, diagnosed in 2004—33 states with confidential name-based HIV-infection reporting.* Atlanta: Author.

Centers for Disease Control and Prevention. (2004b). *HIV/AIDS surveillance report: HIV infection and AIDS in the United States, 2004.* Atlanta: Author.

Centers for Disease Control and Prevention. (2005a). *Health, United States, 2005.* Atlanta: Author.

Centers for Disease Control and Prevention. (2005b). *HIV/AIDS update.* Atlanta, GA: Author.

Centers for Medicare and Medicaid Services. (2003a). *Highlights—national health expenditures—2001.* Washington, DC. Available: http://www.cms.hhs.gov/statistics/nhe/historical/highlishts.asp

Centers for Medicare and Medicaid Services. (2003b). *Where the nation's health dollar came from and where it went.* Washington, DC: Office of the Actuary, National Health Statistics Group.

Centers for Medicare and Medicaid Services. (2006). *Medicare disproportionate share hospital.* Washington, DC: Author.

Children's Alliance Work Group. (2002). *Prevention pays.* Available: http://www.childrensalliance.org/whatwedo/preventionpays.htm

Children's Defense Fund. (2003). *Asthma.* Seattle: Author. Available: http://www.childrensdefense.org/hs_tp_asthmalphp

Children's Defense Fund. (2006). *The state of America's children yearbook, 2005.* Washington, DC: Author. Available: http://www.childrensdefense.org/

Death with Dignity National Center. (2006). *The Oregon Death with Dignity Law.* Available: http://www.deathwithdignity.org/history/facts

Dohrenwend, B. S., & Dohrenwend, B. P. (Eds.). (1974). *Stressful life events: Their nature and effects.* New York: Wiley.

Dziegielewski, S. (2003). *The changing face of health care social work: Professional practice in managed behavioral care* (2nd ed.). New York: Springer Publishing.

Economic Policy Institute. (2006). *Economic snapshots: More children are uninsured.* Washington, DC: Author.

Families USA. (1998). *Hit and miss: State managed care laws.* Washington, DC: Author.

Families USA. (2003a). *The federal budget: Funds for uninsured working families.* Washington, DC: Author. Available: http://www.familiesusa.org/

Families USA. (2003b). *Going without health insurance: Nearly one in three non-elderly Americans.* Washington, DC: Author.

Families USA. (2003c). *State managed care patient protections.* Washington, DC: Author. Available: http://www.familiesusa.org/

Families USA. (2004). *Working without a net: The health care safety net still leaves millions of low-income workers uninsured.* Washington, DC: Author.

Families USA. (2005). *Paying a premium: The increased cost of care for the uninsured.* Washington, DC: Author. Available: http://www.familiesuse.org/resources/publications/reports/paying-a-premium-findings.html

Families USA. (2006). *The 2005 federal Medicaid battle: Where are we now?* Washington, DC: Author.

Available: http://www.familiesusa.org/issues/med-icaid/medicaid-action/federal-battle.html

Federal Interagency Forum on Aging Related Statistics. (2004). *Older Americans 2004: Key indicators of well-being.* Washington, DC: Author.

Flores, G., Abreu, M., & Tomany-Korman, S. (2006). Why are Latinos the most uninsured racial/ethnic group of US children? A community-based study of risk factors for and consequences of being an uninsured Latino child. *Pediatrics, 118*(3), 730–740.

Gandhi, R., Bartlett, J., & Linkinhoker, M. (1999). *Life cycle of HIV infection.* Baltimore: Johns Hopkins. Available: http://hopkins-aids.edu/hiv_lifecycle/hivcycle_txt.html

Germain, C. B. (2002). *Social work practice in health care.* New York: Free Press.

GFOA Federal Liaison Center. (2002). *Health care.* Washington, D.C: Author. Available: http:www.gfoa.org/flc/agenda2002.html

Goldman, D. P., et al. (2004). Pharmacy benefits and the use of drugs by the chronically ill. *Journal of the American Medical Association, 291,* 2344–2350.

Gottlieb, S. (2003). The future of medical technology. In *The New Atlantis,* Number 1, Spring 2003, 79–87.

Havrda, D. E., Omundsen, B. A., Bender, W., & Kirkpatrick, M. A. (2005). Impact of Medicare Modernization Act on low-income persons. *Annals of Internal Medicine, 143*(8), 600–608.

Health Resources and Services Administration. (2003). *Changing demographics: Implications for physicians, nurses, and other health workers.* Washington, DC: Author.

Health Resources and Services Administration. (2004). *Women's health USA, 2004.* Washington, DC: Author.

Health Resources and Services Administration. (2006a). *CARE Act.* Baltimore: Author.

Health Resources and Services Administration. (2006b). *HIV/AIDS Dental Programs.* Baltimore: Author.

Health Resources and Services Administration. (2006c). *Ryan White CARE Act Appropriations.* Baltimore: Author.

Healthy Steps. (2006). *Healthy Steps for children: A national initiative to foster healthy growth and development.* Washington, DC. Available: http://www.healthysteps.org/

Heffler, S., et al. (2005). U.S. health spending projections for 2004–2014. Bethesda, MD. Available: http://content.healthaffairs.org

Herd, P., House, J., & Schoeni, R. (2006). *Income support policies and health among the elderly* (National Poverty Center Working Paper #06-27). Ann Arbor: University of Michigan Gerald Ford School of Public Policy.

Institute of Medicine. (2003). *Hidden costs, value lost: Uninsurance in America.* Washington, D.C: Author.

Israel, B. A., Eng, E., Schulz, A. J., Parker, E. A., & Satcher, D. (2005). *Methods in community-based participatory research for health.* San Francisco: Jossey-Bass Publishers.

Johns Hopkins University. (2006). *Ryan White Care Act.* Baltimore: Johns Hopkins University. Available: http://www.hopkins-aids.edu

Joint United Nations Programme on HIV/AIDS. (2006). *Report on the global AIDS epidemic.* Geneva, Switzerland: Author.

Kaiser Commission on Medicaid and the Uninsured. (2004). *States respond to fiscal pressure: A 50-state update of state Medicaid spending growth and cost containment.* Washington, DC: Author.

Kaiser Commission on Medicaid and the Uninsured. (2006a). *Changes in employees' health insurance coverage, 2001–2005.* Washington, DC: Author.

Kaiser Commission on Medicaid and the Uninsured. (2006b). *The uninsured: A primer.* Washington, DC: Author.

Kaiser Commission on Medicaid and the Uninsured. (2006c). *Why did the number of uninsured continue to increase in 2005?* Washington, DC: Author.

Kaiser EDU.Org. (2006). *Prescription drug benefit under Medicare: Background brief.* Washington, DC: Author. Available: http://www.kaiseredu.org/topics

Kaiser Family Foundation. (1998). *Kaiser/Harvard national survey of Americans' views on consumer protection in managed care.* Menlo Park, CA: Author.

Kaiser Family Foundation. (2005). *Trends and indicators in the changing health care marketplace.* Menlo Park, CA: Author. Available: http://www.kff.org/insurance/7031/print-sec4.cfm

Kaiser Family Foundation. (2006a). *Prescription drug coverage among Medicare beneficiaries.* Menlo Park, CA: Author.

Kaiser Family Foundation. (2006b). *Sexual health statistics for teenagers and young adults in the United States.* Menlo Park, CA: Author.

Kaiser Family Foundation. (2006c). *Current monthly SCHIP enrollment, June 2005*. Menlo Park, CA: Author.

Knab, J., Garfinkel, I., & McLanahan, S. (2006). *The effects of welfare and child support policies on maternal health and wellbeing*. Ann Arbor, MI: National Poverty Center.

Kowelski-Jones, L., & Duncan, G. J. (2002). Effects of participation in the WIC program on birthweight: Evidence from the National Longitudinal Survey of Youth. *American Journal of Public Health, 92*(5), 799–804.

Kübler-Ross, E. (1997). *On death and dying*. New York: Simon & Schuster. (Originally published 1969)

Meilaender, G. (2003). Bioethics and the character of human life. In *The New Atlantis*. Number 1, Spring 2003, 67–78. Available: http://www.thenewatlantis.com/

Meleis, A. F. (2001). (ed.). *Women's work, health, and quality of life*. Binghamton, NY: Haworth Press

Mental Health Resource Foundation. (2005). *And I will make thee whole: Helping families with mental health concerns*. Springville, UT: Cedar Fort Publishers.

Moniz, C., & Gorin, S. (2002). *Health and health care policy: AQ social work perspective*. Boston: Allyn & Bacon.

Nathanson, M., & Ku, L. (2003). *Proposed state Medicaid cuts would jeopardize health insurance coverage for 1.7 million people: An update*. Washington, DC: Center on Budget and Policy Priorities. Available: http://www.cbpp.org/pubs/health.htm

National Association of Chronic Disease Directors. (2005). *Comprehensive and integrated chronic disease prevention: Action planning handbook for states and communities*. Atlanta: Author.

National Association of Community Health Centers. (2005). *Shifting sands: State funding, Medicaid cuts, and health centers* (State Policy Rep. #8). Washington, DC: Author.

National Association of Social Workers. (1994). *Social work speaks: NASW policy statements* (3rd ed.). Washington, DC: NASW Press.

National Cancer Institute (2004). *The majority of cancers are linked to the environment*. Bethesda, MD: Author. Available: http://www.cancer.gov/templates/doc

National Center for Chronic Disease Prevention and Health Promotion. (2006a). *Targeting tobacco use: The nation's leading cause of death*. Atlanta: Author. Available: http://apps.nccd.gov

National Center for Chronic Disease Prevention and Health Promotion. (2006b). *What are some of CDC's key findings related to adult health-related quality of life?* Atlanta: Author: Available: http://www.cdc.gov/hrqo/findings.htm

National Center for Health Statistics. (2002, Sept. 16). Deaths and percent of total deaths for the top 10 leading causes of death, Tables C, E and F. *National Vital Statistics Report, 50*(16).

National Center for Health Statistics. (2003a, March). *National vital statistics reports 51*(5). Hyattsville, MD: U.S. Department of Health and Human Services.

National Center for Health Statistics. (2003b). *Study finds life expectancy in the US rose to 77.2 years in 2001*. Hyattsville, MD: U.S. Department of Health and Human Services.

National Center for Health Statistics. (2004a). *Deaths—leading causes*. Hyattsville, MD: Author.

National Center for Health Statistics. (2004b). *Hospital utilization (in non-federal short-stay hospitals)*. Hyattsville, MD: Author.

National Center for Health Statistics. (2005a). *Births: Preliminary data for 2004*. Hyattsville, MD: Author. Available: http://www.cdc.gov/nchs/releases03news/lifeex/htm

National Center for Health Statistics. (2005b). *Health expenditures*. Hyattsville, MD: Author.

National Center for Health Statistics. (2005c). *Health, United States, 2005*. Hyattsville, MD: Author. Available: http://www.cdc.gov/nchs/hus/htm

National Center for Health Statistics. (2006a). *Health behaviors of adults: United States, 2004–05*. Hyattsville, MD: Author.

National Center for Health Statistics. (2006b). *Life expectancy*. Hyattsville, MD: Author.

National Center for Health Statistics. (2006c). *National ambulatory medical care survey: 2004 summary*. Hyattsville, MD: Author.

National Center for Health Statistics. (2006d). *NCHS definitions: Health maintenance organization (HMO)*. Hyattsville, MD: Author.

National Coalition on Health Care. (2006). *Facts on health insurance coverage*. Washington, DC: Author.

National Conference of State Legislatures. (2006a). *Funding prenatal care for unauthorized immigrants: Challenges lie ahead for states*. Denver: Author. Available: http://www.ncsl.org/statefed/prenatal.htm

National Conference of State Legislatures. (2006b). *Medicaid*. Denver: Author. Available: http://www.ncsl.org/programs/health/h-medicaid.htm

National Institute of Allergy and Infectious Diseases. (2003). *HIV/AIDS statistics*. Bethesda, MD: Author. Available: http://www.niaid.nih.gov/factsheets/aidsstt.htm

Office of Civil Rights—HIPPA. (2003). *Protecting the privacy of patients' health information*. Washington, DC: Author. Available: www.hhs.gov/news/facts/privacy.html

Office of Rural Health Policy. (2006). *Office of rural health policy FY 2005 annual report*. Rockville, MD: Author.

Oregon Department of Human Services. (2005). *Seventh annual report on Oregon's Death with Dignity Act*. Portland, OR: Author.

Park, E., Mann, C., Alker, J., & Nathanson, M. (2003). *NGA Medicaid Task Force's draft proposal shifts fiscal risks to states and jeopardizes health coverage for millions*. Washington, DC: Georgetown University Health Policy Institute, Center on Budget and Policy Priorities.

Rehm, R. (2003). Legal, financial, and ethical ambiguities for Mexican-American families: Caring for children with chronic conditions. *Qualitative Health Research, 13*(5), 689–702.

Save the Children. (2006). *Children in the world of AIDS*. Westport, CT.: Author. Available: http://www.savethechildren.org/health/hiv_aids

Sexuality Information and Education Council of the United States [SIECUS]. (2006). *Teen pregnancy, birth and abortion*. Washington, DC: Author.

Ullman, F., Hill, I., & Almeida, R. (1999). *CHIP: A look at emerging state programs* (Series A, No. A-35). Washington, DC: Urban Institute.

U.S. Census Bureau. (2005). *Health insurance coverage—2005*. Washington, DC: Author.

U.S. Census Bureau. (2006a). *More than 50 million Americans report some level of disability*. Washington, DC: Author.

U.S. Census Bureau. (2006b). *Percentage of people without health insurance coverage by state using 2- and 3-year averages*. Washington, DC: Author.

U.S. Census Bureau. (2006c). *Statistical Abstract of the United States: 2006*. Washington, DC: Author.

U.S. Department of Agriculture. (2004). *Nutrition and health characteristics of low-income populations: Volume II, WIC participants and non-participants*. Washington, DC: Author.

U.S. Department of Commerce. (2002). *Statistical abstract of the United States*. 2002. (122 ed.).

U.S. Department of Health and Human Services. (2001). *Healthy people in healthy communities: A community planning guide using Healthy People 2010*. Washington, DC: Author.

U.S. Department of Health and Human Services. (2003). *Changing demographics: Implications for physicians, nurses, and other health workers*. Washington, DC: Author.

U.S. Department of Health and Human Services. (2006a). *Deaths: Preliminary data for 2004*. Washington, DC: Author.

U.S. Department of Health and Human Services. (2006b). *United States life tables, 2003*. Washington, DC: Author.

U.S. Department of Labor. (2003). *Workplace injury, illness and fatality statistics*. Washington, DC: Bureau of Labor Statistics. Available: http://www.osha.gov/oshstts/work.html

U.S. Department of Labor. (2006). *Workplace injuries and illnesses in 2005*. Washington, DC: Bureau of Labor Statistics.

U.S. Government Accountability Office (GAO). (2006). *Evaluating health care system reforms*. Washington, DC: Author.

U.S. National Center for Health Statistics. (2002) *Fastats*. Hyattsville, MD: Author. Available: http://www.cdc.gov/nchswww/fastats.htm

U.S. Public Health Service. (1977). 200 years of child health. In E. Grotberg (Ed.), *200 years of children*. Washington, DC: U.S. Department of Health, Education and Welfare.

U.S. Surgeon General. (1979). *Healthy people: The Surgeon General's report on health promotion and disease prevention*. Washington, DC: U.S. Department of Health, Education and Welfare, Public Health Service.

U.S. Treasury Department. (2005). *All about HSAs*. Washington, DC: Author.

Williams, D., & Mohammed, S. (2006). *Poverty, migration, and health*. Ann Arbor, MI: National Poverty Center.

World Health Organization. (2003). *WHO definition of health: Preamble to the Constitution of the World Health Organization as adopted by the International Health Conference, New York, 19–22 June, 1946*. Geneva, Switzerland: Author. Available: http://www.who.int/about/definition/en

Suggested Further Readings

Anderson, R. M., Rice, T. H., Kominski, G. F., Afifi, A. A., & Rosenstock, L. (2007). *Changing the U.S. health care system: Key issues in health services policy and management* (3rd ed.). San Francisco: Jossey-Bass.

Bartlett, D. L, & Steele, J. B. (2005). *Critical condition: Health care in America became big business—and bad medicine.* New York: Broadway Publishers.

Behan, P. (2006). *Solving the health care problem: How other nations have succeeded and why United States has failed.* Albany: State University of New York Press.

Bloche, M. G. (Ed.). (2002). *The privatization of health care reform.* New York: Oxford University Press.

Daley, J. B. (Ed.). (2006). *Advances in social work: Special issue on the future of social work.* London, England: Trafford Publishing.

Dolan, P., & Olsen, J. A. (2003). *Distributing health care: Economic and ethical issues.* New York: Oxford University Press.

Gehlert, S., & Browne, T. A. (2006). *Handbook of health social work.* Hoboken, NJ: Wiley.

Isaacs, S. L., & Knickman, J. R. (Eds.). (2005). *To improve health and health care: The Robert Wood Johnson Foundation Anthology.* San Francisco: Jossey-Bass.

Mechanic, D. (2006). *The truth about health care: Why reform is not working in America.* New Brunswick, NJ: Rutgers University Press.

Mechanic, D., Rogut, L. B., & Colby, D. B. (Eds.). (2005). *Policy challenges in modern health care.* New Brunswick, NJ: Rutgers University Press.

Mites, T. P., & Furino, A. (Eds.). (2005). *Annual review of gerontology and geriatrics: Aging health care workforce issues.* New York: Springer Publishing.

Quadango, J. (2005). *One nation uninsured: Why the U.S. has no national health insurance.* New York: Oxford University Press.

Rehr, H., & Rosenberg, G. (2006). *The social work-medicine relationship: 100 years at Mount Sinai.* Binghamton, NY: Haworth Social Work.

Richmond, J. B., Fein, R., & Carter, J. (2005). *The health care mess: How we got into it and what it will take to get out.* Cambridge, MA: Harvard University Press.

CHAPTER 10

The Needs of Children, Youth, and Families

Divorced for 2 years, Ernestine Moore is struggling to survive. Her five children are in a foster home while she tries to stabilize her life. Ernestine is looking forward to the day when she and her children can live together as a family again.

Ernestine comes from a large family. Her father drinks often and beats her mother, her siblings, and Ernestine herself. Pregnant at age 16 and afraid of her father, she eloped with the father of her child, a 19-year-old high school graduate, James Moore, who worked at a fast-food restaurant. The first year was fairly peaceful for the new family, although lack of money was a continual problem. Lacking health insurance, they began to pay the bills for the baby's birth, which would require several years to pay off. Both James and Ernestine were excited about the baby, and Ernestine worked hard to provide a good home for her husband and baby. She wanted desperately to have the kind of home and family she had not had as a child.

During the next 6 years, Ernestine and James had three more children. One of the children had several health problems, which added to the financial pressures, and life became increasingly stressful. James began to drink heavily and started to beat Ernestine. He also physically and verbally abused one of their sons, who was diagnosed as having a developmental disability. When Ernestine became pregnant with her fifth child,

James left her. Since that time, he has paid child support for only 6 months.

After James left, Ernestine moved in with a sister, who has three children of her own. To support her children and contribute to the rent her sister was paying, Ernestine got two jobs—one in a fast-food restaurant and one at night, cleaning a bank. Shortly after her new baby was born, this arrangement ended because of continual arguments between the two sisters over money, space, and childrearing.

At that point Ernestine applied for food stamps and medical assistance and moved into a two-room apartment. She applied for low-income housing and, although she was eligible, she was told there was a 2-year waiting list. Ernestine hired a teenage girl to care for her children while she worked. Tired and overwhelmed, Ernestine had little time or energy left to devote to her children and became increasingly abusive toward them. The older children fell behind in school and were fighting continually. Then they began to steal and vandalize. Neighbors in the apartment complex saw the younger children outside at all hours, unsupervised, often wearing only diapers. The neighbors heard screaming and the baby crying throughout the night.

The babysitter quit because Ernestine fell behind in paying her. After Ernestine missed 2 days of work while she tried desperately to find another sitter, she was fired from her fast-food job.

Afraid that she also would lose her cleaning job, she began to put the younger children to bed at 6 o'clock and leave the oldest child (age 8) in charge until she returned home.

Ernestine and her children were evicted from the apartment because of failure to pay the rent, and for 2 weeks the entire family slept in a friend's van. Finally, when the oldest child came to school with bruises and complaining of a sore arm and revealed the family's living situation to her teacher, the teacher called the local child protective services agency. When the social worker arrived, she observed the bruises and obvious malnourishment. In talking with Ernestine, it was apparent that she was overwhelmed and angry, and she felt extremely guilty about what had happened to her children.

The children were placed in foster care with an older, nurturing couple. With more structure and a stable living situation, the children began doing better in school and were able to develop some positive relationships with others. Ernestine visited the children often and began to see the foster parents as caring people who almost seemed like parents to her.

Ernestine enrolled in a job-training program and was hired as a health-care aide for a local nursing home. She enjoys her job and is talking about getting her high school equivalency certificate and going to nursing school. Her social worker encouraged her to join Parents Anonymous, a support group for abusive parents. For the first time, Ernestine has developed positive, trusting relationships with others. She has located an affordable duplex, and she and her social worker are making plans to have the children return home permanently.

The family is considered to be the most significant social system within which all individuals function. Within the family we first develop trusting relationships, a special identity, and a sense of self-worth. Traditionally, the family has been looked upon as a safe, protective haven where its members can receive nurturing, love, and support. In today's complex and rapidly changing world, however, families are encountering more difficulty. Increasingly, children are affected by the family's financial pressures, the need for one or both parents to work long hours, or the physical or mental illness of a family member.

Unable to cope with the pressures, family members often turn to alcohol or drugs, resort to violence, or withdraw from other family members. Sometimes, because they did not grow up in a loving, nurturing environment, they are unable to provide a healthy environment for their own children. Sometimes parents do not know how to provide for their children because they have not learned what children need or what to expect from them at various ages. Many parents are emotionally unable to meet the needs of other family members during a crisis, such as a serious illness or death.

How well a family is able to meet the needs of its members also depends on other systems with which the family interacts—the neighborhood, community, and broader society. The quality and consistency of these interactions have a tremendous impact on the family's well-being. Many experts who work with children and families suggest that attention to these broader systems rather than only individual family members is essential to effective intervention with families (Berkes, Golding, & Folke, 2002; Bronfenbrenner, 1979; Duncan & Goddard, 2005; Garbarino, 1992, 1999; Maynard & Martini, 2005; Powers, DuPaul, Shapiro, & Kazak, 2003; and Yuen, Skibinski, & Pardeck, 2003).

A family that functions within an unsupportive environment is much more susceptible to family problems than one that functions within a supportive environment. If the family lives in a community that provides few family supports, that also may threaten the family's well-being. Consider Ernestine's situation. Abused as a child, her emotional needs were not met and she learned to distrust others. This left her feeling worthless and inadequate. Individuals with low self-esteem are more likely to become pregnant at an early age. They also are more likely than other parents to abuse their children. Ernestine also learned from her own parents to deal with anger by hitting. And life with an alcoholic father taught Ernestine many dysfunctional behavior patterns that she carried into her own life.

In this chapter we consider general issues and trends involving the needs of children, youth, and families; the types and extent of problems that influence children and adolescents and their families; and factors that place families at risk for encountering problems. Chapter 11 builds on this chapter, detailing services and policies that prevent or alleviate problems of children, youth, and families, as well as the roles of social workers in providing these services and developing and implementing these policies.

What Is a Family?

All families have strengths as well as different ways of coping. No matter how many strengths a family has, however, the impact (past and present) of the broader environment may make it difficult, if not impossible, for the family to cope with crisis without additional support. Actually, all families need support beyond the family to survive and to reinforce their internal strengths. The African saying, "It takes a village to raise a child" is perhaps more true today than ever before.

The typical American family in the 1950s, 1960s, and 1970s consisted of a husband, a wife, and two or more children. That picture looks quite different today. In 2002, 69% of children lived with two parents, 23% lived with only their mother, 5% lived with only their father, and 4% lived in households with neither parent present. Almost half (48%) of African American children were living with a single mother. Some 25% of Hispanic children lived with a single mother, compared to 16% of Caucasian children and 13% of Asian and Pacific Islander children (U.S. Bureau of the Census, 2003). Of all families, 32% were are headed by only one parent, usually a female.

Many family households include extended family members—grandparents, aunts, uncles, or cousins. Others are gay or lesbian couples with children. Still others include adopted or foster children. A growing number of individuals not related by blood or marriage are living together. Some families are headed by one or more grandparents who assume parenting responsibilities because one of their own children is unable or unwilling to do so—a practice referred to as *second-time parenting* (AARP, 2006). More than 2.4 million children in the United States are living in households in which grandparents are responsible for them (U.S. Bureau of the Census, 2003).

Some would argue that it is not possible to come up with a standard definition of a **family.** Others provide a broad definition of a family exemplified by Crosson-Tower (2005) as

> any group of individuals who live together (or at least have regular contact) and who are expected to perform specific functions, especially in reference to the children involved.

When discussing the needs of children and families, a family is referred to within the context of a parent figure or figures and at least one child. Perhaps the most important issue in relation to what constitutes a family is that no two families are alike. Each family may be viewed as its own unique system.

How Are Families of Today Viewed?

Two of the most relevant frameworks for considering the family in the context of the social welfare system are the *systems/ecological framework* and the *life-span development framework*. The systems/ecological framework emphasizes the interactions between family members and other levels of the environment, including extended family members, the neighborhood, the school, places of worship, the workplace, the community, the state, and other larger systems such as the economic system and the political system. (This framework and the life-span development framework are discussed in chapter 3.)

The family as a social system has more impact on the individual than any other system throughout the life cycle. Even before birth, the physical and emotional health of the family in which the child will be born and the environment in which the family functions affect the child's future significantly. How well individuals learn to trust others, develop autonomy, take initiative, be industrious, have a positive identity, be intimate with others, give something of themselves back to others, and face death with integrity—all are shaped extensively by relationships within the family.

Families, too, go through distinct stages of development (Crosson-Tower, 2005). Carter and McGoldrick (2005) discuss the following stages in the family life cycle:

1. unattached young adult,
2. courtship and early marriage/long-term relationship,
3. transition to parenthood and care of young children,
4. raising adolescents,
5. launching the children and moving on, and
6. later life, including involvement in the next generation of marriage/long-term relationship and parenting.

Every family undergoes changes as its members grow and change, and the family's needs and interactions with the social welfare system will differ according to the family's stage of development at the time. Carter and McGoldrick also identified specific changes characteristic of divorced families and families involving the remarriage of a parent.

What Is a Healthy Family?

All families go through some sort of problem at some point during the family life cycle, but some families are better able to cope with family problems because of the availability of financial resources and social support systems and the strong physical and mental health of family members. In any case, though, a major crisis—no matter how healthy the family is—will have a serious impact on the family and is likely to result in at least a temporary need for assistance from the social welfare system in some way.

Among the factors associated with healthy families are the opportunity to express ideas and feelings, absence of family secrets, valuing of everyone's opinions and feelings, rules that are flexible yet enforced with consistency, positive energy, and regular opportunities for growth and change. Children are more likely to grow up to be successful adults if, as a child, they have a positive, nurturing relationship with at least one caregiver; consistent parenting, particularly during their first year of life; well-balanced discipline; at least a 2-year separation in age between siblings; and access to others who can provide emotional support if their immediate families cannot do so (Newman & Newman, 2005).

How Are Family Problems Defined?

What constitutes a family problem depends on the perspective of the individual defining the problem. It also depends on factors such as the cultural context within which the problem takes place; community norms and values; attitudes and professional values of the person defining the problem; legal definitions of the problem; and the availability of resources to address the problem.

CULTURAL CONTEXT

Cultural attitudes, values, and practices shape how family problems are defined. In cultures in which women become sexually active as soon as they reach menses, teenage pregnancy is not likely to be considered a problem. Some cultures think it is abusive to make young children sit in a dental chair and force them to open their mouth and have a tooth pulled out. Some family policy experts suggest that our country's fascination with violence, as exemplified through the media and sports events, strongly influences the high incidence of violence within families, and that the emphasis on sex in the media contributes to the high incidence of teenage pregnancy.

COMMUNITY NORMS AND VALUES

The norms and values of the community also shape the way by which family problems are defined. For example, if all employable community members are unemployed and, as a consequence, their children live in substandard housing and are poorly fed and clothed, the families in that community living under those circumstances are not likely to be seen as neglecting their children. But children in such a family in a wealthy community most likely would be considered neglected.

ATTITUDES AND VALUES

The attitudes, values, personal life experiences, and professional background of the person defining the problem also influence problem definition. For example, a person who grew up in a family in which any alcohol drinking was taboo might define alcoholism differently than a person who grew up in a family in which wine was part of evening meals. A physician may be more likely to define child abuse only in terms of physical characteristics, whereas a social worker may be more likely to take a more holistic approach to defining child maltreatment.

LEGAL DEFINITIONS

Legal statutes also provide a basis for defining family problems. These definitions vary by country and state and often leave a great deal of room for interpretation. For example, the landmark **Child Abuse Prevention and Treatment Act of 1974** defines child maltreatment as

> . . . the physical or mental injury, sexual abuse or exploitation, negligent treatment, or maltreatment of a child by a person who is responsible for the child's welfare, under circumstances which indicate that the child's health or welfare is harmed or threatened. (42 Section 5016g)

Terms such as *mental injury, negligent treatment,* and *threatened* often are difficult to interpret. At the same time, they allow leeway for the protection of children. For example, a child who is constantly threatened with a knife or gun, even though never actually hurt physically, is likely to have serious emotional problems.

AVAILABILITY OF RESOURCES

Availability of resources may be the most important factor in how a problem is defined. That is, the broader the definition, the more children and families will be identified as having the problem and needing assistance; and the narrower the definition, the fewer will be identified as having the problem and needing assistance. The legal definition just given, for example, allows for the inclusion of neglected and emotionally maltreated children.

Resources are stretched so thin in most states today that they are using narrower definitions of child maltreatment. Also, the debate over the proper role of government in intervening with families has resulted in conflicting child welfare policies, which leaves many children vulnerable to child maltreatment in all its forms. As the debate continues, children in the United States,

TABLE 10.1
Indicators of Child Well-Being

Indicators	National Data
Number of low-birth weight babies	324,064
Infant mortality rate for non-Hispanic blacks	14.0
Child death rate/100,000 children ages 1–14 for all groups	21
Child death rate/100,000 children ages 1–14 for African Americans	29
Child death rate /100,000 children ages 1–14 for American Indians	30
Number of teens neither in school nor working	1.3 million
Percent of children in single-parent families	31%
Children in female-headed households who are poor	40%
Female-headed families receiving child support/alimony	33%

Source: Kids Count Data Book, by Annie E. Casey Foundation Greenwich, CT: Author, 2006, pp. 32–50. Reprinted with permission.

particularly children of color, continue to fare poorly when looking at key indicators of child well-being (see Table 10.1 and Box 10.1).

What Causes Families to Have Problems?

Families have problems for many reasons, and some families have similar problems but for different reasons. A given problem has no single cause, which makes a systems/ecological perspective important in addressing family problems. Also, saying that certain factors are *associated* with specific family problems is more appropriate than saying that those factors *cause* those problems. This means that a family with a problem may have other problems as well, but determining which problem caused the other is difficult.

We know that problems often go together. For example, child abuse, spouse abuse, alcoholism, and teenage pregnancy are likely to be found within the same family. Individuals with these problems are more often under stress and worried about financial pressures, have low self-esteem, and come from families in which similar problems existed than are individuals in families without these problems.

Meanwhile, services for children and families often are provided by the "problem area"—for example, alcoholism, child abuse and neglect, spouse abuse—rather than as services for the family as a system. This is largely because of the categorical basis on which state and federal funding generally is allocated. This categorical funding system has resulted in fragmented and duplicated services, as well as gaps in services in which client groups "fall through the cracks."

How Do Cultural and Gender Differences Affect Family Problems?

While statistics show that more children and families who have family problems in the United States are white and headed by two parents, that statement is true only because there are more white, two-parent families than other types of families (Children's Defense Fund, 2006). Thus, it is important to consider not only raw simple numerical counts but also *rates*—the number of individuals of a certain group who are experiencing problems compared to the total population of that group. These comparisons show that some groups are more vulnerable, or at risk, than other groups to have certain problems.

In the United States, single women and people of color with children are more at risk than men and whites to have family problems. Several reasons have been offered for their vulnerability. In 2005, 23.8% of African American families with related children lived below the federal poverty level—nearly three times the rate for Caucasians. The rate for Latino families was 20.6%. In that same year, the poverty rates for female-headed

---

BOX 10.1
How American Children Are Doing

Millions of children thrive in America, but a profile of U.S. children developed by Kids Count, a project of the Annie E. Casey Foundation (2006), reveals a nation failing to keep pace with the needs of its youngest citizens. Nationally, nearly 325,000 babies were born weighing less than 2,500 grams (about 5.5 pounds) in 2003. The percent of low-birthweight babies born to non-Hispanic blacks was twice that of non-Hispanic whites. The infant mortality rate (the number of deaths to persons less than 1 year old per 1,000 live births) for children born into poor families was more than 50% higher than that for children born into families with incomes above the poverty line.

The child death rate (deaths per 100,000 children ages 1 to 14) has declined steadily for the past several years, but the 2003 rates for African American children and American Indian children were much higher than the rates for children in other groups. In 2004 almost 1.3 million teens between the ages of 16 and 19 were neither enrolled in school nor working (disconnected youth). African American and Hispanic youth were about twice as likely as white youth to be disconnected in 2004.

In 2004, more than 24 million children had no parent in the household who worked full time, year-round (lack of secure parental employment). Children from these families are more likely to lack access to health and family benefits made possible by a stable job. Despite the enormous concentration of wealth in the United States, the nation's child poverty rate is among the highest among developed countries. The percent of families with children headed by a single parent (31%) was about the same as it was in 2000. About 40% of children in female-headed households were poor in 2004, compared to 8% of children in married-couple families. Only about one-third of female-headed families reported receiving any child support or alimony payments in 2004.

Source: Kids Count Data Book, by Annie E. Casey Foundation Greenwich, CT: Author, 2006, pp. 32–50.

African American and Latino households with no husband present were 39.3% and 39.0%, respectively. Half of children in America are projected to live in a single-parent family at some point in their childhood, one in three will be poor at some point during their childhood, and one in five is poor today (Children's Defense Fund, 2006; U.S. Bureau of the Census, 2006).

Because people living in poverty conditions are far more likely to undergo stress, they are far more at risk to have other family problems as well. Thus, women and people of color, by the very nature of their positions within the socioeconomic hierarchy, are more likely to develop family problems. In addition, these groups traditionally have had less power than other groups, so they are more vulnerable to being ignored or blamed for causing their problems and also are unable to advocate for solutions and resources to address their problems. Women, for example, are paid less overall than men, and are hired into lower-level jobs. Those who reenter the workplace after or while in more traditional marriages when they have not been employed outside the home ("displaced homemakers") are at a disadvantage in getting jobs that allow them to support their families adequately. They also are forced to bear the brunt of child care and other child-related needs. Traditional attitudes about women and people of color are changing, but because resources available to address their needs are scarce, they continue to be at the bottom of the social structure in our country.

Children growing up in families in which social support is not available are more likely to have problems in development, have low self-esteem, drop out of school, become pregnant at an early age, and have difficulty finding adequate employment. Because they often lack appropriate role models and have grown up in an environment of hopelessness and despair, having children is often the only way for them to feel competent. With few skills and even fewer resources and opportunities, they frequently repeat the cycle of the at-risk family with their own children.

Although some attention is being directed to the special needs of women and people of color and their families, it does not always address the problems from a broad context. For example, with the growing divorce rate and people having children out of marriage, women have been targeted as "America's new poor"—also termed the **feminization of poverty** (DiNitto, 2005). In addition to providing more social supports to women and their families, however, the problem has to be addressed from a systems/ecological perspective. Women alone are not responsible for pregnancy or divorce. Men's responsibility in these situations also must be addressed.

When considering the relationship between family problems and people of color and women, additional factors must be taken into account. At the same time as these families are more likely to experience poverty and stress, and thus are more likely to experience alcoholism or spouse or child abuse or be too overwhelmed by these pressures to parent their children adequately, they also are more likely to be *labeled* as having such problems. An African American or Latino parent who abuses a child, for example, is much

more likely to take the child to a public hospital or clinic for treatment, where the case is likely to be reported to authorities. A Caucasian parent, in comparison, is much more likely to take the child to a private physician, and perhaps to a different private physician, if the child is abused again.

Families of color and single-parent women also are more likely to seek help for family problems at public agencies, such as local community mental health centers, than at private psychological counseling programs. White parents having problems with children are far more likely to be able to afford to send them to private residential treatment facilities for therapy, whereas children of color are much more likely to be sent to juvenile detention centers, where such treatment usually is not available.

Individuals who study social welfare systems must be aware that children who grow up in families headed by people of color and women are more vulnerable than children who grow up in other families. Family problems must be considered within the context of the broader environment, including the impacts of oppression and discrimination, and these considerations are important in shaping the environment to make it more supportive for children and their families.

Changing Family Situations

Issues of diversity have to be taken into account when working with children and their families. Many families today are undergoing changes in composition as a result of separation and divorce, and those transitions are difficult for all family members. More children are growing up in female-headed, single-parent families, which necessitates additional effort from these parents to provide for their children. Many single parents who marry or remarry already have children, creating additional transitions and the development of new relationships for children and adults alike. Increasingly, children are being reared by gay and lesbian parents, often in the face of oppression from the community and society in which they live.

Divorce and Separation

The divorce rate in the U.S. in 2003 was 3.8 per 1,000 population (U.S. Department of Commerce, 2006). One in three marriages ends in divorce, with each marriage involving an estimated two children. Current projections suggest that more than half of today's children will spend at least some time in a single-parent household (Children's Defense Fund, 2006).

Divorce and separation frequently result in crises for family members. For adults, the separation or divorce signifies the loss of an intimate relationship that brought security and support. Separation or divorce also represents a loss of hopes and dreams, as well as feelings of failure. Although the divorce may bring relief, being alone brings fear, anxiety, loneliness, and guilt as well, especially if children are involved. Initially, parents are apt to be so caught up in dealing with their own emotions that they have little energy left to help their children cope with their feelings. Thus, at a time when their children need them most, the parents find themselves unable to reach out and help them.

For children, the divorce almost always is traumatic. If the family fought a great deal, children may feel a sense of relief, but at the same time they feel anger, guilt, fear, and sadness. Typically, children blame themselves for their parents' divorce. They frequently change their behavior, acting either overly good or overly bad, in the hope that this will bring their parents back together. Too, parents often fail to say anything to their children about an impending divorce, because of their own grieving and the belief that their children will cope better if they are not burdened with adult problems. Studies suggest that the most important factor that helps children get

through a divorce is having someone who will listen to and give them support. Parents need to explain that they are divorcing each other and not the child, and that both of them will continue to love and spend time with the child. Some children do not react visibly when they are informed that their parents are separating or divorcing. If children do not react immediately after the divorce, however, they probably are holding their feelings inside and will express them at a later age (Marquardt, 2005; Wolfinger, 2005).

Talking about the divorce and giving children a chance to express their feelings are important in helping them cope with divorce. Children experiencing a divorce in their family usually regress at the time of the divorce. They may have nightmares and exhibit bed wetting, thumb sucking, behavioral problems at school and at home, a drop in academic performance at school, listlessness and daydreaming, changes in eating habits, more frequent illnesses, and, if preadolescents or adolescents, experimentation with alcohol, drugs, sexual activity, and other risk-taking behaviors. If one parent has much less contact than in the past, children may develop extreme fear that the other parent will abandon them or worry about what will happen to them if the parent they are living with dies (Marquardt, 2005).

Although children are likely to cope better with divorce if the adults cope well, children usually take longer to recover, primarily because they have no control over the situation. Various studies show that children require at least 3.5 years to work through their parents' divorce (Marquardt, 2005; Wolfinger, 2005). Some individuals still struggle with the situation two or three decades later. Children fare better after a divorce if they maintain a positive relationship with both parents and if the parents do not speak negatively about each other or use the children to fight their battles with each other.

Custody and visitation problems often have a negative impact on a child following a divorce (see Figure 10.1). Although the situation is changing,

FIGURE 10.1

Depiction by a 9-Year-Old Girl Whose Parents Are Involved in a Custody Battle

mothers are much more likely to obtain custody in a divorce. Courts have emphasized a long-held doctrine that, in a child's "tender years," the mother is more important in the child's life, and unless she is totally unfit, she should receive custody of children in a divorce.

Although in many instances today, fathers want custody and are equally and often more capable of caring for their children, fathers are awarded primary custody in less than 10% of divorces. Because the average woman's income decreases significantly following a divorce and the average man's income increases, children of divorce frequently view their fathers as "Santa Clauses" or "Disney dads." Their fathers may buy them presents and take them special places, let them stay up later, and impose fewer rules than their mothers, who are buying the necessities and maintaining the daily routine, which usually requires more discipline. Mothers may resent not being able to give their children the same fun aspects of life, whereas fathers often find visitation time with their children artificial and awkward.

In some cases, parents expect the child to decide where to live and where to spend holidays, which puts undue pressure on the child, who knows that he or she will hurt one parent no matter what the decision. Child welfare professionals recommend that children be given input into these decisions, but that final decisions should be made either by the parents or, if they cannot agree, by a trained mediator who is skilled in divorce conflicts, or by the court (Folberg, Milne, & Salem, 2004).

Increasingly, parents are opting for **joint custody,** in which both parents share custody equally and, often, the amount of time the child lives with each parent. In some cases, the child alternates between parents, living with each parent 3 or 4 days. In other cases, one parent has the child for 6 months, followed by living with the other parent for the next 6 months. In a few instances, to maintain stability for the child, the parents take turns moving in with the child, who remains in the same home, for a specified time.

The research is inconclusive as to the benefits of different types of custody. Many experts suggest joint custody if the parents have a positive relationship with each other, as this provides the child with two strong role models who love and pay attention to the child, and communicates that the child is wanted and loved by both parents equally. Other experts suggest that joint custody, particularly if it involves a great deal of moving back and forth on the child's part, creates instability and a lack of permanence, and that the child has no place to truly call his or her own.

The need for support to families going through divorce, particularly for children, is receiving increased attention. Many cities have established family **mediation** centers, in which a team of social workers and attorneys work together with families in the divorce process. The aim is to help parents maintain positive relationships with each other in an adult way and to resolve conflicts together rather than take adversarial roles, as is often the case when the parents have separate attorneys and pursue the divorce through court action. Public schools and family service agencies also have established special programs and support groups for children who are involved in divorce and their parents.

Single Parenting

About 23% of families in the United States are headed by a single parent, either because of divorce or separation or, increasingly, because of unmarried women giving birth to children (Children's Defense Fund, 2006; U.S. Department of Commerce, 2006). No evidence suggests that growing up in a single-parent family is inherently positive or negative. Researchers have found that when socioeconomic status is controlled for, children in single-parent families fare as well as those in two-parent families.

Factors that have a significant influence on how children fare include poverty and conflict between parents (Children's Defense Fund, 2006; Jung, 2006; Scott & Ward, 2005). Single-parent families, like other families, should be viewed from a strengths perspective, with attempts to eliminate environmental barriers that place these families at risk and to build on family strengths. The major barrier for most is income. A single-parent woman is more likely to be poor and, if not within the poverty definition of poor, under financial duress. The median income for married households and single-parent, female-headed households in 2003 was $62,281 and $26,550, respectively (U.S. Department of Commerce, 2006). The average income for Caucasian female-headed households ($30,879) was significantly higher than for households headed by women of color ($21,962 and $22,096 for African Americans and Hispanics, respectively).

In addition to financial pressure, single parents have sole responsibility for overseeing the household and childrearing. As a result, children growing up in single-parent families often have different lifestyles than others. A paradox of children growing up in single-parent families is that, on one hand, they are likely to have more freedom than other children and, on the other hand, they must take on much more responsibility.

Children of single parents tend to have more freedom because they must spend more time by themselves while the parent is working. Because child care is so expensive, many children of single parents, especially school-age children, become "latch-key" children, responsible for themselves until their parent gets home from work. Others are responsible for younger siblings while the parent is at work. It is not unusual for a child of a single parent to come home from school alone, do homework and household chores, and prepare the evening meal. And single-parent children must assume more responsibility for themselves because of the absence of supervision.

Single-parent children who are the same gender as the parent who has left the home also may assume many of the roles of the absent parent— for example, mowing the lawn and doing household repairs if the father is gone. And they may serve as companions to their parents, who may be lonely or too busy or hurt to establish adult relationships. Parents may confide in children about money, relationships with the ex-spouse, and other adult matters, and expect children to accompany them on shopping trips, to meetings, and to social events. They may place children in a situation of role reversal, expecting their children to comfort them. Or they may become overly protective, worrying that because they have lost a significant relationship with an ex-spouse, they may lose the relationship with the child as well.

Further, discipline of children in single-parent families is likely to be inconsistent. A parent may be too tired or too stressed to discipline at some times and may over-discipline at other times. Parents' dating and development of opposite-sex relationships also can be stressful to children in single-parent families.

Some children, particularly if they feel abandoned by the absent parent or do not have a positive relationship with that parent, may be anxious for the parent with whom they reside to remarry. Conversely, older children who have been in a single-parent family for a longer time may consider any dating by their parent as a threat to their own relationship with the parent and do everything possible to destroy competing relationships. Of concern to single parents and their families are issues such as how much to tell children about dating, how involved they should be in decision making about serious relationships or remarriage, whether the parent should have "overnight guests" and live-in partners, and how to help children handle a relationship that has ended.

Children growing up in single-parent families, too, generally have fewer options regarding long-range plans for their future. Income and time limitations of these families may preclude college or other post–high school education. Additional issues affecting some children are a fear of being kidnapped by the noncustodial parent, one or more forms of child abuse by the parent or parent's friends, alcoholism or drug abuse by one or both parents, and concerns about the child's own sexuality and ability to establish long-term, opposite-sex relationships.

Increasingly, schools, child-guidance centers, and community mental-health centers are offering special programs for children in single-parent families. These programs provide individual and group counseling, family counseling, and self-help groups for children. Big Brother/Big Sister programs, which match adult role models in one-to-one relationships with children, help children in single-parent families develop healthy relationships with adults of the opposite sex from the custodial parent figure to ensure that children have positive relationships with both male and female adults.

A number of books and other materials are available to help single parents and their children (see, for example, Canfield, Hansen, Hartman, &

Vogl, 2005; Holyfield, 2002; Lessord, 2004; Morrisette, 2006). Longitudinal studies of children growing up in single-parent families are helping to identify strengths, as well as problem areas, of these families, to be better able to help children who find themselves in this family constellation.

Gay and Lesbian Parenting

Many gays and lesbians have been married and have children before declaring their homosexuality (Mohr, 2005). In addition, some gays and lesbians decide to have children while they are in same-sex relationships or as single parents. Difficulties may arise, however, when gay and lesbian parents seek custody of children through the courts. In recent years, men and women alike have had difficulty gaining custody if they are gay or lesbian, in spite of research indicating few differences between parenting in gay or lesbian families and non-gay or non-lesbian families.

Studies have found that children born and/or reared in families in which one or more parents are gay or lesbian are no more likely to be gay or lesbian themselves than children born and/or reared in families in which both parents are heterosexual. Studies also have found that gay and lesbian parents do not influence their children to become gay or lesbian and that children reared by homosexual parents are not emotionally impaired. Researchers have found, too, that a child is more at risk to be molested in a heterosexual household than in a homosexual home (American Academy of Pediatrics, 2002; Bernstein, 2005).

Families with gay and lesbian parents must address some specific issues, however. For example, homosexual parents may not want their employers to know that they are gay or lesbian because they fear being fired. Thus, children may have to keep the homosexuality a secret from others. Many gay and lesbian parents worry about how their children's friends and their parents will react to their being homosexual,

and children may fear this as well, particularly as they become older and more aware.

Gay and lesbian parents may be afraid that their children will be ridiculed or discriminated against. As in any family, children who are dealt with honestly and have open communication with their homosexual parents usually are better adjusted than children who find out about the homosexuality from others or sense the homosexuality but are not allowed to discuss it with their parents.

Stepparenting and Blended Families

Along with increasing numbers of single-parent families, second marriages are on the rise. Of divorced adults, 75% remarry, and 65% of these remarriages involve at least one child. Nearly one-third of Americans are now stepparents, stepchildren, stepsiblings, or some other member of a stepfamily. The most common **stepfamilies** with children are stepfather-families or combined stepfather-stepmother families. These families often are referred to as **blended families** or re-coupled families (Barta, 2001). It is estimated that by 2020, stepfamilies will be the predominant family form in the United States (Stepfamily Foundation, 2006; Winning Stepfamilies, 2006).

Because remarriage typically generates a number of strong feelings in the children and adults involved that are difficult to resolve, more than 70% of second marriages that involve children fail (Partridge, 2006). At first, adults may feel a sense of joy and security but the children are likely to have a sense of loss of relationship to the parent, whom they now must share with the spouse, as well as anxiety over what the addition of another adult will mean to their own well-being. Children may be concerned about balancing the stepparent relationship with that of the birth parent, who is absent from the home. If the new marriage brings other children into the family, relationships between stepsiblings may incite competition and jealousy.

Studies show that there are no differences in children raised by gay and lesbian parents when compared to children raised by parent who are heterosexual.

Bart Geerligs/Taxi/Getty Images

Because developing stepfamily relationships can be difficult, time and effort are required by all family members to make the new family constellation work. The children frequently feel distant from their new stepparent and may see that parent as a replacement for their absent parent. Even if they like the stepparent, conflicts over loyalty to their birth parent may prevent them from establishing a positive relationship with the stepparent. If, prior to the new marriage, the child functioned as more of a "partner" than a child in the family, he or she may feel displaced and jealous of the stepparent.

Further, many children, no matter how old, retain fantasies of their birth parents reuniting, and the remarriage represents a threat to these fantasies. And stepsiblings may mean less attention to birth children, as well as possible competition outside the family boundaries regarding friends, sports, and school.

In addition to developing emotional bonds among family members, children have to adjust to changing family roles, responsibilities, and family identity. Rules often are readjusted, and many times are stricter than they were in the single-parent household. If children are still in regular contact with their birth parent, they now are essentially members of two households, each with its own distinct culture and rules. Problems regarding multiple role models and parental figures can be confusing to children.

Some experts in stepparent family relationships suggest that the stepparent should not in any way undermine the relationship between the child and the absent birth parent but should establish himself or herself as a parental figure in the family and take an active role in immediate family issues such as rules and discipline. Other experts say the parenting should be left completely to the child's birth parents, while the stepparent should work to establish a positive bond with the child, but as an adult friend rather than a parental figure, staying out of decisions regarding rules and discipline.

Although remarriage can increase stability, security, and financial resources for children, working through the implications of the changes takes a great deal of time before acceptance. In many communities, special parent-education classes for stepparents, support groups for stepparents, spouses, and children in stepparent families, and family counseling programs are available to capitalize on the strengths of the families and provide support in working through problem areas.

Family Problems Affecting Children

Families today face increasing pressures from the broader environment. They often live in communities that have limited support available to families. Because today's families are more diverse, the issues to consider when addressing their needs are more complex than in the past. More and more children and families need social support beyond the family because of problems such as substance abuse, spouse abuse, and child maltreatment.

In addition, as increasing numbers of children are growing up in communities rife with poverty and violence and do not receive the nurturing and guidance they need for healthy development, they are more likely to enter adolescence angry, depressed, and searching for attention and acceptance wherever they can find it. The consequences of family conflict can be linked directly to problems associated with youth crime, membership in gangs, violence, and teen pregnancy and parenthood (Office of Juvenile Justice and Delinquency Prevention, 2004). These behaviors are also on the rise among younger children.

Substance Abuse

The National Institute on Alcohol Abuse and Alcoholism (2003) estimated that about 43% of U.S. children were living in households with one or more adults who were **alcoholics** or alcohol abusers at some point in life. Approximately 15% of these children lived in households with an adult during the preceding year. Until recently, **substance abuse** was viewed as an individual disease rather than a family problem, but new studies have found that individuals growing up in these families are five times as likely to become substance abusers themselves. Of juvenile delinquents and children seen in child guidance and mental health clinics, 20% come from families in which **alcohol abuse** is a problem. Other studies show a strong relationship between substance abuse and family violence.

The Substance Abuse and Mental Health Services Administration (2004) estimated that approximately 6 million children in the country were being reared by at least one parent with a substance-abuse problem. Parents who regularly abuse substances are less likely to be able to carry out their parental role effectively. Statistics vary, but between 40% and 80% of child maltreatment cases are said to involve substance abuse (Child Welfare League of America, 2004). Maltreated children of substance-abusing parents are more likely to have poorer physical, intellectual, social, and emotional outcomes and are at higher risk for substance abuse problems themselves. Abused or neglected children from substance-abusing families are more likely to be placed in foster care and more likely to remain there longer than maltreated children from non-substance-abusing families (U.S. Department of Health and Human Services, 2003). Of infants abandoned in hospitals, 70% have parents who are drug addicts, and many of these children are born addicted to drugs.

Children who manage to survive in substance-abusive families seldom escape unscathed (National Institute on Alcohol Abuse and Alcoholism, 2003). **Adult children of alcoholics** manifest coping characteristics that they developed as children within their own families, including a compulsion to control, a need to overachieve, and a need to please others continually (Black, 2002, 2006; Brown & Lewis, 2002; Lashley, 2006; Petit, 2005). They also have many fears—about abandonment, emotional harm, and personal violence to themselves or other family members. They also feel lonely, guilty, angry, shamed, and sad.

Because of messages they receive in their families and the resulting feelings of guilt and shame, they maintain as secrets what is going on in the family and their own feelings as well. In looking at a substance-abusive family from a systems/ecological perspective, one can see how substance-abusing families develop a way of functioning with the abuser as the central family member that, although dysfunctional to outsiders, is functional within the family and facilitates the survival of its members.

ROLES AND CODEPENDENCE

Family members and others who facilitate continuation of substance abuse are called **enablers.**

For example, a spouse may make excuses for the substance abuser's behavior to other family members, friends, or employers. An older child may take on a "hero" role, believing that by being a "perfect" child, the substance abuse will stop or be less likely to disrupt the family. This child is likely to get excellent grades in school, take care of younger children, nurture both parents, and strive to keep family members happy no matter what the costs to the child.

Another child in the family may take on a "scapegoat" role, subconsciously believing that negative attention directed at him or her will take the attention away from the substance-abusing parent. Conflict between the parents over the substance abuse may instead be directed at the child, who continually gets in trouble at home, at school, and in the neighborhood.

Yet another child may assume the role of the "lost child," believing that the family is better able to cope if he or she is out of sight. These children seem to be always in their room or at friends' homes. They seek little attention and actually go out of their way not to call any attention to themselves.

A final role that a child in substance-abusing families may assume is that of "mascot." These children, often the youngest, become the pets or clowns of the family, always available to be cuddled when cuddling is demanded or to entertain when entertainment can alleviate some of the family's pain (Black, 2006).

Some experts in the substance-abuse field take issue with the term *enabler.* They prefer the term **codependent,** a person who relies extensively on others for self-worth and self-definition, focusing more on pleasing or controlling others than creating a healthy sense of self (Black, 2006). The term *codependence,* they propose, defines the problem more clearly as belonging to the codependent person and indicates a need for individual recovery for that person separate from the substance abuser (Mellody & Freundlich, 2004; Mellody & Miller, 2003). All definitions and models of codependence focus on the impact of the behavior on the codependent individual and the long-term consequences, regardless of whether the person remains in a relationship with the substance abuser.

The costs of these roles to the individual family members throughout their lives, as well as the total family, are enormous. These roles actually promote the substance abuse, with family members unknowingly encouraging it. This is why current substance-abuse intervention strategies view the abuse as a family systems problem. If communication patterns and roles within families are not changed concurrently with treatment for the substance abuser, the substance-abusive behavior is likely to return quickly, reinforced by the behaviors of other family members.

PHASES OF COPING

The ways in which families typically cope with substance abuse can be divided into four phases.

1. *Reactive phase.* Family members deny that the substance abuse exists and develop their own coping strategies around the substance-abusing parent, usually—sometimes intentionally—enabling the abuse to continue. These strategies range from nagging to making excuses or covering up the abuse, to staying at home and trying to prevent the substance abuse, to denying emotional feelings.

Children in these families may have birth defects as a result of the mother using drugs or alcohol during pregnancy. They may be torn between parents who demonstrate conflicting and often confusing behavior. They may avoid activities with peers because of fear and shame. They may distrust others, or they may learn destructive and negative ways to get attention (Conyers, 2003).

2. *Active phase.* Family members become aware that there is a substance-abuse problem, that they do not live in a normally functioning family, and that help is available. Family members begin to realize that the abuser does not control the family, that they have the power to make changes in their own behaviors, and that they cannot assume responsibility for the substance abuser. At this point, members may join self-help groups such as Al-Anon or Alateen, in which others going through similar experiences within their own families can lend support.

3. *Disequilibrium phase.* While painful and difficult, all family members must go through this phase if the problem is to be alleviated. It follows family members' awareness that a problem exists and all efforts to change the abuser or the family dynamics have been unsuccessful. During this phase, family members consider openly whether disruption is the only alternative. This may cause polarization of family members and frequently ends in divorce, with subsequent separation of family members if the abuser still will not seek help. Although the family usually fares better in the long run, this outcome is often doubly traumatic for children, who then have to cope with the problems of both alcoholism and divorce.

Approximately 40% of family situations that reach this phase end up in divorce (Lawson & Lawson, 2004; Rotskoff, 2002). In families that do not choose separation, the traditional family communication patterns may be shaken enough that the family begins to change actively. Whether it is disrupted or the substance-abusing member agrees to make a concerted effort to change, the family is forced to reorganize. This entails new and different roles for family members (Black, 2006; Conyers, 2003).

4. *Family unity phase.* Many families with substance-abuse problems do not reach this phase. Being free of substance abuse is central to this phase, but it is not enough. Accepting the family member as a non-substance-abuser and lasting changes in family communication patterns must take place if the family is to remain free of recurring substance-abuse problems.

Spouse Abuse

Although definitions of **family violence** differ from state to state, a general definition that often is used is that it is an act carried out by one family member against another family member that causes or is intended to cause physical or emotional pain or injury to that person. Family violence typically has been separated into two major categories: spouse abuse (also called "domestic violence," "battering," or "relationship abuse") and child abuse. Recent attention also has been directed to elder abuse, children abusing their parents.

Before spouse abuse received national attention during the well-publicized O. J. Simpson trial, most of the attention had focused on the abuse of children, with legislative roots going back to the 1960s. As a result, federal dollars have been appropriated for child abuse, with more limited funds for spouse-abuse programs. Some states have earmarked funding for spouse-abuse programs, but these programs often are either small adjuncts to child welfare/child abuse departments or under the auspices of special women's commissions. This implies that spouse abuse is a woman- or child-related problem rather than a family problem of concern to everyone. Some child-abuse programs have funded spouse-abuse programs only by suggesting that children growing up in a home in which spouse abuse is present are emotionally abused.

Although men are sometimes abused in partner relationships, the large majority of spouse abuse is perpetrated by men (U.S. Department of Justice, 2000). Therefore, we use the male gender (he/him) here, recognizing that women also can be abusers. Attention to spouse abuse was late in developing because of the ways that our society views men and women. Men are regarded in power positions both inside and outside the home, and some still subscribe to the myth that women who are beaten somehow deserve it or that they must enjoy it or they would not put up with it.

Between 2 and 3 million women are estimated to be victims of violence (rape, physical assault, stalking) annually in the United States (U.S. Department of Justice, 2000). Violence against women consists primarily of intimate-partner violence. According to the National Violence Against Women Survey, nearly two-thirds of women who reported being raped, physically assaulted, and/or stalked since age 18 were victimized by a former husband, cohabiting partner, boyfriend, or date (National Institute of Justice, 2000).

The risk of injury increases for victims of female rape and physical assault when their assailant is a current or former intimate. Only an estimated third of injured female rape or assault victims receive medical treatment. Too, there is a relationship between victimization as a minor and subsequent victimization. Women who reported being raped before age 18 were twice as likely to report being raped as an adult. Women who reported that they were stalked before age 18 were seven times more likely to report being stalked as an adult (National Institute of Justice, 2000). African Americans are at greater risk of victimization by violent crime than are Caucasians or persons of other racial groupings. Hispanics have a higher risk for violent victimization than non-Hispanics (National Institute of Justice, 2000; Sokoloff & Pratt, 2005).

FORMS OF ABUSE

Although physical violence has received the majority of attention in the media, other types of spouse abuse have been classified as (Helpguide, 2006):

- *verbal abuse*—yelling, screaming, name-calling; embarrassing, making fun of, or mocking the victim, either alone in the household, in public, or in front of family or friends; criticizing or diminishing the victim's accomplishments or goals; telling victims that they are worthless.
- *nonverbal abuse*—destruction of the victim's personal property and possessions; excessive

possessiveness and isolation from friends and family; excessive checking-up on victims to make sure they are where they said they would be; making victims remain on the premises after a fight, or leaving them somewhere after a fight, just to "teach them a lesson."

- *sexual abuse*—sexual assault (forcing victims to participate in unwanted, unsafe, or degrading sexual activity); sexual harassment, including ridiculing victims to try to limit their sexuality or reproductive choices; sexual exploitation (e.g., forcing someone to look at pornography, or forcing someone to participate in pornographic filmmaking).

- *stalking and cyber-stalking*—harassment of or threatening another person, especially in a way that haunts the person physically or emotionally in a repetitive and devious manner. Stalking an intimate partner can take place during the relationship or after a partner or spouse has left the relationship. The stalker may be motivated to get the partner back or wish to harm the partner as punishment for the departure. Stalking can take place at or near the victim's home, near or in the workplace, on the way to the store or another destination, or on the Internet (cyber-stalking). Stalkers may never show their face, or they may be everywhere.

  Cyber-stalking is defined as the use of telecommunication technologies such as the Internet or e-mail to stalk another person. Cyber-stalking is deliberate, persistent, and personal.

- *economic or financial abuse*—withholding economic resources; stealing from or defrauding a partner of money or assets; exploiting the intimate partner's resources for personal gain; withholding resources such as food, clothes, necessary medications, or shelter from a partner; or preventing the spouse or partner from working or choosing an occupation.

- *spiritual abuse*—using spouses' or intimate partners' religious or spiritual beliefs to manipulate them; preventing partners from practicing their religious or spiritual beliefs; ridiculing the other person's religious or spiritual beliefs; or forcing the children to be reared in a faith with which the partner does not agree.

Two additional forms of spousal or intimate partner abuse often cited by experts are (a) "crazy-making" or placing responsibility for the abuse on the person who is being abused, changing interpretations of the person's reality, and other erratic behavior that leads the abused person to begin to believe that she is crazy, and (b) suicidal and homicidal threats.

CHARACTERISTICS OF ABUSERS AND THOSE WHO ARE ABUSED

A number of factors are associated with spouse abuse. Men who assault their wives generally have low self-esteem and feel inferior. Feeling powerless outside the family, they exert their power within the domain of their homes. Male perpetrators of domestic violence are likely to be young and abuse alcohol or drugs (National Center for Injury Prevention and Control, 2003).

Factors associated with women who are abused are more difficult to interpret. Lenore Walker (2000) identified "learned helplessness" as a trait common in abused women: They become passive and helpless as a way to cope with their violent spouses. In some cases, they blame themselves for their abuse, or they may redefine the event, rationalizing that it wasn't that serious or that it was a rare occurrence. Others (see, for example, Wilson, 2005) have compared the symptoms of battered women to post-traumatic stress disorder, a diagnosis of some individuals who have suffered severe trauma.

Many times, abused women are reluctant to leave violent situations because they have no employable skills and are concerned about being able to survive, particularly if they have children.

But other studies show that battered women are not always passive. Some seek help in dealing with the abuse, but they love their husbands in spite of the violence and stay with them, believing they will reform.

In many violent situations between spouses, the period following the violence is almost like a honeymoon. The abusive spouse is extremely loving and supportive. He often cries and says he is extremely sorry for the episode, even threatening suicide if the spouse leaves him. He promises never to be violent again. At least initially, it is difficult for a woman who loves her husband not to be taken in by this repentant behavior.

Other studies show that women with low self-esteem, particularly those who were physically or sexually abused as children, feel so worthless that they believe they deserve the violent treatment. These women are more at risk than other women to be abused.

It should be noted that in most situations, the woman is passive and the man is abusive, but in some situations both spouses are violent. Because of the typical difference in size and strength between men and women, however, the woman most often is the one who is physically hurt. Finally, factors that place couples more at risk for spouse abuse include substance abuse, financial stress and poverty, and the male's unemployment or underemployment.

RELEVANT LEGISLATION

Several laws have been passed to support spouse abuse programs. The first of note was the Family Violence Prevention and Services Act of 1984, which provided funding for shelters for abused persons. The Victims of Crime Act, also passed in 1984, gave priority to abused spouses in receiving compensation for crime-related costs.

The landmark Violence Against Women Act (VAWA), passed in 1994, makes it a crime to cross state lines to abuse a partner, prohibits individuals who have restraining orders filed against them for domestic violence from possessing firearms, imposes tougher penalties for sex offenders, requires sex offenders to pay restitution to their victims, requires states to pay for rape examinations, and creates protections for survivors of rape from inappropriate inquiries about their personal lives. The act committed more than $1.6 billion over a 6-year period for domestic violence programs, including hiring police, prosecutors, and victim-witness counselors and establishing prevention programs (Violence Against Women Office, 2000).

The Violence Against Women Act of 2000 (P.L. 106-386) improved legal tools and programs addressing domestic violence, sexual assault, and stalking. VAWA 2000 reauthorized critical grant programs created by the original Violence Against Women Act and subsequent legislation, established new programs, and strengthened federal laws. And the latest reauthorization of the Violence Against Women Act, VAWA 2005, provides for the following (National Task Force to End Sexual and Domestic Violence Against Women, 2005, pp. 1–2):

- enhances core programs and policies in the criminal justice and legal systems;
- reaffirms the commitment to reform systems that affect adult and youth victims of domestic violence, dating violence, sexual assault, and stalking;
- expands funding for local groups working with underserved communities;
- develops standards for protecting the confidentiality of victims served by VAWA programs;
- enhances collaboration between victim service organizations and civil legal assistance providers;
- enhances provisions to fully enforce protective orders across state lines;
- develops new services that respond to evolving community needs;
- provides solutions-based remedies that address the concerns of victims generally,

as well as the unique needs of disabled, elderly, Native American, legal immigrant, ethnic minority victims, and victims living in rural communities;

- expands transitional housing options and protects the safety and confidentiality of homeless victims receiving services;
- creates permanent housing solutions for homeless victims of domestic violence;
- provides a comprehensive approach for assisting children, teens, and young adults who have violence in their homes;
- provides cross-training that addresses the co-occurrence of domestic violence and child abuse;
- assists colleges and universities in creating services and policies to address violence on campus;
- provides teens and young adults with appropriate services, ensuring access to court systems and preventing abuse during child visitation;
- strengthens the capacity of American Indian nations to provide tribal-based services to women and close gaps in their ability to track perpetrators of violence against American Indian women;
- provides for training and education of health-care providers and federal health programs to improve their services to victims;
- provides victims reasonable unpaid leave from work to take steps to leave a violent relationship; and
- makes technical corrections to existing immigration law, thereby resolving inconsistencies in the eligibility of services for immigrant victims.

A comprehensive summary of VAWA 2005 legislation can be found at http://www.usdoj.gov/ovw.

Many communities have established safe houses and battered women's shelters, where battered spouses and their children can seek refuge. These programs include counseling for women and children, assistance with legal issues, locating housing and employment, and developing support networks. But many women seeking shelter at these places are turned away because of lack of space. Also, while community outreach programs have been established to provide counseling and other services to survivors and perpetrators of spouse abuse, most of these programs begin to treat the violence after it has reached an intolerable point and any change, particularly for the abuser, is difficult.

Child Maltreatment

As reported cases of child abuse continue to increase, existing resources are unable to serve the many abused and neglected children and their families who come to the attention of available programs. In calendar year 2004 (the latest year for which national data are available) child protective services (CPS) agencies in the United States accepted an estimated 3 million reports alleging maltreatment involving approximately 5.5 million children (U.S. Department of Health and Human Services, 2006). These figures are likely to underestimate the true scope of the problem (see Figure 10.2) because most maltreatment happens within the confines of family privacy, and even when cases are known to others, they often are not reported.

Child maltreatment falls into four main categories: physical abuse, sexual abuse, child neglect, and psychological maltreatment (see Figure 10.3). Neglect is the most frequently reported type of maltreatment; more than half of all reports are of this type. Reports of sexual abuse, however, have increased the most in recent years, possibly because of greater awareness of sexual abuse, which has eliminated some of the secrecy that previously surrounded the problem.

Children of all ages are maltreated. Although infants are most at risk to be severely abused or neglected, most maltreated children are school age. Of the 872,000 children confirmed as

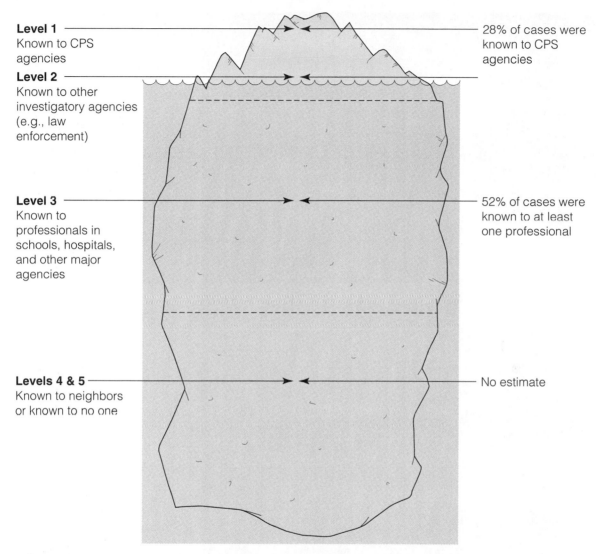

Level 1 — 28% of cases were
Known to CPS — known to CPS
agencies — agencies

Level 2 —
Known to other
investigatory agencies
(e.g., law
enforcement)

Level 3 — 52% of cases were
Known to — known to at least
professionals in — one professional
schools, hospitals,
and other major
agencies

Levels 4 & 5 — No estimate
Known to neighbors
or known to no one

FIGURE 10.2

Knowledge About Maltreated Children: The Tip of the Iceberg

This figure depicts the estimated incidence of cases of child maltreatment and who in the community knows about them. As the figure shows, the child protective services (CPS) agencies mandated to provide services in such cases actually know about only 28% of cases that other professionals know about. This percentage does not include cases that only neighbors or immediate family members know about, suggesting that known cases of actual child maltreatment are only the "tip of the iceberg."

Source: Figure adapted from National Center on Child Abuse and Neglect (Washington, DC: Author, 1996).

It's Up To You

To make a difference
in your child's life.
Get Involved, put your child first.

www.itsuptoyou.org

Texas Department of Protective and Regulatory Services

FIGURE 10.3

Sometimes parents can't provide the right care because they are in trouble themselves, experiencing problems such as depression, drugs, or alcohol. If an adult in your family is in this kind of trouble, the kids may not be safe. Protect your family by finding help.

Source: Courtesy of the Texas Department of Family and Protective Services.

Public awareness campaigns have been developed by national, state, and local organizations to focus attention on positive parenting and child abuse prevention.

maltreated by CPS agencies in 2004, the rates of child maltreatment per 1,000 children under 17 years of age declined with the victim's age and were the highest for children 0–3 years old (16.1) and the lowest for children 16–17 years old (6.1). Girls were slightly more likely than boys to be victims. Rates of child maltreatment were the highest for non-Hispanic, Black-only (19.9), followed by non-Hispanic, Pacific Islander-only (17.6), non-Hispanic, American Indian/Alaskan Native-only (15.5), and multiple-race children (14.6). Rates were the lowest for non-Hispanic, Pacific Islander-only children (2.0), and about the same for non-Hispanic, White-only children

(10.7) and Hispanic children at (10.4) (U.S. Department of Health and Human Services, 2006).

The number and rate of children confirmed as maltreated for the 15-year period 1990 to 2004 followed a roller coaster pattern. The number and rate of children confirmed as abused or neglected peaked in 1994 (1,026,300 and 15.3, respectively), fell to 1,012,000 and 14.7 in 1996, dipped sharply to 829,000 and 11.8 in 1999, and rose slightly to 872,000 and 11.9 in 2004 (U.S. Department of Health and Human Services, 2006). The numbers vary not only because there may be an actual increase in cases but also because of factors such as the availability of resources to address the problem (if resources are not available to respond, people are more likely to report only the most serious cases); public awareness about the problem and how to make a report; and economic conditions.

PHYSICAL ABUSE

Most children who are victims of **physical child abuse** receive bruises, welts, or abrasions. These injuries are caused by parents' whipping or spanking children with objects such as belts, extension cords, hair brushes, or coat hangers. Often, imprints of the objects can be seen on the child's body. When these types of injuries appear on the face, head, or more than one plane of a child's body (such as the back and arms) and are in various stages of healing (for example, bruises in varying colors), child abuse is suspected.

Children also receive broken bones and burns, as well as internal injuries, as a result of physical child abuse. Physicians can use X-rays to determine the types of breaks and when they occurred. In spiral fractures, for example, the bone may have been broken when a caregiver became angry and twisted one of the child's limbs. Often, children who are physically abused with one suspected broken bone or other serious injury have fractures or other injuries in various stages of healing in several areas of the body. This condition, termed **battered child syndrome** by C. Henry Kempe, a physician instrumental in advocating for child abuse legislation, is a diagnosis that now is recognized by medical professionals.

One of the most serious types of child maltreatment is an internal injury to the head, which can result in internal bleeding, brain damage, and death. Shaking a child severely also can cause serious injury, including blindness (resulting from detached retinas), brain injury, and death. Children may be burned on their hands, feet, and other parts of their bodies with cigarettes or lighters. And parents with unrealistic expectations about toilet training have burned children by placing them in extremely hot water when they have soiled themselves.

Among the many factors associated with families who physically abuse children are financial problems such as unemployment and poverty, isolation, unrealistic parental expectations about child development or children's abilities to meet parental needs for love and attention, alcoholism and drug abuse, abuse or maltreatment of the parent himself or herself during childhood, lack of education about nonphysical alternatives to discipline, low impulse control, and inability to cope well with stress. Only about 10% of parents who maltreat their children have a serious psychological disturbance (Crosson-Tower, 2005).

Some children are more at risk than others for physical abuse. These include children who are born prematurely or with congenital problems, children who do not meet parental expectations or whose parents perceive them as different, and children who are the result of unwanted pregnancies. Many parents who abuse children begin with role reversal in the family system, expecting the child, even as an infant or toddler, to meet their emotional needs. When the child resists or is unable to do so, the parent may feel rejected, become angry and frustrated, and abuse the child.

Children who grow up in communities with few economic resources and few support systems available to families also are more at risk to be abused (U.S. Children's Bureau, 2006a)

BOX 10.2
Factors That Contribute to Child Abuse and Neglect

1. **Child has been reported previously:** There have been previous founded or unfounded reports of abuse or neglect of the child or his or her siblings in the family system.
2. **Parent abused as a child:** Children who are maltreated may learn violent behavior and how to justify that behavior.
3. **Age of the parent:** Some studies of physical abuse, in particular, have found that teenage mothers have higher rates of child abuse than older mothers.
4. **Age of the child:** Infants and young children are more at risk of maltreatment than older children and adolescents.
5. **Family composition:** Most at risk are single parents rearing children alone, including a never-married, separated, or divorced parent and children living in an extended family household.
6. **Child-rearing approaches:** Negative attitudes about a child's behavior and inaccurate knowledge about child development may play a contributing role in child maltreatment. Maltreating parents are more likely to use harsh discipline and less likely to use positive parenting practices.
7. **Domestic violence in the home:** Children who witness violence between their parents or caregivers may learn violent behavior as well as justify that behavior.

8. **Separation of a parent or child for a long period:** The child may have been reared by a grandmother or other family member or have been in foster care.
9. **Parent's or caretaker's substance abuse:** Substance abuse is suspected to be a contributing factor for between one-third and two-thirds of maltreated children in the child welfare system.
10. **Physical, mental, or emotional impairment of the child:** The child has been diagnosed or observed to have mental retardation, cognitive limitations, physical or emotional disturbance, or chronic illness.
11. **Physical, mental, or emotional impairment of the parent:** The parent or other caretaker has low self-esteem, a belief that events are determined by chance or outside forces beyond one's personal control, poor impulse control, depression, anxiety, and antisocial behavior.
12. **Low socioeconomic status:** Lower economic status, lack of social support, and high stress levels may contribute to the incidence of child maltreatment, especially for adolescent mothers and young parents.

Source: "Understanding Child Abuse and Neglect," by C. Crosson-Tower (Boston: Allyn & Bacon, 2005); *Factors That Contribute to Child Abuse and Neglect*, by the U.S. Children's Bureau (Washington, DC: Author, 2006a).

(see Box 10.2). Cultural conditions also have an impact on physical abuse. Child abuse is less prevalent in cultures that value children and share parenting with others beyond the nuclear family (Crosson-Tower, 2005).

SEXUAL ABUSE

Sexual abuse is receiving more attention in recent years because of: (a) increased public awareness of the problem, and (b) exposure of children to more adults than in the past, including child-care providers, stepparents, and other adults, which increases the likelihood of sexual abuse. In 2004, CPS agencies confirmed nearly 87,000 victims of sexual abuse in the United States (U.S. Department of Health and Human Services, 2006). Child **sexual abuse** has been defined as

> an act or failure to act by a parent, caregiver, or other person as defined under State law that results in physical abuse, neglect, medical neglect, sexual abuse, emotional abuse, or an act or failure to act which presents an imminent risk of serious harm to a child. (U.S. Children's Bureau, 2006b)

Thus, child sexual abuse can include, in addition to sexual intercourse, acts such as fondling. Legislation mandates, too, that state child abuse laws include child pornography and sexual exploitation. This expands the definition to acts such as taking pictures of children in sexual poses or for purposes of sexual gratification.

Many individuals are unaware until later in life that they have been sexually abused. They repressed their childhood sexual abuse until they became adults or assumed that all children had the same treatment, not realizing what constitutes healthy adult–child interactions. Others have been reluctant to report the abuse because they are ashamed or embarrassed, have been threatened, or are worried about possible repercussions to themselves and their families. Some studies suggest that 25% of women and 10% of men have been sexually abused before reaching the age of 18 (National Center for Post Traumatic Stress Disorder, 2003) but that only 6% to 12% of cases are reported to law enforcement agencies at the time they occur.

Although individuals tend to think of sexual abusers as strangers who accost children in the park, the majority are known and trusted by the children they abuse. There are four categories of sex abusers:

1. *Parents.* Most professionals agree that sexual abuse by birth parents, **incest,** has the most serious personal and social consequences (Crosson-Tower, 2005). Abusers also may be other parent figures such as stepparents.

2. *Family members other than parent figures.* This category includes siblings, grandparents, and uncles or aunts. Of these, sexual relationships between siblings are reported to be the most prevalent. The broadest definition of incest includes sexual relationships between any family members.

3. *Trusted adults.* Among others, they can be teachers, babysitters, neighbors, coaches, leaders of children's groups, or other adults.

4. *Strangers and remote acquaintances.* This is the least frequent category of sexual abusers. An estimated 11% of the cases of child maltreatment involve perpetration by someone outside the child's family (U.S. Department of Health and Human Services, 2006).

Although all children are at risk to be sexually abused, perpetrators often single out those whom they perceive as most vulnerable. Children who are more likely to be sexually abused are those living without their birth fathers, living in stepparent families, having mothers employed outside the home, having a mother who is ill, observing violence between parents, or having a poor relationship with their parents (Crosson-Tower, 2005). Boys are most likely to be abused by non-family members, and girls by family members; 95% of girls and 80% of boys who report being sexually abused indicate that their abuser was a male. Ethnicity is not clearly associated with differences in rates of sexual abuse, but it is associated with differences in related factors such as age of child and type of perpetrator (Wolf, 2002).

Characteristics of perpetrators of sexual abuse include poor impulse control, low tolerance for frustration, low self-esteem, denial, manipulation, social and emotional immaturity, abuse of alcohol and other drugs, and isolation (Crosson-Tower, 2005). About one-fourth of male offenders report having been sexually abused as children, and about half began sexually abusing others during adolescence.

Most abusers engage in a seductive power role with children with whom they become involved. Children, wanting affection and too young to know how to draw boundaries between positive affection and sexual abuse, initially may become involved—and then be too afraid to tell anyone what is going on. Although the sexual abuse acts themselves may not involve physical force on the adult's part, the child is trapped in the situation because adults are in a power position with children. Some abusers within the family tell the children they abuse that the relationship is the only thing that is keeping the family together, or that the abuser is the only one in the family who really loves and understands them. Other abusers threaten physical harm to the child or to other family members if the child refuses to cooperate or tells anyone what is going on. For example, they may say that their mother will "go crazy," that the child will be taken out of the home, or that the adult will sexually abuse a younger sibling.

Studies on the effects of sexual abuse on children agree that it is extremely harmful emotionally and that individuals who have been sexually abused suffer long-term effects. The impact of sexual abuse on children depends on factors such as the following (Crosson-Tower, 2005):

- the child's age when the abuse occurred;
- the form of sexual abuse;
- the relationship of the abuser to the child;
- the duration, over time, when the abuse occurred;
- the length of time between when the abuse occurred and when someone found out that it was going on;
- other characteristics of the child's family and available positive support to the child; and
- reactions from family members and professionals when the sexual abuse is discovered.

Issues faced by survivors of sexual abuse include lack of trust and feelings of betrayal, powerlessness, isolation, blame, and a sense of loss (Crosson-Tower, 2005). Others have problems such as depression, anxiety or panic disorder, and post-traumatic stress disorder. Many individuals who have been sexually abused see themselves as victims because of the trauma of the abuse and have extremely low self-esteem; difficulty establishing intimate, trusting relationships with others; and problems with their own marriages and families when they become adults.

Without intervention, those who have been sexually abused are more at risk than others to turn to alcohol, drugs, or suicide to ease their pain. Many communities have established programs that promote public awareness of sexual abuse and early intervention with families once cases are reported, to address the long-term effects.

CHILD NEGLECT

Neglect is characterized by acts of omission, which usually means that something that should have been done to or for a child was not done (Crosson-Tower, 2005; Horvath, 2007; Howe, 2005). **Child neglect** has been defined as

> a type of maltreatment that refers to the failure of the caregiver to provide needed, age-appropriate care although financially able to do so or offered financial or other means to do so. (U.S. Children's Bureau, 2006b)

Many states include specific categories in their definitions of child neglect:

- failing to provide adequate food, clothing, or shelter for a child (physical neglect);
- leaving a child unattended for inappropriate periods of time (lack of supervision);
- leaving a child alone or not returning when expected to care for a child (abandonment);
- not providing medical care for a child (medical neglect);
- failing to provide an education for a child (educational neglect); and
- not tending to a child's emotional needs (emotional neglect).

In 2004, CPS agencies reported about 523,200 victims of child neglect in the United States (U.S.

Department of Health and Human Services, 2006).

As many children die each year from neglect as from abuse (Crosson-Tower, 2005). Many are burned in fires or drown in bathtubs while left alone or with inadequate supervision. Others die because their parents did not obtain medical care for them soon enough when they became ill. Adults who did not have their physical or emotional needs met as children are much more likely than others to have problems finding and maintaining jobs, developing positive relationships with other individuals, remaining in marriages, and parenting their own children adequately.

One type of neglect that is receiving more attention is **non-organic failure to thrive,** a form of parental deprivation. Failure to thrive is medically described as a child who is 3 percentiles or more below the normal weight for his or her age. The child seems to be fed regularly by his or her caregivers, and nothing organically wrong can be found, yet the child does not gain weight and literally fails to thrive.

When placed in a hospital and given nothing more than regular feedings of the child's normal diet, coupled with love and attention (for example, holding and cuddling), the child begins to gain weight immediately. Bowlby's (1951) classic studies of maternal deprivation and children raised in orphanages in Europe without love and attention found a high death rate and significant differences in intelligence quotient (IQ) and physical and emotional development compared to children in environments where they received love and attention. Similar findings are evident in children diagnosed with failure-to-thrive syndrome.

Although there is a strong relationship between poverty and neglect, not all parents who are poor neglect their children. Typical neglectful parents, compared to non-neglectful parents who also are living in poverty, are more isolated, have fewer relationships with others, are less able to plan and to control impulses, are less confident about the future, and are more plagued with physical and psychological problems.

Neglectful parents also are more likely to say that they did not receive love from, and were unwanted by, their parents. Many were raised by relatives or were in foster care. Neglectful parents often began life lonely, and they continue to live in isolation. The U.S. Department of Health and Human Services (2006) reported that neglectful parents had difficulty identifying neighbors or friends with whom they could leave their children if they needed emergency child care or from whom they could borrow five dollars in an emergency. They are extremely isolated from both formal and informal support networks. Many neglecting parents describe their social workers as being their best or only friends.

Early research by Polansky, Chalmers, Buttenweiser & Williams (1985) identified the following five types of inadequate or neglectful parents:

1. *Apathy-futility syndrome:* These neglecting parents have all but given up on life. They see little hope for the future and view all efforts to try to relate to either their children or others as futile. They convey an attitude of hopelessness and despair. Usually neglected themselves as children, and in many instances beaten down whenever they tried to make a go of life, they lack the physical or emotional energy to relate to their children. A neglectful parent with apathy-futility syndrome is likely to be found lying on the couch in a chaotic household that hasn't been cleaned or cared for, with children unkempt and uncared for, left largely to fend for themselves. Children of this type of neglectful parent suffer from physical, medical, educational, and/or emotional neglect, as well as lack of supervision.

2. *Impulse-ridden behavior:* This type of parent may be loving and caring and provide adequate food, clothing, and medical care most of the time. But these parents have trouble making appropriate decisions and often behave impulsively. They may decide suddenly to go to a party and leave the children alone, or answer the

phone and become so engrossed in the conversation that they forget that their child is unattended in the bathtub. They often get in trouble with employers over impulsive behavior at work, with creditors because of impulsive spending habits, and with friends because they make commitments and then impulsively change their mind and go off with others instead.

Neglectful parents with impulse-ridden behavior are restless, intolerant of stress, and inconsistent. Their children never know exactly what to expect and may be abandoned for long periods by them. Children of neglecting parents of this type are likely to suffer the effects of abandonment, lack of supervision, and emotional neglect. In addition, because of the inconsistency of the parent, these children may have difficulty trusting others, developing positive relationships, and being consistent themselves.

3. *Mental retardation:* Although only a small percentage of neglectful parents have mental retardation, they may neglect their children if they do not receive, or cannot comprehend, parenting information or have adequate supervision to help them care for the child.

4. *Reactive-depressive behavior:* These parents are so depressed that they cannot parent adequately. The depression may be a result of the death or loss of a significant person in their lives or the end of a love relationship, among other possibilities.

5. *Psychotic behavior:* These parents may be in such a delusional state that they cannot parent the child adequately.

Neglectful parents often are more resistant than abusive parents to be helped, particularly those who are apathetic and feel hopeless. Unlike abusive parents, who still have enough spirit to be angry, neglectful parents generally have feelings of despair and futility, which are much more difficult to change. Social workers can make a start in helping these parents develop trust in other individuals and increasing their self-esteem, particularly through links with supportive individuals. This, in turn, will enable them to care for their children more adequately (Crosson-Tower, 2005).

Neglect is affected more by environmental factors than are the other forms of maltreatment. Because of its relationship to poverty, it may be more appropriate to consider the unmet needs of the child and the community and social response to meeting those needs rather than the inappropriate actions of the parents (Crosson-Tower, 2005). Most of the attention and resources in the area of child maltreatment have been directed to physical and sexual abuse at the expense of neglect, which merits much more concern.

PSYCHOLOGICAL MALTREATMENT

Psychological maltreatment, also called **emotional maltreatment,** is the most difficult form to define, the most difficult to substantiate, and the most difficult to obtain resources for. Nevertheless, it is the most prevalent form of child maltreatment and, like other types of child maltreatment, it can result in serious long-term consequences for the child (Crosson-Tower, 2005; U.S. Department of Health and Human Services, 2006). One conceptualization is of two types of emotional maltreatment: emotional abuse and emotional neglect.

Emotional abuse refers to acts of commission, or emotional acts against a child. Emotional abuse often is verbal. It includes telling the child how bad he or she is, perhaps saying that the parents wish the child had never been born, and blaming the child for all the parents' and family's problems.

Almost all parents emotionally abuse their children at one time or another (U.S. Department of Health and Human Services, 2006), but continual emotional abuse can lower self-esteem and undermine a child's feelings of competence. Parents emotionally abuse their children in other ways, too. Some parents, for example, give a child's prized possession to "another child who will appreciate it," telling the child that "you don't deserve special things, because you're bad." Parents have also psychologically abused children by shaving their head or doing other humiliating things as forms of punishment.

Children who are forced to watch parents or others in the family being beaten or otherwise abused also experience psychological abuse. And children who are sexually abused are also psychologically/emotionally abused by that experience. Some experts suggest that the psychological abuse has just as severe, if not more severe, consequences for the sexually abused child than the sexual abuse itself (U.S. Children's Bureau, 2006b).

The other form of emotional abuse, *emotional neglect,* refers to acts of omission, or failure to meet the child's emotional needs. Parents who psychologically neglect their children may provide for their physical needs but interact very little with their children. They do not interact by cuddling or holding the child or engage in activities such as reading, singing, going places together, or just talking together. Children who do not have their emotional needs met are likely, as adults, to be unable to give emotionally to their own children. These adults may psychologically neglect their own children and also subject them to other types of maltreatment.

Garbarino, Guttman, and Seeley (1986, as cited in Crosson-Tower, 2005) provide a broader conceptualization of psychological maltreatment, which they define as "a concerted attack by an adult on a child's development and social competence, a pattern of psychically destructive behavior." They suggest that psychological maltreatment takes five forms:

1. *rejecting,* in which the adult refuses to acknowledge the child's worth and the legitimacy of the child's needs;
2. *isolating,* in which the adult cuts the child off from normal social experiences;
3. *terrorizing,* in which the adult verbally assaults the child, creating an environment of fear and terror;

4. *ignoring,* in which the adult deprives the child of essential stimulation and responsiveness, and
5. *corrupting,* in which the adult stimulates the child to engage in destructive antisocial behavior and reinforces deviance (p. 8).

The conceptualization offered by Garbarino and colleagues is based on a systems/ecological perspective, which suggests that emotional deprivation or emotional trauma in one domain of children's lives increases their vulnerability to similar experiences in other domains.

Problems Associated with Adolescents

Until recently, the literature about children and family problems has paid scant attention to the special needs of adolescents. Youth crime, gangs, violence, and teenage pregnancy are rapidly escalating and drawing extensive media attention. Many family development specialists are quick to point out that prevention and early intervention efforts aimed at young children and families would likely have eliminated many of these adolescent problems. They note that adolescents who enter the juvenile justice system as delinquents, gang members, and runaways, or are pregnant most often come from families with many of the problems discussed in this chapter who have not received appropriate services and support.

THE JUVENILE JUSTICE SYSTEM

Although delinquent adolescents are required by law to be treated differently than adults, the present juvenile justice system does not have the resources to address the numerous family problems and provide the extensive treatment that many juveniles need. Those who are released from the juvenile justice system more often than not quickly enter the adult criminal justice system. As juveniles are committing more severe crimes at younger ages, the issue of how to address

The needs of adolescents are often difficult to get help for because of scarce resources usually targeted at younger children. Many adolescents receive help for the first time after they come to the attention of the juvenile justice system.

© Heinle/Index Stock

their needs effectively and protect them, as well as those they harm, is becoming more pressing. Many states are responding by making the laws relating to juveniles tougher, such as certifying juveniles as adults and sending them to the adult criminal justice system to be prosecuted.

RUNAWAYS

Most runaways do so to escape serious family problems, such as physical and sexual abuse, alcoholism or drug abuse, divorce, or spouse abuse, as well as problems in school. Runaway youth are prone to get involved in crime, assault, rape, robbery, prostitution, and to participate in the development of pornographic materials, and they are susceptible to acquiring sexually transmitted infections and diseases, including HIV/AIDS.

Resources for families are largely targeted toward younger children. Youth shelters and services are a possible resource, but these are limited. One youth advocate suggested that some adolescents get arrested so they could gain shelter, food, and services by being booked into the juvenile detention center. In some cases, adolescents labeled as delinquent can be considered more appropriately as "throwaways" or "push-outs," when families fail to provide for their children's needs and now cannot cope with the problems of their emotionally damaged adolescents (National Coalition for the Homeless, 2006; Children's Defense Fund, 2006).

In the course of a year, an estimated 500,000 to 1.5 million young people run away from or are forced out of their homes, and an estimated 200,000 are homeless and living on the streets. More than half of runaway youths are age 15 or 16. Almost two-thirds of these youth seek assistance from youth shelters because of problems with parental relationships (National Coalition for the Homeless, 2006).

Early on, the Runaway and Homeless Youth Act of 1974 was passed in response to concern about runaway youth, who were exposed to exploitation and the dangers of street life. That act since has been expanded to assist homeless youth in making the transition to independent living and to provide drug education and prevention services to runaway and homeless youth (National Center for Homeless Education, 2006).

ACADEMIC AND EMPLOYMENT PROBLEMS

Many adolescents with problems suffer academically, and some have learning disabilities and other learning problems that undermine their confidence. In short, young people who do not feel good about themselves and are faced with daily problems at home, rather than support and encouragement, are not likely to do well in school. Dropout rates are of increasing concern, and the consequent high illiteracy rates. The 2004 high school completion rate for Caucasians, African Americans, and Hispanics was 85.3%, 80.6%, and 58.4%, respectively (U.S. Department of Commerce, 2006). Adolescents who do not complete high school encounter difficulty in locating suitable employment.

TEEN PREGNANCY

Another problem facing our country today is teen pregnancy. Even with the 13% decline in the percent of children born to teen mothers in the period 2000–2003, births by members of this age group are troublesome for a number of reasons (Annie E. Casey Foundation, 2006):

- Most of the young mothers are unmarried and have not completed high school.
- From 8 to 12 years after birth, a child born to an unmarried, teenage, high school dropout is 10 times as likely to be living in poverty as a child born to a mother with none of these characteristics.
- Most teenage mothers are not settled in a job or career, and many young fathers are not in a position to provide financial help.
- Children born to teenage mothers are less likely to receive the emotional and financial resources that support their development into independent, productive, and well-adjusted adults (p. 40).

In addition, becoming a teenage parent interrupts, sometimes permanently, the teen's successful transition into adulthood.

Teens today are faced with a great deal of pressure from many sources—peers, the media, advertising—to view their primary self-worth in terms of their sexuality. With limited opportunities to be successful in other arenas—family, school, and the workplace—some teens think that producing a baby is the only way they can feel good about themselves and have someone to love them.

Among the many factors associated with teen pregnancy are poverty, low self-esteem, lack of information about reproduction, school failure, lack of appropriate health care and other services, and poor family relationships. The emphasis on pregnancy prevention and intervention, however, has been solely on teenage females, to the exclusion of prevention and intervention with teenage males.

Overall, 63% of sexually active students in grades 9 through 12 reported that they used condoms when they had intercourse. The percentage using condoms for males and females, respectively, was 70% and 50% (Franzetta, Terry-Humen,

Manlove, & Ikamullah, 2006). Although attention to pregnancy prevention often begins only when teens (females) reach age 13, developing positive self-esteem, effective decision-making skills, a strong value system, and a sense of responsibility for oneself and others—all major deterrents to teen pregnancy—are shaped from birth on.

In the past, most teens who became pregnant relinquished their babies for adoption, either formally through agencies or informally through relatives. Today, the majority of teens are choosing to keep their babies. Infants born to teenagers are much more likely than to older mothers to have low birthweight, be premature, or have congenital or other health problems. Their mothers are more likely to drop out of school, remain unemployed or underemployed, and bring up their children in poverty. The cycle often repeats itself. Teen pregnancy is both a cause and a result of poverty.

CRIME

Increased concern is being raised about youth crime. Key findings of the 2006 national report of juvenile offenders and victims are summarized here (Snyder & Sickmund, 2006):

- In 2003, law enforcement agencies arrested an estimated 2.2 million persons under the age of 18.
- In 2003, an estimated 1,130 murders (approximately 9% of all murders) in the United States involved at least one juvenile offender.
- One in every four juveniles who will come to a juvenile court charged with a violent offense will have a court record by the 14th birthday.
- On a typical day in 2003, nearly 97,000 juveniles were being held in a residential facility as a result of a violation of law.
- African American and Latino juveniles are held in residential custody in the United

States at about the same rate, and twice the rate for Caucasians, respectively.
- Allowing one youth to leave high school for a life of crime and drug abuse costs society $2 million.

GANGS

More youth are also joining gangs. The 2004 National Youth Gang Survey revealed the following about gangs (U.S. Department of Justice, 2006, pp. 1–2):

- 29% of the jurisdictions that city and county law enforcement agencies serve had youth gang problems in 2004;
- approximately 760,000 gang members and 24,000 gangs were active in more than 2,900 jurisdictions that city and county law enforcement agencies served in 2004;
- 173 cities with a population of 100,000 or more reported a gang problem in 2004;
- in Los Angeles and Chicago, more than half of the combined nearly 1,000 homicides were considered to be gang-related;
- 36% of the reporting agencies with gang problems in 2004 operated a specialized unit with at least two officers who were assigned primarily to handle gang-related matters; and
- 47% of the responding agencies indicated that their youth gang problem was "getting worse."

Results of this survey highlight the significance of gang problems and the need for a systematic response.

Many youth join gangs to "belong," indicating that gangs are "like families to me." Gangs replace the nurturing, support, and sense of belonging that youth lack in their own families. Gang members often commit crimes or violent acts as part of initiation rites or other gang-related activities. Peer pressure is considerable for youth who join gangs, and gang members have difficulty saying no to their peers when they become involved in inappropriate and/or illegal activities, and to leave gangs once they join them. (Short, 2006).

SUICIDE AND CHILDREN'S MENTAL HEALTH

Children are too often the victims of divorce, family and community violence, substance abuse, and other family, community, and societal dysfunctions. The 2003 National Household Survey on Drug Abuse revealed that 20.6% of persons aged 12 to 17 reported mental health treatment/ counseling in the past year (Substance Abuse and Mental Health Services Administration, 2004).

The two greatest sources of treatment/ counseling were mental health practitioners including social workers (46.1%) and school-based personnel such as counselors and psychologists (48.0%). The categories cited by respondents for seeking treatment or counseling included. thought about killing self or tried to kill self (18.9%), felt depressed (50.2%), felt very afraid or tense (21.4.9%), breaking rules or "acting out" (25.7%), eating problems (9.4%), family/home problems (14.3.9%), social/friend problems (8.8%), school-related issues (10.4%), and other reason/ reasons (21.9%). Males and females sought help in about equal numbers.

Many children and adolescents get involved in substance abuse and become alcoholics or addicts, often at young ages, or suffer serious physical and emotional injuries as a result. In 2002, accidents were the number-one cause of death for adolescents. Suicide was the third leading cause of death for adolescents and the sixth leading cause of death for children 5 to 14 years old (U.S. Department of Commerce, 2006). Substance abuse, accidents, and suicide attempts often are interrelated. Depressed youth are more likely to abuse alcohol and other drugs and when they do, more likely to take unhealthy risks that can result in accidents, and also to attempt suicide.

In 2003, there were 49,639 suicides in the United States (135.2 suicides per day). Of this number, 15% were committed by individuals younger than age 25. Males are more than four times more likely than females to die from suicide, but females are more likely than males to attempt suicide (Centers for Disease Control and Prevention, 2006). Each suicide is estimated to intimately affect at least six other people. Suicidal individuals often try other ways to stop their pain first, frequently with drugs and alcohol as indicated earlier. Children and adolescents who attempt suicide feel helpless, hopeless, and powerless, often in connection with a series of losses in their lives. When they are in an environment over which they feel they have no control, they ultimately may seek suicide as an escape.

Professionals who work with adolescents at risk for mental health problems, including suicide, believe that *mattering*—the extent to which a person believes he or she is important to others— has a significant influence in preventing such problems. Joiner (2006) has identified the following three significant aspects of mattering:

1. feeling that you command attention from others,
2. feeling that you are important to others, and
3. feeling that others depend on you.

Summary

Children, youth, and families in the United States develop problems for many reasons. From a systems/ecological perspective, factors associated with family problems are complex and interactive. Societal and cultural factors, as well as the level of support available to families from the communities in which they reside, have an impact on the nature and extent of family problems.

All families have strengths they can draw upon when they do have problems. Effective intervention and prevention programs can capitalize on these strengths when working with children, youth, and families. Still, effective intervention and prevention efforts must be undertaken within the broader context of understanding the complexities of the family problems discussed in this chapter.

Problems that result from changing family situations, substance abuse, domestic violence, child maltreatment, teen pregnancy, homelessness, and involvement with the juvenile justice system can have a dramatic impact on the well-being of families. Left unchecked, such problems often are passed on from generation to generation and thus are more resistant to family-strengthening interventions. In Chapter 12, we address programs and policies that help families in need and the roles that social workers play in providing these policies and programs.

 Key Terms and InfoTrac® College Edition

The terms below are defined in the Glossary at the end of this text. To learn more about key terms and topics in this chapter, enter the following search terms using InfoTrac or the World Wide Web:

adult children
   of alcoholics
alcohol abuse
alcoholics
battered child
   syndrome
blended families
Child Abuse
   Prevention and
   Treatment Act
   of 1974
child neglect
codependent

custody
cyber-stalking
enablers
family
family violence
feminization of
   poverty
incest
joint custody
mediation
non-organic failure
   to thrive
physical child abuse

psychological
   maltreatment/
   emotional
   maltreatment

sexual abuse
stepfamilies
substance abuse

Discussion Questions

1. What are three issues that must be considered when defining a family problem? How can the systems/ecological framework contribute to this process?
2. Name the four roles that family members play when substance abuse is a problem. How do family dynamics help shape these roles?
3. Describe the dynamics of a violent spousal relationship.
4. Define four types of child maltreatment. What are their characteristics?
5. What are five factors that are likely to be associated with families who abuse or neglect their children?
6. Discuss the reasons that teenagers today are likely to become parents.
7. Why are children from unstable families more likely to become involved with juvenile delinquency and criminal behavior than those who come from stable families?

 **On the Internet**

http://www.calib.com/nccanch/
http://www.acf.dhhs.gov/
http://www.americanhumane.org/
http://child.cornell.edu/
http://childhelpusa.org/
http://www.childrensdefense.org/
http://www.cwla.org/
http://www.preventchildabuse.org/

References

American Academy of Pediatrics. (2002). Co-parent or second-parent adoptions by same-sex parents (Technical report). *Pediatrics, 109*(2), 341–344.

American Association for Retired Persons (AARP). (2006). *State fact sheets for grandparents and other relatives raising children.* Washington, DC: Author. Available: http://aarp.org/research/family/grandparenting/aresearch-import-488.html

Annie E. Casey Foundation. *Kids count data book.* (2006). Greenwich, CT: Author.

Barta, P. L. (2001). Blended families: How to make sense of your new stepfamily. *APS Healthcare, 1*(2).

Berkes, F., Golding, J., & Folke, C. (Eds.). (2002). *Navigating social-ecological systems: Building resilience for complexity and change.* New York: Cambridge University Press.

Bernstein, R. (2005). *Families of value: Personal profiles of pioneering lesbian and gay parents.* New York: Marlowe and Company.

Black, C. (2002). *Changing course: Healing from loss, abandonment, and fear.* Center City, MN: Hazelden.

Black, C. (2006). *Family strategies: Practical tools for professionals treating families impacted by addiction.* Bainbridge Island, WA: MAC Publishing.

Bowlby J. (1951). Maternal care and mental health. *Bulletin of the World Health Organization, 3,* 355–534.

Bronfenbrenner, U. (1979). *The ecology of human development.* Cambridge, MA: Harvard University Press.

Brown, S., & Lewis, V. (2002). *The alcoholic family in recovery: A developmental model.* New York: Guilford Press.

Canfield, J., Hansen, M., Hartman, L., & Vogl, N. (2005). *Chicken soup for the single parent's soul: Stories of hope, healing, and humor.* Deerfield Beach, FL: HCI Publishers.

Carter, E., & McGoldrick, M. (2005). *The expanded family life cycle: Individual, family, and social perspectives* (3rd ed.). Boston: Allyn & Bacon.

Centers for Disease Control and Prevention. (2006). *Homicides and suicides: United states 2003.* Atlanta, GA: Author.

Child Welfare League of America. (2004). *Children of substance abusers fact sheet.* Washington, DC: Author.

Children's Defense Fund. (2006). *The state of America's children yearbook 2005.* Washington, DC: Author.

Conyers, B. (2003). *Addict in the family: Stories of loss, hope, and recovery.* Center City, MN: Hazelden.

Crosson-Tower, C. (2005). *Understanding child abuse and neglect* (3rd ed.). Boston: Allyn & Bacon.

Covey, H., & Menard, S. and Franzese, R. (1997). *Juvenile gangs* (3rd ed.). (1997). Springfield, IL: Charles C Thomas.

Crosson-Tower, C. (2005). *Understanding child abuse and neglect* (6th ed.). Boston: Allyn & Bacon.

DiNitto, D. (2005). *Social welfare: Politics and public policy* (6th ed.). Boston: Allyn & Bacon.

Duncan, S. F., & Goddard, H. W. (2005). *Family life education: Principles for effective outreach.* Thousand Oaks, CA: Sage Publications.

Folberg, J., Milne, A., & Salem, P. (Eds.). (2004). *Divorce and family mediation: Models, techniques, and applications.* New York: Guilford Press.

Franzetta, K., Terry-Humen, E., Manlove, G., & Ikamullah, E. (2006). *Trends and recent estimates: Contraceptive use among U.S. teens.* Washington, DC: Child Trends.

Garbarino, J. (1992). *Children and families in the social environment* (2nd ed.). New York: Aldine de Gruyter.

Garbarino, J. (1999). *Raising children in a socially toxic environment.* San Francisco: Jossey-Bass.

Garbarino, J., Guttman, L., & Seeley, J. (1986). *The psychologically battered child.* Lexington, MA: Lexington.

Helpguide. (2006). *Domestic violence and abuse: Types, signs, symptoms, and effects.* Santa Monica, CA: Author.

Holyfield, L. (2002). *Moving up and out: Poverty, education and the single parent family.* Philadelphia: Temple University Press.

Homelessness Education. (2006). *Summary of McKinney-Vento Act and Title 1 provisions.* Washington, DC: Author.

Horvath, J. (2007). *Child neglect.* New York: Palgrave Macmillan.

Howe, D. (2005). *Child abuse and neglect: Attachment, development and intervention.* New York: Palgrave MacMillan.

Joiner, T. (2006). *Why people die by suicide.* Cambridge, MA: Harvard University Press.

Jung, K. (2006). *The impact of family stressors, interpersonal conflict, and parenting behaviors on children's overt and relational aggression: A focus on Korean families*. Ann Arbor, MI: ProQuest/UMI.

Lashley, M. (2006). *Stress, coping and the severity of depression in African-American adult children of alcoholics*. Ann Arbor, MI: ProQuest/Com.

Lawson, A., & Lawson, G. (2004). *Alcoholism and the family: A guide to treatment and prevention* (2nd ed.). Austin, TX: Pro-Ed Publishers.

Lessord, R. D. (2004). *Put on your oxygen mask first: Physical, emotional, and spiritual healing for single parents and their families*. Frederick, MD: PublishAmerica.

Marquardt, E. (2005). *Between two worlds: The inner lives of children of divorce*. New York: Crown Publishers.

Maynard, A., & Martini, M. (2005). *Learning in cultural context: Family, peers, and school*. New York: Springer.

Mellody, P., & Freundlich, L. (2004). *The intimacy factor: Ground rules for overcoming the obstacles to truth, respect, and lasting love*. San Francisco: HarperSanfrancisco.

Mellody, P., & Miller, A. (2003). *Facing codependence: What it is, what it comes from, how it sabotages our lives*. San Francisco: Harper.

Mohr, R. (2005). *The long arc of justice: Lesbian and gay marriage, equality, and rights*. New York: Columbia University Press.

Morrisette, M. (2006). *Choosing single motherhood: The thinking woman's guide*. New York: Mando Publishers.

National Center for Education Statistics. (2006). *Adult literacy and education in America*. Washington, DC: Author.

National Center for Homeless Education. (2006). *McKinney-Vento data standards and indicators* (rev.). Greensboro, NC: Author.

National Center for Injury Prevention and Control. (2003). *Intimate partner violence*. Atlanta: Author. Available: http:www.cdc.gov/ncipc/factsheets/ipufacts.htm

National Center for Post Traumatic Stress Disorder. (2003). *Child sexual abuse*. White River Junction, VT: Author. Available: http://www.ncptsd.org/facts/specfic/fs_child_sexual_abuse.html

National Center on Child Abuse and Neglect. (1996). *Third national incidence study of child abuse and neglect*. Washington, DC: Author. Available: http://www.calib.com/nccanch/pubs/

National Coalition for the Homeless. (2006). *Homeless youth: NCH Fact Sheet #11*. Washington, DC: Author. Available: http://nch.ari.net/youth.html

National Institute of Justice. (2000). *Full report of the prevalence, incidence, and consequences of violence against women*. Washington, DC: Author.

National Institute on Alcohol Abuse and Alcoholism. (2003). *Children of alcoholics*. Bethesda, MD: Author.

National Task Force to End Sexual and Domestic Violence Against Women. (2005). *The Violence Against Women Act: Re-authorization 2005*. Washington, DC: Author.

Newman, B., & Newman, P. (2005). *Development through life: A psychosocial approach*. Belmont, CA: Wadsworth.

Office of Juvenile Justice and Delinquency Prevention. (2004). *OJJDP statistical briefing book: The national report notebook*. Washington, DC: Author. Available: http://www.ojjdp.ncjrs.org

Partridge, D. (2006). *Blended families can work*. Pleasanton, CA: Author. Available: http://www.blendingfamily.com/article1.html

Petit, R. (2005). *Transformation for life: Healing and growth for adult children of alcoholics and others*. Rushden, England: Bright Horizons Press.

Polansky, N. A., Chalmers, M. A., Buttenweiser, E. W., & Williams, D. P. (1983). *Damaged parents: An anatomy of child neglect*. Chicago: University of Chicago Press.

Powers, T., DuPaul, E., Shapiro, S., & Kazak, A. (2003). *Promoting children's health: Integrating school, family, and community*. New York: Guilford Press.

Rotskoff, L. (2002). *Love on the rocks: Men, women, and alcohol in post-World War II America*. Raleigh: University of North Carolina Press.

Scott, J., & Ward, H. (Eds.). (2005). *Safeguarding and promoting the well-being of children, families, and communities*. London, England: Jessica Kingsley Publishers.

Short, J. (2006). *Studying youth gangs (violence prevention and policy)*. Lanham, MD: Alta Mira Press.

Snyder, H.N., & Sickmund, M. (2006). *Juvenile offenders and victims: 2006 national report*. Washington, DC: U.S. Department of Justice, Office of Juvenile Justice and Delinquency Prevention.

Sokoloff, N., & Pratt, C. (Eds.). (2005). *Domestic violence at the margins: Readings on race, class, gender, and culture*. Piscataway, NJ: Rutgers University Press.

Stepfamily Foundation. (2006). *The stepfamily: The new "silent majority."* New York: Author.

Substance Abuse and Mental Health Services Administration. (2004). *Results from the 2003 National Survey on Drug Use and Health: National findings.* Rockville, MD: Author.

U.S. Bureau of the Census. (2003). *Children's living arrangements and characteristics: March 2002.* Washington, DC: Author.

U.S. Bureau of the Census. (2006). *Income, poverty, and health insurance coverage in the United States: 2005.* Washington, DC: Author.

U.S. Children's Bureau. (2006a). *Factors that contribute to child abuse and neglect.* Washington, DC: Author.

U.S. Children's Bureau. (2006b). *What are the major types of child abuse and neglect?* Washington, DC: Author.

U.S. Department of Commerce. (2006). *Statistical abstract of the United States.* Washington, DC: Author.

U.S. Department of Health and Human Services. (2003). *Substance abuse and child maltreatment.* Washington, D.C: Author.

U.S. Department of Health and Human Services. (2006). *Child maltreatment 2004.* Washington, DC: Administration on Children, Youth, and Families.

U.S. Department of Justice. (2000). *Prevalence, incidence, and consequences of violence against women: Findings from the National Violence against Women Survey.* Washington, DC: Author.

U.S. Department of Justice (2006). *Highlights of the 2004 National Youth Gang Survey.* Washington, DC: Author.

Violence Against Women Office. (2000). *Summary of criminal provisions of the Violence against Women Act.* Washington, DC: Publisher. Available: http://www.ojp.usdoj.gov/vawo/laws/

Walker, L. (2000). *The battered woman syndrome* (2nd ed.). New York: Springer.

Wilson, K. J. (2005). *When violence begins at home: A comprehensive guide to understanding and ending domestic abuse.* Alameda, CA: Hunter House Publishers.

Winning Stepfamilies. (2006). *Stepfamily statistics:* Folsom, CA: Author. Available: http://Winningfamilies.com/statistics.htm

Wolf, M. (2002). *Child sexual abuse.* Berkeley: University of California, Berkeley School of Social Welfare.

Wolfinger, N. H. (2005). *Understanding the divorce cycle: The children of divorce and their own marriages.* New York: Cambridge University Press.

Yuen, F. K., Skibinski, G. J., & Pardeck, J. T. (2003). *Family health social work practice: A knowledge and skills casebook.* Binghamton, NY: Haworth Press.

Suggested Further Readings

Aronson-Fontes, L. (2005). *Child abuse and culture: Working with diverse families.* New York: Guilford Press.

Conyers, P. (2003). *Addict in the family: Stories of loss, hope, and recovery.* Center City, MN: Hazelden.

Marsolini, M. (2006). *Raising children in blended families: Helpful insights, expert opinions, and true stories.* Grand Rapids, MI: Kregel Publications.

Pipher, M. (2005). *Reviving Ophelia: Saving the selves of adolescent girls.* New York: Penguin.

Sokoloff, N. J., & Pratt, C. (Eds.).(2005). *Domestic violence at the margins: Readings on race, gender, and culture.* New Brunswick, NJ: Rutgers University Press.

Walsh, F. (2006). *Strengthening family resilience* (2d ed.) New York: Guilford Press.

White, S. (Ed.). (2006). *Handbook of youth and justice.* New York: Springer.

CHAPTER 11

Services to Children, Youth, and Families

As a social worker with the local family services agency, Juanita Kingbird is involved in a number of activities to prevent families from becoming dysfunctional, as well as activities that help families when they have special needs. Her agency provides a variety of programs, including parenting programs that teach child care to teenage parents, an outreach program that seeks out parents who are under stress or need help with parenting, and individual, family, and group counseling for children and family members of all ages. Recently the agency opened a shelter for adolescents who cannot remain in their own homes, and a respite-care program for families of children with developmental disabilities. The agency also provides homemaker services, child care, and employment services to help families remain economically self-sufficient and stay together.

At the start of a typical day, Juanita returns a crisis call from a mother whose son ran away from home the night before following a family argument. She calls the school social worker and asks her to check and see if the boy is in school and, if so, to talk with him. Then she holds two counseling sessions with adolescents who are staying in the shelter, exploring their feelings about becoming independent and separating from their families.

Juanita then leaves her agency for the high school, where she leads a support group for teen parents. Afterward, she meets individually with several of the parents and helps one of them make an appointment with a specialist for her infant with developmental delays. She has a quick lunch with the school social worker to coordinate services that the two of them are providing to some of her clients, then meets with the runaway boy—who did go to school. He agrees to meet with her and his mother later in the day. On the way back to her office, Juanita stops to make a home visit with a client who has been emotionally abusing her two young children. Juanita interacts with the mother and her children, role-modeling good communication patterns and ways to give feedback and set limits positively.

She returns to the office in time to attend a staffing, with social workers from the five other agencies involved, regarding another family. Although the family has many serious problems, the coordinated intervention plan developed by the agencies seems to be effective, as everyone reports that the family is making progress. Juanita then meets with the runaway boy and his mother. They negotiate family rules and boundaries, and mother and son agree to try to live together without major conflicts, and to return in a week for another counseling session. After a long and eventful day, Juanita leaves the agency for home, glad that she has a supportive family waiting for her so she does not burn out from getting too emotionally involved with her clients.

Juanita enjoys her job very much. Although she finds it difficult to deal with the many needs of the families with whom she is assigned to work, especially when children are suffering, she appreciates even small successes. "If I can make things better in some small way each day for one child or one parent, my job is more than worthwhile," she stated in a recent newspaper interview.

Programs and policies that address the needs of children, youth, and families are as diverse as the types of needs encountered. Traditionally, the system that has provided programs and policies that address child and family concerns has been called the **child welfare service delivery system,** "a group of services designed to promote the well-being of children by ensuring safety, achieving permanency, and strengthening families to successfully care for their children" (U.S. Children's Bureau, 2006b, p. 1).

In this chapter we focus on services that address the children, youth, and family-related needs discussed in chapter 10. We also discuss the roles that social workers play in providing services to children, youth, and families.

Current Philosophical Issues

All policies and programs that address the needs of children, youth, and their families must consider a number of philosophical issues and assumptions in addition to the social and cultural context of the child's family, the community, and the broader environment discussed in the preceding chapters. These are detailed, beginning with the child's right to a permanent, nurturing home life.

The Right to a Permanent, Nurturing Family

Every child has a right to grow up in a permanent, nurturing home, and every attempt must be made to provide such a home. The underlying assumption is that the child's own home is the best option for that child whenever possible. This philosophical position dictates that services should be provided first to the child's family, and that every attempt should be made to keep the child and the family together. This position has led to the development of **family preservation programs,** or services provided to a child and his or her family while they remain together, rather than placing the child in a foster home or other substitute care. Increasingly, emphasis is placed on services that will keep families together rather than removing children from their family settings.

In the past, many children receiving services in an overloaded service delivery system became lost in the system, with no chance to return home, be adopted, or become emancipated. There was no way to determine exactly how many children were in substitute care, and in some instances children were sent to other states because care was less expensive and the responsibility for their care could be shifted elsewhere. Although foster care was, and still is, supposed to be temporary, many children placed in foster care "aged out" of the system when they reached age 18 because no other options or alternatives were available to them. Children often lived in five or more foster homes and had as many or more social workers. Some children moved around so much that they didn't go to the same school for an entire school year.

Concern among many individuals and advocacy organizations led to legislation at both state and federal levels that mandates **permanency planning.** This concept ensures that when a child and family first receive services, a specific plan is developed to help keep that family together if possible and, if not, what will be done to provide a permanent, nurturing home for the child. Specific actions are identified to take place within certain time limits, and these actions are monitored for compliance by the court or a citizen review panel, or both.

If a family receives services without making enough progress to provide for a child's most basic needs, parents' rights can be terminated and the child placed in an adoptive home rather than the child remaining in limbo in the foster-care system. This planning allows agencies to make more realistic decisions about helping children and their families and ensures that families know specifically what they need to do to be allowed to continue to parent their children.

Best Interests of the Child

Decisions about the needs of children and families should be based on what is in the **best interests of the child.** Sometimes, even with the most appropriate intervention, it is questionable whether children's best interests are served by their remaining with their own families. In these circumstances, should decisions regarding where a child is placed (remain with his or her own family or be placed elsewhere) center on the child's best interests, the parents' best interests, or the family's best interests? Although experts agree that the rights of both the parents and their children have to be considered, attention first must go to the child's best interests. This means that before any decision is made, careful attention has to be given to the most beneficial outcome for that child.

The landmark book, *The Best Interests of the Child: The Least Detrimental Alternative* (Goldstein, Solnit, Goldstein, & Freud, 1996) carefully considers this issue. The authors argue that determining what is *best* for a child often places decision makers in a position of rendering a decision for which they have no experience or training. As a result, the interests of a child are best served by choosing the **least detrimental alternative** from a number of available

alternatives. Other researchers have come to a similar conclusion (see, for example, Friedman, 2005; Guggenheim, 2005; Lindsey, 2003).

Legislation now requires that courts appoint a guardian *ad litem* (one who advocates for the minor on a limited and special basis) in certain child welfare situations, such as hearings when a parent's rights are being terminated. The sole purpose of the guardian *ad litem* is to represent the best interests of the child and to make a recommendation to the court with those interests in mind. This is especially important in situations in which the parents and the state child welfare agency disagree about what is in the best interest of a child.

Goldstein and colleagues (1996) also consider *who* should be involved in planning changes in a child's life. Until recently, decisions regarding where a child should be reared usually favored the child's biological mother, and then the father. But often the early childrearing is by a relative or a foster parent, not one or both biological parents. More recent thinking considers the child's **psychological parent,** who is not always the child's biological parent.

Considerations before State Intervention

Under what circumstances should the community or state intervene in family matters? In the past, the family was considered sacred, and intervention in family matters was rare. When allowed, it was based on the doctrine of *parens patriae*—that the state is a parent to all of its children and has the obligation, through regulatory and legislative powers, to protect them and, when necessary, provide them with resources needed to keep them safe.

Many children grow up in unsafe and non-nurturing environments. Some family advocates argue that early intervention is necessary to keep a family together, as well as to protect the child from growing up with severe emotional damage. Others suggest that intervention in families should take place less often because in too many instances the intervention—especially when limited resources do not allow for the family to be rehabilitated—is more harmful than no intervention at all. These advocates suggest that intervention in families should take place only when requested by a parent, such as in child-custody disputes; when a parent chooses to relinquish parental rights and place that child for adoption; or when a parent is seriously maltreating a child.

The issue of when a government entity has the right or the obligation to intervene is increasingly before the courts. Many child advocacy groups have filed class-action suits against state child protective services agencies, charging failure to provide needed services to protect children from serious maltreatment (American Prosecutors Research Institute, 2003; Martell, 2005; Vieth, Bottoms, & Perona, 2005).

Preventing Family Disruption and Dysfunction

Another major issue is whether scarce resources should be targeted toward preventing family problems. And if prevention is chosen, should it be universal or primary, secondary, or tertiary? All three are important in strengthening families. Most intervention with families today occurs *after* problems have occurred, and even then, services are not always available to the families that need them (see Box 11.1).

Because resources are scarce, little attention is given to any type of prevention. Of the few prevention programs available, the focus is tertiary in nature, well after the problems began. In many instances, this means that children must be severely abused or families must be going through a serious crisis before services are available, and by that time, preserving the family is not as likely to be a realistic option.

How Accountable Are Parents?

A final issue receiving attention today is the extent to which parents should be held accountable for providing adequate care for their children and what should be done to parents who fail do so. Some specialists in family dynamics say that punishment is more likely to make parents angry and less likely to teach them how to be better parents. These specialists hold that effective intervention programs should be directed toward meeting the needs of the child, with an emphasis on keeping the child in the home. Others suggest that parents whose family problems pose severe consequences for their children be brought before the court and ordered to receive help, with punishment ordered if they refuse the help.

The relationships between parents' problems and consequences for a child are also coming before the courts. For example, should a woman who fears for her own life if she were to intervene to protect her child be held accountable if the father injures the child? In two high-profile child-abuse fatalities, a battered woman was charged with failing to protect her child from her violent husband. In one case, the mother was found not guilty. In the other case, the woman received a prison sentence that was longer than the sentence her husband received because she was tried separately by a different jury. The court also terminated her parental rights.

The 1995 case of the woman from South Carolina who drowned her two young sons also precipitated extensive debate. Should parents who have experienced severe maltreatment themselves as children and/or who have serious emotional or mental health problems be held accountable for their actions? If so, should those experiences be considered when assessing penalties for their actions? When the South Carolina woman was a young child, her mother committed suicide, as a young teenager she was molested by her stepfather, and she had a history of psychiatric problems. The prosecuting attorney asked that the woman receive the death penalty, but the jury recommended that she receive a life sentence. Tragic situations like these are likely to be repeated without stronger efforts to prevent problems such as domestic violence

BOX 11.1
Tasha and Family Deserve a Good Chance

Tasha loves her children. This is not in question. Tasha holds Patik and Felicia, ages 2 and 4, close to her, pulling their heads to hers, smiling, singing the Barney song, "I love you . . . you love me. . . ."

Her two older children, Robert and Honree ("I was 13 when I had him," says Tasha. "What did I know about spelling a French name?"), are helping women lay out doughnuts, sandwiches, and loaves of bread on a table set up on a sidewalk in inner-city Baltimore. The food is for giving away to hungry people. It has been donated to an organization that does that, and more. For four days, Tasha and her children have stayed in a shelter operated by this organization. While food is being laid out, a taxi pulls up, carrying a woman and a little boy. Both have been beaten by the boy's father. They, too, are looking for shelter. And more.

Honree, at 8, the oldest of Tasha's children, watches the women giving away food, then asks if he, too, may have a pair of the thin, white rubber gloves the women wear to handle food.

The next time someone approaches the table, Honree is right there.

"May I help you?" he says. "You can have one sandwich, a doughnut and three loaves of bread, if you want to. May I get it for you? Here, will you sign this?"

A man takes a second sandwich.

"Please," says Honree, "there isn't enough. You can only have one sandwich."

The man faces down this dignified boy and, after a couple of beats, returns the second sandwich.

For several hours Honree runs the free food table. He is polite and firm. . . . He means to do it right.

Tasha has laid Patik down for his nap. Patik sleeps, curled on a blanket on the sidewalk. His sweet baby face carries in it all the possibilities in the world. He does not yet know how limited his are. Meanwhile, Tasha answers questions from the white, middle-class women who have come to help distribute food, only to find an 8-year-old boy doing it better.

and child maltreatment and to intervene quickly and effectively when they come to light.

Defining Services to Children, Youth, and Families

Traditionally, services to children, youth, and families have been defined as **child welfare services.** Early definitions of child welfare focused on *residual* services—services provided

after family breakdown. In his seminal child welfare book, Kadushin (1980) proposed, as the goals of child welfare services,

> to reinforce, supplement or substitute the functions that parents have difficulty in performing; and to improve conditions for children and their families by modifying existing social institutions or organizing new ones (p. 5).

The Social Security Act of 1935—the cornerstone of American social welfare policy—has a specific section (Title IV-B) that mandates states

"My own mother was a junkie," says Tasha. "She's been clean for six years now. She made me go to a parenting program for a year. My children's fathers? Two are dead from drugs. The other two, they don't do anything for the kids. Nothing at all. Yeah, I did drugs. I'm in the program now. AA, you know?"

Tasha looks at Felicia, who, at 4, already is beautiful. "I've got to do what I can to make sure her life is different. I don't want her to be 13 and make the choices I made. Or only have the choices I had. But it's hard. I can't get a good job because I can't get my GED because I can't get child care. Actually, I can't get any kind of job until I can work out the child-care thing. I'm getting a place to live next Monday. The social worker called and said we'd go look at it. I told her I don't have to look at it. If it's got a roof and walls and locks on the door and windows and a toilet that flushes, I'll take it."

Tasha's children play with one another and with others. Robert and Felicia sing a song about a rabbit and smile at everybody. Their smiles can light a whole day. They hug people, too, probably because they have been hugged. Honree works the food table. It seems clear he's been helping his mother take care of the smaller kids. This is an intelligent boy, alert, interested, quick, kind.

One wants to do something. Something that will give Honree his chance. Something that will give Tasha an opportunity to give Honree—and Robert and Felicia and Patik—a chance.

Something.

One thinks of politics. But politics is theory and politicians take too long to do anything. Tasha, Patik, Felicia, Robert and Honree are not theory—they are people—and they don't have too long.

Two men, old and wasted, approach the free food table. The sandwiches are all gone, Honree tells them. Tasha looks up and, seeing the old men, takes two sandwiches that had been given to her children and says, "Here. Take these. My kids got fed last night. They're not as hungry as you."

And so it goes.

Source: Written by award-winning TV producer and best-selling author, Linda Ellerbee (1995), p. A15. Used by permission of *Austin* (Texas) *American Statesman.*

to provide a full range of child welfare services, defined as follows (Section 425):

[P]ublic social services which supplement, or substitute for parental care and supervision for the purpose of:

1. preventing or remedying, or assisting in the solution of problems which may result in the neglect, abuse, exploitation or delinquency of children,
2. protecting and caring for homeless, dependent, or neglected children,
3. protecting and promoting the welfare of children of working mothers, and
4. otherwise protecting and promoting the welfare of children, including the strengthening of their own homes where possible or, where needed, the provision of adequate care of children away from their homes in foster family homes or day care or other child care facilities.

Because of negative connotations associated with the term *welfare* and the current emphasis on strengthening the family to support the child, child welfare services today more often are referred to as services to children, youth, and families (or as child and family services). They also are viewed more broadly, encompassing the traditional child welfare services of child protection, foster care, and adoption, as well as family preservation and supportive services such as child care and parenting programs.

The History of Services to Children, Youth, and Families

Some historians argue that societal attitudes toward children and families have improved significantly since the United States was settled, as have policies and programs supportive of children and families. Others disagree, saying that little has really changed. They suggest that the debate about the needs of children and families in the late-1800s and early-1900s is not much different from contemporary debate about the same issues. Regardless of whether today's children and families are better off or worse off than in the past, a review of the history of services to children, youth, and families shows clearly the historical base of our present child welfare service delivery system.

Colonial Times

In colonial times, children were considered to be the responsibility of their families, and little attention was directed to children whose families were available to provide for them, no matter how well the family actually met their needs. Children usually came to the attention of authorities only if they were orphaned and relatives were not available to provide for them. Churches and a few private orphanages cared for some dependent children. Prior to 1800, however, most orphans were placed in almshouses or given to families to function as servants. The emphasis during this period was on survival. Fewer than half of all children born in this country prior to the 1800s lived to the age of 18.

The 19th Century

During the 1800s, more attention was aimed at the negative effects of placing young children in almshouses with adults, particularly adults who were criminals or had disabilities. In 1853, Charles Loring Brace founded the Children's Aid Society of New York, which established orphanages and other programs for children. Brace and others believed that these programs were the most appropriate way to "save" children from the negative influences of urban life (Axinn & Stern, 2005). Brace viewed rural Protestant families as ideal for these children, and he recruited many foster families from the rural Midwest to serve as foster parents.

"Orphan trains" carrying hundreds of children from New York City traveled throughout the Midwest, leaving behind children who had been selected by foster families. By 1880, the Children's Aid Society of New York had sent 40,000 children to live with rural farm families (Axinn & Stern, 2005). This was not a universally accepted practice. A number of prominent individuals called attention to the negative effects of separating children from their parents, even if the parents were deemed "unfit," but most of the criticism involved religious conflicts. The majority of children placed in foster homes were from Irish immigrant families who were predominantly Catholic, whereas their foster families were primarily German and Scandinavian Protestants. The outcry led to the development of more Catholic orphanages and foster homes.

Still, the needs of abused and neglected children and their families were not addressed. This changed in the 1870s as the result of a now-famous case involving a young girl in New York named Mary Ellen. Abandoned by her parents at birth, Mary Ellen was living with relatives who beat her severely, tied her to her bed, and fed her meager amounts of food from a bowl—like a dog. A visitor to Mary Ellen's neighborhood was appalled at the girl's abusive treatment and reported the situation to a number of agencies in New York City. When none would intervene, the visitor—reasoning that Mary Ellen fell under the broad rubric of "animal"—finally convinced the New York Society for the Prevention of Cruelty to Animals to take the case to court and request that the child be removed from the family immediately.

As a result of the Mary Ellen case, New York established the Society for the Prevention of Cruelty to Children, and other Northeast cities followed suit. The primary aim of these organizations, however, was on prosecuting parents rather than providing services to children or their families. Charity Organization Societies (COS) and settlement houses established in the late-1800s directed more attention to children and families, as well as the environments in which they lived.

Other efforts in the late-1800s and early-1900s were aimed at children's health needs. Deaths of children were common during this period. Well-off families saw prevention of disease as a way to keep the diseases of immigrants from spreading to their own children (Axinn & Stern, 2005). During this time, various public health laws were passed. Other relevant legislation dealt with preventing child labor as well as mandating compulsory school attendance. More attention was given to the responsibilities of government to provide for children and families, and many states passed legislation establishing monitoring systems for foster care and separating facilities for dependent, neglected, and delinquent children from those for adults.

The Early 20th Century

The most significant effort toward establishing a true service-delivery system for children, youth, and families was the inception of the **U.S. Children's Bureau** in 1912. This was a direct result of the first White House Conference on Children, held in 1910, and the activities of a coalition of child advocates from the settlement houses, COS groups, and state boards of charities and corrections.

The legislation establishing the U.S. Children's Bureau was significant, because it was the first law that recognized the federal government's responsibility for the welfare of the country's children. Julia Lathrop, a prominent member of society and a resident of Hull House in Chicago, was appointed the first chief of the bureau. The bureau's earliest efforts were aimed at birth registration and maternal and child health programs, in an attempt to reduce the high infant mortality rate and improve children's health.

One of the bureau's first publications, *Infant Care,* a booklet for parents, underwent more than 20 revisions and was the most popular document available from the U.S. Government Printing Office for many years. In its current form, the Children's Bureau is responsible for a number of federal programs for children, youth, and families and is under the umbrella of the U.S. Department of Health and Human Services.

During the first three decades of the 1900s, state governments continued to become more involved in services to children, youth, and families, particularly in the South and West, where strong private agencies did not exist. Many states established public departments of welfare that also were responsible for child and family services, including protecting children from abuse and neglect, providing foster homes, and overseeing orphanages and other children's institutions. Establishment of the American Association for Organizing Family Social Work (which later became the Family Service Association of America) in 1919 and the **Child Welfare League of America** in 1920 gave further impetus to the child and family services movement. Both of these organizations stressed the role of the social work profession and established recommended standards for the provision of services.

During the 1920s, attention turned to parenting and facilitating the development of healthy parent–child relationships. Child guidance centers were established, and the emphasis on psychoanalysis led to increased attention to child therapy. During this period, adoption was included as a formal child welfare service, and adoption legislation followed.

Services to children, youth, and families became more formalized when the **Social Security Act** was passed in 1935. This act established mothers' pensions, which later became the Aid to Families with Dependent Children (AFDC) program, and also mandated states to establish, expand, and strengthen statewide child welfare services, especially in rural areas. Child welfare programs incorporated the following trends, which remain in state and federal child welfare services:

- recognition that poverty is a major factor associated with other child and family problems;
- a shift from rescuing children from poor families and placing them in substitute care to keeping children in their own homes and providing supportive services to prevent family breakup;
- state intervention in family life to protect children;
- increased professionalization and bureaucratization of child welfare services; and
- an emphasis on the federal government's responsibility to oversee delivery of child welfare services within states to ensure that all children and families in the United States have access to needed services.

Notwithstanding the Social Security Act, problems persisted in the delivery of services to children, youth, and families. Access to services remained unequal, and many children continued to grow up in poverty. Some child welfare services, such as adoption, were provided primarily to white, middle-class families, and few child welfare services addressed the needs adequately. Many children, particularly children of color, spent their entire childhood in foster care.

The 1960s and 1970s

In the 1960s, the Kennedy and Johnson administrations took a strong interest in children, youth, and families. Services during these administrations were broader and were targeted at preventing and eliminating poverty. Many of these programs were based on the emerging belief that children's lives are influenced by their environment and that heredity plays only a minimal role in individual outcomes. The goal became to "maximize the potential of all individuals" and to help them become productive adults.

One result was the establishment of infant care centers and **Head Start,** a preschool program incorporating physical, social, emotional, and cognitive development. Other emphases were on education, as well as job training and employment programs for youth and their parents. With this broad base, traditional child welfare services received less attention in favor of strengthening families and preventive services.

When President Nixon took office, child and family services shifted from providing maximum resources to meeting minimum standards. Available services to children, youth, and families were narrowed greatly. Funding, programs, and policies reverted to more traditional child welfare services, including child protection, foster care, and adoption.

Because of increased concern about the high costs of child care and the number of children left alone because their parents could not afford child care, Congress attempted to pass legislation that would give states funds for child-care subsidies for low-income working parents. The reasoning was that this approach would keep more children safe and also would reduce the number of women on AFDC and the number of families living in poverty. Not until 1990 was child-care legislation—called the Better Child Care (ABC) Act—introduced in Congress with a wide base of support.

Significant legislation enacted in the 1970s includes

- the Juvenile Justice and Delinquency Prevention Act (1974), which established limited funding for runaway youth programs;
- the Indian Child Welfare Act (1976), to prevent disruption of Native American families; and

- the Education for All Handicapped Children Act (1975), mandating, through public school systems, the provision of educational and social services to children with disabilities.

CAPTA

The most significant piece of child welfare legislation in the 1970s was the Child Abuse Prevention and Treatment Act, or CAPTA (Public Law 93-247). This act established the National Center on Child Abuse and Neglect as part of the Department of Health, Education, and Welfare (now the Department of Health and Human Services). It required that states receiving federal funds strengthen child maltreatment programs in the areas of state definitions and reporting laws regarding child maltreatment. It established research and technical assistance programs to assist states in developing child maltreatment prevention and intervention programs. And it established special demonstration programs that could be adopted later by other states. When the act was renewed 3 years later, a new section was added to strengthen adoption services for children with special needs (children who were waiting to be adopted and considered difficult to find homes for because of ethnicity, age, or developmental disabilities).

ADOPTION ASSISTANCE AND RELATED CHILD WELFARE LEGISLATION

A number of studies (see Maas & Engler, 1959; Vasaly, 1976) indicated that the child welfare services delivery system perhaps was doing more harm than good to children. Researchers in one study (Shyne & Schroeder, 1978) found that although foster care philosophically was (and is) intended to be short-term (6 months or less) while parents were preparing for family reunification through counseling and other types of assistance, this was not the experience of too many children.

The 1977 National Study of Social Services to Children and Their Families (U.S Department of Health and Human Services, Children's Bureau, 1997, pp. 4–5). produced the following key findings:

1. Approximately 1.8 million children were served by public child welfare agencies.
2. 38% of the children served were children of color.
3. More than 500,000 children were in out-of-home placement.
4. The average length of placement in foster care was 2.5 years.
5. Approximately 200,000 foster care children needed permanent homes, and half were already available for adoption, but only half of those who were legally available were receiving adoption services.

The Adoption Assistance and Child Welfare Act (Public Law 96-272), passed in 1980, changed the thrust of services to children, youth, and families. By placing ceilings on the amounts that states could receive for foster care, the act encouraged establishment of **own-home services** and reductions in the number of children in foster care. It also required the development of comprehensive case plans and 6-month reviews for all children receiving child welfare services so they would not languish in foster care, and provided federal funding to subsidize the adoption of children with special needs.

Although Public Law 96-272 authorized more expenditures for services to children and families in their own homes, not enough funding was provided to overcome the imbalance that continued between foster care and child welfare services designed to prevent placement. The final report of the *National Study of Protective, Preventive and Reunification Services Delivered to Children and Their Families,* released by the U.S. Children's Bureau (U.S. Department of Health and Human Services, Children's Bureau, 1997, pp. 1–3), contains five major findings regarding the impact of Public Law 96-272:

1. Between 1977 and 1994, the number of children receiving child welfare services declined

dramatically, from an estimated 1.8 million to 1 million. This decrease reflected a child welfare system that had evolved from a more broad-based child and family services system into a system serving primarily abused and neglected children and their families.

2. The intent of Public Law 96-272 and other federal policies to shift child welfare from a foster care system to an in-home, family-based system was not realized. The number of children in foster care changed little, and between 1977 and 1994 the number of children receiving in-home services declined by 60%.

3. Despite provisions in Public Law 96-272 for conducting an inventory of children in foster care longer than 6 months and for holding administrative and dispositional hearings, foster care drift remained a problem. Although the average length of stay in foster care declined overall, more than one-third of the children placed in foster care remained there for more than 18 months.

4. Children of color, particularly African American children, were more likely than white children to be placed in foster care than to receive in-home services, even when they shared the same problems and characteristics.

5. Children of color also remained in foster care longer than white children. Kinship foster care, or placement with relatives, did not explain the dramatically longer stays in foster care for African American and Latino children when compared to white children.

The Mid-1980s and the 1990s

In 1986, Public Law 99-272 established the Independent Living Program, which provided funding for states to develop or strengthen services for youth age 16 and older who either were in, or had been in, the foster care system. The Abandoned Infants Assistance Act (AIAA), passed in 1988, provided grants to support demonstration service programs to prevent the abandonment of children and identify the needs of infants and young children, particularly those with HIV/AIDS and drug exposure. Other legislation passed during the mid-1980s focused on runaway and homeless youth, provisions for one-time payments to adoptive parents for adoption-related costs such as legal fees, grant programs for family preservation and support services, and the Children's Justice Act.

One of the most significant pieces of child welfare legislation in the 1990s was the Omnibus Budget Reconciliation Act of 1993 (OBRA 1993), which established a new family preservation and family support services program. This act filled an important piece that had been missing from the earlier 1980 Adoption Assistance and Child Welfare Act by providing $1 billion in new funding over a 5-year period for states to prevent foster-care placement.

Creating a separate funding source for family preservation and family support programs was intended to ensure that funds be used to strengthen families, and not for child abuse and neglect investigations and foster-care placements (U.S. Department of Health and Human Services, Children's Bureau, 1997, p. 7). In addition, OBRA 1993 and amendments to the legislation passed in 1994 and 1997

- established funding for state courts to improve handling of foster care and adoption proceedings;
- provided funding for states to develop automated data systems to better track children and families receiving child welfare services and outcomes;
- permanently extended the Independent Living Program for youth 16 and older;
- mandated that judicial hearings for children be held within 12 months after the initial 18-month judicial hearing.

This legislation highlighted family services and prevention as national priorities and provided opportunities for states to implement child welfare reforms.

During the 1980s and 1990s, the debate also was related to the extent to which race and ethnicity should be factors in foster care and adoptive placement. In 1994, Congress passed the Multiethnic Placement Act (Public Law 103-382) to promote the placement of children of color, who remained in foster care much longer than white children and were less likely to be adopted. This act prevents children from being denied placement with a foster or adoptive parent solely on the basis of the race, color, or national origin of either the prospective parent or the child involved. The act also requires states to "recruit and retain foster and adoptive families that reflect the racial and ethnic diversity of the children for whom homes are needed" (*Adoption 2002,* 1997, p. 3). Congress amended the Multiethnic Placement Act in 1996, repealing some of the language in the earlier legislation that could have been used to circumvent the intent of the law, and providing strict penalties for agencies receiving federal funding if they violate the act.

Although child welfare advocates heralded the greater emphasis on supportive services to families and decreasing foster care placements, new concern began to emerge about the balance between foster care and in-home services. In many geographic areas, the foster care numbers decreased and children and families remained together and improved their functioning. In other areas, however, large numbers of children continued to remain in foster care even when assessments showed that they most likely would have done well in their own homes with appropriate supportive services. In still other areas, the increased funding received for fewer children in foster care was coupled with an increase in severe injuries and deaths of children remaining in their own homes.

To address the concerns regarding the balance between safety and permanency, Congress passed the Adoption and Safe Families Act (ASFA) of 1997 (Public Law 105-89) as an amendment to the child welfare section of the Social Security Act. Funding and services provided under this act are based on the following principles (*Adoption 2002,* 1997, pp. 4–5):

1. Safety is the paramount concern that must guide all child welfare services.
2. Foster care is temporary.
3. Permanency planning efforts should begin as soon as a child enters care.
4. The child welfare system must focus on results and accountability.
5. Innovative approaches are needed to achieve the goals of safety, permanency, and well-being.

Under AFSA, the Family Preservation and Support Services Program created by the Omnibus Reconciliation Act of 1993 was renamed the Promoting Safe and Stable Families (PSSF) Program.

The Foster Care Independence Act (John H. Chafee Foster Care Independence Program) was passed in 1999. Title I of this act is intended to ensure that young people who leave foster care get the tools they need to make the most of their lives: better educational opportunities, access to health care, life skills and other training, housing assistance, and counseling.

During the late-1980s and early-1990s, Congress passed legislation in other areas of health and human services that had the potential to affect the child welfare system. These programs include:

- Public Law 99-457 (Special Education for Infants and Toddlers), which provides services, including case management services, to children from birth to age 2;
- Omnibus Budget Reconciliation Act of 1984, which made limited funding available to provide grants to states to develop services for children with emotional disturbances;
- the Developmentally Disabled Assistance and Bill of Rights Act (1990), requiring states to establish services in the least restrictive settings possible;
- the Adolescent Family Life demonstration program, which provides support for pregnancy prevention as well as services to pregnant and parenting teens.

In addition to the limited funding authorized to implement the requirements of each act, one of the drawbacks to these legislative efforts has been the continued categorization of legislation. Such categorization leads to the establishment of programs limited to narrow populations and reinforces the fragmentation of services. More recent sessions of Congress have placed additional ceilings on amounts available for child and family services. Thus, even attention to a newly publicized area deemed important, such as legislation establishing programs targeted at gangs and youth crime, usually has not resulted in increased funding.

Despite the demands of serving a child welfare population of increasing size and complexity, states made significant inroads, particularly in reducing foster care and providing family-centered services during the 1980s and 1990s. Important components of a strong child welfare service-delivery system are the development of family preservation programs, efforts to reduce the length of stay in foster care, emphasis on culturally appropriate casework practice, and expansion of **kinship care** (Geen, 2003; Iwaniec, 2006; Sindone, 2004).

SUPPORT TO GET FAMILIES OFF WELFARE

The federal legislation that had the potential to be the most significant for children and families since the Social Security Act of 1935 was the Family Support Act of 1988 (see chapter 7). Proponents of this legislation argued that this comprehensive package of services would reduce some of the problems with previously fragmented services created by categorical legislation. But funding to provide such services was limited from the beginning. Moreover, implementation of the act at the state and local levels required extensive coordination and services among human services agencies, school districts, community colleges and universities, employment- and job-training programs, child-care programs, health-care providers, transportation programs, and employers in the private and public sectors.

Because of the costs involved in initiating or strengthening welfare reform programs, many states were unable to provide sufficient resources to address the needs of AFDC recipients who wanted to get off welfare. Often-disappointed and otherwise motivated clients were placed on waiting lists for education, job training, and child-care programs. Other clients were placed in jobs that paid the minimum wage so states could meet federal requirements to maintain funding for their programs, but these jobs did not pay enough or provide benefits that would allow clients to become self-sufficient.

In the mid-1990s, the mood of Congress and the rest of the country took a dramatic turn with regard to public welfare programs. Hailing the legislation as "the end of welfare as we know it," President Clinton signed into law the Personal Responsibility and Work Opportunity Budget Reconciliation Act of 1996 (HR 3734). This law, which eliminated AFDC as an entitlement program and replaced it with the Temporary Assistance to Needy Families (TANF) block grant, has serious implications for children. Under TANF, rigid time limits have been imposed as to how long and under what conditions clients can continue to receive assistance for themselves and their children.

The legislation also consolidates separate child-care programs created during the 1980s. In addition, it mandates changes in the Food Stamp Program, SSI for children, benefits for legal immigrants, the Child Support and Enforcement Program, and child nutrition programs (U.S. Department of Health and Human Services, Children's Bureau, 1997).

Moving into the 21st Century

In an executive memorandum dated December 14, 1996, President Clinton said:

> I am committed to giving the children waiting in our Nation's foster care system what every child in America deserves—loving parents and a healthy, stable home. The goal for every child in our Nation's public welfare system is permanence in a safe and

stable home, whether it be returning home, adoption, legal guardianship, or another permanent placement.

While the great majority of children in foster care will return home, for about one in five, returning home is not an option, and they will need another home, one that is caring and safe. These children wait far too long, typically over 3 years, but many children wait much longer to be placed in permanent homes. Each year state child welfare agencies secure homes for less than one-third of the children whose goal is adoption or an alternate permanent plan. I know we can do better. (*Adoption 2002,* 1997, p. 1)

President Clinton directed Secretary of Health and Human Services Donna Shalala to recommend strategies to move children more quickly into permanent homes and to double the number of children adopted or permanently placed during the next 5 years. In 1997, Shalala issued *Adoption 2002: A Response to the Presidential Executive Memorandum on Adoption* as a "blueprint for bipartisan federal leadership in adoption and other permanent placements for children in the public welfare system" (p. 1). The report is based on the following premises:

- Every child deserves a safe and permanent family.
- Children's health and safety are paramount concerns that must guide all child welfare services.
- Children deserve prompt and timely decision making as to their permanent caregivers.
- Permanency planning begins when a child enters foster care; foster care is a temporary setting.
- Adoption is one of the pathways to a permanent family.
- Adoptive families require supports after a child's adoption is legalized.
- The diversity and strengths of all communities must be tapped.
- Quality services must be provided as quickly as possible to enable families in crisis to address problems.

The report calls for the development of model state legislation to advance the goal of giving every child in the U.S. child welfare system a safe, permanent home. The *Adoption 2002* report concludes that

all the nation's leaders collectively share equal levels of responsibility for America's children, whether their sphere of operation is in local communities or in business, the professions, science, education, social services, or any other type of work (p. 8).

The report urges that child welfare reform be broad-based and interdisciplinary. The years ahead will bear witness to how well the country responds to this challenge.

CHANGES UNDER THE GEORGE W. BUSH ADMINISTRATION

The 1996 welfare reform legislation was re-authorized by the **Deficit Reduction Act of 2005,** signed into law by President George Bush in February 2006. The re-authorization maintains the original law's requirement that 50% of states' welfare caseloads fulfill statutory work requirements. It also updates incentives for states to reduce welfare caseloads, expands the pool of families subject to work requirements, and creates a new penalty for failing to comply with work verification procedures (U.S. Department of Health and Human Services, 2006).

Overall, the re-authorization of the Personal Responsibility and Work Opportunity Budget Reconciliation Act of 1996 tightens the focus on work requirements for recipients and strengthens state accountability.

It is clear that this reauthorization is even more restrictive than the original 1996 legislation. Early studies on the negative effects of the 1996 welfare reform law on former welfare clients have failed to convince most politicians and the general public that the United States is pursuing a social welfare policy that has disastrous consequences for millions of children and families (see Figure 11.1).

FIGURE 11.1

Who's Watching Those Kids?

Note: Ben Sargent, an editorial cartoonist with the *Austin American Statesman*, captures the essence of the systems/ecological framework and the need for giving attention to children at all levels of the environment. Reprinted with permission from the *Austin* (Texas) *American Statesman*.

Other activities at the federal level that have had an impact on children and families in recent years include the following.

- The Child and Family Services Improvement Act of 2006 reauthorized the Promoting Safe and Stable Families program for a 5-year period.
- The U.S. Children's Bureau awarded the Adoption Exchange Association in Denver $22 million over a 5-year period to operate the National Adoption Internet Photo-listing Service (AdoptUSKids).
- In an attempt to place more children with relatives rather than in non-relative foster and adoptive homes, kinship foster care was promoted as a viable foster-care placement alternative.

- The U.S. Department of Health and Human Services published a final rule to establish a new approach to monitoring state child welfare programs. Under the rule, states were to be assessed for substantial conformity with the following federal requirements for child protective, foster care, adoption, family preservation and family support, and independent services:

  - Children are, first and foremost, protected from abuse and neglect.
  - Children are safely maintained in their homes whenever possible and appropriate.
  - Children have permanency and stability in their living situations.
  - The continuity of family relationships and connections is preserved for families.

- Families have enhanced capacity to provide for their children's needs.
- Children receive appropriate services to meet their educational needs.
- Children receive adequate services to meet their physical and mental health needs.

- Proposed legislation, the Adoption Equality Act of 2005 (S1539), was introduced. This legislation would provide special federal financial assistance to all families that adopt children with disabilities or special needs.
- The Kinship Caregiver bill (S985) was introduced. This legislation calls for establishing a Kinship Navigator Program to connect families to a wide range of services and resources. The act, if passed, also would create a Kinship Guardianship Assistance program to provide federal assistance for subsidized guardianship programs. Finally, the act would require states to notify grandparents and other relatives when children enter the foster care system.
- Intended to close a loophole in federal law, the Victims of Child Abuse bill would amend the Uniform Code of Military Justice so members of the armed forces accused of child abuse would not be immune from prosecution.
- Using funds from the Department of Justice's Victims of Crime Fund, the Children's Justice Act helps states develop, establish, and operate programs designed to improve the investigation and prosecution of child abuse and neglect cases.
- The Children's Health Act of 2000 reauthorized programs within the jurisdiction of the Substance Abuse and Mental Health Services Administration to improve mental health and substance abuse services for children and adolescents, and implement proposals giving states more flexibility in the use of block grant funds with accountability based on performance. The act also consolidated discretionary grant authorities to provide more flexibility to respond to those who need mental health and substance-abuse services.
- State child welfare legislation was enacted addressing critical issues such as parent and child involvement in case planning, education of children in foster care, kinship care and guardianship, children's exposure to drug manufacturing, and tribal affairs.

Perhaps the most ambitious proposed child welfare undertaking of the new millennium is the legislation, Leave No Child Behind Act (S 448/HR 936). This omnibus legislation combines a number of previous federally-funded programs with new initiatives. The Leave No Child Behind (LNCB) legislation aims at achieving a healthy start, a head start, a fair start, a safe start, and a moral start for the nation's children. Key provisions of the proposed legislation include the following (Children's Defense Fund, 2003):

- Healthy Start: health coverage for all of the more than 9 million uninsured children in the United States, addressing childhood illnesses, and improving the quality of children's health care.
- Head Start: increased funding for child care for 3- and 4-year-olds in the Head Start program and strengthening of the education system by improving teacher training and quality, increasing public school accountability, reducing class size, and modernizing school facilities.
- Fair Start: supports for working parents to remain employed and help lift themselves and their children out of poverty, and tax relief to low-income families that currently earn too little to qualify for many tax benefits.
- Safe Start: assurance that more children are in safe, nurturing, and permanent families by extending support to families before they incur family breakdown, encouraging permanency for children who cannot stay at home safely, strengthening youth-development efforts, and addressing other safety issues such as gun violence and effective delinquency programs.

Preventive Services to Children

Although preventive services receive less attention than other types of services, many programs strengthen families and reduce the chances for family dysfunction. These include natural support systems; home-based services; parent education; child development and child-care programs; recreational, religious, and social programs; health and family-planning programs; and educational opportunities.

Natural Support Systems

Given the scarcity of formal resources, more and more attention is being directed to strengthening **natural support systems.** Many families develop social networks of friends, relatives, neighbors, or co-workers who provide emotional support; share child care, transportation, clothing, toys, and other resources; offer the opportunity to observe other children, parents, and family constellations and how they interact; and provide education about childrearing and other family life situations. But studies show that many families with problems are isolated and lack such support systems.

A key role of social services agencies, churches and synagogues, and other community organizations is to provide support systems for new families and other families who lack natural support systems. For example, some communities have established telephone support programs for various groups, through which individuals can receive information about appropriate resources.

Home-Based Services

A relatively recent focus has been on **home-based family-centered services,** services delivered to children and families in their own homes, with a goal of preserving the family system by strengthening the family to bring about needed change. Comprehensive services, usually overseen by a single case manager assigned to the family, include homemaker services, respite care, child care, crisis intervention, financial assistance, substance-abuse treatment, vocational counseling, and help in locating housing and transportation.

Most home-based service programs include the following features (Crosson-Tower, 2005a):

- a primary worker or case manager who establishes and maintains a supportive, nurturing relationship with the family;
- small caseloads with a variety of service options used with each family;
- a team approach, in which team members provide some services and serve as a backup to the primary worker/case manager;
- a support system available 24 hours a day for crisis calls and emergencies;
- the home as the natural setting, with maximum use of natural support systems, including the family, extended family, neighborhood, and community;
- parents remaining in charge of and responsible for their families as educators, nurturers, and primary caregivers; and
- willingness to invest at least as much in providing home-based services to a family as society is willing to pay for out-of-home care for our children.

Most families receiving home-based, family-centered services are those with multiple needs that have received fragmented services from a number of agencies over time. Typically, children from these families have spent some time in substitute care. Because of the chronic and severe problems in these families and their repeated crises, past efforts have been largely ineffective.

Home-based family-centered services are based on a systems/ecological approach to family intervention, viewing the entire family as the unit of help. Intervention is short-term and goal-oriented, aimed at specific behavioral change. Intensive services usually are provided to families for 60 to 90 days—which averages out to the same number of families a worker providing traditional child welfare services serves during the course of a year.

Providing intensive services to a limited number of families at home has significant benefits. First, it gives workers a chance to stabilize the family so it can function either independently or with fewer services while allowing the children to remain in the home. Second, it allows workers to determine more quickly and with more documentation if the family cannot be stabilized. This enables children to be placed in adoptive homes, if indicated, rather than remain in limbo in either a dysfunctional, life-threatening family situation or the instability of foster care.

Research has shown that, for the most part, short-term gains achieved by family-preservation programs do not persist over time. This suggests that these programs may want to consider a shift from preventing placement to improving family and child functioning, directed to specific groups of families instead of broad groups of families with a wide variety of problems, and offering different durations of service and intensity that address the unique needs of each family (WESTAT and James Bell Associates, 2002; U.S. Children's Bureau, 2003).

Parent Education

While math and English are school staples, little attention is given to one of the most important roles that children are likely to play as adults: being a parent. Many communities offer parenting classes aimed at a wide range of parents: prenatal classes for parents before the birth or adoption of their first infant, classes for parents of toddlers and preschoolers, classes for parents of school-age children, and classes for parents of adolescents. These programs offer education about basic developmental stages of children and adolescents and alternative methods of childrearing and discipline. They also encourage the development of mutual support systems among participants, who often relax about their roles as parents when they realize that other parents have similar concerns and struggles.

An example of a successful parent-education prevention effort is Healthy Families America, launched by the National Committee for the Prevention of Child Abuse in partnership with Ronald McDonald Children's Charities in 1992. The goals of the program are to promote positive parenting, to enhance child health and development, and to prevent child abuse and neglect. Healthy Families America programs are found in more than 430 communities throughout the United States and Canada. Overall, 90% of families invited to participate in the program accept these services (Healthy Families America, 2006, p.1).

Education about the various types of family problems—and, if they occur, about resources available—is a significant form of prevention. And many communities offer programs specifically about sexual abuse of children and how to avoid it by teaching children about types of touch and what to do when they find themselves in an uncomfortable situation with an adult or older child. Finally, some communities offer education in the form of alcohol and drug awareness programs.

Child Development and Child-Care Programs

Accessible, high-quality child-care programs that are affordable for working parents, particularly single parents, can help to prevent family breakdown. These programs provide a safe, comfortable, nurturing environment for children while their parents work, thereby reducing parental stress. Many child-care programs offer additional opportunities for parents, including parenting education classes, babysitting cooperatives, and social programs, as well as the opportunity to develop support systems with other parents and children. But affordable, high-quality, child-care programs often are unavailable to working parents, particularly in inner-city and rural areas. Child care for infants, children with disabilities or other special needs, school-age children during vacations and holidays, and children who are ill also is not widely available in the United States. An additional gap in services relates to evening and night child care for parents who must work two jobs or late shifts.

Although special programs are available for low-income parents, they often are limited in the hours and in the number of children they can serve. Head Start—perhaps the most successful federal program established under the Office of Economic Opportunity in the 1960s—provides a developmental learning program for preschool children, as well as health care, social services, and parent education. Also available to some parents on a limited basis are infant–parent centers that allow parents an opportunity to learn how to interact and play with their children and stimulate their development.

Recreational, Religious, and Social Programs

When discussing programs that strengthen the welfare of children and their families, the broader social, recreational, and religious programs must be included. Faith-based organizations such as churches and synagogues meet the spiritual, emotional, social, and recreational needs of many children, youth, and families. They can play a major role in establishing special preventive services, such as child-care programs, outreach centers, and parent education programs.

Federal faith-based initiatives have come under criticism from groups claiming that these programs violate the separation of church and state provisions of the U.S. Constitution. Other concerns revolve around whether faith-based organizations have the professional staff resources required to deliver services effectively and efficiently. Increasingly, the business community is providing preventive services through the workplace, including informational programs during the lunch hour for working parents, recreational facilities and programs for employees and their families, and the facilitation of co-worker support systems. Many communities offer substantial recreation and family entertainment programs for families without charge. Most communities, however, seem to lack programs geared to adolescents. Some experts attribute increases in adolescent problems, including teen pregnancy and delinquency, to the lack of available programs for this age group.

Health and Family-Planning Programs

Early health screening can reduce child and family problems (Children's Defense Fund, 2006; Federal Interagency Forum on Child and Family Statistics, 2003). Health problems place increased stress on families, and access to affordable health care from prenatal care to adulthood is vital in helping to prevent family breakdown. In addition, programs can assist families in deciding whether to become parents and in exploring options when pregnancy occurs.

In 2003, 324,064 babies were born weighing less than 2,500 grams (about 5.5 pounds). These babies are at high risk for developmental problems and infant mortality (Children's Defense Fund, 2006), but potential problems can be reduced substantially through comprehensive prenatal care (Bavier, 2004; National Committee for Quality Assurance, 2006; U.S. Department of Health and Human Services, 2003).

Educational Opportunities

Most studies identify the strong relationship between difficulties in school and individual and family problems (Epstein, Sanders, Simon, Salwas, Jansorn, & Van Voohis, 2002; Maran, 2000; Patrikakou et al., 2005; Sanders, 2005; Walsh, 2006; Weiss, Kreider, Lopez, & Chatman, 2005). Programs that offer children an opportunity to learn in ways that help them feel good about themselves and develop a sense of competence help to prevent family and child-related problems. As a result, these children are less likely to have children themselves while they are in school, to drop out of school, or to live their lives in poverty. School-based social services allow for close cooperation among children and adolescents, teachers and school administrators, parents, and the community.

School Social Work

A specialized field involving services to children, youth, and families is school social work. **School social work**—social services offered in a school-based setting—provides the opportunity to identify needs of children and their families early and to facilitate early intervention before problems become more serious. Social workers in school settings offer parenting education and facilitate positive mental health for children through special outreach programs in the school.

School social work includes individual, family, and group counseling, as well as crisis intervention services. School social workers deal with suicidal students; students and their families and friends in the aftermath of serious injury or death; and students in conflict with family members, peers, or school authorities (see Box 11.2 for an account of a school social worker in an inner-city elementary school).

School social workers are members of intervention teams that work with children who have developmental disabilities and other special needs, often as liaison to parents and the community when special services are needed. The Education for All Handicapped Children Act has been updated to specify that schools may hire social workers to provide social services to special-needs children. Dropout-prevention legislation in some states also suggests the hiring of social workers. School-based social-work services are advantageous for many reasons, including:

- The social worker sees the child or adolescent in a natural setting, interacting with peers, teachers, and school administrators, which gives the social worker a different perspective than seeing a client in an office or agency.

School-based social services help many children and youth address emotional needs and become successful academically. Here, two social work interns develop plans for a group session they are co-facilitating with fifth graders to help them better manage feelings of frustration and anger.

© Heinle/Index Stock

BOX 11.2
A Day in the Life of a School Social Worker

- 8 A.M.: A student is in my office waiting to talk. He says he is 7 years old and he is crying.
- Last night, he said, his 16-year-old brother took his gun, drove to the park, and shot himself dead. The little boy knew his brother was upset and had tried to talk to him. The family had hidden the gun. The little boy thought he could have stopped it from happening.
- As I am talking with this student, a frantic call comes in from the school office. A 7-year-old girl is bruised and battered. The secretary says the little girl is shaking like a leaf. I ask a social work intern to help the little boy find a quiet place to try to rest, as he had not slept the night before. The girl had got in the middle of a domestic violence episode the night before. Her drunk stepfather came over in the middle of the night, beat her mother, trashed the place, tore out the phone, battered the child, and vowed to return. After comforting the child, I ask her to draw pictures of her feelings while I report the abuse to CPS and check on the boy.

- Another call from the office. An 8-year-old's father had overdosed the previous weekend. He is dead. The little girl had just returned to school.
- The 7-year-old girl draws a 6-page "story" of the night's events. She says she is scared about her stepfather returning. Together we come up with a plan for her, pending investigation of the abuse and a home visit to her mother:

  - Ask to stay at her grandmother's place temporarily. If that can't be arranged, follow the next steps.
  - Crawl out of her bedroom window.
  - Wake the neighbors by screaming "Help! Help!!! Call 911!!"
  - Pound on their door.

- A regular student in the CIS Program* drops by. She is 7 years old and is very sad. She and her mother and sister have been homeless for months. She has not seen her older sister since spring break. Her mother is using drugs again. They are staying at a man's apartment. His name is "Killer."

- The social worker has access to a large number of children and families in need of services.
- The social worker can help parents and school personnel apply a systems/ecological approach to better address the child's needs, encompassing the child, home, school, and broader community.
- The social worker can help school personnel understand the importance of family and community variables in relation to the child's capacity to function in the school setting.

Services to Children and Families at Risk

A lack of coordination among service providers is a problem identified by service providers and recipients alike. Some communities have made special efforts to increase coordination, avoid duplication, and reduce gaps in services available to at-risk children and families. These include

- "first-stop" resource centers where families can receive thorough assessments so they

- A CPS worker arrives to interview a 5-year-old boy who had been found "having sex" with a 7-year-old boy at the babysitter's place over the weekend.
- I talk with the CPS worker about the 7-year-old girl who reported being abused by her stepfather. The CPS worker will see the child today!
- The 4-year-old girl I had just begun to work with has not arrived at school. The day before, I had made a CPS report for medical neglect, as she has open sores all over her head. She has been identified as having a developmental delay. Her height, weight, and head circumference are all below the 10th percentile. She comes to school dirty and wearing inappropriate clothing. Her mom says she has never seen a doctor and the mom refuses to come to any appointments, even for immunizations provided at the school. The other six children appear to be healthy and well fed.
- And finally I make time to talk with the 10-year-old CIS student who the afternoon before had picked up her little brother out

of a pool of blood and called 911. She had been watching him outside, and he was hit in the crossfire by two bullets. He is in a coma. The 10-year-old is in two of our "pre-employment" groups—"child care club" and "nurse assistants."
- 7 P.M.: I end the day by writing this to process the events so I might be able to sleep tonight. I also remind myself of all the children in similar circumstances who have been helped by our program and hope that we can improve the situations for the children I saw today as well.

---

*CIS Program—the Communities in Schools Program directed by the school social worker.

Source: From a report by Deborah Selbin, a school social worker and program manager of an inner-city, social services program at the elementary level. The program is part of Communities in Schools-Central Texas, a dropout-prevention program for at-risk children and their families. Used with permission.

can be referred to appropriate agencies rather than going from agency to agency only to learn that services are not available to them or do not meet their needs;
- computerized databases that contain critical information about the services available to the target population;
- centralized information and referral systems;
- co-location of offices and programs; and
- coordinated multi-agency service networks.

Through such efforts, at-risk families—often reluctant to trust service providers and without

transportation to access services—can receive individual and family counseling, complete forms to receive public assistance, get help in finding employment and housing, and attend parenting classes and parent support groups—all at the same location.

Health and Hospital Outreach Programs

Many health clinics and hospitals have established special programs to address the needs of children and families who are at risk of family disruption or dysfunction. (These and other services to families at risk are shown in Box 11.3.) Some clinics have high-risk infant programs, for example, that provide intensive services to teenage parents, parents of low birthweight or premature infants or infants with disabilities, parents with substance-abuse problems, and parents who have not established appropriate relationships with their children. Clinics offer a variety of services, such as weekly outreach programs conducted by a public health nurse, individual counseling, play groups for children and support groups for parents, role modeling of appropriate child care, and assistance in obtaining other resources as needed.

Hospitals offer similar programs. In some hospitals, specially trained nurses identify at-risk mothers in the delivery room and work with hospital social workers to give those mothers intensive care and support during their hospitalization, in addition to outreach services for both parents after the hospital stay. These programs, in some instances, help parents realize that they do not wish to be parents and assist them in relinquishing the children for adoption or placing them in foster care.

Often, programs in health settings are developed to prevent child abuse and neglect and help parents achieve positive relationships with their children. In response to an identified need, pediatric AIDS programs have been established in many major metropolitan area hospitals, to attempt to stabilize the health of infants and older children infected with HIV. Because many parents do not want to or cannot care for children with HIV and it is difficult to locate foster families that are willing to do so, many children with HIV remain in the hospital for an extended time.

In some areas, special health clinics provide services for adolescents. Clinics offer basic health care; information on adolescent development and puberty and sexually transmitted infections and diseases; and, in some instances, pregnancy tests, contraceptive information, and prenatal care. Some clinics of this type are located in public high schools. Although this has caused some controversy, the results reveal that physical and emotional problems, sexually transmitted infections and diseases, and pregnancies have decreased significantly in these schools.

Child Care

Although most child-care programs are targeted at working parents, child care also is a service for non-working parents. Some parents need respite from their children and from attending to their needs 24 hours a day. Child care for these parents can be either in the home or elsewhere. In any case, it gives parents time to meet their own needs while offering children emotional support that their parents may not be able to provide. This service is less costly than foster care and less traumatic for the child.

Child-care providers in many states receive special training to enable them to work more effectively with at-risk parents and children. In some instances, child-care providers develop surrogate parent or positive role relationships with parents, giving them and their children much needed emotional support.

Parents under extreme stress can reach a point where they will maltreat the child and may lack natural support systems to help them during a crisis. In particular, families with children who have severe developmental disabilities often need extra support. Many communities have established crisis or respite care programs for such families. Some agencies have respite-care programs for parents of children with developmental disabilities, in which specially trained adults care for children evenings or weekends so parents can have time to themselves. Other communities have established crisis nurseries or shelters, where parents under severe stress or in a serious emergency can leave their children for a limited time. Some programs even provide emergency transportation for the children to get out of the home. Most crisis programs require counseling for parents while their children are in crisis care.

BOX 11.3
Support Service Options for Families at Risk

Informal Support to Participants: Opportunities for informal nurturing and interaction among participants and between participants and staff members to facilitate acceptance and support.

Parent Education: Formal and informal instruction, self-development programming, and modeling of healthy parent-child interaction for program participants.

Peer Support Groups and Peer Counseling: Opportunities for parents to share experiences, successes, and frustrations, as well as gain insights into other parents' methods of carrying out their childrearing responsibilities.

Recreation Services: Opportunities to develop new interests, learn new skills, and have fun.

Early Developmental Screening: Early and continuing developmental screening of infants and children to reinforce healthy child development and to identify potential developmental problems or delays.

Enhancement of Child Development: Developmentally appropriate activities that enhance child development, as well as model appropriate adult–child interaction.

Child (Day) Care Services: Developmentally appropriate child care for children during the day.

Home Visits: Visits to the home designed to assist parents in structuring a safe, caring, stimulating home environment for their children.

Referral and Linkage to Appropriate Resources: Assistance to families in obtaining health, mental health, social service, education, employment, and other services they may need, and follow-up to ensure that those services have been received.

Outreach: Outreach in communities to assure that isolated parents are aware of, and have full opportunities to participate in, available programs.

Education and Job Skill Development: Assistance in completing education, obtaining employment, and upgrading job skills.

Specialized Services for Adolescent Parents: Education and discussion groups on sexuality and sexual responsibilities, referral for reproductive health care, assistance in returning to school or obtaining a GED certificate, life-skills education, tutoring or homework assistance, involvement of extended family members and significant others, job orientation and training, parent–child interaction groups, groups for adolescent males and adolescent fathers, and discussion groups on personal growth and development.

Source: Adapted and reproduced by permission of the Child Welfare League of America. From *Child Welfare League of America Standards for Services to Strengthen and Preserve Families with Children* (Washington, DC: Author, 1990), pp. 18–24.

Adolescents often can benefit from specialized services, and some communities offer respite care for adolescents who need time away from their parents. Most emergency-shelter facilities for teens also provide crisis and family counseling to help stabilize the situation so the teen can return home. In many areas, however, special services for teens are lacking. In some communities the only resource available for children as young as 12 or 13 is the Salvation Army's general shelter.

One group that is receiving more attention lately consists of working parents, particularly the working poor, whose inability to find affordable child care can be the last straw before a crisis. These families are more likely to be at risk and under severe stress, and some single parents lose their jobs because of the lack of child care.

Homemaker Services

Many agencies provide homemaker services to families that are at risk or have neglected or abused their children. Homemakers are specially trained individuals, often indigenous to the community, who have been parents themselves and can serve as a nurturing, supportive role model for other parents. Homemakers offer practical suggestions and education about housekeeping, child care, nutrition and cooking, health and safety, shopping, budgeting, and access to community resources. In addition, they often serve as surrogate parents, developing positive, trusting relationships with family members who have been isolated. Homemaker services are far more cost-effective than out-of-home care and may prevent separation of children from their parents.

Crisis Intervention Programs

Various community agencies provide **crisis intervention** services to families, to de-escalate the crisis. This intervention frequently results in a subsequent referral for additional help, such as counseling. Law-enforcement agencies in many communities have crisis intervention teams that handle domestic disputes, including spouse and child abuse. Some youth shelters include crisis intervention for adolescents and their parents. Hospitals, too, provide crisis intervention services in emergency rooms, dealing with child maltreatment, family violence, and other serious family problems.

Intervention frequently is more effective in a crisis situation than in a non-crisis situation, because the crisis throws the family into a state of disequilibrium. Studies show that families are more receptive to change and more readily agree to services such as counseling at these times because their usual defenses and the family balance are no longer intact.

Counseling

In many communities, individual, marital, and family counseling services are available for families with problems. Mental health centers, social service agencies, child and family service agencies, child-guidance clinics, employee-assistance programs, churches, schools, youth services programs, and hospital outreach programs are various types of counseling services (see Box 11.4 for a young woman's experience with her school district's teen parent program). These services often are available on a limited basis, because of scarce resources in relation to the large number of persons needing services, or available only on a fee basis. Specialized counseling to address problems such as family violence or sexual abuse is unavailable in many communities.

For many problems, group counseling has been shown to be more effective than individual counseling, and a combination of the two may be more effective than individual counseling alone. For example, children who have been sexually abused need to hear from other children that they are not the only ones who have had that experience. Sexual and physical abusers, as well as others with family problems, typically deny their problem, and group therapy sessions with others in similar situations are apt to break down their defenses more quickly than individual counseling.

Family counseling is garnering more attention as an effective means of strengthening individual functioning and addressing needs. Family counseling has been shown to be effective in helping families understand behavior and coping patterns, establish more productive communication patterns, identify needs and resolve problems, and support each other as family members. In almost all situations in which a family member has a problem or is undergoing a stressful change, family counseling can help the entire family reinforce positive changes, address negative patterns appropriately, and serve as a source of support to each other.

Some agencies have initiated multi-family groups—groups of families that receive therapy jointly. Individuals frequently can see their own issues and family dynamics more clearly while watching other families interact, because they are too involved when these interactions occur within their own families. Teenagers, for example, are more likely to listen to another parent who offers feedback than to their own parents, and parents, too, may be more likely to listen to other teens or parents than to family members.

Social workers have played an important role in this shift from individual to family counseling. In particular, social workers emphasize the strengths of family members and of the family as a total system, building on those strengths to make the system more supportive of its individual members.

Support and Self-Help Groups

Support groups and **self-help groups** are effective ways of helping children, youth, and families cope with family problems. These groups help individuals realize that they are not the only ones coping with a given problem. They also assist members in developing new ways to cope as they learn from each other. Perhaps most impor-

tant, persons who see themselves as being inadequate have a chance to reach out and give something to someone else. Examples of self-help groups are:

- 12-step programs such as Alcoholics Anonymous for alcoholics, Al-Anon for family members of alcoholics, Alateen for teen family members of alcoholics, Narcotics Anonymous, and Adult Children of Alcoholics;
- Parents Anonymous and Circle of Parents for abusive or potentially abusive parents;
- Parents United for sexually abusive parents;
- Tough Love for parents of out-of-control adolescents; and
- Parents Without Partners for single parents.

Many communities have established support groups for adults, children, or teens dealing with divorce, stepparenting, the death of a loved one or other type of loss, or those living with a family member with a physical or emotional disability. Schools have established support groups for students who have difficulty functioning within the school setting, coping with family problems such as divorce or abuse, and recovering from substance abuse, as well as for students who are teen parents. With constrained resources, social service agencies are realizing that in many instances more individuals and families can be served effectively through support and self-help groups.

Volunteer and Outreach Programs

Most traditional social services agencies are overloaded and can provide only limited services— and those services to only the families with the most severe problems. A number of these agencies have established volunteer components; others use volunteers exclusively to perform the work of the agency. Because they are able to spend more time with families, volunteers can prevent family disruption and can be highly successful in intervention. Most volunteer programs have effective screening mechanisms for recruiting volunteers with good nurturing skills who

BOX 11.4
Impact of Social Work Intervention

Elena Vasquez grew up in an inner-city area with her mother and five brothers and sisters. Her father left the family when Elena was a toddler, and her mother worked long hours to try to keep the family fed and clothed until her diabetic condition prevented her from keeping a job. Forced to go on welfare, Elena's mother became depressed and was in and out of the hospital constantly as her diabetes created additional health problems.

As the oldest girl living at home, Elena took care of her brothers and sisters and tried to maintain the household. Increasingly behind in school and lacking attention from adults and peers her own age, she fell in love with a neighbor boy at age 13 and became pregnant at 14. Although she tried to stay in school, after the baby was born she found it increasingly difficult to care for her infant, her siblings, and her mother.

Leaving her baby with her boyfriend's mother in the afternoons, Elena got a part-time job at a fast-food restaurant so her family could have some additional income. Overwhelmed with life, Elena's boyfriend and his family provided her with emotional support, and 6 months after the birth of her first baby, Elena found herself pregnant again. A short time later, however, her boyfriend found another girlfriend, leaving Elena alone and discouraged.

Desperate, Elena went to her junior high school counselor, who sent her to the school district's special program for teen parents. There she was assigned to meet regularly with a social work intern from a neighboring university. The intern referred Elena's mother to a nearby health clinic that was better able to meet her health-care needs and got her siblings involved with the school social workers at their schools.

Seeing an incredible resiliency in Elena, the intern slowly gained Elena's trust and helped her realize the potential she had to create a viable life for herself, her baby, and her soon-to-be-born child. Elena met with the intern weekly

can relate well to clients. Many have been parents themselves, some are grandparents, and others are students or are involved in human services already. Volunteers usually receive extensive training and are supervised by a social work case manager.

Two examples of states and communities with successful volunteer programs are Suspected Child Abuse and Neglect (SCAN) of Arkansas, and Family Outreach Centers established by the National Council of Jewish Women. Both use highly trained volunteers to work one-to-one with abusive and neglecting families. The SCAN model is based on a re-parenting framework, which aims first to develop trust, then to work through the stages of

psychosocial development that the parents missed during their own childhood. Volunteers in these programs visit often and converse with parents and children, assist in problem solving and gaining access to community resources, and serve as a surrogate parent/role model/friend to parents and family members.

Similar programs have been developed in which volunteers work with teenage parents and abused and neglected children. In the national Big Brothers/Big Sisters program, for example, volunteers are paired with children from single-parent families, as friends and role models. Volunteer programs like the ones mentioned here can help families stay together (Center for Urban for the remainder of the year. Her attendance was almost perfect, and she soon was getting excellent grades. Then, when Elena was 15, she vowed to become a social worker just like the intern and work with teenagers who become pregnant.

Although life wasn't easy for her, Elena graduated from high school and, because of her experiences with her mother's health, got a job at a local health clinic. A hard worker who was highly motivated, Elena moved up through the support staff ranks quickly and became a clinic supervisor. When her children started school, Elena began taking classes at the local community college. Slowly she progressed through school while working full-time, volunteering at the local battered women's shelter and a nursing home, and providing exceptional care for her children, attending their sports events and prodding them to do well academically.

When her children were in junior high school, and her oldest child the same age Elena had been when she first became pregnant, Elena transferred to the social work program at the state university. In her senior year she asked to do her internship at the same agency where she had been a client 15 years ago. After determining that Elena was mature enough to work with pregnant teens without her own personal experiences influencing her work with clients, the university placed Elena in one of the agency's teen parent programs.

While Elena was an intern, the funding for the agency was being reviewed by the state legislature, and she asked to testify on behalf of the program and share with legislators the impact the program had had on her life. As you can imagine, Elena's testimony was powerful and well received. At this point, Elena has graduated and is working with teen parents as a case manager at the agency. Her children are doing well in school and making plans for their own careers.

Policy and Environment, 2003). Given the continuing increase in the number of families needing services and the declining resources available to help them, volunteer programs are likely to assume a larger role in the future (U.S. Department of Labor, 2005).

Programs for at-risk families are funded by federal, state, and local governments, as well as the private sector, of which the United Way is a prominent example, providing assistance to families at risk in many communities throughout the nation. Faith-based organizations, foundations, and private contributions fund other programs. Increasingly, public–private partnerships are being developed with funding from a variety of sources. State and local governments are contracting with private agencies to provide services, and many private agencies receive funding from multiple sources, both public and private.

Which entity should pay for what type of services? This is a complex issue at all levels in the United States as the number of at-risk families continues to expand while federal and state funding programs decline. And local governments, employers, and private contributors are not always able or willing to provide the needed assistance. New ways of providing services, along with new and more effective ways of cost sharing, will have to be explored in more depth during the first decade of the 21st century.

Child Protective Services

The federal Child Abuse and Neglect Prevention and Treatment Act (CAPTA, as amended) mandates that all states designate a single agency to oversee services to abused and neglected children and their families. These services usually come under the rubric of **child protective services (CPS).** Families reported to that agency as being abusive or neglectful must be investigated by the agency to ascertain whether the maltreatment report can be substantiated. All states have statutes establishing a minimum standard of care that caregivers are expected to provide to their children. If the worker investigating the case determines that parents are not meeting this standard, the family is slated to receive protective services. This is an involuntary program—that is, the parents did not request or volunteer to receive the services.

Investigations of Child Maltreatment

In implementing the mandated services, CPS workers cooperate closely with other professionals, including law-enforcement officers, attorneys, health-care providers, and educators. Child protective services workers assume a variety of roles in cooperation or jointly with other agencies. They may offer intake services, in which they screen reports of child maltreatment, interviewing persons who report cases by phone to obtain the information necessary to make a preliminary determination about how serious the report is and if it requires immediate investigation. Most states require that life-threatening situations be investigated immediately or within 24 to 48 hours, and that less serious cases be investigated within 10 days.

CPS workers, by themselves or jointly with law-enforcement officers, conduct investigations of child maltreatment, interviewing children, parents, other family members, and collateral contacts such as teachers and neighbors, to determine the nature and extent of the reported maltreatment. Investigations involve examining and interviewing the child, attending to the child's immediate emotional needs during the investigation, and making a preliminary assessment about whether maltreatment is occurring. If a positive finding is confirmed, investigators determine whether the maltreatment is causing or could cause permanent damage to the child's body or mind, how severe the maltreatment has been, and whether the situation is life-threatening and warrants immediately removing the child to a safer environment.

In some instances, other resources, such as physicians, are asked to assist in gathering the needed information. Investigations of child maltreatment require knowledge and skill in identifying various types of maltreatment, as well as interviewing techniques appropriate with children and adults who may be apprehensive and reluctant to cooperate Achieving a balance between authority and compassion, or between the ability to confront and the ability to be empathic, is one of the challenges of being a child protective services worker (Brittain & Hunt, 2004; Brown, 2002; Crosson-Tower, 2005a).

Determination of Intervention

Following the investigation of child maltreatment, the situation is assessed to determine the most appropriate actions to take. CPS workers are not expected to prove that the maltreatment is a criminal offense or to determine who perpetrated the maltreatment. Those actions are within the domain of the courts. Rather, the role of CPS workers is to determine whether the child has to be protected and what is needed to provide that protection. When assessing a possible situation of child maltreatment, workers have four options:

1. Determine that the child is not being maltreated and withdraw from the case.
2. Offer help to the family.

3. Determine that the child is at serious risk and/or that the parents are uncooperative, and make arrangements to take the family to court.
4. With the court's permission, remove the child from the home immediately and place the child in emergency care (and, later, usually foster care).

Usually CPS workers determine that, although services are required, leaving a child in the home is safe while the services are being provided. When children are removed from the home, this is done most often for the following reasons:

- The child or a sibling has been seriously injured or abandoned.
- The parent/caregiver states that he or she is going to injure or kill the child.
- Evidence suggests that the child has been sexually abused and the perpetrator is still in the home or has easy access to the child.
- A current crisis exists, such as a psychotic parent or a parent in jail because of a crime connected with substance abuse.
- The parents are not cooperative, and the child is at serious risk for substantial harm.

Like other helping professionals, CPS workers are most effective if they identify strengths in their clients and the clients' environment and work to empower clients to make choices that will keep the children safe. But if, after trying to provide mandated services to a family, protective services workers believe that the family is resisting services and is making choices that fail to keep the child(ren) safe, CPS workers may take the case to court and request that the court order services. In so doing, if the family does not comply, the worker can bring the case back into court and request more serious options, such as placing the child in foster care. Some states mandate court involvement with all families receiving child protective services.

The issue of when to involve the court in CPS cases does not have universal agreement.

Advocates for early involvement argue that it gives workers leverage in dealing with families because the authority of the courts is present immediately. Advocates for limited involvement believe that most families are more receptive to services without court action because families feel empowered and thus can maintain a less adversarial relationship with their worker.

A number of states are developing two-track CPS programs: (a) clients who can be charged with criminal charges under the auspices of an investigative unit, and (b) the majority of other clients under the auspices of an assessment/intervention unit. Proponents of this approach believe it will remove the adversarial relationship that arises when a law enforcement investigation is done for families that need family preservation or other supportive services (Madden, 2003; Stein, 2004; Vernon, 2005).

Typical Services Provided

CPS workers provide a variety of services to the families with whom they work, including

- making every effort to ensure that children can be safe in their own homes;
- serving as case managers—arranging for community resources such as housing, employment, transportation, counseling, health services, child care, homemaker services, or financial assistance;
- providing counseling, parent education, and support;
- helping clients get involved in a parent support group or be assigned a volunteer; and
- developing a contract with a parent that delineates specific goals the family must accomplish to be removed from the child protective services caseload.

Providing CPS services is challenging because of the emotional aspects of working with abused and neglected children and the multiple roles that CPS workers must play. A number of national organizations, including the Child Welfare

League of America, the American Association for Protecting Children, and the American Public Human Services Association, have established specialized training for staff, and have explored with states new ways to provide protective services. Many states have adopted a computerized risk-management system that helps workers assess family situations and needs and the safety of children involved.

CPS agencies also are expanding their efforts to collaborate with other systems that come in contact with abused and neglected children, and promoting collaboration between child welfare and domestic violence programs. Domestic violence and child abuse often appear within the same families, and programs targeted at them serve overlapping populations. Collaborative training, shared use of resources, and coordinated case-management efforts can remove many barriers that prevent women from being harmed when their children are under protection, or vice versa. These programs strengthen the concept of family preservation. In some battered women's shelters, for example, a family preservation worker is assigned to the shelter to work onsite with the program's clients and their children (U.S. Children's Bureau, 2006a; Chalk, Gibbons, & Scarupa, 2002).

As reports of child maltreatment continue to increase and involve children who are injured more severely than in the past, the role of CPS as part of the child and family service delivery system is undergoing extensive debate. Because of the scarcity of resources, CPS is the dominating child welfare service in many communities. Although CPS agencies once publicized their role as providing services to children and families to prevent child maltreatment from occurring or recurring, their overriding message at present is that they protect children.

Because of staff shortages, many agencies can barely respond to all the reports they receive and are unable to investigate all except the most serious reports. With increases in child maltreatment, attributed in part to more extensive use of crack and cocaine, poverty, and homelessness, the emphasis of child protective services is more often one of "damage control" rather than intensive services. This shift in philosophy places other community organizations in the role of preventing child maltreatment, as well as providing the extensive services needed to keep it from recurring.

Family Preservation Services

Today the emphasis is on keeping together families that would have been separated in the past. These families have complex needs, often involving some form of child maltreatment, substance abuse, or children exhibiting oppositional behavior or delinquency in the home, school, and community (Crosson-Tower, 2005a). The goals of family preservation programs are to

- allow children to remain safely in their own home,
- maintain and strengthen family bonds,
- stabilize the crisis situation that precipitated any need for outside placement,
- increase the family's coping skills and competencies, and
- facilitate the family's use of appropriate and informal helping resources.

Efforts in family preservation have built on the permanency-planning emphasis of the late-1970s, after several studies found that many children were remaining in foster care with little attention to alternatives.

In reaction to more children—particularly children of color and those living in poverty—being removed from their own homes and placed in foster care, attention turned to finding ways to keep families together or to reunite children with their biological families rather than leaving the children to languish in foster care. In most instances, because of insufficient resources, efforts to work with families were limited and families generally were viewed as a large part of the problem rather than the solution.

The Adoption Assistance and Child Welfare Act of 1980 (Public Law 96-272) required that efforts be made to avoid family disruption, reunify families after separation, and place children in permanent settings if they could not be reunited. The number of family preservation programs grew rapidly in the 1980s. Based on traditional social work practice, they emphasize home visits and intensive approaches with high-risk families. Currently there are more than 400 family preservation programs in the United States.

Horchak-Andino (2003) delineated the following three types of family preservation programs:

1. *family support programs,* which usually are community-based and provide support and education services;
2. *family-centered preventive programs,* which provide case management; counseling, and education for families with problems that threaten their stability; and
3. *intensive family preservation services,* designed for families in crisis when removal of the child is imminent or reunification with the family is under way.

Although the programs vary, they offer crisis intervention, staff members available to provide around-the-clock services if needed, low caseloads, and highly intensive, time-limited services similar to other in-home services described previously.

In working with families, family preservation programs incorporate a family systems perspective. Thus, they view families that need services as being in disequilibrium or out of balance because the needs of various family members are unmet. The emphasis in family preservation programs is on empowering family members to get their needs met and develop new skills in problem solving and communication to stabilize the family system.

Family preservation social workers do not blame families for failure (Biddleman & Doyle, 2002). The model is based on the assumption that the family has a significant influence on children and that separation has detrimental effects on parents and children alike. Through role modeling, counseling, and interactions with family members, the program stresses values, respect, listening rather than giving advice, and help with goal setting, coping, and problem-solving skills.

Social workers try to connect with and get to know all family members in a nonjudgmental way. At the first stage of services, concrete needs, such as housing and food, are addressed. As the social worker develops a relationship with the family, the emphasis is consistent with good social work practice—not on diagnosis and labeling but, instead, on understanding the day-to-day reality of the family and how it functions. Interventions often involve contracting, encouraging, and reframing of issues (Crosson-Tower, 2005a; Horchak-Andino, 2003).

Evaluation of family preservation programs is difficult because families' needs and how they are addressed vary, as do the interventions used. Programs, too, are finding that, although the original program goal was to prevent out-of-home placement of a child or adolescent, the program may not be able to prevent such a placement and that sometimes out-of-home placements are necessary. Other outcome measures, such as an increase in positive communication among family members, have yet to be studied (WESTAT and James Bell Associates, 2002).

Substitute Care

Sometimes the best solution is to remove children from their own homes. Parents may have too many unmet needs of their own, or be too uninterested in parenting to care for their children adequately. In such situations, **substitute care** is located for the children involved. Unless the situation is an emergency—which many state laws define as a life-threatening situation—a child protective services worker cannot remove a child from a family without a court order. Even with emergency removals, court orders must be obtained, usually within 24 hours, and hearings held with parents present.

Substitute care is of different types. In many communities, crisis shelters are available to take in children 24 hours a day until a family situation can be stabilized or other care that best meets a child's needs can be located. Attempts are made to place children with relatives or neighbors so that they can remain in their immediate environment, but this is not always possible. Other types of substitute care include foster homes, group homes, residential treatment facilities, and psychiatric treatment facilities.

Once a child is placed in substitute care, the worker (in collaboration with the family, if possible, and with the child, depending on the child's age) must develop a plan either to return the child to the home or to terminate parental rights and place the child in an adoptive family. Under federal law, the court must review the case every 6 months to ensure that the child is not in limbo in the child welfare system.

If a child does require placement in substitute care, every effort should be made to ensure that the placement is the *least restrictive* option. After first considering relatives, neighbors, and others with whom the child is familiar and those individuals fail to meet the criteria to be positive substitute parents for the child, consideration is given to finding care that is consistent with the child's cultural background, preferably in the same neighborhood or school area. Usually it is deemed important that the birth parents visit the child (if this is in the best interests of the child), so attention must be given to accessibility of the parents.

Foster Care

If appropriate relative or kinship placements or other suitable arrangements are not possible, the child most often is placed in foster care. **Foster care** means that children live in homes with families other than their birth parents until they are returned to their birth parents or adopted. Foster parents are recruited and trained to relate to children and their birth parents. They are often parents already and may take in more than one foster child. Many foster parents keep in touch with their foster children after they leave, and some adopt the children if they become available for adoption.

All states have strict standards regarding foster care, including training that individuals must complete before becoming and continuing as foster parents, the number of children foster parents can take, appropriate discipline and treatment of the children, and supervision of foster parents. A number of states train foster parents to parent certain types of children—for example, adolescents, children with AIDS, or children who have been sexually abused. Foster parents also develop support systems, and many belong to local and national foster parent organizations. Foster parents are paid monthly to care for each child, but they often spend more than they receive, in addition to giving the children love and attention (CWLA, 2006).

Currently, almost all children who require foster care have been abused or neglected. Because more children whose safety is threatened are being removed from their homes, the need for additional foster parents is acute nationwide. Many localities are having difficulty finding foster parents who are willing to parent adolescents or younger children with serious emotional problems that often have resulted from child maltreatment (Barbell & Wright, 2001).

Some children have trouble handling the intimacy of a foster family, particularly if they have been seriously neglected or abused. In other instances, a foster family may not be found for a given child. Adolescents are the foremost example. As an alternative to foster care, group homes have a set of house parents to care for five to ten children or adolescents. These homes attempt to maintain a homelike atmosphere and provide rules and structure to children and adolescents. They also may include regular group

Foster parents undergo special training to understand how to meet the special needs of children whose parents are unable to provide appropriate care for them.

Davic Ellis/Digital Vision/Getty Images

counseling sessions for residents (Fox, Frasch, & Berrick, 2000).

As noted, a major problem with the foster care system is the dearth of adequate foster homes. As a result, children often remain in emergency shelters and institutions for a long time and many foster homes have more children than they can adequately handle. The shortage of foster homes results in children frequently being moved from home to home (National Coalition for Child Protection Reform, 2006; Pew Charitable Trusts, 2004).

According to the U.S. Children's Bureau (2006a), an estimated 513,000 children were in foster care in the United States in September 2005. Of this number, 51% had a permanency goal of reunification, 20% had a goal of adoption, 4% had a goal of living with a relative or guardian, 7% had a goal of long-term foster care, 6% had a goal of emancipation, 3% had a goal of guardianship, and 8% had not yet established a permanency goal. Of the 311,000 children who exited foster care in 2005, 5% had been in care

less than 1 month, 20% had been in care for 1 to 5 months, 17% had been in care for 6 to 11 months, 21% had been in care for 1 to 2 years, 12% had been in care for 2 to 3 years, 11% had been in care for 3 to 4 years, and 14% had been in care for 5 or more years.

From an ethnicity perspective, of the children in foster care in 2005, 41% were Caucasian, 32% were African American, 18% were Hispanic, and 9% were other races. The distribution was about equal between males (52%) and females (48%) in care at that time. About 10% of the children who entered foster care in 2005 were reentering the system within 12 months after discharge.

The federal government is spending approximately $5 billion per year to reimburse states for a portion of their annual foster care expenses (Horn, 2005). This figure was projected to increase to $8 billion in 2008 (U.S. General Accounting Office, 2006). The federal government reimburses states for 50% of eligible administrative costs, with no limit. Thus, *total* expenditures for foster care services in the United States were projected to be $10 billion in 2006 and $16 billion in 2008.

Residential Treatment

Children and adolescents who need more structure than foster care or group homes can provide may be placed in **residential treatment** programs. More expensive to maintain than foster care and group homes, these programs provide consistent structure for children and adolescents, as well as intensive individual and group counseling. Most residential treatment programs help the child establish boundaries that were missing from home, work to build self-esteem and competence, and help the child resolve anger and other issues from his or her family experience.

The goal of residential treatment is for the child to develop enough coping skills to be able to deal with the family situation after returning home. Ideally, the family also undergoes counseling so the parents and other family members do not revert to old roles that may force the child back into previous behaviors. Family counseling does not always take place, however, and the child has to cope with the former problems upon returning to the family and community. In situations where returning home or living with a non-parent relative is not possible, a child exiting residential treatment may be placed in a less restrictive setting, such as a group home or foster care.

Children and adolescents with more serious problems may be hospitalized. In hospital settings, the child typically has more restrictions, more intensive therapy, and possibly, prescription medication. In other instances, children or adolescents, primarily delinquent adolescents, are placed in juvenile detention facilities. Studies suggest that white, middle-class children are more likely to be placed in residential treatment or hospital programs, while poor children and children of color are more likely to be placed in juvenile detention facilities (see for example, Crosson-Tower, 2005a).

Although attempts have been made to strengthen the substitute care system, problems remain. Perhaps the biggest problem is the lack of resources to enable birth parents to reunite with their children. Overloaded service delivery systems often thwart social workers from providing needed services to parents. As a result, social workers may be reluctant to terminate parental rights and free children for adoption. Or, conversely, because they cannot provide the needed services, they may be reluctant to return children to unsafe homes. Thus, children languish in the foster care system. When intensive services are provided to parents, however, even children who have multiple problems and have been separated from their parents for long periods can be reunited successfully with their birth family (National Coalition for Child Protection Reform, 2006).

Adoption

When parents choose not to or cannot provide for their children, the court terminates their parental rights and the child becomes legally free for **adoption.** But many children in the United States, particularly African American children, are adopted informally by relatives without a formal court hearing ever taking place. The whole concept of adoption has changed significantly in recent years. In the past, the aim was to match an adoptive child as closely as possible, according to physical features such as hair and eye color, with parents who could not have children biologically. Today, the emphasis has been redirected to finding a parent who can best meet the child's needs.

ADOPTION ISSUES

The forms of adoption in the United States have changed, too. Until the 1970s, most formal adoptions in the United States involved couples adopting healthy infants. Most adoptions today are by stepparents—a result of the higher rates of divorce and remarriage. Also, there are fewer infant adoptions today because many young women of all ethnic groups are choosing to keep their babies rather than place them for adoption. Still, some traditional maternity homes/adoption agencies remain, providing residential and health care and counseling services before birth and, in some instances, post-adoption counseling as well.

A major issue relating to adoption is the length of time to move children through the child welfare services system once they have been removed from their homes. Because of the priority given to family preservation, efforts are made first to ensure that parents are given the opportunities and resources to provide safe, supportive homes for their children. If children are in substitute care, the initial plan, whenever possible, is to return them to their birth parents.

Reaching a decision to terminate parental rights and sever the parent–child relationship is one of the most difficult decisions anyone has to make. Even when parents are not able to provide for their children's needs, most children who are not reared by their birth parents find themselves dealing with separation and loss issues throughout their lives. The extent to which they address these issues depends on many factors, but no matter how superb their adoptive and foster parents are, these children still question why they did not remain with their birth parents.

Most children who become legally free for adoption because their parents' rights have been terminated spend a number of years in foster care. As of September 2005, 114,000 children in the United States were waiting to be adopted. Almost 21% of them had been in continuous foster care for 3 to 5 years, and a similar number had been in continuous foster care for more than 5 years (U.S. Department of Health and Human Services, 2006).

Social workers in child-placing agencies work with children before placement, preparing them for what adoption is like and helping them address grief and loss issues surrounding their birth parents so they can begin to attach more readily to their adoptive parents. Many children in foster care have parents whose legal rights have not been terminated and have to wait for that legal process to play out.

ADOPTION OF CHILDREN WITH SPECIAL NEEDS

The majority of children who are legally free and available for adoption in the United States are termed **children with special needs.** These children, formerly considered unadoptable in many cases, have been placed successfully in a variety of family settings. Children with special needs are those who are children of color, are older, have physical or emotional disabilities, or are members of sibling groups. In 2005, public child welfare agencies reported that of the 51,000 children adopted from foster care, nearly 90% had one or more special needs (U.S. Children's Bureau, 2006c).

Adoption agencies, too, are looking at potential parents they had not considered before. During the 1960s and 1970s, the emphasis was on trans-racial adoption. Currently, most agencies are seeking parents of the same ethnic or cultural background as the child, if possible. Advocacy by groups such as the Association of Black Social Workers has given impetus to ethnicity in placing children for adoption. A number of agencies have established special outreach programs to African American and Latino communities to recruit adoptive parents.

In the 1980s, Father George Clements, an African American priest in Chicago, worked on the "One Church, One Child" campaign. This effort was based on the premise that if each church in the United States, particularly churches with primarily minority congregations, could work to have one child adopted by a member of its congregation, the adoption of children with special needs would no longer be such a critical problem. This campaign spread throughout the United States as one of many successful efforts to place these children in adoptive families.

Concern about children of color awaiting adoption has raised a number of issues about how and when ethnicity should be considered in child placement. The Howard M. Metzenbaum

Multiethnic Placement Act (MEPA I), enacted by Congress in 1994, prohibits any federally funded program from denying the opportunity to become a foster or adoptive parent based solely on the ethnicity, race, or national origin of the foster parent or the adoptive parent or the child involved. The act also prohibits any federally funded program from engaging in discrimination in a placement decision on the basis of ethnicity. Race, ethnicity, or national heritage can be used as one of a number of factors in making placement decisions, but not as the only factor (Edwards, 2003). The act was amended in 1996 (MEPA II), repealing some of the language in the earlier legislation that could have been used to circumvent the intent of the law and providing strict penalties for agencies receiving federal funding if they violated the act.

Many children have become caught in the middle of arguments about the role of ethnicity in placement—and this is psychologically damaging to the child no matter what the decision. In several situations that have received national attention, children of color have been placed with white foster parents, and remained with them for a long time. Later, when the foster parents have tried to adopt these children, the children have been placed in adoptive homes with parents of the same heritage as the child. Any young child, regardless of ethnicity, goes through separation trauma after being removed from a psychological parent who has been the child's primary caregiver. Conflicts can be mitigated by carefully assessing the child's background and current situation, as well as other demographic variables such as age and ethnicity, when placing children in temporary settings prior to placing them in permanent homes (Fogg-Davis, 2002; Rothman, 2005; Trenka, Oparah, & Shin, 2006).

In addition to trying to recruit more families of color, adoption agencies are recruiting single parents, working parents, foster parents, and parents who already have large families. Experience is showing that all of these individuals can be successful adoptive parents. Also, attempts are being made to place siblings together in the same adoptive family rather than separating them as often was done in the past.

The Adoption Assistance Act, previously noted, allows monthly living allowances and medical expenses for families who otherwise could not afford to adopt children with special needs. More assertive and creative outreach efforts have resulted in children being adopted who previously were considered unadoptable, including many who would have been relegated to a life in a state institution.

Other adoption trends include foreign-born adoptions and open adoptions (see, for example, Alice, 2005; Dorow, 2006; Lears & Farnsworth, 2005; U.S. State Department, 2006; Waters, 2005). During the 30-year period 1971–2001, U.S. citizens adopted more than 265,000 children from other countries (Adoption Institute, 2006). Nearly 60% of these children were from Asia. About 64% of the children adopted were male and 36% were female. Almost 90% of internationally adopted children were under 5 years old. The countries from which most of the adoptive children came in 2002 were, first, China, followed by Russia, South Korea, and Guatemala; together, these countries accounted for about 60% of the total international adoptions that year (Adoption Institute, 2006).

From the time the practice began in the early 1970s, members of the international child welfare community have raised concerns about the wisdom of international adoptions. These concerns culminated in 1993, when 66 countries reached an agreement on the Hague Convention on Protection of Children and Co-operation in Respect to Inter-country Adoption (Hague Convention, 1993). The Hague Convention sets minimum standards and procedures for adoptions between countries that are parties to the Convention (U.S. Children's Bureau, 2006c) that

- seek to prevent abuses such as the abduction or sale of children;
- ensure proper counseling and consent(s) before an adoption placement may proceed;

- require that the prospective adoptive parents be eligible and suitable to adopt and that the child may enter and reside permanently in the receiving country;
- require the accreditation/approval of adoption service providers for Convention adoptions; and
- require the recognition of Convention adoptions by all countries party to the Convention (p. 16).

In the United States, federal legislation was required to implement the provisions of the Hague Convention fully and uniformly. The Intercountry Adoption Act of 2000 (P.L. 106-279) was enacted by Congress to fulfill this requirement. The United States signed the Hague Convention in 1994. When it is ratified, all intercountry adoptions between the United States and parties to the Convention must comply with the Convention, the Intercountry Adoption Act of 2000, and applicable regulations.

Another recent trend, *open adoptions* allow the birth parent(s) to be involved in selecting the adoptive parents and, in some instances, to be able to maintain contact with the child as the child grows up (Crosson-Tower, 2005a; Lears & Farnsworth, 2005; Waters, 2005). Even though adoption services have been strengthened, barriers to successful placements remain, particularly for children with special needs. Agencies and individuals still consider some children unadoptable, and some agencies are reluctant to try to place children across state lines, even when parents (or children) in other states can be located.

As the number of adoptions of children with special needs has increased, agencies and adoptive parents have recognized the need for post-adoption services for children and their adoptive families. Children who have lost their birth parents and have suffered extensive child maltreatment have special needs that often continue or do not surface until long after the adoption is final. Adoptive parent groups have been instrumental in advocating for legislation establishing adoption programs, and support groups for adoptive parents. Currently these groups offer the primary support after placement in many communities.

An additional issue relating to adoption that has gained attention is what should be decided when birth parents want to reclaim their children after the children have been adopted. These incidents are traumatic for everyone involved but, like the conflicts with ethnic placements, usually can be avoided by following sound child welfare practice and using licensed adoption agencies. If the system does fail in some way, however, the courts are required to decide who obtains custody of the child. In many instances, however, Goldstein et al.'s (1996) concept of the psychological parent and the extensive research on attachment and the impact of separation on children have not been considered and children have been moved into new settings with total strangers.

Among the adoption-related issues that will continue to be raised in the next decade are the following:

- Who has priority in gaining custody of children in an adoption dispute after an adoption has taken place?
- What impact will privately arranged adoptions and intercountry adoptions have on the number of children and youth awaiting adoption in the United States?
- How important is ethnicity in determining child placement, and at what point should ethnicity be considered?
- To what extent should adopted children have contact with birth parents and siblings?
- What ethical issues should be considered in paying young pregnant girls for their unborn children without going through an agency?
- What rights should surrogate parents have?

Child Welfare and Cultural Diversity

Whatever the child welfare services provided, they must be responsive to the day-to-day realities of diverse populations. Ideally, this means that the child welfare services system should be culturally competent throughout. That is, federal, state, and local entities, as well as individual social workers who provide child welfare services, must:

- understand the impact of culture on individuals, families, and communities;
- recognize that, although some factors may be more typical of one ethnic group than another, in general, there is vast diversity within groups, and specific factors should not be assumed just because someone is from a given group;
- value the diversity of individuals and cultural groups, and view the diversity as a strength rather than a deviation; and
- recognize the impact of oppression and social and economic injustice on at-risk populations.

Child welfare workers should learn as much as possible about the cultures of the diverse populations with which they work, including history, family structure, family dynamics, religion, language, music and art, traditions, communication patterns, views about seeking help, and about social work and social welfare (Crosson-Tower, 2005a; Fontes, 2005; Samantrai, 2003; Thoburn & Chand, 2004). For example, strengths of African American families identified by various researchers include strong kinship bonds that go beyond the nuclear family, flexibility of family roles, and a strong religious orientation. These strengths are seen from a child welfare perspective in the informal kinship system regarding children's living situations, in which many African American children live with relatives other than their birth parents or non-relatives who are considered kin without going through a formal foster care or adoption process (Everett, Chipungu, & Leashore, 2004).

Until recently, child placement agencies did not consider the possibility of placing a child with relative or kin, which meant that African American children often were placed with non-relatives

when family members were available who could serve in parental roles for them. Child welfare agencies also often overlooked the church as a resource in keeping African American families together or helping children when families could not care for them. In one southern city, a church was awarded custody of a sibling group.

Many Asians, particularly first-generation immigrants, hold traditional Asian values, which place the needs of the family above the needs of the individual and emphasize the importance of bringing honor to a family. Thus, outsiders who make Asian family problems known can be viewed as bringing shame to the family. Similarly, Asian family members may be reluctant to divulge information to social workers about how their children are being cared for or what is needed to help them. They also may hesitate to openly disagree with individuals they view as authority figures, including social workers. This cultural pattern may be seen when an Asian client seems to agree with a social worker but then does not follow through on what was agreed (Coalition for Asian American Children and Families, 2006).

Latino cultures value the family as a means of socializing family members about their culture, as well as sources of social support and coping. Many Latinos have left their jobs and immediate family members and traveled long distances to help other family members in need. In most Latino cultures, males play important roles as protectors, and they consider supporting their families as crucial. The role of mothers in Latino families, too, is defined and respected. Social support systems in many Latino families include not only parents and extended family members but also godparents, who frequently are looked to as a resource. The church, too, is a viable resource for many Latino families (Fontes, 2005; Congress & Gonzales, 2005; Torres & Rivera, 2002).

Native American cultures show vast diversity. Some tribes are matrilineal (the mother's family is looked to first when legal issues such as adoption are addressed, as well as for other types of social support), while other tribes are patrilineal.

Native Americans as a whole value the family, with particular emphasis on cooperation and respect for the elderly. Therefore, they may seek advice from elderly members of the family or the tribe in matters of child welfare issues, and may defer to them (Fixico, 2003; Mihesauh, 2005; Washburn, 2006).

These are just a few examples of how culture can shape interactions with social workers and child welfare agencies and must be placed in the context of the rich heritage of each cultural group. Most important is to view the client from his or her day-to-day reality and from the way that person's culture shapes that reality, rather than to overlook culture completely, misunderstand it, or assume an "expert" role and assign stereotypes at the expense of the uniqueness of each individual. To be culturally competent when dealing with children, youth, and families, social workers first must be self-aware and in touch with their own culture and the ways their culture shapes their beliefs about and interactions with others. Social workers, too, must also become knowledgeable about other cultures and willing to learn from clients, seeing them as knowledgeable in regard to their own lives and needs.

Child Welfare and the Future

A major debate in the child welfare field relates to what direction to take in providing services to children, youth, and families in the future. Some child welfare leaders caution that much more knowledge is needed before we can make significant changes for the better. Others claim that we already have the answers and that the real challenge is to mobilize the political will to implement them. Still others indicate that to be effective, wide-scale change will be required (Daley, 2006; Dominelli, 2004; Morris & Hopps, 2000).

This debate reflects a fundamental flaw in U.S. child welfare policy. Put simply, the country has not yet developed a cogent, consistent, and comprehensive system for addressing the needs of children and their families. The American people remain ambivalent about the role of government in the private lives of its citizens. The market economy and the individualist perspective have resulted in the primarily residual focus of contemporary social welfare programs. We seem to be content with letting families spiral out of control and break down before offering services, and even then, the services provided are often too little, too late.

Patriarchy and the "new Puritanism" have played a strong role in the development of child welfare policy in the United States (Gregory, 2005). The latest attempts at welfare reform have brought us back to the era of personal and family responsibility valued during colonial times (Axinn & Stern, 2005). The middle class has all but disappeared in the United States. In its place, two classes of people have emerged—the "haves" and the "have nots" (sometimes called the "underclass"). Millions of children are living in families at or below the poverty level. A large portion of those families are living in *extreme* poverty, defined as having an income below half of the official poverty level (Ehrenreich, 2002).

The development of social welfare policy, of which child welfare policy is a subset, tends to reflect the prevailing social values of the country. Although most people would agree that "children are the future of the world," we seem reluctant, if not immobilized, as a nation to act on that conviction. And so we study the problem a little more or, through incremental policy making, tinker with the existing system, with the hope that things will improve. Or we blame the victims of poor policy or decision making for things that largely are not of their doing and beyond their control (Day, 2005).

If, indeed, "it takes a village" to raise a child— and most serious-minded child welfare professionals would agree that it does—it is time to act with regard to the future of children and families in the United States. And that action must be both deliberate and decisive. We must work together as a nation to develop a child welfare system that is comprehensive, strengths-based, flexible, culturally competent, based on the premise that all children truly are created equal and should have equal opportunities in life, and invests in children as human capital. Social workers at all levels of the environment—agency, community, state, nation, and world—are in a unique position to advocate for improving services to children, youth, and families.

The Role of Social Workers in Providing Services to Children, Youth, and Families

Social workers play many roles in providing services to children, youth, and families. In fact, this is the most traditional area of social work practice. The "child welfare worker," first a volunteer during the 1800s and then a trained social worker in the 1900s, is most often the stereotype of social workers. But the roles of social workers in this area have expanded significantly, and social workers at the BSW, MSW, and PhD levels are actively involved in providing services to children, youth, and families. At the BSW level, social workers are involved as

- child care workers in group homes and residential treatment centers;
- women's and children's counselors at battered women's shelters;
- counselors at youth shelters;
- crisis counselors in law enforcement agencies; and
- child protective services and foster care workers in public social services agencies.

An entry-level position in the area of child and family services usually offers broad-based experience that gives social workers a great deal of flexibility to move to other jobs in working with children and families (in either direct services

or supervisory positions) or other areas of social work. Some states require a minimum of a BSW degree for certain child and family positions, such as child protective services and foster care staff.

A growing number of social workers are specializing in child protective services, investigating reported cases of abuse and neglect and intervening when necessary. They work closely with the courts, law-enforcement agencies, and community-based family intervention, self-help, and volunteer programs. Foster care staffs recruit foster families and oversee their training, and they often work with the child and foster family while the child is in foster care, helping the child adjust (see Box 11.5).

Many BSW graduates are employed as child-care workers in residential treatment and psychiatric care facilities, serving as members of treatment teams and working directly with children and adolescents to implement the team's plan. This experience is valuable in learning the skills necessary for working with children who have emotional disturbance and their families. Other social workers are employed in agencies such as Big Brothers and Big Sisters of America, assessing children and potential volunteers and monitoring the matches afterward.

Increasingly, BSW graduates are being hired as social workers in family preservation programs, family support programs that assist families in getting off public assistance, and programs that provide services to children with developmental disabilities and their families. Social workers at the BSW level also are hired as substance-abuse counselors in inpatient and community-based adult and adolescent treatment programs. Special certification in the area of substance abuse often is required for these jobs.

School social workers often require special state certification, which varies from state to state. In some states, BSW graduates can be hired as school social workers, whereas other states require teaching experience and graduate-level courses or an MSW degree. With more attention to school dropouts and increases in problems

---

BOX 11.5
Do You Have the Characteristics to Be a Competent Social Worker?

A number of researchers have studied what constitutes an effective client–worker relationship.* According to the research, child welfare clients want social workers who are

- Willing to listen and help
- Accurately empathic
- Genuine and warm
- Respectful and nonjudgmental
- Fair
- Accessible

- Supportive and practical
- Experienced and competent

Many of these characteristics relate to social work values and skills learned in BSW social work programs.

---

*See, for example, *Social Work: A Profession of Many Faces* (11th ed.), by A. Morales, B. Sheafor, & M. Scott (Boston: Allyn & Bacon, 2006).

---

such as school violence and teen pregnancy, school social work is a rapidly growing area. School social workers:

- provide individual, parent, and family counseling;
- lead groups of students who are teen parents, are on probation, are recovering from substance abuse, are experiencing family problems such as divorce or abuse, or are having problems relating to teachers and peers;
- provide crisis-intervention services such as suicide intervention;
- organize parent education and parent support groups;
- advocate for the needs of children and families within the school system and the community; and
- network with other social services agencies in the community to assist parents and their children in accessing appropriate services.

The National Association of Social Workers has a school social work division, and two school social work journals are published nationally.

Other BSW graduates become employed in advocacy or policy-related positions as legislative

assistants or staff members of state or federal child and family services organizations or agencies, such as the Children's Defense Fund. An MSW degree may be required for some of these positions, particularly those related to policy analysis.

A number of other social work jobs in the child and family services arena require an MSW degree, partly because of the standards established by the CWLA, which many agencies follow, and partly because some child and family services are highly specialized. In almost all instances, an MSW is required of an adoption worker. Most child guidance centers and child and family service agencies also require an MSW degree. Many social work or therapist positions in residential treatment centers require an MSW, as do clinical social work positions in adolescent and child psychiatric treatment programs. Most schools of social work have child and family or child welfare concentrations at the graduate level, which provide special coursework in this area, as well as field placements in child and family services settings.

With implementation of the PhD degree in social work, some child guidance or child and family services agencies are attempting to hire agency directors at this level. In addition, persons who want more highly specialized clinical experience are earning the PhD degree, enabling them to undertake more intensive therapy with children, youth, and families.

If students are interested in a social work career in the area of child and family services, a number of child welfare and child and family journals, as well as numerous books on all areas discussed in this chapter, are readily available. In addition, many child and family services programs have volunteer programs. Volunteer experience is highly recommended, as it helps students determine whether they are interested in this area and also provides sound social work experience. Box 11.5 asks, "Do you have the characteristics to be a competent social worker?"

Summary

Policies and programs directed to the needs of children, youth, and families are developed and implemented within the context of society, as well as community attitudes and values, awareness about the needs, and the availability of resources. The preferred emphases at present are prevention and early intervention, keeping families together, and making decisions based on the least harm to the children. Nevertheless, the lack of prevention and early intervention resources, as well as a focus on the most serious situations, places large numbers of families with children at risk of family breakdown, often leading to placement of children in foster care and adoption. Many of these placements could have been avoided if the family had received comprehensive family preservation services designed to help the family function in ways that do not place their children at risk of child maltreatment, failure in school, juvenile delinquency, and criminal behavior.

The needs of families with children are complex and diverse. Available programs designed to address these needs are limited in both number and the scope of services offered. Thus, plenty of employment opportunities are available in both the public and private sectors for social workers who are interested in children, youth, and family services.

Key Terms and InfoTrac® College Edition

The terms below are defined in the Glossary at the end of this text. To learn more about key terms and topics in this chapter, enter the following search terms using InfoTrac and the World Wide Web:

adoption
best interests of the
  child
child protective
  services (CPS)
Child Welfare League
  of America (CWLA)
child welfare service
  delivery system
child welfare services
children with special
  needs
crisis intervention
Deficit Reduction Act
  of 2005
family preservation
  programs
foster care

Head Start
home-based family-
  centered services
kinship care
least detrimental
  alternative
natural support
  systems
own-home services
permanency planning
psychological parent
residential treatment
school social work
self-help groups
Social Security Act
substitute care
U.S. Children's Bureau

Discussion Questions

1. What is meant by the concepts "best interests of the child," "least detrimental alternative," and "psychological parent"?
2. Describe briefly at least three prevention programs used with children and their families.

3. Compare home-based family-centered services with substitute care and adoption. What are the advantages and disadvantages of each?

4. What are two areas in which social workers at the BSW and MSW levels might be employed in a child and family services position?

5. What is meant by special-needs adoption?

6. Select one of the "family problem areas" discussed in this chapter. Identify one prevention program and one intervention program that you would suggest to address that problem area.

7. Identify three problems with the current children, youth, and families service delivery system. What are some possible solutions?

8. Debate the following arguments, giving a rationale for both pro and con positions:

   a. Child abuse is a "red herring" that has directed attention away from the more critical child welfare issue of poverty.

   b. The knowledge to make things better for children and families is within our reach; we just have to begin to put the tools in place to do so.

On the Internet

http://www.acf.dhhs.gov/

http://www.cwla.org/

http://www.childrensdefense.org/

http://guthrie.hunter.cuny.edu/socwork/nrcfcpp/

http://www.nreadoption.org/

http://www.nicwa.org/

References

Adoption 2002. (1997). Washington, DC: U.S. Department of Health and Human Services, Children's Bureau.

Adoption Institute. (2006). *International adoption facts.* New York: Author. Available: http://www.adoptioninstitute.org/FactOverview/international_print.html

Alice, T. (Ed.). (2005). *Cultures of transnational adoption.* Durham, NC: Duke University Press.

American Prosecutors Research Institute. (2003). *Investigating and prosecution of child abuse* (3rd ed.). Thousand Oaks, CA: Sage Publications.

Axinn, J., & Stern, M. (2005). *Social welfare: A history of the American response to need* (5th ed.). Boston: Allyn & Bacon.

Barbell, K., & Wright, L. (Eds.). (2001). *Family foster care in the next century.* Somerset, NJ: Transaction Publishers.

Bavier, K. (2004). *The impact of barriers to prenatal care in rural and urban teenage pregnancies.* Durham, NC: Duke University School of Nursing.

Biddleman, M., & Doyle, A. (2002). Supporting families makes a difference: A partnership for prevention and well-being. *Protecting Children, 17*(2), 32–39.

Brittain, C., & Hunt, E. (Eds.). (2004). Helping in child protective services: *A competency-based casework handbook.* New York: Oxford University Press.

Brown, V. A. (2002). *Child welfare: Case studies.* Boston: Allyn & Bacon.

Center for Urban Policy and the Environment. (2003). *Family volunteering: An exploratory study of the impact of families.* Indianapolis: Indiana University-Purdue University, Indianapolis.

Chalk, R., Gibbons, A., & Scarupa, H. (2002). *The multiple dimensions of child abuse and neglect: New insights into an old problem.* Washington, DC: ChildTrends.

Children's Defense Fund. (2003). *Background materials on key sections of the act to Leave No Child Behind.* Washington, DC: Author.

Children's Defense Fund. (2006). *The state of America's children, 2005.* Washington, DC: Author.

Child Welfare League of America (CWLA). (1990). *Standards for services to strengthen and preserve families with children.* Washington, DC: Author.

Child Welfare League of America (CWLA). (2006). *CWLA Standards of Excellence for family foster care services.* Washington, DC. Author. Available: http://www.cwla.org/

Coalition for Asian American Children and Families. (2006), *Understanding the issues of abuse and neglect and Asian American families.* New York: Author.

Congress, E., & Gonzales, M. (Eds.). (2005). *Multicultural perspectives in working with families* (2nd ed.). New York: Springer.

Crosson-Tower, C. (2005a). *Exploring child welfare: A practice perspective* (5th ed.). Boston: Allyn & Bacon.

Crosson-Tower, C. (2005b). *Understanding child abuse and neglect* (5th ed.). Boston: Allyn & Bacon.

Daley, J. G. (Ed.). (2006). *Advances in social work: Special issue on the futures of social work.* Victoria, BC, Canada: Trafford Publishing.

Day, P. J. (2005). *New history of social welfare* (5th ed.). Boston: Allyn & Bacon.

Dominelli, L. (2004). *Social work: Theory and practice for a changing world.* Williston, VT: Polity Press.

Dorow, S. K. (2006). *Transnational adoption: A cultural economy of race, gender, and kinship.* New York: NYU Press.

Edwards, R. L. (Ed.). (2003). *Encyclopedia of social work 2003 supplement.* Washington, DC: NASW Press.

Ellerbee, L. (1995, June 23). Tasha and family deserve a good chance. *Austin American-Statesman,* p. A15.

Epstein, J. L., Sanders, M. G., Simon, B. S., Salinas, K. C., Jansorn, N. R., & Van Voorhis, F. L. (2002). *School, family, and community partnerships: Your handbook for action.* Thousand Oaks, CA: Corwin Press.

Ehrenreich, B. (2002). *Nickel and dimed: On (not) getting by in America.* New York: Owl Books.

Everett, J., Chipungu, S., & Leashore, B. (Eds.), (2004). *Child welfare revisited: An Africentric perspective.* Piscataway, NJ: Rutgers University Press.

Federal Interagency Forum on Child and Family Services. (2003). *America's children: Key national indicators of well-being.* Washington, DC: Author.

Finance Project. (2003). *TANF reauthorization.* Washington, D.C: Available: http://www.financeproject-info. org/TANF/

Fixico, D. (2003). *The American Indian mind in a linear world.* Oxford, England: Routledge.

Fogg-Davis, H. (2002). *The ethics of transracial adoption.* Ithaca, NY: Cornell University Press.

Fontes, L. A. (2005). *Child abuse and culture: Working with diverse families.* New York: Guilford Press.

Fox, A., Frasch, K., & Berrick, J. (2000). Children's experiences in out of home care: A review of the literature. In *Listening to children in foster care: An empirically based curriculum.* Berkeley, CA: Child Welfare Research Center.

Friedman, L. M. (2005). *Private lives: Families, individuals, and the law.* Cambridge, MA: Harvard University Press.

Geen, R. (Ed.). (2003). *Kinship care: Making the most of a valuable resource.* Washington, DC: Urban Institute Press.

Goldstein, J., Solnit, A., Goldstein, S., & Freud, A. (1996). *The best interests of the child: The least detrimental alternative.* New York: Free Press.

Gregory, J. (2005). *Puritanism in the old world and in the new from its inception.* Whitefish, MT: Kessinger Publishing.

Guggenheim, M. (2005). *What's wrong with children's rights?* Cambridge, MA: Harvard University Press.

Hague Convention. (1993). *The Hague Convention on the Protection of Children and Co-operation in Respect to Intercountry Adoption.* Geneva, Switzerland: Author. Available: http://child-abuse.com/childhouse

Healthy Families America. (2006). *About us: Overview.* Chicago: Author. Available: http://healthyfamiliesamerica.org/about_us/index.shtml

Horchak-Andino, K. (2003). *Family preservation and preventive programs—Alternatives to foster care placement.* New York: National Resource Center for Foster Care and Permanency Planning.

Horn, W. (2005). *Testimony before the Subcommittee on Human Resources of the House Committee on Ways and Means.* Washington, D.C: Author. Available: http://waysandmeans.house.gov/hearings.asp?formmode=printfriendly&id=2761

Iwaniec, I. (Ed.). (2006). *The child's journey through care: Placement stability, case planning, and achieving permanency.* New York: John Wiley and Sons.

Kadushin, A. (1980). *Child welfare services* (3rd ed.). New York: Macmillan.

Lears, L., & Farnsworth, B. (2005). *Megan's birthday: A story about open adoption.* Morton Grove, IL: Albert Whitman & Co.

Lindsey, D. (2003). *The welfare of children.* New York: Oxford University Press.

Maas, H., & Engler, R. (1959). *Children in need of parents.* New York: Columbia University Press.

Madden, R. G. (2003). *Essential law for social workers.* New York: Columbia University Press.

Maran, M. (2000). *Class dismissed: A year in the life of an American high school, a glimpse into the heart of a nation.* New York: St. Martin's Griffin.

Martell, D. R. (2005). *Criminal justice and the placement of abused children*. New York: Lfb Scholarly Publishing.

Mihesauh, D. A. (2005). *So you want to write about American Indians? A guide for writers, students, and scholars*. Lincoln, NE: Bison Books.

Morales, A., Sheafor, B., & Scott, M. (2006). *Social work: A profession of many faces* (11th ed.). Boston: Allyn & Bacon.

Morris, R., & Hopps, J. (Eds.). (2000). *Social work at the millennium: Critical reflections on the future of the profession*. Northampton, MA: Free Press.

National Coalition for Child Protection Reform. (2006). *Foster care vs. family preservation: The track record on safety*. Alexandria, VA: Author.

National Committee for Quality Assurance. (2006). *The state of health care quality 2006*. Washington, DC: Author.

Patrikakou, E., et al. (Eds.). (2005). *School-family partnerships for children's success*. New York: Teachers College Press.

Pew Charitable Trusts. (2004). *Home at last: Moving in foster care to safe, permanent families*. Philadelphia: Author.

Rothman, B. K. (2005). *Weaving a family: Untangling race and adoption*. Boston: Beacon Press.

Samantrai, K. (2003). *Culturally competent public child welfare practice*. Belmont, CA: Wadsworth Publishing.

Sanders, M. G. (2005). *Building school-community partnerships: Collaboration for student success*. New York: Corwin Press.

Shyne, A., & Schroeder, A. (1978). *National study of services to children and their families*. Washington, DC: U.S. Children's Bureau, Department of Health, Education, and Welfare.

Sindone, M. (2004). *Raise the blue: The practical and humorous guide to foster and kinship care*. Baltimore: Bookman Publishing.

Stein, T. J. (2004). *The role of law in social work practice and administration*. New York: Columbia University Press.

Thoburn, J., & Chand, A. C. (2004). *Child welfare services for minority ethnic families: The research reviewed*. London, England: Jessica Kingsley Publishers.

Torres, J. B., & Rivera, F. G. (2002). *Latino/Hispanic liaisons and visions for human behavior in the social environment*. Binghamton, NY: Haworth Social Work.

Trenka, J., Oparah, J., & Shin, S. Y. (Eds.). (2006). *Outsiders within: Writing on transracial adoption*. Cambridge, MA: South End Press.

U.S. Children's Bureau. (2003). Evaluation of family preservation and reunification. *Children's Bureau Express, 4*(6).

U.S. Children's Bureau. (2006a). *The AFCARS report: Preliminary FY 2005 estimates as of September 2005*. Washington, DC: Author.

U.S. Children's Bureau. (2006b). *How does the child welfare system work?* Washington, DC: Author.

U.S. Children's Bureau. (2006c). *Major federal legislation concerned with child protection, child welfare, and adoption*. Washington, DC: Author.

U.S. Children's Bureau. (2006d). *Overview of systems of care*. Washington, DC: Author.

U.S. Department of Health and Human Services. (1997). *National study of protective, preventive and reunification services delivered to children and their families*. Washington, DC: U.S. Government Printing Office.

U.S. Department of Health and Human Services. (2003). *Prenatal care*. Washington, DC: Author. Available: http://www.4woman.gov/Pregnancy/pg.cfm?page=264

U.S. Department of Health and Human Services. (2006). *Welfare reform: Interim final regulations*. Washington, D.C: Author. Available: http://www.act.hhs.gov/programs/ofa/regfact.htm

U.S. Department of Labor. (2005). *Volunteering in the United States, 2005*. Washington, DC: Author.

U.S. General Accounting Office. (2006). *Federal oversight needed to safeguard funds and ensure consistent support for states' administrative costs*. Washington, DC: Author.

U.S. State Department. (2006). *International adoption*. Washington, D.C: Author. Available: http://travel.state.gov/family/adoption/notices/notices_473.html

Vasaly, S. (1976). *Foster care in five states*. Washington, DC: U.S. Department of Health, Education, and Welfare.

Vernon, S. (2005). *Social work and the law*. New York: Oxford University Press.

Vieth, V., Bottoms, B., & Perona, A. (Eds.). (2005). *Ending child abuse: New efforts in prevention, investigation, and training*. Binghamton, NY: Haworth Press.

Walsh, F. (2006). *Strengthening family resilience* (2nd ed.). New York: Guilford Press.

Washburn, F. A. (2006). *Elsie's business (Native stories: A series of American narratives).* Lincoln, NE: Bison Books.

Waters, J. (2005). *Arms open wide: An insight into open adoption.* Bloomington, IN: Authorhouse Publishing.

Weiss, H. B., Kreider, H. M., Lopez, M. E., & Chatman, C. M. (2005). (Eds.). *Preparing educators to involve families: From theory to practice.* Thousand Oaks, CA: Sage Publications.

WESTAT and James Bell Associates. (2002). *Evaluation of family preservation and reunification programs: Final report.* Washington, D.C: Author. Available: http://www.aspc.hhs.gov/hsp/evalfampres94/final/

Suggested Further Readings

Child Welfare. A bimonthly journal published by the Child Welfare League of America, New York.

Children's Defense Fund. (Annual). *Children's defense budget: Analysis of the federal budget and children.* Washington, DC: Author.

Crenshaw, W. (2004). *Treating families and children in the child protective system: Strategies for advocacy and family healing.* London, England: Routledge.

Dolgoff, R., & Feldstein, D. (2006). *Understanding social welfare: A search for social justice* (7th ed.). Boston: Allyn & Bacon.

Downs, S. W., Moore, E., McFadden, D. J., Michano, S. M., & Costin, L. B. (2004). *Child welfare and family services: Policies and practice* (7th ed.). Boston: Allyn & Bacon.

Freymond, N., & Cameron, G. (Eds.). (2006). *Towards positive systems of child welfare: International comparisons of child protection, family service, and community caring.* Toronto, Ontario, Canada: University of Toronto Press.

Goldstein, S., & Brooks, R. (Eds.). (2005). *Handbook of resilience in children.* New York: Springer.

Krebs, B. (2006). *Beyond the foster care system: The future of teens.* Piscataway, NJ: Rutgers University Press.

Petr, C. G. (2003). *Social work with children and their families: Pragmatic foundations.* New York: Oxford University Press.

Shirk, M., & Stangler, G. (2006). *On their own: What happens to kids when they age out of the foster care system?* New York: Perseus Books Group.

Weiss, H. B., Kreider, H. M., Lopez, M. E., & Chatman, C. M., (Eds.). (2005). *Preparing educators to involve families: From theory to practice.* Thousand Oaks, CA: Sage Publications.

CHAPTER 12

Older Adults:
Needs and Services

Sam Parker is an 85-year-old widower who lives alone in a northern state. He has been unable to care for himself, and his home lacks an adequate heating system. Sam lives on a limited income derived from his social security benefits plus a small Supplemental Security Income benefit. He has been the object of concern to many in the community for quite some time, and he has frustrated all those who have attempted to assist him. His personal appearance and home are cause for serious concern. Besides being unkempt, Sam has many large sores on his hands, face and legs. Communication is difficult because he is unable to hear. He also has difficulty seeing without glasses. His conversation often consists of delusional and paranoid comments about his neighbor, whom Sam claims is responsible for the condition of his home.

Sam has two daughters who live several hundred miles away, making it difficult for them to look after their father on a regular basis. Both daughters think their father should be in some type of protective environment such as a nursing home, but they have been unwilling to force him to enter such a living environment. Efforts by community agencies have been rebuffed, and the dilemma over whether to intervene forcibly and provide Sam with adequate health care in a protective environment continues.

Recently an adult protective services social worker has been assigned to the case and is working with Sam and his daughters to find a solution that will best meet Sam's needs. The social worker is slowly gaining Sam's trust, and Sam has agreed to go with the social worker to the local health clinic. The social worker and the daughters hope that Sam finally will agree to obtain the services and living situation that can provide the care he needs.

Sam's experience is not typical of most older adults, although far too many share similar experiences. In general, older adults experience life satisfaction, purpose in life, good health, and contentment. For those with problems similar to those of Sam's, however, the struggle to survive often limits their ability to enjoy life. Unfortunately, the myth that all older persons are alike obscures the reality that there is as much variation among the elderly as there is between the young and the old.

The number and percentage of people reaching old age are greater than they have ever been throughout recorded history. This is in part because life expectancy has been extended dramatically since 1900. In 1900, for example, the life expectancy for individuals was approximately

47 years; by 2003, it was almost 78 years (U.S. Department of Commerce, 2006). Viewing this phenomenon from the perspective of age distribution—in 1900, only 4% of Americans were older than age 65; in 2004, just over 12% of Americans were 65 and older. The percent of Americans age 65 and older is projected to grow to 21.2% by 2011, to 25.3% by 2020, and to 31.5% by 2030 (U.S. Department of Commerce, 2006). Not only are more individuals reaching age 65, but they also are living longer. Table 12.1 shows the population projections by age.

Overall, in 2004, more than 36 million Americans were age 65 and older. Almost half of the over-65 population was older than age 75 (U.S. Department of Commerce, 2006), and to many experts this increase in individuals older than 75 suggests that there are really two groups of older adults— the "old" (age 65 and older) and the "oldest-old" (age 80 and older). One consequence of extended longevity is that many adults in their 60s are caring for their parents who are in their 80s and 90s.

Aging viewed from an international perspective is instructive. Statistics released by the U.S. Census Bureau (2004a, pp. 49–52) reveal the following trends in the global elderly population:

- In 2002, 7.1% of the world's total population consisted of elderly people; the elderly population is projected to comprise 16.5% of the world's population in 2050.
- The rapid growth in numbers of elderly people worldwide is attributable primarily to historical declines in fertility coupled with the general aging of the population.
- Over the next 25 years, the elderly population is projected to grow more rapidly than the total population in all parts of the world.
- By 2050, women are expected to outnumber men throughout the world.
- In 2050, the population of individuals 80 and older is projected to make up a considerable proportion of the total population worldwide.

Although most of us aspire to live a long life, the consequences to society of a larger older population have catastrophic potential. Assuring that essential resources are available to meet the health, social, and economic needs of the older population places a heavy burden on government and private resources, including families. Middle-aged Americans are being referred to as the "sandwich generation," as they are having to provide for their children while they also are providing for their aging parents. But many families cannot offer such support, especially when major health problems occur, and many older people do not have families available to give even emotional support. Thus, there is an increasing reliance on federal and state governments to provide for such needs.

TABLE 12.1

Population Projections by Age: 2010–2030 (Percent of Total Population)

Age 65 and Older	
Year	Percent
2010	21.2
2020	25.3
2030	31.5

Age 75 and Older	
Year	Percent
2010	8.1
2020	9.0
2030	11.9

Age 85 and Older	
Year	Percent
2010	2.0
2020	2.2
2030	2.6

Source: *Statistical Abstract of the United States*, U.S. Department of Commerce (Washington, DC: U.S. Government Printing Office, 2006).

For example, in 2003, public expenditures for health care in the United States amounted to $765.7 billion, or 46% of total health-care expenditures in the country. The cost of health-care services provided through Medicare, the country's oldest and largest public health-care program for individuals age 65 and older, represented the largest single component of public health-care expenditures ($283.1 billion, or 37%). National health-care expenditures are expected to rise to $3.6 trillion in 2014, with the public–private split being about equal. Again, Medicare is expected to account for the single largest component of public health-care expenditures ($746.9 billion, or 42%). Although the share of public health-care funds consumed by the Medicare program is expected to increase by only 5% between 2003 and 2014, this increase amounts to hundreds of millions of dollars (Heffler, Smith, Keehan, Borger, Clemens, & Truffer, 2005). With continually increasing numbers of older adults in our society (see Figure 12.1), even larger government allocations will be necessary in the future.

In this chapter we examine the more salient issues and problems of older people, review their problems of adaptation, and identify physical and social support systems and resources designed to meet their needs.

Physiological Aging

Physiological changes, through growth and physical maturation, continue throughout the life cycle. During midlife (around age 45), we go through a stage of physical change termed *senescence,* defined as the onset of the degenerative process. At this stage, individuals undergo significant bodily changes—graying or loss of hair, wrinkling of the skin, slower pace—and become aware that old age eventually will be a reality.

Typically, aging is accompanied by sensory losses. With less visual acuity, bifocals may

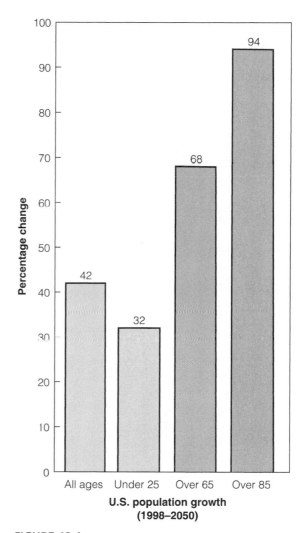

FIGURE 12.1

U.S. Aging Population

Source: Statistical Abstract of the United States, U.S. Department of Commerce (Washington, DC: U.S. Government Printing Office, 2006).

become necessary. Many older adults need hearing aids to compensate for hearing loss. In very late life, tactile (touch) and olfactory (taste) senses are much less acute. These changes do not happen at any specific age, nor do they affect all individuals to the same extent. In some, the losses are minor and hardly detectable, and in others, the losses represent major dysfunctions. Unless sensory losses are profound, they usually do not limit the older person's social interactions and ability to live a normal and fulfilling life. Even when older people have more serious sensory debilities, the proper prosthetic supports often allow the older person to maintain a productive life.

More significant changes occur internally. Changes in the cardiovascular system often are reflected in elevated blood pressure and loss of elasticity in the lungs. Renal (kidney) capacity is reduced, and the bladder loses approximately a third of its capacity. There is a loss of brain weight, as well as muscular strength. Estrogen and testosterone levels are lowered, and other hormonal changes occur. For most, these factors can be mitigated by a change in diet, a program of regular exercise, surgical procedures, a therapeutic drug regimen, or some combination of these. In the latter case, the cost of prescription drugs has risen dramatically in recent years. Further, the proliferation of managed-care health plans and significant changes in the Medicare program have made it difficult for older Americans to reap the benefits that modern medicine can offer.

Scientists have yet to determine *why* we age. A number of theories—including those regarding wear and tear (organisms wearing out), autoimmune responses (less effective immune system in warding off invaders), cellular changes (fewer cells and less ability to replicate lost cells), and cross-linkages (changes in collagen, with subsequent loss of elasticity in body tissue)—have been proposed as viable theories of aging (Masoro & Austad, 2005; Moody, 2006).

Students who plan to work with older adults should familiarize themselves with these theoretical perspectives, and social workers who specialize in working with older adults should be sensitive to the physiological changes that reflect the normal aging processes. When placed in the proper perspective, these changes should not be viewed negatively but, rather, as part of the life continuum.

Behavior and Adaptation to Old Age

Social workers should be aware that aging is not a fixed dimension of the life cycle. Young children are aging, as are older adults. All societies attach significance to various stages of the life cycle. **Aging** is not just a chronological process; it has symbolic meaning as well. Cultures determine, for example, the age at which their members should enter school, marry, begin careers, enter the military, have children, become grandparents, and retire. Norms for behavior are prescribed at various developmental stages of the life cycle. Too often, old age has been viewed as a period of dramatic decline. Thus, older adults are expected to be less active, require fewer resources, contribute less to society, and become more content and serene.

Many of the symbolic definitions assigned to old age are buttressed by scientific data. Physiological changes, including the loss of muscular strength, sensory losses, and reduced lung elasticity, are but a few of the measurable differences between younger and older adults. But many of the presumed losses associated with cognitive functioning have been shown to have little substance in fact. Intelligence and intellectual functioning, once thought to decline appreciably in old age, are not measurably reduced. Behavior in old age is an individual matter and not attributable to aging alone. Any accurate assessment of adaptation in late life must consider the effects of the environment on behavior, as well as the physiological and cognitive characteristics within the behavioral context.

Theories of Aging

Several theories of aging have emerged to explain or describe adaptation in late life. Among the more prominent ones are continuity theory, activity theory, exchange theory, and developmental theory (Eyetsemitan & Gire, 2003; Joseph, 2006; Tornstam, 2005; Newman & Newman, 2005).

Continuity Theory

Continuity theory emphasizes that a person's personality, formed early in one's life, changes little over the life span. How a person adjusts to old age is largely a product (or extension) of adaptive patterns developed in earlier years (Hillier & Barrow, 2006). Continuity theory stresses the maintenance and integrity of one's personality and social experiences over the life span as generally effective in adjusting to old age.

Activity Theory

Activity theory stresses the importance of maintaining adequate levels of activity, including social activity, if people are to age successfully (Hillier & Barrow, 2006). Presumably, more active older adults will achieve greater satisfaction, and thus age more adaptively. Activity theory has provided the basis for a number of programs developed for older adults, such as the Retired Seniors Volunteer program (RSVP), Senior Luncheon programs, Foster Grandparents program, Green Thumb program, and activity programs in nursing homes.

Developmental Theory

Developmental theory emphasizes positive adaptation and life satisfaction based on mastering new tasks as the individual moves through the life cycle, including old age. Life span development is viewed as a normal process that encompasses new challenges, new tasks, and flexibility in incorporating changes into the repertoire of behaviors. Older adults must accept the physiological changes, reconstruct their physical and psychological life accordingly, and integrate values that validate their worth as older adults (Newman & Newman, 2005).

This theory postulates that the psychological crises of late life are "integrity versus despair" and "immortality versus extinction" (Newman & Newman, 2005). *Integrity,* according to Newman and Newman, is "not so much a quality of honesty and trustworthiness . . . as it is an ability to integrate one's sense of past history with one's present circumstances and to feel content with the outcome" (p. 551). *Despair* suggests the opposite of integrity—the inability to integrate past history with the present or to achieve contentment with the outcome.

Confrontation with the psychosocial crisis of immortality versus extinction occurs in very late life. *Immortality* refers to the extension of one's life through one's children, contributions to social institutions, spirituality, and positive influences that one has had on others. *Extinction* suggests a lack of connectedness and attachment and the fear that death brings nothingness (Newman & Newman, 2005).

Exchange Theory

Exchange theory attributes social withdrawal of the aged to a loss of power. Having once exchanged their expertise for wages, the aged must comply with mandatory retirement in exchange for pensions, Social Security payments, and Medicare. Thus, the power advantage has shifted from them as individuals to society. The effect of this loss of power results in withdrawal from meaningful social interaction and more dependence on those who hold power over them.

The role of society in creating the behavioral and value context for older adults must be examined to gain insights into the problems and issues implicit in understanding adaptation in later life. Our society, for example, stresses productivity and distributes rewards and power in relation to it.

Retirement disengages older adults from socially recognized productive efforts. Instead of being consumers of products from their own currently productive efforts, elderly people are forced to be consumers of products from others' efforts. As we now turn our attention to the problems and issues confronting older adults, we must keep in mind that there are no simple solutions. Social work with older adults who have problems may bring some relief to the individuals who are helped, but it does not address the causes of those problems. Changing the social systems that produce the problems is a more tenable solution, albeit more difficult.

Attitudes toward Growing Old

Among the many harsh realities that people face in aging are negative attitudes toward the elderly. Despite a positive turn in recent years, these attitudes persist. Our society has been characterized by an emphasis on youth and productivity, stressing independence that is enabled by financial support gained through employment. Retirement often drastically reduces the person's available income and may contribute to dependency. As a result, older adults often are considered to be of less value to society.

Negative attitudes also are expressed through exclusion. The media, for example, have avoided using older adults in television commercials altogether or have cast them in stereotypical roles as doting, kind and benevolent, irascible, or dependent. Advertisements in newspapers and magazines rarely use older persons to convey messages because they do not resonate with the younger population to which the ads are directed. The media, however, do seem to be changing their stance, as one of the most populous generations of Americans—those born in the years immediately following World War II (the so-called baby boomers)—is about to enter retirement. This has given rise to an explosion in marketing a wide array of highly profitable products and services to a population that is willing and able to afford them.

Collectively, societal practices have reinforced negativism toward old age. Many of these practices, such as mandatory retirement, have supported the idea that older adults are less capable of making contributions through work and to society. Various rules and regulations governing employment limit the opportunities for them to make such contributions. Discrimination or differential treatment based on age alone is called **ageism.** Like other forms of discrimination, ageism is institutionalized and, as a result, often subtle (Nelson, 2004; Palmore, Branch, & Harris, 2005). Individuals frequently are unaware that they reinforce ageism through their attitudes and practices. Negative attitudes toward older adults sometimes are expressed by professional practitioners as well as the general public. In a classic study, Riley (1968) identified nurses, medical doctors, attorneys, the clergy, and social workers, among others, as giving preference to younger individuals as clientele. Little evidence indicates that this situation has changed.

Negative attitudes toward older adults often result in their loss of social status, with accompanying diminished self-concept. And real-life issues compound the problem. For example, as adults grow older, they invariably lose significant others through death, and they must deal with their own physical decline, which may limit their activities and opportunities for mobility. Although the majority of older adults are independent and find life satisfying, these changes (or losses) invariably affect their quality of life (Shenk & Groger, 2006).

As we review other problem areas of older adults, we must keep in mind that attitudes, although not always linked directly with behavior, tend to shape our priorities and practices. Viewing the older population as "excess baggage" is not the bedrock on which positive responses to the needs of older adults will be achieved.

Retirement

The impact of **retirement** on human behavior continues to be a topic of major interest. The relationship between retirement and old age has

Retirement brings new opportunities to contribute to family and community for many but also increased concern, even among the middle class, about whether finances and other needed support will be available. For those who are poor, being elderly adds additional risk to getting needs met.

David Young-Wolff/Stone/Getty Images

swung like a pendulum over the years. Traditionally, retirement and aging were viewed as one and the same: People retired from work to enter into the "golden age" of life. A combination of private retirement and Social Security benefits made it possible for most retired persons to live comfortably.

This view of retirement changed dramatically beginning in the 1980s and continues to the present. The Information Age, which emerged in the late-1970s and early-1980s, forever changed the landscape of American industrial dominance. Blue-collar workers in heavy industries such as steel-making suddenly were displaced as American companies were unable to compete with low-cost labor from abroad, given the high labor costs and associated benefits that labor unions had negotiated since the time they were introduced in the United States in the 1930s. This economic shift affected entire generations of families.

Workers no longer were able to depend on the retirement benefits to which they were entitled, forcing them to postpone retirement and try to find employment elsewhere.

Another phenomenon that began in the late 1980s, and continues, is the increasing use of contract workers in a wide variety of businesses throughout the country, especially those engaged in computer-related industries. In an attempt to reduce costs to stay even with low-cost competition from abroad, American companies began to outsource work to independent consultants who worked under contract and did not receive any employee benefits, including retirement benefits. These workers were expected to self-fund health-care and retirement benefits from the monies they earned as contractors. Because of the high cost of self-funding benefits such as health-care and private retirement plans, many of these contract workers simply did not invest in these benefits, thereby disrupting the traditional retirement paradigm once again.

During the decade of the 1990s, the "dot-coms" spawned a large cadre of young people who worked for and invested heavily in penny stocks of nascent computer hardware and software companies, only to become millionaires in their 30s. Many of these newly minted millionaires chose to retire from work early to pursue personal, non-work interests. Once again, the traditional retirement paradigm shifted, even after the crash of the dot-coms. A historical event that also has changed the traditional retirement paradigm in the United States is the globalization of the economic marketplace, which has forced American business and industry to cut operating costs substantially and look elsewhere across the globe for low-cost alternatives to support their business interests. Increasingly, American companies are relocating to countries in India, Mexico, China, and Southeast Asia, to take advantage of the favorable business climate, as well as skilled workers who are willing to work at substantially lower wages than their American counterparts. Many American workers today are happy just to have a job, let alone worry about their retirement benefits.

Because wages and employee benefits for American workers have slowly eroded over time, many workers are having to work well into their 70s and extend the age at which they could officially retire. Consider, for example, that in 1980, only 2.9%, or about 3.1 million workers 65 years and older, were part of the U.S. civilian labor force. Comparable figures for 2012 are projected to be nearly 4.0%, or some 6.4 million workers (U.S. Department of Commerce, 2006).

The traditional retirement paradigm in the United States has been altered forever. There is no guarantee that a lifetime of work will result in adequate retirement benefits that will allow older Americans to live out their lives in some measure of comfort. One of the primary functions of retirement in the past was to clear out workers from one generation to make way for workers from the next. If this is no longer possible—as it appears to be—will older workers be forced out of the workplace regardless of their need or desire to continue working? What will happen to these workers? What changes in federal and state laws would be required to ensure a decent quality of life for older Americans after leaving the workforce? Who should bear the costs of these changes? Is the concept of retirement in the United States so out of kilter that it is no longer operative? If so, what role does society have in correcting this picture?

As the pendulum swings, employers are beginning to see, as valuable assets to their organizations, older persons who have retired from the workforce. For one thing, employers do not have to pay for expensive employee benefits such as health care because health-care benefits are often covered by the employee's retirement benefits. In addition, older persons are recognized as being agreeable, dependable, and knowledgeable. Many also are part of the institutional history of the organization that is at the heart of the organization's culture (Chester, 2002; Lancaster & Stillman, 2003; Martin & Tulgan, 2002; Meredith & Schewe, 2002).

Further, many companies are concerned about the "brain drain" that is expected to occur when millions of highly skilled and experienced workers (baby-boomers) retire in large numbers a few years from now. Employers are concerned about finding new workers to replace the seniors exiting the workforce (Penner, Perun, & Steuerle, 2003).

At the same time as there is a growing interest in retaining older workers in the workforce, there are many economic, legal, and institutional barriers to achieving more flexible work arrangements for them. Chief among these obstacles are out-of-date employee compensation systems, rigid employee benefit plans, and legal restrictions on phased retirement plans (Penner, Perun, & Steuerle, 2003). Reaching solutions to these problems is not insurmountable, but existing laws will have to be changed and new ones introduced to implement those solutions. This may be easier said than done, as considerable political will is necessary to bring about reform in this area. Which political leaders, if any, will be willing to champion this cause? What role does the social work community have in advocating for such changes? How can social workers learn more about this situation to be more effective advocates?

Primarily because of the definitional problems just described, it is difficult to ascertain how many individuals are added to the retirement pool each year, but it certainly must be large. Persons 65 and older comprise almost 4% of the total workforce, or 6.4 million individuals (U.S. Department of Commerce, 2006). Table 12.2 indicates the percentage of individuals age 65 and older in the labor force by gender and ethnic status.

For many retirees, income resources often are reduced drastically upon their retirement. Few would disagree that quality of life is related to disposable income. The luxurious lifestyles and world cruises that appear in magazines targeted for the retired "over-50" population and sponsored by organizations such as the American Association of Retired Persons (AARP) are within reach of only a relatively small percentage of

TABLE 12.2

Percentage of Those 65 and Older in Labor Force by Gender and Ethnic Status, 2004 and 2012 (Projected)

	2004		2012	
	Male	**Female**	**Male**	**Female**
Caucasian	12.6	8.2	13.8	8.9
African American	12.1	7.4	13.8	8.4

Source: Statistical Abstract of the United States, U.S. Department of Commerce (Washington, DC: U.S. Government Printing Office, 2006).

retirees. Understandably, many retirees remain concerned about the stability of the Social Security system, the government-sponsored retirement system in the United States.

Income is not the only factor affecting positive adjustment to retirement. Health is a matter of great importance and concern. As the population grows older, good health becomes more problematic. Few survive beyond their 70s without some health problem, such as arthritis, high blood pressure, poor digestion, or other conditions. For most, the problems do not severely restrict their mobility or daily activities. For others with more severe conditions, the role of patient eclipses preferred retirement activities. Concerns about meeting medical expenses, or anticipated expenses, may curtail spending patterns and, in turn, reduce options and activities.

Most older adults rely primarily on Medicare, a federal health insurance program available to the elderly and persons with disabilities. Medicare provides health insurance coverage for 35.4 million elderly people and 6.3 million non-elderly people with permanent disabilities. The number of beneficiaries doubled between 1966 and 2004 and is expected to double again by 2030 (Kaiser Family Foundation, 2005). In 2002, Medicare covered only about 45% of beneficiaries' total and long-term care expenses. Also in 2002, beneficiaries paid an average of $2,223 in out-of-pocket expenses, with the greatest increase associated with prescription drug benefits. Beginning in 2006, Medicare beneficiaries were able to access prescription drug coverage through private plans (see chapter 9 for a detailed discussion on this benefit offering).

The costs of Medicare benefits are expected to soar as the baby-boom generation enters retirement. Most forecasters predict that major changes to Medicare will be required in the near future to accommodate significant increases in costs associated with the program. (Medicare's share of the **gross domestic product** [GDP]— 2.3% in 2000—was expected rise to 6.8% of the GDP by 2030.) For retirees who are in poor health, health-related problems may diminish satisfaction in their world away from work.

The need for research on retirement continues to be pressing. Although social scientists have made great strides over the last several decades, the potential value of retirement-related research becomes more manifest as the number of retirees rises. The emerging body of knowledge and understanding of the effects of retirement on individuals is helpful, but much remains to be learned. Appropriate and valid social policies must be guided by a sound knowledge base.

Over the past decade, considerable emphasis has been given to preparation for retirement. Called **pre-retirement planning,** it is based on the notion that people who prepare adequately for retirement adjust better to the lifestyle changes that accompany retirement. Many major corporations, as well as public agencies, have developed pre-retirement training programs for their employees. These programs usually emphasize estate planning; forecasting of income; identifying federal, state, and private resources for older adults; and strategies for dealing with issues such as relocating, living alone, and planning for leisure-time activities. Although no compelling evidence indicates that pre-retirement planning affects adaptation to retirement positively, a mounting consensus indicates that it does. Logic alone suggests that life changes can be managed more successfully with adequate preparation.

The Families of Older Adults

Facts refute the myth that older adults are abandoned by their families. Family members continue to be the primary source of emotional support and, in times of illness, care for their elderly members. Following is a snapshot of family caregivers in the United States (Johnson & Wiener, 2006; McKune, Andresen, Zhang, & Neugaard, 2006; National Family Caregivers Association, 2006).

Caregiving populations:

- More than 50 million people are participating in family caregiving during any given year.
- Women make up about 60% of the caregiving population in the United States.
- The typical family caregiver is a 46-year-old woman who is both married and employed, caring for her widowed mother who lives on her own.
- About one-third of family caregivers of elderly persons are 65 years of age and older.
- The estimated value of services that family caregivers provide is $306 billion a year.

Economics of caregiving:

- The median incomes of caregiving families are lower than those of non-caregiving families.
- Women who are family caregivers are significantly more likely than their non-caregiving counterparts to live in poverty.
- Non-reimbursable medical expenses for caregiving families are significantly higher than for non-caregiving families.
- In 2000, family caregivers who provided full-time care at home lost $109 per day in wages and health benefits.

Family impacts of caregiving:

- The stress of family caregivers has been shown to have a negative impact on the caregiver's immune system (and, thus, susceptibility to chronic illness), especially when caring for a member with dementia.

- Depression is fairly common in family caregivers who provide care for 36 hours or more a week.
- Extreme stress by family caregivers has been shown to lead to the caregivers' premature aging.

Caregiving and work:

- About 13% of the American workforce is engaged in some form of family caregiving.
- Two in five human resource directors expressed concern that their organizations were not doing an adequate job of informing employees about help they could get in managing work and family responsibilities.
- On average, women who spend time out of the paid labor force to care for an elderly member or one with disabilities forgo about $400,000 in earnings and health benefits.
- American businesses lose more than $30 billion in productivity and absenteeism annually because of family caregiving.
- Caregiving responsibilities require that the caregivers make significant adjustments to their work schedules, such as coming to work late, leaving work during the day, or leaving work early.

Caregiving and health care:

- Most of the long-term care services in the United States are provided by family caregivers.
- One in five family caregivers has difficulty communicating with physicians.
- More than 40% of family caregivers give medications, change bandages, manage equipment, and monitor vital signs—tasks normally assigned to a professional nurse.
- Often, family caregivers who change dressings or manage equipment have received no formal instructions on how to do so.

Additional information on the extent and scope of family caregiving in the United States can be found at the Rosalynn Carter Center for Caregiving (www.RosalynnCarter.org).

Introduced in Congress in June, 2005, the Lifespan Respite Care Act (S. 1283) proposed to amend the Public Health Service Act to establish a program that would expand and enhance respite-care services to family caregivers; improve statewide dissemination about and coordination of respite care programs; and provide, supplement, or improve access and quality of respite care services to family caregivers (National Respite Coalition for Lifespan Respite Task Force (2006). Under the act, funds would be provided on a competitive basis to state agencies, other public or private nonprofit entities capable of operating on a statewide basis, political subdivisions of states with a population of more than 3 million, or already recognized state respite-care coordinating authorities, to implement programs and services that have a high likelihood of enhancing life span respite care services statewide. Under separate authority, the act also would establish a National Resource Center on Lifespan Respite Care. Family caregiver advocates worked diligently to help ensure that the proposed legislation was actually enacted.

The family caregiver statistics summarized above have enormous policy and practice implications for the social work profession. In the future, social workers will have more career opportunities to work with older Americans in the areas of direct service to elderly individuals and their families, family education and support, educating the public about the nature and extent of the issues surrounding family caregiving, advocating for additional resources for caregiving families, and helping state and federal lawmakers understand the importance of enacting legislation that provides support to caregiving families. The future of the family caregiving movement will depend in large part on the contributions of social work professionals and the organizations to which they belong, such as the National

Association of Social Workers and the National Council on Social Work Education. Schools of social work can expand their degree programs in **gerontology**—the scientific study of aging, the aging process, and the aged—and related fields. They also can increase the extent to which they work with community-based agencies that provide assistance to family caregivers, with the goal of developing meaningful field experiences for social work students who are interested in this area.

Families continue to be a viable resource for older adults, giving them comfort and self-identity. The **family caregiving** research continues to provide inconclusive findings about the overall quality of intergenerational relationships, but it does suggest that, for the most part, older people maintain regular contact with their family members, who are the primary source of assistance when needed.

Dying and Death

Although a person can die at any point in the life cycle, death rates rise dramatically in individuals age 50 and older. Unlike deaths in younger people, deaths in later life are more often the product of disease than accidents.

Every culture shapes its attitudes toward death as well as life. Our society tends to overemphasize a rational view of death as being a natural, yet highly individualized event. Because most of us are not engaged with the dying process, we have little experience to prepare us for coping with either the death of others or our own death. Consequently, too many people are uncomfortable when confronted with dying individuals, and apprehensive about their own death.

In a classic work, Elisabeth Kübler-Ross (1975/1997) laid the groundwork for helping dying persons come to grips with the remaining part of their lives. Her contribution, along with others, created a framework for social workers

and other professionals to provide assistance for the dying as well as their families, often through the aid of a **hospice,** a program or facility designed to help individuals in the process of dying remain in comfortable environments that allow for dignity and support their physical and emotional needs. The hospice movement originated in England, and the first U.S. hospice was established in Connecticut in the 1970s. This movement has grown rapidly since that time, and now hospices are found in major cities as well as some rural areas. Few dying persons, however, are served by a hospice because of a lack of financial resources, health-care coverage, or knowledge that these services are available.

Controversy has been introduced into the dying process in the form of "voluntary" or "involuntary" euthanasia (see chapter 9 for a discussion of this topic). The medical community has long embraced the philosophical tenet that life should be preserved as long as medically possible, including the use of artificial means such as respirators. Taking a contrary position, supporters of the "right-to-die" movement believe that the individual should have the right of choice in governing the time and circumstance under which his or her death should occur. Proponents of the right-to-die position promote the **living will,** a legal device in which the individual delineates the conditions under which he or she would refuse artificial means to maintain life. Organizations such as the Hemlock Society support the concept of the living will and also the right of individuals to induce their own death under circumstances in which they are in great pain and suffering without hope of recovery.

Social workers who work with older adults invariably will work with those who are dying and their loved ones. Applying their clinical skills, social workers can assist individuals and families in handling interpersonal losses and protect the dying person's dignity, integrity, and right to choices. Social workers also can act as advocates alone or in conjunction with an established advocacy group such as the National Family

Caregivers Association, to promote state and federal legislation that will provide assistance to family caregivers. They also might work with insurance companies to be sure that hospice care is covered in their health-care policies. Finally, social workers can assist in the design and implementation of public information campaigns aimed at increasing the public's knowledge and understanding of end-of-life issues.

Aging and Mental Health

Contrary to popular belief, the state of mental health in older adults is not appreciably different from that of the general population. Myths regarding inherent disorientation, memory loss, excessive dependency, and senility in older people are pervasive. Certainly, some older adults have problems of a mental nature that result in dysfunction, but, as with younger people, these problems generally are responsive to treatment. Late in life, mental health problems may be a result of interpersonal loss, organic deterioration, or some traumatic event. By way of prevention, being active and having a future orientation are associated with good mental health. Maintaining enthusiasm and working toward goals are deterrents to dysfunctional behavior.

Problems of old age may be analyzed using the systems/ecological perspective, discussed in chapter 3. The way in which an individual interacts within the environment strongly influences the quality of that person's mental health. Many of the symptoms of dysfunctional behavior that appear in old age are attributable to environmental factors. Social isolation and loneliness, in particular, seem to produce maladaptive behaviors. And overmedication can result in loss of appetite, loss of vigor, memory loss, or disorientation.

Depression—one of the more common mental health problems in late life—may be caused by bereavement, anxiety related to income security, a limited social friendship network, health concerns, relocation, and similar factors. Ageism and lack of attention to problems of the elderly have led to increased concern about this group's high suicide rate. In 2003, the suicide rate for the population in general was 10.8 per 100,000 people. By comparison, the rate per 100,000 for adults age 65–74 was 12.7; for those 75–84 years, 16.4; and for those 85 years and older, 16.9 (American Association of Suicidology, 2006). Elderly adults 75 years and older have rates of suicide close to 50% higher than that of the nation as a whole.

Alzheimer's disease has emerged as one of the more publicized of the mental/brain conditions in later life, afflicting an estimated 4.5 million Americans—more than double the number in 1980. By 2050, the number of individuals with Alzheimer's disease in the United States could range from 11.3 million to 16 million (Alzheimer's Association, 2006b). Alzheimer's is an insidious, progressive disease that results in increasing maladaptation. Among the symptoms are disorientation, memory loss, and inappropriate behavior. In the later stages, the person requires total care, including feeding, bathing, and all routine maintenance activities. Alzheimer's disease imposes heavy demands on family members, who are the primary caregivers in the initial stages.

Scientific advances in neuroimaging and DNA research offer hope for early diagnosis, prevention, and treatment of the disease (Alzheimer's Association, 2006c). A study conducted by the Lewin Group for the Alzheimer's Association concluded that an annual investment of $1 billion in Alzheimer's research could yield results that would significantly reduce Medicare and Medicaid costs, achieving annual Medicare savings of $51 billion by 2015, $126 billion by 2025, and $444 billion by 2050. The same investment is projected to result in annual savings in Medicaid spending on nursing-home care for Alzheimer's patients of $10 billion by 2015, $23 billion by 2025, and $70 billion by 2050 (Alzheimer's Association, 2006a).

The physical and emotional demands related to caring for a loved one with Alzheimer's disease increase as the disease progresses. Social workers can play a significant role in establishing community-based Alzheimer's support groups to provide emotional support for caregivers, as well as an opportunity to share effective techniques in caring for the person. Social workers also can work side by side with Alzheimer's advocates to implement public information campaigns about the disease, as well as promote state and federal legislation providing assistance to family care-givers of those with Alzheimer's disease. Too, they can engage in political advocacy, encouraging Congress to appropriate funding aimed at early diagnosis, prevention, and treatment of the disease.

Dramatic changes in mental health seldom are caused by aging alone. Individuals who have well-integrated personalities, who prepare themselves for changes related to retirement, who develop leisure-time interests, and who plan for the future are less vulnerable than others to age-related stress factors and debilities.

Income Security

One of the more persistent anxieties for older adults relates to income security. As a person grows older, the ability to secure income through employment declines while reliance on pensions, savings, investments, and Social Security increases. For the majority of older adults, income available after retirement is below what they received while working full-time.

For some, income is less than half of what it was before retirement. Few of our present-day older adults earned sufficient income to be able to reserve money for retirement. Also, retirement-incentive plans such as IRAs, tax-deferred annuities, and Keogh plans did not exist during the time of their employment. As a result, many retirees are forced to live on Social Security payments alone. Table 12.3 details the sources of income for retirees in 2004.

TABLE 12.3
Retirement Income Sources, 2004 (Percentage Receiving Income from Major Sources by Ethnicity)

	Percent of Total		
Source	White	African American	Hispanic
Social Security	91	83	77
Assets	59	26	26
Pensions	42	30	19
Earnings	23	18	20
Public assistance (SSI)	3	10	13

Source: *Income of the Population 55 and Older: 2004* (Washington, DC: Social Security Administration, 2006a).

As Table 12.3 reflects, the percent of elderly persons in the United States receiving income from pensions ranges from a low of 19% for Hispanics to a high of 42% for whites (Social Security Administration, 2006a). Thus, a large share of older Americans are not covered by any kind of pension plan. This, coupled with the fact that Social Security was not designed to be a "complete" retirement system, creates a financial dilemma for the vast majority of retirees.

Table 12.4 shows the median household incomes for adults older than 65 in 2002, by ethnic group. As can be seen, the median household income for whites is almost twice that for Latinos and African Americans.

Table 12.5 shows that poverty rates for people age 65 and older were about the same in 2005 as they were in 2000, despite a slight increase in overall income for this population during the same time period (U.S. Department of Commerce, 2006). Thus, the plight of the older poor remains about the same, despite improvements in the economy and the fact that overall income for this group increased slightly during the 6-year period 2000 to 2005. As Table 12.5 clearly shows,

TABLE 12.4

Median Income of Households Containing Families Headed by Persons Older Than 65 Years of Age, 2002, by Ethnic Group

Ethnicity	Median Income
White	$20,104
African American	$12,000
Latino	$11,376

Source: Statistical Abstract of the United States, U.S. Department of Commerce (Washington, DC: U.S. Government Printing Office, 2006).

elderly Latinos and blacks are much more likely than whites to be poor.

Table 12.6 shows changes in Social Security and Medicare benefits between 2000 and 2005. As can be seen, some benefits have remained the same, but the vast majority of benefits have increased substantially (U.S. Department of Health and Human Services, 2006; Social Security Administration, 2000, 2006b). For example, the cost of Medicare Part B monthly premiums for the two reporting years rose by nearly 75%. These increases add to the financial burden that elderly persons already face while trying to make ends meet on a limited, fixed income.

The Social Security Act serves as a clear disincentive to work for individuals between the ages of 65 and 67 (those considered to be below normal retirement age, or NRA) (Michaud & van

TABLE 12.5

Percentage of Aged below Poverty Line, 2000 and 2005

Ethnicity	2000	2005	Difference
White	8.7	8.7	0.0
Black	21.8	23.3	+1.5
Latino	0.9	19.9	−1.7

Source: U.S. Census Bureau (Washington, DC: U.S. Government Printing Office, 2006).

Soest, 2006). These recipients find that earnings over $12,000 are taxed at the rate of $1 for every $2 earned—a 50% tax rate (applies in 3 years before attaining NRA). For recipients who have reached NRA, the rate of taxation is 33% (or $1 for every $3 earned over $30,800 (applies in the year of attaining NRA, for months prior to such attainment).

This "tax" comes through a reduction in Social Security checks. Although federal regulations prohibit discrimination based on age, the Social Security system clearly does so, as evidenced here. Before 2000, when Congress passed legislation eliminating the earnings penalty for Social Security recipients, the earnings test tax rate was 33% for those who had attained NRA until the time they stopped working altogether. The change was good news for older Americans who desire to continue working beyond age 65 (now age 67).

Many older citizens are becoming concerned about the future of Social Security. The Social Security "trust fund" has long been tapped by Congress to offset shortages in national general revenue expenditures. Older adults fear that their benefits will be reduced. Proposals and discussions about privatizing some or part of Social Security, raising the age at which an individual would become eligible for Social Security benefits, and means-testing eligibility for benefits have caused skepticism as to if, or in what form, Social Security will be available in the future.

Although money does not equate to happiness, money is related to satisfaction in later life. The notion that older adults need less income to meet their living needs has little basis in fact. The needs for food, clothing, shelter, recreation, transportation, and the ability to engage in discretionary spending, such as buying gifts for family members, does not decline with age while the cost of health care usually increases, often significantly. Lowered standards of living, unmet needs, and the inability to meet those needs adequately may result in feelings of inadequacy, despair, loss of self-esteem, and poor health.

TABLE 12.6
Social Security and Medicare Changes between 2000 and 2005

Benefit Category	2000	2005
2000 cost-of-living adjustment (COLA)	2.40%	2.70%
Tax rate for employees (unchanged)	7.65%	Unchanged
Social Security portion	6.20%	Unchanged
Medicare portion	1.65%	Unchanged
Tax rate for self-employed (unchanged)	15.30%	Unchanged
Maximum taxable payroll earnings		
Social Security	$72,600	$90,000
Medicare	No Limit	Unchanged
Retirement earnings tax exemption		
Under age 65	$10,080	$12,000
Age 65–69	$17,000	$31,800
Maximum Social Security monthly benefit for worker retiring at age 65 in January 2000	$1,433	$1,939
Maximum monthly Social Security benefits		
All retired workers (after COLA)	$804	$955
Couple, both receiving benefits	$1,348	$1,574
Widow(er)	$775	$920
Maximum SSI monthly payments		
Individual	$512/month	$579
Couple	$769/month	$869
Medicare Part B monthly premium	$45.50/month	$78.20/month
Part A deductible for hospital stay—1st 60 days	$776	$912
Co-payment for days 61–90	$194/day	$228/day
Co-payment for lifetime reserve days	$388/day	$456
Co-payment for skilled nursing facility—days 21–100	$ 97/day	$114/day

Sources: *Medicare Deductible, Coinsurance, and Premium Payments* (Washington, DC: U.S. Department of Health and Human Services, 2006); *Social Security Changes* (Washington, DC: Social Security Administration, 2000, 2006b).

Income is an enabling resource that affects the options available in life. As income declines, so do those options, with a resulting loss of independence.

Many of the support and social services designed to assist older adults with their unmet needs might not be necessary if retirement incomes were sufficient to enable the nonworking aged to meet those needs. The United States continues to lag behind other industrialized nations in replacement (retirement) income for its aged, ranking fourth in payments to couples and eighth in income benefits for the single older adult (U.S. Department of Commerce, 2006).

Health and Health-Care Services

In later life, the probability of developing health problems becomes more pronounced. Older adults are more prone than the population in general to develop illnesses such as pneumonia, influenza, and gastrointestinal complications. Also more common in old age are chronic diseases, including heart disease, hypertension, cancer, arthritis, diabetes, emphysema, osteoporosis, and visual impairments (Hillier & Barrow, 2006). Table 12.7 shows the leading causes of death for older adults.

Only 5% of the older adult population is affected by health problems so severe as to limit their mobility. Most are able to remain mobile even though they may have one or more disease symptoms. Health-care resources for the elderly are provided primarily through Medicare and Medicaid. **Medicare** is a government health insurance program designed to pay for hospital care and related medical expenses for individuals age 65 and older. Because of the high costs of medical care, benefits paid by Medicare have decreased to approximately half of the total cost of the care. The inability of older adults to pay the portion of medical fees not covered by Medicare (supplemental insurance or "Medigap" insurance) has resulted in large numbers not seeking necessary medical attention (Centers for Medicare and Medicaid, 2006).

Both Medicare and **Medicaid** (health insurance for the poor) have enabled many older adults to obtain needed medical treatment. Because of personal cost-related factors, however, many older adults are forced to delay seeking treatment until their health conditions become severe or life-threatening. Prescription drug benefits for the elderly in this country have undergone major changes. (Chapter 9 details these changes.) Neither Medicare nor Medicaid is designed to provide for preventive health-care services.

TABLE 12.7
Leading Causes of Death for Persons Age 65 and Older (Deaths Per 100,000 Population > 65)

Cause of Death	65–74	75–84	85+
Heart diseases	615.9	1,677.2	5,446.8
Malignant neoplasms	792.1	1,311.9	1,723.9
Cerebrovascular diseases	120.3	431.0	1,445.9
Pulmonary diseases	163.0	386.7	—
Diabetes	91.4	182.8	—
Alzheimer's disease	—	—	752.3
Influenza and pneumonia	—	—	696.6

Source: *Statistical Abstract of the United States,* U.S. Department of Commerce (Washington, DC: U.S. Government Printing Office, 2006).

Doubtless, many serious illnesses could be averted or become less problematic if attention were given to preventive health measures.

As with other government-funded benefit programs, Medicare and Medicaid funds are rapidly approaching deficit-spending levels. Various solutions to the financing of health care have been implemented or are under consideration. These include changes in Medicare coverage of prescription drugs, reduction of benefits, higher co-payments for care, more stringent eligibility requirements, and an expansion of government coverage for catastrophic cases, among others. We must find creative solutions to financing and providing health-care services for America's elderly to meet the increasing health needs of this population.

Abuse and Neglect

As is the case with battered children, the vulnerable elderly population has been subjected to abuse and neglect—antithetical to our social morality. **Elder abuse** has been defined as

Although increased longevity has resulted in many older adults being able to remain active, limited financial resources have raised concerns about access to health care and other needs for many others.

"any knowing, intentional, or negligent act by a caregiver or any other person that causes harm or a serious risk of harm to a vulnerable adult" (National Center on Elder Abuse, 2006, p. 1). Although state statutes vary, elder abuse can be considered to fall into one or more of the following categories

- *Physical abuse:* inflicting or threatening to inflict physical pain or injury on a vulnerable elder, or depriving him or her of a basic need
- *Emotional abuse:* inflicting mental pain, anguish, or distress on an elder person through verbal or nonverbal acts
- *Sexual abuse:* nonconsensual sexual contact of any kind
- *Exploitation:* illegal taking, misuse, or concealing of funds, property, or assets of a vulnerable elder

- *Neglect:* refusal or failure by those responsible to provide food, shelter, health care, or protection for a vulnerable elder
- *Abandonment:* desertion of a vulnerable elder by anyone who has assumed the responsibility for care or custody of that person.

A national survey of abuse of adults 60 years of age and older (Teaster, Dugar, Mendiono, Abner, & Cecil, 2006, pp. 5–6) revealed the following findings:

- Self-neglect (hoarding, failing to take essential medications or refusing to seek medical treatment for serious illness, leaving a burning stove untended, poor hygiene, not wearing suitable clothing for the weather, confusion, inability to attend to housekeeping, and/or dehydration) was the most common category of investigated reports

(26.7%), followed by caregiver neglect (23.7%), and financial exploitation (20.8%).

- Self-neglect was the most common category of substantiated reports (37.2%), followed by caregiver neglect (20.4%) and financial exploitation (14.7%).
- Nearly two-thirds of elder abuse victims were female.
- Nearly 43% of victims were 80 years of age or older.
- The majority of victims were Caucasian.
- Nearly 90% of elder abuse reports occurred in domestic settings.
- 53% of alleged perpetrators of abuse were female.
- More than three-fourths of alleged perpetrators were under the age of 60.
- The most common relationships of victims to alleged perpetrators were adult child (32.6%) and other family members (21.5%).
- More than half (53.2%) of cases of elder abuse were closed because the client was no longer in need of services or the risk of harm was reduced.

The primary risk factors for elder abuse are social isolation, mental impairment (e.g., dementia or Alzheimer's disease), and a history of domestic violence. Warning signs of elder abuse include the following (National Center on Elder Abuse, 2006, p. 1):

- bruises, pressure marks, broken bones, abrasions, and burns
- unexplained withdrawal from normal activities; sudden change in alertness; unusual depression
- bruises around the breasts or genital area
- sudden changes in financial situation
- bedsores, unattended medical needs, poor hygiene, and unusual weight loss
- belittling, threats, and other uses of power and control by spouses
- strained and tense relationships, frequent arguments between the caregiver and elderly persons.

Precise estimates of the number of older Americans who are being abused, neglected, or exploited are difficult to obtain because definitions of elder abuse differ, state statistics vary widely, there is no uniform reporting system, and comprehensive national data are not collected (National Center on Elder Abuse, 2005). Notwithstanding these caveats, it is estimated that between 1 and 2 million incidents of elder abuse and neglect occur in a given year. Only about 25% of all incidents (between 250,000 and 450,000) are actually reported to adult protective services agencies, and 35% of these (between 87,500 and 157,500) are substantiated (National Center on Elder Abuse, 2005; Teaster, Dugar, Mendiondo, Abner, & Cecil, 2006).

Many states have enacted legislation to protect older adults from abuse and neglect. Family violence is an unfortunate and dehumanizing product of our society that generally is directed toward those who are dependent on others for some aspect of their care. Adult protective services are designed to shield older adults from further harm. Such services, however, do little to alleviate the causes of the problem.

Long-Term Care

Most older Americans enjoy reasonably good health, with only 5% experiencing health problems so debilitating that they require long-term care (often thought of as nursing-home care). The contemporary long-term care industry has emerged primarily as a result of Medicare and Medicaid legislation, which allows third-party payments to the providers of health-care services.

Nursing homes and other long-term care facilities typically are licensed by state health departments, which have the responsibility of reviewing these facilities periodically to ensure minimal standards of care. In addition, all states require that administrators of long-term care facilities be licensed, although administrator-licensing requirements vary considerably among the states.

The media quite often portray nursing homes as dehumanizing warehouses where residents are neglected and abuse is common. Staff members of these facilities often are characterized as incompetent, uncaring, and uninterested in providing high-quality care for the residents. For some nursing homes and other long-term care facilities, these allegations are valid. Even though most of these facilities make every effort to provide quality care, caring for debilitated, aging residents is both physically and emotionally demanding.

High rates of staff turnover are common, which places further stress on long-term care facilities in the selection and training of nursing-care staff. In recent years, more stringent state standards and skillful investigation and evaluation techniques by state regulatory agencies have resulted in a higher level and quality of services. The Nursing Home Reform Act, part of the **Omnibus Budget Reconciliation Act (OBRA) of 1987,** introduced major nursing home reforms, including strengthening residents' rights, establishing written care plans, providing staff training, and requiring the employment of certified social workers. These efforts were designed to create a safe and secure environment for residents, with appropriate medical and nursing care administered by a caring staff.

The Nursing Home Reform Act also established the following rights for nursing-home residents:

- the right to freedom from abuse, mistreatment, and neglect;
- the right to freedom from physical restraints;
- the right to privacy;
- the right to accommodation of their medical, physical, psychological, and social needs;
- the right to participate in resident and family groups;
- the right to be treated with dignity;
- the right to exercise self-determination;
- the right to communicate freely;
- the right to participate in the review of one's care plan, and to be fully informed in advance about any changes in care, treatment, or change of status in the facility; and
- the right to voice grievances without discrimination or reprisal.

Most nursing homes and other long-term care facilities in the United States are proprietary; that is, they are private, profit-making businesses. Some facilities are nonprofit, usually operated through the auspices of religious organizations or units of state or local governments. The quality of care of private profit-making facilities and nonprofit ones seems to be about the same. Although privately owned facilities are more vulnerable to "shaving" services to maximize profit, strict enforcement of standards minimizes any significant differences in the services provided to residents.

Without question, nursing-home care has improved since the Nursing Home Reform Act was passed in 1987. For example, the number of citations for deficiencies issued by official monitors who survey nursing-home facilities dropped by nearly 50% in the 10 years following passage of the act, despite the increasing nursing home population of those with disabilities and cognitive impairments, who require more rigorous care. After passage of the act, nursing-home facilities were allowed time to correct deficiencies before civil penalties were imposed, and the term "widespread problems" was redefined to apply only when a violation affects every resident of the facility. The federal government has been encouraging states to limit circumstances that would lead to the imposition of civil penalties, while the nursing-home industry has undertaken efforts to weaken enforcement (American Society on Aging, 2006). Thus, concern remains for the future.

Long-term care facilities will continue to be the most viable resource for the debilitated elderly. Many facilities, particularly those that wealthier elderly people can afford, offer a wide range of living options. An individual or couple can move into a private apartment that is part of the facility and maintain independence if

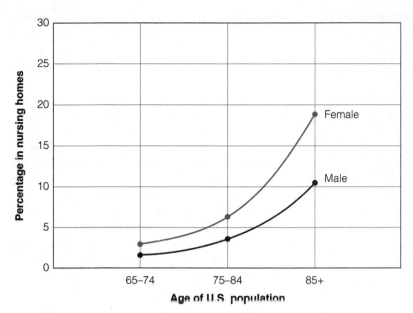

FIGURE 12.2

Percentage of Residents in Nursing Homes in U.S. Population Age 65 and Over, 1999

Note: This is the most recent year for which these figures are available.

Source: Statistical Abstract of the United States, U.S. Department of Commerce (Washington, DC: U.S. Government Printing Office, 2002).

desired, although meals in a central dining area, educational and recreational activities, and some health care may be available to them, often at an increased cost.

As their health deteriorates and their independence diminishes, nursing care, meals, and other services are readily available without the individual having to move. If the person's health deteriorates to the point at which he or she cannot be alone in an apartment, a facility more like the traditional nursing home is sometimes located on the same property. This option is preferable to many elderly individuals because they can remain in the same familiar location with a minimum of disruption if their health deteriorates.

Alternatives such as home health care, visiting nurses, and personal-care homes enable older adults to reside in the community longer, but they tend to defer, not replace, the need for nursing-home care (see Figure 12.2). Because of more alternatives, however, the percentage of people 65 and older living in nursing homes is decreasing—from 5.1% in 1990 to 4.5% in 2000. This percentage, however, rises steeply by age: 1.1% for persons age 65–74; 4.7% for persons 75–85; and 18.2% for persons 85 and older (National Coalition on Aging, 2002).

As the need for additional nursing home/long-term care beds increases, financing will become more critical. More cost-effective plans must be developed to assure that the debilitated elderly receive essential health-care services. In a number of communities, faith-based organizations, unions, and private profit-making organizations are establishing residential facilities for the elderly.

Housing

About 80% of older adults are homeowners, and nearly 75% of these homeowners own their homes free and clear. The U.S. Census Bureau (2004b) reported that only 7.8% and 4.2% of all houses owned by persons age 65–74 and 75 or older in 2001, respectively, were built after 1990. About 12% and 17% of the homes owned by persons age 65–74 and 75 or more, respectively, were built before 1920.

Older homes are attractive to low-income homeowners because they generally are more affordable to purchase, but older homes typically have higher utility and maintenance costs. As a result, many of these homes become dilapidated over the years, and in later life the ability of their owners to maintain or repair them becomes more and more difficult, so the homes deteriorate further. In addition, older adults have difficulty securing home-repair loans. Thus, they are faced with living in homes that provide inadequate protection from the elements, as well as a host of other problems, and they become safety hazards.

Another factor that makes it more difficult for older persons to stay in their homes, even if they own them outright, is *gentrification*—the restoration and upgrading of deteriorated urban property by middle-class or affluent people, which often results in displacement of low-income people. At the beginning of the **gentrification** process, property values and property taxes are generally low. As the process unfolds, property values skyrocket and the taxing authorities impose a sharp rise in property taxes. Low-income homeowners who reside in areas undergoing gentrification find that they no longer can afford to pay their property taxes and are forced to sell their houses at well below market value and move out of their neighborhoods, sometimes where generations of their family have lived.

To make matters worse, the displaced persons do not have enough money to purchase a new home outright and do not qualify for a home mortgage, so they may have to move in with a family member, or live in an undesirable part of town, or move to a rural area where the cost of living is affordable. Disruption and displacement may cause older people to become confused, develop stress-related medical problems, or withdraw and become isolated—all of which are antithetical to a healthy lifestyle.

Government housing for older people typically is difficult to secure because of the high demand for low-cost housing by younger persons, especially those with children. Even when available, low-cost housing may be unattractive, impersonal, and lacking in privacy; often in areas with a high crime rates; and too noisy. Without question, more affordable housing options are needed for older adults, but this is not likely to happen because of other government spending priorities, as well as the lack of government incentives to homebuilders to construct more affordable housing units.

Meanwhile, housing alternatives for more economically secure elderly people have expanded. Self-contained apartment complexes have been developed through the auspices of religious organizations and private sponsorship. These facilities typically are attractive, provide all the amenities for comfortable living, and assure peer interactions and essential social supports. Many of these facilities, as discussed, also provide medical care, nursing services, and meals, if individuals become unable to care for themselves in their own apartments. These facilities, however, are much more costly, and many require a substantial down payment before an individual is accepted as a resident.

Although housing communes are not abundant, this option is growing in popularity and provides a family-type living experience for older participants. This is a housing arrangement in which several older adults pool their resources to rent or purchase a dwelling and share in its upkeep. Basic living costs for things such as food and utilities are shared, enabling participants to spend less on basic living needs.

Transportation

Transportation is essential for grocery shopping, attending church services, keeping appointments with doctors and dentists, visiting friends, and maintaining contact with families. Most older adults must travel some distance to procure the necessities for daily living, and this likely is difficult for them. Many who once drove are no longer able to do so, and the costs of maintaining a vehicle and buying insurance are beyond their means. Consequently, they depend on alternative sources of travel. Public means of transit—buses and trains—have been geared primarily to ambulatory individuals who typically use these forms of transportation to get to and from work during the week. For older people, navigating the public transportation system can be problematic, as the nearest bus stop may be some distance from their home, riding times may be long, and transfers may be needed from one line to another. Further, older adults may have trouble getting grocery bags on and off a bus, then carrying them several blocks from the stop to their residence.

A few transit systems have developed specialized services for the elderly and people with disabilities, operating on a door-to-door basis by appointment. Few, however, are available to serve the elderly on-call. Users must anticipate their needs (often as long as 2 weeks in advance), make the appointment, and hope they are not forgotten.

On the positive side, volunteers have been engaged in providing transportation services for the elderly in some communities, and public transportation has taken into account the needs of many older adults to secure needed goods and services. Nutrition programs have provided transportation to lunch programs, and some have extended their transportation services to include shopping and social visits. These transportation alternatives, however, are available to only a comparatively few older adults in need. The absence of transportation has resulted in many older adults' becoming homebound. Frequently, the result is social isolation, which leads to a loss of incentive, less activity, self-deprecation, and eventually psychological and physical deterioration.

Older People of Color

The problems of aging discussed in this chapter are applicable to older people of color, but to a much greater extent. Life expectancy for African Americans is appreciably less than for whites for persons 65 and older (see Table 12.8). Because neither genetics nor heredity has been a factor contributing to a shorter life expectancy for these groups, social and cultural factors are more likely to account for this differential in longevity.

As a result of social discrimination, a large proportion of non-white populations have lower incomes, more physically demanding work, and fewer opportunities to achieve essential life-support services. This has led to more severe and unattended health problems, inadequate nutrition, fewer opportunities for social advancement, below-market wages, and an oppressive cultural environment. Growing old under these adverse conditions is stressful, accelerating the aging process for these individuals.

Although the figures have been dropping in recent years, the percentage of elderly people in the United States who are living below the poverty level is still high, especially for persons of color. For example, in 2005, the percentage of elderly white persons living below the poverty level was 10.1%, compared to 24.9% for elderly

TABLE 12.8
Life Expectancy* at Selected Ages for White and African American Persons, 2000

| Age | Male | | Female | |
---	White	Black	White	Black
0	74.8	68.2	80.0	74.9
65	16.3	14.5	19.2	17.4
70	13.0	11.7	15.5	14.1
75	10.1	9.4	12.1	11.2
80	7.6	7.3	9.1	8.6
85	5.5	5.7	6.6	6.5
90	4.0	4.5	4.7	4.8

*Average number of additional years persons will live by age.

Source: *Statistical Abstract of the United States,* U.S. Department of Commerce (Washington, DC: U.S. Government Printing Office, 2006).

African Americans and 21.8% for elderly Latinos (U.S. Department of Commerce, 2006). Without regard to age, these figures are dramatically higher for households headed by women: 24.0% for whites, 36.9% for African Americans, and 37.0% for Latinos.

Many of the necessary support services are not available to older people of color because of discrimination, language differences, complex or confusing eligibility requirements, limited entitlement, and limited outreach efforts, as well as their own pride, which prevents them from seeking services. Poverty, limited options, and discrimination mean that many elderly people of color cannot attain the security, contentment, and life satisfaction of most other elderly Americans.

Services for Older Adults

A wide array of social, health, and related support services have been developed or extended to provide for the needs of older people in the United States. At the federal level, these programs are based largely in the Social Security Act—social insurance and SSI—and health services through Medicare or Medicaid. And the Older Americans Act provides supplementary services through funding of nutrition programs, transportation, social services, and coordination of services for older people.

Through both government-sponsored and private sources, older-citizen participation programs such as Foster Grandparents, Green Thumb, and the Retired Seniors Volunteer Program, as well as a variety of self-help programs, have been developed. Older adults in the Foster Grandparents program, for example, are employed part-time to work with children in state schools, hospitals, and child-care centers, as well as with pregnant teenagers and abusive and neglectful parents. Senior centers in many communities offer a place where older adults can interact, eat nutritious meals, participate in recreational activities, and pursue hobbies or crafts.

Under the auspices of the Older Americans Act, areawide agencies on aging (AAAs) have been established throughout the country to coordinate services to older people. Among their many functions are activities such as assessing the needs of the older population, providing or contracting for congregate meals programs, developing transportation services, serving as information and referral resources, and acting as advocates to assure that communities will be attentive to the needs of older people. Meals-on-Wheels programs provide hot meals for the homebound elderly and essential social contact for older adults who have difficulty leaving their homes because of limited mobility.

Adult day care centers enable older adults to remain in the community. Often, older people with a working son or daughter cannot be monitored during the day, so day care centers assume caregiving responsibilities at those times. These centers usually offer a variety of activities and provide health checkups and supervision for participants. Mental health services are provided through mental health outreach centers, and counseling services usually are available to older people and their families through local social services agencies. In rural areas, all of these services may not be readily available, although nutrition and transportation resources usually are offered.

Although community services are helpful in meeting many needs of older adults, these are not widely available in proportion to the numbers in the community who potentially could benefit from them. Outreach efforts have been reasonably successful in securing participation; however, funding levels of available resources limit the number who can be served. Often, agencies are not located strategically and, therefore, exclude the participation of many older adults. Also, outreach efforts would be more effective if older adults were employed as care providers.

Social Work with Older Adults

The U.S. Bureau of Labor Statistics (2006) projects an increase of at least 27% for social workers and social and human service assistants jobs between 2004 and 2014. A bachelor's degree is the minimum requirement, and a master's degree in social work or a related field has become the standard for many positions in social work. Competition for jobs is expected in cities, and opportunities should be plentiful in rural areas. As a result of the aging of the U.S. population, a growing proportion of these jobs is expected to involve services to persons 65 and older.

Many schools of social work have developed specializations in gerontology and social work research has focused on problems of adaptation and life satisfaction in old age. As a result, research and literature on this topic have developed rapidly, and a knowledge base for intervention is being established. Older adults, we now recognize, have many of the same problems that are evident at other stages in the life cycle:

personal adjustment problems, marital problems, relocation, family conflict, adjustment to separation and loneliness, anxiety about limited income, mental illness, and interpersonal loss, among others. Along with this recognition is the acknowledgment that the aged are responsive to social work change efforts.

The most common form of social work intervention with the elderly population is generalist practice at the micro-level. This includes working with older adults and their families on specific problems, such as enhancing personal adjustment, securing resources to meet their needs, providing emotional support in decision making, dealing with death and dying, and managing family conflict. Intervention often employs a counseling and guidance approach, stresses problem clarification and the development of options and priorities, and provides an opportunity for the client to express anxiety and emotion.

Community-based practice is directed to exo-level community systems as targets for creating a more responsive opportunity structure for the elderly. In an advocacy approach, social workers identify issues such as poor housing and lack of transportation and health care and mobilize community resources to bring about change by developing resources to meet these needs (Kirst-Ashman & Hull, 2005).

With an older adult clientele, social workers must be aware of the special problems that this population encounters. Many older people have been self-sustaining members of society and have developed problems of adaptation only at an older age. Without support, accumulated interpersonal losses (such as the loss of a spouse, friends, familiar environment, job, income, physical health) threaten the fulfillment of daily living needs and life satisfaction.

Social workers are employed in a variety of agencies that serve the elderly, including mental health centers, family service agencies, nursing homes, nutrition programs, recreational centers, hospitals, health and nutrition centers, volunteer programs, transportation and housing programs, protective services programs, and community planning agencies. As the theoretical knowledge base expands, social work activity with older adults will continue to be intensified and intervention techniques refined, resulting in more effective services to the ever-increasing older population.

Summary

A dramatic increase in the number of Americans age 65 and older is expected in years to come as millions of baby-boomers enter retirement and advances in medicine and medical technology allow individuals to live longer. The projected growth will strain our contemporary health and welfare delivery systems and require additional resources to manage. This growth will create expanded job opportunities for employment in human services organizations. In turn, this will create a need for additional educational opportunities for those who are interested in becoming employed in one of the health or social services fields. A cadre of trained and knowledgeable social work staff will have to be developed to maintain a high quality of life for older adults as they continue to increase in numbers.

To formulate effective interventions, social workers who work with older adults must be aware of the physiological, psychological, and social changes that accompany aging. Of particular concern are problems related to income inadequacies, health-care costs, housing and transportation, abuse and neglect, family support, and the availability and efficiency of various community programs that assist older adults with their living needs and are culturally sensitive, recognizing the diversity among the elderly.

Far too many older adults suffer from deprivation related to limited resources and unattended health problems. Social workers can assist by developing knowledge and skill, and understanding, when working with older individuals.

They also can work within the community in developing and using resources that will enrich the quality of life for vulnerable elderly people.

Key Terms and InfoTrac® College Edition

The terms below are defined in the Glossary at the end of this text. To learn more about key terms and topics in this chapter, enter the following search terms using InfoTrac or the World Wide Web:

activity theory	gross domestic
ageism	product (GDP)
aging	hospice
Alzheimer's disease	living will
continuity theory	Medicaid
developmental theory	Medicare
elder abuse	Omnibus Budget
exchange theory	Reconciliation Act
family caregiving	(OBRA) of 1987
gentrification	pre-retirement planning
gerontology	retirement

Discussion Questions

1. In what manner does physiological aging affect adaptation in late life?
2. Compare the social theories of aging discussed in this chapter. What are the strengths and limitations of each theory? How does each fit with the systems/ecological framework?
3. What are some of the major issues with which adults must cope as they grow older?
4. What is the role of a generalist social work practitioner in identifying needs and resources for older adults?
5. How could a generalist social work practitioner contribute to a better quality of life for residents in a long-term care facility?

6. As the population continues to grow older, what effect do you think this will have on our society? On social work practice?

On the Internet

http://www.aoa.dhhs.gov/

http://www.aarp.org/

http://www.ssa.gov/

http://www.alzforum.org/

http://ninds.nih.gov/

http://www.alzheimers.com/

http://www.elderweb.com/

References

Alzheimer's Association. (2006a). *Saving lives, saving money: Dividends for Americans investing in Alzheimer research.* Chicago: Author.

Alzheimer's Association. (2006b). *Statistics about Alzheimer's disease.* Chicago: Author. Available: http://alz.org/AboutAD/Statistics.asp

Alzheimer's Association. (2006c). *The year in Alzheimer science: 2005.* Chicago: Author.

American Association of Suicidology. (2006). *Suicide in the USA.* Washington, DC: Author.

American Society on Aging. (2006). *Problems beset nursing home reform.* San Francisco: CA: Author. Available: http://www.asaging.org/at/at-193/nhreform.html

Centers for Medicare and Medicaid. (2006). *Medicare supplement insurance: "Medigap."* Baltimore: Author.

Chester, E. (2002). *Employing generation why.* Palo Alto, CA: Chess Press.

Eyetsemitan, F. E., & Gire, J. T. (2003). *Aging and adult development in the developing world: Applying western theories and concepts.* Westport, CT: Praeger.

Heffler, S., Smith, S., Keehan, S., Borger, G., Clemens, M., and Truffer, C. (2005). U.S. health spending projections for 2004–2014. *Health Affairs, 24*

74–85. Available: http://content.healthaffairs.org/cgi/content/abstract/hlthaff.w5.74v1

Hillier, S. M., & Barrow, G. M. (2006). *Aging, the individual, and society* (8th ed.). Belmont, CA: Wadsworth Publishing.

Johnson, R. W., & Wiener, J. M. (2006). *A profile of frail older Americans and their caregivers.* Washington, DC: Urban Institute. (Occasional Paper Number 8)

Joseph, P. (2006). *The science of aging: Theories and potential therapies (The new biology).* Emeryville, CA: Checkmark Books.

Kaiser Family Foundation. (2005). *Medicare chartbook* (3rd ed.). Menlo Park, CA: Author.

Kirst-Ashman, K., & Hull, G. (2005). *Generalist practice with organizations and communities* (3rd ed.). Pacific Grove, CA: Brooks/Cole.

Kübler-Ross, E. (1997). *Death: The final stage of growth.* Upper Saddle River, NJ: Prentice Hall. (originally published 1975)

Lancaster, L. C., & Stillman, D. (2003). *When generations collide: Who they are. Why they clash. How to solve the generational puzzle at work.* Mississauga, Ontario, Canada: Crisp Learning.

Martin, C. A., & Tulgan, B. (2002). *Managing the generation mix: From collision to collaboration.* Amherst, MA: HRD Press.

Masoro, E., & Austad, S. (Eds.). (2005). *Handbook of the biology of ageing* (6th ed.). New York: Academic Press.

McKune, S. L., Andresen, E. M., Zhang, J., & Neugaard, B. (2006). *Caregiving: A national profile and assessment of caregiving services and needs.* Americus, GA: Rosalynn Carter Institute for Caregiving. Available: http://www.Rosalynncarter.org

Meredith, G. E., & Schewe, C. D. (2002). *Managing by defining moments: America's 7 generational cohorts, their workplace values, and why managers should care.* Hoboken, NJ: Wiley.

Michaud, P., & van Soest, A. (2006). *How did the elimination of the earnings test above the normal retirement age affect retirement expectations?* Ann Arbor: University of Michigan Retirement Research Center.

Moody, H. R. (2006). *Aging: Concepts and controversies.* Boston: Pine Forge Press.

National Center on Elder Abuse. (2005). *Elder abuse prevalence and indicators.* Washington, DC: Author.

National Center on Elder Abuse. (2006). *Frequently asked questions.* Washington, DC: Author.

National Coalition on Aging. (2002). *American perceptions of aging in the 21st century*. Washington, DC: Author.

National Family Caregivers Association. (2006). *Caregiving statistics*. Kensington, MD: Author.

National Respite Coalition for Lifespan Respite Task Force. (2006). *Summary of Lifespan Respite Care Act of 2005, S. 1283*. Annandale, VA: Author.

Nelson, T. D. (Ed.). (2004). *Ageism: Stereotyping and prejudice against older persons*. Cambridge, MA: MIT Press.

Newman, B. M., & Newman, P. R. (2005). *Development through life: A psychosocial approach* (9th ed.). Belmont, CA: Wadsworth Publishing.

Palmore, E. B., Branch, L., & Harris, D. (Eds.). (2005). *Encyclopedia of ageism (religion and mental health)*. Binghamton, NY: Haworth Press.

Penner, R. G., Perun, P., & Steuerle, E. (2003). *Letting older workers work*. Washington, DC: Urban Institute.

Riley, M. W. (1968). *Aging and society*. New York: Russell Sage Foundation.

Shenk, D., & Groger, L. (Eds.). (2006). *Aging education in a global context (gerontology and geriatrics)*. Binghamton, NY: Haworth Press.

Social Security Administration. (2000). *Income of the aged chartbook, 2000*. Washington, DC: Author.

Social Security Administration. (2002). *Income of the aged chartbook, 2002*. Washington, DC: Author.

Social Security Administration. (2006a). *Income of the population 55 and older, 2004*. Washington, DC: Author.

Social Security Administration. (2006b). *2005 Social Security changes*. Washington, DC: Author.

Teaster, P., Dugar, T., Mendiondo, M., Abner, E., & Cecil, K. (2006). *The 2004 survey of adult protective services: Abuse of adults 60 years of age or older*. Lexington: University of Kentucky Graduate Center for Gerontology.

Tornstam, L. (2005). *Gerotranscendence: A developmental theory of positive ageing*. New York: Springer Publishing.

U.S. Bureau of Labor Statistics. (2006). *Career guide to industries*. Available: http://www.bls.gov/oco/ocos060.htm

U.S. Census Bureau. (2004a). *Global population profile: 2002*. Washington, DC: Author.

U.S. Census Bureau. (2004b). *These old houses: 2001*. Washington, DC: Author.

U.S. Census Bureau. (2006). *Historical poverty tables*. Washington, DC: Author.

U.S. Department of Commerce. (2002). *Statistical abstract of the United States, 2002*. (122nd ed.). Washington, DC: U.S. Government Printing Office.

U.S. Department of Commerce. (2006). *Statistical abstract of the United States, 2006*. (126th ed.). Washington, DC: U.S. Government Printing Office.

U.S. Department of Health and Human Services. (2006). *Medicare deductible, coinsurance and premium amounts, 2005*. Washington, DC: Author.

Suggested Further Readings

Atchley, R., & Barusch, A. (2003). *Social forces and aging—An introduction to social gerontology* (6th ed.). Belmont, CA: Wadsworth Publishing.

Baars, J., Dannefer, D., Phillipson, C., & Walker, A. (Eds.). (2006). *Aging, globalization and inequality: The new critical gerontology*. New York: Springer Publishing.

Berkman, B. (Ed.). (2006). *Handbook of social work in health and aging*. Amityville, NY: Baywood Publishing Company.

Berkman, B., & Harootyan, L. (Eds.). (2006). *Social work and health care in an aging society: Education, policy, and research*. New York: Oxford University Press.

Birren, J. E., & Schaie, K. W. (Eds.). (2005). *Handbook of the psychology of aging* (6th ed.). New York: Springer Publishing.

Cummings, S. M. (2003). *Diversity and aging in the social environment*. New York: Springer Publishing.

Herdt, G., & DeVries, B. (Eds.). (2004). *Gay and lesbian aging: Research and future directions*. New York: Springer Publishing.

Hunter, S. (2005). *Midlife and older GLBT adults: Knowledge and affirmative practice for the social services*. Binghamton, NY: Haworth Press.

Wilmoth, J. M. (Ed.). (2005). *Gerontology: Perspectives and issues*. Binghamton, NY: Haworth Press.

Wykle, M. L., Morris, D. L., & Whitehouse, P. J. (Eds.). (2004). *Successful aging through the lifespan: International issues in health*. New York: Springer Publishing.

CHAPTER 13

Criminal Justice

Ray is a 32-year-old man whose current address is Huntsville State Prison. He is serving a 20-year sentence for armed robbery. This is not Ray's first prison term, but he hopes that it will be his last.

Ray first came to the attention of the justice system at age 14, when he was arrested for stealing a car. The third child in a family with six children, he grew up with his mother and siblings in a poverty-stricken area of a large eastern city. He was physically abused by his mother during his childhood and received little positive attention from her. From first grade on, Ray had difficulty in school. He had a short attention span, disrupted the classroom regularly, and rarely completed his schoolwork.

At the time of his first arrest, Ray was in the seventh grade for the second time. He was placed on juvenile probation, and his family was referred for counseling. Because his mother worked long hours, however, she was not able to attend the counseling sessions. Ray became more of a problem in school and in his neighborhood. He began skipping school, experimenting with drugs, and committing a series of burglaries. His mother could not handle his frequent bursts of anger or get Ray to respond to the limits she set for him.

When Ray was 16, he spent 3 months in a juvenile detention facility, where he responded well to the program structure. When he left the program, he was assigned a probation officer and returned to live with his family. The conditions of his probation stipulated that he attend school consistently, maintain a strict curfew, and report to his probation officer monthly. Ray followed these conditions for several months but continued to have difficulty in school and dropped out 4 months after returning home.

He held a series of jobs at fast-food restaurants but had difficulty going to work regularly and became frustrated because he was not earning much money. Increasingly, he gravitated toward older young adults, who hung out on the street and seemed to have the freedom and the money for which he yearned. Ray's new friends liked him, and he felt accepted and enjoyed being with them. Ray soon became involved with them in selling drugs and committing burglaries.

At that point, Ray had a series of arrests for drug dealing, burglary, and assault, which resulted in several stays in various detention facilities. Just before his last arrest, Ray married a 19-year-old, who recently had their baby. He is anxious to get out of prison and begin to get to know his son and support his family. Frustrated by the lack of educational opportunities and counseling at the prison, he has enrolled in a prison program to try to earn his high school equivalency certificate. He hopes to be released to a community halfway house and enroll in a job-training program, knowing that he will need job skills and help in dealing with his anger if he is to maintain a successful marriage, keep a job, and stay out of prison.

In this chapter we look at the four components of the criminal justice system: legislative, law enforcement, judicial, and corrections. Although social workers play some role in all of these, our attention will be directed to the corrections component and social work roles involved in rehabilitation. Consistent with the overall focus of this text, we will look at rehabilitation strategies in light of the competing views of criminal behavior and the role the environment plays in shaping behaviors that lead to both crime and rehabilitation.

The Criminal Justice System

In its broadest sense, the **criminal justice system** refers to the means used to enforce the standards of conduct required to protect individuals and property and to maintain a sense of justice in the community. A system of criminal justice creates the laws governing social behavior, attempts to prevent violations of these laws, and apprehends, judges, punishes, and makes efforts to rehabilitate those who violate the laws. **Crime** is a legal concept with political origins. Crimes are acts that are considered to be a threat to individual or community well-being—and some acts are more serious than others.

Criminal behavior has two principal restraints: (1) *morality,* enforced by an individual's social conscience; and (2) *law,* enforced by the police and the courts. Any decline in the former usually is matched by a rise in the latter. That is, if traditional restraints on behavior are eroded (e.g., disapproval of family, friends, and others we love and respect; informal discipline within social institutions such as schools and places of employment; and private lawsuits), legal restraints must be placed on that behavior (Abadinsky, 2007, Samaha, 2005; Schmalleger, 2007).

The criminal justice system consists of the following four components:

1. The *legislative component,* which deems certain acts to be criminal;

2. The *law enforcement component,* which seeks to deter crime and to apprehend and prosecute lawbreakers;
3. The *judicial component,* which determines if the laws are valid under our Constitution and prescribes penalties for the illegal behavior; and
4. A *corrections component,* which administers the penalties and performs the rehabilitative functions.

Each of these components is discussed next.

Legislative Component

Criminal codes define the types of conduct that are considered to constitute crimes and establish a range of penalties for such behavior. Three basic kinds of crime are measured by the major criminal statistics in the United States (Samaha, 2005, p. 28):

1. violent or personal crimes or actions that hurt or threaten to hurt people;
2. property crimes or actions that take, damage, or destroy or threaten to take, damage, or destroy people's property; and
3. other crimes or behavior such as disorderly conduct, public drunkenness, drug use, and prostitution.

In the United States, each state is allowed to enact its own criminal laws or statutes, as long as they conform to the restrictions dictated by the U.S. Constitution. The U.S. Congress, state legislatures, and local bodies such as city councils are constantly defining or redefining criminal behavior to reflect social and political change.

Social workers may be involved in political action to persuade legislative bodies to classify certain behaviors as criminal, such as abusing or neglecting a child; or to declassify certain prohibited behaviors as non-criminal, such as homeless people sleeping on the streets. Some people oppose social workers' intentions or actions and their commitment to social and economic justice, so social workers in these roles should be prepared for opposition. The ideal legislative system attempts to define and enact a consensus criminal code—one that forbids, or extracts penalties for, behavior that most of us find threatening to the community while protecting the rights of the minority to express their own lifestyles.

Law Enforcement Component

Law enforcement has the functions of preventing crime, investigating crime, apprehending criminal suspects, and assisting in criminal prosecution (Abadinsky, 2007). Law enforcement officers are bound to enforce all criminal statutes with equal emphasis (that is, full enforcement). Rarely, however, do law enforcement efforts attempt to enforce every criminal statute all of the time. Instead, they use their discretion, enforcing some laws sometimes against some people, called **selective enforcement.** The amount of discretion is inversely related to the severity of the crime; the less the severity, the more discretion that is applied, and vice versa. Little discretion typically is associated with behaviors such as public drunkenness, threatening behavior and harassment, and street prostitution.

Law enforcement officers are legally "empowered" to make an arrest when they have probable cause to believe that an individual has violated a law. Arrested persons generally are taken into custody until arraignment, at which time a trial judge or a grand jury determines whether probable cause exists for the arrested person to stand trial. As shown in Figure 13.1, the law enforcement process has many "stops," from suspicion that a person has committed a crime to trial.

Social workers can have a significant influence on the law enforcement process. For example, what discretion, if any, should law enforcement officers have in dealing with domestic-disturbance cases? Most law enforcement officers agree that intervention in domestic cases is the most dangerous part of their job. How might this belief influence law enforcement's handling of these situations? Are more women harmed or killed as a result?

Law enforcement officers also have a responsibility to identify people with mental illness who are a threat to themselves or others and take them to a hospital. How much discretion, if any, should law enforcement officers exercise when dealing with people with mental illness? Who makes that decision? How do we ensure that law enforcement officers are trained adequately to deal with them? These examples constitute important areas for social workers in law enforcement.

Judicial Component

Following arrest, individuals charged with a crime become defendants, and decision making regarding their future shifts from law enforcement to the criminal courts. Strictly speaking, courts are legal institutions in which lawyers play the leading roles and make most of the decisions. In reality, that is not the case. Most decision making takes place behind closed doors and in the corridors of the courthouse. **Courts** are political and social institutions as much as they are legal institutions; they are sensitive and respond to the needs and demands of the public, special-interest groups, and individuals. They use discretionary decision making to balance the law and extralegal, professional, organizational, and societal goals. Thus, formal court proceedings simply ratify what lawyers and other criminal justice personnel already have decided informally (Abadinsky, 2007; Samaha, 2005; Schmalleger, 2007).

The three levels or tiers of criminal courts (Berman, Greiner, & Saliba, 2004) are:

1. **lower criminal courts** (also referred to as superior, municipal, county, justice of the peace, and magistrate courts): courts with the power to decide minor cases and to conduct pretrial proceedings;

2. **trial courts:** courts with the power to conduct pretrial and trial proceedings in all criminal cases; and

3. **appellate courts:** courts with the authority to review the decision of trial courts and lower criminal courts.

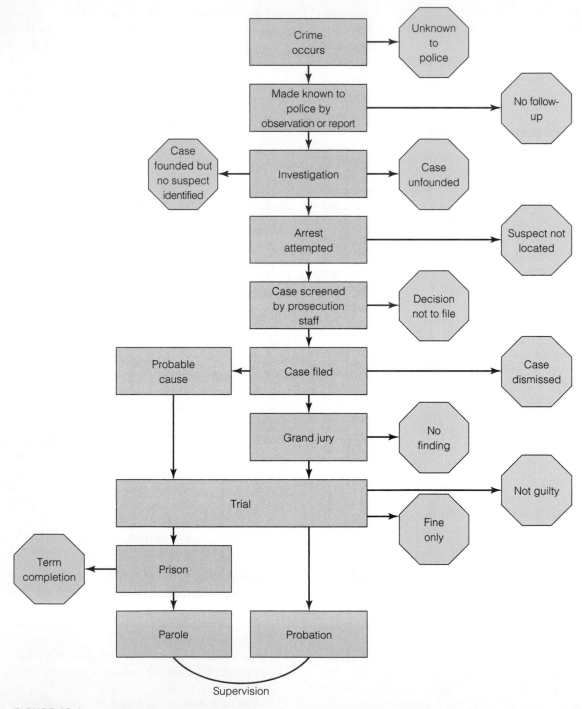

FIGURE 13.1

The Path through the Criminal Justice System

Note: The stop signs show how a crime drops out of the system. Rectangles represent stages in the system.

LOWER COURTS

The lower courts decide the majority of criminal cases involving minor crimes such as traffic offenses, drunk and disorderly conduct, shoplifting, and prostitution. These are the only contacts that most people have with the criminal courts. Lower courts are courts of limited jurisdiction; their authority is limited to trying misdemeanor cases and conducting preliminary proceedings in felony cases.

Defendants in lower courts have the same rights as defendants in trial courts; however, lower court judges try most cases less formally than trial courts and they try them without juries. Lower courts perform a number of additional tasks, including deciding bail; assigning lawyers to defendants who cannot afford them; and conducting pretrial hearings, including preliminary hearings, to decide the legality of confession, searches, and seizures.

The U.S. Constitution does not require that lower court judges have legal training (Schmalleger, 2007). And in about two-thirds of lower court systems, judges are not required to be members of the state bar. Although some states require lower court judges to pass an examination or attend training courses, as a general rule the judges in lower courts have less training than the lawyers with whom they deal daily. Some would argue that lower court judges are only minimally qualified to rule on complex legal issues, decide guilt or innocence, or pass sentences, and that they should be held to a higher standard of competence.

TRIAL COURTS

In contrast, trial courts are courts of general jurisdiction; they have the authority to decide all criminal cases, from capital felonies to petty misdemeanors. Adjudication or court proceedings begin in trial courts (original jurisdiction), and only trial courts can adjudicate felony cases (exclusive jurisdiction). Not surprisingly, trial courts adhere to formal rules more than lower courts do. Only members of the state bar are allowed to preside as judges.

APPELLATE COURTS

Appellate courts hear and decide appeals of trial court decisions. Thus, proceedings in appellate courts are more formal than those of lower criminal courts or trial courts. In most states, intermediate appellate courts hear the bulk of initial appeals, deciding whether the government has proved its case beyond a reasonable doubt, and whether defendants have established their defenses adequately. Supreme courts (courts of last resort) review the decisions of intermediate appellate court decisions, as well as complicated questions of law and the constitutional rights of criminal defendants (Abadinsky, 2007; Berman, Greiner, & Saliba, 2004).

The U.S. Constitution does not guarantee the right to a review of a lower-court decision; however, all jurisdictions by law allow defendants to have the decisions of lower courts reviewed by courts of appeals. Overturning a decision of a lower court does not close a case automatically. In many cases in which a lower court decision is overturned by an appellate court, the government proceeds with retrying the defendant.

More than 90% of all criminal cases do not reach the formal trial stage; they are adjudicated by way of guilty pleas in a process known as plea bargaining. **Plea bargaining** involves negotiations among the prosecutor, the defendant, and the defendant's counsel that lead to the defendant's entering a guilty plea in exchange for a reduction in charges or the prosecutor's promise to recommend a more lenient sentence. The process may take place at the arraignment, at the preliminary hearing (if there is one), or during the trial itself. A defendant who agrees to a plea bargain may not receive the trial to which he or she has a constitutional right. Plea bargaining does, however, relieve the courts, which could not possibly handle the trials of all accused persons. Prosecutors often are willing to accept plea bargaining when they believe that a trial could otherwise result in an acquittal.

Social workers must have a working knowledge of the judicial system in the United States because many of their clients are involved with or at risk of becoming involved with that system at some level. Social workers also may be called as special witnesses in trial court proceedings, either for the prosecution or for the defense. As such, social workers must clearly understand their obligations under the NASW Social Work Code of Ethics when it comes to criminal behavior or alleged criminal behavior on the part of their clients (Kirst-Ashman & Hull, 2005).

Corrections Component

Once convicted, criminals are sentenced and passed on to the corrections component of the criminal justice system. The term *corrections* is based on the idea that the state can reform or correct criminals. Convicted criminals in the United States are supervised by corrections agencies in one of three settings: the community; jails and prisons; or a combination of incarceration and community supervision (Samaha, 2005).

Most people convicted of crimes in the United States are not in prison. According to the Bureau of Justice Statistics (2005), about 4.1 million men and women were on probation in this country at the end of 2004, a slight increase from the previous year.

PROBATION
Probation is not the same as parole. Probation replaces incarceration, and parole follows incarceration. Another difference between probation and parole is that counties typically administer probation, whereas states are responsible for administering parole. Probation is a criminal sentence that substitutes community supervision for incarceration. Those who receive probated sentences are in the custody of the state and have limited freedom and privacy.

About half of those on probation in 2004 had committed minor offenses such as driving while intoxicated (DWI) (Bureau of Justice Statistics, 2005). The rest were felons who had committed violent and serious property offenses. Most minor offenders receive probation because they are not considered to be a high risk to public safety. Probation was not set up for, nor is it intended to deal with, repeat felony offenders.

Individuals on probation typically are required to obey the law, work, go to school or get vocational training, pay child support, and refrain from using or selling drugs. They also must obtain written permission from their probation officer to change residence, change employment, or travel outside the community. Further, they are required to notify their probation officer of any arrests or criminal investigations. The requirements for felony probationers typically are more stringent: Submit to regular drug testing, participate in drug or alcohol treatment, perform community service work, obtain mental health counseling, and reside in a community facility or be under house arrest. They also are required to help pay the cost of probation (Samaha, 2005).

Probation ends when the probationer completes the term of probation successfully or the court cancels or revokes the probation. Probation can be revoked when the probationer is either arrested for or convicted of a new crime, called **recidivism,** or in cases of a technical violation of probation such as failing to notify the probation officer of a change of address or a change in employment status. The percentage of probationers discharged successfully has remained at about 60% since 1995. Although nearly half of all probationers commit technical probation violations, only about 20% of those violations actually result in revocation of probation (Bureau of Justice Statistics, 2005).

INTERMEDIATE PUNISHMENT
Intermediate punishments, in which offenders remain in the community under strict supervision (community corrections), are increasingly replacing both probation and parole in response to a rapidly expanding prison population, reduction in state and federal funding to construct new jails and prisons, a shift in criminal justice policy from rehabilitation to retribution, and the desire to

Many social work graduates become probation or parole officers. Here, a probation officer counsels his young client about employment opportunities.

© Heinle/Index Stock

have a middle ground between either/or choices of probation or parole. Community corrections are gaining in popularity because they allow for better protection of community members, reduce the costs of incarceration, and help offenders reintegrate into the community.

The community corrections movement is compatible with a philosophy of restorative justice, which works to heal victims, communities, and offenders who have been injured by crime (Samaha, 2005; Sullivan, 2006; Zehr & Toews, 2004). Examples of intermediate sanctions programs include intensive supervised probation; home confinement (also referred to as house arrest or home detention); correctional boot camps; and day reporting centers (Samaha, 2005).

INCARCERATION

The number of inmates confined in federal and state prisons or in local jails in the United States increased from 1,585,586 in 1995 to 2,186,230 in 2005—an average annual increase of about 3%. The female inmate population continued to grow at a rate of nearly twice that of their male counterparts. The incarceration rates for black males

of all ages were five to seven times greater than those for white males in the same age groups (Bureau of Justice Statistics, 2006). California, Texas, Florida, New York, and the federal system held about 31% of all prisoners in the nation. At year-end 2004, state prisons were operating at between 1% below and 15% above rated capacity, while federal prisons were operating at 40% above rated capacity. This increase has produced a serious shortage in prison and jail capacity. In some states, prisons and jails have become the primary industries in many rural areas, creating a strong lobby to keep correctional facilities full so they can remain a source of employment for area residents.

In fiscal year 2003, federal, state, and local governments spent more than $185 billion for civil and criminal justice, a 10% increase over 2001. For every person in the United States, the three levels of government together spent $640. For the 20-year period 1982 to 2002, increases in expenditures for civil and criminal justice for states, municipalities, and the federal government amounted to 480%, 347%, and 607%, respectively. Local governments funded about half of all justice-system expenses. Another third of justice funding came from the states (Bureau of Justice Statistics, 2003).

Longer sentences and more frequent **incarceration** were expected to reduce crime and recidivism. Research has not confirmed this to be the case. Violence in crime often is linked to participation in other criminal activities such as drug use. Thus, the incarcerated offenders are replaced quickly on the streets by other offenders. Incapacitation of the one offender does not necessarily reduce the propensity of others to commit the same offense. Prison time seems to have been used as an expression of public outrage with little thought to its deterrent or incapacitation effect on other criminals (Golash, 2005; Travis & Visher, 2005; Western, 2006).

The Juvenile Justice System

Whether juvenile offenders should be treated differently than adult offenders remains a topic of extensive debate. State definitions of juveniles vary considerably. Most exclude children under age 8 from juvenile justice jurisdiction, but the states differ in the upper age, with some using 16 and others 18 for determining juvenile or criminal justice jurisdiction (Champion, 2006; Ryder, 2005). **Juvenile delinquency** can refer to a youth who has committed a crime, a status offense (e.g., truancy, underage drinking, curfew violation, running away, incorrigibility), or both.

Several facts stand out regarding juvenile delinquency (Sickmund, 2003):

- Youths are substantially more crime-prone than adults.
- The juvenile arrest rate is six times the adult rate for serious property crimes and twice the adult rate for violent crimes.
- Most youth arrests are for property crimes such as theft and burglary and youth-only offenses such as truancy and curfew violations.

- Younger offenders commit crimes in groups with four or more members five times more often than adults.
- Serious juvenile crime is concentrated in urban areas, with the highest arrest and conviction rates among youths of color.
- Youths are frequently armed.

How to handle youthful offenders has been debated throughout the history of the United States. Until the late-1800s, youthful offenders were treated in the same way as adult offenders—for example, imprisoned with adults and even sentenced to death. **Juvenile courts** in the United States were first established in Cook County, Illinois, in 1899 (Axinn & Stern, 2005; Ryder, 2005). The philosophy of juvenile courts has been that they should act in the child's best interest. Juvenile courts, thus, have had a treatment and rehabilitation orientation instead of a focus on a specific crime as in adult criminal proceedings. The focus of juvenile courts is on the child's psychological, physical, emotional, and educational needs rather than the child's guilt. But the increase in youth crimes—particularly violent crimes committed by very young offenders—has put pressure on the juvenile justice system to rethink the efficacy of the treatment and rehabilitation emphasis that has been the hallmark of that system for so long.

The Gault Decision

In the 1960s, Gerald Gault, age 15, was tried in the Arizona juvenile court for allegedly making an obscene phone call to a neighbor. Neither the accused nor his parents were given advance notice of the charges against him. He was not informed of his legal rights and, if found guilty, could have been held within the criminal justice system until he reached the age of majority. The procedures used by the Arizona officials in the Gault proceeding were not unreasonable. They were in accord with the thinking of the times—namely, that advance notice and formal trial are likely to stigmatize a child and violate many confidentialities. The concern was with the state as a parent rather than the state as the embodiment of a social conscience. Thus, Gault was brought before the juvenile court and tried without proper safeguards.

In 1967, the case went to the Supreme Court. The majority opinion, written by Justice Abe Fortas, vehemently criticized the juvenile correctional establishment and made it clear that regardless of intent, juveniles should not be deprived of their liberty without the full set of due-process rights available to an adult. This case restored to juvenile procedures safeguards that often had been ignored, including notification of charges, protection from self-incrimination, confrontation and cross-examination (Cohen, 2006).

The wisdom of the *Gault* decision is still disputed today. It undoubtedly gives minors the same basic constitutional rights enjoyed by adults, but the return to a focus on whether a young person has or has not committed a crime often masks the need for help exhibited by young persons caught up in the court processes. The *Gault* case has brought about a critical reassessment of juvenile procedures and has suggested that the treatment and rehabilitative role of the juvenile correctional system must be secondary to protecting the rights of the juvenile before the criminal justice system.

Juvenile Justice Agencies

Many entities deal with juvenile delinquency: lawmaking bodies, police departments, prosecutors, defense attorneys, correctional facilities, treatment centers, halfway houses, and social service agencies. Lawmaking bodies define the scope of legal authority of these entities. They also determine when older juveniles can be transferred to the adult criminal justice system in a process called *certification*. Finally, lawmaking bodies determine the budgets needed to support agencies administering juvenile justice programs and services (Champion, 2006).

Juvenile Courts

Juvenile courts in the United States have several, often competing, goals: helping children in need, treating and/or punishing juveniles who commit crimes, and protecting society from juvenile crime. The juvenile court process typically involves intake, adjudication, and disposition (Martin, 2005; McShane & Williams, 2002).

INTAKE

Intake takes place after police referrals to juvenile court and usually involves detaining juveniles during case investigation, filing a petition for a formal court hearing, and dismissing cases altogether. Status and property offenses account for most referrals to juvenile court. Only a small proportion of referrals involve crimes against persons, and most of these are minor assaults (Puzzanchera et al., 2004).

ADJUDICATION

Adjudication, which takes place after intake, is the legal process that judges conduct in juvenile court with assistance from probation officers. If the judge determines that the allegations in a petition are proven, the juvenile for whom the petition was filed is considered to be formally delinquent (Martin, 2005).

DISPOSITION

Disposition follows adjudication and is the legal process by which judges decide how best to resolve delinquency cases. Juvenile court judges choose from a wide array of dispositions, from dismissing the case to committing the juvenile to a secure juvenile correctional facility (Champion, 2006; Samaha, 2005).

Juvenile Corrections

Juvenile corrections can be divided into community corrections and institutional corrections. **Community corrections** can be defined as all correctional activities in the community. Probation is the most widely used form of community juvenile corrections. Juvenile probation is an informal probation supervised by the police. Under this type of probation, juveniles usually are required to report periodically to police departments and to follow police-established conditions for behavior (McShane & Williams, 2002).

Juvenile correctional institutions range from short-term, non-secure facilities serving a limited geographic area to long-term, highly secure facilities serving large geographic areas. (McShane & Williams, 2002; Rosenheim et al., 2002; Samaha, 2005):

- *Foster homes* are used at all stages in the juvenile justice process.
- *Shelters* (non-secure residential facilities) hold juveniles who are temporarily assigned to them, usually in lieu of detention or returning home following arrest, or after adjudication while awaiting more permanent placement.
- *Group homes* (non-secure, relatively open community-based facilities) hold primarily juveniles who have been adjudicated as delinquent. Larger and less family-like than foster homes, group homes allow more independent living in a more permanent setting. Residents of group homes usually attend school—in the home or in the community—or work. Group homes provide support and structure in unrestrictive settings that facilitate reintegration into the community.
- *Halfway houses* (large, non-secure residential centers) provide both a place to live and a range of personal and social services that emphasize normal group living, attending school, securing employment, working with parents to resolve problems, and participating in community events.
- *Ranches and camps* (non-secure facilities, almost always located in rural and remote areas), emphasize outside activity, self-discipline, and the development of vocational and interpersonal skills. Juveniles adjudicated

as delinquent usually are placed in camps and ranches as an alternative to more secure facilities such as training schools.
- *Detention centers* (temporary custodial facilities) are secure institutions that hold juveniles both before and after adjudication.
- *Training schools* house the most serious delinquents—those who are security risks, those who have substantial prior records, and those who have exhausted other juvenile court dispositions.

Dual System of Justice

Every jurisdiction in the United States operates separate systems for responding to juvenile and adult criminal behavior. Each system is governed by a different set of laws and procedures. Juvenile courts typically handle cases for individuals under age 18 and adult criminal courts handle the others. This **dual system of justice** has received considerable scrutiny recently as the proportion of serious youthful offenders has increased (Martin, 2005). Juveniles were involved in 15% of all arrests in the Violent Crime Index in 2003 (Snyder, 2005).

GET-TOUGH POLICIES

Various get-tough policies that would change the way that serious youthful offenders are treated were introduced in the 1990s, in response to what was considered an epidemic in serious juvenile crime and violence (Human Rights Watch, 2005; Krisberg, 2004; Mendel, 2000; Sheldon & Hussong, 2001):

- reducing the juvenile court's maximum age limit from 18 to 16;
- increasing the use of juvenile records, particularly in adult courts, to help identify high-risk offenders and treat them accordingly;
- replacing the juvenile court's rehabilitation philosophy with a policy in which the sentencing objective becomes punishment that fits the crime;

- making mandatory the sentencing of juveniles charged with specific, violent crimes;
- prosecuting juvenile career criminals; and
- replacing the two-track system with a three-track system: a family court for neglected and dependent youths under 14 years of age; a juvenile court for 14- to 18-year-olds whose crimes are not particularly serious; and a criminal court to handle offenders age 18 and older and juveniles whose crimes are serious.

TRYING AND SENTENCING YOUTHS AS ADULTS

Upward of 250,000 teens under the age of 18 are sent into the criminal justice system each year. More than half of the cases of youths in adult criminal court have been charged with nonviolent drug or property offenses. Some of those who have been transferred to adult court are as young as 12 or 13 years of age (Coalition for Juvenile Justice, 2005).

Since the beginning of the juvenile court system more than 100 years ago, juvenile court judges have been able to assess a youth's circumstances, offense record, and potential for rehabilitation and, when necessary, transfer a chronic, violent teen offender to adult criminal court. Many states have replaced this practice with broad-based laws that require automatic transfer of juvenile offenders into adult court based on the type of offense or age of the offender, without the benefit of individualized assessment (15 states automatically transfer youthful offenders to criminal court based on age and crime criteria). In some states, prosecutors are *required* to file certain juvenile cases in adult courts, at times against their better judgment (American Bar Association, 2004; Coalition for Juvenile Justice, 2005; Hubner, 2005; Humes, 1997; Physicians for Human Rights, 2006; Siegel, Welsh, & Senna, 2005).

Services generally available to youth in the adult criminal justice system are not geared to meet teens' educational, emotional, physical, and social needs. Many youths who end up in the adult criminal justice system come into the system with undiagnosed and untreated mental health disorders that get worse as a result of the stress of being confined, especially with adults. Teenagers in adult institutions are five times more likely to be sexually assaulted, three times more likely to be beaten by prison staff, and eight times more likely to commit suicide than youths held in a juvenile facility.

Advances in brain research show that the area of the brain that permits anticipation of consequences, consideration of alternatives, planning, setting of long-range goals, and organization of sequential behavior does not fully mature until *well past the age of 18* (Physicians for Human Rights, 2006). Research on the impact on community safety of trying and sentencing youths in adult criminal court reveals that prosecuting juveniles in the adult criminal system actually increases the likelihood that they will re-offend, and upon re-offense, commit more serious crimes than their counterparts in the juvenile system (Coalition for Juvenile Justice, 2005; Physicians for Human Rights, 2006). Also, the majority of youth who are under age 18 when admitted to the criminal justice system are released to probation before the age of 22. Without age-appropriate services and supports to help them become productive citizens, they return to their communities hardened and angry, with an increased number of criminal skills (Coalition for Juvenile Justice, 2005).

In *Childhood on Trial: The Failure of Trying and Sentencing Youth in Adult Criminal Court,* the Coalition for Juvenile Justice (2005, p. 4) made the following recommendations regarding transferring juveniles to the adult criminal system:

- All organizations and individuals invested in child and family health, and community well-being, should adopt a formal position calling on policymakers to revisit and reform state laws that inappropriately send far too many youths under the age of 18 (including first-time and nonviolent offenders) into the adult criminal justice system.

- States must reexamine their practices related to youths sent into the adult criminal court to gain a clear picture of the circumstances and characteristics of youths who are treated like adults.
- Policymakers, law enforcement officers, and justice officials need to take a hard look at whether "adult-time" policies in their jurisdictions truly fulfill the public safety mandate.
- Policymakers and justice administrators cannot continue to use cost savings as the principal rationale for continuing to try and sentence youths in adult criminal court rather than juvenile court.
- Policymakers and juvenile justice professionals should call for changes in state and federal laws to restore the authority of juvenile court judges to assess a juvenile's fitness for adult court and hold the boundary between childhood and adulthood at age 18.

As of 2005, 40 national organizations that represent and serve millions of children, youth, and families throughout the United States have signed the *National Resolution Regarding Trying and Sentencing Youth Offenders in Adult Criminal Court* (see Box 13.1). As noted above, however, so-called youthful offender "reforms" have proved to be ineffective in addressing the problems of serious juvenile delinquency and violence, as they treat only the symptoms and not the causes of this behavior. While appealing to many who support a get-tough approach to dealing with youth crime, this approach serves little purpose in preventing the crime from happening in the first place (Mendel, 2000).

Differential Treatment of Minority Youth in the Justice System

Several authors have addressed the issue of differential treatment of minority youth in the juvenile system, indicating that their overrepresentation often reflects decisions made at critical points throughout the justice system (Bonavita, 2001; Gabbidon, 2005; Males & Macallair, 2004; Mann & Zatz, 2006; Martin, 2005; Mooradian, 2003; Parry, 2004; Poe-Yamagata & Jones, 2000; Walker, Spohn, & DeLone, 2006. In what has become known as the "cumulative disadvantage," the overrepresentation of minority youth in the juvenile justice system tends to accumulate as youth are processed through the system.

The get-tough policies described above have resulted in a disproportionate number of minority youths being processed through adult criminal courts and incarcerated in adult jails and prisons. Unless federal and state governments do something to eliminate the causes of the differential treatment of minority youth brought about by a broad range of current practices, the criminal justice system will continue to have a negative and disproportionate impact on minority youth.

The Juvenile Detention Alternatives Initiative (JDAI), funded through the Annie E. Casey Foundation (2006), represents a major step in the right direction to reduce the overrepresentation of minority youths in the juvenile justice system. The JDAI was developed as a demonstration that jurisdictions across the country could control the destiny of their youth-detention practices. The four key objectives of JDAI are:

1. to eliminate the inappropriate or unnecessary use of secure detention;
2. to minimize failures to appear and the incidence of delinquent behavior;
3. to redirect public finances from building new facility capacity to responsible alternative strategies; and
4. to improve conditions in secure detention facilities.

Several reports on reforming the juvenile justice system in the United States were published by JDAI, including a report titled *Reducing Racial Disparities in Juvenile Detention* (Annie E. Casey Foundation, 2006). This report includes a synthesis of the experiences (successes as well as

BOX 13.11
National Resolution Regarding Trying and Sentencing Youth Offenders in Adult Criminal Court

WHEREAS, policies and practices providing "adult time for adult crime" are often harmful—rather than helpful—to community safety, as evidenced by research demonstrating that prosecuting juveniles in the adult criminal system increases rather than decreases the likelihood that they will re-offend, as compared with handling them in the juvenile justice system;

WHEREAS, 75% of youth under age 18 sent to adult facilities will be released by the age of 22 and most will have been denied adequate education, mental health, drug treatment and employment skills training;

WHEREAS, trying and sentencing youth in adult court is not reserved for the most serious, chronic and violent juvenile offenders, but inappropriately includes more than half of the cases involving only nonviolent drug and property crimes.

WHEREAS, there exists serious human rights, as well as physical and emotional health concerns when youth held in adult facilities are sexually assaulted five times more often, commit suicide eight times more often, and are assaulted with a weapon 50% more often than youth held in juvenile facilities;

WHEREAS, there exists serious civil rights concerns given that youth of color are disproportionately represented in cases sent to adult court—as shown in 18 of the largest court jurisdictions where 82% of juvenile cases filed in adult court involved youth of color;

WHEREAS, research continues to establish and reaffirm that the adolescent brain—particularly the part that makes judgments, reins in impulsive behavior and engages in moral reasoning—is not fully developed until age 19 or 20, laying the foundation for laws that prohibit youth under age 18 from taking on major adult responsibilities such as voting, jury duty, and military service;

WHEREAS, the use of statutes or procedures that automatically exclude youth from the juvenile court without assessment of individual circumstances deny them basic fairness;

WHEREAS, more than 250,000 offenders under the age of 18 are sent each year to adult criminal courts across the United States, including an estimated 218,000 excluded from juvenile court jurisdiction, not because of the severity of their crimes, nor because they are habitual offenders, but because states have lowered the age of adulthood in the criminal code;

BE IT RESOLVED that the national organizations listed herein will work to build broad acceptance for reform, as well as to create reform, in state policies and practices, so as to significantly reduce the number of youth sent to adult criminal court and to ensure that young offenders are appropriately adjudicated in ways that enhance community safety and vitality.

Source: *Unlocking the Future: Detention Reform in the Juvenile Justice System,* by the Coalition for Juvenile Justice (Washington, DC: Author, 2003).

failures) of the various sites that participated in the JDAI initiative. These experiences are captured in the following set of 10 "lessons learned" intended to "flatten the learning curves" of JDAI sites:

1. Without a commitment to juvenile detention reform in general, reducing racial disparities is unlikely.
2. An explicit focus on reducing racial disparities is essential.
3. Reducing racial disparities requires authoritative leadership.
4. Define the problem in terms that can be changed.
5. Emphasize action, not just discussion or training.
6. Broad, diverse coalitions can facilitate disproportionate minority contact reduction.
7. Individual agencies can make a difference.
8. Keep the police in the work.
9. Data really helps.
10. It *is* [emphasis added] possible to reduce racial disparities in juvenile detention. (pp. 65–70)

It is hoped that efforts such as JDAI will encourage others to make significant investments to reduce racial disparities in the country's juvenile justice system and thereby build a brighter future for youths who come into contact with that system in their formative years.

Alternatives to Get-Tough Policies

Several alternatives to get-tough policies aimed at reducing youth crime have been identified. A landmark study spearheaded by the American Youth Policy Forum in collaboration with the Child Welfare League of America, Coalition for Juvenile Justice, National Collaboration for Youth, National Crime Prevention Council, National League of Cities, and National Urban League identified four areas for which significant investments must be made to effectively reduce juvenile crime in America (Mendel, 2000, pp. 65–69):

1. *Prevention in early childhood:* home-based visitation services for high-risk families

2. *School-based prevention:* nationally recognized school-based violence and substance-abuse prevention programs that are evidence-based and are implemented with strong training and technical support
3. *Effective child welfare:* increased funding, worker training, and family support services
4. *Intervening with behaviorally troubled children:* family-focused intervention strategies for families with troubled youth.

The study identified the following strategic action areas that are considered to offer the most promise for reducing juvenile crime and violence in the United States (Mendel, 2000, pp. 71–76):

- *End overreliance on corrections and other out-of-home placements.* States are encouraged to revise their funding formulas to reward localities for serving youths in their homes and communities whenever possible.
- *Invest in research-based interventions for juvenile offenders, as well as research-based prevention.* The federal government should invest heavily in the replication and further refinement of proven strategies, as well as in continuing research efforts to develop even better strategies for reducing delinquent conduct by troubled youths. This investment should include funds for training and technical assistance and matching funds for implementation. Both process and outcome evaluations should be required for all funded projects.
- *Measure results, fund what works, and cut funds to what doesn't work.* Developing new knowledge must be a core goal for all federal spending to reduce juvenile crime and violence. States must provide the leadership necessary to support ongoing data collection and program evaluation, and this should be a national effort.
- *Engage community partners.* Youths should be reconnected to their communities through innovative, restorative justice initiatives such

as family-group conferencing, teen courts, drug courts, and youth aid panels. State and local juvenile justice authorities should increase their efforts in these areas. Juvenile courts and probation agencies should be encouraged or even required to strengthen partnerships with community residents and organizations. Local courts and probation departments should consider funding set-asides for contracts with community-based service providers. States should support "systems of care" reforms that reward and support multi-agency partnerships to provide case management and intervention treatment services for delinquent youth. The federal government should expand funding for community mental health services to children with severe emotional problems.

- *Mobilize whole communities to study, plan, and implement comprehensive strategies for combating youth crime.* Congress should continue to expand funding for comprehensive, community analysis; planning; and mobilization. States should require local jurisdictions to create local policy boards and to develop and submit community plans as a condition for receiving state funds and federal pass-through funds for juvenile justice and delinquency prevention programming.

Juvenile justice reform advocates also recommend the following as a means of reducing juvenile crime and violence:

- increased accountability and improved quality assurance in public and private agencies mandated to provide essential resources for infants, toddlers, and school-age children;
- knowledgeable advocates who are able to help caregivers and adolescents circumvent bureaucratic barriers in agencies mandated to provide essential resources;
- neighborhood-based organizations that provide sustained and comprehensive support

and opportunities needed for wholesome youth development from early childhood through the teen years;
- hands-on parenting classes for offenders with babies and young children;
- perinatal care for pregnant offenders;
- comprehensive services for children with incarcerated parents and their caregivers utilizing a "wrap-around" or "systems of care" approach;
- referral and advocacy for health, nutrition, and related services for children of parents under juvenile/criminal justice system supervision or conditional release;
- accessible educational services and employment-skills training for young mothers, especially in tandem with developmentally appropriate child care for their infants, toddlers, and preschool-age children;
- recruitment of stable extended family members to care for the children of offenders—especially in cultural groups in which the extended family traditionally has played a key role in childrearing;
- neighborhood-based programs that emphasize provision of basic needs for infants and preschool children and positive youth development services for older children during non-school hours;
- referrals of 10-, 11-, and 12-year-olds detained by the police to neighborhood organizations that provide sustained activities during non-school hours—the types of support and opportunities from which young adolescents and their families can benefit and enjoy;
- for older teens who have been engaging in persistent delinquent behavior, placement in communal detention settings where they gradually earn status and privileges through vocational achievement and through contributions to the welfare of all in the community—followed by supervised participation in similar activities after they earn their way out of detention.

Gang Peace is a youth organization in Massachusetts that works with teens active in gangs or at risk of becoming gang members. The organization helps empower youth to identify positive goals and develop the skills to realize them.

Kristin Finnegan/Stone/Getty Image

A number of other authors (see, for example, Acorn, 2005; Strang & Braithwaite, 2002; Strang & Braithwaite, 2001; Vos, Coates, Brown, & Umbreit, 2003; Zehr, 2004) have addressed alternatives to get-tough policies. They suggest designing policies and programs that hold juvenile offenders accountable for their actions, helping them to empathize with those affected by their actions, and making changes in their lives so they are less likely to reoffend and put others at risk in the future.

Social workers can play a significant role in implementing these strategies, because they require the sustained political will of Congress, as well as individual state legislatures, to move forward. In advancing these strategies, the social worker can engage in a variety of individual roles—as educator, advocate, mediator, researcher,

teacher, community organizer, mobilizer, and policy analyst (Kirst-Ashman & Hull, 2005). Solutions also will mean an unwavering commitment by society at large to ensure that each child born in this country has the opportunity to grow and thrive.

Rehabilitation

Rehabilitation programs for criminal offenders serve many purposes:

- reduce offenders' further criminal activity;
- improve prison management;
- help mete out humane punishment; and
- give prisoners something meaningful to do.

Programs aimed at the rehabilitation of offenders include vocational training, work release, financial assistance, prison industries, and therapeutic treatment (Samaha, 2005).

Vocational Training

Vocational training is important to prisoner rehabilitation, as most prisoners have few, if any, skills that qualify them for legitimate work. The results of vocational rehabilitation programs, however, have been disappointing because prison budgets are not geared to support these programs; unions do not accept workers who have finished prison-based apprenticeship programs; most prisoners do not serve long enough sentences to fulfill apprenticeship requirements; or their training is interrupted (Samaha, 2005). Notwithstanding these problems, vocational training enjoys more public support than academic education programs, stemming from the belief that vocational training programs are more practical and useful than academic learning.

Work Release

Work release has numerous positive rehabilitative effects: Offenders are provided with a stable work record and job experience, the opportunity to support their dependents while in prison, new job skills, money at the time of release and often with a job, the ability to maintain positive contact with the free community, and an improved attitude toward themselves, as well as toward society. Providing support to offenders who participate in work release programs is another fruitful area of involvement for social workers. Many social workers are employed by organizations that provide case-management services to soon-to-be released prisoners to help them to navigate the reentry process successfully. The work begins while the offender is still in prison and continues for a period of time (usually 6 months to 1 year) after release into the community.

Among the most pressing needs of offenders released from prison are getting a job (60% of ex-offenders are unemployed), finding a place to live, reconnecting with family members, participating in a substance-abuse treatment program if applicable, seeking help for health and mental health problems, and meeting the requirements of parole. Because most prisoners return to the community in which they committed the crime(s) that put them in jail in the first place, making these services available is critical to helping them deal with stressors that easily could lead to their reoffending and going back to prison.

Financial Assistance

Some rehabilitation programs provide financial assistance in the form of employment to offenders who are released from prison. Released prisoners receiving such assistance have been arrested less frequently and are better able to find better jobs than those not receiving assistance.

Prison Industries

During the early 1900s, prison industries were considered to be a major component in the rehabilitation of prisoners in the United States. Prison reformers of the time argued that work was not only useful but also therapeutic. Despite their popularity, however, prison industries were scaled back substantially because of ethical questions about using prison labor, competition with private industry, the belief that prisoners are supposed to suffer and not do something worthwhile during their incarceration, and the opposition of labor unions and small businesses.

Prison industries regained popularity beginning in the 1980s. The major justification for returning prison industries was the idea that prisoners should pay for their imprisonment. Prison industries were believed to support the goal of creating work, reducing idle time, and helping to manage prisons. The National Center for Policy Analysis (1997) estimated that during the 5-year period 1997 to 2002, if half of all prisoners in the United States were to participate in some kind of prison industry program, the cost of supporting the adult prison system would be reduced by almost $9 billion.

Treatment

Treatment programs in prisons most often include either counseling or some type of behavior modification. Counseling programs assume that the cause of criminal behavior is an underlying emotional problem, whereas behavior modification programs focus on how people behave in social situations that get them in trouble and on changing that behavior. Often, treatment services are provided by licensed social workers who are employed by a local, state, or federal prison authority or who work under contract to one of these entities. Sometimes social workers volunteer their services on a pro bono basis along with those from other community-based organizations and the faith community.

Issues in Rehabilitation

Prison rehabilitation programs have been controversial from their inception. Two primary questions fuel this controversy: Should we rehabilitate prisoners? Can we rehabilitate prisoners? Often, strongly held ideological beliefs regarding the rehabilitation of prisoners have confounded major prison rehabilitation evaluation efforts. Results of studies evaluating rehabilitation are decidedly mixed if one considers whether the programs actually rehabilitate the offender. As noted above, however, rehabilitation programs serve purposes other than preparing offenders to work hard and play by the rules when they leave prison. Rehabilitation programs also keep prisoners busy, and keeping them busy keeps them out of trouble. Finally, rehabilitation programs are viewed as consistent with orderly, safe, and humane

confinement (Crow, 2001; Magnani & Wray, 2006; Prison Research Education Action Project, 2006; Russell, 2006).

Crime Prevention

In what has become a landmark study, the National Institute of Justice (1998) conducted a systematic review of more than 500 scientific evaluations of crime-prevention practices in the United States. The study revealed that most crime-prevention programs have not yet been evaluated with enough scientific evidence to draw defensible conclusions. The study concluded, however, that enough evidence is available to create provisional lists of what works, what doesn't, and what's promising. Key promising prevention initiatives included the following (pp. 6–12):

In Communities:

- gang offender monitoring by community and probation and police officers
- community-based mentoring by Big Brothers/Big Sisters of America
- community-based after-school recreation programs
- dispersing inner-city public housing residents to scattered-site suburban public housing

In Schools:

- schools-within-schools that group students into smaller units
- training or coaching in thinking skills for high-risk youths
- teaching of social competency skills
- communication and reinforcement of clear, consistent norms
- building school capacity to initiate and sustain innovation through organizational-development strategies
- improved classroom management and instructional techniques

In Families:

- battered women's shelters aimed at reducing the rate of repeat victimization for women who take steps to seek help beyond staying in the shelter

In Labor Markets:

- Job Corps (intensive residential training programs for at-risk youth)
- prison-based vocational programs for adult inmates
- enterprise zones with tax-break incentives in areas of extremely high unemployment

By Criminal Justice Agencies after Arrest:

- drug courts that order and monitor a combination of rehabilitation and drug treatment
- intensive supervision and after-care of minor and serious juvenile offenders
- fines for criminal acts in combination with other penalties
- drug treatment in jails followed by urine testing in the community

In Places:

- adding a second clerk to potentially reduce robberies in already-robbed convenience stores
- redesigning the layout of retail stores to reduce shoplifting
- improving training and management of bar and tavern staffs
- metal detectors to reduce weapon carrying in schools
- street closures, barricades, and rerouting

By Police:

- proactive arrests for carrying concealed weapons
- proactive drunk-driving arrests
- **community policing** with meetings to set priorities
- policing with more respect for offenders
- field interrogations of suspicious persons

- mailing arrest warrants to domestic-violence suspects who leave the scene before police arrive
- more police officers in cities.

A number of authors have identified building blocks for successful community **crime prevention** initiatives (see for example, Champion, 2006; Du Cane, 2006; Hughes, McLaughlin, & Muncie, 2002; Lab, 2004; Sherman, Farrington, & Welsh, 2002):

- community-based partnerships that draw upon the knowledge and experience of all stakeholders;
- programs that build community capacity to address local problems;
- integrated programs that nurture families and communities;
- comprehensive efforts that support parenting, prevention of child abuse and domestic violence, victim assistance, child-support enforcement, truancy, conflict resolution, youth mentoring, teen pregnancy prevention, and other child development and supervision programs;
- knowledge base of best practices to share across disciplines and communities; and
- process and outcome evaluations of community-based crime-prevention efforts.

The U.S. criminal justice system is evaluated not only by its capacity to prevent and contain crime but also by the justice meted out by the system. Its dual responsibility to protect the citizenship rights of criminals as well as those of their victims constitutes the core of the criminal justice system. Law-abiding citizens want to be protected from criminal behavior but also want protection from unwarranted intrusion of the criminal justice system into their private lives. The duality of these demands imposes costs and constraints on police, court officers, and prison and parole officials. In the final analysis, then, law-and-order proponents and civil libertarians want the same things. So the policy problem lies in emphasis and balance, and the latter seldom seems to exist.

Views of Criminal Behavior

A number of views of criminal behavior have been set forth to explain why people commit crimes. The **etiology of crime** can be viewed as psychologically aberrant behavior, or socially induced behavior, or a consequence of rational thought in which criminals see crime as just another way to make a living, or as a complex interactive process of an individual's personal characteristics and the many factors that constitute his or her environment.

Psychological Views of the Criminal Personality

One school of psychological thought suggests that criminals differ from non-criminals in some fundamental way—other than the obvious one of having been convicted. Over the years the distinguishing trait has been proposed to reside in the body or head shape, skull size, chromosome structure, specific patterns of response to projective tests, or in the complex labeling process of psychiatric diagnosis. All of the psychological/physiological attempts to establish a criminal type demonstrate a circular reasoning process. The notion of a criminal type brings a kind of satisfaction because crime policy then becomes, simply, segregating criminals from the rest of society.

A second psychological interpretation of the etiology of crime is only slightly more sophisticated. Crime is seen simply as a manifestation of a compulsion derived from unresolved conflicts between the superego (Freud's personality component that serves as one's conscience), and the id (Freud's personality component that serves as one's free spirit). Someone with a criminal personality—by definition a defective ego—is unable to overcome the desire to defy social taboos, yet the conflict is reflected in an unconscious desire to be caught.

Anecdotal evidence suggests that criminals do operate this way. They may deliberately, albeit unconsciously, leave the clues that lead to their arrests. Were it not for the seriousness of the incidents, this behavior often would be truly comic. One young criminal brought a pair of slacks to the cleaners and, after being presented with the claim check, pulled a gun and robbed the attendant. He returned 3 days later with the stub of the claim check to pick up his slacks and was patient enough to wait when the same attendant went to retrieve them. The young man waited calmly until the police came and arrested him. Another pair of criminals left the motor running in the getaway car, but because they had failed to check the fuel gauge before the robbery, their car ran out of gas while they were holding up the bank.

A more sophisticated psychosocial theory also contains in its assumptions the prescription for a proper anti-crime policy. As the theory goes, criminal behavior is learned. The type of criminal behavior that individuals learn is related to their socioeconomic status in society. That is, certain classes of persons learn different criminal ways. The processes involved in learning criminal behavior are the same as those in learning other behavior that entail learning a technique as well as values.

This psychological view of criminality is less encompassing than the simpler etiological-psychological views of crime. It does not attempt to explain which people will commit crimes—an impossible task—but, rather, why and how those who have committed crimes are systematically different from those who do not.

Social Views of Criminal Behavior

Another perspective suggests that crime is not caused by individual physical or mental deficiencies but, instead, by societal breakdown. Proponents of this perspective identify industrialization, racism, poverty, and family breakdown as major factors in creating social disorganization, and, in turn, increases in crime. Sociological inquiries into crime frequently are based on statistical correlates, such as the analysis of traditional family or variations in unemployment and crime rates. The more sophisticated inquiries fall short of establishing a direct path of causation. Crime is seen as a result of many factors within the context of the offender's society. Street crime and white-collar crime are viewed as very different expressions of social maladjustment. Regardless of specifics, the essence of the sociological perspective is that general **deterrence factors** (things that are likely to stop people from committing crimes), rehabilitation, and reeducation of offenders constitute the best safeguards against repeated crimes.

The social view of crime advocates a criminal justice system that offers a variety of social intervention strategies. One of these—of particular importance to social work practitioners—is collaboration between social workers and police officers at the earliest intervention point. When the suspected offender is in police custody initially, social workers and police officers are expected to concur on the case disposition. The argument is made that, despite their disparate professional orientations, social workers and police officers alike are experienced in dealing with troubled people at crisis points in their lives. Individualization of response is considered essential. No one sociological perspective is seen as dominant. Consider, for example, the following typology of crime:

- violent personal crimes (e.g., murder);
- sexual offenses;
- occupational/white-collar crimes;
- political crimes;
- organized crimes;
- professional crimes; and
- crimes without victims.

Each of these types of crime has its own sociological pattern, and each places a unique set of demands on the criminal justice system.

Economic Rationale of Crime

A final perspective is that crime is simply another form of entrepreneurship that happens to be illegal. Proponents of this view see the criminal as an amoral person who calculates the costs and benefits of a crime, much as a businessperson calculates the costs and benefits of opening a new store. In the economic formulation, potential criminals assess the costs of getting caught and sentenced against the probable benefits of completing the crime successfully. Depending on the outcomes of their calculations, they decide to be criminal or not. People who are not poor commit fewer crimes because the costs of going to prison (in lost wages, deprivation of status, amenities of life, and so forth) are too high. If we subscribe to this theoretical perspective, all we need to do to contain crime is to increase the probability of being caught, sentenced, and sent to jail. This theory has little or no empirical evidence as a valid basis to support it.

Each of these views of crime—and we have described only three—provides a policy paradigm for the criminal justice system, from the role of the arresting officer to the responsibilities of the parole and probation workers. One's beliefs about *why* some people commit crimes are the obvious source of ideas about how to contain crime.

Program Alternatives

For every 36 crimes committed, one person is sentenced to prison. Only one crime in every four that are reported results in an arrest of a suspected offender. There is roughly one arraignment for every three arrests, and although nearly 95% of all criminal arraignments result in criminal conviction or guilty pleas, only one in three ends up in a prison term (Samaha, 2005). These numbers mislead as much as they reveal, because tracking a given crime (acknowledging that crimes are greatly underreported) to a specific sentence is a Herculean statistical task. One thing that is unambiguous in these numbers is the enormous amount of discretion operating within the criminal justice system. Figure 13.1, presented earlier, portrays the complex pathways in the criminal justice system. Each new stage (represented by the rectangles) signifies an opportunity for dropping out of the criminal justice system. Only a small percentage of all crimes results in criminal convictions.

The U.S. criminal justice system has largely British roots, but it includes some innovations that are unique to the United States. These innovations are those in which social work is involved most explicitly: probation, parole, and juvenile procedures. The U.S. system perhaps is more fragmented than the criminal justice system in most countries. The criminal justice system can be seen first as composed of three parts—police, courts, and correctional arrangements. With federal, state, and local involvement at each level and separation into adult and juvenile divisions, a multipartite system emerges. More dramatic, no subsystem views the criminal problem from a total perspective. Each is busily resolving its own problems. The result is a highly fractured system that is difficult to describe, evaluate, or control.

Despite the lack of cohesion and the internal tensions, actions within one subsystem clearly reverberate throughout the entire system. "Success" or "failure" in one part may generate significant problems for another part. If state and local police, by virtue of more personnel or better investigation, were to apprehend 25% more offenders, both the courts and the correctional system would have to absorb more defendants and prisoners. If the prison system were to release a higher proportion of recidivists, police and the courts would have to deal with a larger population of criminals. But overcrowded prisons generate backups in local jails. All elements of the criminal justice system must respond to the factors in the larger society that accelerate criminal behavior. Because the criminal justice system is not examined or funded as an entity, each component accepts and adopts its own strategies.

The fundamental adaptation for one part often produces problems for another entity within the system.

The Role of Social Work in the Criminal Justice System

The role of the social work community in the criminal justice system has been relegated almost exclusively to the correctional components of the system. Only recently have police agencies begun to use social workers. These social work functions have low priority in law enforcement budgets and often fall quickly to budget cuts. Adult courts have made relatively little use of professional social workers. Therefore, social workers most frequently work in the criminal justice system in juvenile courts, rehabilitation centers, prisons, and parole programs. These uses of social workers, however, should be assessed in a systemwide context.

Some law enforcement officials suggest that the most police calls are family- or crisis-oriented rather than crime-related. When crimes occur, they frequently are the result of family problems. Many homicides, for example, are perpetrated by family members rather than by someone outside of the family. Increasingly, crime is associated with other social problems, such as alcohol or drug abuse.

Social workers play various roles in law enforcement agencies. Many departments have crisis intervention teams, consisting of police officers as well as social workers who respond to domestic violence calls or calls to assist victims of rape or other violent crimes. Some law enforcement agencies have established special victim-assistance programs. Often staffed by social workers, these programs provide follow-up services to victims of crime, such as child and family counseling, support groups, information and referral, and case management. They also help victims locate emergency funding, shelter, employment, counseling, and other needed services.

Many police departments have special child abuse or sex crimes units, which sometimes include social workers on their staffs. The social workers assist in investigating reported cases, interviewing children and other individuals involved, contacting child welfare departments and hospitals, and arranging for emergency services when needed. A number of police departments also hire social workers to work in youth programs. In Pittsburgh, for example, social workers operate inner-city recreation programs. In Austin, Texas, the police department has had a social worker who manages a dropout prevention program in the public schools. These social workers provide counseling and drug and alcohol education, and serve as positive law enforcement role models to youths at risk for becoming involved in crime.

The role of the social worker in prison and prison life is peripheral. The social worker most likely is involved only when convicts enter or leave prison. The classification and assignment process at entry point is influenced heavily by social work practice. The pardon and parole recommendation also is influenced by social workers. Probation or parole officers often are BSW graduates, helping youth and adults learn new skills and behaviors that will deter them from committing additional crimes and recommending stricter penalties to the court if they violate probation or parole. Others work in youth correction facilities, including halfway houses and community-based programs. Although social services in prisons for problems such as substance abuse are limited, some BSW graduates work within prisons as well.

Summary

In the history of crime and punishment, reform is always just beyond the horizon. This chapter paints a dreary picture of practice and current procedures. Police practices do not deter crime, the courts do not dispense justice, the corrections system does not correct, and the parole system does not facilitate ex-prisoners' reentry into society as law-abiding citizens. Part of the problem is that while large sums of money are spent, the emphasis is on building more prisons and jails to house criminals rather than spending that money on crime-prevention efforts.

Funds alone are not the problem. Despite a considerable and growing body of knowledge of what works and what does not work in police, court, and correctional settings, insufficient attention is directed to integration within the system. Each unit of the system seeks to improve its operation and to clarify its mission, but at the expense of other components within the system. More effective integration of police, court, and prison practices is required.

Failure of the criminal justice system also stems from uncertainty about what it is expected to deliver: Is it safe streets, a just system, effective rehabilitation, or simple containment? Effective policies require clarity, choice, commitment, and closure. The segmented structure of the criminal justice system precludes all of these. As a consequence, during some periods, society throws money at aspects of the overall problem; during other periods it funds other aspects. Clearly, careful diagnosis and prescription are needed.

Key Terms and InfoTrac® College Edition

The terms below are defined in the Glossary at the end of this text. To learn more about key terms and topics in this chapter, enter the following search terms using InfoTrac or the World Wide Web:

adjudication	courts
appellate courts	crime
community corrections	crime prevention
community policing	criminal codes

criminal justice system
deterrence factors
disposition
dual system of justice
etiology of crime
incarceration
intake
intermediate
  punishments
juvenile correctional
  institutions

juvenile courts
juvenile delinquency
lower criminal
  courts
plea bargaining
probation
recidivism
rehabilitation
selective enforcement
trial courts

http://ojjdp.ncjrs.org/
http://juvenilejustice.com/
http://abanet.org/crimjust/juvjus/home.html/

Discussion Questions

1. To what extent is the policy dilemma of the criminal justice system reflected in the juvenile justice system? To what extent does the juvenile justice system have its own unique policy dilemma?

2. Which of the three views of crime, if any, is most consistent with social work practice theory?

3. Discuss the relationships between crime and other social problems.

4. If systems integration is the central problem of the criminal justice system, how can the contemporary social worker further integration?

5. Identify possible differences in worldviews of social workers and others working in the criminal justice field, and discuss strengths and problems that might arise in work settings or collaborative efforts because of those differences.

 ## On the Internet

http://www.ojp.usdoj.gov/bjs/
http://www.crime.org/links_nat.html/
http://www.fbi.gov/ucr/ucr.htm

References

Abadinsky, H. (2007). *Law and justice: An introduction to the American legal system* (6th ed.). Upper Saddle River, NJ: Prentice Hall.

Acorn, A. (2005). *Compulsory compassion: A critique of restorative justice.* Vancouver, BC, Canada: UBC Press.

American Bar Association. (2004). *Youth in the criminal justice system: Guidelines for policymakers and Practitioners.* Chicago: Author. Available: http://abanet.org/crimjust/pubs/reports/introduction.html

Annie E. Casey Foundation. (2006). *Reducing racial disparities in juvenile detention.* Baltimore: Author. Available: http://www.aecf.org/initiatives/jdai

Axinn, J., & Stern, M. J. (2005). *Social welfare: A history of the American response to need.* Boston: Allyn & Bacon.

Berman, H. J., Greiner, W., & Saliba, S. N. (2004). *The nature and functions of law.* Belmont, CA: Thomson Publishing Company.

Bonavita, N. (2001). *Disproportionate minority representation in the juvenile justice system.* Denver: National Conference of State Legislatures.

Bureau of Justice Statistics. (1999). *Time spent in prison by federal offenders, 1986–97.* Washington, DC: Author. Available: http://www.ojp.usdoj.gov/bjs

Bureau of Justice Statistics. (2003). *Local governments spend more on criminal justice than state governments or the federal government.* Washington, DC: Author.

Bureau of Justice Statistics. (2005). *Probation and parole in the United States, 2004.* Washington, DC: Author. Available: http://www.ojp.usdoj.gov/bjs

Bureau of Justice Statistics. (2006). *Prison and jail inmates at midyear 2005.* Washington, DC: Author. Available: http://www.ojp.usdoj.gov/bjs

Champion, D. J. (2006) *Crime prevention in America.* Upper Saddle River, NJ: Prentice Hall.

Coalition for Juvenile Justice. (2003). *Unlocking the future: Detention reform in the juvenile justice system.* Washington, DC: Author.

Coalition for Juvenile Justice. (2005). *Childhood on trial: The failure of trying and sentencing youth in adult criminal court.* Pittsburgh: Author.

Cohen, L. (2006). *The Gault case and young people's rights: Debating Supreme Court decisions.* Berkeley Heights, NJ: Enslow Publishers.

Crow, D. G. (Ed.). (2001). *The treatment and rehabilitation of offenders.* Thousand Oaks, CA: Sage Publications.

Du Cane, E. F. (2006). *The punishment and prevention of crime.* Kila, MT: Kessinger Publishing.

Gabbidon, S. L. (Ed.). (2005). *Race, crime, and justice.* London: Routledge Publishers.

Golash, D. (2005). *Case against retribution: Crime prevention, and the law.* New York: NYU Press.

Hubner, J. (2005). *Last chance in Texas: The redemption of criminal youth.* New York: Random House.

Hughes, G., McLaughlin, E., & Muncie, J. (Eds.). (2002). *Crime prevention and community safety. New directions.* Thousand Oaks, CA: Sage Publications.

Human Rights Watch. (2005). *Juvenile justice trends in the United States.* New York: Author.

Humes, E. (1997). *No matter how loud I shout: A year in the life of juvenile court.* New York: Simon & Schuster.

Kirst-Ashman, K., & Hull, G. H. (2005). *Understanding generalist practice.* Belmont, CA: Wadsworth/Thomson.

Krisberg, G. (2004). *Juvenile justice: Redeeming our children.* Thousand Oaks, CA: Sage Publications.

Lab, S. P. (2004). *Crime prevention: Approaches, practices, and evaluations* (5th ed.). Conklin, NY: Anderson Publishing.

Magnani, L., & Wray, H. L. (2006). *Beyond prisons: A new interfaith paradigm for our failed prison system.* Minneapolis: Fortress Press.

Males, D., & Macallair, M. (2004). A failure of good intentions: An analysis of juvenile justice reform in San Francisco during the 1990s. *Review of Policy Research, 21*(1), 63–78.

Mann, C. R., & Zatz, M. S. (Eds.). (2006). *Images of color, images of crime.* Los Angeles: Roxbury Publishing.

Martin, C. (2005). *Juvenile justice: Process and systems.* Thousand Oaks, CA: Sage Publications.

McShane, M. D., & Williams, F. P. (2002). (Eds.). *Encyclopedia of juvenile justice.* Thousand Oaks, CA: Sage Publications.

Mendel, R. A. (2000). *Less hype, more help: Reduce juvenile crime, what works—and what doesn't.* Washington, DC: American Youth Policy Forum.

Mooradian, J. K. (2003). *Disproportionate confinement of African-American delinquents.* New York: LFB Scholarly Publishing.

National Center for Policy Analysis. (1997). *The economic impact of prison labor.* Washington, DC: Author.

National Institute of Justice. (1998). *Preventing crime: What works, what doesn't, what's promising.* Washington, DC: Author. Available: http://www.ojp.usdoj.gov/nij/

Parry, D. L. (2004). *Essential readings in juvenile justice.* Upper Saddle River, NJ: Prentice Hall.

Physicians for Human Rights. (2006). *Juveniles in adult prisons.* Cambridge, MA: Author. Available: http://www.phrusa.org/campaigns/juv_justice/how.html

Poe-Yamagata, E., and Jones, M. (2000). *And justice for some: Differential treatment of minority youth in the justice system.* Washington, DC: Youth Law Center.

Prison Research Education Action Project. (2006). *Instead of prisons.* New York: Critical Resistance.

Puzzanchera, C., Stahl, A., Finnegan, T., Snyder, H., Poole, R., & Tierney, N. (2004). *Juvenile court statistics 2000.* Washington, DC. Available: http://ojp.usdoj.gov/ojjdp

Rosenheim, M. K., et al. (Eds.) (2002). *A century of juvenile justice.* Chicago: University of Chicago Press.

Russell, C. (2006). *Alternatives to prison: Rehabilitation and other programs (Incarceration issues: Punishment, reform, and rehabilitation).* Broomall, PA: Mason Crest Publishers.

Ryder, R. S. (2005). *Juvenile justice: A social, historical and legal perspective* (2nd ed.). Sudbury, MA: Jones and Bartlett Publishers.

Samaha, J. (2005). *Criminal justice* (7th ed.). Belmont, CA: Wadsworth/Thomson Publishing Company.

Schmalleger, F. (2007). *Criminal justice: A brief introduction* (7th ed.). Upper Saddle River, NJ: Prentice Hall.

Sheldon, R. G., & Hussong, K. (2001). *Juvenile crime, adult adjudication, and the death penalty: Draconian policies revisited:* Las Vegas: University of Nevada–Las Vegas.

Sherman, L. W., Farrington, D. P., & Welsh, B. C. (Eds.). (2002). *Evidence based crime prevention.* London: Routledge Publishers.

Sickmund, M. (2003). *Juveniles in* court. Washington, DC: Author. Available: http://www.ojp.usdoj.gov/ojjdp

Siegel, L. J., Welsh, B. C., & Senna, J. J. (2005). *Juvenile delinquency: Theory, practice, and law*. Belmont, CA: Wadsworth Publishing Company.

Snyder, H. (2005). *Juvenile arrests 2003*. Washington, DC: Author. Available: http://www.ojp.usdoj.gov/ojjdp

Strang, H., & Braithwaite, J. (Eds.). (2001). *Restorative justice and civil society*. New York: Cambridge University Press.

Strang, H., & Braithwaite, J. (Eds.). (2002). *Restorative justice and family violence*. New York: Cambridge University Press.

Sullivan, D. (2006). *The handbook of restorative justice: A global perspective*. London: Routledge Publishers.

Travis, J., & Visher, C. (Eds.). (2005). *Prisoner reentry and crime in America*. New York: Cambridge University Press.

Vos, B., Coates, R. B., Brown, K. A., & Umbreit, M. S. (Eds.). (2003). *Facing violence: The path of restorative justice and dialogue*. Monsey, NY: Criminal Justice Press.

Walker, S., Spohn, C., & DeLone, M. (2006). *The color of justice: Race, ethnicity, and crime in America*. Belmont, CA: Wadsworth Publishing Company.

Western, B. (2006). *Punishment and equality in America*. New York: Russell Sage Foundation Publications.

Zehr, H. (2004). *Critical issues in restorative justice*. Monsey, NY: Criminal Justice Press.

Zehr, H., & Toews, B. (Eds.). (2004). *Critical issues in restorative justice*. Monsey, NY: Criminal Justice Press.

Suggested Further Readings

Barak, G., Leighton, P., & Flavin, J. (2006). *Class, race, gender, and crime: The social realities of justice in America*. Lanham, MD: Rowman & Littlefield Publishers.

Bartollas, C., & Miller, S. (2007). *Juvenile justice in America* (5th ed.). Upper Saddle River, NJ: Prentice-Hall Publishers.

Bazemore, G., & Schiff, M. (2005). (Eds.). *Juvenile justice reform and restorative justice: Building theory and policy from practice*. Portland, OR: Willan Publishing Company.

Bohm, R. M. (2005). *Introduction to criminal justice*. Hightstown, NJ: McGraw-Hill Publishers.

Bosworth, M., & Flavin, J. (Eds.) (2007). *Race, gender, and punishment: From colonialism to the war on terror*. New Burnswick, NJ: Rutgers University Press.

Champion, D. J. (2006). *The juvenile justice system: Delinquency, processing, and the law*. Upper Saddle River, NJ: Prentice-Hall Publishers.

Cole, G. F., & Smith, C. E. (2007). *Criminal justice in America* (5th ed.). Belmont, CA: Wadsworth Publishing.

Cook, D. M. (2007). *Criminal and social justice*. (2007). Upper Saddle River, NJ: Prentice-Hall Publishers.

Del Carmen, R. V., & Trulson, C. R. (2005). *Juvenile justice: The system, process, and law*. Belmont, CA: Wadsworth Publishing Company.

Gabbidon, S. L., & Greene, H. T. (2005). *Race and crime*. Thousand Oaks, CA: Sage Publications.

Grisso, T. (2006). *Double jeopardy: Adolescent offenders with mental disorders*. Chicago: University of Chicago Press.

Grisso, T., Vincent, G., & Seagrave, D. (Eds.). (2005). *Mental health screening and assessment in juvenile justice*. New York: Guilford Press.

Hallworth, S. (2005). *Street crime*. Montpelier, VT: Brill Publishers.

Jordan, K. L. (2006). *Violent youth in adult court: The decertification of transferred offenders*. New York: LFB Scholarly Publishing.

Meyers, D. L. (2005). *Boys among men: Trying and sentencing juveniles as adults*. New York: Praeger Publishers.

Morash, M. *Understanding gender, crime, and justice*. Thousand Oaks, CA: Sage Publishers.

Pollock, J. M. (2007). *Ethical dilemmas and decisions in criminal justice*. Belmont, CA: Wadsworth Publishing.

Reichel, P. L. (2006). *Comparative criminal justice systems: A topical approach* (5th ed.). Belmont, CA: Wadsworth Publishing.

Taylor, W. T., Fritsch, E. J., & Caeti, T. J. (2006). *Juvenile Justice: Policies, programs and practices*. Hightstown, NJ: McGraw-Hill Publishers.

Winston, J., & Pakes, F. (Eds.). (2005). *Community justice: Issues for probation and criminal justice*. Devon, UK: Willan Publishing.

CHAPTER 14

Social Work in Rural Settings

Joe and Linda McDowell live on a 160-acre farm in southern Missouri. Joe inherited this farm from his father. His grandfather originally obtained the farm in the early 1900s, and three generations of McDowells have eked out their living on this farm and raised their families there. Joe and Linda both dropped out of high school in the 10th grade and were married on Linda's 18th birthday. They now have four children: Tommy, 9; Grace, 7; Sue, 6; and Jimmy, 4.

Over the past few years, the McDowells have had increasing difficulty producing farm products sufficient to meet the family's basic needs. They are heavily in debt for farm equipment loans and owe back taxes on the farm. They find themselves unable to compete with large farm operations.

The children are attending school sporadically, and they do not wear clothing appropriate to the weather (a luxury the McDowells cannot afford). Tommy has severe dental problems. Linda's health problems have limited her ability to help with the crops. Living 85 miles from a small city has not allowed Joe to try to supplement the family's income through gainful employment, and, even if he could locate a job, he would be able to earn only minimum wages because of his limited skills.

Joe and Linda are deeply invested emotionally in their farm, its family traditions, and the rural way of life. Considering their indebtedness, the back taxes they owe, and limited opportunity to make their farming operations productive, they likely will lose the farm through foreclosure. Joe and Linda worry about their future and that of their children.

Wherever social workers practice, they have to work within the context of the broader environment and the unique aspects of the community and geographic location. Although social work as a profession has some general values, a common body of knowledge, and a common skills set, certain aspects of the profession vary by the location in which social workers practice. Social workers in rural settings face issues different from those who practice in urban settings and have other social workers nearby.

In its most recent update, the federal government indicated that 17% (almost 50 million) of the nation's population live in non-metropolitan or rural areas, although they are spread out across three-fourths of the land area of the country. By contrast, more than 80% of the nation's population live in metropolitan or urban areas, concentrated in one-fourth of the country's land area (U.S. Department of Agriculture, 2003a).

In this chapter we will review some of the more salient characteristics of rural life in America, identify social welfare and social work resources available in rural communities, and discuss unique aspects of social work in rural settings.

Operational Definitions

What is considered "rural" and what is considered "urban" is often debated, with official definitions changing in recent years. In 2003, the U.S. Census Bureau released new definitions for what was rural and what was urban. These definitions shifted some U.S. counties that previously had been considered rural to an urban classification because they had become absorbed in rapidly growing metropolitan areas. The U.S. Census Bureau classifies as **urban** all urbanized areas regardless of total area population. Non-urban areas are grouped in two categories—micropolitan and noncore or non-inner city—emphasizing the diversity found in non-metropolitan areas of the United States.

Areas classified as **rural** include open country and small towns with populations of fewer than 2,500. Small towns and small cities that adjoin each other, however, are defined as urban clusters (for example, a town of 2,300 adjoining a town of 900 would be considered an urban cluster with a population of 3,200). Statistically, then, any small community of 2,499 or fewer people is classified as rural (U.S. Department of Agriculture, 2003a). (See Table 14.1 for a breakdown of urban and rural populations by state.)

TABLE 14.1
Urban and Rural Population for Selected States

State	Percent Urban	Percent Rural
Alabama	55.4	44.6
Arkansas	52.5	47.5
California	94.4	5.6
Florida	89.3	10.7
Illinois	87.3	12.2
Kentucky	55.8	44.2
Maine	91.4	8.6
Mississippi	48.8	51.2
Nebraska	69.8	30.2
Nevada	91.5	8.5
New Jersey	94.4	5.6
North Carolina	60.2	39.8
Ohio	77.4	22.6
South Dakota	51.9	48.1
Texas	82.5	17.5
Wyoming	65.1	34.9
U.S. Total	79.0	21.0

Source: *Statistical Abstract of the United States, 2006* (Washington, DC: U.S. Census Bureau, 2006).

Limitations of Rural and Urban Classification Systems

This classification system has limited utility in that it enables us only to separate communities statistically identified as rural or urban from those that are not. For example: Is a small isolated community in southwestern Kansas equivalent to a similarly sized, incorporated "bedroom community" 30 miles from Chicago? This is not to say that bedroom communities are any more resource-sufficient than isolated rural towns. The advantage lies in their proximity to larger cities, which places them within commuting distance for employment, health services, shopping alternatives, and related resources that are not available to the more isolated rural towns and villages.

Defining What Is Rural

Small towns have been struggling to maintain their "persona" and traditions. With the advent of regional shopping and discount centers moving into remote rural areas, many towns have become virtual ghost towns as shops have closed. The social discourse that once was prevalent on Main Street has been transplanted to large discount centers. Government grants designed to restore downtown areas have met with limited success. Although federal monies have provided subsidies for electric cooperatives and rural water systems and, thus, provided incentives for people to remain in rural areas, much remains to be accomplished to restructure downtown areas in rural communities into viable resource opportunities.

In addition, millions of Americans live on farms and ranches some distance from villages, towns, or cities. In many of these areas, small farms are close together, and in others, miles may separate families from each other. Rural inhabitants often are identified as rural-farm or rural non-farm to further clarify and differentiate the nature of rural residency. Clearly, the daily living requirements and patterns of farm dwellers are different from those of small-town residents.

To identify rural life as a primarily statistical anomaly is to miss the essence of rural existence. One can gain a better understanding of rural life experiences by reviewing the cultural ethos, environmental characteristics, and the means through which the people are able to provide sustenance for themselves and their families. These characteristics, reflected in the discussion that follows, are contrasted with urban issues. The reader must keep in mind that the life of a small farmer in Missouri is likely to be appreciably different from that of a cattle rancher in Montana, and the Missouri farmer may have more in common with a St. Louis urbanite than the cattle rancher would.

Definitions of urban or rural are not subject to the behavioral attributes of population groups but, instead, to population size. Such definitions do not take into account the complexity of life in either place.

Characteristics of Rural Populations

Approximately 50 million Americans currently live in rural areas in the United States. Farming is no longer central to the rural economy as it once was. Agriculture no longer dominates rural America, and the economy in rural areas has become diverse. In 1950, approximately one-third of those employed in rural areas worked in a job related to farm produce. Today, fewer than 10% of those living in rural areas live on farms and only about 6.5% are employed in jobs related to farm produce. In 2003, almost 70% of farm families reported that the farm operator or partner worked off the farm and almost 90% of their household income was from non-farm sources (U.S. Department of Agriculture, 2006).

Today, seven in eight rural counties are dominated by industries involving agricultural inputs, processing and marketing of agricultural goods, wholesale and retail trade of agricultural products, and agribusiness (U.S. Department of Agriculture, 2003a, 2003b). Manufacturing now accounts for more than 25% of private-sector earnings in rural areas, and the rural counties that have grown in population are those that rely on income from natural resources and climate for recreation and retirement or are close to urban areas (U.S. Department of Agriculture, 2006).

Rural areas, with their characteristic small towns, farms, and ranches of varying sizes, offer an appreciably different environment and lifestyle than metropolitan areas. Although some rural residents are able to access the resources of major cities, isolation and long distances to the resources of cities pose problems for others. As a whole, people living in rural areas have more limited resources than urban residents. Poverty rates are higher, and per-capita income is lower.

Using data from a variety of federal sources, Hamrick (2003) highlights the most recent indicators of social and economic conditions in rural

Migrant workers and their families often face extreme hardship and discrimination, including low wages, substandard housing, and limited access to education, health care, and other needed services.

© Jonathan Blair/CORBIS

areas for use in developing policies and programs to assist rural areas:

- Growing numbers of Hispanics are settling in rural America, accounting for the largest percentage of the non-metro population growth in recent years.
- The rural West grew by 20%, twice the national average.
- Average weekly earnings for non-metro workers were about 80% of the metro average in 2001.
- Half of the 1.9 million non-metro workers without high school degrees work in low-wage jobs.
- The non-metro median household income of $34,654 in 2000 continues to be well below the metro median of $45,257 (U.S. Department of Agriculture, 2004).
- Rural poverty is the highest in the South (17.5% in 2002, compared to 12.7% for urban areas) and lowest in the Northeast (10.7% in 2002, compared to 10.9% in urban areas) and Midwest (10.7% in 2002,

compared to 10.1% in urban areas) (U.S. Department of Agriculture, 2004).
- Poverty rates for African Americans were 33.2% in rural areas compared to 22.7% in urban areas in 2002; for Hispanics, 26.7% compared to 21.4% in urban areas; and for whites, 11% compared to 7.2% in urban areas (U.S. Department of Agriculture, 2004).
- Children in metro and non-metro areas alike have substantially higher rates of poverty than adults; nearly 20% of children age 18 and under in rural areas lived in poverty in 2002, compared to 16% in urban areas (U.S. Department of Agriculture, 2004).
- In 2000, the rate of food insecurity was higher in non-metro areas than in metro areas.
- Many rural areas have not participated in the success of welfare reform as defined by moving people from the welfare rolls into unsubsidized employment (Weber, Duncan, & Whitener, 2002).

Other, less measurable characteristics often define rural areas. Jennings (1990) identified the following characteristics that describe rural communities:

- basic trust
- basic friendliness
- isolation
- resistance to change
- suspicion toward newcomers or outsiders
- tendency for children to take on the identity of their parents
- independence of spirit, yet vulnerable
- similarity to a family system, especially regarding roles
- financial and experiential poverty
- reliance on informal and/or natural helping systems first for assistance
- concrete thinking and more reserved behaviors
- traditional values and conservatism
- more holistic, less compartmentalized lives

The strength and intensity of any (or all) of these characteristics vary, depending on the organization and density of the population of the rural area as well.

Table 14.2 presents a comparison of urban and rural areas of the United States for selected socioeconomic variables. When compared to their urban counterparts, rural residents are more likely to be older, make less money, live in poverty, and "make do" with an inadequate or functionally deficient transportation infrastructure.

Social Organization of Rural Communities

Unlike major metropolitan areas, social networks in rural communities are more personalized and informal than those typically found in urban communities. Many prominent and powerful community leaders are descendants of early settlers, often large landowners, and leaders in community affairs. Residents, affluent and poor alike, tend to be known by many people in the community. Residents seldom achieve privacy and anonymity. News, both good and bad, travels

TABLE 14.2
Selected Comparisons of Rural and Urban Communities in the United States

Characteristic	Value
Per-capita income (2000 dollars)	
Urban areas	$31,364
Rural areas	$21,856
Percentage persons living at or below poverty level	
Urban areas	11.1%
Rural areas	14.2%
Unemployment rate	
Urban areas	5.7%
Rural areas	6.2%
Median age of population	
Urban areas	34.0
Rural areas	38.0
Share of population with Medicare coverage	
Urban areas	12.7%
Rural areas	16.2%
Number of physicians per 100,000 residents	
Urban areas	308.5
Rural areas	110.4

Sources: America at a Glance, by Hamrick, K. (Ed.) (Washington, DC: U.S. Department of Agriculture, 2003). Available: http://www.ers.usda.gov/publications/rdrr94-1; "Rural Health Issues for the Older Population," by C. Rogers, in *Rural America* (2002), *17*(2), 32.

through the informal community network with amazing speed. Residents gain reputations that are changed only with great effort. Newcomers often find themselves in an out-group category and, regardless of their interest or endeavor, have difficulty being accepted fully into the inner circles of community life. Judgments concerning the character, ability, and competency of individuals tend to be based on subjective assessments.

The success or failure of community residents usually is attributed to personal effort and motivation. Hence, the poor, unemployed, and downtrodden are viewed as lacking the determination to achieve. Divorce and poverty typically are thought to be a reflection of personal failure, and strong negative sanctions serve as constant reminders that deviation from the norm is accompanied by increasing social distance and exclusion from free and full participation in community life.

Often politically conservative, rural communities are characterized by resistance to innovation and skepticism concerning modern technological innovations. Outsiders, particularly those from metro areas, are met with suspicion and disdain. They are considered to be uninformed as to rural residents' needs and not to be trusted.

At the same time, responses to people in need are often quick and personal. A death in the family or a farm failure stimulates neighbors to respond with goods and services to assist the needy through the crisis. Droughts, floods, tornadoes, and other natural disasters create a bond among farmers and ranchers, engendering a unity of purpose with shared concern. People often show reciprocity by sharing labor for the harvesting of crops, helping others in times of need, and organizing to counteract threats to community life. Honesty and strong character are valued traits.

The action hub of rural communities is composed of the church, the local bank, the county extension office, small businesses, the feed store, and the local school system. As a consequence, the local banker, ministers, county agricultural agent, store owners, and school administrators usually have a powerful influence on community life. County government typically is relegated to the county judge and county commissioner. The sheriff's office often handles law enforcement, although many small towns also have a police force. Violations of the law are considered to be a personal offense against the community, and mitigating circumstances usually are downplayed or viewed as irrelevant. The social organization of rural communities is as varied as their locations. Although a community in any setting has common threads of roles and relationships that knit it together, each locale has its own character (U.S. Department of Agriculture, 2003b).

Support Services in Rural Communities

Support services in rural areas may be scarce or nonexistent. Doctors, nurses, social workers, dentists, and attorneys typically are lacking in small rural towns. Adequately staffed hospitals with state-of-the-art equipment often are not found in small communities because they lack the resources to finance their development and ongoing support. As a consequence, many health-related problems go unattended, or people rely on traditional cures or folk medicine. Resources for treating mental illness are particularly lacking, but individuals who exhibit "peculiar" behavior often find acceptance in rural areas, and their families may benefit from considerable understanding and social support from neighbors. Because of the community's mores or limited financial support, social work and social services tend to be distributed sparsely in rural areas.

As noted, the church is a significant institution in rural life. Congregations respond quickly to those in need and set the pace for community action in times of crisis. The church also is the center of community activities, sponsoring social get-togethers and recreational opportunities. Religion plays a vital role in setting the moral tone and in meeting the spiritual needs of rural residents. Ministers are viewed as more than spiritual advisers; they are considered as community leaders as well.

In agricultural areas, the county extension office, funded by the **U.S. Department of Agriculture (USDA),** provides many services that the farm community values, and the county liaison office provides a variety of community and family services. Technical assistance is made available for crop planting and harvesting, ranch management, disease control, care of livestock, food preparation, home canning, and other activities related to farm, ranch, and home management.

Informally, the **county agent** often becomes aware of personal problems and serves as counselor, case manager, and resource finder. He or she also often functions as an advocate or a broker (with the local banker or other lending agencies) for farmers undergoing financial disaster. The USDA also provides vital funding for rural community initiatives such as creating affordable housing opportunities and community service centers where residents can obtain information or critical services (see Box 14.1).

An additional link to obtaining information has been the introduction of computer technology in rural areas. Virtually all small businesses, service agencies, and school systems are computer-equipped with access to the Internet. Most small, rural school systems provide instruction in technology, and many are linked to statewide networks that help residents access information. This technology has enabled a closer link with urban areas in acquiring essential information, along with its potential use as a problem solving resource. Many residents of rural areas are increasingly knowledgeable about health issues, for example, because of their access to the Internet. In some rural areas, access to such technology is not yet available, which furthers the **digital divide** and adds to the employment and educational barriers.

Recreational activities, too, may be limited in rural areas. The absence of a local movie theater, skating rink, park, library, and other outlets for children and teenagers severely restricts opportunities for leisure-time activities. Many small communities "roll up the sidewalks" at dark. As a consequence, the local school has become a prominent source for recreational get-togethers, dances, and holiday programs. Athletic events usually are well attended, and are a central focus for young people and adults to meet and socialize.

BOX 14.1
U.S. Department of Agriculture Rural Development Program: A Success Story

Alfred and Betty Muzer were living in an old mobile home with a leaking roof, holes in the floor, and mildew on everything they owned. They were paying $450 per month in rent on a fixed income of Social Security and retirement benefits. The family visited our office, interested in purchasing a home of their own.

How Rural Development Helped

Mr. and Mrs. Muzer were determined to be eligible for the Section 502 housing program. Rural Development assisted the family in purchasing and updating a three-bedroom home in Bertie County.

The Results

The family now has a decent, safe, and sanitary home in which to spend their retirement years, and their payment is less than the rent they were paying previously. Mr. and Mrs. Muzer now have room for family members to visit and added funds in their pocket to enjoy their retirement. The Muzers are proud of their new home. They could not have obtained this dream without Rural Development Assistance.

Source: U.S. Department of Agriculture (2005a). http://www.rurdev.usda/rd/stories/nc-20051019-muzer.html

In addition to the church, the school is a primary institution for social organization in the rural community.

The importance of **natural helping networks,** many of which have been mentioned, should not be minimized in **rural social work.** Historically, networks of friends, relatives, congregations, clubs, civic groups, and related entities have constituted the backbone of assistance to those in need. These networks can be readily seen in many rural communities that are largely African American or Latino, accompanied by a strong sense of collective identity. In many African American and Latino communities, the church is the center of the community and the priest or pastor is an important leader. Avant (2004) talks about informal kinship care in rural African American communities as contrasted with formal foster care or adoption, and notes that individuals rally around community members and support each other by sharing resources including food, shelter, and transportation. Cordova (2004) describes life in a rural colonia ("neighborhood" or "community" in Spanish) in Texas, communities of primarily Mexican immigrants who share many of the same struggles as underdeveloped countries and may lack running water, an adequate sewer system, electricity, and paved roads.

In spite of these conditions, residents support each other, often bringing a network of extended family members who live together until they can afford to live in their own residences. They also share food, electricity, child and elder care, and they help each other bridge the barrier to the broader, primarily English-speaking community in making necessary transactions. Celebrations, especially those involving children and youth, are important traditions in many African American and Latino rural communities.

The rural culture of values and mores that involves assisting each other in times of need and crisis remains intact to a large extent—particularly in the more isolated areas. Social service workers who understand this culture and are skillful at identifying relevant natural groups often find that their efforts are enhanced by incorporating natural helping networks into the helping process.

Social Problems and Needs in Rural Areas

Many people have a romantic view of rural areas as peaceful, serene, and devoid of the problems in large cities and metropolitan areas. These views fail to portray the reality of rural life. Rural areas are not devoid of social problems, and the impacts on rural residents are likely to be greater than on those living in cities because of the lack of transportation or the absence of support services. A few of the more prominent problems are discussed next.

Mental Health

People living in rural areas have the same kinds of mental health problems and needs for services as individuals who live in urban and suburban areas, yet rural areas have unique characteristics that present barriers to mental-health care. Access to and availability of mental health specialists is extremely limited. Poverty, geographic isolation and cultural differences, lack of transportation, staff shortages, inadequate facilities, few treatment alternatives, and the high cost of medications further limit the amount and quality of mental-health care available to people in rural areas (National Institute of Mental Health, 2003). Rural areas, for example, have far fewer psychiatrists than urban areas to serve the population, and even if residents can obtain an appointment, they may have to drive hundreds of miles, which can be a problem, especially for ill and elderly people who do not have access to reliable transportation.

Overall, residents of rural areas are more likely than urban residents to have mental

Rural life often involves having to travel long distances for services, education, and jobs.

© Jim Craigmyle/Corbis

health-related problems. Rates of suicide, child maltreatment, and mental illness are higher in rural areas. In addition to these more severe problems, the psychological and emotional anguish associated with marital discord and parent–child conflicts has intensified in many rural areas as increasing numbers of residents are replacing farming with other sources of income. For instance, child abuse, once thought to be a primarily urban problem, is found in rural areas with increasing frequency.

Too, many have considered drug abuse to be primarily an urban problem. Now, methamphetamine ("meth") production and use are becoming a concern in rural communities. Initially produced in rural areas because of the availability of abandoned barns and farmhouses in remote locations, as well as a key ingredient used in producing the illegal drug also used as a fertilizer, methamphetamine has devastated thousands of rural families and many communities because of its addictive nature and the resulting debilitation, which often leads to unemployment, child maltreatment, and serious health problems. Rural

areas with meth labs have had to deal with problems of toxic waste from the labs' contaminating fields and household drains.

In 2003, the rise of arrests of meth users in rural areas of the United States was associated with 3,000 children being removed from parents who were addicted in 2003. Law-enforcement officials also report that 60% of children removed from lab sites had methamphetamine in their system (Rural Assistance Center, 2006). The federal government and a number of states have established special programs to deal with this growing problem in rural areas, as treatment for methamphetamine addiction is much more difficult to access in rural locations than in urban areas.

Abuse of other drugs, including alcohol, and local youth gangs traditionally have been viewed as symptoms of economic and social unrest. These problems, too, have become more significant in rural areas, reflecting the ecological instability of rural life today.

The National Institute of Mental Health and other national and state programs have attempted to draw attention to rural mental health needs.

They have called for internships and training programs directed specifically to mental health service delivery in rural areas—hiring more staff in rural areas and ensuring that they are trained to work effectively with rural populations, offering "wrap-around services" that provide holistic care for rural families, developing networks of multi-disciplinary teams that can work collaboratively to address needs in rural areas, and using technology as a tool for assessment, intervention, and coordination (Scales & Streeter, 2004).

Health Care

As in urban areas, health care is of great concern to people who live in rural America. Health indicators reflect that the rates of infant mortality and chronic disease are higher in rural areas than in urban areas. The rural elderly suffer from chronic illness and poor health in far greater numbers than their urban counterparts. Diabetes, as one example, is more likely to be untreated in rural areas than in urban areas, which results in more serious problems when it does come to the attention of health-care providers.

Rural hospitals are funded on the same per-service basis as urban hospitals, but, because of the smaller capacity of rural hospitals, the costs to deliver services are higher. Many rural hospitals also do not have the ability to purchase the expensive equipment that larger urban hospitals do. Thus, rural residents may go to more distant urban hospitals to receive more extensive care. These factors lead to inadequate financial capability to continue operations—a factor that all too often results in the hospital's having to close. Thus, rural residents are left without nearby access to health care.

Considering the high costs for gasoline, rural residents tend to postpone necessary care that often is far away and beyond their financial means. Although most rural areas do have emergency medical services (EMS), these services typically are not prepared to handle life-threatening diseases or severe traumatic injuries.

In addition, recruiting doctors, nurses, and other health-care professionals for rural areas has been relatively unsuccessful.

Although solutions to rural health problems are not easy to come by, the health needs of rural residents must become a priority for policymakers. The **Omnibus Health Care Rescue Act of 1989** was designed to provide relief in the form of additional health-care resources, but major gaps in service remain. Some of the more recent health-care concerns, such as HIV/AIDS, place even more demands on rural health resources. Demands on rural health providers will continue to escalate while resources to meet the needs are limited.

The shortage of medical doctors and specialists also imposes limited choices from which to select treatment options for disease and illness in many rural areas. Patients who require kidney dialysis and other complicated health problems often must travel long distances for treatment or, in some cases, even move to a location where treatment facilities are easily accessed. Further, turnover rates among medical practitioners tend to be higher in rural areas, and attracting and retaining qualified medical personnel are difficult (Ormond, Wallin, & Goldenson, 2001).

One innovative approach to improving the quality of care for rural residents is the product of our high-tech society. Mobile vans equipped with state-of-the-art equipment and health practitioners are making health care more accessible in many rural areas. And, through **telecommunications,** rural medical practitioners have immediate access to large medical centers, where consultation is available for both diagnostic and treatment regimens. Technology also enables rural patients to have electronic equipment in their homes, to transmit data such as blood pressure and blood sugar levels to health practitioners for monitoring. **Telemedicine** has rapidly expanded throughout rural areas of the United States, with the capacity to enhance the quality of care for clients who lack the capacity to receive care in a major medical center (Norris, 2002).

Poverty

In the rural population—which makes up about 17% of the total U.S. population—almost 14% live below the poverty level. Residents in some parts of the country, such as Appalachia and the area along the Texas-Mexico border, experience poverty rates of 30% to 50%. As noted earlier, poverty rates for rural areas are higher than those for urban areas, and income is approximately 30% lower for rural residents than for their urban counterparts (U.S. Department of Agriculture, 2004).

People of color living in rural areas are more likely to be poor than their white counterparts: About 33% of all rural African Americans and 27% of all rural Latinos live in poverty, compared to 11% of whites (U.S. Department of Agriculture, 2004). The rural poor tend to have primarily low-wage jobs; and their ability to attain higher-paying jobs is curtailed because they generally are less well educated than their urban counterparts. Their income-earning capacity is affected further by seasonal employment, illness, and injury.

Most of the rural poor are involved with crop harvesting, which is characteristically unpredictable, pays poor wages, and frequently requires that families move from place to place to secure employment. Although many of these families no longer travel long distances to harvest crops, they retain the terminology of *migrant workers*.

Other types of employment, such as working in a feed store, being a nurse's aide, clerking at a hardware or department store, and similar types of jobs, generally pay only minimum or near-minimum wages. This income, often at poverty level, is insufficient to meet the family's financial needs. Career mobility is severely limited, too, and many workers with 20 or 30 years of experience continue to earn only a minimum wage.

As mentioned, the children of these workers, like their parents, have less education than their counterparts in urban areas. Higher rates of disease and infant mortality reflect the substandard conditions under which many live. Small-town school systems, already strained for financial resources, often are not diligent in enforcing mandatory school-attendance laws. School personnel also have trouble convincing youth and their families that attending school is important in the long run when the efforts of as many family members as possible are needed just for the family to survive. As a result, many children are not encouraged to pursue an education and, instead, work alongside their parents to help the family earn enough money to survive. Consequently, a vicious cycle is set in motion, perpetuating intergenerational patterns of farm laborers who are poor and lack the necessary resources to break out of poverty.

Older Adults

Another group that receives less attention in rural areas consists of older adults. This population is growing at a faster rate in rural areas than in urban areas, accounting for 14.6% in non-metro areas compared to 11.9% in urban areas. The median age is 37.2 in rural areas compared to 34.9 in urban areas, reflecting the higher proportion of elderly (U.S. Department of Agriculture, 2006).

Because women in general live longer than men, they also constitute a larger proportion of the rural elderly population. Women represent 51.8% of adults ages 65–74 and 65.9% of those age 85 and older (U.S. Department of Agriculture, 2005b).

Ethnic Composition

Rural communities are more segregated than urban areas. Racial segregation, limited political participation, and impoverishment continue to characterize the plight of people of color in rural communities. Attempts to organize farm labor and implement civil rights legislation have met with only limited success, primarily because of the resistance of large landowners and commercial farmers who seek to maintain the status quo and exert sufficient power to foil reform efforts.

Immigrants have increased the population in many rural areas that had been declining, where primarily elderly residents remain. In Minnesota, for example, immigrants have replaced young adults who leave rural areas seeking better job and social opportunities (Minnesota Advocates for Human Rights, 2006). In the Minnesota River Valley—a farming area that long has been part of the migrant trail—the Latino population increased by 600% between 1985 and 2001. This influx in population kept schools from closing or consolidating and also brought $8 million dollars to rural school districts. Immigrants are employed not only on farms and ranches in rural areas but also in food-processing plants and other jobs where English proficiency is not vital and low wages prevail. This helps to keep plants open that had been having difficulty finding employees who were willing to remain in the area.

In the Minnesota River Valley, in 2006, Latino workers made up one-third of the workforce, generated an additional 7,800 jobs for non-Latinos, and contributed $484 million annually to the economy. While state and local governments have funded social service needs of new immigrants, the $45 million generated in tax revenue from immigrant workers more than offset the $24.5 million spent on services.

As evidenced by continuing debates about immigrants and immigration policy at state and federal levels, many people view undocumented persons negatively, believing that they compound problems in the farm labor market through their willingness to work for lower wages. Experience has shown, however, that they take jobs that otherwise would not be filled. Because most undocumented persons are concerned with being detected by federal immigration officials (and being returned to Mexico), they are vulnerable to exploitation by landowners who seek cheap labor. The decline in the value of the peso has exacerbated the problem, prompting large numbers of undocumented persons to cross the border seeking work and better living conditions in the United States.

Nearly 75% of agricultural workers do not have health insurance, complicated by the fact that agricultural workers are at greater risk for chronic diseases, including stroke, diabetes, asthma, high blood pressure, and heart disease. The 1996 federal Health Insurance Portability and Accountability Act (HIPPA) was intended to protect farm workers and others who move from job to job, or have preexisting health conditions, from loss of health insurance. The act, however, did not include portability of Medicaid benefits within and between states for migrant farm workers, making continuity of health care exceedingly difficult for this at-risk population (California Institute for Rural Studies, 2006).

Poor white farm workers have many of the same problems as farm workers of color. Typically less educated than urban whites, they are viewed stereotypically as people with less incentive and motivation to succeed. Limited resources and skill levels keep them on the farm. Illiteracy rates are higher and poverty is more pervasive among rural whites than urban whites. When rural whites do migrate to cities, they often are relegated to low-paying jobs and have considerable difficulty assimilating into the urban environment.

Perhaps the conditions of the poor are best described in an article by Colby (1987), who cites an anonymous poor rural resident:

> Poverty is dirt. You say in your clean clothes coming from a clean house, "Anybody can be clean." Let me explain housekeeping with no money. For breakfast I give my children grits with oleo, or cornbread with no eggs or oleo. What dishes there are, I wash in cold water with no soap. . . . Look at my hands, so cracked and red. . . . Why not hot water? Hot water is a luxury. Fuel costs money. . . . Poverty is . . . remembering quitting school in junior high because "nice" children had been so cruel about my clothes and my smell. . . . Poverty is a chisel that chips on honor until honor is worn away. (pp. 9–10)

The problems of the rural poor are compounded by a lack of community support services—public water and sewage, fire and police protection, transportation, employment opportunities, and related services.

The Rural Family

The notion that rural families are harmonious, are problem-free, and enjoy life to its fullest is not borne out by fact. This idyllic view is an illusion that filters out the reality of existing conditions. Just as in urban areas, the negatives related to strained relationships, substance abuse, divorce, child abuse and neglect, sexual exploitation, and a myriad of related problems are found in rural areas. Certainly the rural environment has much to offer its residents, and most of them find contentment and satisfaction within the context of family solidarity. Unlike urban families, however, solutions may be more elusive for rural families when problems do emerge. Needed support programs are generally lacking for rural children with special problems such as physical, mental, or learning disabilities.

Marital discord and related interpersonal relationship issues may go unattended. Teen pregnancy has become more prevalent, as have single-parent families. Among the poorest (although not limited to them), early marriage, coupled with limited education, locks younger couples into a life with low wages and barriers to career mobility.

Even where limited support services are available, rural families tend to be reticent about calling upon them. For example, one small Southwest town of 3,500 people seldom used a mental health service except for court-ordered substance-abuse cases. Careful community analysis reflected strong values tied to self-help and self-management of problems. The residents treasured anonymity, deterring them from utilizing available mental health assistance. Only after an innovative plan was implemented in which a social worker was housed in the local medical clinic did matters change. Prospective clients first visited the medical center, where the doctor referred them to the social worker when mental health or family-related problems were detected. Within a relatively short time after the plan was implemented, the social worker had a full caseload, including persons with marital conflict, spousal alcoholism, family violence, depression, and related dysfunctional behaviors (Shuttlesworth, 1993).

The Crisis of the Small Farmer

Like the McDowells at the start of the chapter, many small farmers are facing a similar crisis. Low farm prices, high production costs, imports, and a convergence of related factors have created a crisis for the small farmer. Reemerging in the 1990s, farm and ranch foreclosures again have skyrocketed, which has resulted in the displacement of large numbers of farmers and ranchers who depended on agricultural production for their livelihood.

Like the McDowells, intergenerational farms and ranches are being lost through foreclosure. Displaced farmers and ranchers often lack the skills required to become absorbed readily into other parts of the labor market, particularly in the instance of older farmers and ranchers. Major commercial farm operations (sometimes called "mega farming" or "precision farming") have contributed to the demise of small farm operations through volume production, which lowers the unit prices for products. The small operator, even under optimum conditions, has great difficulty competing (Ohio State University, 2003; Tobler, 2002).

Currently, few resources are available to assist small farmers and ranchers in maintaining their property and purchasing the equipment essential to compete successfully. The federal government priority of reducing deficit spending has taken its toll on farm supports. Along with these problems, the stress and tension associated with the loss or probable loss of one's farm or ranch create havoc for these families. Problems such as increased family conflict—including spouse and child abuse—alcoholism, and depression are common in rural areas populated by ranchers and farmers operating as single-family businesses.

The increase in stress and the accompanying problems serve as disincentives for prospective new farmers to engage in agricultural operations. Some individuals who once were productive and self-sustaining must turn to public assistance as a means of survival. Urbanites must be reminded that their survival depends on a healthy agricultural industry.

Social Welfare in Rural Communities

The United States has many more small communities and towns than cities or major metropolitan areas. These communities vary in size and in their proximity to major metropolitan areas. For example, Tilden, Texas, a county-seat town of approximately 350 residents, is situated in a county that covers approximately 1,400 square miles. It is the largest town in the county. What type of organized social welfare programs are available in this community? What is needed? To what extent could the community support social welfare services?

Generalizations about the nature and extent of organized social welfare programs in small towns and rural areas should be avoided, because they vary greatly in size, nature, and ability to finance needed services. Many rural areas have few services, and those tend to be basic. Typically, public welfare services, mental health and developmental disabilities outreach centers, and public health services are available, although they usually have minimal staffs, offer limited assistance, and often are accessible only by a drive of several hundred miles. Counties sometimes offer a limited welfare assistance program and few county administrative officials (usually the county judge) to administer benefits along with their other duties.

A few rural communities have Community Action Agencies (first developed during the 1960s as part of the War on Poverty programs), although attempts to organize rural areas have been unsuccessful in general. Senior citizens' lunch programs may be provided by a branch of an areawide agency on aging. Employment agencies, family planning services, and family counseling agencies and related services typically are not found in rural areas.

A number of authors have suggested some innovative changes that would increase the service capacity to meet the needs of rural populations (Carlton-Laney, Edwards, & Reid, 1999; Scales & Streeter, 2004; Smith & Nelson, 1999). They include the following.

- Integrate services into a single, seamless service delivery system in recognition of the transportation problems that residents of rural communities often encounter. Capitalize on informal networks of exchange that frequently exist in rural areas to supplement limited formal services.
- Draw upon the spirit of cooperation, neighborliness, and helping, which often characterizes rural communities, to enhance available services.
- Be sensitive to cultural issues that might prevent people in need from accessing appropriate services.
- Utilize organizations such as the county agricultural extension service to promote social programs for individuals and families in need. The traditional function of these programs is to provide consultation on agricultural activities to farmers and ranchers, as well as homemaking information to rural women. They have the added potential for expanding their functions to include

community improvement and development programs in areas as diverse as housing, drug-abuse treatment, and social welfare planning, among others.

As suggested earlier, public social services generally are extended to rural areas through the auspices of state agencies. For example, state mental health programs usually have satellite offices in rural areas, implemented through regional offices, as do state departments of human services that offer public-assistance programs. Regional Education Service Centers provide resource assistance for rural schools.

If services equivalent to those in urban areas are to exist, additional resources must be developed in rural areas. In the past decade, efforts have been made to update and improve rural social services. Projects such as the Great Plains Staff Training and Development for Rural Mental Health in Nebraska, the information and advocacy efforts of the National Association of Rural Mental Health, and the caucus of national rural social workers and rural human service workers are all active in promoting higher levels and quality of service in rural areas.

More attention is being directed at the state and federal level to sustainability in rural areas. The U.S. Department of Agriculture's rural development programs assist rural areas in financing local water and wastewater systems, alternative energy systems, access to technology, housing, community facilities, electricity generation and distribution, conservation of natural resources, and research into new uses for agricultural products. Other federal agencies such as the Small Business Administration, Environmental Protection Agency, Health and Human Services Department, Department of Labor, and the Department of Commerce have rural development programs. In FY 2005, the USDA invested $4.24 billion to help nearly 45,000 rural families obtain homes and an additional $66 million to rehabilitate the homes of more than 11,700 low-income families (U.S. Department of Agriculture, 2006).

The U.S. Department of Agriculture (2006), in the planned 2007 reauthorization of the Farm Bill, called for

- targeting programs to be funded based on empirical data rather than perceived need, net impact on rural areas receiving funds, and sustainability of targeted programs;
- focusing on new-business development with at least partial financing by individuals and communities, incorporating the development of an equity plan to aggregate rural capital to stretch dollars; and
- proposing greater regionalized funding, requiring rural areas to develop planning regions for health care, education, waste and water resource management, transportation, and others. Planning regions then could receive block grants to address the most critical regional priorities and ensure that they go to the rural areas in the region that need them the most.

Social Work in Rural Settings

The practice of social work in rural communities is both similar to and different from that practiced in urban areas. The core of knowledge, methods, and skills of social work practice is the foundation for practice efforts in both environments (Phillips & Straussner, 2002). The nature of rural settings, the problems experienced, and the lack of resources confront the social worker with a unique set of challenges. Creativity, innovation, and the ability to influence community members to mobilize in meeting their needs are crucial skills for successful practice in rural settings. Social workers must be involved at the individual client level and also in the revitalization of rural areas, identifying community strengths to create healthy communities that use everyone's capabilities. No other type of social work compares with rural social work practice in intervening within the total environment.

Although many of the skills needed to practice social work are the same as those that urban social workers use, an important difference is the emphasis on informal and personal relationships in rural settings. Social workers Michael Daley and Freddie Avant (2004) suggest that the two concepts of Gemeinschaft and Gesellschaft, which you might have studied in a sociology course, can be applied when contrasting social work in rural and urban settings. Rural social work is consistent with Gemeinschaft, with its emphasis on family, geographic place, friendship, and the dynamics of informal relationships and social status. In contrast, urban social work is more consistent with Gesellschaft, which emphasizes more impersonal, formal transactions.

Rural social workers often must provide rural dwellers with services, support, and hope while helping simultaneously to change the environment to provide better transportation, improved medical care, and a more responsive community. Unlike urban social workers, the social worker in a rural area may feel frustrated by the absence of the company and support of fellow social work professionals, as well as the absence of a formal social service network. Opportunities for consultation and feedback on one's work are limited, so rural social workers may be left to make critical decisions on their own.

Social workers who both live and practice in rural areas find themselves as neighbors as well as professional practitioners. Almost everyone in the community knows who they are, and they may be called at home as well as the office to provide a wide range of services. Their service constituency may consist of children, adults, those with mental illness, the incarcerated, the bedridden, the distressed, and the abandoned. At any one time, a social worker may be helping a family locate a nursing-home placement for an older parent, securing resources for a child with a disability, counseling with a pregnant teenager and her family, collaborating with local ministers in developing leisure-time activities for youth, assisting school personnel in developing management techniques for a hyperactive child, or working with the court to secure rehabilitation resources for a delinquent child. These varied demands require that the social worker be flexible, have good communication skills, engage both private and public resources, and have a basic understanding of community values and practices.

Practicing social work in a rural setting subjects the social worker to "life in a fish bowl." Everyone seems to know the social worker both professionally and personally. His or her private life is closely scrutinized. Because social workers, like everyone else, have problems, the way these problems are managed becomes a matter of community concern. Like ministers, their work is expected to meet high personal and moral standards, and any deviation may lower the esteem in which they are held in the community. In rural communities, the ability to separate personal life from professional competence is difficult. Often, the social worker's credibility is at stake if a personal problem goes unresolved.

Maintaining the client's confidentiality when practicing in rural settings can be difficult. Residents typically know when anyone in the community is having problems and when someone is seeking professional assistance. A casual encounter at the grocery store may prompt a resident to inquire about a client whom they know through the grapevine is receiving services.

Social workers who have periodic assignments in the rural area but do not reside there encounter other problems. Typically, they are regarded as outsiders. In some instances, they have not had the opportunity to become aware of community priorities and values. Often, they are viewed as having little vested interest in the community and, as a result, respond to client problems out of context. Community resistance may become an additional barrier to problem solving.

An old social work axiom suggests that "change comes slowly." Although this premise is open to debate, it is valid most obviously in rural social work practice. Timetables and pace of life tend to be slower. Urgency is offset by practicality and patience. Waiting out matters may be given more credence than intervention. Social workers must learn to stifle their frustration and impatience while retaining their persistent efforts in the helping process. As their credibility and competence become better established, community resistance will turn into support and social workers' contribution to the community will be enhanced.

Interpersonal relationships with community leaders are essential in gaining support for change efforts in rural areas. As mentioned, small communities are as varied in culture and values as they are in number. Ethnic settlements often cling to traditional values and practices—an important factor in getting to know the community. Values and traditions often are identified as its "pulse"—the driving dynamic of community life. Understanding this phenomenon enhances the social worker's ability to communicate effectively with community leaders.

One of the authors, a long-time rural resident, has found that visiting the local café regularly provides informal opportunities to meet with farmers, ranchers, judges, police officers and sheriffs, teachers, the clergy, and a wide variety of community members—all sources of valuable information about the cares and concerns of the community. A further benefit is getting to be known as a person as well as a professional. As a result, trust is established and communication greatly enhanced.

The social work profession has long been concerned about the needs in rural areas and how best to address them. In the mid-1970s, the Rural Social Work Caucus was created to direct attention to practice and research issues related to rural communities and social work practice (Hickman, 2004). The caucus meets regularly and has been instrumental in developing policy statements on rural social work adopted by both the National Association of Social Workers (NSAW) and the Council on Social Work Education (CSWE). Caucus members submitted a new policy statement to NASW in 2002, which was adopted by the organization (see Box 14.2 for a summary of this statement).

By now you should be aware of some of the more salient differences between social work practice in rural areas and in areas characterized as urban or suburban. The models of intervention used in urban and suburban areas generally are not transportable to rural areas because of the nature, culture, diversity, and resource limitations of rural areas.

Rural Social Work as Generalist Practice

The variety and diversity of the tasks inherent in rural social work practice can best be accomplished by the generalist practitioner. Haulotte and Oliver (2004) identified six steps critical for a social worker who is entering a rural community. Note the parallel with the concepts of generalist practice discussed earlier in the text:

1. Know the geographic area (study maps, learn the names of roads and counties, learn where rural settlements are located).
2. Know the demographics (learn about the age, ethnicity, and income levels of residents and places of employment in the community).
3. Know the local culture (learn about political groups, religious affiliations, informal networks, civic groups, and relationships among them).
4. Know the formal resources provided by federal, state, and local entities (go to offices and learn what they do and who they are intended to serve).
5. Know the informal resources, including religious organizations, community civic and service groups, and the informal community nurturers and supporters.
6. Practice ethically, using social work values and principles.

BOX 14.2
NASW Professional Policy Statement in Rural Social Work

This statement was approved by NASW's Delegate Assembly in 2002. Excerpts from the policy statement are presented below:

Social work practice in rural communities challenges the social worker to embrace and effectively use an impressive range of professional intervention and community skills. It is critical that the social worker have practice expertise in multiple areas. Like all subcultures, rural populations must be understood to be effectively engaged. The difficulties associated with experiencing social problems are magnified in rural areas because close social and personal relationships coexist with a low population base. This and other unique features require the social worker to apply professional ethical constructs more consistently to protect confidentiality, analyze relationship issues, and otherwise behave in the best interests of clients.

Rural areas suffer disproportionately when urban-based policies are forced upon them. Corporate mergers, centralization, managed care, globalization, and similar cost-saving strategies based solely on urban models are disadvantageous to rural areas, where distance and time are the enemies of efficiency and of access to social services, health care delivery, and health maintenance. . . . .

Public and social policy must take into account the unique nature of rural areas and residents. Equitable policy formation should be the goal, so that urban and rural populations and jurisdictions are not pitted against each other over issues of livelihood, lifestyle, economy, or ecology. . . .

The skills of professional social workers are uniquely suited to helping rural people organize their lives, families, communities, and organizations to overcome adversity, identify and develop resources, and change lives for the better. . .

Source: From NASW Professional Policy Statement in Rural Social Work, edited by T. L. Scales & C. L. Streeter, *Rural Social Work: Building and Sustaining Community Assets* (Belmont, CA: Thomson Brooks Cole, 2004, Appendix), pp. 354–359.

Social workers in rural settings are called upon to work with individuals, families, and groups and in community organizations. Administrative and management skills are essential in rendering needed services (see Box 14.3). The abilities to define problems operationally, collect and analyze data, and translate findings into practical solutions are requisites for enriched practice. The rural social work practitioner is a multi-method worker who appropriately facilitates the problem-solving process. Knowledge of resources, resource development, methods of linking clients with resources, and case management is required of the rural social worker.

The Baccalaureate Social Worker and Rural Social Work Practice

Social work in rural communities is both challenging and rewarding. To function effectively, rural social workers must be self-reliant and have the ability to work apart from social work support systems. Many undergraduate social work programs are located in small cities or large towns adjacent to rural areas and specialize in rural social work practice. Field placements typically call

BOX 14.3
Some Characteristics of Effective Rural Social Workers

- They embody the generalist perspective of social work practice and link people with resources, both traditional and non-traditional, to address client needs.
- They are skillful at networking with a variety of traditional and non-traditional resources to address client and community needs.
- They are quick to understand the nuances of the rural communities in which they work, including traditions, values, culture, and formal and informal sources of support, and adapt their practice methods accordingly and with sensitivity to best meet client needs.
- They are able to establish informal mechanisms of communication with clients and other community members, yet maintain appropriate professional boundaries.
- They are creative in determining effective strategies to address client and community needs.
- They are comfortable with use of technology to link the communities they serve with the broader environment.

- They are able to work independently and make critical decisions about client and community needs within the boundaries of agency guidelines without ready access to immediate supervision.
- They have a strong sense of identity with the social work profession and are able to exemplify the values and methods of the profession without constant reinforcement from other social workers.
- They are able to gather and use feedback effectively to evaluate their professional work.
- They are strong advocates for the needs of rural areas.
- They are comfortable working across all levels of the environment and at becoming actively involved at the community level and beyond to create needed change.
- They understand the value of evidence-based practice and share what they learn about best practice in rural areas.

upon rural agencies to familiarize students with the skills essential for practicing in those settings.

The BSW social worker's generalist practice perspective will prove invaluable in working with rural populations. The opportunity to engage existing formal and informal organizations in extending or developing resources to meet community needs is a continuing challenge that the BSW social worker can address competently. Also, knowledge and expertise in problem identification, outreach, linking of target systems with resources, resource development, education, and problem solving enrich the lives of rural inhabitants and strengthen community support systems as well. The abilities to understand community value systems and to experiment with innovative techniques in working with community residents are essential assets for productive practice.

Until recently, social workers have not been inclined to engage in rural social work practice. Fortunately, this attitude is changing. Job opportunities in rural communities are increasing, and the potential for a satisfying and rewarding career in rural social work practice is greater now than ever before.

Summary

Approximately 20% of the nation's population live in non-metropolitan or rural areas on four-fifth's of the country's land. Rural areas differ from urban areas in social organization, lifestyle, informal and formal helping networks, and the types of problems that are more likely to be experienced. Rural areas are becoming increasingly Hispanic, with most of the growth in rural areas in the West. Household incomes in rural areas are below those of household incomes in urban areas. Communities in rural areas are characterized by trust, independence of spirit, and basic friendliness; isolation, resistance to change, and traditional values; informal social networks, and a personal response to human need.

Unique issues related to rural social welfare delivery systems relate to diversity and availability of resources to meet human needs. Because the scarcity of organized social services may require hours of travel, rural dwellers depend more on local churches and county extension offices, as well as natural helping networks of friends, relatives and civic groups.

The impact of social problems is often greater on rural residents than their urban counterparts. These problems include mental health disorders, child abuse and neglect, family violence, and poverty. Generalist practice is well suited to addressing rural social issues, and an ideal fit for the BSW, with emphases on linking clients with informal resources, the need to be innovative and creative, and working with individuals and families while influencing community members to meet identified needs. Job opportunities in rural areas are increasing, and the challenges of a successful social work career in providing needed services for rural communities are attracting social workers in greater numbers to rural communities.

Key Terms and InfoTrac® College Edition

The terms below are defined in the Glossary at the end of this text. To learn more about key terms and topics in this chapter, enter the following search terms using InfoTrac or the World Wide Web:

county agent	rural social work
digital divide	support services
natural helping	telecommunications
networks	telemedicine
Omnibus Health Care	urban
Rescue Act of 1989	U.S. Department
rural	of Agriculture

Discussion Questions

1. Review the case study at the beginning of this chapter. How might a generalist social worker help the McDowell family? How would geographic location shape the social work skills this family needs?

2. How are social problems in rural areas different from those in urban areas?

3. To what extent is generalist social work practice viable in working with individuals and families in rural communities? Why?

4. With fewer formal social welfare programs available in rural areas, how are natural helping networks useful to the social worker in providing services in these areas?

5. Why is it important to understand the culture, traditions, and values of rural communities, and how would you learn about them as a social worker in a rural area? How does this

understanding enable social workers to be more effective?

6. How are the problems facing rural Americans today different from those facing urban Americans? How are they similar?

7. What kind of plan would you develop in a rural community to move toward sustainability? Who would you involve in the plan?

On the Internet

www.cirsinc.org

www.cardi.cornell.edu/

www.ncth.org

www.research.marshfieldclinic.org/nfmc/

www.nrharural.org/

www.ruralinstitute.umt.edu/

www.rupri.org

www.uncp.edu/home/marson/rural/

www.rwhc.com

www.ruralwomyn.net

www.worh.org

www.wfan.org

www.ers.usda.gov/

www.nalusda.gov/ric/richs/elderpg.htm/

www.kumc.edu/instruction/medicine/NRPC/

References

Avant, F. (2004). African Americans in rural areas: Building on assets from an Afrocentric perspective. In T. Scales & C. Streeter (Eds.), *Rural social work: Building and sustaining community assets*. Belmont, CA: Brooks Cole.

California Institute for Rural Studies (2006). *Farmwork and rural health and safety*. Davis, CA: Author. Available: www.cirsinc.org/recent.html

Carlton-Laney, I. B., Edwards, R. L., & Reid, P. N. (Eds.). (1999). *Preserving and strengthening small towns and rural communities*. Washington, DC: National Association of Social Workers.

Colby, I. (1987). The bottom line: A personal account of poverty (anonymous author). *Human Services in the Rural Environment, 11*(1), 9–11.

Cordova, W. (2004). Life in a Colonia: Identifying community assets. In T. Scales & C. Streeter (Eds.), *Rural social work: Building and sustaining community assets*. Belmont, CA: Brooks Cole.

Daley, M., & Avant, F. (2004). Rural social work: Reconceptualizing the framework for practice. In T. Scales & C. Streeter (Eds.), *Rural social work: Building and sustaining community assets*. Belmont, CA: Brooks Cole.

Hamrick, K. (Ed.). (2003). *America at a glance*. Washington, DC: U.S. Department of Agriculture. Available: http://www.ers.usda.gov/publications/rdrr94 1

Haulotte, S., & Oliver, S. (2004). In T. Scales & C. Streeter (Eds.), (2004). *Rural social work: Building and sustaining community assets*. Belmont, CA: Brooks Cole.

Hickman, S. (2004). Rural is real: Supporting professional practice through the Rural Social Work Caucus and the NASW Professional Policy Statement for Rural Social Work. In T. L. Scales & C. L. Streeter (Eds.), *Rural social work: Building and sustaining community assets*. Belmont, CA: Brooks Cole.

Jennings, M. (1990). *Community mobilization*. Presentation to National Association of Rural Mental Health Workers, Lubbock, TX.

Minnesota Advocates for Human Rights (2006). *Immigrants in rural and urban communities fact sheet*. Minneapolis: Author. Available: energyofanation.org.8f536509-bb39-4157-bc9a-04e8flaeff87.html?NoedeId

National Institute of Mental Health. (2003). *Rural mental health research agenda: Building on success and planning for the future*. Available: http://www.nimh.nih.gov/scientificmeetings/ruralmentalhealthjune03.pdf

Norris, A. C. (2002). *Essentials of telemedicine and telecare*. New York: John Wiley and Sons.

Ohio State University. (2003). *Columnist defends "large farming operations."* Columbus: Ohio State University Extension. Available: http://clark.osu.edu/ag/largeoperations.htm

Ormond, B. A., Wallin, S., & Goldenson, S. M. (2001). *Supporting the rural health care safety net.* Washington, DC: Urban Institute. Available: http://www.urban.org/url.cfm?ID=309437

Phillips, N. K., & Straussner, S. L. A. (2002). *Urban social work: An introduction to policy and practice in the cities.* Boston: Allyn & Bacon.

Rogers, C. (2002). Rural health issues for the older population. *Rural America, 17*(2), 32.

Rural Assistance Center (2006). *$10 million awarded to fight methamphetamine in rural America.* Available: www.raconline.org/news/news_details.php?news_id=5101

Scales, T. L., & Streeter, C. L. (2004). *Rural social work: Building and sustaining community assets.* Belmont, CA: Brooks Cole.

Shuttlesworth, G. (1993). The rural medical social worker: A pilot project. *Human Services in the Rural Environment, 15*(4), 26–29.

Smith, J., & Nelson, M. K. (1999). *Working hard and making do: Surviving in small town America.* Berkeley: University of California Press.

Tobler, W. (2002). *Are "mega" farms really the only future?* Ann Arbor, MI: Great Lakes Information Network. Available: http://www.great-lakes.net/lists/enviro-mich/2002-10/msg00017.html

U.S. Census Bureau (2006). *Statistical abstract of the United States.* Washington, DC: Author.

U.S. Department of Agriculture (2003a). *Measuring rurality: New definitions in 2003.* Available: www.ers.usda.gov/Briefing/Rurality/NewDefinitions/2003

U.S. Department of Agriculture. (2003b). *Rural America: Opportunities and challenges.* Available: http://www.ers.usda.gov/Amberwaves/Feb03/features/ruralamerica.htm

U.S. Department of Agriculture (2004). *Rural poverty at a glance.* Rural Development (Research Rep. No. 100). Washington, DC: U.S. Government Printing Office.

U.S. Department of Agriculture (2005a). *How rural development helped.* Washington, DC: Author.

Available: www.rurdev.usda/rd/stories/nc-20051019-muzer.html

U.S. Department of Agriculture (2005b). *Rural population and migration: Rural older population.* Available: www.ers.usda.gov/briefing/Population/Older/

U.S. Department of Agriculture (2006). *Rural development 2006: 2007 Farm Bill theme papers.* Available: www.usda.gov/documents/Farmbill07ruraldevelopment.pdf

Weber, B. A., Duncan, G. A., & Whitener, L. A. (2002). *Rural dimensions of welfare reform.* Kalamazoo, MI: W.E. Upjohn Institute.

Suggested Further Readings

Butler, S., & Kaye, L. (Eds.). (2004). *Gerontological social work in small towns and rural communities.* Binghamton, NY: Haworth Press.

Ginsberg, L. H. (1998). *Social work in rural communities* (3rd ed.). Alexandria, VA: Council on Social Work Education.

Lohmann, N., & Lohmann, R. (2006). *Rural social work practice.* New York: Columbia University Press.

Rural Social Work, journal available at www.labrobe.edu.a/socialwork/rsw.html

Nyman, K. (2004). The complex challenges of building assets in rural communities and strategic bridging solutions. In T. L. Scales & C. L. Streeter (Eds.), *Rural social work: Building and sustaining community assets.* Belmont, CA: Thomson Brooks Cole.

Saltman, J., Gumpert, J., Allen-Kelly, K., & Zubrzycki, J. (2004). Rural social work practice in the United States and Australia. *International Social Work, 47*(4), 515–531.

Wilkinson, K. P. (1991). *The community in rural America.* New York: Greenwood Press.

CHAPTER 15

Social Work in the Workplace

A typical couple, Bill and Meredith Hunt, both 32 years old, live in a small house in a rapidly deteriorating part of the city with their three children, ages 2, 4, and 8. Bill is one of several workers who monitor a largely automated assembly line at a large manufacturing plant. Meredith is a computer programmer for a large company. The Hunts' two youngest children attend a child-care center, and their oldest child attends public school.

Until recently, Bill's job has been the most important aspect of his life. He is well liked as an employee, as well as in his neighborhood, but he is finding that his job is a lot less meaningful to him than in the past. His raises are less frequent, and not enough to pay even for necessities. Last year, Bill and the other assembly-line workers were laid off for 2 months because of a production slowdown. Most manufacturing companies in the area are buying their parts from abroad, and Bill's company increasingly is automating its operations, which reduces the need for employees. There is even talk of shutting down the plant and moving it to Mexico. Bill is frustrated about the recent layoff and the lack of pay and is concerned about how long his job will last. Although he knows that his wife has to work to make ends meet, Bill is resentful that she has less time for him and he feels badly that he can't provide for his family on his own.

Recently Bill has begun drinking heavily. During these drinking bouts, he has hit Meredith several times, and he yells at the children and spanks them. Bill's supervisor has noticed a change in his job performance and is ready to give him formal notification that his performance has to improve or he risks being fired. Bill feels constantly tired, financially pressured, and emotionally defeated.

Meredith also feels emotionally drained. In addition to her job, she maintains primary responsibility for the house and the children. She gets up at 5:30 a.m., and finally, after midnight, everything is done and she collapses into bed. Because the child care for the Hunts' two children costs more than half of Meredith's take-home pay, they can't afford child care for their oldest son before and after school. Meredith worries about him being at home alone and calls him several times each afternoon.

Neither of the companies the Hunts work for allows employees to take leave when the children are sick, and all three children have been sick a lot lately. Meredith has missed 6 days of work in the last 2 months to stay home and care for her sick children. On three other occasions she has kept her oldest son home from school to take care of the younger children.

Meredith's mother, who lives in a neighboring city, recently was diagnosed with cancer and is scheduled to have major surgery. Meredith would like to spend several days with her mother during and after the surgery, as her siblings live out of state. But she has used all of her vacation days for her children's illnesses, and her company doesn't have any policies that provide for leave in situations like this.

Recently, Meredith has been having trouble sleeping and has developed stomach problems. Her doctor prescribed tranquilizers, which she takes more often than the prescription calls for. Meredith's co-workers are worried about her, but at the same time they resent having to do extra work when she is absent or not able to work as efficiently as usual. Her boss has commented on the decline in her job performance. Meredith likes her job very much but is worried about her husband, her children, and her mother. She feels guilty because her working places extra pressures on her family. Her oldest son is not doing well in school, and Meredith is too tired to help him. All three children vie constantly for her attention. Both Meredith and Bill feel caught between the pressures of work and their family, and they are becoming increasingly overwhelmed by the demands on them.

Most individuals who are older than 18 have two major domains in which they interact: the family and the workplace. Attention to social problems and individual needs usually centers on the family and rarely considers the relationship between the individual and the workplace. This omission has resulted in social workers not helping individuals and their families as effectively as they could.

Consider again the systems/ecological perspective to understanding problems discussed in chapter 3, particularly the way in which the systems overlap and interact with each other and the individuals who function within those systems. Think about this perspective in relation to the Hunt family. Though until recently the Hunts have been a close-knit family, work has become the focal point in their lives. Work produces the economic resources needed to provide food, clothing, shelter, and the recreational activities that are affordable to them.

When we meet someone, our first question frequently is not, "What about your family?" but, rather, "Where do you work?" In U.S. society, a person's status in life is defined largely by occupation. The type of work we do defines much of our self-respect, self-fulfillment, identity, and status. Until recently, both Bill and Meredith had received positive fulfillment in their workplaces. They got along well with co-workers and received raises, recognition for jobs well done.

At first their two jobs allowed the Hunts to support their family adequately. The positive aspects of work spilled over into the family, allowing them to maintain positive support within the family. But the overlap between the two domains began to create additional pressures for both Bill and Meredith. Conflicts arose about which has to come first—home or work—when they are drained of energy for both. What should be done when a child or relative gets sick? How much money should be spent on child care? Who is going to prepare the meals when both parents are tired? What jobs and career paths should be pursued in the rapidly changing workplace? All of these issues have an impact on Bill and Meredith's relationships and ability to function, both at home and at work.

For Bill and Meredith, work currently has many negative implications. Ideally, they will seek help from some social service program before either their family or their jobs become jeopardized further. A social worker or other helping professional who becomes involved with the Hunts' problems must consider work issues in the total intervention.

In this chapter we explore current and projected workforce demographics, the changing nature and meaning of work, problems created by work and family tensions, and the roles the workplace and social workers can play in attempting to prevent these problems from occurring or recurring.

A Historical Perspective on Work and Family Relationships

In most Western countries, particularly in the United States, the roots of society can be traced to the Protestant work ethic, which stems from the Protestant Reformation of the 17th century. This ethic suggests that work is an expectation of God and laziness is sinful. Attitudes toward paupers during the early colonization of the United States and toward welfare recipients today are derived from the impact of the work ethic on our society. For women, however, the emphasis was different: The primary role of women was to maintain the family and to support the ability of men in the family to work outside the home.

Until the 1970s, this pattern changed only during wartime, when women were needed in the factories while men were away at war. But as soon as peace was restored, the women returned to the home and men to the workplace. The women who did work outside the home—because of necessity, interest, or both—often were considered to be outside their appropriate role. Until the 1970s, most studies regarding work concentrated on the negative impact of the *unemployed* male on his family or on the negative impact of the *employed* female on her family (Pitt-Catsouphes, Kossek, & Sweet, 2005).

In recent years, much has changed in regard to the relationship between the individual and the workplace. Probably the biggest change has come from the large number of women who are working, including women with children. Other changes include a more diverse workplace, not only in gender but also in ethnicity. African Americans, Latinos, and other people of color are comprising a greater portion of the workforce.

Between 2004 and 2014, the U.S. civilian labor force is expected to change in the following ways (U.S. Bureau of Labor Statistics, 2006a):

- 9.1% increase in men age 16 and older;
- 10.9% increase in women 16 years of age and older;
- 49.1% growth in persons age 55 and older;
- 16.8% increase in African Americans age 16 and older;
- 32.4% increase in Asians and Pacific Islanders, American Indians, and Alaska Natives 16 years old and older; and
- 33.7% growth in Latinos 16 years of age and older.

Employees' expectations about work have changed as well. Individuals today expect more from the workplace than just a paycheck. They seek recognition, a voice in decision making, benefits, and flexible working hours. Numerous studies have found that many workers today have placed other priorities ahead of their jobs. Additional problems that are receiving more attention in the workplace include substance abuse; higher costs of health care and other benefits; maternity, paternity, and sick leave; and the overall increase in employees' stress.

Because work for pay is such an important facet of our society, fluctuations in the U.S. economy in recent years have raised concerns about the unemployment and **underemployment** of many individuals. The unemployed and underemployed are much more likely to be women and people of color, most often with children. Unemployment and underemployment—and the fear of both—cause added stress to individual employees and to their families.

A growing number of experts view the relationship between work and family life as one of the most critical policy issues to be addressed during this decade (Akabas & Kurzman, 2007). In many instances, special social services and other programs have been established in the workplace to help employees and their families maintain or increase productivity (Bianchi, Casper, & King, 2005). Increasingly as well, social services programs in the workplace are helping workers deal with layoffs and business closings (Pitt-Catsouphes, Kossek, & Sweet, 2005).

Occupational social work (sometimes called "industrial social work") has emerged as a growing field for social workers. Occupational social workers usually work in the human resources department or health unit of a company. They help employees cope with job-related pressures and personal problems that affect the quality of their work. They provide counseling to employees whose performance is hindered by emotional or family problems or substance abuse. They also develop educational programs on a variety of quality-of-life issues and refer workers to community programs for assistance (U.S. Bureau of Labor Statistics, 2006e). By applying a systems/ecological perspective, social workers have the potential to play a major role in strengthening relationships among individuals, their families, and the workplace.

The Current Workforce

Today's workforce is considerably different from what it was even a decade ago. In the past, most employees were white males employed in business and industry who often stayed with one company until retirement. Today, a large number of women and people of color are employed in often low-paying, service-related jobs. The median annual earnings of service workers in the United States in 2004 were $21,371 for males and $17,096 for females U.S. Census Bureau, 2006).

In addition, as a result of technological and economic changes, many workplaces have closed, **downsized** their operations, or modified the nature of their work and the type of resources needed, including personnel. Employees today are more likely to change jobs frequently and go through several career moves before they retire. Being terminated from a job for reasons other than job performance also will become much more common as global changes affect the workplace (Berger, 2005; Mann & Kirkegaard, 2006).

More Women in the Workforce

Many of today's work-related programs and policies are based on work and family demographics existing during the 1950s—an almost exclusively male workforce and a male breadwinner supporting his stay-at-home wife and an average 2.6 children. Currently, few American families can be classified in this way. In nearly 65% of two-parent families with children under 18, both parents were employed full time in 2004. The proportion of families maintained by women who had children under age 18 was 80%; children between 6 and 17, it was 83%; and under 6, it was 74.45% (U.S. Census Bureau, 2006). The rate of workforce participation by female heads of household exceeds that of two-parent families regardless of ages of children in the household.

The increase in the number of women employed outside the family has been fairly sudden, leaving employers and families alike unprepared to deal adequately with the resulting implications. Many argue that the reason for this phenomenon has been primarily economic—that the majority of women work as an economic necessity rather than by choice. Others argue that the women's movement and the realization that women have choices other than remaining at home created this influx. Still others believe that the women's movement took hold because women were forced by economics to enter the workforce and, once there, they faced unfair conditions and began lobbying for improvements and more options. Still others counter that more women are working because of the greater emphasis on self-fulfillment and consumption in both genders (Akabas & Kurzman, 2007).

Recent welfare reform measures also have had the result of increasing the numbers of women in the workplace. Though the *economic* status of these women has improved, some would argue that, because of their primarily low-wage, dead-end jobs, the overall quality of their lives has not (Albeda & Withorn, 2002; Hays, 2004; Shipler, 2005).

Whatever the reason or reasons for more women in the labor force, this factor more than any other has drawn attention to the relationship between work and family. When only one family member left the home each day for work, there was less necessity for overlap or interaction between the work and family systems and it was fairly easy to keep them separate. But when two family members become involved in the work system, the two systems cannot be kept separate (Akabas & Kurzman, 2007).

Single-Parent Families

In 2004, the percentage of all family households in the United States maintained by a female was 22.8%. The percentage of family households maintained by a female within the African American and Hispanic population was 52% and 24%, respectively (U.S. Census Bureau, 2006). Nationally, in 2004 women in general earned nearly 20% less than their male counterparts in the workforce (U.S. Women's Bureau, 2006). Progress in achieving pay equity for women in the United States has been slow (a 4% improvement from 2001), despite women representing more and more of the total workforce.

It will be interesting to see if this trend accelerates over the next decade, as women are expected to comprise nearly half of the workforce by 2014 (U.S. Women's Bureau, 2006). In 2003, the percentage of persons in the United States with incomes below $10,000 that year (at less than the federal minimum of $5.15 per hour) was 23.1% for men and 40.1% for women. Part-time workers, Latinos, and African Americans were

TABLE 15.1
Single-Parent Families' Median Income by Ethnicity and Gender, 2005

Family Type	White	Black	Hispanic
Male-headed	$46,757	$39,275	$41,440
Female-headed	$30,672	$25,699	$27,185

Source: U.S. Census Bureau. *Statistical Abstract of the United States* 2006 (125th Edition). Washington, DC: Author. Available: www.census.gov/statab/www

paid at a rate of $5.15/hour more often than whites were (U.S. Census Bureau, 2006).

Low wages with limited or no benefits make survival extremely difficult, particularly for those with families. Although advocates for a living wage recommend that no more than 30% of take-home pay be spent on housing, many poor families have to spend as much as 70% on housing, thereby cutting into the money they have left for food, clothing, and other essential items. Some 50 million persons in this country do not have private health insurance of any kind. Others cannot afford to pay for health insurance, even if it is available through their place of work.

In 2005 the median income in the United States was $66,067 for all married households, $40,277 for all single-parent, male-headed families, and $27,525 for all single-parent, female-headed families. These differences are even more pronounced for single-parent black and Hispanic families (U.S. Census Bureau, 2005). When both ethnicity and gender are accounted for, white males earn the highest wages and black women, the lowest (see Table 15.1).

Emerging Issues

For women and their families, crucial issues, in addition to salary, benefits, and pensions, include patterns of childrearing and availability and accessibility of affordable child care, flexible working hours, access to reliable transportation to and from work, and job training. For their employers, critical factors are absenteeism and tardiness, sick leave, and employee stress. As more and more women enter the workforce, the following changes are expected:

- expanded child-care options;
- elimination of the cap on child-care deductions on federal income tax returns;
- two-career families becoming less willing to relocate;
- achievement of pay equity between men and women;
- more job flexibility (e.g., part-time, flexible, and stay-at-home jobs) and fewer total work hours per employee;
- restructuring of private benefit policies to reflect the needs of two-income families and single-parent workers; and
- standardization of health care and other benefits available to low-income earners and the unemployed.

The civilian labor force for persons 16 years and older was projected to increase by 10% between 2004 and 2010. The projected increase for individuals age 55 and older was nearly five times that figure (49%). The median age of the labor force was projected to continue to rise, even though the youth labor force was expected to grow faster than the overall labor force. The women's labor force was expected to grow faster than the men's, reaching 47% by 2014. Women were expected to account for more than half of the increase in total growth in the labor force between 2004 and 2014 (U.S. Bureau of Labor Statistics, 2006d).

While the overall U.S. population between 2000 and 2010 is projected to grow by about 10%, population growth for persons age 45 to 64 is expected to increase by nearly 30% (U.S. Census Bureau, 2006). The aging of the workforce and of society in general is likely to have the following impacts:

- The workforce will be more experienced, stable, and reliable.

- The average age of retirement is likely to rise to accommodate the financial strain on the Social Security system.
- Older workers will be at risk of being displaced by younger workers as companies seek to reduce costs to remain competitive. Ironically, even younger workers may face the same risk, as American companies continue to move their operations offshore to save money and compete in the global marketplace.
- Workers who leave or lose jobs will have a difficult time finding new jobs at their previous salary and benefit levels.

Greater Ethnic Diversity within the Workforce

The demographic composition of the labor force has been projected to change over this decade because of changes in the demographic composition of the population and in the rates of workforce participation across demographic groups. The share of the labor force for non-Hispanic whites was expected to decline from 73% in 2000 to 69% in 2010. The share of the labor force for all ethnic groups was projected to rise, with the most rapid growth by Asians (44.1%) and Hispanics (36.73%) (U.S. Bureau of Labor Statistics, 2001).

The number of immigrants entering the United States also is expected to increase. If immigration patterns continue, even under the most conservative estimates, Hispanic and Asian populations in the United States will grow by 25% to 30% between the years 2000 and 2010 (U.S. Census Bureau, 2002). This shift in population will be most significant in the South and the West, particularly Texas, Arizona, and California. Given the changing nature of work in this country (strong backs and nimble fingers are no longer primary assets), immigrants will have a difficult time finding work that pays enough to make ends meet, particularly if they are unable to access education and job-training programs.

The increased ethnic diversity in the workforce has the following implications:

- People of color will continue to be discriminated against, work in lower-paying jobs, and be promoted to management positions less often than whites.
- People of color will continue to earn less than whites, and unemployment rates and earnings may actually worsen for them. In 2004, the median household income for blacks was 64% of the median household income for whites, while the median household income for Hispanics was 73% of that for a white household (U.S. Census Bureau, 2006).
- Unemployment rates will continue to be higher for people of color in comparison to whites. The unemployment rate for blacks was about twice that for whites in 2001, and the rate for Hispanics was about one and-a-half times higher during that same period (U.S. Census Bureau, 2006). See Table 15.2.
- Blacks and Hispanics will continue to be overrepresented in low-wage, dead-end jobs and in declining occupations.
- Blacks and Hispanics will continue to live in inner-city core areas with severe financial and infrastructure problems that place them more at risk for unemployment.

- Immigrants will represent the largest increase in both the population and the workforce since World War I and also will face barriers related to language and lack of education.

Employment analysts are concerned that unemployment and low wages will worsen for people of color because they also have disproportionately high school dropout rates and low literacy proficiency compared to whites. These issues indicate that the changing nature of the workforce will have significant implications for employers and employees alike, particularly for companies that historically have employed white males of all ages.

Types of Jobs Available

The types of jobs in which workers are employed have changed, too. Through the 1960s, most workers were employed in blue-collar jobs. But as the United States has changed from a manufacturing-based economy to a service-based economy (all activities not involved with producing something physical, or "goods"), fewer and fewer workers are employed in blue-collar positions. In 2004, the service sector accounted for 83% of the non-agricultural civilian workforce (U.S. Census Bureau, 2006). For the period 2000–2010, the trend toward a service-based economy is expected to continue.

The *service industry* is a subset of the service sector. Examples of jobs in the service industry include health services, legal services, engineering and architectural services, computer and data-processing services, the motion picture industry, the amusement and recreation industry, the hotel and lodging industry, and the car repair, service, and parking industry.

Women constitute the majority of workers in both the service sector and the service industry. As in the goods-producing sector, men earn more than women, even in occupations dominated by women, such as registered nurses and teachers. By 2010, it was projected that three in every five

TABLE 15.2
Seasonally Adjusted Unemployment Rates by Ethnicity: 2003–2005

Ethnicity	2003	2004	2005
White	4.3%	8.3%	6.4%
Black	3.9%	8.1%	5.7%
Hispanic	3.5%	7.5%	4.8%

Source: U.S. Census Bureau, *Statistical Abstract of the United States* 2006 (125th Edition). Washington, DC: Author. Available: www.census.gov/statab/www

jobs in the United States would be in the services industry, with business, health, and social services constituting more than two-thirds of these jobs (U.S. Bureau of Labor Statistics, 2006d). Jobs in the least-skilled job classifications were expected to continue to grow more slowly, while the number of white-collar and skilled professional jobs would see the most growth.

Between 2000 and 2010, the services industry was expected to add 13.7 million new wage and salary jobs, or 62% of the total job growth during that period. Employment in computer and data-processing services was projected to grow by 86%, the fastest growing industry in the economy.

New jobs will require higher levels of education and higher-level skills in mathematics and language. Education will be essential in getting and keeping a high-paying job. Most of the new jobs will require at least an associate degree, and many will require at least a bachelor's degree. Labor force groups with less than average educational attainment, including Latinos and African Americans, will continue to have difficulty obtaining a share of the high-paying jobs unless they attain a better education (U.S. Bureau of Labor Statistics, 2006d).

The types of jobs available are likely to lead to a dual workforce: more jobs available in the white-collar and skilled areas, primarily in services, which require high levels of education, coupled with fewer jobs available in manufacturing and low-level service jobs, which require less education and skill. These changes are likely to make the workforce even more segregated, with more people of color, immigrants, and women in the less-skilled, lower-paying jobs and more white males in the jobs requiring more education and skill.

The service industry is a major source of **contingent employment** in the United States. Contingent work arrangements include temporary and part-time employees, consultants, leased employees, subcontractors, and short-term, life-of-the-project employees (AFL-CIO, 2006, p. 10). Contingent work arrangements typically offer

less economic security than full-time, core, or permanent wage jobs, as they do not provide health, pension, and other benefits such as paid vacation and sick leave.

The shift in jobs away from major industrial centers in the North and East to the Sunbelt and West Coast, as well as the shrinking small-farm agricultural production, have had a significant impact on workers and their families. Many individuals and families who remained in industrial centers or farm areas have been forced to move or to take lower-paying jobs or seek financial assistance for the first time in their lives. They often have lost their homes, farms, and businesses and face an unpredictable future.

The Changing Nature of Work and the Workplace

During the 1990s, workplaces of all kinds continued to change to remain competitive in the expanding global marketplace. Workplaces that have been able to survive have had to be increasingly innovative and flexible. As a result, many workers have lost jobs, have had to take new roles within the organization, or have had to become contract workers for the organization with which they were employed previously. Increasingly, in an effort to remain competitive, organizations have streamlined their operations by eliminating the hierarchy and the positions associated with it. Instead, organizations are seeking to be leaner and more agile to take advantage of changing market opportunities.

Cross-functional work teams are becoming more common in today's workplaces. These teams are formed to meet a specific organizational goal and then are dismantled once that goal has been achieved. In some organizations, salaries and raises are based on the performance of the entire team rather than on individual performance.

All of these changes have affected employees significantly in all sectors of business and commerce. The key to being a successful employee today is to be flexible and willing to work at multiple tasks, and be able to switch to new tasks quickly. Interpersonal skills are more important than in the past, as is knowledge of new technology. Today's workers have to find new ways to measure their job performance, as salary increases often are less frequent because organizations have to remain economically competitive. Promotions now are based on how well an employee can add value to his or her organization, as well as its customers.

In addition, because the costs of employee benefits have grown so rapidly, many workplaces are eliminating benefits or requiring workers to pay a larger share of the benefits. The trend to add new benefits to keep employees on the job also has ended in most workplaces as more and more qualified applicants are applying for positions when they become vacant. These changes have created additional stress for employees at all levels of work organizations, including top-level managers, as job security is becoming a thing of the past.

These issues have important implications when addressing employee concerns and the roles that social workers and others can play in dealing with them. Because of the many changes in the workplace and the nature of work, it is difficult to predict accurately the future needs of employees and their families, how those needs will surface in the workplace, and which strategies are most likely to meet them (see Box 15.1).

Unemployment and Underemployment

Although being employed often creates numerous problems for employees and their families, and vice versa, the ramifications of unemployment are far more serious. Layoffs and unemployment are expected to increase along with changes in the nature of work. Between January 2003 and December 2005, 3.8 million workers were displaced from jobs they had held for at least 3 years (U.S. Census Bureau, 2006). **Displaced workers** are defined as persons age 20 and older who lost or left jobs because their plant or company closed or moved, the work was insufficient, or their position or shift was eliminated. Of these 3.8 million workers, 49% lost their jobs because their plant closed or their company shut down or moved. An additional 22% lost their jobs because of insufficient work for them to do, and 29% lost their jobs because their position had been abolished. Displacement from manufacturing industries accounted for a much smaller share of the total, while displacement from non-manufacturing industries such as services, trade, and finance, insurance and real estate accounted for the larger share.

Because work provides economic support to families and also defines an individual's self-worth, increased unemployment is a double-edged issue of national concern (Cottle, 2003; Dooley & Prause, 2003; Hannington, 2006; Mirra, 2004). Unemployment and low economic status are associated with weak family cohesion and family deterioration (Groot, 2004).

Although official unemployment rates have been relatively low for the past few years, the rates can be said to be artificially low because they do not reflect individuals who are not actively seeking employment and those who have given up looking for employment. Unemployment rates for African Americans are about twice those for whites (U.S. Census Bureau, 2006).

Underemployment—placement in jobs that are at a lower level than the person is qualified for—is another growing problem. A third of Americans in one study reported that they were underemployed in their present jobs (Dooley & Prause, 2003). When faced with unemployment or underemployment, many individuals and their families relocate to what they believe is a more opportune area. These areas, however, may be largely unprepared to address the many needs created by a rapidly expanding population. Housing and other

---

BOX 15.1
The Changing Work Paradigm

What It Used to Be (Pre-1970s)

- The workforce is predominantly white and male—with few women and people of color.
- Companies are paternalistic, yet they don't always act in the best interests of employees.
- Companies meet the most basic needs of employees.
- Employees have little say in the workings of the organization.
- Benefit programs are traditional and limited.
- Most employees work for the same organization for their entire work lives.
- In many instances, generations of families work for the same organization.
- Employees do what they are told to get ahead—the company comes first.
- Organizations are highly structured with a rigid chain of command.
- The only talk about families is to ensure that top executives have one (marriage is assumed to be a virtue).
- Big is definitely better.
- The only economy is the U.S. economy.

What It Became (1970s, 1980s, and 1990s)

- The "new-breed worker" replaces the "organization man"; quality of work life becomes more important than simply getting ahead.
- Women and people of color enter the workforce in increasing numbers.
- Employees begin to demand more say in what happens at work.
- The dual wage-earning family is common.
- Employee loyalty to the company is no longer unquestioned.
- The global economy emerges—companies can no longer be concerned only with what goes on at home.
- New "perks" are created to retain highly sought-after employees.
- Leveraged buyouts become popular.
- Average employee tenure drops significantly.
- Many companies falter because they do not adapt to the global economy or cannot change quickly enough to meet new and different markets.
- The information age explodes.

---

necessities either are unavailable or are more expensive than anticipated; the availability of work for certain types of workers is inflated or exaggerated; and transportation, utilities, and education often are lacking or underdeveloped. Those relocating to new areas to find work miss the support from family and friends; and social services agencies, overwhelmed by the population influx, may be unable to provide sufficient resources to meet many employee and family needs.

For employees and their families who remain in unproductive areas, as well as those who relocate to new areas, stress levels rise significantly (Cottle, 2003; Dooley & Prause, 2003; Mirra, 2004).

Social services agencies in these areas report significant increases in family financial problems, suicides, family violence, substance abuse, marital problems, juvenile delinquency, and other mental health–related problems.

Changing Attitudes and Values toward Work

Demographic changes in the workforce have had a considerable impact on attitudes and values toward work. Although most employees continue to be fairly satisfied with their jobs, discontent is growing in certain segments of the labor force

- Increasingly, companies merge, downsize, or do both to become more competitive
- The service industry grows by leaps and bounds.
- Workers with limited skills and little education are increasingly displaced.
- Companies start to realize that past success guarantees nothing.

What It Is Now (2000 and Beyond)

- Women and people of color constitute more than half of the workforce, but their presence in executive and management positions is still disproportionate.
- Successful organizations are flexible and able to change their focus quickly.
- Advances in information technology are making the global marketplace the only marketplace.
- Traditional employee benefits are replaced with a menu of benefits, many of which require significant employee contributions.
- Organizations are flatter and leaner.
- Current success guarantees nothing.

- Only those organizations that can adapt to constantly changing market conditions are able to survive.
- Having satisfied customers is not enough; organizations must provide additional value to retain their customers.
- Increased use of contract labor and outsourcing is displacing many traditional employees.
- Strategic planning is redefined.
- Outside of legal protections, employee entitlements are a thing of the past.
- There are no job guarantees.
- Employees are asked to "give at the office" in new ways.
- Faster is better.
- Product development cycles decline significantly.
- What makes sense today may have no relevance tomorrow.

Source: *The Changing Work Paradigm,* by R. J. Ambrosino (Austin: University of Texas at Austin, 2006).

concerning the nature and meaning of work. Employers today see a new type of worker, first described by policy analyst Daniel Yankelovich (1979) as the "new breed worker."

Yankelovich contrasted today's worker with the "organization man" of the 1950s (Whyte, 1956). This term would be considered sexist today, but it was appropriate at that time because the workforce was primarily male. Whyte's organization man was one who put the needs of the organization for which he worked above all else. He came to the company intending to remain there for his entire career, worked long hours, willingly traveled and relocated for the company,

and viewed his paycheck as his primary reward for his loyalty and hard work.

Today's worker is much different. Concerns about quality of life and willingness to express these concerns to employers have forced employers to offer incentives beyond the paycheck. Insistence on individual accomplishment and self-fulfillment, priorities given to interests outside the workplace, and personal recognition on the job suggest that employees expect work to have meaning beyond the extrinsic rewards of a paycheck.

Less support from family members and lack of time to develop supportive relationships with people outside the workplace have resulted in many individuals' maintaining a strong identity with the workplace. These individuals typically expect their work to meet most of their needs. Thus, employees frequently seek help from co-workers, rather than neighbors, friends, or others with whom they have little contact, when dealing with marital and other family problems. In addition, a growing number of younger, more educated workers, especially in high-tech fields, expect high salaries, rapid promotions, and challenging jobs. Because of the increased acceptance of alternative lifestyles and the large number of families in which more than one individual is employed, the traditional work ethic has diminished significantly.

Another phenomenon in the contemporary workplace is the employment of mixed generations under the same roof. Researchers have identified four generational types in today's workplace (Tulgan, 2006):

1. *seniors*—those currently older than 65 years;
2. *boomers*—those born between 1946 and 1964;
3. *X'ers*—those in their late-teens to mid-30s; and
4. *generation Y, echo boomers, or the millennium generation*—those between the ages of 5 and 20.

The values and perceptions of each of these groups are quite different and sometimes conflicting (Beck & Wade, 2004; Chester, 2002; Hu, 2006; Tulgan, 2006; Twenge, 2006).

- S*eniors* are reported to understand well-defined boundaries, to be dependable and reliable, and to have a good work ethic. They are said to be more tolerant of "marginal" working conditions and to be highly committed to the organization.
- *Boomers* are reported to have somewhat rigid work habits, to be "workaholics" (work is their life), and to be rather formal (they like agendas, meetings, schedules, lists, and

being on time). Also, they often are taking on the burden of caring for their parents, which in turn affects their work and retirement decisions.
- *X'ers* are said to be bold, savvy, confident, and often demanding. They are less understanding of the concept of teamwork, defend the right to a full life outside of work, and are unafraid to ask for something they want. They are willing to switch careers to accommodate their personal needs but unwilling to change their personal lives to satisfy work demands.
- *Generation Y, the millennium generation,* or *echo boomers* are said to be radically diverse (one in five is not Caucasian, one in four lives with a single parent, and three in four have working mothers), to have grown up in a media-saturated, brand-conscious world (and thus to respond to the world differently); and to be more likely to respond to humor, irony, and the unvarnished truth. They are confident beyond their years and have access to an almost unlimited array of material goods.

The types of workers in today's workforce and their attitudes toward work have changed so rapidly that the workplace, for the most part, has been unable to adjust at a comparable pace. Many workplaces still expect the loyalty of Whyte's organization man, to which they were accustomed, yet they are faced increasingly with employees for whom loyalty to one's workplace is not always a high priority (Applegate, Reuss, Hart, Grist, & Caraway, 2005; Deal, 2006; Tulgan, 2006).

The Impact of Changes on Employees and Their Families

Most of the attention relating to changes in the types of individuals now in the workplace has been directed toward the impact on the family rather than on the workplace. This attention has centered largely on two-parent families, although these conflicts also are the purview, perhaps more so, of employees who are single parents. As suggested earlier, when work and family domains begin to overlap, in many instances this overlapping creates conflicts including the following (Akabas & Kurzman, 2007; Epstein & Kalleberg, 2004; Gambles, Lewis, & Rapoport, 2006; Halpern & Murphy, 2005; Jacobs & Gerson, 2004; Presser, 2005; Zimmerman, 2002):

- individuals' lack of time for themselves and family members,
- stress caused by balancing work and family schedules and priorities,
- problems in obtaining adequate child care and other parenting issues,
- feelings of isolation because of lack of time and energy to develop friendships and support systems, and
- financial difficulties.

Balancing Work and Family Life

Several studies addressing the impact of work on family life have stemmed from Wilensky's (1960) early work in this area suggesting that people undergo a **spillover effect,** in which feelings, attitudes, and behaviors from the workplace enter their leisure life, and vice versa. The spillover effect is one of five possible work–family relationships that emerged from these studies:

1. *spillover effect,* in which one domain affects the other in either a positive or a negative way; for example, if you really like your job, this will add satisfaction to your family life;
2. *independent,* in which work and family life exist side by side but are independent from each other, allowing you to be satisfied and successful with your job but not your family, for example;
3. *conflict,* in which work and family are in opposition to each other and cannot be reconciled; in a conflict relationship, sacrifices are required in one area to be satisfied and

successful in the other—for example, spending less time at home with family members to be successful at the job;

4. *instrumental,* in which one domain is primarily a means to obtain something for the other; for example, a job is seen only as a way to earn money to maintain a satisfying family life; and
5. *compensation,* in which one domain is a way of making up for what is missing in another; for example, a recently divorced man puts all of his energies into his job, works long hours, and socializes only with co-workers.

In helping employees and their family members alike understand how they can better balance work and family life, social workers and other helping professionals have to get them to look at how they view their work–family relationships. Sheila Akabas and Paul Kurzman (2007) at Columbia University found that the quality of employees' jobs and the supportiveness of their workplaces are predictors of job satisfaction, commitment, performance, and retention. In this context:

- *job quality* includes attributes such as the ability to manage one's work, the availability of personal and professional learning opportunities, meaningful work, opportunities for advancement, and a semblance of job security.
- *workplace support* incorporates attributes such as flexible work schedules, support from supervisors, a workplace culture that acknowledges the dynamics of work–family relationships, the absence of discrimination of any kind, an atmosphere of mutual respect among employees and between management and employees, and a commitment to equal opportunity for all workers, regardless of their backgrounds.

Based on the preceding discussion, one could conclude that if employers want to maximize satisfaction, commitment, performance, and retention, they must provide high-quality jobs in a supportive environment, regardless of the industry involved.

When examining the impact of work on the individual and family, one additional perspective that deserves attention is the importance of life events. Rapoport and Rapoport (1980) advocated the use of a **life-span model,** in which the meaning of work and family changes as individuals move through childhood, adolescence, youth, adulthood, midlife, and old age. Individuals often are pressured to give full attention to both work and family life at the same period of life—for example, learning and beginning a successful career at the same time that they have married recently and are beginning to have children. Some policy analysts suggest that companies should not emphasize promotions and climbing the career ladder for their employees until they are middle-aged and have dealt with the childrearing years already. The importance of looking at life-span stages also can be seen when considering the many individuals who make midlife career changes, not because they are necessarily unhappy with their jobs but, rather, because they are dealing with personal, developmental issues that are age-related.

Most of the attention given to the impact of work on the family has been directed to working wives and mothers. For all families in which mothers work, the impact on the family, particularly the children, is a well-researched issue. Taken by itself, though, a mother's employment outside the home has not been found to have any negative effects on the child. Factors that may affect children of working mothers include (Galinsky, 2000):

- the quality of child care the child receives while the mother is working,
- the overall stability of the family itself,
- the type of employment,
- the family's socioeconomic status, and
- the quality and quantity of time that either parent spends with the child.

Increased Stress

The issue identified most often in studies focusing on work and family issues is the increased stress on the employed family member and the family itself. Some mental health experts suggest that the tremendous growth in the number of individuals seeking mental health services can be attributed to heightened pressures faced by individuals who are trying to balance the demands of job and family.

Recent studies have also focused on **dual-career families**—in which both spouses are pursuing their own careers—particularly in relation to the changes in family roles and responsibilities when both parents work. Although both parents in dual-career families experience stress and have less time for themselves and family members, most studies find that the wives and mothers feel these pressures the most. In many dual-career families, the husbands are sharing more in childrearing responsibilities, but most of the childrearing responsibility still falls on the wife. Even if husbands are taking on more of the parenting tasks, the housekeeping responsibilities fall almost totally on the wives, even in families in which both husbands and wives view themselves as being less traditional than other couples in the division of household tasks.

Men and women from dual-career families list, among advantages, additional income, more opportunities for meaningful communication and growth because both individuals are stimulated by jobs, and more sharing in parenting roles. But women in these families face numerous role conflicts, citing lack of time to accomplish tasks both at home and at work, lack of time for self, lack of time for spouse, and lack of time for children (Jacobs & Gerson, 2004; Moen, 2003; Schneider & Waite, 2005).

Relocation

Increases in the number of dual-career families also have resulted in problems when one spouse has a job opportunity in another geographic location. Determining which spouse's job should prevail, and under what conditions, presents conflicts in many marriages when opportunities arise (Pascoe, 2003; Roman, Bickel, & Cadieux, 2006). These dilemmas have resulted in more employers providing relocation services that include help in finding employment for spouses, as well as an increase in the number of **commuter families**—families in which spouses are employed in different locations, often in different parts of the country. Many more workers also are refusing promotions that require relocation.

Financial Problems

In many families, even though both parents are employed outside the home, their incomes still are below or barely above the poverty level. Financial pressures are especially severe for women, people of color, and other workers who are less likely to be well educated or trained—and, as a result, more likely to be employed in low-paying jobs. Single parents (also most likely to be women and people of color) are particularly vulnerable to financial pressures.

"Working poor" is becoming one the largest categories of poor people in the United States. In 2003, of poor people (those who were living at or below the federal poverty level), 16 years of age and older, only 18.6% worked full-time year-round. In contrast, of all people 16 years and older, 47.3% worked full-time year-round (U.S. Census Bureau, 2006). Even those who work full-time at the federal minimum wage (currently $5.15 per hour), or $10,712, find it difficult to support themselves and their families. A single parent with a full-time job earning the minimum wage in 2006 and supporting three children under 18 years old earned a salary nearly $5,288 below the poverty level.

Advocates for the working poor and those moving from welfare assistance to employment argue that continuing to ignore this population will result in substantial costs to families as well as to the U.S. economy. The following are strategies for promoting job retention and advancement among the working poor (including welfare clients) (Campbell, Maniha, & Rolston, 2002; Crandall, 2004; Jarchow, 2003; U.S. Department of Health and Human Services, 2006):

- Provide intensive, team-based case-management services to help clients secure employment and retain employment.
- Develop effective post-employment services such as financial assistance in emergency situations, mentoring and community-support programs, reemployment assistance, and career-advancement initiatives.
- Integrate job retention and advancement with job placement efforts.
- Use intermediaries that have established relationships with employers to deliver post-employment services aimed at job retention and advancement.
- Provide wage supplements and work incentives to reward behaviors and outcomes associated with steady employment.
- Improve access to support services such as child care, transportation, health care, and housing.
- Provide intensive, family-based support services.
- Provide pre-employment services that prepare clients for the world of work, help them find a job, and expose them to possible career choices.
- Focus on job placement aimed at getting good jobs, not just any job.
- Promote the use of federal and state earned income tax credits.
- Improve access to education and training in the workplace as well as outside of work.
- Help individuals achieve growth in earnings, and access career ladders/pathways.

About 30% of the U.S. workforce is not covered by employee health insurance. Among those who are covered, only about half actually participate in one of the plans that are offered. Increasingly, employees are being required to share the cost of employee health coverage. A study by the U.S. Bureau of Labor Statistics (2006c) revealed that the medical care plans that most employees utilize require employee contributions for both single and family coverage—an average of $76.05 per month ($912.60 per year) for single coverage and $266.50 per month ($3,198 per year) for family coverage. Most employees with families who are engaged in full-time, low-wage work (most often women and people of color) cannot afford to pay these costs and, thus, go without health coverage.

When these families do have health crises, they are likely to face severe financial problems in paying the full cost for the care they receive. In the same study cited above, employer premiums for medical care plans ranged from $266.50 per month ($3,198 per year) per participant for single coverage to $618.18 per month ($7,418.16 per year) per participant for family coverage. In attempting to avoid these costs, many employers continue to hire workers as temporary or part-time workers so they will not have to pay part of their health insurance and other benefits.

Family and Medical Leave Act

One of the most significant pieces of legislation in regard to work and family issues, the **Family and Medical Leave Act,** was passed by Congress in 1993 after several previously unsuccessful attempts. The act requires employers with more than 50 employees to provide up to 12 weeks of unpaid leave to eligible employees for the following reasons (U.S. Bureau of Labor Statistics, 2006c):

- for the birth and care of an employee's newborn child;
- for placement with the employee of a son or daughter for adoption or foster care;
- to care for an immediate family member (spouse, child, or parent) with a serious health condition; or

- to take medical leave when the employee is unable to work because of a serious health condition.

The act also specifies that most employees must be able to return to their original jobs or equivalent positions with equivalent pay, benefits, and other conditions of employment.

Accidents and Other Occupational Hazards

Accidents and other on-the-job health hazards create additional problems for employees and their families. Coal miners who come into contact daily with coal dust can contract black lung disease; workers in chemical plants can contract cancer and miscarry or produce children born with congenital deformities; and construction workers may be hurt by heavy equipment—placing themselves and their families in jeopardy. A number of individuals have successfully sued employers for mental anguish that they or their family members experienced as a result of situations like these.

The United States has a high rate of industrial health and safety accidents (U.S. Department of Labor, 2004). In 1970 the federal Occupational Safety and Health Act was passed to address this problem. The act sets health and safety standards in industrial workplaces through onsite inspections and citations for violations. The regulatory function is housed in the U.S. Department of Labor, and research and technology are addressed through the **National Institute of Occupational Safety and Health (NIOSH)** within the Department of Health and Human Services. NIOSH also sets standards related to hazardous materials.

Approximately 20 deaths each workday result from industrial accidents, according to the **Occupational Safety and Health Administration (OSHA)** (2004). African Americans and Latinos are likely to be employed in the most dangerous jobs and occupations and are most at risk to incur accidental injury or death while on the job (U.S.

Census Bureau, 2006). Although occupational hazards such as exposure to asbestos and other dangerous chemicals have received more publicity of late, efforts to deal effectively with these concerns have been limited at both state and federal levels.

Violence in the Workplace

Employers and employees are increasingly identifying **workplace violence (WPV)** as a problem. Some employees are bringing their family problems to work or are harassed by others, often family members, while at work. On average, 1.7 million workers are injured each year, and more than 800 die as a result of workplace violence (National Institute for Occupational Safety and Health [NIOSH], 2004). Factors that place workers at risk for violence in the work place include interacting with the public, exchanging money, delivering services or goods, working late at night or during early morning hours, working alone, guarding valuable goods or property, and dealing with violent people or volatile situations (NIOSH, 2004).

To better understand the causes and possible solutions, the University of Iowa Injury Prevention Research Center (2001, p. 4) identified four categories of workplace violence:

- Type I—*Criminal intent:* The perpetrator has no legitimate relationship to the business or its employees and usually is committing a crime in conjunction with the violence. Typical crimes in this category are robbery, shoplifting, and trespassing;
- Type II—*Customer/Client:* The perpetrator has a legitimate relationship with the business and becomes violent while being served by the business. This category includes customers, clients, patients, students, inmates, and any other group for which the business provides services;
- Type III—*Worker-on-Worker:* The perpetrator is an employee or past employee of the business who attacks or threatens another employee(s) or past employee(s) in the workplace.
- Type IV—*Personal Relationship:* The perpetrator usually does not have a relationship with the business but has a personal relationship with the intended victim. This category includes victims of domestic violence assaulted or threatened while at work.

In efforts to confront workplace violence through prevention and research, NIOSH (2004, pp. 24–26) identified the following partners or types of partners necessary to WPV-prevention and research efforts:

- *federal partners with NIOSH:* coordinating the national WPV effort over the next decade, forging a common definition of WPV and identifying the range of behaviors that constitute WPV, gathering data on the federal workforce, implementing WPV prevention programs in the federal workplace, ensuring and maintaining up-to-date statistics on WPV, and adapting a partnership model to develop regulations addressing WPV;
- *state agencies:* collaborating with federal partners to develop a common definition of WPV, collecting WPV statistics among state workers, and determining strategies for prevention in state government;
- *private-sector companies, corporations, and alliances:* contributing to the effort to develop common WPV definitions, sharing data on WPV events, as well as successes, problems, and methods to overcome barriers in implementing WPV-prevention programs and strategies, and adopting WPV-prevention strategies that federal agencies have recommended and verified;
- *business and community organizations:* bringing together factions of the community to engage in dialogue about WPV and forging a coordinated response to WPV prevention, sharing prevention programs and strategies,

and assisting government, the media, and educational institutions to increase public awareness of WPV risks and prevention;

- *insurers:* providing incentives for employers who implement WPV-prevention programs that lower workers' compensation costs, and supporting research that seeks to demonstrate the cost–benefit of investing in WPV prevention;

- *law enforcement:* collecting more detailed data and standardizing definitions, disseminating evidence-based prevention information, providing assistance to businesses in taking prevention steps, participating in research efforts to address WPV prevention, and focusing on community-oriented policing;

- *the legal profession:* balancing the need for collecting accurate WPV data with overlapping privacy-interest laws, securing exemptions or waivers from existing privacy restraints to collect data, and training attorneys to be sensitive and provide outreach to affected clients;

- *academic research institutions:* training new researchers in WPV issues, promoting evidence-based WPV-prevention strategies, taking a proactive role in accessing private-industry data, and emphasizing in its law, business, and management curricula the dynamics of WPV and its impact on workers, families, and organizational health;

- *the media:* providing public service announcements (PSAs) in support of WPV public information campaigns;

- *the medical community:* improving recognition and reporting of potential cases of injury or stress from WPV;

- *worker assistance programs:* improving screening and recognition of potential WPV issues, and being involved in response to WPV incidents to serve victim, witness, and co-worker needs;

- *social advocacy organization:* contributing to the effort to create WPV definitions in common with federal, state, business, and labor partners, and developing media campaigns following the model provided by Mothers Against Drunk Driving (MADD); and

- *other national organizations:* having safety and security specialists and organizations interact with research and regulatory communities to enable WPV research-to-practice linkages, and having academic schools of architecture, urban planning, and civil engineering provide input to research and regulatory efforts and to incorporate safety and security considerations into their designs.

Social workers at all levels can play a number of roles to assist the partners referenced above in promoting WPV prevention. For example, a social worker could serve as an advocate for victims of WPV in either a public or a private setting. A social worker could act as a convener of community-based stakeholders who currently are involved or could provide valuable assistance to WPV prevention. A social worker could serve as a teacher by providing information to a variety of audiences about WPV and its effects on individuals, workplaces, and the community. Finally, a social worker could be a mediator between parties who have different views about WPV and how it can be prevented.

Sexual Harassment

Sexual harassment is another concern in the workplace. The costs of sexual harassment can be extremely damaging to employees, both emotionally and from a cost perspective, and employers are legally responsible to ensure that sexual harassment does not occur (Boland, 2005; Gregory, 2004; Marshall, 2005). Obtaining accurate figures about the actual incidence of sexual harassment in the workplace is difficult because it is thought that about half of those who are harassed do not report it. They may fear that they will lose their jobs or be subjected to other retribution, that they will not be taken seriously, or that they somehow have contributed to the harassment.

Title VII of the Civil Rights Act of 1964 specifies that discrimination that violates individual rights occurs when (MacKinnon & Siegel, 2003):

- individuals are offered rewards in return for sexual favors, or threatened with punishment if they do not provide them;
- a hostile environment is created that interferes with employees' ability to concentrate on their job tasks because of behaviors such as making lewd comments and telling inappropriate sexual jokes, displaying inappropriate artwork and other materials, and touching or threatening to touch individuals in inappropriate ways;
- an employee's job or job opportunities are jeopardized because of another person who is responding positively to requests for sexual favors.

Social workers in the workplace often provide employee training regarding what constitutes sexual harassment and how to handle it if it does occur, assessment and conflict resolution if incidents are reported, and counseling to those who have been sexually harassed. Social workers also advocate and encourage employee empowerment to ensure that the workplace culture does not support such behavior.

Child Care for Working Parents

Of the 76 million families in the United States in 2004, about 20% had one relative child under age 18, 18% had two relative children under 18, and 10% had three or more relative children under 18. Of these families, 17 million married couple families with both wife and husband in the labor force and 3.3 million female-headed families with the woman in the labor force can be considered likely to have work-related child care requirements (U.S. Census Bureau, 2006). In 2001, half of all preschoolers had mothers in the labor force (Children's Defense Fund, 2006).

In a report titled, *Breaking the Piggy Bank: Parents and the High Price of Child Care,* the National Association of Child Care Resource and Referral Agencies (NACCRRA, 2006) revealed the following dramatic findings about child care in the United States:

- *Child care is part of the daily lives of millions of American families with young children.* Nine in ten parents consider leaving the labor force to stay home with their children but decide to continue working for economic reasons.
- *Child care, especially high-quality care, is expensive.* A family in the United States with a 4-year-old child pays average prices of $3,016 to $9,628 a year in child-care fees. The price of care for an infant ranges from $3,083 to $13,480 a year.
- *Child-care prices are high compared to other family/household expenses.* In every region of the country, average child-care fees for an infant are higher than the average amount that families spend on food each year; average child-care fees for two children at any age exceed the median rent cost.
- *Working families earning low incomes, especially, struggle to afford child care.* Families earning $18,000 (slightly above the poverty rate for a family of three) or less each year would have to spend 30% or more of their annual income to afford the average price of child care for an infant in 38 states; in New York, Connecticut, Minnesota, Massachusetts, and New Jersey, the average price of child care for two children exceeds $18,000 per year.
- *High child-care prices force parents to make sacrifices.* To afford care at all, most parents, especially those with low incomes (less than 200% of the federal poverty level, or $40,000 for a family of four) are faced with compromising on the quality of care that their children receive, and even then, they pay more for child care than they think they can afford.

The implications of this report are far-reaching for today's families. Although most families agree that they want the best child care available for their children, they simply cannot afford to pay for that care. In short, their children do not have access to the benefits of developmentally appropriate care that nationally certified child-care agencies provide. To be able to work, most low-income families are faced with placing their children in substandard child-care arrangements. Women who have exited the welfare system to enter the low-paid workforce have even fewer choices. Being aware that the child-care arrangement they have chosen for their child is marginally beneficial and perhaps even dangerous for their child is stressful for low-income parents, which saps their strength to face other challenges in their lives.

Finally, children who are able to benefit from high-qualify child care have an advantage over children who do not have access to this care as it relates to school achievement. Access to quality child care is important for *all* families, not just those that can afford it.

Care of Elderly Parents

Care of elderly parents is another problem that increasingly affects employees. In 2006, Some 44 million Americans, mostly women, provided unpaid care for a dependent adult, usually aging parents. Almost 60% of these caregivers either worked or have worked while providing care. A similar percentage of women have had to make adjustments in their work life or give up work entirely (ElderWeb, 2006). A study conducted by the MetLife Mature Market Institute® and the National Alliance for Caregiving (2006a) estimated the total cost to employers of all full-time employed caregivers to be $33.6 billion. This figure included costs lost because of the need to replace employees, absenteeism, workday disruptions, supervisor time, unpaid leave, and the cost of switching from full-time to part-time employment.

A survey of caregivers conducted by Evercare in collaboration with the National Alliance for Caregiving (2006b, pp. 5–7) revealed the following health risks of caring for an older loved one:

- The caregivers found themselves in a downward spiral of health as a result of giving care.
- Half of those surveyed reported that their decline in health also affected their ability to provide care.
- Despite caregivers' health problems, their caregiving responsibilities did not subside.
- The deterioration in caregivers' health increased in relation to the amount of time they spent providing care, as well as the intensity of the caregiving.
- The most common health-related problems reported by caregivers were problems with energy and sleep, stress and/or panic attacks, pain or aching, depression, headaches, and weight gain or loss.
- Nearly all of the caregivers surveyed indicated that they suffer from depression, and 60% said that their depression was moderate or severe.
- Half of the caregivers surveyed said they put off personal preventive care such as getting their teeth cleaned, having a periodic vision test, or getting a routine medical exam.

Formal elder-care services vary tremendously. Types of elder care include the following (National Institutes of Health, 1997):

- *adult day care* provided in a home or a center-based setting;
- *home health care,* which allows the elderly person to remain in a familiar environment and to maintain a certain level of independence;
- *group homes,* which offer a residential setting for elders who need only limited assistance (nursing care and other arrangements are available from outside agencies); and
- *skilled nursing facilities,* which offer 24-hour residential services in a nursing home setting.

Changing Expectations about Work and Family Life

Changing expectations regarding what is important in life have implications both for families and for the workplace. More individuals are reassessing tradeoffs between work and family life. Assuming that no financial hardship exists, many people today are willing to reduce their salaries to have more personal or family time. Others are willing to turn down a promotion if it seriously jeopardizes the amount of time they could spend with their families or pursuing personal interests. The term **downshifting** refers to voluntary limitation of job demands so employees can devote more time to their families or to themselves.

Implications for the Mental Health of Employees and Their Families

Increasingly, employees and their families who lack a support system and are unable to cope with life's pressures succumb to divorce, family violence, substance abuse, suicide, or other health or emotional problems. For workers and their families facing such pressures, however, the options often are limited. Many individuals work because they must support their families, often as the sole source of support for those families. For those who earn low wages and cannot rely on other family members to offer emotional support or assistance in family needs such as child care, the toll on them and their families can be extensive (refer to the Hunts, the family described at the beginning of the chapter). Even for those who have more options, such as being able to afford child care or rely on relatives, or who work different hours than other family members, balancing work and family pressures is difficult.

Implications for the Workplace

The problems that have an impact on the individual employee and his or her family also have a significant effect in the workplace. The United States currently ranks *eighth* in productivity among Western countries. Job turnover, absenteeism, and other costs created by employee and family problems are expensive to the workplace as well as consumers, who ultimately are forced to absorb these costs.

COSTS OF SUBSTANCE ABUSE

Available data on drug and alcohol abuse from the Office of National Drug Control Policy (2001) indicate that in 2000, alcoholism and drug abuse cost the United States approximately $259 billion. Table 15.3 shows selected outcomes of alcohol and drug use on the workplace. In addition, the money spent on drugs saps the country's

TABLE 15.3 Workplace Outcomes by Drug and Heavy Alcohol Use	
Outcome	**Current Illicit Drug/Heavy Alcohol Use (%)**
Worked for three or more employers in the past year	32.1
Taken an unexcused absence from work during past month	12.1
Voluntarily left an employer in the past year	25.8
Fired by an employer in the past year	4.6
Had a workplace accident in the past year	4.7

Source: *General Workplace Impact (of Alcohol and Drug Abuse) in America,* U.S. Department of Labor (Washington, DC: Office of National Drug Control Policy, 2001).

economic power. In 2000, U.S. users were estimated to spend $64 billion annually on cocaine, heroin, marijuana, and other illegal drugs (Office of National Drug Control Policy, 2001).

OTHER PROBLEMS THAT COST EMPLOYERS

Other health and mental health problems also are expensive, particularly if they are not addressed early. National health-care expenditures in the United States in 2003 were projected to reach $1.7 trillion, or $5,313 per capita (National Center for Health Statistics, 2006). Mental illness results in $17 billion in lost productivity each year. Workplace stress also can lead to higher rates of worker illness and injury (Ettner & Grzywacz, 2001; Probst & Brubaker, 2001; Rosskam, 2005).

A special issue of *Managed Care Magazine* titled "Depression in the Workplace" (Spring 2006) claims that the per-capita annual cost of depression to employers is $5,415, a figure that is more than that for hypertension or back problems, and comparable to that of diabetes or heart disease. In addition, employees with depression missed an average of nearly 10 days of work a year, the most days missed among a group of problems that compared depression to hypertension, back problems, diabetes, and heart disease.

Increased Demands on Employers

Many studies suggest that emotionally based individual and family problems exact a heavy toll on both the individual and the workplace in relation to health-care costs. In 2004, employer costs for employee compensation for civilian workers (private industry and state and local government) in the United States averaged $24.17 per hour worked (U.S. Census Bureau, 2006). Wages and salaries accounted for about 70% of these costs, and benefits accounted for the remaining 30%.

In 2004, labor unions covered 12.5% of the U.S. workforce, a nearly 8% reduction from similar coverage in 1983 (U.S. Census Bureau, 2006). Historically, labor unions have wielded significant collective bargaining powers on behalf of union members, including efforts to keep employee costs for benefits low and the extent of benefits available high. However, their presence in the U.S. workplace today is hardly a factor in negotiations between labor and management. The high cost of employee health-care benefits is a major issue facing employers today. In response, many employers are increasing the employee-paid costs of health care and also reducing the extent of benefits available.

Affiliation Needs

As more and more workers are looking to the workplace to meet their need for affiliation, additional concerns arise on the job. Co-workers and supervisors find themselves spending work time listening to employees' problems ranging from marital disputes to more serious problems such as substance abuse and family violence. A supervisor who oversees 15 employees noted that in one day she had helped find temporary shelter for a female employee who had suffered spouse abuse, listened to another employee whose son was in jail for cocaine abuse and theft and referred him to a counseling center, confronted an employee regarding a job error and learned that he was in the midst of a divorce after a 25-year marriage, and covered for another worker who had to leave early because she had a sick child.

Addressing Work and Family Problems: Whose Responsibility?

Given the serious costs to workers of employee- and family-related problems, their families, and the workplace, strategies are being developed to address these challenges. When working with individuals and family members, social services counselors today are much more likely to address job-related factors than they have in the past. Many communities have initiated task forces and programs to provide affordable child care and transportation for employees. A number of public schools have established before-school and after-school child-care programs, and some schools schedule parent–teacher conferences and other events during evening hours when most working parents can attend. Social services agencies in some communities have come into the workplace to provide noontime seminars and other programs relating to topics such as coping with divorce, substance abuse, and parenting.

A growing number of employers have recognized their social responsibility to address these problems. Today, personnel departments have been replaced largely with human resources departments, which have expanded roles, including a more holistic approach to employee needs. Human resources departments oversee personnel, social services, and health and wellness, along with other employee-related programs. Some employers have called upon social workers as consultants to assist managers in determining how they can better meet their employees' needs. In a systems/ecological approach, appropriate interventions can be directed to all levels of the workplace, from the individual employee to the total corporate environment.

Some companies have established employee assistance programs (EAPs) which provide counseling and other social services to employees, and often to their families, through the company. (EAPs are discussed in detail in the next section.) Of all employees in medium and large firms, 40% were covered by EAP programs in 2005 (U.S. Bureau of Labor Statistics, 2006c). Others have expanded health coverage to include treatment for substance abuse, mental health counseling, and dental care.

A number of public and private employers have established flexible working hours for their employees, called **flextime,** which allows employees to work hours that vary from the traditional 8 a.m. to 5 p.m. workday. For example, an employee might work four 10-hour days each week, or work hours different from other employees, perhaps 6 a.m. to 3 p.m.

Other employers offer **job sharing,** a system that allows two people to share the same job—which means that each person usually works half-time. Another alternative for employers is to create permanent part-time positions. Some employers also allow employees to work in their homes. Particularly, some workers with disabilities and workers with children can access employers' computer networks to complete word-processing and other tasks without leaving their homes. This practice is sometimes called **flexiplace.**

Still other employers have stress-reduction and health promotion programs, including on-site fitness centers where employees and their families can exercise. Of all employees in private industry, 40% were covered by wellness programs in 2005 (U.S. Bureau of Labor Statistics, 2006c). Some employers also provide onsite child care for employees or other child-care programs; and companies even have established special programs that provide care for school-age children during the summer or when the children are sick.

Employee Assistance Programs

A number of organizations have established formal **employee assistance programs (EAPs)** to provide counseling to their employees. The U.S. Bureau of Labor Statistics (2006c) provided the following information regarding worker access to health-promotion benefits in 2005:

- Of all workers, 40% had access to employee assistance programs, 23% had access to wellness programs, and 13% had access to fitness centers.
- With regard to size of establishment, employees who worked in establishments with

100 or more workers had easier access to employee assistance programs, wellness programs, and fitness centers than employees who worked in establishments with 1 to 99 workers.

- With regard to wages earned, employees with average wages of $15 per hour or more had greater access than employees with average wages of less than $15 per hour to employee assistance programs, wellness programs, and fitness centers.
- With regard to type of worker, employees in white-collar occupations had more access to employee assistance programs, wellness programs, and fitness centers than employees in blue-collar occupations.
- With regard to hours worked, full-time employees had greater access to employee assistance programs, wellness programs, and fitness centers than part-time employees.

EAPs are mandated in federal government agencies, including the military, and in most state, county, and city governments as well. A related group of programs known as **membership assistance programs (MAPS),** provided under the auspices of labor unions, offers similar employee support services to union members (Kelly, 2001).

Originally, EAPs were established to provide counseling and treatment for employees with alcohol problems, and a recovering alcoholic—often one of the company's own employees—was the program coordinator. Today, a wide variety of EAPs are available. Although many are still primarily alcohol-related, others are "broad-brush" programs, addressing a wide range of employee issues including divorce, childrearing, family violence, and financial problems. Many innovative programs have been developed for employees and their families through EAPs. More EAPs now are offering services relating to the care of elderly parents. EAPs also are called upon when workers are relocated or laid off and when companies close.

Social workers employed in EAPs become involved in a wide range of situations involving employees—discrimination, including unfair treatment of people of color, women, new immigrants, and persons with AIDS; the needs of workers with disabilities; the effects of toxic chemicals and pollutants on employees; and the effects of the physical and emotional demands of the workplace on employees. Four major types of EAPs have been identified in the literature (Emener, Hutchison, & Richard, 2003):

1. *internal programs:* those provided in-house by professional staff members who are employees of the organization;
2. *external programs:* those provided through referral to an outside contractor who actually provides the services, usually off the worksite (this model has seen the most growth in recent years);
3. *consortium programs:* several employers pooling resources to provide "group coverage" (this model is less expensive for its members, who can share the costs of operating an EAP with other consortium members, and may work better for smaller organizations); and
4. *association programs:* occupational associations (such as the Association of Airline Pilots) and professional organizations (such as state bar associations and NASW) providing EAP services. Advantages of this model are that the EAP can accommodate the unique aspects of the profession/occupation served and possible reduced stigma because the EAP is not directly connected with the employee's workplace.

Most workplaces that use models other than the internal model have a full-time or part-time coordinator (employed by the company) who trains supervisors in how to recognize troubled employees and make referrals and who publicizes the program within the company. This coordinator provides the initial screening of employees to ensure that the EAP services are appropriate; however, a referral then is made to a contracting social services agency or trained professional outside the company that provides the services.

EAPs have a proven track record in reducing employee absenteeism, decreasing health-care costs, and increasing employee productivity (Attridge, Herlihy, & Maiden, 2006). Examples of successful interventions include reduction of absenteeism stemming from alcoholism; programs that improve family relations, resulting in improved employee productivity; and the introduction of site-based fitness programs that result in substantial savings in health insurance-related claims (Davies, 2000; Roberts & Greene, 2002).

Also, EAPs oversee managed health care and mental health care for employees, in an attempt to reduce inadequate and ineffective services (Feldman, 2002; Winegar, 2002). In this role, EAP staffs conduct assessments of employee needs, determine the most appropriate type of care needed, and refer the employee or family member to the most appropriate resource. EAP personnel also often serve as case managers in these situations, ensuring that the services are received and monitoring the case until it is terminated. Employees receive an incentive in reduced co-payments for using these services. This role has raised ethical issues for social workers in some instances if the emphasis is on saving costs for the employer at the expense of providing the most appropriate services for the client.

Another critical issue that EAP workers confront is confidentiality, with more EAPs adopting clear guidelines about the circumstances under which information about employees is given to management. Most programs advocate total confidentiality between the EAP and employees unless a crime has been committed or the employee is deemed dangerous to himself or herself or others.

Dependent-Care Programs

Companies and organizations are responding to the needs of employees by establishing a variety of child-care programs. Child-care options currently include the following (Families and Work Institute, 2005, p. 15):

- access to information to help locate child care in the community;
- child care at or near the worksite;
- payment for child care with vouchers or other subsidies that have direct costs to the company;
- Dependent Care Assistance Plans, which help employees pay for child care with pre-tax dollars;
- reimbursement of child-care costs when employees work late;
- reimbursement of child-care costs when employees travel for business;
- child care for school-age children on vacation from school;
- back up or emergency care for children of employees when the regular child care arrangements fall apart;
- sick care for children of employees; and
- financial support of local child care through a fund or corporate contributions beyond the United Way.

A growing number of corporations have responded. The following are examples from the "100 Best Companies for Working Mothers" (2006).

- About 65% of employees at Abbott Laboratories use some form of alternative work arrangement, and most have been supplied with the computers, software, and remote access that allow them to work from home.
- At Accenture, 60% of employees have flex hours or telecommute.
- The American Express Company allows employees to utilize flextime, compressed work weeks, telecommuting, and job sharing.
- The Bank of America subsidizes 65% of the cost at its three onsite child-care centers at its headquarters.
- Children's Memorial Hospital in Jacksonville allows flexible schedules, including staggered

Many employers offer on-site child care programs or other types of child care benefits to support working parents.

Lawrence Migdale/Stone/Getty Images

shifts, compressed work weeks, and part-time hours.

- Deloitte, a large management consulting firm, provides child care at 69 back-up care centers across the country when emergencies arise.

Other companies have worked with communities in establishing child-care referral systems, helping employees locate appropriate child care that best meets individual needs, or they offer flexible spending packages in which employee benefits can be designed for the care of elderly dependents.

Some companies provide vouchers for child care, which permit parents to contribute a portion of their employee benefits for child care of their choice. Others offer a variety of after-school and summer child-care programs and programs for sick children. Recognizing the amount of money lost every time a child is sick, some companies provide nurses to go to parents' homes and care for children, paying a portion of the cost for this service ("100 Best Companies for Working Mothers," 2006).

The National Child Care Information Center (2006) provides a list of organizations and publications that have information about the costs and benefits of employee-sponsored child care. Although few companies actually have conducted formal cost–benefit analyses, businesses have posited the following reasons as to why child care can have a significant impact on their bottom line:

- Lack of access to affordable, quality child care may make it difficult for businesses to hire qualified employees.
- Productive and valued employees may leave their jobs because of child-care problems, which increases hiring and training costs.
- Employees may be forced to take time off because of child-care problems or spend time at work handling child-care concerns.
- Companies with employer-supported child-care services have reported improved employee morale, reduced absenteeism, increased productivity, and lower turnover.

Because so many employers were finding that their employees had problems with dependent care for their elderly parents as well as children, a number have expanded their efforts to include this population. For example, IBM, a founding member of the American Business Collaboration for Quality Dependent Care, has provided funding to improve the quality and availability of dependent care for the elderly since the early 1990s.

Some firms have implemented programs to increase productivity, including flexible work schedules, health and wellness programs, transportation systems, recreation teams, and employee work groups, that together attempt to improve the workplace environment. Co-workers, too, are turning to their fellow employees for support—helping with child care and transportation and offering advice about coping with teenagers, among many examples. Co-workers are increasingly assuming this role, which traditionally has been the province of neighbors, friends, or relatives.

Despite significant inroads, the need for affordable, accessible child care for working parents has been identified as the most critical need for families. In the United States, 29 million children currently need child care, but many parents—particularly those at or near the poverty level—cannot afford the costs of good care. Child-care costs are less than 10% of total expenditures for the average family but often more than a third of total expenditures for the working poor (Lindsay & Chase-Landsdale, 2002).

Social Work in the Workplace

Social work is expanding its provision of social services in the workplace, known as *industrial* or *occupational social work.* Although many view this specialization as relatively new, this is not the case. Actually, the profession of social work owes its name to industry. The term *social work,* introduced in the United States in the early 1890s (apparently a direct translation of the German phrase *Arbeiten sozial*), referred to housing, canteens, health care, and other resources provided to employees by Krupp munitions plants to support the industrial workforce (Carter, 1977).

Industrial Social Work

In many other countries, industry is the largest field for social work practice. In the United States, industrial social work developed and was practiced between 1890 and 1920, then was largely dormant until it reemerged in the 1970s.

The development of welfare and social work programs in industry began with the mutual aid societies and volunteer programs accompanying many of the progressive reform movements during the late 1800s and early 1900s. Positions of "social secretary," "welfare manager," and "welfare secretary" were found in many American industries, including textile mills in the South, as well as Kimberly Clark and International Harvester. Welfare secretaries had backgrounds primarily in religious or humanitarian work, with little previous experience in either social work or industry. In general, they were responsible for overseeing the physical welfare (safety, health, sanitation, and housing), cultural welfare (recreation, libraries, and education programs), economic welfare (loans, pensions, rehabilitation, hiring, and firing), and personal welfare, which included social work (then called *case work*), of employees and their families (Carter, 1977).

According to a U.S. Bureau of Labor Statistics survey, by the mid-1920s, most of the largest companies in the United States had at least one type of welfare program and about half had comprehensive programs (Axinn & Stern, 2005). Sociologist Teresa Haveren (1982) reviewed old records and conducted a historical study of work and family relationships at the Amoskeag Textile Mill in New Hampshire in the late 1800s and early 1900s. Like many other industries during that time, this company provided the following for employees:

- corporate housing close to the mill for working parents;
- boarding houses for young, single employees;
- English, sewing, cooking, and gardening classes;
- nurses who provided instruction in housekeeping, health care, and medical aid and visited the sick and elderly regularly to provide food and assistance;

- a charity department to provide needy families with clothing, food, and coal, and assistance to widows with large families if their husbands died or were injured on the job or were former employees;
- a hospital ward for employees injured on the job;
- a dentist for employees' families;
- a child-care program and kindergarten;
- a children's playground with attendants to supervise the children;
- a swimming pool and ice-skating rink;
- an Americanization program;
- an athletic field and showers;
- lectures, concerts, and fairs; and
- a Boy Scouts program.

Although many companies were generous with assistance, services were denied if an individual refused to work. Thus, the system was designed to encourage loyalty to the organization, not simply to provide benefits to employees. Because many industries employed entire families, often in the same work unit, it can be argued that this system made it easier for workers to make the transition from family to factory, with many family members seeing little difference between work life and family life.

During the late 1920s, opposition to these programs came from a number of fronts, including employees themselves. Many employees, including women, were immigrants. As they became more acculturated within the United States, they saw the welfare programs as paternalistic. The rise of the labor movement also increased opposition to corporate welfare programs. Labor leaders considered the programs anti-union, believing that the welfare secretary diffused employee unrest without bringing about changes that would improve working conditions for employees.

The emergence of scientific management of the workplace redirected attention to improving workers' efficiency. Later, scientific management and welfare work merged into a new field—personnel management. At the same time, public and private social services agencies became more prevalent, lessening the need for businesses to offer many of their previous services. Thus, corporate welfare programs declined.

During World War II, the National Maritime Union and United Seaman's Service operated an extensive industrial social work program, providing assistance to the families of the more than 5,000 union members who had been killed during the war. Because unions feared that social workers hired by companies would not be sympathetic to unions, other unions initiated industrial social work programs. Until recently, unions were responsible for most of the social work programs in the United States (Carter, 1977).

Occupational Social Work

With the decline in manufacturing and other heavy industries and the shift to a service economy, the term *industrial social work* has been replaced by **occupational social work.** Historically, occupational social work has served a variety of functions in business and industry. Profit often has been a major motivation of employers who provide social work services, with the hope that these services would increase productivity and morale. But social workers have affected the workplace in ways other than providing social services to employees and their families. Social workers also have played a role in

- integrating new groups of inexperienced workers (such as women, people of color, and immigrants) into the work world;
- consulting with businesses on how to increase diversity in the workplace and to be sensitive to the needs of diverse groups; and
- strengthening relationships between the corporate world and the community; and in organizational development through redesign of work to make the workplace more humane for employees.

In addition to expertise in working with troubled individuals and families, social workers are trained in effective communication and negotiation—skills that lend themselves well to advocating for employee needs or working to improve conditions within a workplace and increase understanding between employees and employers.

It seems logical that social workers should become more actively involved in the workplace. Occupational social work lends itself to providing services within a natural setting. After all, the majority of adults are employed. The opportunity for a universal service-delivery system that goes beyond services to the poor, the elderly, and the sick also is ideal for providing preventive services—an area that is almost negligible from the broader perspective of total services provided.

Social work as a profession is strengthening its interests and capabilities in the area of occupational social work (see Box 15.2). The two major professional bodies that guide the profession—the National Association of Social Workers and the Council on Social Work Education—have established task forces, developed publications, and held conferences dealing with occupational social work.

In some instances, university social work programs offer courses in occupational social work and related areas, sometimes in collaboration with other departments such as business administration. All programs provide future occupational social workers with knowledge and skill in dealing with substance abuse, marriage and family problems, and other individual and family problems. They also offer courses relevant to working in organizations and the corporate world.

To be successful in the workplace, social workers need additional knowledge and skill in business principles, planning and management, marketing, financial management, human resources administration, family counseling, and organizational behavior. And students in

---

BOX 15.2
The Occupational Social Worker

A job description for an occupational social worker might include the following:

- Linking individuals and family members to entitlements and other public and private resources
- Conducting short-term counseling involving a full range of job-related and non-job-related psychosocial and health/disability concerns
- Providing specialized emergency services in areas such as substance abuse, disability management, and mental health
- Identifying and addressing the needs of special populations within the workplace, such as older workers and retirees, workers with disabilities, chemically dependent workers, relocated workers, unemployed individuals, dislocated and underemployed workers,

ethnic and racial groups, workers exposed to hazardous conditions, and workers with mental health problems
- Addressing issues such as violence in the workplace
- Collaborating with others to identify and address issues of workplace health and safety
- Working with management to minimize problems encountered by part-time and temporary employees
- Assisting workers in accessing vocational and educational opportunities.

Source: Social Work in the 21st Century, by M. Reisch and E. Gambrill (Thousand Oaks, CA: Pine Forge Press), pp. 226–238. Copyright © 1997 by Pine Forge Press. Reprinted with permission.

---

occupational social work programs also are placed in field internships in corporations and unions, where they work directly with troubled employees and their families or are involved in administration and planning activities.

Although social work as a profession must recognize the importance of work within the individual's life, the emphasis of occupational social work has been primarily at the individual casework level through EAPs and other forms of one-to-one counseling or information and referral services. The focal point seems to be the relationship of work to emotional problems. Social workers also have played a role in addressing work-related social policy issues such as the appropriate division between corporate and social welfare sectors in providing services; the relationships between work and family roles for men and women; the impact of affirmative action

programs on women, people of color, and individuals with disabilities; and unemployment. But little attention has been given to the role that social work might play from an organizational-change perspective.

Social Work in the Changing Workplace

Since the 1990s, many workplaces are making changes that are not new to social workers. The emphasis on empowering employees to take responsibility for initiative and product design and completion, for example, is consistent with the social work focus of client empowerment. The use of task groups to make decisions and complete projects also is not new to social workers. Social workers are skilled at understanding group dynamics, leadership styles, and the use of a systems/ecological perspective in achieving synergy among systems, including groups. The need for occupational social work continues to be supported by legislation relating to civil rights and equal opportunities for employees, safe work conditions, and the financial and legal protection of at-risk populations through programs such as workers' compensation, unemployment insurance, and income support programs (National Association of Social Workers, 1997).

Social workers can play key roles at all levels of the workplace. They can incorporate these new directions into the workplace culture from both employer and employee perspectives, and to balance individual and organizational interests.

Applying a Systems/Ecological Perspective

Because social workers focus on the interactions between the individual and his or her environment, they are well equipped to develop strategies of intervention at various levels of the systems within which the individual functions (see Box 15.3) (Akabas & Kurzman, 2007). Consider again the Hunt family discussed at the beginning of this chapter. Social work intervention could consist of individual counseling for Bill and Meredith relating to their respective jobs. Because the problems the Hunts face, however, are associated with their relationship to each other, a social worker might propose marital counseling for the couple, seeing both of them together. Remember, though, that the Hunt children, too, were having difficulties in the family. Therefore, the social worker should provide counseling for the entire Hunt family.

Other individuals within the systems in which the Hunts function may have to be involved, too. Co-workers and supervisors with whom they interact may be exacerbating their problems. The oldest son's teacher might offer insight into the boy's problems, and the social worker might work with other individuals who interact with the Hunts to be more supportive of the family's needs. The social worker might tap into resources within the community such as low-cost after-school child care, a recreational program for the son, parenting classes, Alcoholics Anonymous, or a family violence program.

Thus, the role of a social worker can go beyond individual and family interventions. The social worker might recognize that many individuals in the workplace have the same kinds of problems as the Hunts. Therefore, he or she might establish support groups for employees with similar concerns and needs. An additional role could be to advocate with management for company policies that better support the needs of employees like the Hunts.

Social workers might work with others within the workplace to implement child-care programs, flexible work hours, and adequate sick-leave policies. Finally, they might stretch beyond the workplace in developing state and federal legislation to mandate policies that are more supportive of employees and their families, such as expanding family-leave and sick-leave policies that allow leave for family-related issues beyond the employee's illness to include all workplaces.

Service Models

The following three models of service have been identified for occupational social workers, incorporating a variety of roles inherent to the profession of social work (National Association of Social Work, 1997):

1. *Employee service model:* focuses primarily on the micro level of the systems within which employees and their families function. In this model, social work functions include counseling employees and their families, providing educational programs to employees, referring employees to other agencies, implementing recreational programs, consulting with management regarding

BOX 15.3
Client Assessment Incorporating Work and Family Domains

I. **Employee Perceptions**
   a. Employment history, including education and training
   b. Current employment situation—culture of organization, hours worked, responsibilities, relationships with supervisors and co-workers, stresses of job, strengths of job and workplace
   c. Performance expectations and how well employee is meeting them
   d. Adequacy of income and benefits
   e. What employee values regarding workplace (autonomy, relationships, pay) and how well organization is meeting expectations
   f. Career goals of employee
   g. Value employee places on job and workplace in comparison to other life domains
   h. Opportunities within the workplace that help employer better understand family needs and demands

II. **Workplace Expectations and Perceptions**
   a. Culture of organization and expectations of its employees
   b. Demographics of organization—size, geographic location, structure, setting
   c. Policies and practices and fit with employee needs and concerns, i.e., health insurance and other benefits, child care, flex time
   d. Opportunities available to employee for upward mobility or horizontal growth
   e. Specific concerns about employee, including job performance, employee relationships, inappropriate use of

alcohol or other drugs, potential for workplace violence/harm to self or others

III. **Workplace/Family Interaction**
   a. Expectations of employee regarding work and family
   b. Expectations of other family members regarding employee's job and family
   c. Fit between workplace support, i.e., salary, benefits, time on job, and family needs
   d. Ways that job stresses and job satisfaction of employee impact employee within family and other family members (partner, children, other relatives)
   e. Negative impacts of employment on employee and family members, including inappropriate use of alcohol or other drugs, potential for workplace or family violence/harm to self or others
   e. Other benefits of work/employment to employee and family
   f. Opportunities for employee and family members to participate in workplace activities or leisure activities that help family members better understand workplace and its demands

---

Source: Content from S. H. Akabas & P. A. Kurzman (2007). *Work and the workplace: A resource for innovation practice and policy.* New York: Columbia University Press and J. Cohen and B. McGowan (1982). What do you do? An inquiry into the potential of work-related research, in *Work, workers, and work organizations: A view from social work,* edited by S. Akabas and P. Kurzman. Upper Saddle River, NJ: Prentice Hall.

individual employee problems, and training supervisors to recognize and deal appropriately with employee problems.

2. *Consumer service model*: emphasizes intervention at a broader level within the same systems. This model views employees as consumers and assists them in identifying needs and advocating to get those needs met. Social workers work with consumers/employees in assessing their needs, developing strategies to best meet the needs identified, locating and providing community resources to meet the needs, serving as a liaison between consumer/employee groups and social services agencies, and developing outreach programs to meet employee needs.

3. *Corporate social responsibility model*: intervenes at the exo-level and macro-level within the various systems in which employees and their families function. Within the realm of this model, social workers are found in the workplace, community, and society in general, developing and strengthening programs that support individual employees and their families. They consult about human resources, policy, and donations to tax-exempt activities within the workplace and to community organizations such as the United Way; analyze relevant legislation and recommend additional legislation; administer health and welfare benefits; conduct research to document needs and evaluate programs and policies; and serve as community developers, providing a link among social service, social policy, and corporate interests.

These models often overlap, with social workers in workplace settings providing tasks that fall within more than one model. Most of the social work activity in the workplace to date has followed the employee service model. It is anticipated that as a growing number of social workers practice in occupational settings, more of their activity will reside within the other two models.

Summary

A systems/ecological approach to social problems focuses on the interactions between individuals and their environments. Until recently, little attention has been given to the interactions among the individual, the individual's place of employment, and the individual's family. But as more women, both with and without children, enter the workplace, and as rapid social change continues to affect many individuals negatively, the relationship between the workplace and the family cannot be ignored. Individuals with workplace stresses invariably bring those stresses home, and vice versa. The costs of employee and family substance abuse, marital discord, parenting problems, and other mental health problems are extensive to the family and the workplace alike.

A number of communities and workplaces have developed programs that assist individual employees and their families to better balance work and family pressures. These include employee assistance programs (EAPs), as well as child-care, transportation, and health and wellness programs. Studies show that these programs are effective in preventing family and workplace dysfunction.

The field of occupational social work is an emerging area that can have some impact through intervention in the workplace to improve family functioning, as well as to increase profitability and productivity for the work organization. Social work as a profession will play a major role in developing programs within the workplace, as well as advocating for appropriate policies and legislation to support employees and their families.

 ## Key Terms and Infotrac® College Edition

The terms below are defined in the Glossary at the end of this text. To learn more about the key terms and topics included in this chapter, enter the following search terms using InfoTrac or the World Wide Web:

commuter families
contingent
    employment
cross-functional work
    teams
displaced workers
downshifting
downsized
dual-career families
employee assistance
    programs (EAPs)
Family and Medical
    Leave Act
flexiplace
flextime
job sharing
life-span model

membership assistance
    programs (MAPS)
National Institute of
    Occupational Safety
    and Health (NIOSH)
Occupational Safety
    and Health
    Administration
    (OSHA)
occupational
    social work
spillover effect
underemployment
working poor
workplace violence
    (WPV)

Discussion Questions

1. In what ways has the composition of the workplace changed over the past three decades? What effect have these changes had on the workplace?
2. From a systems/ecological perspective, what are the relationships among individuals, their workplaces, and their families?
3. What are three types of employee- and family-related problems, and how do these problems affect the workplace?
4. What are three types of work-related problems for an employee? How might these problems affect an employee's family?
5. What are five types of programs that employers have established to address employee and family needs?
6. Describe the three models on which an industrial social work program might be based. List at least three of the roles an industrial social worker employed in a workplace setting might play.

On the Internet

http://www.stats.bls.gov
http://www.dol.gov/wb/
http://www.osha.gov
http://www.neas.com/
http://www.naswdc.org/

References

Ambrosino, R. J. (2006). *The changing work paradigm.* Austin: University of Texas.

Akabas, S. H., & Kurzman, P. A. (2007). *Work and the workplace: A resource for innovative practice and policy.* New York: Columbia University Press.

AFL-CIO. (2006). *The service sector.* Washington, DC: Department for Professional Employees.

Albeda, R., & Withorn, A. (Eds.). (2002). *Lost ground: Welfare reform, poverty, and beyond.* Boston: South End Press.

Applegate, B., Reuss, P., Hart, J., Grist, A., & Caraway, J. (Eds.). (2005). *Renaissance 5807: Leading multiple generations* (Leadership toolkit: Leadership in the evolving workplace). Seattle: Renaissance Professional Training.

Attridge, M., Herlihy, P. A., & Maiden, R. P. (Eds.). (2006). *The integration of employee assistance, worklife, and wellness services.* Binghamton, NY: Haworth Press.

Axinn, J., & Stern, M. (2005). *Social welfare: A history of the American response to need* (6th ed.). Boston: Allyn & Bacon.

Beck, J. C., & Wade, M. (2004). *How the gamer generation is reshaping business forever.* Cambridge, MA: Harvard Business School Press.

Berger, S. (2005). *How we compete: What companies around the world are doing to make it in today's global economy.* Boston: Currency Press.

Bianchi, S. M., Casper, L. M., & King, R. B. (2005). *Work, family, health and well-being.* Mahwah, NJ: Lawrence Erlbaum Associates.

Boland, M. L. (2005). *Sexual harassment in the workplace.* Naperville, IL: Sphinx Publishing.

Bond, J. T., Galinsky, E., & Swanberg, J. E. (1998). *The 1997 national study of the changing workforce.* New York: Work and Families Initiatives.

Campbell, N., Maniha, J. K., & Rolston, H. (2002). *Job retention and advancement in welfare reform.* Washington, DC: Brookings Institution.

Carter, L. (1977). Social work in industry: A history and a viewpoint. *Social Thought, 3,* 7–17.

Chester, E. *Employing generation why.* Philadelphia, PA, and Vacaville, CA: Chess Press.

Children's Defense Fund. (2006). *The state of America's children yearbook, 2005.* Washington, DC: Author.

Cottle, T. J. (2003). *Hardest times: The trauma of long term unemployment.* Amherst: University of Massachusetts Press.

Crandall, S. R. (2004). *Promoting employer practices that increase retention and advancement.* Washington, DC: Welfare Information Network Issue Notes (Vol. 8, Number 1). Available: www.financeproject.org/Publications/

Cross, M. (2006). Employers take the lead in fighting depression: Innovative business around the country are screening and educating employees, and enlisting the help of primary care physicians. *Managed Care, 1*(1), 13–20.

Davies, M. (Ed.). (2000). *The Blackwell encyclopedia of social work.* Boston: Blackwell Publishing.

Deal, J. J. (2006). *Retiring the generation gap: How employees young and old can find common ground.* San Francisco: Jossey-Bass Publishers.

Dooley, D., & Prause, J. (2003). *The social costs of unemployment: Inadequate employment as disguised unemployment.* New York: Cambridge University Press.

ElderWeb. (2006). *Statistics on the size and scope of eldercare issues.* Edmonton, Alberta, Canada: Grant MacEwan College. Available:www.elderweb.com

Emener, W. G., Hutchison, W. S., & Richard, M. A. (Eds.). (2003). *Employee assistance programs: Wellness/enhancement programming* (3rd ed.). Springfield, IL: Charles C Thomas Publishers.

Epstein, C. F., & Kalleberg, A. L. (Eds.). (2004). *Fighting for time: Shifting boundaries of work and social life.* New York: Russell Sage Foundation Publishers.

Ettner, S. L., & Grzywacz, J. G. (2001). Workers' perceptions of how jobs affect health: A social ecological perspective. *Journal of Occupational Health Psychology, 6*(2).

Families and Work Institute. (2005). *2005 national study of employers.* New York: Author.

Feldman, S. (Ed.). (2002). *Managed behavioral health services: Perspectives and practice.* Springfield, IL: Charles C Thomas Publishers.

Galinsky, E. (2000). *Ask the children: The breakthrough study that reveals how to succeed at work and parenting.* New York: Harper Paperbacks.

Gambles, R., Lewis, S., & Rapoport, R. (2006). *The myth of work-life balance: The challenge of our time for men, women, and societies.* Upper Saddle River, NJ: John Wiley & Sons Publishers.

Gregory, R. F. (2004). *Unwelcome and unlawful: Sexual harassment in the American workplace.* Ithaca, NY: ILR Press.

Groot, L. F. M. (2004). *Basic income, unemployment and compensatory justice.* New York: Springer Publishing.

Halpern, D. F., & Murphy, S. E. (Eds.). (2005). *From work-family balance to work-family interaction: Changing the metaphor.* Mahwah, NJ: Lawrence Erlbaum Associates.

Hannington, W. (2006). *The problem of the distressed areas: An examination of poverty and unemployment.* London: Hesperides Press.

Haveren, T. (1982). *Family time and industrial time.* Cambridge, MA: Harvard University Press.

Hays, S. (2004). *Flat broke with children: Women in the age of welfare reform.* New York: Oxford University Press.

Hu, Lung-Teng. 2006. *Toward a human-centered knowledge transfer in the public sector: Discrepancies and commonalities in perceptions between different generations of employees.* Ann Arbor, MI: ProQuest/UMI.

Jacobs, J. A., & Gerson, K. (2004). *The time divide: Work, family, and gender inequality.* Cambridge, MA: Harvard University Press.

Jarchow, C. (2003). *Job retention and advancement strategy.* Denver: National Conference of State Legislatures.

Kelly, W. (2001). *Employee and member assistance programs: What they were, what they are, and what they will look like in the future.* Charleston, SC: Book Surge Publishing.

Lindsay, G., & Chase-Lansdale, P. L. (Eds.). (2002). *For better or for worse: Welfare reform and the well-being of children and families.* New York: Russell Sage Foundation.

MacKinnon, C. A., & Siegel, R. B. (Eds.). (2003). *Directions in sexual harassment law.* New Haven, CT: Yale University Press.

Manage Care Magazine (2006). *Depression in the workplace.* 1 (1), Spring, 2006, pp. 1–20.

Mann, C. L., & Kirkegaard, J. F. (2006). *Accelerating the globalization of America: The next wave of information technology.* Washington, DC: Institute for International Economics.

Marshall, A. (2005). *Confronting sexual harassment: The law and politics of everyday life.* London: Ashgate Publishing.

Mirra, K. (2004). *The unemployed man and his family: The effect of unemployment upon the status of man in fifty-nine families.* Lanham, MD: AltaMira Press.

Moen, P. (Ed.). (2003). *It's about time: Couples and careers.* Ithaca, NY: ILR Press.

National Alliance for Caregiving. (2006a). *The Metlife caregiving cost study: Productivity losses to U.S. business.* Westport, CT: MetLife Mature Market Institute.

National Alliance for Caregiving & Evercare. (2006b). *Caregivers in decline: A close-up look at the health risks of caring for a loved one.* Bethesda, MD: Author.

National Association of Child Care Resource and Referral Agencies (NACCRRA). (2006). *Breaking the piggy bank: Parents and the high price of child care.* Washington, DC: Author.

National Association of Social Workers. *Encyclopedia of Social Work: 1997 Supplement.* Washington, DC: Author.

National Center for Health Statistics. (2006). *Health, United States, 2005.* Washington, DC: Author. Available:www.cdc.gov/nchs/hus/htm

National Child Care Information Center. (2006). *Cost of child care in the United States.* Washington, DC: Author. Available:www.ncic.acf.hhs.gov

National Institute for Occupational Safety and Health. (2004). *Workplace violence prevention: Strategies and research needs.* Washington, DC: Author.

National Institutes of Health. (1997). *NIH child and elder care.* Washington, DC: Author. Available: http://www.nih.gov

Office of National Drug Control Policy. (2001). *What America's drug users spend on illegal drugs.* Washington, DC: Author.

"100 Best Companies for Working Mothers." *Working Mother.* New York: Working Mother Media, Inc., 2006. Available: www.workingmother.com

Pascoe, R. (2003). *A moveable marriage: Relocate your relationship without breaking it.* Houston, TX: Expatriate Press, Limited.

Pitt-Catsouphes, M., Kossek, E., & Sweet, S. (Eds.). (2005). *The work and family handbook: Multidisciplinary perspectives and approaches.* Mahwah, NJ: Lawrence Erlbaum Associates.

Presser, H. B. (2005). *Working in a 24/7 economy: Challenges for American families.* New York: Russell Sage Foundation Publications.

Probst, T. M., & Brubaker, T. L. (2001). The effects of job insecurity on employee safety outcomes: Cross-sectional and longitudinal explorations. *Journal of Occupational Health Psychology, 6*(2).

Rapoport, R., & Rapoport, R. (1980). Balancing work, family and leisure: A triple helix model. In C. Derr (Ed.), *Work, family, and career: New frontiers in theory and research.* New York: Praeger.

Reisch, M., & Gambrill, E. (1997). *Social work in the 21st century.* Thousand Oaks, CA: Pine Forge Press.

Roberts, A. R., & Greene, G. J. (Eds.). (2002). *Social workers' desk reference.* New York: Oxford University Press.

Roman, B. D., Bickel, D. R., & Cadieux, M. J. (Eds.). (2006). *Relocation: Making the most of your move* (2nd ed.). Wilmington, NC: BR Anchor Publishing.

Rosskam, E. (2005). *Work-related stress: A 21st century global disease.* Geneva, Switzerland: International Labour Office.

Schneider, B., & Waite, L. J. (Eds.). (2005). *Being together, working apart: Dual-career families and the work-life balance.* New York: Cambridge University Press.

Shipler, D. (2005). *The working poor: Invisible in America.* New York: Vintage Press.

Tulgan, B. *Managing the generation mix* (2nd ed.). (2006). Amherst, MA: HRD Press.

Twenge, J. M. (2006). *Generation me: Why today's young Americans are more confident, assertive, entitled—and more miserable than ever before.* New York: Free Press.

University of Iowa Injury Prevention Research Center. (2001). *Workplace violence: A report to the nation.* Iowa City: University of Iowa.

U.S. Bureau of Labor Statistics. (2001). *BLS releases 2000–2010 employment projections.* Washington, DC: Author. Available: http://www.bls.gov/emp

U.S. Bureau of Labor Statistics. (2006a). *Civilian labor force by sex, age, race and Hispanic origin, 1990, 2000–2010.* Washington, DC: Author. Available: ttp://www.bls.gov/news.release/ecopro.t05.htm

U.S. Bureau of Labor Statistics. (2006b). *Compliance assistance—Family and Medical Leave Act (FMLA).* Washington, DC: Author. Available: www.dol.gov/esa/whd/fmla/

U.S. Bureau of Labor Statistics. (2006c). *Emerging benefits: Access to health promotion benefits in the United States, private industry, 1999 and 2005.* Washington, DC: Author. Available: www.bls.gov

U.S. Bureau of Labor Statistics. (2006d). *Labor force (demographic) data.* Washington, DC: Author. Available: http://www.bls.gov/emp

U.S. Bureau of Labor Statistics. (2006e). *Occupational outlook handbook.* Washington, DC: Author. Available: http://www.bls.gov

U.S. Census Bureau. (2002). *Statistical abstract of the United States* (122th ed.). Washington, DC: Author. Available: www.census.gov/statab/www

U.S. Census Bureau. (2005). *Median income in past 12 months (in 2005 inflation-adjusted dollars).* Washington, DC: Author.

U.S. Census Bureau. (2006). *Statistical abstract of the United States* (125th ed.). Washington, DC: Author. Available: www.census.gov/statab/www

U.S. Department of Health and Human Services. (2006). *The employment retention and advancement project.* Washington, DC: Author.

U.S. Department of Labor. (2004). *OSHA Facts—December 2004.* Washington, DC: Occupational Safety and Health Administration.

U.S. Department of Labor. (2006). *General workplace impact (of alcohol and drug abuse) in America.* Washington, DC: Author. Available: www.dol.gov.

U.S. Women's Bureau. (2006). *20 leading occupations of employed women: 2004 annual averages.* Washington, DC: Author. Available: www.dol.gov/wb/wb_pubs/20lead2001.htm

Winegar, N. (Ed.). (2002). *Employee assistance programs in managed care.* New York: Haworth Press.

Whyte, W. (1956). *The organization man.* New York: Doubleday.

Wilensky, H. (1960). Work, careers and social integration. *International Social Science Journal,* 7(4), 543–560.

Yankelovich, D. (1979). Work, values, and the new breed. In C. Kerr & J. Rosow (Eds.), *Work in America: The decade ahead.* New York: Van Nostrand Reinhold.

Zimmerman, T. S. (2002). *Balancing family and work: Special considerations in feminist theory.* Binghamton, NY: Haworth Press.

Suggested Further Readings

Blair-Loy, M. (2005). *Competing devotions: Career and family among women executives.* Cambridge, MA: Harvard University Press.

Davis, M., Jordan, C., & Weissbach, J. (2005). *7 demographic trends driving employee communication: How to reach and engage the changing workforce.* New York: H.B. Davis & Company Publishers.

Lancaster, L., & Stillman, D. (2003). *When generations collide: Who they are, why they clash, how to solve the generational puzzle at work.* Chino Hills, CA: Collins Publishing.

Moses, D. (2004). *A descriptive study of issues associated with sexual harassment in the workplace.* London: Cork Hill Press.

Raines, C. (2003). *Connecting generations.* Mississauga, Ontario, Canada: Crisp Learning.

Smedley, H. W. (2006). *Age matters: Employing, motivating, and managing older employees.* London: Ashgate Publishing.

Waitley, D. (2003). *Psychology of success: Finding meaning in work and life.* New York: McGraw-Hill.

CHAPTER 16

The Globalization of Social Work

Sonia is a social worker working in a refugee re-settlement camp in Eastern Europe. Her tasks are many and demanding, and she is forced to work with limited resources in less than optimal conditions. She has been working with a network of social workers from the region and around the world to connect children and families separated from each other as a result of one of the many civil wars in the area. This is a difficult task as the children and families she seeks to reunite speak many different languages, communications in and out of the camp are limited, and few people are available to assist her in her work. Many of the children Sonia is working with will never see their parents again. The parents either are dead or have been forced to settle in another region or country. Others may be reunited with their families but will suffer the emotional scars of war and violence for the rest of their lives.

Sonia also works closely with representatives of the International Red Cross, a variety of faith-based organizations, and other refugee resettlement agencies to ensure that the basic health needs of the refugees are met. Together, they are trying desperately to avoid an outbreak of contagious and sometimes deadly diseases caused by the crowded and unsanitary living conditions in the camp. Even though the refugee camp is located in a so-called neutral country, Sonia and her colleagues are exposed constantly to the dangers of war.

Shawn, a social worker and Peace Corps volunteer from Ireland, is hard at work in an ill-equipped medical clinic in the heart of a small African country. He works side by side with representatives from a variety of international relief organizations to clothe and feed thousands of people suffering from malnutrition. Many face imminent death from starvation. Shawn's compassion for his fellow human beings is tested daily in the decisions he must make on behalf of his clients. Some are so weak or sick by the time they reach the clinic that they die shortly thereafter, leaving families and loved ones behind. He is helpless to do anything for them except perhaps to console them or their loved ones who accompanied them on their journey to the clinic.

The resources available to Shawn and his colleagues are meager in comparison to the need. He also must wrangle daily with local authorities who sometimes prevent relief cargo from being unloaded, divert that cargo for some other purpose, or demand bribes in exchange for access to the cargo. If he pushes too hard for what he believes to be the right thing to do for his clients, Shawn faces time in jail or even summary execution.

Kristin and Mario, recently married and both social workers from the United States, are working at a rural outpost high in the mountains of the Oaxaca region of Mexico. They are part of a multidisciplinary team of medical personnel and other volunteers who have come to the region to provide basic medical care, including immunizations, for the local peasant population, The team also promotes preventive health-care practices in this population, but it is difficult because of the severe poverty conditions in which its residents live. Many of the people Mario and Kristin treat have spent days traveling to the outpost, walking over terrain that is barely passable, to seek help for themselves and their loved ones.

In trying hard to establish positive relationships with members of the community, Kristin and Mario are working with a group of women to develop a cooperative to make crafts and clothing from specially dyed and hand-woven cloth. They also are helping to establish a school and a child development program for preschoolers. No money changes hands for these services; the local residents are so poor that such an exchange would be out of the question. The payment that Mario and Kristin receive is in the knowledge that they have helped preserve the life of a child, reduced the pain and suffering of a person who would have died without the medical care provided, and helped the residents of the area become more self-sufficient through education and enterprise.

Sonia, Shawn, and Mario and Kristin are examples of different roles in international social work, with the common aim of achieving social, economic, and political justice throughout the world. These social workers play a key role in improving the quality of life for persons who are victims of persecution, war, famine, dislocation, and political strife. They work side by side with social work and other professionals to improve the quality of life for marginalized populations throughout the world. They work in highly volatile political environments, and their physical well-being frequently is in danger. They often work in isolated, out-of-the-way places that have little communication with the outside world. They have come together to ensure that basic human rights are honored and to do what they can to normalize the lives of individuals who, through no act of their own, have been forced to live a life of abject poverty. Despite language barriers, cultural differences, and the threat of violence and being jailed, these individuals work tirelessly to advance the cause of social work across the globe.

In this chapter, we discuss international social work and global issues currently addressed by social workers throughout the world. We also briefly identify the major issues relating to the future of social welfare and social justice in the United States and the world and probable directions that the profession of social work will take in addressing them.

A Changed World

The future of the world has changed significantly from what it was before the terrorist attacks on the United States on September 11, 2001; the subsequent global war on terrorism waged by the United States and its allies; and the social, political, and economic aftermath of the war in Iraq for the United States and the world. Since 2001, we also have seen loss of the lives of thousands of soldiers and civilians, other tragic human rights violations, and the displacement of 2 million civilians in the Darfur region of Sudan. Ethnic and racial bias, as well as religious and economic differences, divide hemispheres, nations, communities, and neighborhoods.

The role of the United States as a world power has changed at the same time that the country faces a number of serious issues at home, such as a growing homeless population; a public school system that is largely ineffective in achieving its primary goal of educating students; the lingering effects of welfare reform and its impact on the country's underclass; the large-scale exporting of jobs to countries such as India; the escalating costs of going to college, making access to the higher education system by traditionally undeserved populations increasingly difficult to achieve; and the debate about what to do with the millions of undocumented immigrants entering the country each year. Our international, national, local, and personal priorities are being debated by religious, government, and civic leaders, as well as individual citizens. The resources available to us as social workers, the attitudes and values of other people and those who shape our own personal and professional belief systems, and the sense of community that is critical to making a difference in the clients we serve—all have significant impact on us and on our profession.

As more attention is directed nationally and internationally to social welfare and social and economic justice issues—and the roles that various segments of society should play in meeting unmet human needs—the social work profession is receiving increased importance. The future of social work is challenging, with numerous opportunities for the profession across the globe.

International Social Welfare and Globalization

International social welfare is the field of practice concerned with promoting basic human well-being in a context in which cross-national efforts are involved. Sari (1997) discussed a number of reasons why social workers should have knowledge of international social work practice, as well as skill in working in other countries or with international populations within the United States.

- An international cross-cultural social welfare education can broaden one's horizons about alternative economic, political, and social welfare systems.

- A cross-cultural emphasis helps one to understand and appreciate diverse cultures from other countries as well as to gain added insight about one's own values, ideologies, and cultural preferences.
- An international approach exposes one to divergent thinking so one can view social policies and services more critically and in a comparative perspective because there usually are alternative options.
- Cross-national collaboration between social workers and other human service professionals opens up many possibilities for innovation and change (pp. 390–391).

This international perspective will allow social workers to practice more effectively in a world that is increasingly interdependent along economic, political, and social lines, as well as to contribute in meaningful ways to reduce conflict and exploitation throughout the world.

Social welfare practice in an international context focuses on the study of social problems between and among nations. Such problems include, but are not limited to, the following (Amnesty International, 2003; UNICEF, 2006):

- deaths from war;
- global governance that deals with problems that affect all peoples;
- social justice;
- the rights of women and children;
- religious, economic, and political oppression;
- the rights of immigrants and those seeking asylum from political persecution;
- displacement of persons because of war, political strife, and natural disasters;
- marginalization of people through marketplace globalization;
- the distribution of wealth;
- poverty; and
- human and environmental exploitation.

Global governance that has clearly defined and limited authority and deals with global problems that affect all peoples is also central to achieving a **global village** of social and economic justice, lasting peace, and a sustainable environment (Afulezi, 2005; Follesdal & Pogge, 2006; McFaul, 2006). The time must come when people will accept international law to settle global disputes as they now accept their national government in settling disputes between states and provinces as evidenced by the *Universal Declaration of Human Rights,* adopted by the United Nations in 1948 (see Box 16.1).

Achieving a global village is seriously hindered by the inequitable distribution of power and wealth throughout the world. Today, with little more than 10% of the world's population, wealthy countries and their multinational corporations make virtually all of the world's economic decisions, and most of the military ones, without any consultation from the world community. For example, the global arms trade involves billions of dollars of weapons sales every year. The United States leads this business with more than half of such sales.

World peace cannot be accomplished unless every country is allowed only enough military capability to defend its borders and never enough to wage aggression against its neighbors. Along with this fulfillment of international law is the complete elimination of nuclear, chemical, and other weapons of mass destruction that serve no valid purpose in maintaining a world community in which social and economic justice exist (Association of World Citizens, 2006a, 2006b; Human Rights Watch, 2005; Mattern, 2006).

The social work profession has long embraced the notion that justice, particularly social justice, is a critical component in creating the global village. The global village cannot be achieved without overcoming the many historic prejudices and fears that divide the peoples of the world. Nor can there be peace and lasting stability in the world without achieving a reasonable degree of economic justice. Today, less than 20% of the world's people hold 80% of the world's wealth, while more than 80% hold the rest (Global Issues, 2006). The same relationship exists when it comes to consumption of the world's resources. The richest 50 million people in Europe and

North America have the same income as 2.7 billion people. The gap between the rich and the poor continues to widen every year. Nearly *3 billion* people in the world live on less than $2 a day.

The Gross Domestic Product (GDP) of the poorest nations (a quarter of the world's countries) is less than the wealth of the world's three richest people combined. Nearly 11 million children under 5 years of age die each year as a consequence of poverty. The wealthiest nation on earth, the United States, has the widest gap between the rich and the poor of any industrialized nation (Global Issues, 2006).

These facts are staggering—even to those who are the most cynical about world poverty. They also point out how much work has to be done to close the income gap between the rich and the poor and between wealthy countries and poor countries across the globe.

The concept of **world citizenship** is also central to achieving the global village. Technologically, we have achieved a world community, as evidenced by modern communications, travel, and international trade. But the world remains a place that is dramatically divided into political, social, religious, and ethnic tribes. Although a number of proposals have been advanced to overcome the divisions, the only concept that comes close to conquering them is the idea of world citizenship, or people accepting their responsibility in this interdependent world by thinking and acting as citizens of that world (Brown & Isaacs, 2005; Hansen & Stepputat, 2005; Hoffman, 2004; O'Byrne, 2003; Tan, 2005).

Responding to the Challenge of Globalization

Is the social work profession prepared to respond to the challenges and opportunities of globalization? James Midgley (1997), author of eight books on international and comparative

BOX 16.1
Universal Declaration of Human Rights

Preamble

Whereas recognition of the inherent dignity and of the equal and inalienable rights of all members of the human family is the foundation of freedom, justice and peace in the world,

Whereas disregard and contempt for human rights have resulted in barbarous acts which have outraged the conscience of mankind, and the advent of a world in which human beings shall enjoy freedom of speech and belief and freedom from fear and want has been proclaimed as the highest aspiration of the common people,

Whereas it is essential, if man is not to be compelled to have recourse, as a last resort, to rebellion against tyranny and oppression, that human rights should be protected by the rule of law,

Whereas it is essential to promote the development of friendly relations between nations,

Whereas the peoples of the United Nations have in the Charter reaffirmed their faith in fundamental human rights, in the dignity and worth of the human person and in the equal rights of men and women and have determined to promote social progress and better standards of life in larger freedom,

Whereas Member States have pledged themselves to achieve, in cooperation with the United Nations, the promotion of universal respect for and observance of human rights and fundamental freedoms,

Whereas a common understanding of these rights and freedoms is of the greatest importance for the full realization of this pledge,

Now, therefore, The General Assembly, Proclaims this Universal Declaration of Human Rights as a common standard of achievement for all peoples and all nations, to the end that every individual and every organ of society, keeping this Declaration constantly in mind, shall strive by teaching and education to promote respect for these rights and freedoms and by progressive measures, national and international, to secure their universal and effective recognition and observance, both among the peoples of Member States themselves and among the peoples of territories under their jurisdiction.

Article 1

All human beings are born free and equal in dignity and rights. They are endowed with reason and conscience and should act towards one another in a spirit of brotherhood.

Article 2

Everyone is entitled to all the rights and freedoms set forth in this Declaration, without distinction of any kind, such as race, colour, sex, language, religion, political or other opinion, national or social origin, property, birth or other status. Furthermore, no distinction shall be made on the basis of the political, jurisdictional or international status of the country or territory to which a person belongs, whether it be independent, trust, non-self governing or under any other limitation of sovereignty.

Article 3

Everyone has the right to life, liberty, and security of person.

Article 4

No one shall be held in slavery or servitude; slavery and the slave trade shall be prohibited in all their forms.

Article 5

No one shall be subjected to torture or to cruel, inhuman or degrading treatment or punishment.

Article 6

Everyone has the right to recognition everywhere as a person before the law.

Article 7

All are equal before the law and are entitled without any discrimination to equal protection of the law. All are entitled to equal protection against any discrimination in violation of this Declaration and against any incitement to such discrimination.

Article 8

Everyone has the right to an effective remedy by the competent national tribunals for acts violating the fundamental rights granted him by the constitution or by law.

Article 9

No one shall be subjected to arbitrary arrest, detention or exile.

Article 10

Everyone is entitled in full equality to a fair and public hearing by an independent and impartial tribunal, in the determination of his rights and obligations and of any criminal charge against him.

Article 11

1. Everyone charged with a penal offence has the right to be presumed innocent until proved guilty according to law in a public trial at which he has had all the guarantees necessary for his defence.
2. No one shall be held guilty of any penal offence on account of any act or omission which did not constitute a penal offence, under national or international law, at the time when it was committed. Nor shall a heavier penalty be imposed than the one that was applicable at the time the penal offence was committed.

Article 12

No one shall be subjected to arbitrary interference with his privacy, family, home or correspondence, nor to attacks upon his honour and reputation. Everyone has the right to the protection of the law against such interference or attacks.

Article 13

1. Everyone has the right to freedom of movement and residence within the borders of each State.
2. Everyone has the right to leave any country, including his own, and to return to his country.

Article 14

1. Everyone has the right to seek and to enjoy in other countries asylum from persecution.
2. This right may not be invoked in the case of prosecutions genuinely arising from non-political crimes or from acts contrary to the purposes and principles of the United Nations.

Article 15

1. Everyone has the right to a nationality.
2. No one shall be arbitrarily deprived of his nationality nor denied the right to change his nationality.

Article 16

1. Men and women of full age, without any limitation due to race, nationality or religion, have the right to marry and to found a family. They are entitled to equal rights as to marriage, during marriage and at its dissolution.

Continued

BOX 16.1—*Continued*
Universal Declaration of Human Rights

2. Marriage shall be entered into only with the free and full consent of the intending spouses.
3. The family is the natural and fundamental group unit of society and is entitled to protection by society and the State.

Article 17
1. Everyone has the right to own property alone as well as in association with others.
2. No one shall be arbitrarily deprived of his property.

Article 18
Everyone has the right to freedom of thought, conscience and religion; this right includes freedom to change his religion or belief, and freedom, either alone or in community with others and in public or private, to manifest his religion or belief in teaching, practice, worship and observance.

Article 19
Everyone has the right to freedom of opinion and expression; this right includes freedom to hold opinions without interference and to seek, receive and impart information and ideas through any media and regardless of frontiers.

Article 20
1. Everyone has the right to freedom of peaceful assembly and association.
2. No one may be compelled to belong to an association.

Article 21
1. Everyone has the right to take part in the government of his country, directly or through freely chosen representatives.
2. Everyone has the right to equal access to public service in his country.

3. The will of the people shall be the basis of the authority of government; this will shall be expressed in periodic and genuine elections which shall be by universal and equal suffrage and shall be held by secret vote or by equivalent free voting procedures.

Article 22
Everyone, as a member of society, has the right to social security and is entitled to realization, through national effort and international cooperation and in accordance with the organization and resources of each State, of the economic, social and cultural rights indispensable for his dignity and the free development of his personality.

Article 23
1. Everyone has the right to work, to free choice of employment, to just and favourable conditions of work and to protection against unemployment.
2. Everyone, without any discrimination, has the right to equal pay for equal work.
3. Everyone who works has the right to just and favourable remuneration ensuring for himself and his family an existence worthy of human dignity, and supplemented, if necessary, by other means of social protection.
4. Everyone has the right to form and to join trade unions for the protection of his interests.

Article 24
Everyone has the right to rest and leisure, including reasonable limitation of working hours and periodic holidays with pay.

Article 25
1. Everyone has the right to a standard of living adequate for the health and wellbeing of

himself and of his family, including food, clothing, housing and medical care and necessary social services, and the right to security in the event of unemployment, sickness, disability, widowhood, old age or other lack of livelihood in circumstances beyond his control.

2. Motherhood and childhood are entitled to special care and assistance. All children, whether born in or out of wedlock, shall enjoy the same social protection.

Article 26

1. Everyone has the right to education. Education shall be free, at least in the elementary and fundamental stages. Elementary education shall be compulsory. Technical and professional education shall be made generally available and higher education shall be equally accessible to all on the basis of merit.
2. Education shall be directed to the full development of the human personality and to the strengthening of respect for human rights and fundamental freedoms. It shall promote understanding, tolerance and friendship among all nations, racial or religious groups, and shall further the activities of the United Nations for the maintenance of peace.
3. Parents have a prior right to choose the kind of education that shall be given to their children.

Article 27

1. Everyone has the right to participate freely in the cultural life of the community, to enjoy the arts and to share in scientific advancement and its benefits.

2. Everyone has the right to the protection of the moral and material interests resulting from any scientific, literary or artistic production of which he is the author.

Article 28

Everyone is entitled to a social and international order in which the rights and freedoms set forth in this Declaration can be fully realized.

Article 29

1. Everyone has duties to the community in which alone the free and full development of his personality is possible.
2. In the exercise of his rights and freedoms, everyone shall be subject only to such limitations as are determined by law solely for the purpose of securing due recognition and respect for the rights and freedoms of others and of meeting the just requirements of morality, public order and the general welfare in a democratic society.
3. These rights and freedoms may in no case be exercised contrary to the purposes and principles of the United Nations.

Article 30

Nothing in this Declaration may be interpreted as implying for any State, group or person any right to engage in any activity or to perform any act aimed at the destruction of any of the rights and freedoms set forth herein.

Source: United Nations, 1948.

social welfare, would answer *no* to this question. He has identified the following problems that inhibit the profession's readiness for these challenges and opportunities:

- lack of international content in social work courses;
- failure to emphasize the importance of an international outlook;
- absence of international exchanges of scholars, practitioners, and other individuals;
- low level of participation of social workers in the activities and programs of international agencies;
- lack of international influence of professional social work organizations;
- lack of authentic commitment to internationalism as a value system;
- low level of understanding of the role of international events in social work practice; and
- a need to make international exchanges of ideas, staff, and other resources truly reciprocal.

Midgley (1997) concluded that "a stronger commitment by the profession as a whole is urgently needed. Only in this way can social work successfully cope with the demands of the new international order of the future" (p. 66).

A number of authors have stepped forward to address the concerns expressed by Midgley (see, for example, Drachman & Paulino, 2004; Healy, 2001; Hill, 2006; Hockenstad & Midgley, 2004). The Council on Social Work Education's (CSWE) *Educational Policy and Accreditation Standards,* which establishes guidelines for social work curriculum across the United States, mandates that international content be integrated across the curriculum (CSWE, 2006b). Social work educators across the globe are working together on a number of projects to globalize the social work curriculum by increasing international research on social welfare practice and policy issues and arranging student and faculty exchange and linkage projects. One

effort that is under way and coordinated by CSWE is the launching of a special website (see end of chapter for web address) that is collecting links to international social work-related resources.

Children and Human Rights

According to UNICEF (2006),

> millions of children make their way through life impoverished, abandoned, uneducated, malnourished, discriminated against, neglected, and vulnerable. For them, life is a daily struggle to survive. . . . For these children, childhood as a time to grow, learn, play and feel safe, is, in effect, meaningless (p. 1).

Children suffer many of the same human rights abuses as adults but also may be targeted simply because they are dependent and vulnerable. Examples of this mistreatment include:

- torture by state officials;
- unlawful or arbitrary detainment, often in appalling conditions;
- death, maiming, or being forced to flee their homes because of armed conflicts;
- death or abuse in the name of social or ethnic cleansing;
- work at exploitative or hazardous jobs;
- exploitation as combatants by armed forces and armed opposition groups;
- child trafficking and forced prostitution; and
- threats or abuse to punish family members who are not so accessible.

Often the rights of children are disregarded by the very institutions responsible for their protection. Children often suffer abuse, neglect, and violence in the administration of juvenile justice. According to Amnesty International (1999, p. 4), they frequently are beaten and humiliated, their legal rights ignored, and their parents not informed of their whereabouts. They are held in degrading conditions and often are incarcerated with adults. Some are denied their right to fair trial and are given sentences that disregard the key objectives of juvenile justice—the child's rehabilitation and reintegration into society. According to UNICEF (2006), poverty, armed conflict, and HIV/AIDS are among the greatest threats to childhood throughout the world, but in particular in the least developed countries (LDCs).

Poverty

Children in LDCs are most at risk of becoming excluded and invisible. They are represented disproportionately among the poor, are more likely to be engaged in labor, to experience extreme deprivation, and to die before the age of 5 (UNICEF, 2006).

Armed Conflict

Millions of children live in the midst of war every day of their lives. For many, this is the only existence they have ever known. Others are forced to flee and end up as refugees or displaced persons, often separated from their families. During the decade of the 1990s, 2 million children were killed as a result of armed conflict, 4 to 5 million were disabled, 12 million were left homeless, another million were orphaned or separated from their parents, and 10 million were traumatized psychologically (Global Issues, 2003).

HIV/AIDS

HIV/AIDS in family members undermines adults' ability to protect and provide for their families, increasing the risk to all members and restricting access to essential services. Worldwide, some 15 million children have lost one or both of their parents to AIDS. Millions more children have become vulnerable, as the disease presents challenges to the health and development of families as well as the maintenance of viable communities

and provinces, and in the worst areas, entire nations.

> The protracted illness and eventual death of parents and other caregivers exert enormous pressure on children, who often have to assume adult roles in treatment, care, and support. Surviving siblings can suffer stigma and discrimination in their communities and societies, experience greater exposure to violence, abuse and exploitation, and drop out of school for a variety of reasons (UNICEF, 2006, p. 16).

Other Risks Faced by Children

Children all over the world are forced to work in fields, sweatshop factories, mines, and brothels, and other such dangerous and unhealthy environments, and they are accorded few or no rights. Many are sold or forced into labor. In some countries, children are forced by the government into dangerous or inappropriate work. Most of the 250 million child workers are engaged in domestic labor. Child domestics often are forced to work long hours for little or no salary, endure permanent or long-term isolation from their families and friends, and rarely have the chance to attend school (Amnesty International, 2003).

The illegal transport and sale of human beings for their labor are serious violations of human rights. Every year, thousands of women and girls around the world are lured, abducted, or sold into forced labor, prostitution, domestic service, and involuntary marriage. Trafficked children often end up detained by authorities because they have no money for bail, or they return home (Amnesty International, 2003).

An estimated 100 million children live and work on the streets throughout the world—begging; peddling fruit, cigarettes, or trinkets; shining shoes; or engaging in petty theft or prostitution. Many have been abandoned, rejected, orphaned, or have run away from home. Many are addicted to drugs. Street children are often victims of "social cleansing" campaigns, in which local business owners pay to have them chased away or even killed (Amnesty International, 2003).

International Efforts to Alleviate the Plight of Children

In 2000, 189 countries adopted the *Millennium Declaration* (see Box 16.2 for a list of its values and principles), which resulted in the develop-

ment of a set of Millennium Development Goals (MDGs) that established specific targets to address extreme poverty and hunger, child and maternal mortality, and HIV/AIDS and other diseases, while promoting universal primary education, gender equality, environmental sustainability, and a global partnership for development by the year 2015 (UNICEF, 2006, p. vii). Each of the MDGs is related directly to the well-being of

---

BOX 16.2
Values and Principles of the United Nations Millennium Declaration

We consider certain fundamental values to be essential to international relations in the twenty-first century. These include:

- **Freedom.** Men and women have the right to live their lives and raise their children in dignity, free from hunger and from the fear of violence, oppression or injustice. Democratic and participatory governance based on the will of the people best assures these rights.
- **Equality.** No individual and no nation must be denied the opportunity to benefit from development. The equal rights and opportunities of women and men must be assured.
- **Solidarity.** Global challenges must be managed in a way that distributes the costs and burdens fairly in accordance with basic principles of equity and social justice. Those who suffer or who benefit least deserve help from those who benefit most.
- **Tolerance.** Human beings must respect one another, in all their diversity of belief, culture, and language. Differences within and between societies should be neither feared nor repressed, but cherished as a precious asset of humanity. A culture of peace and

dialogue among all civilizations should be actively promoted.

- **Respect for nature.** Prudence must be shown in the management of all living species and natural resources, in accordance with the precepts of sustainable development. Only in this way can the immeasurable riches provided to us by nature be preserved and passed on to our descendents. The current unsustainable patterns of production and consumption must be changed in the interest of our future welfare and that of our descendants.
- **Shared responsibility.** Responsibility for managing worldwide economic and social development, as well as threats to international peace and security, must be shared among the nations of the world and should be exercised multilaterally. As the most universal and most representative organization in the world, the United Nations must play the central role.

Source: United Nations Millennium Declaration., New York, 2000, p. 2.

children. Failure to achieve them would have a dramatic effect on the well-being of children throughout the world and for the adults they will become if they make it through childhood.

> The MDGs are a catalyst for improved access to essential services, protection, and participation for children, but they are not an end in themselves. Children around the globe deserve our commitment and dedication to helping provide them with a better world in which to live (UNICEF, 2006, p. vii).

The Plight of World Refugees

In common terms, a refugee is any person in flight from dire circumstances in search of a safe haven. In a strict sense, according to the 1951 United Nations Convention on the Status of Refugees, a **refugee** is a person who,

> owing to well-founded fear of being persecuted for reason of race, religion, nationality, or membership in a particular social group or political opinion, is outside the country of his [her] nationality and is unable or, owing to such fear, unwilling to avail himself/herself of the protection of that country (United Nations, 1951).

Any person without the protection of at least one nation is a concern to the international community. Social workers who work with refugees assist nations and voluntary organizations to provide early warning, protection, maintenance, rehabilitation, and guided reestablishment of a protective relationship via safe return to one's original country (repatriation), integration in the country of refuge, or, in some instances, relocation and resettlement in a third country. Refugee movements and the presence of displaced persons anywhere in the world generate humanitarian and often political responses from the international community.

In many instances, despite humanitarian intervention, there are tragic consequences for refugees including:

- deliberate persecution and/or lack of protection within the national borders of refugee-producing nations;
- the inability or unwillingness of governments of countries receiving refugees to fulfill their treaty responsibilities of assuring protection to the legitimate asylum-seekers who come within their territory;
- the inability or unwillingness of countries receiving refugees to accept the financial responsibility of providing assistance to the United Nations and its voluntary agency partners and those countries willing to take in refugees; and
- the inability or unwillingness of the international community to press for sanctions against those entities that produce refugees as a result of persecution and violence.

By the end of 2005, the refugee population worldwide was 8.4 million. Of that number, Afghans constituted the largest group, followed by Colombians, Iraqis, Sudanese, and Somalis (United Nations High Command on Refugees [UNHCR], 2006). About half of all refugees benefit from UNHCR assistance programs, with nearly 90% of this group located in developing countries. Overall, about half of the refugees were female, but this statistic differs for countries depending on the nature of the refugee situation, the region of asylum, and age. About 44% of the refugees are children under 18, 50% are between the ages of 18 and 59, and 6% are 60 years of age and older (UNHCR, 2006).

If the doors to refugees are closed, millions of displaced persons throughout the world will be prevented from reaching safety outside of their homelands and will require protection in safe havens within their homelands. A number of international social work organizations and their members are working tirelessly to strengthen policies and services for the increasing number

Paula Bronstein/Reportage/Getty Images

Social work transcends geographic boundaries and political ideologies. Social work professionals play many critical roles in helping make the world a better place so today's children can enjoy a successful future.

of refugees throughout the world. But ideal international mechanisms designed to address these issues do not exist.

Immigration in the United States

Working with recent immigrants and addressing immigration-related policy and practice issues have long been within the domain of social workers. The influx of immigrants across the United States, coupled with concerns by citizens about who should have access to resources already perceived as scarce, have escalated discussions about how easily, if at all, immigrants should be allowed to come to the United States and if they do come, what services they should receive. Immigration policy in the United States serves the following

four fundamental purposes (U.S. Congressional Budget Office [CBO], 2006, p. vii):

1. reuniting families by admitting immigrants who already have family members living in the United States;
2. admitting workers with specific skills to fill jobs that have labor shortages;
3. providing a refuge for persons who face political, racial, or religious persecution in their country of origin; and
4. ensuring diversity by admitting people from countries with historically low rates of immigration.

Lawful Entry

Non-citizens (or *aliens*, as the federal government refers to them) may achieve lawful entry into the United States by being accorded the status of "lawful permanent resident" (LPR) by U.S.

immigration authorities. Those admitted in this manner are classified formally as "immigrants" and are given a permanent resident card, called a *green card*. Non-citizens admitted in this manner are eligible to work and apply for U.S. citizenship. In 2004, LPR status was granted to about 362,000 new immigrants, as well as to some 584,000 non-citizens already in the country (Office of Immigration Statistics, 2006).

Non-citizens also may achieve lawful entry into the United States by being granted temporary admission. These individuals are allowed to enter the country for a specific purpose on a time-limited basis (e.g., tourism, diplomatic missions, education, or temporary work). By law, these individuals are classified as *non-immigrants*. As such, they may be permitted to visit, study, or work for a limited time, but they must apply for LPR status if they wish to remain in the country permanently (U.S. Congressional Budget Office, 2006).

In 2004, the U.S. State Department authorized temporary admission to the United States for some 5 million non-citizens. Another 15.8 million non-citizens were allowed to remain in the country for no more than 90 days (Office of Immigration Statistics, 2006). These figures do not reflect the flow of non-citizens out of the United States. It is estimated that some 217,000 LPRs exit the country annually, presumably to reenter their country of origin (Office of Immigration Statistics, 2006).

Unlawful Entry

An estimated 7 to 10 million unauthorized persons are living in the United States in a given year (Office of Immigration Statistics, 2006). Unauthorized persons who have violated U.S. immigration laws may be removed from the country through a process that can include fines, incarceration, or prohibition against future entry, or they may be offered the chance to depart voluntarily (U.S. Congressional Budget Office, 2006). In 2004, approximately 200,000 unauthorized persons were removed from the country formally, and some 1 million others left the country voluntarily (Office

of Immigration Statistics, 2006). Table 16.1 shows the requirements for naturalization in the United States according to the characteristics of the applicant and certain preconditions at the time of application.

A Brief History of U.S. Immigration Policy and Legislation

Immigration policy first emerged in the United States in 1790 when Congress established a process for enabling people born abroad to become U.S. citizens. The first federal law limiting immigration, passed in 1875, prohibited the admission of criminals and prostitutes. The U.S. Immigration Service was established in 1891 in response to the millions of immigrants who came into the country throughout the 19th century to fuel the Industrial Revolution (Axinn & Stern, 2005; CBO, 2006; Zinn & Arnove, 2004).

Concerned about how to support the social and economic needs of the millions of immigrants entering the country, Congress established a national-origins quota system as part of the Quota Law of 1921. This law was revised in 1924 to restrict immigration by assigning each nationality a quota based on its representation in past U.S. census figures. The Quota Law of 1921 as revised favored family reunification, in which immediate relatives of U.S. citizens and other family members either were exempted from numerical restrictions or were granted preference within the restrictions (U.S. Congressional Budget Office, 2006; Fiske, 2005).

The Immigration and Nationality Act Amendments of 1965 (Nationality Act), in place today, replaced the national-origins quota system with a categorical preference system. That provided preferences for relatives of U.S. citizens with job skills considered to be useful to the country. Neither the preference categories nor country-specific caps applied to immigrants from the Western Hemisphere. Amendments to the Nationality Act in 1976 and 1987 extended the categorical preference system to applicants from

TABLE 16.1

Requirements for Naturalization in the United States

Characteristics of Applicant	Preconditions			
	Time as Lawful Permanent Resident (LPR)	Continuous Residence in the U.S.[a]	Physical Presence in the U.S.	Time in District or State[b]
LPR with no special circumstances	5 years	5 years	30 months	3 months
Married to and living with a U.S. citizen for the past 3 years[c]	3 years	3 years	18 months	3 months
In Armed Forces for at least 1 year	Must be an LPR at the time of interview	Not required	Not required	Not required
In Armed Forces less than 1 year, or in Armed Forces less than 1 year and discharged more than 6 months earlier	5 years	5 years	30 months	3 months
Performed active military duty during WW I, WW II, Korea, Vietnam, Persian Gulf, on or before 9/11/01	Not required	Not required	Not required	Not required
Widow or widower of a U.S. citizen who died during active duty	Must be an LPR at the time of interview	Not required	Not required	Not required
Employee of or under contract to U.S. government	5 years	5 years	30 months	3 months
Performing ministerial or priestly functions for a religious organization with a valid U.S. presence	5 years	5 years	30 months	3 months
Employed by certain U.S. research institutions, a U.S.-owned firm involved with development of U.S. or foreign trade or commerce, or public international organization of which the U.S. is a member	5 years	5 years	30 months	3 months
Employed at least 5 years by a U.S. nonprofit organization supporting U.S. interests abroad through communications media	5 years	Not required	Not required	Not required
Spouse of a U.S. citizen who is a member of the Armed Forces, or in one of the four previous categories, and who is working abroad under an employment contract with a qualifying employer for at least 1 year	Must be an LPR at the time of interview	Not Required	Not required	Not required

[a] Trips outside of the U.S. for 6 months or longer are considered a break in continuous U.S. residency. Exceptions are made for members of the armed forces whose service takes them out of the country.

[b] Most applicants must be a resident of the district or state in which they are applying.

[c] Spouse must have been a citizen for the past three years.

Source: *A Guide to Naturalization,* Department of Homeland Security, U.S. Citizenship and Immigration Services (February 2004), as cited in U.S. Congressional Budget Office, Washington, DC, 2006.

the Western Hemisphere and combined Eastern and Western Hemisphere restrictions into a single annual worldwide ceiling of 190,000 (U.S. Congressional Budget Office, 2006).

The Refugee Act of 1980 created a comprehensive refugee policy in which the President, in consultation with Congress, had the authority to determine the number of refugees who would be allowed to enter the United States yearly. This act adopted the internationally accepted definition of "refugee" contained in the U.N. Convention and Protocol Relating to the Status of Refugees (U.S. Congressional Budget Office, 2006).

The Immigration and Control Act of 1986 addressed the issue of unauthorized immigration and sought to strengthen enforcement of unauthorized immigration as well as create new opportunities for legal immigration. For the first time, employers who knowingly hired or recruited unauthorized persons were subject to financial and other penalties. The act also provided for two amnesty programs for unauthorized immigrants—the Seasonal Agricultural Worker amnesty program and the Legally Authorized Workers amnesty program—and created a new classification for seasonal agricultural workers.

The Seasonal Agricultural Worker amnesty program allowed individuals who had worked for at least 90 days in certain agricultural jobs to apply for permanent resident status. The Legally Authorized Workers amnesty program allowed current unauthorized immigrants who had lived in the United States since 1982 to legalize their status. Under the two programs, some 2.7 million undocumented persons living in the United States became lawful permanent residents (U.S. Congressional Budget Office, 2006).

The Immigration Act of 1990 added a new category of admission based on diversity and raised the worldwide immigration ceiling to the current "flexible" cap of 675,000 per year. That cap allows for transferring unused immigration visas from one year to the next. Concerns about continued unauthorized immigration led to passage of the Illegal Immigration Reform and Immigrant

Responsibility Act of 1996, which increased the number of border patrol agents, broadened border-control measures, reduced government benefits available to immigrants, and established a pilot program whereby employers and social service agencies could check by telephone or electronically to verify the eligibility of immigrants applying for work or social service benefits (U.S. Congressional Budget Office, 2006).

The Homeland Security Act of 2002 restructured the Immigration and Naturalization Service (INS), transferring immigration services, border enforcement, and border inspection to a newly created Department of Homeland Security (DHS). The immigrant services and enforcement functions were combined under the INS, but these functions have been split up among different bureaus of DHS. Some immigration officials have challenged the wisdom of these changes, citing concerns about the new organizational structure, as well as the leadership at DHS, which had little knowledge or experience in dealing with immigration issues (U.S. Congressional Budget Office, 2006).

No Consensus on Immigration Problem or Proposed Fixes—a joint survey by the Pew Hispanic Center and the Pew Research Center for the People and the Press (Pew Hispanic Center, 2006)—reveals that Americans are increasingly concerned about immigration (i.e., that immigrants take jobs and housing and create strains on the health care system), yet the public remains largely divided in how it views the overall effect of immigration (p. 1).

The survey showed that the public is about equally divided regarding the three main approaches for addressing concerns about illegal immigrants in the United States (Pew Hispanic Center, 2006, pp. 1–2):

- 32% thought they should be able to stay permanently,
- 32% indicated that some should be allowed to stay under a temporary worker program under the condition that they leave eventually, and

- 27% thought that all undocumented persons in the country should be required to go home.

The survey also revealed significant disagreement between college graduates and those who did not attend or complete college, between people who were struggling financially and those who were well off, between liberals and conservatives, and along ethnic lines (p. 7).

The public, too, is deeply divided about how to handle undocumented immigrants already in the United States and how to curtail the flow of undocumented immigrants in the future. The two main approaches to reducing the flow of undocumented immigrants are:

1. greater enforcement along the border between Arizona, California, New Mexico, Texas, and Mexico, and
2. greater enforcement of the 1986 law that prohibits the employment of undocumented persons.

In May, 2006, President Bush unveiled a $1.9 billion border-enforcement plan that would send 6,000 more National Guard troops to the Mexico border to bolster current enforcement efforts of the U.S. Border Patrol, build new detention spaces for those caught trying to enter the country illegally, and use high-tech identification cards to verify workers' status.

Congress continues to consider a variety of other options for stemming the flow of undocumented immigrants into the country. Proposals include building a fence along 700 miles of the U.S.–Mexico border; imposing stricter penalties on employers of undocumented workers; making it a felony to be an undocumented worker; and making it a crime for humanitarian groups to help undocumented immigrants.

A study about what America's immigrants have to say about life in the United States today (Public Agenda, 2003) revealed an initial outpouring of affection for the United States, followed by candid talk about the slights and difficulties immigrants often encounter. Most of the immigrants concluded, however, that, "problems notwithstanding, there's no place better than the U.S. to build [our] homes" (p. 10).

The immigration debate in the United States is not likely to be resolved soon because of the magnitude and complexity of the problem and the deep divisions among the people it affects. Notwithstanding these caveats, all social workers should become familiar with this issue because of the accompanying social, economic, and political justice implications.

The International Federation of Social Workers

Problems such as those described in this chapter demand the attention and active collaboration of all nations if they are to be resolved satisfactorily. This is the focus of the **International Federation of Social Workers (IFSW),** founded in 1956. The aims of IFSW (2006a) are to

- promote social work as a profession through international cooperation, especially regarding professional values, standards, ethics, human rights, recognition, training, and working conditions;
- promote the establishment of national organizations of social workers or professional unions for social workers and, when needed, national coordinating bodies (collectively "social work organizations") where they do not exist; and
- support social work organizations in promoting the participation of social workers in social planning, and the formulation of social policies, nationally and internationally, recognition of social work, enhancement of social work training and the values and professional standards of social work.

To achieve these aims, the Federation (IFSW, 2006a, p. 1) engages in the following activities:

- encourages cooperation among social workers of all countries;
- facilitates opportunities for discussion and the exchange of ideas and experiences through meetings, study visits, research projects, and publications; and
- establishes and maintains relationships with, and presents and promotes the views of, social work organizations and their members to international organizations relevant to social development and welfare.

Following the September 11, 2001, attacks in the United States and other terrorist attacks throughout the world, the IFSE and the International Association of Schools of Social Work (IASSW) asked all members worldwide to work together to advocate for a nonviolent approach to resolving conflict. These groups called for dialogue about the distribution of wealth throughout the world, the impact of war on vulnerable populations in underdeveloped countries where the vast majority of civilians are women and children, and safeguarding core human rights (Council on Social Work Education, 2002).

The IFSW is divided into five geographical regions: (1) Africa; (2) Asia and the Pacific; (3) Europe; (4) Latin America and the Caribbean; and (5) North America (IFSW, 2006b). Regions arrange their own meetings and conferences and elect representatives to regional organizations and the IFSW Human Rights Commission and Permanent Committee on Ethical Issues. Only one national professional organization in each country may become a member of the Federation. This organization may be a national association or a coordinating body that represents two or more national associations. Each member association or coordinating body must observe the IFSW Constitution.

Member organizations require their membership to engage in regular professional training that reflects an organized sequence of social work education and incorporates ethical standards of practice and a body of knowledge compatible with social work principles. Member organizations also are prohibited from discriminating against groups of social workers or individual social workers on grounds of race, color, ethnic origin, gender, language, religion, political opinion, age, or sexual orientation. Admission is decided by the general meeting and is based on information required by the Federation (p. 1).

IFSW partnerships include the following organizations (IFSW, 2006c):

- *Amnesty International,* a worldwide organization working to support human rights globally, both in general and for individuals;
- *CONGO,* the Conference of Non-governmental Organizations (NGOs) in Consultative Relations with the United States—an independent international organization that facilitates the participation of NGOs in UN debates and decisions;
- *Council of Europe* with 46 member states, set up to defend human rights, parliamentary democracy, and the rule of law; to develop continent-wide agreements to standardize social and legal practices, and to promote awareness of a European identity;
- *European Union,* an organization focusing on political, social, and economic cooperation among its 15 European member states;
- *International Association of Schools of Social Work* (IASSW), an international community of schools and educators in social work promoting quality education, training, and research for the theory and practice of social work, administration of social services, and formulation of social policies;
- *International Council on Social Welfare* (ICSW), an international and nongovernmental organization operating throughout the world for the causes of social welfare, social justice, and social development;
- *United Nations Children's Fund* (UNICEF), an organization dedicated to assisting—

particularly the developing countries of the world—in the development of permanent child health and welfare services; and

• *United Nations,* an international organization formed to promote peace, security, and cooperation throughout the world.

One purpose of the IFSW is to provide social workers throughout the world with practical as well as philosophical guidelines on many key issues. The IFSW has developed a series of 14 policy papers that represent a consensus of professionals from different geographic and professional backgrounds. Topics covered include health, HIV/AIDS, human rights, migration, older persons, protection of personal information, refugees, conditions in rural communities, women, youth, peace and social justice, displaced persons, globalization and the environment, and indigenous peoples.

Acknowledging that ethical awareness is a necessary part of the professional practice of any social worker, the IFSW adopted a two-part document, *The Ethics of Social Work—Principles and Standards,* at its July 1994 general meeting in Colombo, Sri Lanka. This document was updated and replaced by a five-part document in October, 2004 (IFSW, 2006d):

Part I: lays out the origin and purpose of the document

Part II: contains the internationally-accepted definition of social work

Part III: contains international human rights declarations and conventions that are particularly relevant to social work practice and action

Part IV: contains the actual principles themselves organized according to the themes of human rights and human dignity and social justice

Part V: provides guidelines on professional conduct

Today, the IFSW represents nearly half a million social workers in 84 different countries. Its affiliate in the United States is the National Association of Social Workers (NASW).

International Social Work Organizations and Agencies

International social work encompasses refugee programs, relief efforts, community development, intercountry and international adoption, education, family planning, substance abuse, post-traumatic stress, and mental health care. Numerous opportunities also are available to work with national government organizations, international government organizations, and voluntary organizations to provide technical assistance in implementing new programs and strengthening existing efforts and developing and enhancing social welfare policy (National Association of Social Workers, 2006). The following categories of organizations and agencies employ social workers in an international social work capacity (Glusker, 1999):

• *International intergovernmental organizations (IGOs).* The best-known IGO is the United Nations with its 12 specialized agencies (e.g., UN Development Program, World Health Organization, UN High Commissioner for Refugees, and International Labour Office). Often, employees of these organizations come from the ranks of senior members of national governments. Positions in these organizations require extensive experience, linguistic abilities, and political contacts. Entry-level positions are available, but they are difficult to obtain and often require a 2-year application period.

• *International nongovernmental organizations (NGOs).* Like their IGO counterparts, NGOs are international in membership and scope; however, they tend to be relatively free of governmental restrictions and bu-reaucracy. NGOs are more likely than IGOs to focus on specialized issues or take spe-cific political or philosophical stances. Ex-amples of NGOs are Amnesty International, International Planned Parenthood Federa-tion, International Red Cross, International Salvation Army, and the Women's Interna-tional League for Peace and Freedom. NGOs are a good place for less experienced social workers to look for international positions. NGOs strongly prefer prior expe-rience living abroad and having relevant language skills for persons desiring profes-sional positions. Prospective applicants may want to consider serving in an international volunteer capacity to build their credibility and increase their chances of securing a paid position with this type of organization.

- *United States government agencies.* These agencies perform services to Americans vis-iting abroad, as well as to the local popu-lace. Obtaining positions in these agencies requires careful planning, as well as the op-timum combination of skills and experi-ence. Persons assuming these positions also must be comfortable with being an official representative of U.S. government foreign and domestic policies. Examples of agen-cies in this category of international social work employment include the U.S. Agency for International Development, U.S. Infor-mation Agency, Peace Corps, and U.S. State Department.

- *U.S.-based nongovernmental organizations (NGOs).* These organizations may offer some of the most fruitful opportunities for international careers for social workers, ei-ther as volunteers or in entry-level positions with little or no prior experience. Examples of agencies in this category of international social work employment are the American Friends Service Committee, Direct Relief International, Save the Children, and World Vision.

- *Professional organizations and associa-tions with major international commit-ments.* These organizations usually are located in the United States but have a substantial commitment to international problems and issues. Positions at all levels are available within these entities, and often individuals will begin their careers in these organizations and work their way up over time to the highest levels within them. Ex-amples of organizations and associations in this category of international social work employment are the Council for the Inter-national Exchange of Scholars, the National Association of Social Workers, and the Soci-ety for International Development.

- *University-based programs.* Universities in many countries have active research and service connections with their surrounding communities, especially if they offer social work degrees. Social workers who are con-sidering pursuing doctoral studies, and those who already hold doctoral degrees, may wish to consider applying for either short- or long-term faculty or research posi-tions in universities and research centers in other countries.

- *Foundation programs.* Foundations en-gaged in international projects of a human services nature employ social workers as consultants, field representatives, and coun-try directors for programs that the founda-tion supports. The best way to obtain an entry-level position in a major international grant-giving foundation is to work either as part of a project-implementation team or as a member of the core professional staff. Ex-amples of large foundations in this category of international social work employment are the Carnegie Foundation, the Ford Founda-tion, and the Rockefeller Foundation.

- *Religious groups and organizations.* Reli-gious groups and organizations sponsor thousands of human service programs around the world. Most of these programs are located in the developing countries of Africa, Asia, and Latin America, and most are targeted toward the poor, women, and children. Rarely is the religious preference of the professional considering working for a religious organization's human service program considered in employment.

- *Social work in international corporate settings.* Social work positions within corporate contexts are numerous, especially for social workers with the sought-after mix of qualifications and interests. As a general rule, these positions involve providing support services to local personnel or to a company's national personnel assigned abroad. Most multinational corporations prefer to base their personnel in their home country for extended time periods before considering them for international assignments. Work experience, language skills, and good interpersonal skills are important qualifications for these jobs.

Finally, social workers are increasingly speaking out about violations of human rights and acting to ensure that rights of individuals throughout the world are protected (Daley, 2006).

A Look to the Future

Social work has a historical commitment to helping people cope with change, and if the last 10 to 15 years are any indicator, change—both positive and negative—will become a way of life in the 21st century. The ambiguity and strain that have existed in the United States since its founding regarding how to address the unmet needs in our society have intensified during recent years. Many Americans are dissatisfied with the way things are but do not relish the thought of change. At a time when the world is an uncertain place for all of us, many want to focus on their families and their own needs and are either too

overwhelmed or fearful of taking risks to do more than reach out to those they know and trust (Loeb, 1999, 2004; Putnam, 2001).

As a nation, we tend to be generous and compassionate when it comes to helping one or two individuals in need but limiting and suspicious in helping large groups of individuals. How our country balances individual freedom versus collective responsibility is a theme that has been present since colonial times and continues into the 21st century. Recent economic and world events have jeopardized the trust and commitment of many people to assume collective responsibility, especially in the face of moral and political confusion about what and whom we should be responsible for collectively—others in our neighborhood, only in certain parts of the world, or groups that represent some values but not others. Who are we, and what do we stand for? What does the future hold, and how will it be shaped by the actions we take, as individuals, as a nation, as a world, as a profession?

Any attempt to forecast future trends must be tentative at best. History has shown us that change does not progress at an even rate, nor is its direction predictable. The events of September 11, 2001, were testament to that. Nevertheless, we can identify certain trends that suggest factors that will have an impact on the profession of social work and the social welfare system, at least in the near future. And regardless of the future, the profession of social work and its core values can play a major role and make a significant difference at all levels of society.

The Past as Prologue

In order to comprehend the difficulty of predicting the effects of social change on social work and social welfare, it is helpful to review the earlier chapters of this book. The history of the social work profession is related integrally to the unpredictable nature of the world in which we live. The social work profession is called to respond as social change alters the economic base and values of society, as well as other basic social institutions including the family, education, religion, and political and social organizations. The rapid growth of the social work profession in the latter part of the 19th century was related directly to the emergence of large urban communities and the associated problems. During those times, common problems included displaced persons, high rates of unemployment, large-scale migration from rural areas into the cities, slums, a rise in poverty, and increasing health-related problems.

To reduce or eliminate the sources of these problems and to provide support for the displaced people and their families, trained helpers had to become an integral part of the solution. The social work profession emerged in response to the need for a cadre of professionals with an understanding of human behavior, awareness of how social organizations function, and sensitivity to the effects of the environment on individual growth and development.

When the American Industrial Revolution erupted, the stability inherent in a primarily agrarian society began to disintegrate rapidly. Change intensified as new ways of manufacturing gave way to new ways of thinking, leading to what has been termed the Information Age. Moreover, the structure and function of the family, once stable and secure, have been affected by the stresses and tensions produced by the economic marketplace, which calls for greater mobility, division of labor outside of the home, and consequent restructuring of family priorities. As a result, families have become less stable, the divorce rate has increased dramatically, multiple marriages are more common, and child abuse, spouse abuse, and various forms of neglect at all levels of society have emerged as more visible problems.

As the nature of work has become more unpredictable, the long-sought goal of financial security has become more difficult to achieve for many people. The poor have continued to be victimized by the lack of opportunity and

increasingly blamed for their condition. With recent fiscal crises, hundreds of government workers at state and local levels, as well as employees of high-tech firms and other businesses, are losing their jobs to outsourcing or international competition, which limits the scarce resources and cannot begin to help those who already were the poorest of the poor.

Increasingly, individuals' health and mental health needs have been neglected. The residual effects of the terrorist attacks of September 11, 2001, the war in Iraq and global strife in other areas, and the continuing spread of HIV, and AIDS-related deaths throughout the world have had far-reaching effects on the health and mental health of society. On the domestic front, the U.S. population has grown older and more individuals have become detached from meaningful production, resulting in a lack of sufficient supports to provide for their needs. Violence, crime, delinquency, substance abuse, homelessness, and a variety of related problems have become sources of constant societal concern.

The Challenges of Today

The organization of social welfare services is far different today from that during colonial times. Gone are the almshouses, the poorhouses, and "indoor" relief. Since passage of the Social Security Act of 1935, the social welfare system in the United States has expanded to meet the proliferation and magnitude of new needs, and then contracted in response to welfare devolution and current welfare reform efforts, and it now requires substantial societal resources to maintain.

Social workers have done their best to step up to this challenge, actively assisting a wide variety of individuals whose personal resources cannot provide an adequate level of social functioning and life satisfaction. Today, social workers are skilled in working with the homeless and the displaced, the poor, substance abusers, single parents, and juvenile and criminal offenders. They also are actively involved with helping those beset by marital conflict, family violence, mental illness, and problems associated with later life, as well as a myriad of other personal and social problems.

In addition, the roles of social workers as promoters of social and economic justice and as advocates for disenfranchised populations—the poor, women, people of color, gays, lesbians and transgender individuals, people with disabilities—have become increasingly important as society tends more and more to marginalize or reject these groups. As new problems have emerged, the capacity of the social work profession to incorporate the knowledge and skills essential to providing assistance has been forthcoming. Our profession's emphasis on empowerment, collaboration and problem solving, and open discussion about issues from multiple points of view challenges us to use these skills and model our values as we work in our many roles as social workers, and as individuals, family members, and citizens.

The positions that members of society take toward social problems and the resolution of those problems invariably relate to the availability of resources. Not all members of society, however, take an unequivocally progressive stance on this issue. For example, federal government indebtedness and reluctance to raise taxes have resulted in reductions in funding to address social problems. Monies for social welfare services have been cut significantly, and populations at risk have not received the assistance they need to become or remain productive citizens. This problem has been exacerbated after the terrorist attacks of September 11, 2001, when billions of dollars shifted to defense and security programs while many public and private social welfare agencies are either downsizing their operations or closing.

The reduction of public monies for social welfare services has resulted in a cry for the private sector to "take up the slack." However noble they may be, private efforts have fallen far short of their intended goals because of the magnitude of the need and the drastic reduction of available resources. The line in the sand has been drawn: Unless we do something to overturn this chain of events—and soon—it may be too late to make much of a difference in the lives of millions of people in need of critical services.

In a materialistically oriented society like that of the United States, the definition of need paradoxically is related to the amount of resources that society is willing to allocate (Gilbert & Terrell, 2004). Thus, in times of monetary scarcity or when demands are made on individuals to share (through the taxing process) more of their earned incomes, the tendency to redefine need levels is inevitable. In this manner, the true need becomes relative need and everyone seems to feel better. Today we stand at a crossroads. Do we continue to advance a global military policy of "preemptive democracy," or do we reorganize our priorities to assure that the basic needs of all members of society are met?

A related challenge is to determine which of the myriad of societal and individual problems properly fall within the domain of the social welfare system. We know that the social welfare system cannot be all things to all people—a panacea that addresses all needs not being met by other systems. There is a need to define and limit the boundaries that encompass the social welfare system so its services can be effective and sustained by available resources. Regardless of this argument, social workers constantly face value conflicts over if and when to address human needs when no one else is meeting them.

How does one deny benefits, for example, to a woman with four young children with no housing, no food, and a temporary part-time job, who makes $5 more each month than the income eligibility guidelines allow for receiving cash assistance under the Temporary Assistance to Needy Families (TANF) program? If the federal government or states refuse to provide for certain groups (for example, teen parents, mothers whose public assistance time limits have run out but who are still not self-sufficient), who should provide for them, and in what ways? Should children be removed from parents who cannot afford to care for them and placed in other settings? And, if this is the case, who should pay for that care? How does one determine whether limited funding should be allocated to the elderly, children, or individuals with disabilities? How does one decide who should have first priority for heart and other organ transplants, whether limited dollars should be spent on neonatal care for premature infants whose prognosis is poor, or at what point resources no longer should be provided to families with little potential to be rehabilitated?

If limited resources do not allow for a full range of preventive and remedial/rehabilitative services, which should be chosen? Should the goal be to try to prevent problems such as child maltreatment, knowing that in the short run this may limit the resources for those already abused but in the long run may prevent more abuse? We seem to be stuck with a classic "pay now or pay later" dilemma. That is, if we pay now to implement a wide range of preventive social welfare programs, the expectation is that we will not have to pay later to address the remedial or rehabilitative needs of those who did not benefit from such preventive programs. But one might ask: Is this simply a political issue, or does it reflect mainstream thinking about the value of prevention?

Metaphorically, there is an increasing trend in the United States to lease things rather than buy them outright. The terms of the leases are fixed, and when they expire, most people return the product to the leasing agent and renew the cycle. In doing so, the lessee is absolved of any preventive maintenance on the product being leased.

Rapidly changing technology, too, has affected the way that members of society think about product longevity. The technological gadget you buy today has practically no shelf life at all, even though it was marketed as "state of the art" or "cutting edge." In actuality, that product became obsolete the day after it was invented. Thus, a person's political ideology, sense of social consciousness, and perspective on technology and change all have an impact on whether he or she supports social welfare programs with a preventive focus. The main difference for social workers is that we are talking about people or human capital, not some resource that can be readily renewed when it becomes used.

Also, as technology continues to generate new knowledge, the social work profession increasingly will have to grapple with emerging ethical issues. Issues including genetic engineering, cloning, assisted death, destruction of the environment, and technological measures to prolong life—all are matters of growing concern for social workers in the 21st century.

Leaders in the social work profession point to a number of critical issues that the profession faces in the 21st century. First, the profession must value the diversity within the profession while not abandoning its roots. Two social work educators, Harry Specht and Michael Courtney, wrote a thought-provoking book shortly before Specht's death. In *Unfaithful Angels: How Social Work Has Abandoned Its Mission* (1994), the authors chastise the profession for its attention to clinical issues at the micro-level of the environment. Even though this book was written more than a decade ago, the message continues to resonate with social workers worldwide.

Specht and Courtney argued that social work as a profession has to work at all levels of the environment in an overall commitment to promoting social and economic justice and eliminating oppression and discrimination. According to these authors, social work has abandoned this commitment by ignoring the poor, abused and neglected children, the homeless, and other vulnerable populations. Further, they wrote that the profession has not directed enough attention to empowering individuals, families, groups, and communities to improve their own lives. They advocated for the profession to pay more attention to community-based programs that educate individuals about how to solve problems so they are empowered to address their own needs. In this manner, the community's problem-solving capacity can be increased.

Others, too, while perhaps not as dire in their statements as Specht and Courtney, project that social work will lose ground as a profession if it abandons its previous perspective and its uniqueness. Morris and Hopps (2000) have raised similar questions and have suggested that because social workers will function in an even more diverse and complex environment in the coming years, more attention must be paid to interventions at community and societal levels.

Many leaders of the social work profession caution that social workers will have to play a more significant role in providing health and mental health services and in shaping the changes needed to make managed care more responsive to client needs. They point out that, just as the profession values diversity in its clients, it must value diversity within its own group. They further argue that while debating the future of the profession is healthy, the debate diverts attention from the necessity to view social needs along a continuum in which social workers play critical policy, research, and service roles at all levels.

Social work educator June Hopps (as cited in Morris & Hopps, 2000) provides an excellent perspective on the profession of social work in the 21st century:

> Although social work has had a long history of concerns (for example, child welfare, poverty, and family relations) it has not developed sufficient theoretical and empirical foundations and skills to address social ills comprehensively in an effort to impact and ameliorate problems. The profession must be attuned to its context of time, place and public awareness if it is to be effective. Precisely because of this contextual immediacy, we cannot simply invoke history for solutions to contemporary problems (p. 4).

The social work profession and the issues facing us are challenging—whether the work is with individuals, families, groups, or organizations, at the community, state, national, or international level. Social work practitioners must increase their involvement at the legislative and policy levels and become more involved in the political arena, where key social welfare decisions are made. As society becomes ever more complex, the number of social workers will continue to grow, with broadened roles at all levels of practice.

Trends in Social Work Careers

As we indicated in earlier chapters, social workers today function in a variety of job settings and fields of practice and hold degrees at the undergraduate (BSW), master's (MSW), and doctoral (PhD or DSW) levels. As of 2006, the Council on Social Work Education (CWSE) accredited 458 BSW programs and 179 MSW programs. The Group for the Advancement of Doctoral Education (GADE, 2006) listed 81 doctoral programs for PhDs in social work or DSWs (Doctor of Social Work), including six in Canada and one in Israel. Since the late-1980s, enrollment in schools of social work at both the undergraduate and the graduate levels has increased substantially as more young people commit themselves to joining the profession.

Social workers held approximately 562,000 jobs in 2004. Of these jobs, 48% involved work as a child, family, and school social worker; another 20% involved work as a medical and public health social worker; and 20% involved mental health and substance abuse social work; the remaining 12% represented social workers in all other types of jobs (Bureau of Labor Statistics, 2006). About 90% of jobs held by social workers in 2004 were in health care and social assistance industries, as well as state and local government agencies, primarily in departments of health and human services (Bureau of Labor Statistics, 2006).

Median annual earnings in the industries employing the most child, family, and school social workers in 2004 are shown in Table 16.2.

TABLE 16.2

Median Annual Earnings in Industries Employing the Largest Number of Child, Family, and School Social Workers in 2004

Industry Earnings	Median Annual Earnings
Elementary and secondary schools	$44,300
Local government, except education and hospitals	$40,620
State government, except education and hospitals	$35,070
Individual and family services	$30,680
Residential care	$30,550

Source: Social Workers 2004 (Washington, DC: U.S. Bureau of Labor Statistics, 2006). Available: http://www.bls.gov/oco/ocos060.htm

TABLE 16.3

Median Annual Earnings in Industries Employing the Largest Number of Medical and Public Health Social Workers in 2004

Industry	Median Annual Earnings
General, medical, and surgical hospitals	$44,920
Health and allied services, not elsewhere classified	$42,710
Local government, except education and hospitals	$39,390
Nursing and personal care facilities	$35,680
Individual and family services	$32,100

Source: Social Workers 2004 (Washington, DC: U.S. Bureau of Labor Statistics, 2006). Available: http://www.bls.gov/oco/ocos060.htm

TABLE 16.4

Median Annual Earnings in Industries Employing the Largest Number of Mental Health and Substance-abuse Social Workers in 2004

Industry	Median Annual Earnings
Psychiatric and substance-abuse hospitals	$36,170
Local government, except education and hospitals	$35,720
Outpatient care centers	$33,220
Individual and family services	$32,810
Residential care	$29,110

Source: Social Workers 2004 (Washington, DC: U.S. Bureau of Labor Statistics, 2006). Available: http://www.bls.gov/oco/ocos060.htm

Median annual earnings in the industries employing the most medical and public health social workers in 2004 are shown in Table 16.3. Median annual earnings in industries employing the largest number of mental health and substance-abuse social workers in 2004 are given in Table 16.4.

According to the U.S. Bureau of Labor Statistics (2006), employment of social workers is expected to increase faster than the average for all occupations through the year 2014. Gerontology social workers, in particular, will be in high demand to address the social service needs of the rapidly expanding elderly population in the United States. Social workers also will be needed to address the mental health concerns of the baby-boom generation as they deal with concerns stemming from midlife, career, and other personal and professional difficulties. Social workers also will be needed to address issues related to crime and juvenile delinquency; and assist individuals with mental illness, mental retardation, and other disabilities; persons with HIV/AIDS; and individuals and families in crisis.

The number of social workers in hospitals and long-term care facilities is expected to increase in response to the discharge needs of these individuals and to provide follow-up services for them in the community. The employment of social workers in the home health-care industry is also growing, as hospitals are releasing patients earlier than in the past, and, as mentioned, the elderly population is continuing to increase.

Employment of social workers in state and local government is expected to grow only marginally as many of the services provided by government agencies will be contracted to private agencies. More social workers will be employed in child protective services as more and more families crumble under the pressures of poverty, unemployment, and welfare reform. Steady employment in child protective services is almost guaranteed because of the high staff turnover experienced in that field.

Social workers also will be required to address the needs of more families for which one or more family members is incarcerated, as well as individuals who are being released from prison with the hope of reuniting with their families. Social workers, too, will be in demand to address the needs of substance abusers who are placed in community treatment programs rather than being sentenced to prison.

Employment of social workers in school settings also is expected to grow as school administrators recognize the connection between family life and academic performance. Social workers are well-suited for programs that deal with truancy, school dropout, juvenile delinquency, adolescent pregnancy, and involvement with gangs. The Education for All Handicapped Children Act provides for hiring social workers in school settings to work with children with disabilities. The actual growth of jobs for social workers in school settings will depend in large part on the availability of state and local funding.

Finally, opportunities for social workers in private practice are expected to expand, but this growth will be tempered by funding cutbacks and the restrictions that managed-care organizations place on services. Some demand for private practitioners will be created by the growing

popularity of employee assistance programs in business and industry, services that are contracted out to individual providers or groups of providers in the community.

The commitment of the social work profession to social and economic justice provides opportunities for social workers at all levels of society to become more culturally competent and to empower diverse groups to advocate for their share of resources. This challenge means that social workers, individually and collectively, must continue to educate themselves about the various cultural groups and to advocate for hiring more social workers who reflect the diversity of the populations that the profession serves.

The social work profession is becoming younger and less experienced as many long-term social workers enter retirement (Morris & Hopps, 2000). Currently, schools of social work and social work employers are attempting to recruit more diverse student bodies and workforces. Whatever the field of practice or the setting, social workers today and in the future face many challenges—as well as many opportunities for professional and personal growth. We hope that you will consider joining us as members of the social work profession.

Summary

Global issues affect social work clients, individually and collectively, on a daily basis. The basic mission and role of social workers are being challenged as never before. Two primary questions face the social work community in the first decade of the 21st century: What role will the social work profession play in this new world? What should social work do to promote equitable societies? The social work profession is in a pivotal position to articulate and develop alternatives to the new social order.

Social workers around the world are actively engaged in a wide variety of community-development activities and national movements and organizations as people everywhere struggle to survive. Social workers come together internationally to develop a global village or world community that supports the right of all individuals to grow and develop to their fullest potential. If social workers are committed to promoting equitable societies, we must promote inclusion and the empowerment of people. We must strengthen links among education, technology, the environment, and progressive change in a global economy. We must strive to maintain individual cultures and cultural identity in the face of global pressures to become homogeneous. We must actively exchange information and experiences about innovative projects. We must be willing to share lessons learned so that successful ideas and programs can be applied across communities. Finally, we must build on the promise of information technology that made the global village a reality that touches everyone and make the world a truly better place to live for everyone.

In this book we have addressed the current state of the art in social work and social welfare. Throughout each chapter, the effects of social problems on various segments of the population have been identified and the societal responses through the social welfare system described. We also have explored the many roles that social workers play in addressing social welfare problems. The significant and dramatic modifications in both the social welfare system and the social work profession since the early days of organized helping efforts are apparent. Armed with knowledge and understanding of human behavior and complex organizations, and bringing a systems/ecological perspective to bear, the contemporary professional social worker is uniquely capable of skillful intervention in the resolution of problems. The social worker of the future will have many challenging opportunities to make major contributions to society.

Key Terms and Infotrac® College Edition

The terms below are defined in the Glossary at the end of this text. To learn more about key terms and topics included in this chapter, enter the following terms using InfoTrac or the World Wide Web:

global village
International
   Federation
   of Social
   Workers (IFSW)

international social
   welfare
refugee
world citizenship

Discussion Questions

1. Choose one of the problems or social issues discussed in an earlier chapter in the text. How might this problem/issue be addressed differently if you were a social worker in another country?

2. What are some ways an international social worker might intervene from a generalist practice standpoint: working with individuals, with families, with groups, with organizations, with communities, as an administrator, as a social policy expert, as a researcher?

3. If you were a social worker in a country operating under a different values base than your own, what perspective would you take in working with clients from that country? Where, if anywhere, would you draw the line between respecting cultural differences and advocating for basic human rights?

4. What do you see as the three major social welfare issues the United States is facing during the first decade of the 21st century? What major issues do you think will have

the greatest impact on the social work profession? What will your role be in addressing these issues?

5. In which *settings* are social workers employed most often? In which *fields of practice* are social workers employed most often? Where are most BSW social workers employed?

6. Discuss some of the future employment opportunities for social work professionals. Which career areas interest you most? Why?

7. What can the profession of social work do to promote social and economic justice? What can you do, both individually and as a social work professional to further social and economic justice?

8. How do you think our increasingly global society impacts social work as a profession and your life? What should the role of social work be from a global perspective?

On the Internet

http://www.nas.edu/pd
http://www.brook.edu/
http://onlineethics.org/
http://www.DigitalDivideNetwork.org/
http://www.undp.org/
http://www.cswr.org

References

Afulezi, U. (2005). *Global village citizen*. Philadelphia: Xlibris Publishing.

Amnesty International. (1999). *Children's rights: The future starts here*. New York: Author. Available: http://www.amnesty.org/

Amnesty International. (2003). *Amnesty International report 2003*. New York: Author. Available: http://www.amnesty.org/shop/index/ISBN_0862103290

Association of World Citizens. (2006a). *A human manifesto*. San Francisco: Author. Available: http://www.worldcitizens.org/manifesto.html

Association of World Citizens. (2006b). *Resolution: No later than 2010*. San Francisco: Author. Available: http://www.worldcitizens.org/resolution2010.html

Axinn, J., & Stern, M. (2005). *Social welfare: A history of the American response to need* (6th ed.). Boston: Allyn & Bacon.

Brown, J., & Isaacs, D. (2005). *The world café: Shaping our futures through conversations that matter*. San Francisco: Berrett-Koehler Publishers.

Council on Social Work Education. (2002). IASSW, IFSW call for nonviolent approach to resolving world crisis. *Social Work Education Reporter, 60* (1) (winter), 17–22.

Council on Social Work Education (2003). Globalizing the social work curriculum. *Social Work Education Reporter 51*(2) (spring/summer), 17–22.

Council on Social Work Education. (2006a). *Directory of accredited social work degree programs*. Alexandria, VA: Author.

Council on Social Work Education. (2006b). *Educational policy and accreditation standards*. Alexandria, VA: Author. Available: http://www.cswe.org

Daley, J. G. (Ed.). (2006). *Advances in social work: Special issue on the futures of social work*. Victoria, BC, Canada: Trafford Publishing.

Drachman, D., & Paulino, A. (Eds.). (2004). *Immigrants and social work: Thinking beyond the borders of the United States*. Binghamton, NY: Haworth Social Work.

Fiske, J. (2005). *A history of the United States*. Whitefish, MT: Kessinger Publishers.

Follesdal, A., & Pogge, T. (Eds.) (2006). *Real world justice: Grounds, principles, human rights, and social institutions*. New York: Springer Publishing.

Gilbert, N., & Terrell, P. (2004). *Dimension of social welfare policy* (6th ed.). Boston: Allyn & Bacon.

Global Issues. (2003). *Children, conflicts, and the military*. Available: http://www.globalissues.prg/Geopolitics/children.asp

Global Issues. (2006). *Poverty facts and stats*. Available: http://globalissues.org/TradeRelated/Facts.asp?p=1

Glusker, A. (1999). *A student's guide to planning a career in international social work*. Philadelphia: University of Pennsylvania, School of Social Work. Available: http://ssw.upenn.edu/

Group for the Advancement of Doctoral Education (GADE). (2006). *Membership directory.*

Tuscasloosa, AL: Author. Available: http://www. web.uconn/edu/gade

Hansen, T. B., & Stepputat, F. (Eds.). (2005) *Sovereign bodies: Citizens, migrants, and the states in a postcolonial world.* Princeton, NJ: Princeton University Press.

Healy, L. M. (2001). *International social work: Professional action in an interdependent world.* New York: Oxford University Press.

Hill, M. J. (2006). *Social policy in a modern world: A comparative text.* Malden, MA: Blackwell Publishing.

Hockenstad, M. C., & Midgley, J. (Eds.). (2004). *Lessons from abroad: Adapting international social work innovations.* Washington, DC: NASW Press.

Hoffman, J. (2004). *Citizenship beyond the state.* Thousand Oaks, CA: Sage Publications.

Human Rights Watch. (2005). *US: ICC best chance for justice in Darfur.* Washington, DC: Author. Available: http://hrw.org/english/docs/2005/01/21/sudab100% _txt.htm

International Federation of Social Workers. (2006a). *Aims of the IFSW.* Berne, Switzerland: Author. Available: http://www.ifsw.org/

International Federation of Social Workers. (2006b). *IFSW Membership.* Berne, Switzerland: Author. Available: http://www.ifsw.org/

International Federation of Social Workers. (2006c). *IFSW Partnerships.* Berne, Switzerland: Author. Available:http://www.ifsw.org/

International Federation of Social Workers. (2006d). *Ethics in social work, statement of principles.* Berne, Switzerland: Author. Available: http://www.ifsw.org/

Loeb, P. R. (1999). *Soul of a citizen: Living with conviction in a cynical time.* New York: St. Martin's Griffin.

Loeb, P.R. (Ed.). (2004). *The impossible will take a little while: A citizen's guide to hope in a time of fear.* New York: Basic Books.

Mattern, D. (2006). *Looking for square two: Moving from war and organized violence to global community.* Salt Lake City, UT: Millennial Mind Publishing.

McFaul, T. R. (2006). *The future of peace and justice in the global village: The role of the world religions in the twenty-first century.* Westport, CT: Praeger.

Midgley, J. (1997). Social work in international context: Challenges and opportunities for the 21st century. In M. Reisch & E. Gambrill (Eds.), *Social work in the 21st century* (pp. 59–67). Thousand Oaks, CA: Pine Forge Press.

Morris, R., & Hopps, J. G. (Eds.). (2000). *Social work at the millennium: Critical reflections on the future of the profession.* New York: Free Press.

National Association of Social Workers (NASW). (2006). *Careers in social work.* Washington, DC: NASW Press.

O'Byrne, D. (2003). *The dimensions of global citizenship.* London: Routledge Press.

Office of Immigration Statistics. (2006). *2004 yearbook of immigration statistics.* Washington, DC: Author.

Pew Hispanic Center. (2006). *America's immigration quandary: No consensus on immigration problem or proposed fixes.* Washington, DC: Author.

Public Agenda. (2003). *Now that I'm here: What America's immigrants have to say about life in the U.S. today.* New York: Author.

Putnam, R. D. (2001). *Bowling alone: The collapse and revival of American community.* New York: Simon & Schuster.

Sari, R. (1997). International social work at the millennium. In M. Reisch & E. Gambrill (Eds.), *Social Work in the 21st century* (pp. 387–395). Thousand Oaks, CA: Pine Forge Press.

Specht, H., & Courtney, M. (1994). *Unfaithful angels: How social work has abandoned its mission.* New York: Free Press.

Tan, S. (Ed.). (2005). *Challenging citizenship: Group membership and cultural identity in a global age.* Hampshire, UK: Ashgate Publishing.

UNICEF. (2006). *The state of the world's children 2006: Excluded and invisible.* New York: Author.

United Nations. (1948). *Universal declaration of human rights (General assembly resolution 217A (III)).* New York: Author. Available: http://www.um. org/overview/rights.html

United Nations. (1951). Convention relating to the status of refugees. *UN Treaty Series, 189, #2545.* Geneva, Switzerland: Author.

United Nations. (2000). *United Nations millennium declaration.* New York: Author.

United Nations Development Programme. (2003). *Human development report 2003 (Millennium development goals: A compact among nations to end human poverty).* New York: Oxford University Press.

United Nations High Command on Refugees (UNHCR). (2006). *2005 global refugee trends: Statistical overview populations of refugees, asylum-seekers, internally displaced persons, stateless persons, and other persons of concern to UNHCR.* Geneva, Switzerland: Author.

U.S. Bureau of Labor Statistics. (2006). *Social workers 2004*. Washington, DC: Author. Available: http://www.bls.gov/oco/ocos060.htm

U.S. Congressional Budget Office. (2006). *Immigration policy in the United States*. Washington, DC: Author.

Zinn, H., & Arnove, A. (2004). *Voices of people's history of the United States*. St. Paul, MN: Seven Stories Press.

Suggested Further Readings

Barry, C., & Pogge, T. (Eds.). (2006). *Global institutions and responsibilities: Achieving global justice*. Malden, MA: Blackwell Publishers.

Cox, D., & Pawar, M. (2005). *International social work: Issues, strategies, and programs*. Thousand Oaks, CA: Sage Publications.

DeGreiff, P., & Ciaran, P. (Eds.). (2002). *Global justice and transnational politics*. Cambridge, MA: MIT Press.

Dominelli, L., & Thomas, W. (Eds.). (2003). *Broadening horizons: International exchanges in social work*. London: Ashgate Publishers.

Ife, J. (2001). *Human rights and social work: Rights-based Practice*. New York: Cambridge University Press.

Lyons, K., Manion, K., & Carlsen, C. (2006). *International perspectives on social work: Global conditions and local practice*. New York: Palgrave Macmillan.

Metteri, A., Teppo, K., & Pohjola, A. (Eds.). (2005). *Social work visions from around the globe: Citizens, methods, and approaches*. New York: Haworth Social Work.

National Association of Social Workers. (1997). *Encyclopedia of Social Work*. Washington, DC: NASW Press.

A Final Word to Our Readers

This book reveals the need for social services for individuals from birth through death in a variety of settings. Some individuals, by the nature of their age, gender, ethnicity, social class, and sexual orientation, are more likely to need social services than others. We have described the many settings in which social workers are employed—government poverty programs, mental health clinics, hospitals, prisons, schools, faith-based organizations, long-term care facilities for the elderly, and communities throughout the world—and have suggested the almost limitless opportunities for social work practitioners in different settings and with diverse populations.

As you reflect on the chapters you have read and the issues raised, we hope you will develop a vision for the future and the social work profession. You can have a role in making our world a more just and more humane place.

Glossary

AA *See* Alcoholics Anonymous.

Acquired immunodeficiency syndrome (AIDS) A usually fatal disease that attacks the body's natural immune system.

Activist Individual who believes strongly in social change and works to try to create it; important social work role.

Activity theory A theory relating to aging based on the premise that social activity is the essence of life for all ages and that all people must maintain adequate levels of activity if they are to age successfully.

Addams, Jane Social worker in the late 19th century who was instrumental in creating the settlement house movement as a resource for preparing immigrants to live in a new society.

ADA *See* Americans with Disabilities Act.

Addiction A physical or psychological dependence on mood-altering substances or activities, including but not limited to alcohol, other drugs, pills, food, sex, and gambling.

Adjudication The legal process that judges conduct in juvenile court with assistance from probation officers.

Adoption A process by which a child whose birth parents choose not to or cannot care for him or her is provided with a permanent home and parents who are able to provide for the child; legal adoptions can take place only when the court terminates the parental rights of the birth parents, but many adoptions, particularly in minority communities, are informal and do not involve the court.

Adult children of alcoholics Adults who as children lived in a family in which one or both parents was an alcoholic.

Adult protective services Protects the physical and emotional well-being of vulnerable adults who may be abused, neglected, or financially exploited.

Advocate Individual who intercedes or acts on behalf of another person or group; important social work role.

Affirmative action program A legally mandated program established within education, business, and industry to improve opportunities for people of color and women.

Ageism Discrimination against the elderly because of their age.

Aging The process of growing old.

Aid to Families with Dependent Children (AFDC) A public assistance program that provides cash assistance to families with children in need because of the loss of financial support as a result of death, disability, or the continued absence of a parent from the home (changed to Temporary Assistance to Needy Families [TANF] in 1996).

AIDS *See* acquired immunodeficiency syndrome.

Alcohol Oldest and most commonly abused substance in the world, usually functioning as a depressant but for some persons can also serve as a stimulant or hallucinogen.

Alcohol abuse *See* alcoholism.

Alcoholics *See* alcoholism.

Alcoholics Anonymous (AA) Self-help group for alcoholics based on abstinence and a 12-step philosophy of living; similar programs exist for family members of alcoholics and addicts and for persons with other types of addictions.

Alcoholism Use of alcohol that interferes with personal life, including family and friends, school, job, health, spiritual life, or the law.

Alzheimer's disease Degenerative disease of the central nervous system characterized by premature mental deterioration.

Americans with Disabilities Act (ADA) Federal legislation that provides protections for persons with disabilities, including employment and accessibility of accommodations.

Amnesty International Organization that promotes social justice and human rights throughout the world.

Analyst/evaluator Individual who determines the effectiveness of programs or agencies; important social work role.

Apathy futility syndrome Term used to describe a set of behaviors exhibited by a neglecting parent who is severely depressed and apathetic toward her or his immediate environment, including her or his children.

Appellate courts Courts with the authority to review the decisions of trial, lower, and criminal courts.

Assessment The process of making tentative judgments about how the information derived from a client system affects the system.

Assimilation The expectation that members of non-dominant groups in society will adopt the values and behaviors of the dominant group.

Association A relationship between two or more factors that occur together but are not necessarily causative (such as alcoholism and child abuse.)

Battered child syndrome A medical term used to describe a child with physical injuries in various stages of healing, indicating the child has been physically abused on a number of occasions.

Behavior modification An action intervention, based on the assumption that all behaviors are learned and can be changed, that focuses on reinforcing present positive behaviors to eliminate inappropriate behaviors.

Best interests of the child A standard of decision making used by courts and child welfare agencies that emphasizes what is best for a specific child as opposed to what is best for other family members or persons.

Bioethics Moral and ethical decisions associated with advanced technology in the health care field.

Blended family A family formed by marriage or long-term relationship between partners in which at least one partner brings children from a previous relationship into the new family system.

Boundary The limit or extent of a system; the point where one system ends and another begins.

Brain-based economy An economy that is driven primarily by the intellectual capabilities of its workers.

Broker A social worker who assists clients in locating appropriate resources.

Case management Actions taken by social workers to manage the various aspects of cases they are working on.

Casework Services provided to individuals, families, groups, organizations, and the community to strengthen social functioning, based on assessing the client situation, identifying client needs, determining appropriate interventions to address identified needs, and monitoring and evaluating the process to ensure that outcomes address needs identified.

Catastrophic illness A chronic and severely debilitating illness that results in high medical costs and long term dependence on the health care system.

Categorical assistance Cash assistance programs given to individuals and families under the provision of the Social Security Act, which established specific categories of persons in need of cash assistance including the aged, blind and permanently disabled (Supplemental Security Income), and children (Aid to Families with Dependent Children, now Temporary Assistance to Needy Families).

Cause-and-effect relationship A relationship between factors in which one or more factors can be shown to directly cause a change in an additional factor or set of factors.

Charity Organization Society (COS) The first relief organization in the United States that developed a systematic program to help the needy; promoted "scientific philanthropy" that incorporated individual assessment and development of coordinated service plans before providing services.

Child abuse legislation The enactment by a federal or state legislative body of laws that affect the physical and emotional well-being of children.

Child Abuse Prevention and Treatment Act (CAPTA) of 1974 Federal legislation first enacted in 1974 to increase identification, reporting, investigation, prevention, and treatment of child abuse and neglect.

Children's Health Insurance Program (CHIP) Federal program enacted as Title XXI of the Social Security Act that expands health insurance coverage for low-income children up to age 19; financed jointly by federal and state governments and administered by states.

Child neglect A condition in which a caretaker responsible for a child either deliberately or by extraordinary inattentiveness fails to meet a child's basic needs, including failure to provide adequate food, clothing, shelter, medical assistance, or education and/or to supervise a child appropriately.

Child protective services Mandated services provided by state social services agencies to families who abuse or neglect their children, for the purpose of protecting children whose safety is seriously endangered by the actions or inactions of their caretaker.

Child Welfare League of America (CWLA) A national organization consisting of agencies, professionals, and citizens interested in the well-being of children and families; CWLA promotes standards for services, advocates for child welfare policies and programs, conducts research, and provides publications related to child welfare issues.

Child welfare service delivery system A network of agencies and programs that provides social services to children, youth, and families.

Child welfare services Social services that supplement or substitute for parental care and supervision when parents are unable to fulfill parental responsibilities and that improve conditions for children and their families.

Children with special needs Children of color, who are older, who have physical or emotional disabilities, or who are members of sibling groups; term used in reference to adoption.

Civil Rights Act Federal legislation passed in 1964 and amended in 1965 that prohibits discrimination based on race, gender, religion, color, or ethnicity in public facilities, government programs or those operated or funded by the federal government, and employment.

Civil rights movement Far-reaching struggle that sought the full and equal participation of minorities, women, and other marginalized groups in the social and economic arenas of our society.

Class The stratification of individuals and groups according to their social and economic assets.

Classism Discrimination toward members of a group because of their economic status.

Client system Individuals, families, groups, organizations, or communities at whom intervention is directed to enhance social functioning.

Client-centered therapy Intervention based on the perspective that the client knows most about his or her problems and needs; the therapist seeks to provide an acceptable emotional climate where the client can work out solutions with support and reflection from the therapist.

Clinical social workers Persons whose major focus is to provide clinical social work services, usually individual, group, or family counseling; often in a psychiatric, hospital, residential treatment, or mental health facility; usually requires an MSW (also called *psychiatric social worker* in some settings).

Closed system A system with a boundary that is difficult to permeate; such systems are usually unreceptive to outsiders.

Coalition building Process of creating a multi-organizational power base large enough to influence program direction or draw down resources.

Codependent A person who lets someone else's behaviors control her or his functioning and focuses on meeting that person's needs, controlling that person's behaviors instead of his or her own.

Collectivist perspective Holds that social problems reflect fundamental socioeconomic circumstances, barriers to access, and lack of opportunity.

Community A group of individuals who usually live near each other; share a common environment, including public and private resources, and identify themselves with that community.

Community corrections Practice of supervising convicted criminals in a community setting rather than in jails or prisons.

Community development A social work approach to working with communities that considers and respects the diversity of a community's population and uses those differences to achieve positive outcomes for all of its citizens.

Community mental health programs Mental health services provided in the community, usually through a community mental health center.

Community organization A method of social work practice that involves the development of community resources to meet human needs.

Community policing A philosophy of personalized policing where assigned officers patrol and provide outreach in a geographic area on a permanent basis, working in a proactive partnership with area residents to identify and solve problems.

Community practice Activities engaged in by social workers designed to improve conditions in the community.

Community social and economic development
Community intervention designed to assist in the development of community programs and to prepare citizens to make use of social and economic investments (e.g., Earned Income Tax Credit, low-interest housing loans, and weatherization programs).

Communities of diversity Communities usually made up of members of marginalized groups who often struggle to navigate within an oppressive, discriminatory environment.

Communities of identification and interest Communities that are formed around shared concerns and deeply held beliefs and values that sometimes bring them into conflict with other communities.

Commuter families Families with spouses employed in different locations, often in different parts of the country.

Comparable worth The concept that persons should receive measurably equal pay for the same type of work, regardless of their gender.

Comparative social research Approach that enables one nation to build on the policy design initiatives of others, thereby avoiding the need to start afresh.

Comparative social work The comparison of what social workers do in nations other than one's own.

Compassionate conservatism George W. Bush ushered in a new era of social welfare policy when he became the President of the United States in 2000, arguing that government cannot solve every problem, but it can encourage people and communities to help themselves and to help one another. He termed his philosophy and approach "compassionate conservatism," compassionate to actively help fellow citizens in need yet conservative to insist on responsibility and on results.

Competencies Skills that are essential to perform certain functions; social workers must have competencies in a number of areas to be effective professionals.

Consumer price index (CPI) A measure of the average change in prices over time for a fixed "market basket" of goods and services purchased by a specified group of consumers.

Contingent employment Work arrangements that include temporary and part-time employees, consultants, leased employees, subcontractors, and short-term, life-of-the- project employees.

Continuity theory Theory of aging that emphasizes how a person adjusts to old age is largely a product or extension of adaptive patterns developed in earlier years.

Contracting A process of formulating a verbal or written agreement with a client system of established goals based on identified needs, usually including the steps that will be taken to meet those goals, the entities involved, and target dates for completion.

COS *See Charity Organization Society.*

Council on Social Work Education (CSWE) The national organization of schools of social work that focuses on social work education and serves as the accrediting body for professional social work undergraduate (BSW) and master's (MSW) programs.

County agent An employee of a county extension office funded by the U.S. Department of Agriculture; provides technical assistance to persons living in rural areas, including agricultural and home management, as well as community and family services.

Courts Legal institutions in which lawyers play the leading roles and make most of the decisions.

CPS *See* child protective services.

Crime An act that is considered to be a threat to individual or community well-being; a violation of a law.

Crime prevention Any effort designed to reduce the incidence of criminal behavior.

Criminal codes Define the types of conduct that are criminal and establish a range of penalties for such behavior.

Criminal justice system The means used to enforce those standards of conduct required to protect individuals and property and to maintain a sense of justice in the community.

Crisis intervention Intervention provided when a crisis exists to the extent that one's usual coping resources threaten individual or family functioning.

Cross-functional work teams Work teams comprised of members from multiple functions within the organization.

Cultural diversity The coexistence of various groups whose cultural differences are respected as equally valid. Group membership can be based on ethnicity, race, gender, class, religion, ability or disability, or sexual orientation.

Cultural divide The "distance" between different cultural belief systems.

Cultural pluralism The existence of two or more diverse cultures within a given society where each maintains its own traditions and special interests within the confines of the total society.

Culture shock Feelings that may occur when moving to an unfamiliar cultural environment; often results in temporary or long-lasting effects such as anxiety or depression.

Custody A legal charge given to a person requiring her or him to provide certain types of care and to exercise certain control in regards to another individual, as in parental child custody.

CWLA See Child Welfare League of America.

Cyber-stalking Stalking that takes place using the Internet.

Deficit Reduction Act of 2005 Signed into law by President George Bush in 2006, legislation designed to restrain federal spending and leave more money in the hands of the American people (also reauthorized the Personal Responsibility and Work Opportunity Budget Reconciliation Act of 1996 for an additional five years).

Deinstitutionalization A philosophy that advocates for care of individuals with mental health problems and developmental disabilities in local community outpatient programs whenever appropriate to the client's needs, as opposed to hospitalization in an institution.

Delinquency Behavior of juveniles that would be criminal in adults.

Depressant An agent that reduces a bodily functional activity such as staying awake or an instinctive desire such as eating.

Depression Overwhelming feeling of incapacitation that, in the extreme, may result in a person not being able to function.

Deterrence factors Those things that are likely to stop people from committing crimes.

Developmental delay Delay in communication, self-help, social-emotional, motor skills, sensory development, or cognition in comparison to skills typically observed in other individuals within the same age range.

Developmental disability A severe, chronic disability resulting from physical or mental impairment, usually prior to age 21, which results in substantial limitations of the individual's social, emotional, intellectual, and/or physical functioning.

Developmental theory A theory of human development that emphasizes psychological adjustment to the demands from the environment; these demands change as the individual moves through the life cycle.

Devolution The transfer of responsibility for social welfare programs from the federal government to state and local governments.

Diagnostic and Statistical Manual of Mental Disorders (DSM) A classification system of types of mental disorders that incorporates both organic and environmental factors, developed by the American Psychiatric Association for assessment and intervention purposes (now in its fourth edition, referred to as the *DSM-IV*).

Digital divide The gap between the technological competence of people with ready access to technology compared to those with limited or no access to technology.

Direct practice A method of social work involving face-to-face contact with individuals, families, groups, and organizations and actual provision of services by the social worker for the purpose of addressing unmet needs; also referred to as *casework* or *social casework*.

Disability insurance A government fund established by the U.S. government in 1957 that provides cash benefits to workers who become totally and permanently disabled; note that some employers also now offer private disability insurance.

Disciplinary research Studies designed to expand the body of knowledge of a particular discipline; also called *pure* or *basic research*.

Discrimination Action that maintains and supports prejudice.

Disengagement theory A theory related to aging based on the premise that as adults decline physically, they have less need and desire for social interaction and progressively become disengaged from social roles.

Displaced workers Persons age 20 and older who have lost or left jobs because their place of employment closed, there wasn't sufficient work for them to do, or their position or shift was eliminated.

Disposition The legal process by which judges decide how best to resolve delinquency cases.

Diversion A process by which persons coming to the attention of the criminal justice system are diverted to other programs such as social services, community services, or educational (defensive driving) programs, rather than going through the court process.

Dorothea Dix A philanthropist and social reformer who observed the care given the "insane" in the U.S. and sought to convince President Franklin Pierce to allocate federal and land grant monies for establishing federal institutions to care for the mentally ill. Dix's work was successful in raising public awareness about the problems of the mentally ill and set the tone for an era of significant reform during the mid- to late-1800s.

Downshifting The voluntary limiting of job demands so employees can devote increased time to their families and to themselves.

Downsizing Reduction in workforce and/or scope of goods and services produced or delivered to remain economically competitive and/or manage decreasing resources.

DSM *See Diagnostic and Statistical Manual of Mental Disorders.*

Dual-career family A family in which both partners/ spouses have careers outside the family.

Dual diagnosis A determination that an individual has other diagnosable emotional problems in addition to substance abuse.

Dual system of justice Separate systems of justice for juveniles and adults.

Dysfunctional Impaired or abnormal functioning.

Earned Income Tax Credit A provision of the federal income tax system to give a cash supplement to working parents with low incomes; parents file a tax statement, and if their taxable earnings are below a specific amount, they receive a check for a percentage of their earnings regardless of whether they paid that amount or less in taxes.

Economic justice Fair allocation of resources.

Educational group A group formed for the purpose of transmitting knowledge and enabling participants to acquire more complex skills, such as parenting.

Educator Person who provides information and/or teaching skills to facilitate change.

Egalitarianism A belief in human equality, especially with respect to social, political, and economic rights and privileges.

Ego psychology A theoretical perspective that emphasizes ego growth and development.

EITC *See* Earned Income Tax Credit.

Elder abuse Term referring to any intentional or negligent act by a caregiver or any other person that causes harm or a serious risk of harm to a vulnerable older adult.

Elizabethan Poor Law Legislation passed in England in 1601 that established categories of the poor, including the deserving poor (orphans, widows, and others) and the non-deserving poor (able-bodied males), and the treatment they were to receive from national and local governments; this law established precedents for policies toward the poor in the United States.

Employee assistance program (EAP) A workplace sponsored program providing mental health and social services to employees and their families; services may be provided directly at the workplace or through a contractual arrangement by a social service agency.

Empowerment A process to help others increase their personal, interpersonal, or political power so they can take action themselves to improve their lives.

Enabler A person whose behavior facilitates another person's behavior to continue; used most often to describe situations in families in which substance abuse is a problem and other family members enable the substance abuse to continue by their reinforcing behaviors.

Encounter group A group oriented toward assisting individuals in developing more self-awareness and interpersonal skills through in-depth experiential activities and extensive group sharing.

Entitlement A social welfare program that any individual is entitled to if certain eligibility requirements are met; such programs are based on numbers of individuals in need of the services rather than other limitations, such as resources available or caps put on funding by government bodies.

Entropy Unavailable energy in a closed system that creates dysfunction within that system and eventually results in the system's inability to function.

Equal Rights Amendment (ERA) A proposed amendment to the U.S. Constitution to assure the complete and equal rights of all citizens without regard to race, color, creed, or gender; the amendment was not ratified by the number of states necessary for its adoption.

Equifinality   The idea that the final state of a system can be achieved in many different ways.

Ethics   A framework for determining what is right and wrong and how specific situations should be handled; the National Association of Social Workers Code of Ethics relates to the moral principles of social work practice.

Etiology of crime   Theories relating to the origins or causes of crime, including physiological, psychological, and sociological perspectives.

Evaluation   A method of showing how a client system or a program has achieved or failed to achieve established goals.

Evaluative research   Research undertaken to show how a program achieves (or fails to achieve) its goals.

Exchange theory   Theory based on the premise that relationships are exchanges of goods and services, with those in power having the goods and services; in relation to aging, this theory attributes the social withdrawal of the elderly to a loss of power as they lose their income and move to pensions and Medicare.

Exosystem level   The level of social environment that incorporates community factors in which an individual does not participate directly but that affects the individual's functioning, such as school board and city council actions.

Facilitator   Person who brings participants together to promote change through improved communication.

Family   A group of individuals bonded together through marriage, kinship, adoption, or mutual agreement.

Family care-giving   Emotional support, and, in times of illness, care for elderly parents by one or more of their children.

Family and Medical Leave Act (FMLA)   Requires employers with more than 50 employees to provide up to 12 weeks of unpaid leave to eligible employees for certain medical or family reasons such as the birth of a child or the serious illness of a child, spouse, or parent.

Family preservation programs   Family intervention programs whose goal is to keep families together by increasing the coping skills and competencies of family members.

Family roles   Roles taken on by family members as a way to cope with the behaviors of other family members and maintain the family system's patterns of functioning.

Family Support Act   Mandated that states provide job opportunities and basic skills (JOBS) programs for most AFDC recipients (some, such as those with very young children or health problems, were exempted from participation). The act also provided up to 12 months of Medicaid (health care) and child care after recipients found jobs to ease the transition from welfare to work without loss of income; mandated that states provide AFDC benefits for a limited time to those families with previously employed males unable to find employment; and required stronger enforcement of child support payments by absent parents.

Family violence   The use of force by one family member against another, usually by a family member who is more powerful against a member who is less powerful.

Federal poverty income limit   The amount of money required for individuals and families to satisfy their minimal living needs, published by the federal government each year.

Feminism   Theory based on of the economic, political and social equality of the sexes.

Feminist therapy   Intervention that empowers individuals who may be members of an oppressed group to find their own voice and view themselves as equals as they make decisions about their lives.

Feminization of poverty   A term used to describe the result of the increasing numbers of single-parent women being classified as poor.

Flexiplace   A system that allows employees to work at alternate work sites as opposed to a standard workplace (for example, working in their own homes).

Flextime   A system that allows employees to have varied work hours as opposed to standard work hours (for example, working from 6 A.M. to 3 P.M. rather than from 8 A.M. to 5 P.M.).

Food stamps   In-kind assistance program funded by the U.S. Department of Agriculture designed to supplement the food-purchasing power of eligible low-income households to allow families to maintain nutritious diets and to expand the market for agricultural goods

Foster care A form of temporary substitute care in which children live with a family other than their birth family until they are able to be returned to their birth family, adopted, or placed in a more permanent setting that best meets their needs.

FPIL *See* Federal poverty income limit.

Gender equity/equality Social, political, and economic equality between men and women.

Gender gap A reference to gender inequality in society.

General assistance Public assistance programs that provide financial aid to persons who are in need but do not qualify for federally authorized programs; usually administered by county and local government and also referred to as *relief programs.*

General manager Person who assumes administrative responsibility for an agency at some level.

Generalist A social worker who operates from a systems/ecological perspective, using multiple interventions in working with client systems at the individual, family, group, organizational, community, or societal level and using the strengths of those systems to empower them to change their environment.

Generalist practice Orderly sequence of progressive stages in engaging a client (or client system such as a family) in activities and actions that promote agreed-on goals.

Gentrification Restoration and upgrading of deteriorated urban property by middle class or affluent people, which often results in displacement of low-income people.

Generalizable The ability of a theory to use what happens in one situation to explain what happens in other situations.

Geographic or territorial communities Places that have clearly-defined geopolitical boundaries.

Gerontology The study of aging and the aging process.

Global village A place where social and economic justice, lasting peace, and a sustainable environment are achieved.

Goal setting A process used by social workers and other helping professionals with client systems to identify ways to meet their needs; usually includes the identification of specific goals, steps to be taken in meeting those goals, resources needed, and a time frame for completion.

Great Depression The stock market crash of 1929 resulted in a drastic economic downturn that led to the Great Depression. Businesses closed, banks declared bankruptcy, and millions of individuals lost jobs and savings, creating economic disaster and chaos.

Great Society A social reform program proposed by the Johnson administration in the 1960s to improve the quality of life for all Americans, with emphasis on the poor and disenfranchised; the War on Poverty was one of the major Great Society programs.

Gross domestic product (GDP) The total monetary value of a nation's annual output of goods and services.

Group A social unit consisting of individuals who define status and role relationships to one another; it possesses its own set of values and norms and regulates the behavior of its members.

Group work A process that seeks to stimulate and support more adaptive personal functioning and social skills of individuals through structured group interaction.

Hallucinogen A substance that induces hallucinations.

Hate crimes Crimes (such as assault or defacement of property) motivated by hostility against individuals because they are members of a social group, such as one based on race, ethnicity, religion, gender, or sexual orientation.

Head Start A comprehensive early childhood education program, initially established as a Great Society program, which provides developmental learning for preschool children with health care, social services, and parent education components.

Health A state of complete physical, mental, and social well-being that is not merely the absence of disease or infirmity.

Health and welfare services Programs providing services that facilitate individual health and welfare, such as maternal health and child care, public health, family planning, and child welfare services.

Health care Services provided to individuals to prevent or to promote recovery from illness or disease.

Health care system reforms Measures taken to address problems associated with the health care delivery system, usually legislative in nature.

Health maintenance organization (HMO) Prepaid medical group practice for which individuals pay monthly fees and receive specific types of health at no cost or minimum cost per visit.

Health risk factors Factors that affect a person's health and place her or him at risk for serious health problems (for example, smoking).

Health savings accounts (HSAs) Used in conjunction with high-deductible health plans in which insurance does not cover "first dollar" (e.g., Medicare) medical expenses except for preventive care.

HIV-positive The first stage of acquired immunodeficiency syndrome (AIDS), also called the *seropositive state,* which occurs when a person has tested positively for AIDS and has HIV (human immunodeficiency virus) antibodies in his or her blood.

Holistic health care Views all aspects of an individual's health in relation to how that individual interacts with family members, the workplace, and the community.

Home health care Health care provided in a person's home as opposed to a hospital or other institutional health care setting; made available through outreach visits by social workers, nurses, physicians, and other health practitioners.

Home-based, family-centered services Services delivered to children and families in their own homes, with a focus on preserving the family system and strengthening the family to bring about needed change in an effort to prevent family breakup.

Homeless Having no fixed, adequate, regular nighttime residence.

Homophobia A fear of homosexuals and homosexuality.

Hospices Programs for terminally ill individuals and their families that enable them to die with dignity and support, often away from a hospital.

Hull House Patterned after Toynbee Hall in London, Jane Addams established Hull House in 1869 in one of the worst slum neighborhoods of Chicago. By addressing the problems of poor housing, low wages, child labor, juvenile delinquency and disease, Hull House and other settlement houses became major social action agencies.

Humanitarianism Promotion of human welfare and social reform.

Hypothesis A tentative assumption, derived from theory, that is capable of empirical verification.

IDEA *See* Individuals with Disabilities Education Act.

IFSW *See* International Federation of Social Workers.

Implementation strategy A plan for carrying out steps required to put a program or plan into practice.

Impulse-ridden behavior Behavior exhibited by neglecting parents with low impulse control, including acting inconsistently, leaving a child alone or in an unsafe situation without realizing the consequences to the child, or giving higher priority to a new activity.

Incarceration The placing of someone in prison.

Incest Sexual abuse between family members.

Inclusive The ability of a theory to consistently explain events in the same way each time they occur.

Individualist perspective Belief that individual problems are the result of bad choices, personal dysfunction, or a culture of poverty.

Individuals with Disabilities Education Act (IDEA) Federal legislation that mandates that school systems provide educational and social services for children with a range of disabilities, including emotional disturbance, mental retardation, and speech, vision, hearing, and learning disabilities.

Indoor relief Assistance given to the poor and the needy through placement in institutions, such as poorhouses, orphanages, and prisons.

Infant mortality rate The number of infants who die at birth or before they reach a certain age compared to the total number of infants, both living and not living, within that age range, within a specified geographic location and a specified time frame.

Inhalants Class of toxic chemicals whose vapors are inhaled as a form of "getting high" (e.g., gasoline, Freon, aerosol products, paint, and glue).

Initiator/coordinator Person that brings people together to help them organize for change.

Institutional discrimination Discrimination that occurs as the result of accepted beliefs and behaviors and is codified in societal roles and policies.

Intake The process that follows police referrals to juvenile court.

Intermediate punishments A middle ground between either/or choices of probation or parole.

International Federation of Social Workers (IFSW) An organization founded in 1956 to promote social work as a profession through cooperation and action on an international basis and to work toward social and economic justice throughout the world.

International social welfare The field of practice concerned with promoting basic human well-being in a context involving cross-national efforts.

International social work The practice of social work to meet social welfare needs from an international perspective.

Intervention Planned activities designed to improve the social functioning of a client or client system.

Intra-psychic Being or occurring within the mind, psyche, or personality.

Job sharing The sharing of one full-time job by two or more individuals; this practice is increasingly being allowed by employers and advantageous to women with young children and persons with disabilities who do not want to work outside the home on a full-time basis.

Joint custody Divorce arrangement where both parents share child custody equally.

Juvenile correctional institutions Secure and non-secure facilities used to detain juveniles who have committed status or other offenses.

Juvenile courts Courts structured to act in a child's best interest.

Juvenile delinquency Refers to youth who have committed a crime, a status offense (e.g., truancy, underage drinking, curfew violation, or running away), or both.

Kinship care The full-time parenting of children by kin.

Laissez-faire An economic theory developed by Adam Smith that emphasizes persons taking care of themselves and limits government intervention.

Least detrimental alternative A decision-making premise that places priority on making decisions regarding children based on which decision will be least damaging or upsetting to the child.

Least restrictive environment A living environment for an individual that maintains the greatest degree of freedom, self-determination, autonomy, dignity, and integrity for the individual, often while he or she participates in treatment or receives services.

Life span model A framework that focuses on relationships between individuals and their environments with major emphasis on where persons are developmentally and what transitional life processes they are experiencing (for example, marriage, retirement).

Living wage Three times the amount of money needed in a given location to rent an apartment of a given size; rental costs (fair market rents) are established by the U.S. Department of Housing and Urban Development (HUD).

Living will A formal written statement made by an individual specifying the individual's wishes about how her or his death should be handled, including delineation of which medical procedures and life support systems, if any, should be used and under what conditions.

Long-term care facility A program that provides long-term care to individuals, including the elderly and people with disabilities; state and federal regulations have established specific requirements that facilities must meet to be classified as long-term care facilities.

Lower criminal courts Courts with the power to decide minor cases and to conduct pretrial proceedings.

Macrosystem level The level of social environment that incorporates societal factors affecting an individual, including cultural ideologies, assumptions, and social policies that define and organize a given society.

Managed care Health care delivery that limits the use and costs of services and measures performance.

Managed care system A system of health care delivery that limits the use and costs of services and measures performance.

Market basket concept A way of measuring the number of people in poverty based on a formula that includes the estimated costs a family spends to provide a minimum nutritional diet, with adjustments for family size, and a set proportion of income families generally spend for food; families spending less than this proportion of their income are considered below the poverty line.

Mediation Intervention between a divorcing or divorced couple to promote settlement of child custody and property issues to reconcile differences and reach compromises; mediation teams usually include an attorney and a social worker.

Mediator Person who helps factions work out their differences.

Medicaid   Federally and state-funded public assistance program that provides health care to low-income individuals and families based on a means test using strict eligibility guidelines.

Medical model   A model that considers those with emotional problems as sick and thus not responsible for their behavior; focuses on deficits and dysfunction of client and family rather than their strengths, with little attention given to environmental aspects.

Medical social work   The practice of social work in medical settings.

Medical social workers   Social workers that are employed in some type of a medical setting.

Medicare   Federal health insurance program for the elderly.

Membership assistance programs   Employee support services for union members under the auspices of labor unions.

Mental health   A state of successful performance of mental function, resulting in productive activities, fulfilling relationships with other people, and the ability to adapt to change and to cope with adversity.

Mental health services   Range of services provided in the community or in an institutional setting to persons with mental health problems.

Mental illness   Term that refers collectively to all diagnosable mental disorders.

Mesosystem level   The level of social environment that incorporates interactions and interrelations among those persons, groups, and settings that comprise an individual's microsystem.

Microsystem level   The level of social environment that includes the individual, including intra-psychic characteristics and past life experiences, and all the persons and groups in his or her day-to-day environment.

Migrant workers   People engaged in jobs such as crop harvesting that require workers and their families to move from place to place to secure employment.

Minority group   A category of people distinguished by physical or cultural traits that are used by the majority group to single them out for differential and unequal treatment.

Mobilizer   Person who identifies and convenes resources to address unmet community needs.

Moral treatment   A philosophy among professionals and advocates working with the mentally ill in the late 1700s and early 1800s that advocated a caring, humane approach, as opposed to a punitive, repressive environment.

Multidisciplinary team   A group of professionals from a variety of disciplines working with clients.

Multidisciplinary team approach   An approach to working with clients that involves the shared expertise of professionals from a variety of disciplines, such as social workers, health professionals, educators, attorneys, and psychologists.

NAMH   *See* National Association of Mental Health.

Narcotics   Drugs such as opium and its derivatives, morphine, and heroin that dull the senses, relieve pain, and induce profound sleep.

NASW   *See* National Association of Social Workers.

National Association of Mental Health (NAMH)   A national association of professionals, individuals with mental health problems and their families, and organizations concerned about mental health issues and care of persons with mental health problems; provides education, advocacy, and research.

National Association of Social Workers (NASW)   The major national professional organization for social workers, which promotes ethics and quality in social work practice; stimulates political participation and social action; and maintains eligibility standards for membership.

National Institute of Mental Health (NIMH)   A federal agency created by the U.S. Congress in 1949 to address mental health concerns; now a part of the U.S. Department of Health and Human Services.

National Institute of Occupational Safety and Health (NIOSH)   Federal government program housed within the U.S. Department of Health and Human Services that addresses research and technology issues relating to occupational health and safety and sets federal standards for safe storage, use, and disposal of hazardous materials.

Natural group   A group in which members participate as a result of common interests, shared experiences, similar backgrounds and values, and personal satisfactions derived from interaction with other group members (for example, a street gang).

Natural helping networks   An informal system of support available to individuals as opposed to a professional service delivery system; includes individuals such as family members, friends, neighbors, coworkers, and members of organizations in which an individual may be involved, such as a church or synagogue; also called *natural support systems.*

Natural support systems Informal systems of support available to individuals in contrast to professional service delivery systems; examples of natural support systems include family members, friends, neighborhoods, coworkers, and members of organizations in which an individual may be involved, such as a church or synagogue; also called *helping networks.*

Neighborhood   and   community   organizing Process designed to develop the capacity of community members to organize around quality-of-life issues in the community such as air quality and noise pollution.

Negotiator Intermediary who helps to resolve conflicts.

New Deal Emergency legislation created after the Depression that provided assistance for the jobless and poor; coined the "New Deal," this legislation marked the first time in history that the federal government became engaged directly in providing relief and also provided an interpretation of the health and welfare provisions of the Constitution that established a historical precedent mandating the federal government to assume health and welfare responsibility for its citizens. This policy opened the door for later federal legislation in the areas of civil rights, fair employment practices, school busing, public assistance, and a variety of other social programs.

NIMH *See* National Institute of Mental Health.

NIOSH *See* National Institute of Occupational Safety and Health.

Non-organic failure to thrive A medical condition that results when a child is three percentiles or more below the normal range for height and weight and no organic reason can be determined; placing a child in a hospital and providing an adequate diet and nurturing will cause the child to gain height and weight, suggesting a lack of parental care as the cause.

Occupational Safety and Health Act Sets health and safety standards in industrial workplaces through onsite inspections and citations for violations.

Occupational Safety and Health Administration (OSHA) Federal agency that oversees workplace health and safety.

Occupational social work Social work services provided through the workplace that focus on the relationships between work stresses and other systems within which individuals function; also called *industrial social work.*

Official poverty A way of measuring poverty that provides a set of income thresholds adjusted for household size, age of household head, and number of children under 18 years old.

Old Age Survivors Disability Insurance (OASDI) A Social Security insurance program established as part of the Social Security Act of 1935 that provides limited payments to those eligible elderly persons and/or their dependents who have been employed and have had taxes deducted from their wages matched by their employer paid into a funding pool.

Omnibus Budget Reconciliation Act of 1987 (OBRA) Federal legislation that mandated major nursing home reforms, including increased rights for residents, written care plans, training for staff, and the employment of certified social workers.

Omnibus Health Care Rescue Act of 1989 (HB 18) Legislation designed to provide additional health care resources with emphasis on rural areas.

Open system A system whose boundaries are permeated easily.

Opportunities Factors within the environment that encourage an individual to meet his or her needs and to develop as a healthy, well-functioning person.

Opportunity structure The accessibility of opportunities for an individual within that individual's environment, including personal and environmental factors such as physical traits, intelligence, family, and availability of employment.

Oppression Unjust use of power against non-dominant groups by the dominant group.

Organizing functional communities Community organizing technique where the scope of concern is advocacy for a specific issue or population, such as marriage rights for gays, and the system targeted for change is the general public and government institutions.

OSHA *See* Occupational Safety and Health Administration.

Outdoor relief Cash or in-kind assistance given to persons in need, allowing them to remain in their own homes (for example, public assistance payments for food and fuel).

Outsourcing The practice by U.S. businesses of having portions or all of their production carried out outside of the United States and its territories.

Own-home services *See* home-based, family-centered services.

Paradigm Commonly-accepted or established way of thinking about things.

Pastoral counselor A person who provides counseling service under the auspices of a religious organization, which usually includes an emphasis on spiritual wellbeing; usually a member of the clergy.

Permanency planning An idea stating that all child welfare services provided for a child should be centered around a plan directed toward a permanent, nurturing home for that child.

Person-environment fit The fit between a person's needs, rights, goals, and capacities and the physical and social environment within which the person functions.

Physical child abuse A physical act of harm or threatened harm against a child by a caretaker that results in physical or mental injury to a child, including beating, hitting, slapping, burning, shaking, or throwing.

Physician-assisted suicide Term used to describe the process whereby terminally-ill patients obtain and use prescriptions from their physicians for self-administered, lethal medications.

Planned change An orderly approach to addressing client needs based on assessment, knowledge of the client system's capacity for change, and focused intervention.

Plea bargaining Negotiations among the prosecutor, the defendant, and the defendant's counsel that lead to the defendant entering a guilty plea in exchange for a reduction in charges or the prosecutor's promise to recommend a more lenient sentence.

Policy research Research that focuses on evaluating the effects of proposed or existing social policy on constituent populations.

Political and social action Community organizing in which the scope of concern is to build political power and institutional change (get the message to those who can do something about the issue or problem).

Populations at risk Groups that experience prejudice, discrimination, and oppression from the dominant group.

Poverty A determination that a household's income is inadequate, judged by a specific standard.

Prejudice An irrational attitude of hostility directed against an individual, a group, a race, or their supposed characteristics.

Pre-retirement planning Process of planning for retirement in advance of the actual retirement date.

Primary prevention A program targeted at the total population to prevent a problem from occurring.

Primary setting A setting in which the types of services a professional provides match the primary goals of the setting (e.g., a hospital is a primary setting for a nurse but a secondary setting for a social worker).

Private health insurance Health insurance available to individuals and families through the workplace or through purchase of policies with private insurance companies.

Private nonprofit agency Nongovernmental agencies that provide social services, spending all of their funds to meet the goals of the agency with no financial profit earned by agency owners, directors, or employees.

Private practice In social work, the delivery of client services for pay on an independent, autonomous basis rather than under the auspices of an agency; social workers in most states have an MSW degree, receive supervision by an advanced practitioner, and pass a licensing or certification examination before establishing a private practice.

Private sector/private voluntary sector Includes programs and agencies funded and operated by non-public entities (for instance, voluntary and proprietary agencies and private businesses).

Probation Replaces incarceration, in which those convicted face supervised release into the community.

Problem-solving approach A common intervention used by social workers, based on client's motivation and capacity for change and opportunities available to the client to facilitate the change. The client and worker assess needs, identify problems and needs to be addressed, develop a plan to address problems and needs, and implement and monitor the plan, revising as needed.

Pro bono Provision of services at no cost; professionals such as lawyers and social workers do pro bono work with low-income clients for the public good.

Program development and community liaison A form of community organizing in which the desired outcome is the expansion or redirection of agency programs and the system targeted for change consists of agency funding sources and beneficiaries of agency services.

Psychiatry A branch of medicine that deals with mental, emotional, or behavioral disorders.

Psychoanalysis A method of dealing with emotional problems that focuses on inter-psychic functioning (internal conflicts with the individual).

Psychobiology A term describing the interactions between biological and environmental factors in understanding human behavior.

Psychological maltreatment/emotional maltreatment Acting out against a person emotionally or psychologically, such as verbally belittling or attacking a person constantly; or failing to meet emotional needs through acts of omission, such as not providing love, attention, and/or emotional support to a person.

Psychological parent A person viewed by a child as being his or her parental figure from a psychological or emotional standpoint rather than a birth relationship; if a boy were raised by his grandparents and rarely saw his mother, his grandparents would be his psychological parents. Many court decisions are being made based on the concept of a psychological parent.

Psychology A science based on the study of mind and behavior; involves many subspecialties.

Psychologist Individual who practices psychology.

Psychometric instruments Tests used to measure psychological functioning.

Psychotropic drug A type of drug used in the treatment of mental health problems, including depression and psychoses, that has resulted in major reductions in numbers of individuals with emotional problems needing long-term hospitalization.

Public assistance Programs that provide income, medical care, and social services to individuals and families based on economic need, paid from state and local taxes, to provide a socially established minimum standard usually set by the state; Temporary Assistance to Needy Families (TANF), food stamps, and Medicaid are public assistance programs.

Public health insurance Insurance provided by the public sector to those in need who are not covered by private insurance programs and meet eligibility requirements, such as Medicaid.

Public sector Programs and agencies funded and operated by government entities, including public schools, agencies, and hospitals.

Racial profiling Practice of law enforcement officers or others treating a person as a suspect because of his or her race.

Reactive depressive behavior Behavior resulting from depression, often due to a loss, that can affect the ability to parent and lead to child neglect.

Reality therapy An intervention, based on the assumption that people are responsible for their own behavior, that effects change by confronting individuals about irresponsible behaviors and encouraging them to accept responsibility for their behaviors and to develop positive self-worth through positive behavior.

Recidivism Return to previous behaviors; for example, when persons released from prison commit new crimes.

Recreation group A group of individuals who engage in recreational activities in a monitored environment.

Recreation skill group A group designed to promote development of a skill within a recreational or enjoyment context.

Refugee A person who flees to a foreign country or power to escape danger or persecution.

Rehabilitation Philosophy of punishment that aims at preventing future crimes by changing individual offenders.

Relative poverty Poverty measured by comparing the unit being measured (for example, individuals or families) to a set standard for that unit, such as income, with those falling below that standard identified as being in poverty.

Residential treatment Treatment provided in 24-hour care facilities for persons with mental health or substance abuse problems or developmental disabilities; such programs are usually considered less restrictive than psychiatric hospitals.

Resilience Ability to recover or adapt successfully to adversity.

Retirement Leaving paid employment, usually based on age; retirees may receive pensions or Social

Security benefits depending on their work history and eligibility for such programs.

Richmond, Mary A major contributor to the Charity Organization Society movement and considered by many to be the founder of the professional clinical social work movement. Richmond inaugurated the first training program for social workers at the New York School of Applied Philanthropy, the forerunner of schools of social work, and formulated the concept of social casework.

Risks Direct threats to healthy development, or the absence of opportunities that should facilitate healthy individual development.

Root causes Underlying cause of a social problem.

Rural A social, occupational, and cultural way of life for persons living in the country or in rural communities with fewer than 2,500 persons.

Rural social work Social work provided in rural areas usually based on a generalist practice model that involves the actual provision of many services rather than linking individuals with other social service resources.

Same-sex marriage Legal union between couples of the same sex.

School social work A social work approach that involves working with children, youth, and their families within a school setting; school social workers deal directly with children, youth, and their families as well as teachers, school administrators, and other community resources.

Secondary prevention Targeted at specified groups within a larger population that are determined to be "at risk" or more likely to experience a specific problem than the larger population to prevent the problem from occurring, i.e. intervention on prevention of alcoholism targeted at teens with a parent who is an alcoholic.

Secondary setting A setting in which the types of services a professional provides differ from the primary focus of the setting (for example, a social worker in a hospital works in a secondary setting, while a social worker in a social services agency works in a primary setting).

Selective enforcement The use of discretion to enforce some laws sometimes against some people.

Self-concept The image a person has of herself or himself in relation to appearance, ability, motivation, and capacity to react to the environment; derived primarily through feedback from others.

Self-help group A group of individuals with similar problems that meets for the purpose of providing support and information to each other and for mutual problem solving—for example, Parents Anonymous and Alcoholics Anonymous.

Settlement house Physical structure where community-based services and advocacy for the poor and disenfranchised are carried out.

Sexism Discrimination against an individual because of gender.

Sexual abuse The use of a child by an adult for sexual or emotional gratification in a sexual way, such as fondling, exposure, sexual intercourse, and exploitation, including child pornography.

Sexual harassment Unwelcome sexual advances, requests for sexual favors, and other verbal or physical conduct of a sexual nature when submission to or rejection of this conduct explicitly or implicitly affects an individual's employment, unreasonably interferes with an individual's work performance, or creates an intimidating or hostile or offensive work environment.

Sexual inequality Inequality between men and women based on gender attributes.

Sexual orientation An enduring emotional, romantic, sexual or affectional attraction to another person. Sexual orientation exists along a continuum that ranges from exclusive homosexuality to exclusive heterosexuality and includes various forms of bisexuality. Sexual orientation is different from sexual behavior because it refers to feelings and self-concept. Persons may or may not express their sexual orientation in their behaviors.

Single-case/single-subject designs Research designs that evaluate the impact of interventions or policy changes on a single client or case.

Social action A social work approach to working with communities that stresses organization and group cohesion in confrontational approaches geared to modify or eliminate institutional power bases that negatively impact the community.

Social agencies Organizations whose primary focus is to address social problems.

Social casework A social work method involving face-to-face contact with individuals, families, groups, or organizations, by which the social worker provides services directly to clients for the purpose of addressing unmet needs; also referred to as *direct practice.*

Social group work A social work method involving intervention with groups of individuals that uses structured interaction to promote individual and group functioning and well-being.

Social inequality Unequal treatment of social groups based on factors such as economic and social status, age, ethnicity, sexual preference, or gender.

Social insurance Financial assistance for those whose income has been curtailed because of retirement, death, or long-term disability of the family breadwinner; paid to former working persons or their dependents through a tax on earned income.

Social justice Fairness and equity in the protection of civil and human rights, the treatment of individuals, the distribution of opportunity, and the assurance of personal and economic opportunity.

Social movements Form of community organizing in which the desired outcome is action for social justice and the system targeted for change is the general public or political systems.

Social planning A social work approach to working with communities that emphasizes modification of institutional practices through the application of knowledge, values, and theory; a practical, rational approach.

Social Security An insurance program established as part of the Social Security Act that provides limited payments to eligible elderly persons who have been employed and have had taxes deducted from their wages, matched by their employers, and paid into a funding pool, or to their dependents.

Social Security Act Major social welfare legislation passed by the U.S. Congress in 1935, establishing social insurance programs based on taxes paid by working persons; public assistance programs to provide for those who do not qualify for social insurance programs and cannot provide for themselves or their families financially; and health and welfare services for children, families, the disabled, and the aged such as child welfare services, maternal and child health services, and services for the disabled.

Social study The process of obtaining relevant information about the client system and perceived needs.

Social welfare Efforts organized by societies to facilitate the well-being of their members, usually focused on activities that seek to prevent, alleviate, or contribute to the solution of a selected set of social problems.

Social welfare policy A specific course of actions taken to address an identified social problem, with emphasis on the decisions and choices that help determine those actions.

Social welfare theory A type of theory in which the area of concern in social welfare.

Social work The major profession that implements planned change activities prescribed by social welfare institutions through intervention with individuals, families, and groups or at community, organizational, and societal levels to enhance or restore social functioning.

Social worker A member of the social work profession who works with individuals, families, groups, organizations, communities, or societies to improve social functioning.

Socialization group A group of individuals whose goal is to help participants develop socially acceptable behavior and behavioral competency.

Socialization The process of learning to become a social being; the acquisition of knowledge, values, abilities, and skills that are essential to function as a member of the society within which the individual lives.

Sociologist An expert who studies society, its organization and demographic structure, and patterns of human interaction, including norms, values, and behavior.

Solution-focused therapy Short-term cognitive behavioral intervention that emphasizes the present situation rather than events in the client's past; strategies focus on very specific situations and tasks that are assigned to clients to work on between sessions.

Specialization Practice of social work focused on a specific population or field of practice requiring specialized knowledge and skill; contrasts with *generalist practice.*

Specific deterrent A program or sentence targeted at an individual to discourage him or her from repeating inappropriate/illegal behavior.

Spillover effect A term describing the situation when feelings, attitudes, and behaviors from one domain in a person's life have a positive or a negative impact on other domains (such as from the workplace to the family).

SSI   *See* Supplemental Security Income.

Steady state   Constant adjustment of a system moving toward its goal while maintaining order and stability within.

Stepfamilies   *See blended families.*

Stereotype   A standardized mental picture of a group attributed to all group members.

Strengths perspective   An approach to social work that focuses on the strengths of the client system and the broader environment within which it functions rather than on the deficiencies.

Stereotypes   Beliefs that members of certain groups behave in specific ways.

Stimulants   Drugs that stimulate the central nervous system, creating a sense of heightened euphoria.

Substance abuse   Improper use of mood-altering substances such as drugs that results in detrimental effects on an individual's personal life, including school, job, family, friends, health, spiritual life, or the law.

Substitute care   Out-of-home care provided for children when parents are unwilling or unable to provide care in their own homes; types of substitute care include foster care, group home care, and residential treatment and are determined based on the child's needs.

Suicide   The act or instance of taking one's own life voluntarily and intentionally.

Supplemental Security Income (SSI)   A program administered in conjunction with the Social Security Program to provide cash assistance to needy aged, blind, and/or people with permanent and total disabilities who meet certain eligibility standards established by state and federal regulations.

Support services   Services that provide support to individuals and families, such as health care, legal assistance, housing, and social services.

Synergy   The combined energy of smaller parts of a larger system that is greater than the sum of the energy of those parts if they functioned separately.

System   A social unit consisting of interdependent, interacting parts.

Systems/ecological framework   A major framework used to understand individual, family, community, organizational, and societal events and behaviors that emphasizes the interactions and interdependence between individuals and their environments.

Task-centered method   A short-term therapeutic approach to intervention that stresses the selection of specific tasks to be worked on within a limited time frame to address the needs of a client system.

Telecommunications   A way of communicating electronically that allows remote sites to have access to information and consultation.

Telemedicine   The use of telecommunications by medical health practitioners to gain immediate access to large medical centers where consultation is available for both diagnostic and treatment regimens; increased use of telemedicine is occurring in rural areas.

Temporary Assistance to Needy Families (TANF)   A public assistance program that provides cash assistance to families (primarily single-parent women) with children in need because of the loss of financial support as a result of death, disability, or the continued absence of a second parent from the home; assistance is available on a time-limited basis and requires participation in programs that prepare adults in the family for participation in the workforce; TANF replaced the AFDC program.

Tertiary prevention   Efforts targeted at individuals who have already experienced a specific problem to prevent that problem from reoccurring.

Testable   The ability of a theory to be measured accurately and validly.

Theory   A way of organizing facts or sets of facts to describe, explain, or predict events.

Therapeutic group   Group requiring skilled professional leaders who assist group members in addressing intensive personal and emotional problems.

Traditional communities   Communities in which community members attempt to maintain their separateness, uniqueness, cultural integrity, and historical identity (e.g., Amish, Native Americans, Hasidic Jews, and aborigines).

Trail courts   Courts with the power to conduct pre-trial and trial proceedings in all criminal cases.

Underclass   The lowest socioeconomic group in society characterized by chronic poverty and the inability to pull themselves out of their condition, often due to barriers and societal obstacles including oppression.

Under-employment   Work in a job for which one's qualifications exceed those established for the position.

Unemployment compensation   A program established by the Social Security Act that is funded by taxes assessed by employers and is available to eligible unemployed workers

Universal health care   Access to health care by all citizens.

Urban   Term used by the U.S. Bureau of the Census to designate cities of a certain size.

U.S. Children's Bureau   The first department established by the federal government in 1912 to address the needs of children and families; federal programs addressing problems of abuse and neglect, runaway youth, adoption and foster care, and other child welfare services are currently housed within the U.S Department of Health and Human Services.

U.S. Department of Agriculture   A federal department that oversees the food stamp program and houses the Agricultural Extension Service, which provides services targeted to rural areas.

U.S. Department of Health and Human Services   A federal department that oversees the implementation of legislation relating to health and human services, including public assistance programs, child welfare services, and services for the elderly.

Values   Assumptions, convictions, or beliefs of a person or group in which they have an emotional investment; values influence opinions about the ways people should behave and the principles that should govern behavior.

Voluntary sector   A third sector of society, along with the public and for-profit proprietary sectors, that includes private, nonprofit social agencies.

Welfare devolution   Transfer of responsibility for public welfare programs from the federal government to individual states and localities.

Welfare reform   Reform of the public welfare system by policy makers and legislators who believe that it is ineffective in achieving its stated goals.

Workers' compensation   An insurance program that is funded by taxes assessed to employers and is available to eligible workers who are injured on the job or who experience job-related injuries or illnesses.

Working poor   Persons who maintain regular employment but fall below the federal poverty level because of low wages.

Workplace violence   Acts of violence, including harassment by family members, that occur in the workplace.

World citizenship   People accepting responsibility in this interdependent world by thinking and acting as citizens of that world.

Worldview   One's perspective on the way the world works.

Index

TO THE OWNER OF THIS BOOK:

I hope that you have found *Social Work and Social Welfare, Sixth Edition,* useful. So that this book can be improved in a future edition, would you take the time to complete this sheet and return it? Thank you.

School and address:_____

Department:_____

Instructor's name:_____

1. What I like most about this book is:_____

   _____

   _____

2. What I like least about this book is:_____

   _____

   _____

3. My general reaction to this book is:_____

   _____

   _____

4. The name of the course in which I used this book is:_____

   _____

5. Were all of the chapters of the book assigned for you to read?_____

   If not, which ones weren't?_____

6. In the space below, or on a separate sheet of paper, please write specific suggestions for improving this book and anything else you'd care to share about your experience in using this book.

   _____

   _____

   _____

DO NOT STAPLE. PLEASE SEAL WITH TAPE.

FOLD HERE

NO POSTAGE
NECESSARY
IF MAILED
IN THE
UNITED STATES

BUSINESS REPLY MAIL
FIRST-CLASS MAIL   PERMIT NO. 34   BELMONT, CA

POSTAGE WILL BE PAID BY ADDRESSEE

Attn: Social Work/Lisa Gebo

BrooksCole/Thomson Learning
10 Davis Drive
Belmont, CA   94002-9801

FOLD HERE

OPTIONAL:

Your name: _____ Date: _____

May we quote you, either in promotion for *Social Work and Social Welfare, Sixth Edition,* or in future publishing ventures?

Yes: _____   No: _____

Sincerely yours,

Rosalie Ambrosino
Joseph Heffernan
Guy Shuttlesworth
Robert Ambrosino